Post-conflict Cultures
A Reader

edited by Cristina Demaria

CCCP

Critical, Cultural and Communications Press
London
2020

Post-conflict Cultures: A Reader, edited by Cristina Demaria
Series: Studies in Post-Conflict Cultures, no. 11.
Series Editor: Bernard McGuirk
The books in this series are refereed publications.

First published in Great Britain by Critical, Cultural and Communications Press, London, 2020.

The cover shows a reproduction of "A roadside cemetery near Neuve Eglise" by George Edmund Butler (1917), a public domain work available from Archives New Zealand under the records number NCWA 471 and under the record code R22498088.

Cover design by Hannibal.

ISBN 9781905510672

For Silvana

Contents

Introduction

Visual and Performance Cultures

Genres of testimonies/genres of reconstruction

Introduction

What is a Post-conflict Culture?
Temporalities and Agencies of Post-conflict Memories

Cristina Demaria

> Wars – hot and cold – are like love affairs.
> They don't just end. They fizzle and sputter;
> sometimes they reignite... For a post-war
> era lasts as long as people affected by
> conflict employ that painful or exhilarating
> experience to assess their own current
> relationship and aspirations [...] The
> morning after is always an ambiguous
> moment. What just happened? Who
> benefited from it? It is not always crystal-
> clear that today, the day growing out of the
> morning after, is a fresh, new day.
>
> (Enloe 1993, 2-3; 252-3)

To compile a Reader on the subject of post-conflict cultures, as if it were an established field of research, is, it might be argued, a rather daring undertaking; or else, a not-so-brave move that puts together yet another collection of essays by using a different label for an already existing field of studies on memories of collective violence and conflicts. However, on the one hand, within the vast literature dealing with aftermath of wars, such as in the social and political science fields of peace and securities studies, conflict resolution and international relations,[1] it has indeed been common to concentrate on post-conflict situations/scenarios, with little mention or consideration, at least until not so long ago, of their links to cultures. On the other hand, within the human sciences, as in the ever-growing field of memory and trauma studies,[2] works on memories and postmemories of

---

[1] It is rather difficult to list all the different labels and field of studies that focus on the managing of conflict and its aftermath, yet the ones mentioned here are among the most recurrent and significant.

[2] The ever-growing field of memory studies is founded on a body of literature too vast to summarize. See the quite recently established Memory Studies Assoc-

conflicts have been numerous, and they have explored the ways in which the representation of individual and collective memories are closely linked to the building and rebuilding of national and transnational, local and diasporic, cultures. Yet, even within such studies, rarely has the category of post-conflict been associated directly with that of culture, that is to an interpretation of conflicts, collective violence and wars, centred on the disruption of symbolic systems of cultural reproduction, whereby meaninglessness becomes one of the more enduring existential legacies of conflicts; its sometimes very conflictual reconstruction or silencing, one of the main goals of the agents involved.

This cultural dimension is what the CCCP-published series on post-conflict cultures has been investigating since its first volume, from different angles and perspectives, from that of practices of reconstruction after a conflict (Gonçalves Miranda and Zullo 2013) to writing under socialism (Jones and Nehru 2011); from the genres of testimonies (Demaria and Daly 2009), to the specificity of Latin American post-dictatorship societies and their possible lesson for Europe (Sharman *et al.* 2017). Rarely, again, except for the sole and rather concise attempt made in the Introduction to the first volume of this series (Demaria and Wright 2006), have the authors participating in the series directly addressed the shifting and growing meaning of the category of post-conflict cultures. Just as infrequently have they attempted a dialogue with the fields of conflict resolution or peace-building studies, especially those engaged in definitions of post-conflict scenarios and the most effective ways towards achieving reconciliation, a process that, ideally, as Luc Huyse (2003, 19) in a handbook on *Reconciliation after Violent Conflict* explains, should prevent "once and for all, the use of the past as the seed of renewed conflict... Reconciliation consolidates peace, breaks the cycle of violence and strengthens newly established or reintroduced democratic institutions". I shall return to a less idealistic idea of reconciliation once it meets with the actual predicaments of collective suffering.

The aim of this introductory essay is therefore twofold: to discuss the category of post-conflict cultures and further to clarify its understanding;

iation's website for main references and lines of inquiry: **https://www. memory studiesassociation.org/memory-cloud/**. See also the different essays hosted in the Journal *Memory Studies*, published by Sage since 2011. And, amongst the many Readers exploring topics related to Memory Studies, cf. Radstone and Schwartz (eds., 2010); Assmann and Conrad (2010).

and to propose an itinerary through this Reader aimed not only at outlining its various contributions but also at summing up the main intellectual challenges posed by the volumes of this series, to both conflict resolution studies *and* memory studies.

As for the first purpose, my intention is certainly not to draw further disciplinary boundaries and distinctions, but to elaborate on some of the concepts and questions that define a post-conflict culture precisely at the crossroads where the predicaments of a post-conflict situation – as expressed by conflict resolution and transitional justice approaches – meet a human sciences stance on memory, the act of witnessing and its trans-generational transmission. I want to argue that, at this intersection, one may find precious tools for a better understanding of the links between cultures, conflicts and their representation, and for an in-depth recollection of their different temporalities and agencies.

As Colin Wright and I wrote in the above-mentioned Introduction, today we witness the chaotic instability of international power relations in a globalized world, in which "the modes of sovereignty appropriate to the modernist conception of war have given way to partially deterritorialized and de-regulated forms of government or, to use Michel Foucault's seminal distinction, governmentality" (Demaria and Wright 2006, 5; see Foucault 1986). Our shared assumption was, and is, that conflicts lay bare the normative mechanisms of a cultural system *and* the vulnerable, incomplete and provisional character of that normativity since, as a cultural phenomenon, conflict is a way in which the organized act of violence which is war, and the management of it, are "expressed as a border condition, as the paradoxical state of possible change in a system, its reconfiguration" (Demaria and Wright 2006, 10). Conflicts help the understanding of how cultures work, of how individual, collective, ethnic, national and transnational identities, and the memories on which they are founded, are constantly constructed and de-constructed, recognized or mis-recognized, transformed and used not only to define the present, but also to project future possible scenarios, their re-mediation and pre-mediation.[3]

---

[3] In an era many authors define as a post-media one – post-media surely not because the media have lost their centrality, but because of their pervasiveness – images and narratives of wars are constantly re-mediated. This means that they circulate, and are translated and adopted, either shortened or expanded, from one

Moreover, approaching conflict situations from a cultural perspective, one is struck by two dominant processes: firstly, the ways in which a cultural system successfully reproduces and even consolidates itself by inscribing conflict into its dominant practices and, secondly, the ways in which a conflict constitutes a symbolic encounter that threatens deeply to affect, even to transform, the meanings that make up the fabric of any culture. These phenomena become most apparent in the immediate and dazed aftermath of a conflict, when a community is given a moment to "pick up the pieces". In the process of trying to rebuild and repair a riven community, of attempting to understand "what happened", and who are the subjects that can possibly answer this question, the tensions between cultural continuity and discontinuity make themselves felt. Yet, the aftermath of conflicts as events capable of lacerating the texture of social and cultural containment, made by all those rules, frames and shared norms, which allow people to live together, may last for a very long time. Their effects may survive buried deep in the memories of both victims and perpetrators or, on the contrary, lie exposed in museums, re-enacted through forms of commemorations supported by diverse, and often competing, politics of memory.

Hence, conflicts – their regulation, their repression, and, particularly, their representation in the "post" conflict phase – constitute privileged loci for cultural analysis, whether the focus is on how conflicts challenge and rearrange pre-existing systems of cultural control, or on their modes of historicization, linked closely to unifying discourses of national or ethnic identity. As the editors of a recent series published by Springer and dedicated to "Culture and Conflict" reiterate on their website:

> Culture and conflict unavoidably go together. The very idea of culture is marked by the notion of difference and creative, i.e. conflictual, interaction that inevitably support the key themes of the study of culture such as identity and diversity, memory and trauma, the translation of cultures and globalization, dislocation and emplace-ment, mediation and exclusion. How the representation of conflict

device to another, from one platform to another, as from official TV News to Instagram. Yet, scenarios of war and of violence are not only re-mediated, but also pre-mediated, with stories, illustrations, data and images that tell us what has happened and what we might expect to happen, paradoxically projecting an already consumed "future". See Grusin (2010).

works, how it relates to the past and projects the present and how it frames scholarship within the humanities.[4]

In order further to expand this first working definition of post-conflict cultures, I now take a side turn to look at how the term "post-conflict" has firstly been discussed outside the realm of cultural and semiotic practices, only to come back to their relevance for both the understanding of conflicts *tout court*, and for any attempt to solve them and "move forward".

Post-conflict scenarios; post-conflict situations
Although the essays collected in this Reader do not deal strictly with policies and institutional strategies envisaged to foster peace in post-conflict scenarios, I argue that to explore how conflict resolution studies and international relations came to define their main objects and categories, is a way to think of how the category of post-conflict cultures may represent an heuristic perspective in the contemporary apprehension of the experience of our traumatic historical time.

Until the beginning of this century, that is still up until the aftermath of 9/11, both as a cultural trauma and a milestone in any academic debate on the nature of conflicts and wars, post-conflict scenarios, situations or environments – with no clear distinctions made between these definitions of time-space relations – were treated as a recognizable time period. These labels, in other words, have been used to point to a supposedly already existing "context" within which different mandatory steps had to be implemented, all of them adding up to the final resolution and reparation of the (previous) scenarios of violence. Each step was considered as part of "multiple transition processes [...] including the transition from war to peace [...] often accompanied by democratisation, decentralisation, and market liberalisation" (Brown, Langer and Stewart 2008, 2). In this thinking, there existed already defined phases of transformation during which war-torn societies would turn into "stable and more prosperous ones"; yet, nevertheless "susceptible to contradictory pressures and concomitant risks of a relapse into violence" (2-3; see also Reychler and Langer 2006, 1-2). Post-conflict scenarios referred to different stages of

---

[4] The quotation is taken from the website dedicated to the *Culture and Conflict* series at **https://www.degruyter.com/dg/viewseries/serial$002f1824 80**. The series started in 2012 and is edited by Isabel Capeloa Gil, Caterina Nesci and Paulo de Medeiros.

development during which countries that had been at war had to develop "policies intended to bring about reconstruction, promote sustainable recovery and to reduce the likelihood of conflict recurrence" (3). Yet, even within these rather deterministic positions, there emerged the doubt that a "post-conflict" situation is not "as easy to define as it sounds" (4).

It is, indeed, extremely difficult, first of all because in the last fifty years the very forms and practices of war have dramatically changed. "Big international wars" have been substituted by new wars that do not end with a formal surrender, or a negotiated cessation of hostilities, and/or peace talks, followed by a peace treaty that would mark possible "ends" to conflicts. Conflicts nowadays are intra-state or transnational (as it has been with the war on terror or the one against ISIS), and "hostilities do not normally end abruptly, after which there is complete peace. There may be an agreed 'peace' but fighting often continues at a low level or sporadically, and frequently resumes after a short period" (4).

From wars characterized as a territory to be conquered or defended, and from contenders defined and recognizable, today we most of all witness, as media consumers, de-territorialized wars in which the terrain of conflict is everywhere: they are "diffused" wars with an uncertain beginning, and for which it is impossible to indicate a certain end, because the final moment is situated in an indeterminate future.[5] The very possibility of picking one or the other condition to define the beginning and end of a conflict, and so much more of a post-conflict phase, is being substituted by "a more productive approach to conceptualizing the post-conflict scenario", now treated as a "process that involves the achievement of a range of peace milestones and all the steps that are necessary for an economic stabilization" (5).

Taking a process-oriented approach means that "post-conflict" countries should be seen as lying along a transition continuum (in which they sometimes move backwards), rather than placed in more or less arbitrary boxes, of being "in conflict" or "at peace". Yet, a process-oriented approach should, nevertheless, "select a time period for the end of 'post-conflict' categorisation to avoid endless *pathologising of such countries*" (7), this period being one of ten years.

Here we are quoting studies that were aimed at guiding effective

---

[5] I am referring here to the debate on "new wars", not always intersecting the one on post-conflict scenarios, within which Mary Kaldor's work is still a point of reference: see Kaldor (2012) and Montanari in this volume.

policies and stake-holders, and within a thinking for which post-conflict phases had to be calculable and have recognizable time-periods; something that, once we look at the cultural contexts in which the democratization and the economic stabilization have to take place (now, then, and tomorrow), is almost impossible to establish. Without these contexts, without taking into consideration the different temporalities at stake, depending on the different subjectivities at play, all those "designated steps", albeit located in a continuum – which they should punctuate – run the risk of being only abstract milestones listed in many handbooks honestly envisaging the ways optimal peace-building and the best path to reconciliation can be found.

Far from the intention of pathologizing post-conflict countries, a post-conflict culture stance chooses, instead, to look at a much longer and less linear period, since the re-construction and the re-interpretation of "what happened" in order to move forward, is more often than not exploited by different politics of national or transnational memory, responding to the urgencies of different political, social and cultural presents.

Moreover, and again, far from denying the importance of scientific and intellectual struggle aimed at finding best practices to foster peace and reconciliation, nowadays – in a post-media phase of new wars – one can wonder if it is really possible to divide the perception and meaning of a conflict and a post-conflict environment, from the ways conflict resolution and practices of reconciliation, such as truth commissions, amnesty, or pardoning, are pursued. With the latter, we enter the terrain of transitional and restorative justice, the aim of which is to address wrongdoings of repressive predecessor regimes, "in order to combat denial and promote justice, accountability and transparency through strengthening the rule of law" (Mueller-Hirth, Rios Oyola 2018, 2; see also Teitel 2003). However, trials, amnesty, pardons and apologies are all rituals and cultural practices entailing a set of assumptions about winners and losers, power dynamics, justice, identity and, again, the relationship between the past and the future.

Tempos and temporalities

A cultural stance on post-conflict scenarios proposes that all the actions needed to "solve" conflicts are also actions represented and comm-unicated; and that all represented and communicated actions are also, in themselves, forms of action; and that the subjects involved are not mere actors of different institutions, with different goals and "missions", but subjects with complex and ambiguous identities, and different conceptions of both the past and the expected future. Representations, as in all practices of witnessing that attempt to work through traumatic memories – now filtered and translated through the ever changing cultural and mediascape – intervene in the very meaning of conflict and post-conflict situations, in the postmemories they trigger and in the ways they are transmitted. How each culture and its media works through its conflicts comprises a set of complex and intertwined practices whose effects and affects have been deeply transformed by the development of ubiquitous media technologies and global risk (Frosh and Pinchevski 2014), influencing not simply how the media work, but the very construction of any social bonds by the emergence of different agents, that is by networks tying together people, objects, representations. In an era defined by media witnessing, post-conflict cultures are the result of a new configuration of mediation, representation and experience, stemming from "the dynamic realignment of lines of influence and connection between technologies, persons, texts and social forms" (Frosh and Pinchevski 2014, 595; see also Boudana, Cohen and Frosh 2017).

This scenario brought about deep changes in our relation to historical significance and to our experience of time that still need to be explored further. These changes have been acknowledged also within the literature on conflict resolution and international relations briefly described above, in which we now find a growing trend of studies that admit a more nuanced and less linear gaze on post-conflict scenarios and its competing, official and unofficial narratives. In these works we encounter a new awareness of all the factors at play in a post-conflict society, as well as in the representation and communication of its collective suffering, that goes beyond the focus on economic stabilization and national reconciliation and reparation politics.

As Huyse (2003) concedes, emotions caused by and arising from traumatic experience, at both individual and collective levels, are one of the most important factors to be taken into account in post-conflict phases, as they constitute pervasive psychological, social and cultural obstacles to conflict resolution and reconciliation. These emotions, such as fear, humiliation, mistrust, anger and lack of empathy for the former enemy, become part of what Jeffrey Alexander (2003; see also Eyerman *et al.* 2016), from a cultural and semiotic perspective, calls the symbolic representation of social suffering. This is a cultural process able to channel "powerful human emotions", and, depending on the political and social forces at stake, also one able to generate feelings of victimization, to construct fixed stereotypes of "the other", or to fuel the desire for revenge in victims. Moreover, Huyse adds, "these feelings characterize people and communities in which the other is demonized, where historical narratives are such that no mutual acceptance of national or other identities seems possible" (Huyse 2003, 15).

> The mainstream discourse of peace-building and post-conflict reconstruction has thus opened up to the necessity of dealing with these emotions, "by addressing the trauma and legitimizing it, creating an emotionally safe environment in which to express it, and moving on to a stage in which lessons learned in dealing with the trauma are validated and transformed in actual healing practices". (12)

Working through one's recent traumatic past – or traumatic present – is now a recognized precondition for "fostering security and enabling durable peace processes":

> Without an in-depth understanding of what has happened, comparison and reciprocal sharing of different memories of the past by all parties involved, a virtuous cycle of forgiving and reconciliation cannot be ensured. (13)

However, and again, to work through one's traumatic past, and to understand what really happened, is not such a straightforward process as the quotation above seems to suggest. To interrogate a politics of memory, its militarization (or de-militarization), is a complex operation, starting from the fact that it triggers unforeseeable processes. To recognize and, thus, to re-build a past, should in fact imply abandoning oneself to the "other" (the distant "You") in the present, to yield to its difference, having welcomed and understood it. Yet this possibility remains more of a project than a practice. It happens, for example, that individual memories refer to a collective memory that does not find any reconciliation in the cultural and historical remembering of a nation. More generally speaking, it happens, as Tzvetan Todorov suggested, that "in the modern world the 'cult' of memory does not always serve good causes, and we should not be too bewildered by that" (1995, 43). The problem is that of the creation of a public discourse, of the elaboration of that which is normally defined as the "official version" of the "facts": "what we blame the perpetrators for is not that they select only specific elements of the past, but that they claim the right to control the choice of the elements to be retained" (43).

As Robin Wagner Pacifici and Meredith Hall (2012, 189) also argue, discussing possible strategies of resolution of social conflict:

> The experience of a brutal past makes the search for peaceful coexistence a delicate and intricate operation. Reconciliation is not an isolated act, but a constant readiness to leave the tyranny of violence and fear behind. It is not an event but a process, and as such usually a difficult, long and unpredictable one, involving various steps and stages. Each move demands changes in attitudes (e.g., tolerance instead of revenge), in conduct (e.g., joint commemoration of all the dead instead of separate, partisan memorials) and in the institutional environment (e.g., integrating the war veterans of both sides into one national army instead of keeping ex-combatants in quasi-private militias).

Reconciliation is therefore more of a desideratum for periods of post-conflict; a set of performative and ritual gestures mapping a symbolic landscape of transition, always at risk of being shadowed by a politics of regret (Olick 2007). Or, better, as again Wagner Pacifici and Heller state: "reconciliation requires representational, demonstrative and performative features in its transactions" (2012, 190). Here we find again a post-conflict cultures perspective, once "a more robust concept of reconciliation is advanced by scholars emphasizing the roles of symbols, narratives, dramas, rituals, art, and cultural performance in temporally extended resolutions of social conflicts" (2012, 90).

The temporalities – the different transitions and transactions – of "extended" resolution of conflicts are indeed what "was lacking as a systematic perspective in the fields of transitional justice and peacebuilding". Drawing from Mueller-Hirth's (2017) essay on temporalities of victimhood, Nastasha Mueller-Hirth and Sandra Rios Oyola explore how time and temporality are constructed and used by people and institutions, in order to develop a deeper understanding of the role time plays in overcoming violent pasts and, "theoretically, to contribute time-sensitive perspectives to the fields of transitional justice and peacebuilding" (2018, 2). A time-sensitive perspective opens up the investigation to the many ways time and temporal relations are lived and experienced in cyclical and circular manners, as "clusters of temporal features" (Adam 2004), including various signifying practices that underline the ways we express and recount what happened, what happens, and what might happen in the future: "time frames, tempo, timing, sequence and patterns, whose relationships and relative importance are dynamic and contextually dependent" (Mueller-Hirth and Rios Oyola 2018, 3). The paradigm of transitional justice as a "Janus-faced" enterprise that contributes towards accountability measures that deal with the past, as well as with mechanisms that seek to assert stable futures, here intertwine the issue of traumatic memories, their recollections and transmissions. The backward-looking and forward-looking, the retrospective and prospective stances that characterize law (Teitel 1997, 2014), is at the core, also, of any study on post-conflict culture.

This renewed paradigm, affecting both the terms "transitional" and "post-conflict", thus abandons its clear temporal referents, its implicit teleological temporality, the promise of transformation built upon a notion of linear progress, whereby one can easily "leave the past behind" and "move toward democracy", since "transition" implies an assured "change in a liberalizing direction" (Teitel 2000, 13). Mueller-Hirth and Rios Oyola (2018, 3-4) further elaborate along the very lines we have discussed above:

> Moreover, this rhetoric requires a clear setting of boundaries between past and present, as well as future. Amid the chaos of lengthy conflicts, or conflicts that have risen out of chronic deprivation and inequality, setting such boundaries for the past or for the beginning of a conflict in the official discourse is a political act in itself. Indeed, we might argue that, by designating a country a "post-conflict society", violence is relegated to the past and treated as a temporary episode rather than as an ongoing structural concern.

Violence and suffering are not necessarily temporary ruptures, but wounds in the social fabric characterized by tensions, clashes, and negotiations between different temporalities in the context of transitional justice, and with respect to both the victims' and perpetrators' experiences of lived time. This new perspective brings strategies of reconciliation to address several new challenges, including some that we find discussed and analyzed in this Reader, such as "how collective memorialisation becomes a vehicle to transmit memories of the past through the lenses of the present" (Mueller-Hirth and Rios Oyola 2018, 4).

The relevance of disrupting the linear sequence of any post-conflict transition is indeed what trauma studies have argued since their development and up to their current "thinking trauma future". Since trauma has been understood as an unclaimed experience, many authors have discussed how trauma might have an impact on our experience of time, temporality and its structure as *afterwardsness* (Freud's idea of *Nachtraghkeit*). *Reading* trauma, or what one can label as a possible representation of it that tries to express a structure for a not-any-longer unclaimed experience,[6] means looking at the coming together of different times, as the past reappears in the present, and it moves towards the future. In re-thinking its own temporality, therefore, trauma studies sees the category of trauma as not pointing only to the disruption of how we experience time but also of how we write about it, represent it: these are the complexities of *afterwardsness* (Eaglestone 2014) weaving into the structure of experience within which the trauma is made manifest: questions of narrative and time woven into ethical questions. In the recent debate animating this field, we do find many of the questions pertaining to the study of post-conflict cultures: how does a state colonize a disruptive temporality into sovereign chronologies (it happened after 9/11 in the USA, but not only there); or how is the changing bio-political horizon, in which trauma is both produced and policed, affecting its very experience? And how the already mentioned technological transformations of subjectivity and its many identities (social media) have changed or will change the idea of trauma? What is the relationship between trauma and other disruptive social forces?

However, while contemplating the cultural and historical specificity of the concepts of trauma and post-conflict-cultures, they both ought to trouble the historicist gesture of much contemporary criticism as well as its concomitant notions of history and culture. In this respect, any studies of a post-conflict culture follow "the future" of trauma theories as invoked

---

[6] Trauma as an "unclaimed experience", that is an event that will be never fully processed and comprehended by an affected subject, is a definition proposed by Cathy Caruth in a work that has become one of the main references of trauma studies. See Caruth (1996).

by Michael Rothberg (2014; see also Rothberg 2009), whereby trauma is something involving the dislocation of subjects, histories and cultures. And even though there could be different and multiple forms of dislocation, there is a continuity, and the task of "theory" is to find it, to look for connections, overlaps and similitude across the cultural and historical contexts under scrutiny; connections and similitude that have to take into consideration the nowadays climate of *History* whereby there are forms of violence involving different scales of temporality and modes of subjectivity that are there for us to address.

We have, then, to re-think and re-write how we connect events of extreme violence, the structure of subjective and collective experience, and discursive and aesthetic forms. This is a challenge that threatens, moreover, to undermine the assumption of secure and privileged subject-positions by, for example, trying to answer yet another question: what are the risks of over-generalizing trauma and the disruption of a post-conflict phase, when this move could lead to a strengthening of *immunitary* tendencies that perpetuate, rather than diminish, the perception of a collective traumatized post-conflict culture, encouraging a politics of revenge and retaliation? Also, they force us to face new challenges yet to be fully explored, such as how technological acceleration, along with the acceleration of social change and the acceleration of the pace of life of a technologically-driven neo-liberalism, involve a very different temporal logic than the one underlying victim support and reparations policies, which are often aimed at redressing the legacies of many years of violence and discrimination.

> Social acceleration has characterized the development of modernity, although the emergence of a technologically driven neoliberalism and the increasing networking of societies has more recently led to increasing time scarcity and the "shrinking of the present". (Mueller-Hirth and Rios Oyola 2018, 10)[7]

Post-conflict cultures now and then

The developments of the debate on post-conflict scenarios, along with the many layers intervening in the definition of post-conflict cultures, the

---

[7] See also Rosa (2003), and Rosa and Scheuerman (2009).

transformations of contemporary cultures, of conflicts and their possible forms of resolution, all actually strengthen our point of departure, that is how, by introducing the term "culture" into the study of post-conflict situations, the very construction of history and its temporalities is put into question. Through this questioning, Colin Wright and I have argued, a different kind of cultural mapping could emerge, accounting for the ways forms of power both regulate and repress conflicts; what strategies are used to manage fears and pursue security; and what dynamics of memory may be deemed to operate in the wake of a conflict. The map we drew in the first volume of this series is now rendered even more complex by the technological-social acceleration evoked above, and by the recent political changes in local, national and global modes of sovereignty and governmentality; by the ever increasing apparent relevance of traditions and memories, and their simultaneous forgetting; by the deep transformation undergone in the very norms and normativity that used to define a community, and whose lacerations defined a post-conflict scenario. Running the risk of sounding too cynical, one could wonder: what of Truth Commissions in the era of post-truth and fake news?

Moreover, what is worth investigating further is one of the paradoxes that underlines all reflection on conflict and its cultural filtering: that it belongs to a given culture and a given period, but it is simultaneously exportable, able to inform analyses that can also be used in other contexts. Without thinking of a fixed model of war or post-war, of an ontology, but rather of possible forms that migrate through different cultural manifest-ations, how can we still detect the forms of post-conflict?

For representation of conflicts and their testimonies have contributed to the re-conceptualization of the very category of the event (of collective violence and suffering), as both singular and repeatable. Drawing from Jacques Derrida's (1988) insight about the twofold nature of witnessing, that is the singularity of the event is not external or prior to its repetition, but rather its singularity emerges from its repeatability, what other approaches might yield greater insight today, and at the same time do justice to the unreal hiatus that a society occupies in the wake of conflict, like the deafening silence which follows the detonation of a bomb?

Such questioning has been the aspiration of all contributors selected for the present Reader. Their re-engagement with the silences and violence residing in the notion of the "post-conflict" exposes further the contradictions always latent, and often lying, within the term as within the spheres of former and on-going confrontation and struggle. The subsequent-to or consequent-upon entailed in the "post-" can be understood only in and by what is veiled by the replays, the deferrals and the slippages of the conflict and its still combative or would-be conciliatory discourses. As Bernard McGuirk and Constance Goh (2007, 3) predicted in their introduction to *Happiness and Post-conflict*, "the posting of the script will ever gain further momentum in and because of the conflicted space and the conflictual time, whether in aggression, retaliation or reconciliation, in which the embattled subject performs".

The battles many of the authors have engaged with are discourses and representations of conflicts to be thought of as events, as spaces in which strategic thinking is inscribed and produced, and meaning communicated and negotiated. The texts or the discursive regimes they have analyzed are to be thought of as lenses, as a cultural retina, whereby conflict as an object of study becomes a cultural meta-system, a macro-text, which interprets and translates other texts of a culture.

In the object(s) the authors of this Reader are isolating and constructing we find not only history and law reworked by contemporary culture, but also the problem of empathy and belonging of memory, the possibility of establishing, in the visual as well as in writing, a "contract of listening", and not only one of reading or watching, which emerges through the attempt to construct literary, visual, syncretic languages capable of staging and also performing inter-subjective bonds, processes of *transduction* between the pre-individual, the individual and the collective.

There are no definitive answers as to how these processes really work, or could work or might work, in the representation of conflicts made by different kinds of witness and in our writings. Probably, what we have to deal with, or look for, in the limited theorizing space of academe, is a "nervous writing, that is of utterance embracing its status as stutterance [...] In seeking comfort in the process of recovering trauma for culture", we "need to ride our consolations between two echoes [...] The poiesis of culture itself is a narcotic, and as such it summons us to respond to Emily Dickinson's charge that 'Narcotics cannot still the tooth/That nibbles at the soul'" (Yaeger 2002, 42-49).

By drawing on numerous post-conflict situations over a wide temporal and spatial range, and by providing a cross-cultural, international and/or transcontinental perspective, the studies collected here go to great lengths to tease out the conditions and effects of post-conflict cultures and writings. They also travel elsewhere, both geographically and geo-culturally, to go beyond a mono-cultural orientation, to move to another affect-world, in order better to apprehend its impact, and to test its future-tense.

The Essays in this Reader

With the exception of the essays by Federico Montanari and Daniel Filmus, both of which have been updated for this Reader, the present essays have been published in volumes of the series Studies in Post-conflict Cultures, begun in 2006.[8] They deal with different case studies belonging to the fields of media, law, historiography, literature, art, photography, theatre, etc.; and they address the predicaments of quite diverse post-conflict cultures, from that of Portugal and Angola after the fall of the Empire, to Chile and Argentina post-dictatorship; from the role of gender and identity, to that of education and human rights organizations. Given the broad spectrum of the objects they investigate, and the multidisciplinary perspective they effectively put to work, to divide them into neat and well-defined sections based on a category, a genre, a topic, or geographies has proved to be a difficult task. Hence, albeit grouped in six sections (Media and Law, Histories, Visual and Performance Cultures, Genres of Testimonies/ Genres of Reconstruction, Portugal and its lost Empire, Post-dictatorship times and archives in Argentina and Chile), their sequencing mainly reflects the order in which they have been published, which, in itself, mirrors the research interests developed over the years by the once Centre for the Study of Post-Conflict Cultures, now the International Consortium for the Study of Post-Conflict Societies.

Media and Law

In his challenging and informed new essay, "The New Narrative Form of Post-conflicts: New Wars as World-Wide War", Federico Montanari discusses one of the main topics of the study of post-conflict cultures, namely how practices of war are nowadays strictly linked to their representation and, in particular, to their narrative forms and formats.

---

[8] All of the essays have been editorially revised, with minor corrections as necessary, and in particular to render their style, format and bibliographical conventions consistent throughout this volume. They have also been re-indexed, so that the present index is now considerably more expansive than those in the several original volumes in which they appeared.

Montanari's work thus traces the changes and transformations that occurred in the ways in which wars have been defined, conceived, imagined and "visualized" during the last two decades, from Kosovo's and the former Yugoslavia's wars, to the wars of expedition and retaliation, conducted by the US and its allies, to the transformations brought by the advent of ISIS and terrorist attacks in Europe. As the essay meditates on conflict in relation to images and the discursive forms that circulate within the media, old and new, social as well as mainstream, it also explores a socio-semiotics methodology and a model of analysis that looks at systems of subjectivization, forms of enunciation and styles of discourse that are currently modifying our very perception of war. These wars, Montanari argues, are not just "new": their current form is that of a continuous "post-war".

Colin Wright's essay analyzes the encoding of 9/11 by the American media in the immediate aftermath of the attack, showing how it was strongly related to a logic of sovereignty at work within American national identity. By arguing that 9/11 made visible a mutual complicity between media representations and interventionist military policy, the author looks at how this event in its immediate aftermath was represented with images and metaphors of previous conflicts encoding, framing, and indeed translating a contemporary conflict or crisis into recognizable paradigms, that is with meanings and forms belonging to a shared cultural memory (on this, see Zelizer 2011). The essay thus argues that, by reacting to an event that derived its violence also from its forcible insertion into a cultural and technological mediascape, informed by a sense of a global society of the spectacle, it is still ultimately regimes of sovereignty that regulate the semiotic mobilization of affect, and put that affect into the service of pre-existing political agendas. The media reaction to 9/11 was a consolidation of the US-imagined community, an *internal* nation-building which increasingly took the form of a militarization of social life that rejected terrorism as a radicalized difference/other, a different difference, which justified both this militarization, and the logic of the permanent exception which suspended the juridical sovereignty of both local and international entities, thereby paving the way for the profusion of global conflicts we are witnessing today.

This logic of exception is further explored, from a legal point of view, in David Fraser's essay that, starting from the acknowledgement of the rhetorical slippage which, after 9/11, turned a discourse of crime and criminality to one of war, thus establishing the primacy of "war talk", explores what the author defines as the possibility of another possibility, "one which takes into account the traditional dichotomy of war versus crime as the way in which the legal nature of the war on terror can be understood by asserting the unity of the two". This possibility, that is a jurisprudence of the "state of exception", attempts to problematize traditional dichotomous notions such as crime *vs* war, or legal *vs* illegal, by considering "a paradoxical third way", whereby "law appears to destroy itself in order to save itself". The war on terror allowed the sovereign power to use its legal powers in order to define an outlaw space populated by individuals and groups who by the force of law have been removed from the effective force of law. Yet, as Fraser demonstrates, this is a mechanism that did not start with post-9/11 war talk, and whose outcomes were, and still are, manifold, from the legally sanctioned torture and killing by the French in Algeria (then a colony of France), to the conflicts in the former Yugoslavia to, I shall add, the various measures against asylum seekers and refugees in nowadays populist-driven Western countries. In all these examples we find the dual creation of a subject Other, the *homo sacer*, to whom the norms of exception apply, and who has no sovereign protection as a citizen; and a delimited territory in which the *homo sacer* is enclosed and excluded. This is how a body politic immunizes itself, by carrying away, or rejecting, unwanted subjects to places where they can be properly dealt with, "all under the watchful eye of the sovereign power of the law".

Histories

Jeremy Lawrance's scrupulously detailed and historically informed essay examines the rhetoric of the most powerful work of the sixteenth century missionary Bartolomé de Las Casas, *A Brief Relation of the Destruction of the Indies*, a *testimonio* that set out to document a genocide and which, in its subsequent translations and commentary by Protestant polemicists, furnished with illustrations, was used and abused to produce the "Black Legend", that is, the idea that the Spanish Empire was uniquely cruel and rapacious, based on an iconography which remained embedded in the popular imaginary. By reading Las Casas' text as a very peculiar testimony, Lawrance explores and articulates many of the themes which are central to all reflections on the writing of memory and trauma: how may a trauma afflict not only the losers but also the victors of conflict; how acts of violence can be reported in a style that is not objective but affective, that is, a language of feeling and not facts. In the case of *Brief Relation* cumulative strategies of hyperbole depicting the harrowing violence the Indians had to suffer, result in a "tragic pathology of despair" that brought Las Casas not to lie, but to testify to the truth as he "saw" it, in an *ex-post* attempt to rationalize traumatic experience and guilt. Lawrance's essay demonstrates how such a testimony, in dealing with the problem of its truth and authenticity, was based on writing which appealed to the senses, on a rhetoric which showed a link to the body as the only guarantee of that which is lost in language; on emotions that brought into play subjective techniques of representation. Moreover, it is an essay that, in showing how the progressive misrepresentation of *Brief Relation* made the Black Legend shift from a religious-political hostility to ethnic demonization, brings evidence to the crucial role images maintain in the construction of a shared memory. It is the images, whose power rested on an appeal to the obscene alliance of sadism, horror and lust, and not the verbal text, which accounted for Las Casas' impact, arousing, but not engaging, the audience of the early modern time, and of the centuries to come.

Nicholas Hewitt's "Le Poids des mots, le choc des photos: Conflict and the News Magazines *Picture Post* and *Paris Match*" discusses insightfully the visual impact of war photography. Hewitt relates conflict and news coverage in magazines by looking at the historical development of war and photography. According to Hewitt, *Paris Match* was able to call upon unprecedented resources, both from its own photographers and journalists and from news agencies. Also, in both wars (the Six Day War and the Vietnam War), "the magazine was apparently able to break away from some of the controls of embedded journalism which had restricted the operations of *Picture Post* in World War II and which was to become such an issue in the first, but especially the second, Gulf War". He concludes by exploring the complexity inherent in the relationship between the viewer and the object. On the one hand, the pictures are meant to jolt and discomfort the viewer and, on the other, in order to maintain a strong readership, there must be photographs to reassure the readers that the horrors of war visually encountered are external to the happy homes they inhabit, "a complicated menu of concern and happiness which contributed a winning formula".

Patrizia Violi's "Remembering the Future: the Construction of Gendered Identity in the Balkans" is a piercing and semiotic-orientated insight into and analysis of the construction of gendered identity based on the diversities discovered in what was formerly known as the Balkans. Violi's stance in terms of identity construction relates to the multiple temporalities which underscore the notion of "memory", as she argues that the past gains significance only in view of the present and, especially, the future. Her study, conducted in conjunction with the Women's Centre of Bologna, includes an archive of thirty-four life stories of Kosovo women of varied origins: Albanian, Serbian and Roma, collected from 1999 to 2000 in Kosovo and Italy. Tying what she refers to as gender competence to genre construction, the autobiographical details can be read as a form of preservation and transmission of the specific culture to which the individuals belong, an elaboration of the post-conflict cultures' concern with identity, belonging and possible cultural reconstructions. What is particularly noteworthy in Violi's analysis of the shifting positions in the post-conflict narratives is her emphasis on gendered singularity, along with the potentiality of a particular textual genre, i.e. the autobiographical life-story interview pertaining to the practices of oral history that can voice what is generally hidden in official histories, especially everyday knowledge and experiences forgotten by "official" histories of international relations, wars and treaties.

Macdonald Daly's "The Dialectic of Conflict and Culture: Leon Trotsky and Less Fortunate Statesmen" is a meditation on histories and on Trotsky as a proponent of post-conflict culture proper, since he saw that the culture which might be made possible by the cessation of the conflicts he participated in would be the ultimate triumph over those conflicts. The essay takes further the fundamental thesis that the strict demarcation between what are apparently oppositional elements is only a matter of convenience for the parties in power and this postulate is made obvious. In Daly's sagacious reading, Leon Trotsky, is "the seeming combination of man of action with man of aesthetic inclination and intellectual ability", whose *Literature and Revolution* is a figurative correspondence which can be read against the lack of such a phenomenon in British parliamentary history. With a critical analysis of the two histories, that of Russia during the October and February Revolutions and that of contemporary Britain, Daly effectively demonstrates that "the twin foci" of culture as (post)conflict(ed) in Trotsky's Russia and the *savoir faire* of a capitalist economy operating in and through culture in modern Britain are effectively flipsides of the same coin.

The fundamental ambivalence contained in the very idea of becoming animal, within the mimetic-identification as mortification or abasement – a gesture that may stands as a mark of power but also as a way to escape it – lies at the centre of Andrea Borsari's dense and challenging philosophical meditation on power and its effects, which the author develops through a Benjaminian reading of Elias Canetti's discussion of the nexus of power and metamorphosis in Franz Kafka. Here we move away from testimony as a genre in order to explore post-conflict cultures through the lenses of an anthropology of power pointing to "the dreadful things that people do to one another" (Canetti) as elaborated in Kakfa's writings as testimony of the fulfilment and dissolution of a modernity relentlessly facing the humiliation that human beings inflict upon each other. The becoming small, an insect, a mole, a dog – all images to which Kafka keeps returning – does recall not only the submissiveness of those who are sacrificed, of the victims, but also a deeper and more general confrontation with power and the ambiguities of abjection as that movement through which primitive societies have marked out the area of their culture as distinct from the world of animalism. And if, as Walter Benjamin noted, being animal for Kafka meant to have renounced being man, "for some sort of shame", the creatural dimension stands as a space for pensive reflection: a space from which to confront and read the gesture which haunts many of Kafka's stories, that "of the man who bows his head far down his chest"; that of the victim who is an accomplice of his executioner, as in *The Metamorphosis*, but also that of the subject who has destroyed himself in order to overthrow the will of the machine of power, as in *The Trial*.

Evgeny Dobrenko's essay title, "'Entertaining History': Socialist Realism in Search of the 'Historical Past'" already introduces us to the author's exploration of Stalinist historical consciousness, and the way Soviet history became an actual weapon of political action and propaganda. What was then presented by "official" historian as Marxist history had to be created in a lively and entertaining form, recuperating its narrative roots and the centrality of a fictionalized depiction of historical figures. The very writing of history became a deeply political dispute that forced historians to follow the principle of continuous historical synthesis, whereby "dialectical equivalence meant that Soviet ideological doctrine could combine seemingly opposing positions". Dobrenko thus describes how Soviet post-conflict culture deeply transformed its revolutionary background, allowing endless mutations in the succession of "thaws and frost", with the constant feeding of an historical consciousness founded on both legacy and synthesis. The result was a new reading of the past that Dobrenko describes as a "kind of historical schizophrenia", whereby liberation movements could become bourgeois nationalism, and proletarian internationalism turned into rootless cosmopolitanism, ultimately reducing the actors on the stage of Soviet history to three main characters: The Ruler, Historical Law, and the Masses.

Visual and Performance Cultures

Parvati Nair's essay interrogates one of the possible practices of figuring a specific trauma, that of the Rwandan genocide, by looking at the artwork *The Eyes of Gutete Emerita*, in which the Chilean (now US-based) photographer and installation artist Alfredo Jaar captures the gaze of one Tutsi survivor – a victim who has lost her entire family during that slaughter. Nair analyzes this particular photograph in the context of Jaar's artwork by looking at the ways in which, by focusing on the Rwandan context as a site of silence or forgetting, Jaar's work mobilizes politicized responses. Meditating on how the postmemory of the Holocaust continues to command academic focus, and on how, therefore, we should move beyond the geo-political contours of the West, Nair illustrates Jaar's call for an ethics of vision, whereby that pre-discursive moment of encounter with alterity via still photography becomes the ground on which to build collective remembering amongst those who did not live through or witness trauma. In so doing, Nair illustrates that "the photograph becomes the frame within which historical narratives can germinate and collective oblivion can be countered". Moreover, in trying to capture how art installations might mitigate the losses of a conflict as great as that of Rwanda, the author discusses how trauma-related art is best understood as transactive rather than communicative, which implies an idea of aesthetics as a field that negotiates the sentient with the logical or rational. The historical and political value of an artwork thus derives from the way in which affective responses can be translated into conceptual engagement. In other words, artwork like Jaar's does not relay the traumatic experience, but it does convey a mini-shock of trauma generated by the temporal collision between the eye (and the I) of the one who has suffered, the work of testimony conveyed by the gaze inscribed in the image and through it, and how both eyes (those of the victim and that of the camera) relate to our bodies, our minds.

If there are occasions when pictures may indeed be worth more than a thousand narrated words, conflict is certainly one such situation. Nevertheless, one would be naïve to view photographs and the situation to which they attest as an immediate representation of reality. Cristina Demaria unfurls the "testimonial vocation" of photo-reportage by looking at the conditions of production and circulation of photographs created by and for (as well as reproduced in) international humanitarian NGOs' websites. In her critical engagement with discussions surrounding the testimonial and documental character of this photographic sub-genre, Demaria sets out to investigate the "peculiar documental nature" of photographs of women and children available on websites, ranging from Amnesty International and Human Rights Watch to UNICEF and Médecins Sans Frontières. By departing from Michael Rothberg's notion of "traumatic realism" in dealing with the obscene, Demaria ultimately reflects on the role of photographs not only in "bearing witness" but also in providing an "act of testimony". In her analysis, Demaria addresses both the local context of the "production" of photographs and the global contexts of their "reproduction", seeking to understand how traumatized victims are represented and whether such victims are categorized or framed into recurrent topoi; how such photos may bear witness to the suffering of victims and how they may affect those who view them.

María José Contreras Lorenzini explores the theme of the staged collapsing of the boundaries between art and life. She examines a well-known art/memory project that was developed to commemorate the fortieth anniversary of the Chilean coup. Claudia Di Girólamo and Rodrigo Pérez's *Aquí están* begins with a reading of testimonies provided by relatives of *desaparecidos*, moves to children's drawings of the missing, and ends with public readings of testimonies by well-known actors. On the one hand, *Aquí están* naïvely presents the testimonies as if they were the direct recounting of reality, and thereby dissimulates the mediations that characterize each and every collective construction of memory (in this case, the work of adult relatives, research assistants, famous actors). On the other hand, it precisely draws attention to the proliferation of layers of mediation that are combined in the mobilization of memories. And insofar as children are involved in the process, the performance not only foregrounds the question of how the younger generation understands the dictatorship but also points up the creative process by which the past is filtered not just by multiple mediators from the older generation but by the imagination of the new one, now turned into agents of memory. In so doing, Contreras argues, the project points towards an alternative work of commemoration: not the official museumification of memory (bronze statues, stone plinths), but the creative intimacy of inter-subjective interactions producing a dynamic and multiple collective memory.

Genres of testimonies/genres of reconstruction

Roger Bromley's touching and informed piece explores some of the trajectories of "post-apartheid" South Africa's extensive range of narrative forms that have attempted to create a different political imaginary in the country. By commenting on work such as Mark Behr's *The Smell of Apples*, or the account written by one of the cruellest perpetrators of apartheid violence, Eugene de Kock's *A Long Night's Damage: Working for the Apartheid State* (1998), which he balances with Pumla Gobodo-Madikizela's *A Human Being Died That Night: A South African Woman Confronts the Legacy of Apartheid*, based partly on interviews with de Kock in his maximum security prison cell, Bromley demonstrates how these narratives can be considered as potential cultural resources, as projects of anamnesis, as examples of the writing of a critical memory that have emerged once the Truth and Reconciliation Commission had allowed a "restoration of narrative", the opening up of a discursive field concerned with the possibilities and impossibilities of reconciliation. By working against structures of forgetfulness and deniability, and by engaging with forms and genres which extend, de-familiarize and subvert existing paradigms, Bromley discusses how such narratives act as a framework and a methodology by which South African society recalls the past and places it in a dynamic and formative relationship to the interpretation of the present, resulting in explorations of the relationship between power, discourse and the symbolic. In particular, these are narratives which interrogate what Antjie Krog has called the "second narrative" of apartheid, that is how much it was not only white, but also male, how much it concerned a pathological masculinity which these texts reveal and also, as in the case of Gobodo-Madikizela, aims at questioning the possibility of forgiving not only as a personal, but also as an inherently political act, in that it seeks to re-associate the individual with its belonging. Bromley hence manages to open up important examples of testimonial accounts he calls "inclusive narratives" which "extend to both the terrorized and the previous agents of terror in new forms of co-existence in the social domain of language and memory", pointing to forgiveness not as forgetting but as a means of "re-entering time and reclaiming space".

Tomás Albaladejo addresses the time and space of post-conflict by looking at a classical paradigmatic post-conflict scenario: post-Civil War Spain. His study considers the longevity of the post-conflict period in Spain, identifying two large spaces, each of them constituted by several stages. Albaladejo articulates the first space, that of oblivion and memory void, with the second space of memory and reconstruction, and analyzes the relation between literary and cinematic texts and the underlying historical and political context in order to address the issues of cultural memory and cultural rhetoric. From the film-makers' and writers' position of enclave, frustrated by lack of political will, the post-conflict situation is expressed by "means of silence and void" only in the first instance. Franco's death in 1975 and the process of Spanish *transición* would allow for a new space to emerge in which authors sought to recreate memory and "defend an active role of memory in the reconstruction of a divided society". This chapter suggests that a third space may be discerned in this very complex post-conflict landscape with the passing of the *Ley de Memoria Histórica* (Law of Historical Memory) in 2007, acknowledging the victims of fascism and an attempt at the "reconstruction of recon-struction".

In "(Post-)Urbicide: Reconstruction and Ideology in Former Yug-oslavia's Cities", Francesco Mazzucchelli approaches, through a "semiotics of reconstruction", instances of reconstruction which involve bricks and mortar and yet are nevertheless interwoven with a host of ideological symbols and narratives. One is reminded that cities are a "knotty fabric" of practices, "objects" and "discourses" ever shifting and renewing meanings. The study combines aspects of spatial and urban semiotics with insights from cultural geography, urban ethnography and architectural theory in the study of the architectonic and urban renewal and restoration projects in the cities of Sarajevo, Mostar, Dubrovnik and Belgrade. The politics of urban reconstruction in areas of post-conflict brings into evidence the fact that space – urban architecture and monuments in particular – is inextricably linked to power, simultaneously as an agent and as a product. Mazzucchelli's comparative perspective demonstrates the persisting tensions and contradictions which are characteristic of post-conflict situations. If reconstruction and reconciliation can be pointed out as more valid and effective processes, one must nevertheless remain vigilant to the solutions (with blatant or hidden agendas, not seldom seeming to appear as a post-ideological and apolitical objectivity) which are put forward and implemented without public consultation and at the service of very specific interests of the ruling power. More than demonstrating an unproblematic perception of space and urban architecture, the cynicism of public leaders demonstrates that, far from a lack of awareness regarding the validity and the potential for a public discussion which would involve the contribution and inclusion of minorities, there remains a utilitarian perspective of public space and architecture in the expression of official narratives constructed at the expense of historical accuracy, cultural merit and values, as well as socio-political demands.

Portugal and its Empire
Through an exploration of the figurations of the Portuguese Empire and its colonial experience, as well as its self-representative narrations, Roberto Vecchi underlines their importance for a reconsideration of the historical structures that articulate its constructions and deconstructions. These figurations depict the "empire as imagination of a centre" both in the relation of the metropolis to Africa or to other colonies, and on the side of the periphery in relation to Europe, producing a duality that holds on to a massive investment in the imaginary and in processes of representation, in the attempt to build the "cultural empire" evoked by Fernando Pessoa in *Mensagem*. Vecchi's reflections invest directly in the links between conflict and post-conflict as a kind of genealogy – more than a dialectic where crises and fractures punctuate the wartime *continuum*, the "Colonial War" being just one of them. The non-sociability of a common and shared memory about that experience is coupled with a lack of a history dealing with the circumstances which have produced it, and an ideological revisionism embedded in the ways the past is remembered. This is why cultural representations of the war in the Portuguese post-revolutionary context of the second half of the nineteen-seventies are essentially discussions about the feasibility of representation itself, with a strong critical and meta-critical charge as aesthetic objects. And the growing revisionist-negationist wave is firmly at the heart of the discourses, as testified by one of the novels discussed by Vecchi, António Lobo Antunes' *Os cus de Judas* (1979), explicitly denouncing the revisionism already in progress at the time. We are left, then, with questions that still haunt contemporary Portugal: which are *de facto* the casualties of a war that are not supposed to exist – not even as discourse? Which labour is necessary

36

to compensate for its losses, to work out its mourning?

Many of the authors here deal with the writer or the film-maker struggling with ways to speak about a collective suffering as a particular witness, able to issue warnings about his or her own warnings. Thus, as both academics and readers, we also cannot escape the call to be attentive to the paradoxes which entangle not only every act of testimony, but also its plays and amusements, as Bernard McGuirk amply shows in his distinctively ludic meditation on the manner in which recent post-colonial *cum* intra-colonial discourses suffuse the new fiction of sub-Saharan Africa, as filtered through his analysis of José Eduardo Agualusa's *O vendedor de passados/The Book of Chameleons*. In the lineage of Dostoyevsky, Kafka, Guimarães Rosa and Saramago, Agualusa deploys protagonists or narrators "prone" to be less *porte-paroles* than *animots*. Jacques Derrida's "Ecce animot [...] assuming the title of an autobiographical animal, in the form of a risky, fabulous, or chimerical response to the question 'But me, who am I?'" is appropriated in order to trace the re(p)tiling of history in and on the mosaic of Angolan memory. The eponymous protagonist of *The Book of Chameleons*, Félix Ventura, "is a man with an unusual occupation. If your lineage isn't sufficiently distinguished, he'll change that for you. If your family isn't quite as glorious as you'd like, Félix Ventura can make you a new one. Félix Ventura is a seller of pasts". But who is watching him? Who is telling his tale? Who, or what, is on his tail? *L'animot juste* or *juste l'animot*? McGuirk hears in Agualusa's chit-chat narrator the geckoing not of animosity in respect of, and for, the past, but rather the re-animating word of a gentle – transmogrified – ironist *à la* Borges, as Angolan fiction reaches out, resonates, across the Atlantic in a difficult-to-identify "national" literature in which the bookman or booked woman perform in an actantial sphere already and always pre-scripted by devilish precursors.

Rui Gonçalves Miranda's point of departure is yet another of Jacques Derrida's analyses and questionings of the European philosophical tradition of envisaging Europe as a privileged cape, in order to explore a Western European variant of this phenomenon by addressing the discourse of Portuguese exceptionalism. This manifests itself in the tracing of imaginary topographies which map out and assign a "special" and "unique" place for Portugal in its relationship with its former colonies and with Europe. The chapter aims both to dismiss this exceptionalism, by framing it in a larger philosophical, cultural and historical Eurocentric context, and to dismantle the phallogocentrism and Lusotropicalism inherent in (post-)imperial discourses, such as the ideological represent-ation which claimed the possession and the location of territories that Portugal could not otherwise materialize from 1492 until the post-2008 European monetary crisis.

Post-dictatorship times and archives in Argentina and Chile

Several of the essays discuss the post-dictatorship temporalities of both Chile and Argentina. As Adam Sharman (2017, 13-14) reminds us in the introduction to *MemoSur/MemoSouth*:

> Forty years or more have gone by since the coups and a little under forty since the high watermark of the most violent repression. New generations are remembering. Contested, imperilled even by recent government attempts to redefine the politics of memory, there is nevertheless a new sociability of mourning [...] in which those who were not directly affected by violence could [...] adopt grief as a personal commitment to a new way of being together. This contested politics of friendship [...] involves, though is not reducible to, a new sociability in which new generations and new social movements [...] open up the possibility of a politics of affect.

In the Cono Sur, the quality of memory has indeed shifted and changed in a number of ways thanks to changes in public and political discourse and the media. The diverse processes of transition have not been synchronous: for many of the victims it has proceeded from silence, to speaking out immediately after the end of the dictatorship, then again back to silence. In Argentina, for example, the silence has been followed by a period in which the counter-memory of human rights associations has slowly but inexorably become a normative memory, and the individual memories of the victims have turned into a new authoritative account of the nation's past, transforming the nation's self-image as a community.

Cecilia Sosa pursues the question of the disappeared in Argentina and its cultural undertaking, asking whether we can learn anything from experiences of suffering. Analyzing *Aparecida* (Appeared) (2015), Marta Dillon's account of the discovery in 2011 of her missing mother's remains in a mass grave, she explores the possibility of an experience of loss in which the past is not simply obliterated, but rather worked through in unconventional ways. Sosa turns to the "affective turn", apprehending the text not just as cognitive form but as a *concrete and material one* which is able to touch, move and *affect* us. *Aparecida* helps us to read the intensities of a particular moment in Argentina's process of mourning , for Dillon's book is embedded in the Kirchner years, which involved a particular way of *being* and *doing* with others. The new way of mourning, Sosa says, involved those who were not directly affected by violence and yet who adopted grief as a political commitment. Formerly, only those related by blood to the missing had the authority to demand justice. The Kirchner period changed that. Adopting loss as a *state* matter, it challenged the unspoken entanglement between bloodline victims and truth, which had marked Argentina's human rights landscape for more than 30 years. This is a generational affair: H.I.J.O.S. succeed Madres, but avoid positioning themselves "in an endless childhood", and it is a feminist, queer affair. Argentina's experience of trauma allows us to glimpse, Sosa suggests, an ethics that does not reside in individual subjects as atomistic silos, but rather in the collective ties of a new political family.

With Norma Fatala we move to a consideration of narratives of survivors of the clandestine detention centres in Argentina. Her contribution registers, above all, the multiple nuances of survival, most apparent in the different status given to different prisoners. Even a terrorist state had to account for legal prisoners, whereas the *desaparecidos* had no "entity", as the dictator Jorge Videla infamously, albeit correctly, put it. The actions of certain survivors are far from clear, some who were considered traitors by former comrades turning out to have saved tens of lives. Collecting information about their captors was the only possible means of reversal for human beings subjected to the almost total power of others. As Fatala says, information becomes the gift which survivors would bring back from their descent into hell. Nevertheless, living to tell the tale of thousands is not an easy task. While self-justification may play a role in the discourse of the returning subjects, giving testimony not only fulfils an ethical imperative, but in it the intensity of personal feelings provides us with some kind of measure of the irreconcilable nature of the crimes. However, if survivors' testimonies are invaluable, they may have a negative impact on collective memory when politicized. Survivors proclaim themselves not only the memory of genocide, but also, and all too readily, the memory of defeat. In order to demonstrate the military's aberrant quality, and to justify their own survival, they reproduce the effects of terror and risk suggesting that no alternative form of politics is possible.

Daniele Salerno revisits the Provincial Memory Archive of Córdoba to explore the under-studied topic of LGBT people. He analyzes a small corpus of interviews from the Oral History Archive which detail repression of LGBT people before, during and after the Argentine dictatorship. The analysis points up the unsettling fact that the archive is a complex enunciative device which, through the life story interview, throws up the paradox that questions now asked of the interviewees overlap with the interrogation to which they were subjected in the same place decades ago. In a certain sense, they are once again called upon to "confess" their sexuality. Second time around, however, the interview-confession allows interviewees to reconfigure their own subjectivity and to gain political agency. The detention centre that was once the place of human rights violations becomes a place for the struggle for human rights. But, Salerno cautions, the reconstruction of political agency is not straightforward. The case studies analyzed show a tendency on the part of some LGBT people to deploy the human rights organizations' trope of "restoring victims' humanity", but at the expense of their *politicality*. In other words, they were guilty of *being*, not of doing.

Anna Maria Lorusso studies a Chilean television series, *Los archivos del cardenal* (2011), and a Chilean cinema documentary, *Habeas corpus* (2015), which deal with an organ of the Catholic Church, the Vicaría de la Solidaridad, that tried to denounce the dictatorship's crimes and provide succour to its victims. The TV series has nothing "real" in it and yet has such a mimetic force – not least in the detail of its historical reconstructions – that it elevates itself, as Lorusso puts it, to the *status of document*, so much so that the last episode, screened live in the nation's Museum of Memory and Human Rights, became a genuine political action. The documentary film, in contrast, and despite real witnesses and documents, is punctuated by fictional interludes which suspend realism and mark a retreat from reality. The series is aesthetically conventional and yet its memory of the dictatorship presents examples of those who have risked their lives to oppose the regime, exempla that are timeless and universally applicable. As such, the series offers a "model script for dictatorship and resistance", while the more experimental documentary offers the suspension of all schemes. With its "dramatic realism" and belief in the referential efficacy of fiction, *Los archivos del cardenal* cuts deep into Chilean life. With its "traumatic realism" and mistrust of the possibilities of representing reality, *Habeas corpus* blocks the connection to social and political life. In the first, a *historia magistra vitae*; in the second, the subjective time of a tortuous mental experience struggling with the question of how – or even whether – to speak of trauma.

Adam Sharman addresses the relationship between history and memory through the vehicle of documentary film in Argentina. His question is whether there is a radical break in post-dictatorship Argentine documentary filmmaking between an older generation's "classical" view of history and a younger generation's postmodern "postmemory" view. As test cases, he takes two emblematic films dealing with the armed revolutionary groups of the 1970s, David Blaustein's *Cazadores de utopías* (1995) and Nicolás Prividera's documentary *M* (2007). On questions of history and generations, Nietzsche, he claims, remains our surest guide. If, in the older film by the generation of the *guerrilla*, witnesses' memories of Peronist militancy, armed and unarmed, are ordered into something resembling a classical historical narrative, in order to account for what their generation did, and in order that they have their say at a moment when few seemed interested in listening, the film also has critical elements that do not belong to the world of objective history-telling. In contrast, the much more formally experimental and questioning *M*, which charts siblings' search to discover what happened to their disappeared mother, like many probably abducted from the union stronghold that was the INTA (the National Institute for Agricultural Technology), films the younger generation filming the older generation, that is to say, draws attention to the creative appropriation of memory by a later generation. However, in the midst of this postmemory performance there is a strange reversal. The newcomer, Prividera, becomes the rationalist historicist – too many memories, he says, and not enough history – while the older generation become the relativists. What is called "postmemory", Sharman suggests, still has some explaining to do.

"By way of epilogue: new winds of forgetting are blowing"...
... And it is indeed probably the case, if one considers, amongst the many possible intervening factors participating in the trans-generational transmission of violent pasts, the role of education and government politics. This challenge is what Daniel Filmus' contribution considers, first of all by asking what should the Argentine education system teach the

coming generations about the dictatorship and the disappeared. An academic and politician heavily involved in the Fernández de Kirchner government, Filmus – in one of the two revised essays in this Reader – argues that the country's education system, while traditionally, and also deliberately, had "forgotten" whole areas of history and experience in accordance with the interests of the dominant classes during the dictatorship of 1976, took this measure a step further: it "disappeared" authors, texts and entire subjects from the curriculum just as it was disappearing individuals it regarded as threatening the social order. It was not until the Kirchner governments that bold changes were introduced. Schools, it was decided, should transmit the traumatic events of the recent past; not just teach them in instrumental fashion, but impart the experience that lay behind them. While aware of the risks of rendering remembering mechanical, such that it invites only forgetting, and of prescribing memory as an unquestionable legacy, the revised essay Filmus wrote for this Reader expands on a third risk currently being run by the government of President Mauricio Macri, elected in 2015: that of reinstating a politics – and a schooling – of forgetting. In a paragraph entitled "By way of epilogue: new winds of forgetting are blowing", he further elaborates on how current national politics pitched at recovering social memory and keeping alive the task of guarding human rights have altered profoundly in the last four years. Not only has a strong media campaign begun to delegitimize the struggles of human rights organizations, but also these same organizations are suffering the withdrawal of state support. And as the minister of culture of the city of Buenos Aires questioned the emblematic number of 30,000 victims of forced disappearances, collective memory as the result of years of struggles and criminal trials and attempts at reparation for the victims is undermined. All these politics are thus fomenting a national forgetting which has strong collateral effects in the education system. By compiling the sad lists of all the measures taken to prevent schools from carrying forward their capacity to develop critical thinking, Filmus reminds us how any post-conflict culture will always be at risk of being blown by old and new winds of forgetting.

In fine, all the essays in this volume, albeit from different angles and interests, give to both the study and the construction of memory a power *for* and *in* the future, by trusting acts of witnessing and commemoration with the possibility to create new frames of action. This power, always mediated and also often belated, does not assign memory an agency: remembering and forgetting have to be linked to human actors within cultural, political, institutional and social frames, actors and factors that impinge upon the transition process, that are not synchronous: "human buildings, objects, values, emotions, memories, all of these exist in *discrepant temporalities*, changing at different pace" (Assmann and Shortt 2011, 5). Again, memory studies here meets the same concerns that transitional justice and international relation scholars working on conflict resolution are now facing. In a time when conflicts and collective fears do not seem to abate, our little hope is to continue to think critically and, if not to stop, at least to diffuse the winds of forgetting that are fuelling the nationalisms of too many post-conflict cultures.

References

Adam, B. (2004). *Time*. Cambridge: Polity Press.

Alexander, J. (2003). *The Meanings of Social Life. A Cultural Sociology*, Oxford and New York: Oxford University Press.

Assmann, A., and Conrad, S. (eds.) (2010). *Memory in the Global Age. Discourse, Practices and Trajectories*. London and New York: Palgrave Macmillan.

Assmann, A., and Shortt, L. (2011). "Introduction", in A. Assmann, L. Shortt (eds.), *Memory and Political Change*, London and New York: Palgrave Macmillan.

Boudana, S., Cohen, A. C., and Frosh, P. (2017). "Reviving icons to death: when historic photographs become digital memes". *Media, Culture and Society*, 39, 8, 1210-1230.

Brown, G., Langer, A., and Stewart, F. (2008). "A Typology of Post-conflict Environments: An Overview", *CRISE Working Paper*, 53. Available at **https://www.gov.uk/dfid-research-outputs/a-typology-of-post-conflict-environments-an-overview**.

Buelens, G., Durrant, S., and Eaglestone, R. (eds.) (2014). *The Future of Trauma Theory. Contemporary Literary and Cultural Criticism*. London and New York: Routledge.

Caruth, C. (1996). *Unclaimed Experience: Trauma, Narrative and History*. Baltimore and London: The Johns Hopkins University Press.

Demaria, C., and Daly, M. (eds.) (2009). *The Genres of Post-conflict Testimonies*. Nottingham: Critical, Cultural and Communications Press.

Demaria, C., and Wright, C. (eds.) (2006). *Post-conflict Cultures: Rituals and Representations*, Nottingham: Critical, Cultural and Communications Press.

Derrida, J. (1988). *Limited Inc.* Evanston, Illinois: Northwestern University Press.

Eaglestone, R. (2014). "Knowledge, 'afterwardsness' and the future of trauma theory". In G. Buelens, S. Durrant, R. Eaglestone, (eds.) (2014). *The Future of Trauma Theory*. London and New York: Routledge, 11-21.

Enloe, C. (1993). *The Morning After. Sexual Politics at the End of the Cold War*. Berkeley and San Francisco: University of California Press.

Eyerman, R., Alexander, J., and Butler Breese, E. (eds.) (2016). *Narrating Trauma. On the Impact of Social Suffering*. London and New York: Routledge.

Foucault, M. (1986). "Governmentality", *Ideology and Consciousness*, 6, Summer, 5-21.

Frosh, P., and Pinchevski, A. (2014). "Media Witnessing and the Ripeness of Time". *Cultural Studies*, 28, 4, 594-610.

Gonçalves Miranda, R., and Zullo, F. (eds.) (2013). *Post-conflict Reconstructions. Re-mappings and Reconciliations*. Nottingham: Critical, Cultural and Communications Press.

Grusin, R. (2010). *Premediation: Affect and Mediality After 9/11*. London and New York: Palgrave Macmillan.

Hoskins, A. (2011). "7/7 and Connective Memory: Interactional Trajectories of Remembering in Post-scarcity Culture", *Memory Studies*, 4, 3, 269-280.

Huyse, L. (2003). "The Process of Reconciliation". In D. Bloomfield, T. Barnes, and L. Huyse (eds.), *Reconciliation After Violent Conflict. A Handbook*. Stockholm: International IDEA, 19-39.

Jones, S., and Nehru, M. (eds.) (2011). *Writing Under Socialism*. Nottingham: Critical, Cultural and Communications Press.

Kaldor, M. (2012). *New and Old Wars* (3rd ed.). Cambridge: Polity Press.

Landsberg, A. (2004). *Prosthetic Memory. The Transformation of American Remembrance in the Age of Mass Culture*. New York: Columbia University Press.

McGuirk, B., and Goh, C. (eds.) (2007). *Happiness and Post-conflict*. Nottingham: Critical, Cultural and Communications Press.

Mueller-Hirth, N. (2017). "Temporalities of victimhood: Time in the study of postconflict societies". *Sociological Forum* 32, 1, 186–206.

Mueller-Hirth, N., Rios Oyola, S. (2018). "Introduction: Temporal Perspectives on Transitional and Post-conflict Societies", in N. Mueller-Hirth, S. Rios Oyola (eds.). *Time and Temporality in Transitional and Post-Conflict Societies*. London and New York: Routledge.

Olick, J. K. (2007). *The Politics of Regret: On Collective Memory and Historical Responsibility*. Abingdon: Routledge.

Radstone, S.; Schwartz, B. (eds.) (2010). *Memory. Histories, Theories, Debates*. New York: Fordham University Press.

Reychler, L., Langer, A. (2006). *Researching Peace Building Architecture, Cahiers Internationale Betrekkingen En Vredesonderzoek*, 75, 24. Leuven: Centre for Peace Research and Strategic Studies, 4-76.

Rosa, H. (2003). "Social acceleration: Ethical and political consequences of a desynchronized high-speed society". *Constellations* 10, 1, 3–33.

Rosa, H. and Scheuerman, W. E. (2009). "Introduction". In H. Rosa and W. E. Scheuerman (eds.), *High-Speed Society: Social Acceleration, Power and Modernity*, University Park: Pennsylvania State University Press, 1–29.

Rothberg, M. (2009). *Multidirectional Memory: Remembering the Holocaust in the Age of Decolonization*. Stanford, CA: Stanford University Press.

Rothberg, M. (2014). "Preface: Beyond Tancred and Clorinda. Trauma Studies for Implicated Subjects". In G. Buelens, S. Durrant, and R. Eaglestone (eds.). *The Future of Trauma Theory*. London and New York: Routledge, 2-9.

Sharman, A., Grass Kleiner, M., Lorusso, A. M., and Savoini, S. (eds.) (2017). *MemoSur/MemoSouth: Memory, Commemoration and Trauma in Post-Dictatorship Argentina and Chile*. London: Critical, Cultural and Communications Press.

Teitel, R. (1997). "Transitional jurisprudence: The role of law in political transformation". *Yale Law Journal*. 106, 2010–2080.

Teitel, R. (2000). *Transitional Justice*. Oxford: Oxford University Press.

Teitel, R. (2003). "Transitional justice genealogy". *Harvard Human Rights Journal*, 16, 69–94.

Todorov, T. (1995). *The Morals of History*. Minneapolis and London: University of Minnesota Press.

Wagner Pacifici, R., and Hall, M. (2012). "Resolution of social conflicts". *Annual Review of Sociology*, 38, 181-199.

Yaeger, P. (2002). "Consuming Trauma; or, The Pleasure of Merely Circulating". In N. K. Miller and J. Tougaw (eds.). *Extremities.*

Trauma, Testimony, and Community. Urbana and Chicago: University of Illinois Press, 25-51.

Zelizer, B. (2012). "Cannibalizing Memory in the Global Flow of News". In M. Neiger, O. Meyers and E. Zandberg (eds.). *On Media and Memory*. London and New York: Palgrave Macmillan, 27-36.

Media and Law

The New Narrative Form of Post-conflicts:
"New Wars" as World-Wide Wars

Federico Montanari

The transformations of War

This essay seeks to examine the cultural and semiotic changes that have occurred in the vision and conception of war during the last few decades, with particular reference to the turn of the millennium. How are we to think, today, the question of conflict in relation to images, communication and discursive forms that circulate within the media, old and new, social as well as mainstream? The link between images, media and war is a subject that is at the same time vast, very topical but difficult to face, precisely because it is "inflated" and trivialized. Yet, because it is a subject that has been treated by many authors, it should, for this very reason, be addressed from new perspectives.

Let us think, first, of the events in the last twenty years that have characterized the transformation of the perception of war itself: from Kosovo's and the former Yugoslavia's wars, from the First Gulf War, to 9/11, to the wars of expedition and retaliation, or revenge, conducted by the United States and its allies, which have gradually been bogged down in Iraq and Afghanistan, until the transformation represented by the advent of ISIS and terrorist attacks, from Paris, to Baghdad, to Brussels. Each of these events represents a potential transformation and deserves further and deepening analysis. We should consider, in this regard, also the accusation of "Eurocentrism" or "Occidentalism", that is the tendency to talk more about attacks in Europe or in the USA than the massacres that occur daily in Iraq or in Syria. More generally, the question hence becomes that of how to carry out a critical work by analyzing images and communication practices in relation to the media, and how to work not only on the images themselves, but also on their connections and assemblages. Hence the importance of using analytical tools that are "fine-grained" – in a trans-disciplinary work among Media Studies, Sociology, Socio-semiotics and Cultural Studies – which should allow us to deepen the investigation of the multiple relationships between war, conflict and narrative, discursive and thematic dimensions (and, therefore, to show the underlying value systems and ideologies of images); as well as examining the visual-plastic layer of images, that is to say the internal components of the images themselves, their basic mechanisms and frameworks.

From World War I Images to Recent Wars: the Closure of the "War-narrative" Circuit

The idea I want to start from in sketching this research path is that the practices of war are inseparable from their representation and narrative form. Today this argument might sound as obvious as any truism, especially after decades of television and other media footage on war. Yet there is no linear evolution concerning such processes of "mediatization" of war and conflict, and the mere existence of new and better technologies and of digital media does not mean that there are more wars represented through images, as the lack of pictures from, to cite just one example, the conflict in Libya amply demonstrates. At the same time, World War I was extensively covered by film-makers and reporters, with millions and millions of photographs taken not only by professionals but also by the soldiers themselves. It was the first "global war" as well as the first "media war". Speaking about the Great War as the first global conflict, it is no coincidence that, in those years, new film production companies such as Gaumont, or Pathé produced and disseminated, at the same time, fiction movies and the first examples of documentaries and "visual journals" from the battlefield. The serial narrative connects fiction and non-fiction, imageries and footage, with the new tale of total and industrial war, contributing to making conflicts, from the First World War on, "serialized" and "cinematic".

A cinematic vision of that war deals with a change of perception of an event. Some authors speak of "cinematic memory" with regard to the First World War (Williams 2009). Such a concept would be like a semio-cultural form that has changed the very way in which memory and event narratives are constituted: a form in which the visual media, then emerging, found themselves, in their process of inventing their own grammars, as if kneaded into creating events themselves. Williams (2009) further emphasizes that a way of seeing is a new rhetorical weapon. A "canon" of the Great War is, on the one hand, part of "a long history of memory" in connection with the technologies of writing and narration; precisely, of mediation. However, the hypothesis is that the Great War constituted the beginning of a new matrix, in which we find the semio-cultural origins of contemporary media. Williams quotes the extraordinary example of the terrible battle of the Somme (1 July – 18 November 1916) which, in a few days, caused hundreds of thousands of deaths on both sides. It was, in a sense, the first "direct coverage" event in history. Cinemas, first in Britain and later all around the world, projected the documentary of the battle, commissioned by the Propaganda Office of the British headquarters, the British Topical Committee for War Films, and British newsreel producers, and supported by the War Office. The film was based on materials taken during the battle and was screened shortly afterwards in hundreds of theatres. It seems to have been one of the most popular films in the history of British cinema, watched, at the time, by more than 20 million people. We can therefore speak, almost, of "real time" (the film was released on 21 August 1916, during the battle), as the documentary was shown a few weeks later and, in any case, at the height of the War, only a few hundred kilometres from the place of the battle. It was watched by the British with an immense and, at the same time, literally terrifying success. A film, certainly, of propaganda but which, in fact, provides the sense of this "short circuit" between the War and history, media and events, and their re-mediation, with real as well as staged scenes. Williams (2009) quotes the testimony of Frances Stevenson, the secretary and later second wife of Prime Minister Lloyd George, who had lost her brother in the battle: "I felt something of what the ancient Greeks felt when they were in their crowds, those ancients purged in their minds with a thrilling pity and horror."

This is not the place to explore further the question of culture, memory and representation of the Great War. However, it seems important to underline this singular coincidence: the technological and digital remediation of the First World War[1] is linked to an original matrix that has given birth to the techno- and semio-cultural devices we are surrounded by today. The matrix born at that time seems connected with the current "matrix" that is given by the digital media format.

Yet what happens, if we are to follow this direction, not only with visual representation of memory and historical wars, but also once we look at recent conflicts? The virtual weapons of communication and manipulation converge more and more with the technologies of war. The construction and the placing into discourse of these representations and narrations – which actuate themselves in their own time through heterogeneous

---

[1] See the recent examples about the huge quantity of media and cross-media projects, produced either by official international as well as non-official institutions, or governments, concerning the centenary of World War I.

practices – react with the concrete forms of war themselves according to diverse socio-cultural formations. And a further hypothesis, with regard to current wars, takes the form of an apparent paradox: today, there is no distinction between war and post-war. The current form of war presents itself more and more and continuously as a "post-war". Observing once again the transformations of war during the last century and the new millennium, it is possible to observe, today, some telling and critical transformations. According to the Italian former army General and scholar in war studies, Fabio Mini (a Commander-in-chief of NATO forces in the 1999 Kosovo War), these transformations are many. It is true that, starting from the late 1990s to the first years of the new millennium, war appears to take more and more the form of "a war that follows the war": from the peace-keeping and peace-enforcing interventions of the 1990s, up to the mediatized, "titled" wars – in a "movies or TV series style" – of the different military expeditions carried out by the United States and Western allies under the direction of the U.S., from "Restore Hope" to "Enduring Freedom". Or, let us take the nowadays classic concept (although paradoxical as well as oxymoronic and humorous) of "humanitarian wars". According to Mini (2017), after the two world wars and after the period of the "great theories", concepts and "doctrines" that guided the era of the Cold War (such as Deterrence, or "MAD": Mutual Assured Destruction), and during which they had contributed to maintaining a form of order controlled by the great superpowers (U.S. and Russia), at the turn of the new millennium there has been a chaotic proliferation (Mini 2017; see also Joxe 2002) and, at the same time, a privatization of interests, both of power and symbolic kinds, as well as of the economic one. This chaos has produced different genres and related representations of wars, in which the panoply of "semiotic" weapons and their deployment has become ever more important. Further, "humanitarian wars" are part of this new complex map, composed of different poles and directions. Yet, there is a possible misunderstanding here. Wars, from ancient times to nowadays (from ancient Greek *hoplite* formations, to "ship in the line" formations and modern linear battlefields: see O'Connell 1989; Mini 2017), are a continuous mix of material and immaterial contents, of practical and symbolic weapons. What has changed is the differentiation in dimension and intensity of two phenomena: (a) the "virtualization" of war (enhanced during the Cold War, and developed at different layers, from macro to micro, with the importance of "rhetorical" gestures, such as menaces, threats, forms of manipulations, etc.); and (b) the hyper-mediation work, with several mechanisms, such as the concrete representation on media screens, or public address as well public relations activity.

Let us then go back to some typical examples and characteristics of current forms of conflict. Above all, today, in the face of the media-influenced war – a phenomenon that cannot be reduced to the commonplace of a conflict "seen through" the media – we have to confront "stories of war", the narrative forms that in the past had the forms of the memorial or the chronicle or, in a broader sense, myth. We certainly cannot say that the dimension of the representation or the narrative of war is less important today. On the contrary, this dimension has grown so much as to become hypertrophic. One could argue that in the current wars this becomes part of the planning of tactics and of strategy itself. It even contributes to rendering an intermediate dimension, which some studies define as "operational", between the intervention on the field and the level of planning and doctrine, even more important.

This operational level invests itself in either the traditionally military field of operations (logistics, information, control, acquisition and management of data) or in the terrain of the media, which was the old role of propaganda, and which now assumes different forms of planned communication, of the dissemination of news, of preventative commun-ication. Indeed, typical of the new forms of war is continually to make one field pass through the other. Thus we will have strategies, tactics and logistics of communication, just like the control and management of information on the field of battle. An example is the case of the *embedded* journalists following the U.S. troops in Iraq or in Afghanistan; or again, of the recordings taken by the video cameras of soldiers themselves engaged in combat, and the attempts to manage those images – somehow the "spectacular" dimension of war itself – which sometimes escape the net of the information censor. Today, however, after the wars in Iraq and Afghanistan, and with the prolongation of the war in Syria,[2] the issues seem to be further transformed. Today the "battlefronts" are broken up

---

[2] I want to recall that this war stemmed from the "Arab springs", in an attempt at a democratic revolution, and after it had been captured by other dynamics, with its militarization and, subsequently, with the break-in of ISIS, and the Kurdish struggle, and with the new presence of Russia in an unprecedented form of bipolarity with the U.S.

and scattered even more.

Here we find again not only what scholars like Mini or Joxe have stated, but also what Pope Francis declared: we live in a "fragmented world-war situation", distributed into small bits and pieces. For this reason communication and "media at war", during recent years, are becoming even more scattered and disseminated. The "front lines" today appear to be increasingly uncertain and cross many spaces and many different regions. The temporality of war, in particular after the advent of ISIS terrorism, is made much more of sudden and fragmented events with long periods of suspension, of waiting or even inattention, not least by the media.

In any case, all such aspects, related to the "strategic use" of communication and images, have been theorized by scholars and acted out by strategists and military personnel. It was done in one of the most sensational cases or, if one prefers, a case of experimentation-in-the-field during the Kosovo War (1999). In the course of this war the press officers of NATO, the spokespersons, and the various civil experts in strategies of marketing and in campaigns of political communication, mobilized in order to construct a true and proper planning of war communication. It was a question of preparing "attractive, ready-to-go stories" for the press and the public, to "refresh" the communication of the briefings for the journalists.[3]

More generally speaking, in the study of international relations, of political theory, as in the social sciences, there tends to be a growing debate on narrative models as forms of construction and representation of reality. This idea becomes much more important as it is connected with practices on and of "the terrain", with strategic planning of communication. This idea is surely not new, as the concept – developed a long time ago by Lyotard with regard to the "postmodern condition" – of "the end of grand narratives" demonstrates. Within semiotics and socio-semiotics (Montanari 2012) and in social psychology the narrative model has been generalized, and is now used in various frameworks, not least in the ways these models – even if trivialized and simplified – are exploited by marketing and communication studies with the use of the concept of

[3] In relation to this case see Pozzato 2000. See also the article by Massimo Pietroni, "La Nato comunicatrice imperfetta", 1999, in the dossier "La macchina dell'informazione" at **www.sissa.it**; Chilton 2004 and Mini 2003; 2017.

"storytelling". This idea of narrativity assumes, however, also a strategic and operative application.

So, Why Semiotics and Socio-Semiotics, again?

Allow me now a quick theoretical-methodological detour: "Why semiotics?" I believe that a semiotic gaze enables us to help render more pertinent and intelligible all the questions mentioned above. The semiotic field, in particular the structural-narrative branch (and discourse analysis applied to the forms of political discourse and war: see Chilton 2004) has focused on a multi-level model of analysis (of systems of subjectivization, of their organization and narrative activation, of forms of enunciation and styles of discourse), that guides us in the direction of an investigation of the forms and discourses of war within a wider "semiotic and textual turn" in the social sciences.[4] This turn allows us to see how meaning and the forms any content is shaped into are not isolated, intertwining in social phenomena considered as forms of textuality.

Yet, the question really is the change in the nature of war: how has it concretely changed? War, today, is characterized, as already said, by a close link between images and war practices, between these practices and their forms of representation. More generally, today's war is a "semiotic war" whose mechanisms we need to find. Hence, before trying to define yet again new models of conflict, I want to go back to some recent examples relative to that which seems to be the closure of the "war-recount" circuit.

Forms of tactical media gesticulation

In the first months of 2002, in the course of one of the episodes following the "second Palestinian Intifada" – in the context of the Israeli-Palestinian conflict, now neglected also by media coverage, and before the involution of the situation that led to the current stalemate of the Gaza siege – a horrific lynching occurred. An event impossible to justify, even taking into account the context of violence, of oppression and of the killings that the Palestinian people undergo daily, was the lynching of two Israeli soldiers by a crowd of demonstrators, and of militants and Palestinian militia. This episode serves as an example dramatically paradigmatic of the current forms of war, a war that is above all hybrid: it is urban, ethnic, political,

---

[4] We can speak not only of a "semiotic" or "textual" turn (Fabbri, 2001) but also, largely, of a "power turn" (or "power analysis") in the human and social sciences and Cultural Studies, triggered by the work of Foucault, Deleuze and Guattari.

civil and military at the same time, conducted by a regular army and by militiamen, part of a war both local and global. It is emblematic of struggles that spread throughout the world and keep their meaning up to date; and, finally, it is "media-influenced", but in a peculiar way. This lynching appeared to have been carried out with the consent of the police of the Palestinian National Authority, and in fact occurred within the vicinity of a police station in Ramallah. These are the "raw facts" which have been given ample prominence on public and private television throughout the world on the international circuit of images.[5]

Here the consequences of the use of information and images of war do not simply concern a deontology of the media. The question here is different, and it regards a practical, concrete form of conflict. Similar problems and situations have often occurred in the context of civil wars, when the struggling actors are not easily identifiable, such as in the ethno-civil wars of the former Yugoslavia, or in the conflict in Northern Ireland.

In this case the use of TV and other media becomes part of the conflict itself: the media have become instruments of manipulation and counter-manipulation in the hands of the political-military powers as they plan and conduct the war. However, it is not only about this particular medium. One may suppose, in more general terms, that new forms of conflict foresee an organized utilization, diffuse and massive, of social and civil actors; the means of information become themselves an active part of these conflicts, true and proper protagonists (whether willing or unwilling) of the game. Always at war, civilian populations become time and again prey to and hostages of politicians and military men; now, however, the question seems to be of another kind because the speed of dissemination of news, of information and of counter-information, endowed with a variable status of truth, is increasing. True or close-to-true, half true and half false, is the news that circulates.

Indeed, war is always accompanied by the spreading of rumours and news, so much so that, in times of war, communication is intrinsically unstable, diffusive and contagious. Rumours and half-truths will be exploited by those who plan the war, such as military men and Intelligence

---

[5] Images that provoked, in Italy, harsh polemics between the Italian public television, RAI, and the Mediaset private channels – belonging to the former, at that time, prime minister, Berlusconi – regarding their distribution and their use: it appears in fact that, thanks to these, the Israeli intelligence services later captured some of the participants in the lynching.

operatives (Fussell 1975). However, today, the difference consists in the extreme level – of intensity, of speed, and of mass circulation, of information, stories and rumours – that such phenomena have reached, either on the field or thanks to current technologies and the advent of the internet, blogs, and social media. One could hypothesize, in socio-semiotic terms, a change in the mechanisms of enunciation of wars. "Saturation" is one effect of these discursive and rhetorical practices (see, for example, Fontanille 1998); an effect of a quantitative and rhythmic kind, and not only linked to the "themes" or "genres" or their communication. Above all there arises the creation of a space and a time in which the addressee of the communication (which coincides, for example, with the spectator or, making the appropriate changes, a given participant in an action) comes to be inserted into a type of discourse that is constructed for the accumulation and memorization of utterances, usually objective and impersonal (from one side the opinions of experts and journalists, from the other the "it is said" and the "it appears that" of the different press agencies).

Specifically, according to Fontanille, we should look at our "daily representations of affect, which we are used to thinking about in terms of intensity" (1998, 204-205) either of gradients, or of qualitative variations. Moreover, we should also consider the often undervalued aspect of "quantitative" production: the processes through which we perceive the accumulation of forms and occurrences – of whatever type (not only thematic, figurative and so forth, up to "perceptions" and sensations, like the accumulation of emotional characteristics) – within a given "spatial-temporal organization" of the discourse. This addresses the problem of the extension ("*étendue*") that, according to Fontanille, would be at an equal intensity, the fundamental variable of a "tensive" paradigm in semiotics. It is worth saying that such a paradigm takes into consideration phenomena of a gradual type, and not only of categories and oppositions in the production of meaning and communication; and, according to this hypothesis, also our mode of perceiving and conceiving emotions within organizations of meaning like texts or discourses.

We can think, therefore, with more justification, that effects of saturation and accumulation of information – producing in turn "numbness", "intoxication" – function appropriately also in situations of action, of communication and information; and they act within the manipulation of communication, in particular in situations of war and conflict nowadays informed by new technological devices.

In relation to war, weapons and technologies – and also technologies of information – come to be considered as true and proper "materialized utterances" (Latour 1996) inseparable from their systems of socio-anthropological values (Joxe 1991). Indeed, these technological objects and weapons come to be considered as true and proper "texts", containing narrative programmes, intentions and orientations of action. In this sense a French theorist of the Cold War such as General Poirier asks himself: "How images – according to which those making the decisions represent the origins, the conditions, the modalities of an eventual nuclear action – participate in their evaluations and managing decisions?" (Chaliand 1990, 1474).

I believe that this is really the main question we are facing here. We have inherited from the Cold War the idea of "imaging", of imagery, because of its "virtualization". The Cold War was made of defined forms of "strategic gesticulation" (anticipations, forms of threat, of threatening, the ultimatum, making believe, etc.). A virtualization of war transforms its dimensions and its content. The most recent consequences of this transformation are that war becomes only one of the possible modes of armed violence (Poirier 1997, 38). More generally, war now becomes possible in this process of its "relativization".

Now, the possibility of recourse to force is "trivialized" and, at the same time, it is only one of the possible options within a strategic field of manoeuvres made by "semiotic weapons", such as those of dissuasion, ultimatum, manipulation, promising, etc.; but also, mixing actions and gesticulation, menaces and facts. One could think, for instance, of the recent Ukrainian crisis, with the Russian response to a perceived menace being invasion of the Crimea, or its so-called "reappropriation", conducted provocatively, and in a symbolically emphatic, and almost inverted ironic way, with soldiers without identification markers. In other words, we do find in actual forms of war the legacy of the Cold War, in the virtualization of war and the importance of communicative gestures.

Today, even civil technologies like the mobile telephone or the internet and social media can be considered in the same mode, as "action programmes", and as anticipations of action (Marrone 1999); in other cases as actors, as participants in actions. Or, again, they can function as scenarios in which the actions take place. And this is because media and technologies are also vectors of stories, of narratives (considered again as organizers of actions): stories that can provide either models of actions, or induce dangerous stereotypes that may lead to the repeating of similar possible errors or a falling into potential traps.[6] From another point of view, numerous other studies underline how the separation between military and civil technologies is becoming weaker and weaker.[7] It is worth quoting an historian of war such as O'Connell, who considers arms as true and proper "self-fulfilling prophecies" (1989, 7), as immediate material-izations of these prophecies, as displays of practices or actions foreseen or announced within the very planning of the use of a particular weapon and/or technologies. According to O'Connell, this has always been the case (from traditional weapons to information technologies), since the war vessels and the geometric forms of the naval battle can migrate to other kinds of the "expression" of war, like the battles on land. Never before has such a concept assumed such efficacy, speed and generality in its effects.

Such capacity and potentiality – relative, for example, to the weapons typical of the current forms of war, the management of information – within diverse contexts of action, transform themselves immediately into tactical-strategic resources for new forms of conflict. Hence it is important to evaluate the semiotic mechanisms underpinning these processes of management and dissemination of information that are able to transform themselves into levers in the operative means of war. We are dealing here with forms of planning of time and of space, of a true and proper "logistics" of information and communication, with how in modern war information can be transformed, according to Virilio (1991), in "energy" (power) and in "matter" (concrete weapons).

Moreover, it needs to be understood that each action, and its strategic

---

[6] For a cognitive and neuro-cognitive approach on the fact that "believing in" past stories and narratives as models of action can induce errors for future behaviours, see Rosenberg 2018. Yet there is also research which shows that, particularly with regard to conflicts and revolutions, previous narratives can work as devices of "warning", attention and alarm, in relation to possible errors for future actions.

[7] The wife of one of the two lynched Israeli soldiers was made aware of the massacre by mobile phone. See also more recent examples of the use of social media and social platforms such as Twitter, in different war situations: the siege of Kobane (2014-2015) and the defence organized by Rojava's Kurd Militias, YPG, supported by the USA and other allied nations, in which tweets and social messages played a crucial role not only in information, but also in supporting "in real time" the Kurds' battle and sympathizing with them, in a context of a totally "blurred war" like that of the Syrian conflict.

programming, occurs "in" a time and "in" a space. Yet we are dealing with evaluating these dimensions not as abstract categories but within a specific semiotics (historically and culturally located together), which displays a particular production and *ad hoc* treatment of spatiality and temporality. Then we can also discover that, all in all, the current forms of warfare are perhaps not, in many ways, very different from other, older forms. Yet, as we have said, we are not discussing here the establishment of the absolute novelty, or linear evolution, of these current aspects of war, but rather the comparative similarity of general forms.

For some scholars the models of war (particularly those conducted in recent decades by the U.S.) would correspond to forms of an "imperial" type (Hardt and Negri 2000; Joxe 1991; Luttwak 1976). Such a model of "imperial war" expresses itself properly in the conception and the management of space, but also of time. And examples such as those cited – only seemingly incongruous with such general models, and the fruit of local struggles – would not be another superficial indication of such a tendency.[8]

Going back to the specific case of the lynching of two Israeli soldiers, one can see that there occurred something that is disconcerting in a peculiar way. In the following days – first on the Web through different mailing lists, then through diplomatic declarations (for example from the Italian Ambassador at the UN) followed by half-denials, polemics and accusations, and the official declaration which came to be given as "rumours" – the news circulated that this lynching was, if not orchestrated *ad hoc* by the Israelis,[9] at least exploited by the secret services to obtain a victory in what we can call the "parallel war" of the media. In the days preceding this, the image travelling around the world was in fact that of the murder of a Palestinian boy and his father.

---

[8] We recall here the arguments of Hardt and Negri (2000) on the basis of a vast literature ranging from the history of the Roman Empire, to studies on the economics of globalization, to authors who are concerned with the cultural processes of globalization like Jameson or Said. The authors talk explicitly of a vision that rereads Marx in the light of Foucault and of Deleuze and Guattari, and therefore it is "Capital that makes itself Empire". But, citing Braudel, they emphasize that capitalism triumphs only when it comes to be identified with the state, when in fact it is the state.

[9] And here one is at the limits of conspiracy theories, with tones that in certain moments have touched on an attitude with, even if involuntary, anti-semitic force. But this provides no justification, naturally, for the Israeli attitude.

Dissemination of Communication and Current Forms of War: Management of Space and Time

Thanks to a widespread use of "systems of disseminated communication" (mobile phones, the internet, email, blogs, social media, or with the recent use of drones on the battlefield as systems in which communication, recognition, weapons, converge), these phenomena take on even more radical characteristics. Continuing with our examples – it is also the case of the wars in Kosovo and in Afghanistan, or in the more recent war in Syria – we may observe how the effect of the sources of information and of communication directly present on the ground are at the same time stronger and indisputably more efficient but, at the same time, more and more ambiguous; leading, in certain cases, to dramatic effects of "direct from the field" communication; or provoking retroactive effects on the manoeuvreing abilities of the actors on the ground.[10] Things get even more blurred with the advent of the possibility, thanks again to personal media and smartphones, with every spectator or person, of becoming a "reporter", and the rapidity of dissemination of images that are chased down on the ground. As Virilio suggests, the "newshounds" would be like the "wolf packs" (we would add, "media packs") that disperse themselves, attack, compose and recompose in the hunt for images. Perhaps today we could talk of models of a "mediated mass" versus a "media pack", concerning the construction and dissemination of news, in particular, but not exclusively, in times of war (for many scholars war is assumed to be the paradigm of the constitution of the means of communication). The first model would clearly regard the system of traditional media, and the second, the "broadsides", "rumours", and news, perhaps digital or social media, that clot, proliferate and connect each other, themselves producing new spaces of re-mediation.

We can therefore hypothesize that it is not so much the availability of "news" and "images" in itself, but the fact that news becomes an element in a game conducted during a conflict in order to cause a multiplier effect.

---

[10] See the interview with Virilio in *Ctheory* (18 October 2000, available at **http://www.ctheory.net/articles.aspx?id=132**) about, at that time, the emergent phenomenon of independent reporters, sometimes collaborators with CNN or international video-agencies – the so-called "newshounds" – equipped with digital mini-video cameras or telephones, ready to capture, always and everywhere, events and situations.

On the Web and the mailing lists, one can speak of true and real waves of news that then, sometimes, vanish or, on the contrary, feed themselves with the possibility of rising again from sources that are "inversely proportional" to this weight of news. But what is relevant for the new wars is the contagious and widespread impact of this weight of information.

The strategist, or the planner, decides to exploit the opportunities offered in the field, instantly, thanks to the presence of the media. The tactical and strategic activities related to communication and images have become, in current wars, more and more contingent (and in real time) with immediate effects of feedback, and with the construction and activation of narrative structures faster and more instantaneous action. The problem that is raised here, however, seems not only to involve the visible effects that everyone can see on TV, but also the deepest way in which action and conflict, history and narratives, can be rethought from the strategic point of view, in this changing context, thanks also to the use of socio-semiotic analytical tools.

From a political communication point of view, one can no longer talk of a simple "representation" of given ideas or of concepts and values that sustain certain actions, or of a mere instrumental use of the media. What seems to have been, at least in part, undervalued is the fact that the "media" are at the same time actors in the field: actors who give themselves the responsibility of managing the ethical-emotional apparatus of justification shown on the terrain of the engagement; but in many cases they transform themselves and can also become, at the same time, the actors, the space, the scenario, the environment of this encounter.

However, even semiotics seems not to have confronted sufficiently the problem of the efficacy of representation. Certainly, such apparatuses are composed of nothing other than the collection and sequences of heterogeneous utterances (images, declarations, reportage, news reports, etc.). These, in their turn, encompass other types of heterogeneous discourses and diverse formats, like threats, negotiations, visits by heads of state and rulers, declarations or diplomatic games; and these connect themselves at various levels and in different modes, producing intricate "textual networks". We are dealing here with discursive forms which come to constitute the global "political" discourse, a collection of texts that justify, accompany and mix themselves with a given action or collection of actions.

What we are saying is, then, that the media neither possess a privileged status nor a role of subjection: they are actors in the global arena of conflicts. And like all the actors within a discursive construction, they can delegate some utterances or, on the contrary, they can entrust themselves or come to be entrusted with placing on the scene certain characteristic elements. We are dealing, however, with understanding fully the role of the media itself, but without attributing any sort of omnipotence to them, without falling into the trap of the myth of "all is media" and "all is communication"; and we are also searching at the same time to evaluate the role and the impact of the means of information on wars and conflict. There is no need to believe in the myth of total manipulation, according to which the untrustworthy military – with its centres of intelligence placed ahead of all communication and media analysis – would be omnipotent in the conduct of campaigns of manipulation. The problem becomes then the general form this type of new war assumes.

The "Connectivity Machine" of Actual Wars: Narration and Imaging

If we go back to the idea of the Cold War theorist, General Poirier, we can talk of a "strategization of images" and of the representations of war itself. According to Poirier, this process substantially consists of the virtuality of the "ballistic-nuclear panoply" in addressing itself towards scenes and visions that form part of the course of great decisions (in the form of doctrines and "future possibilities" like, as already mentioned, Mutual Assured Destruction etc., in a *Doctor Strangelove* style). But what happened in a post-Cold War world, in a post-apocalyptic, post-Armageddon vision which proposes a new wave of warfare? Alain Joxe, concerning post-9/11, "permanent war" and "Enduring Freedom" (in particular, with regard to the situation in Afghanistan, Iraq and the war on terrorism), has spoken of the "crematistic" of the war, taking this ancient concept from the "Politica" of Aristotle (Joxe 2003). *Crematistica* is, in Aristotelian thought, the art of using wealth to produce wealth, to use money to produce money itself, in opposition to the practice of manufacturing, of producing goods. So, if the task becomes the exchange in itself then there is no longer a limit to that exchange. Today the aim of war is to produce itself, to reproduce war.

Therefore, we can say that the same war produces itself and the aim of war is war. Hence today we witness a form of war which presents itself without objects and without aims: permanent total war (under the cover of tasks and objectives such as the struggle against terrorism, democracy, etc.) because of its lack of the limits of time and space. If we find, from the definition of Clausewitz, the chameleonic feature of war, this concept today has assumed the character of a realized prophecy: today the war machine, derailed from its tracks, has spread into everything, and has become confused with everything. Or, using another metaphor, war theatre, with its mixture of action and representation, with its hybrid actors, is confused with non-war. Post-war becomes a part of war. Michel Foucault (1990), referring to Clausewitz's famous aphorism, hypothesized its complete reversal. If power is war, struggle, politics would be the continuation of war by other means; more precisely war would be the historical moment in which the relations of force affirmed themselves.

The role of power would be, for Foucault, that of "silently inscribing" itself in all the places of a society and in all the social relations, in bodies, in images, in economic inequality, up to language itself, these relations of war. War decides the relations. It is a political act. The war, for another philosopher (Philonenko 1976) is the moment of "semiurgy" (production of new signs) of the construction of meaning, the constituent moment. Do we exaggerate? There are historical epochs in which this has happened. Today, it seems that this same thing is ocurring: in the current forms, certainly, of communication, of media and their technologies. The post-war is none other than the war under other guises, with other means: control, coercion, stabilization, threat.

References

Arrighi, G. (1994). *Il lungo XX secolo*. Milano: Il Saggiatore.

Bartos, O. J., Wehr, P. (2002). *Using Conflict Theory*. Cambridge: Cambridge University Press.

Bozzo, L. (ed.) (2012). *Studi strategici. Guerra, politica, economia, semiotica, psicoanalisi, matematica*. Milano: Egea-Bocconi.

Carruthers, S. J. (2000). *The Media at War*. New York: Palgrave.

Chaliand, G. (ed.) (1990). *Anthologie mondiale de la strategie*. Paris: Laffond.

Chilton, P. (2004). *Analysing Political Discourse*. New York: Routledge.

Deleuze, G., and Guattari, F. (1980). *Mille plateau. Capitalisme et schizophrénie*. Paris: Minuit; (1987) *A Thousand Plateaus: Capitalism and Schizophrenia*. Minneapolis: University of Minnesota Press.

Fabbri, P. (2001). *La svolta semiotica*. Bari: Laterza.

Fabbri, P., Montanari, F. (2000). "Semiotica della comunicazione strategica", in Bozzo 2012.

Fontanille, J. (1998). *Sémiotique du discours*. Limoges: Pulim.

Foucault, M. (1990). *Il faut défendre la société*, Cours au Collège de France (1975-76). Paris: Gallimard; (2003) *Society Must be Defended*. London: Penguin.

Fussell, P. (1975). *The Great War and Modern Memory*. Oxford: Oxford University Press.

Gray, S. C. (2005). *Another Bloody Century*. London: Weidenfeld and Nicolson.

Hardt, M., Negri, A. (2000). *Empire*. Cambridge, MA: Harvard University Press.

Jameson, F. (1990). *Signatures of the Visible*. London: Routledge.

Joxe, A. (1991). *Voyage aux sources de la guerre*. Paris: PUF.

Joxe, A. (2002). *L'empire du chaos*. Paris: La Découverte.

Joxe, A. (2003). "Dilution ou métamorphose du concept de guerre", unpublished paper presented in the seminar "Forme e parole della guerra", organized by the "Scuola Superiore in Scienze Umanistiche", Università di Bologna.

Latour, B. (1996). *Petite réflexion sur le culte moderne des dieux faitiches*. Paris: Synthélabo groupe.

Luttwak, E. T. (1976). *The Grand Strategy of The Roman Empire*. Baltimore: Johns Hopkins University Press.

Marrone, G. (1999). *C'era una volta il telefonino*. Roma: Meltemi.

Migliore, T. (ed.) (2016). *Rimediazioni 2*. Roma: Aracne.

Mini, F. (2003). *La guerra dopo la guerra*. Torino: Einaudi.

Mini, F. (2017). *Che guerra sarà*. Bologna: Il Mulino.

Montanari, F. (2004). *Linguaggi della guerra*. Roma: Meltemi.

Montanari, F. (2012). "Actants, Actors, and Combat Units. The problem of conflict revisited: a semio-cultural viewpoint", *Versus*, 114.

Montanari, F. (2016). "Deep remixing WW1. Rimediazione, media digitali e il caso del centenario della Grande guerra, fra immagini e memoria", in Migliore 2016.

O'Connell, R. (1989). *Of Arms and Men. A History of War, Weapons, and Aggression*. Oxford: Oxford University Press.

Philonenko, A. (1976). *Essais sur la philosophie de la guerre*. Paris: Vrin.

Pietroni, M. (1999). "La Nato comunicatrice imperfetta", at **www.sissa. it.** Accessed 23/5/15.

Poirier, L. (1997). *Le chantier stratégique*. Paris: Hachette.

Pozzato, M. P. (ed.) (2000). *Linea a Belgrado*. Roma: Vqpt/Nuova ERI.

Rosenberg, A. (2018). *How History Gets Things Wrong*. Cambridge, MA: MIT Press.

Said, E. (1993). *Culture and Imperialism*. New York: Alfred A. Knopf.

Virilio, P. (1991). *Guerre et cinéma I. Logistique de la perception*. Paris: Editions Cahiers du Cinéma.

Williams, D. (2009). *Media, Memory and the First World War*. Montreal: McGill-Queen's University Press.

Zolo, D. (1995). *Cosmopolis*. Milano: Feltrinelli.

Media Representations of 9/11:
Constructing the Different Difference

Colin Wright

To begin by stating the obvious, it is very difficult to say anything new about 9/11. Few events in history can have received such intense and sustained attention, and even fewer have had such resoundingly *global* repercussions. Rather than rehearse the familiar platitudes about 9/11, however, I want to attempt to do three things: firstly, to concentrate on the encoding of 9/11 by the American media; secondly, to situate this encoding within the context of economic and cultural globalization; and thirdly, to relate this encoding to a certain logic of sovereignty which I claim is at work within American national identity. Since my analysis will employ somewhat macro-scale arguments, allow me to state three corresponding claims at the outset: firstly, that 9/11 makes visible a certain mutual complicity between media representations and interventionist military policy today; secondly, that the apparently spontaneous encoding of news which is figured as live and breaking nonetheless deploys signifiers from a shared cultural memory, *and* that this encoding determines or at least influences the future response to that event; and thirdly, that despite the altered forms of the nation-state in the context of globalization, it is still ultimately regimes of sovereignty that regulate the semiotic mobilization of affect, and put that affect into the service of pre-existing political agendas.

American media representations of the terrorist attacks of Septem-ber 11, 2001, foreground a tension, arguably endemic to all representation, between pre-existing representational resources on the one hand, and the regulative ideal of fidelity to an immediate present on the other. This tension becomes particularly palpable in the case of 9/11, which, on the level of what might be called "propositional content", has been figured as an unprecedented event, a paradigm shift, something that came completely out of the blue (Wright 2002). And yet on the level of semiotic encoding, of the signifiers required to construct that signified, 9/11 has necessarily drawn on a rich iconic history. The political agenda of the propositional level is obvious: framing 9/11 as an event without context, only consequences, without a past, only a future, narrates the inauguration of a new era in which America *must* consolidate its self-appointed role as Global Police Force. However, the semiotic level of American representations of 9/11 illustrates the inscription of that event into an historical and political *continuity* that betrays the "Big Bang" version of 9/11, which would persuade the world that a new political universe exploded forth on that infamous day from a formerly empty void.

Before even turning to specific representations, it is possible to argue that the very *form* of the attack indicated an awareness of this semiotic level on the part of the terrorists themselves. That is to say, part of the violence of the act was its forcible insertion into the culturally and technologically mediated appropriations through which it would be understood: the very notion of flying commercial aircraft into the Twin Towers and the Pentagon was clearly informed by a sense of a global society of the spectacle. The resultant photographic and filmic images have undoubtedly succeeded in both colonizing, and constituting, a global visual imaginary. Yet the starkness of these images should not blind us to the pull of history. An indication of this historical influence can be gleaned from newspaper headlines on the day of, or immediately following, the attack. *Tulsa World*, for example, carried the headline, "A Day of Infamy" (12/11/01), echoing Roosevelt's description of the Japanese bombing of Pearl Harbour in 1944, an event which of course prompted America to enter the Second World War. *The News Gazette* (9/11/01) referred more directly to "A Second Pearl Harbour", while the *Staten Island Advance* cited "The Longest Day" (12/9/01), thereby deploying associations with the D-Day landings. Dispensing with such connotative subtleties, the *Daily News* announced, simply, "It's War" (12/9/01). This appeal to images and metaphors of previous conflicts immediately encodes, enframes, and indeed translates this contemporary conflict or crisis into recognizable paradigms. However, while the past always functions – consciously or not – as an heuristic device for comprehending the present, in the case of 9/11, it also clearly functions as a preparation for the future. The semiotic militarization of this event was practically instantaneous, and as we know, it paved the way for more concrete expressions of military might in Afghanistan, and then Iraq.

Such internally displaced militarization is clearly evident in the widely reproduced image shown in fig 1. As a symbol of the reiteration of national identity in and through heroic defiance, this image both comforts its traumatized audience, and subtly *instructs* them in how best to respond to that trauma. Deploying the "We Shall Overcome" trope ironically used against the American state during the Civil Rights movement, it clearly indicates that the appropriate reaction to acts of terror is defiant self-assertion. Yet these therapeutic and pedagogical values are predicated upon a deeper iconic resonance hard-wired into the American psyche, which weaves these paternal threads into a militarized history. For this depiction of all-American firefighters is of course a transparent reference to Joe Rosenthal's canonical 1945 image, which shows American soldiers raising a star-spangled banner atop Mount Suribachi on the island of Iwo Jima after sustaining terrible casualties against the Japanese (Fig. 2).

The fact that Rosenthal's photograph was a carefully re-staged version of what had happened spontaneously but moments before, though aesthetically less effectively, is unimportant on the semiotic level on which we are concentrating. The kind of iconic history which I would argue underpins such encoding is of a different nature than conventional, fact-based historiography whose extreme form is positivism, as its power derives not from truth-claims, but from *a capacity to mobilize affect*. That such iconic signifiers play into the construction of a national mythology, and the political capital accruing to such a mythology, is evidenced by the famous Iwo Jima Memorial statue in Washington, D.C. (Fig. 3) which faithfully and in three dimensions replicates Rosenthal's artificial but emotive tableau.

While the image of the 9/11 firefighters (Fig. 1) is certainly parasitic on the visual language and the semantic associations of the Iwo Jima image (Fig. 2), I would argue that its most important semiotic function is the transposition of *military* unity into a domestic space within America's borders. New York's firefighters were explicitly figured as something like civilian soldiers at this time. *Newsday* magazine on September 16, 2001 showed firefighters carrying a flag-draped coffin out of the wreckage of the Twin Towers over the headline, "The Last Roll Call: NYC Firefighters Bury First Three of their Fallen Comrades". The web site of the official retail arm of the New York Fire Department even enables the online purchase of a "support our troops" T-shirt which combines the department's crest with a blessing for American soldiers abroad (see **www.nyfirestore.com**). As if to make this semantic conflation yet more apparent, the city of New York initially proposed to build, outside the Fire Department's Brooklyn headquarters, a 19-foot bronze version of the flag-raising at Ground Zero (Fig. 4).

(Fig. 1)

(Fig. 2)

(Fig. 3)

(Fig. 4)

However, and significantly for the argument to be unfolded in a moment, this project was abandoned after it sparked a row about historical accuracy being compromised by political correctness: in the proposed statue, the three white firefighters were to be replaced by one white, one African-American, and one Hispanic firefighter. A petition delivered to New York City Council in protest against this proposed statue suggests a revealing anxiety about the constructed, and also politicized nature of memorialization-as-historiography:

> This event is of great historical significance and has united the American people like no other [...] The only way to continue the unification created by those horrible events is to present them accurately and truthfully. To do otherwise will only promote disunity and aid the cause of our enemies. [1]

There is much to say about this particular controversy, but for the moment I want to concentrate on the semiotic encoding of the firefighters as civilian soldiers, and to suggest that this semiotic work is a component of a broader "militarisation of social life" (Enloe 1983, 3).

Before simply embracing that thesis, however, it is perhaps productive to mention apparent obstacles to this process of militarization. One need be neither an historian nor an Americanist to assert with some confidence that pre-eminent among those obstacles is undoubtedly Vietnam. Not only was this a failed military campaign, but it was also a major disintegration of American *domestic* unity. Indeed, conservative analysts continue to indulge a metaleptic inversion, suggesting it was the disintegration of domestic unity that led to the failure in Vietnam, rather than that unity being splintered under pressure from the spectacle of that unfolding failure. It is therefore predictable that the re-militarization of domestic space post-9/11 has been accompanied by an attempt to "work through" the repressed memory of Vietnam – to use the psychoanalytic vocabulary which Dominick LaCapra uses in the field of Trauma Studies. Of course, such "working through" is not a new phenomenon. At the time of the first Gulf War for example, *Newsweek* carried the following caption: "Exorcizing Demons: After 48 days of fighting and winning, America's

---

[1] See **www.petitiononline.com/flgraise/petition.html.**

troops exorcized the ghosts of Vietnam. U.S. soldiers came away looking like crack troops led by genius generals Powell and Schwarzkopf. The pain remained, but there was newfound glory for those who endured it" (11/3/91). Ten years later, in the very same publication, a New Yorker who volunteered to help in the wake of 9/11, but who is explicitly introduced as a "draft-dodger", is quoted as saying: "I felt kinda guilty that I never fought for my country, so maybe that's why I do search-and-rescue for free" (30/11/01). While one may have theoretical objections to the ahistorical application of the psychoanalytic paradigm to complex social formations, it is nonetheless difficult *not* to sense here a cathartic acting out. Indeed, "acting out" may be the more accurate term, since the therapeutic teleology implicit in the notion of a "working through" certainly fails to describe the continuing potency of the Vietnam signifier precisely in demanding ever greater domestic unity. It may be more accurate to view that signifier and its strategic deployment post-9/11 as a form of repetition compulsion motivated by a death-instinct (Freud 2003), and therefore as a symptom maintained in and through its repression along Foucaultian lines (Foucault 1981).

So, we have seen the instantaneous semiotic militarization of the events of 9/11, and I have argued that this was preparatory to both the subsequent military action in Afghanistan and Iraq, and to the domestic unity sufficient to maintain that action. But what forms do this "militarization of social life" take post-9/11, and how do they relate to the processes of globalization to which the terrorist attacks were a response, and of which they were also symptomatic? Clearly, this is a prohibitively vast question, but in attempting to answer it one can do away very quickly with that delirious and improbable discourse on globalization which proclaims the end of the nation-state. Firstly, there are good structural reasons why the nation-state looks set to remain, such as capitalism's basis in property rights and the concomitant requirement of the rule of law, as well as the need to regulate capitalism's inherent tendency towards monopoly. But secondly, the post-9/11 era is clearly characterized by a *tightening*, not a loosening, of the state's regulatory powers. The mantra of "post-9/11" has been used to justify profound legal changes, such as the Patriot Act in the U.S. and the amendments to the Terrorism Act in Britain, both of which seriously threaten basic civil rights. The rights of assembly, association, and freedom of both speech and movement have been significantly curtailed. We have witnessed a general tightening up of immigration law and the asylum application process, particularly across Europe. Border security has been increased, as has surveillance once inside those borders. A new terminology has been invented to describe actors in this new era, such as "enemy combatants" or "unlawful combatants", as well as "rogue states". Unprecedented and legally liminal zones have arisen to administer the human embodiments of this era, such as Camp X-Ray in Guantánamo Bay, Cuba, where hundreds are detained without hope of a fair hearing in a civil court. And of course, 9/11 is offered as the explanation for massive increases in the already swollen military budgets of various states, the U.S. being prominent among them: Bush Jr. has presided over a 13% increase in military spending, which now stands at 396 billion dollars *per annum*. That is 15% higher than the average expenditure throughout the Cold War, and it looks set to reach 2.1 trillion dollars by 2010.

Therefore, just as the U.S. and its allies retain the right to intervene in the so-called "rogue states", so individual states now assert the right to intervene into their citizen's private lives in ways which suggest the limits of *laissez-faire* liberalism, even at the height of an aggressive global and economic neo-liberalism. It is true that nation-states are increasingly buffeted from below by NGOs, corporations and even private individuals, and from above by international bodies like the WTO and IMF and, albeit in a different way, by judicial entities like the Court of Human Rights. Yet the "war on terror" represents a way of both sidestepping the awkward legal stumbling blocks set up by national and supranational bodies, and of justifying ever tighter regulatory mechanisms on the domestic level. It enables states to treat their own citizens as potential "enemy combatants" precisely by fulfilling their primary delegated function of protecting those very citizens. To put this aphoristically, one could claim that the deregulation of war – that is, the removal of all rules, aims and codes of conduct which characterizes the "war on terror" – which is clearly related to the economic deregulation of corporate globalization, is also paradoxically related to the *re*regulation of social and cultural life for national subjects today.

If it is accepted that the nation-state, far from disappearing, is actually the most effective vehicle for the realization of the aims of global capital, but that in that realization, its own structures are being irrevocably altered – eroded in some ways certainly, but reasserted in others – then the role of logics of sovereignty in the deployment of *national* iconic histories for the manufacturing of hegemonic consent becomes crucial. As already signposted by the controversy over the firefighter memorial statue (Fig. 4), it is possible to make a link between the multicultural ideal of American sovereignty at home and its interventionist foreign policy abroad.

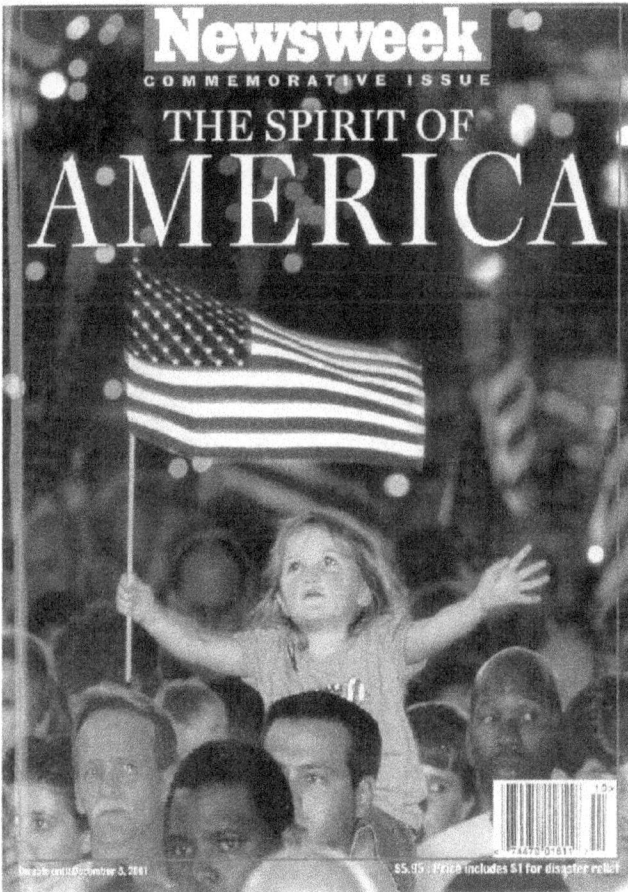

(Fig. 5)

Fig. 5 shows the front cover of a commemorative issue of *Newsweek* published one month after the terrorist attacks. One month on, I would suggest the tropes at work here have evolved from simple militarization. This image is ostensibly an attempt to recuperate the traumatic events of that day into a pre-existing national narrative of unity and shared collective grief. That is, 9/11 starts to be constructed as a "founding trauma". LaCapra defines such "founding traumas" as "traumas that paradoxically become the valorized or intensely cathected basis of identity for an individual or group rather than events that pose the problematic question of identity" (2001, 23). The particular emphasis now is on America-as "melting pot". We see the very deliberate racial and cultural diversity here, with African-American, Anglo-American, and Hispanic-American faces being arranged in a kind of United Colours of Benetton format, although note also that what Barthes would call the punctum of the image is still the flag in the little *white* girl's hand. One of the articles in this issue even shows an American Sikh wearing his turban in his own temple, for which the caption is "E PLURIBUS UNUM" – or "Out of Many, One". I would argue that this rendering of unity from multiplicity is a driving concern of American national sovereignty, and one that has a complicated relation to its famous frontier mentality (recent evidence of this mentality can be seen not only in the "liberation" of Iraq but equally in Bush's proposed conquest of Mars). Moreover, it is crucially the representation of difference that enables the alchemical transformation of multiplicity into unity. Indulging for a moment a vulgar schematic reduction, the relation of the representation of difference to logics of sovereignty, and by extension to logics of intervention, can be explained as follows.

A simple model of sovereignty would involve the spatialization of the reciprocal constitution of sameness and difference (Fig. 6).

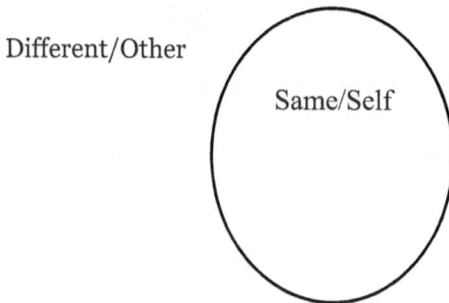

Different/Other

Same/Self

(Fig. 6)

However, given the empirical racial and ethnic diversity of the American population, but more importantly the discursive *ideal* of the "melting pot", sameness contains, indeed celebrates, internal difference (African-

American, Hispanic-American, Chinese-American, Anglo-American, etc.) (Fig. 7). Such multicultural celebration of difference, however, has an impact on the inside-outside topology of the border.

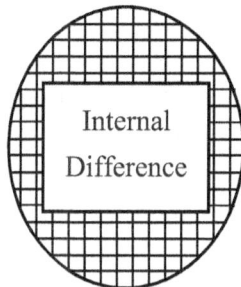

(Fig. 7)

For if the sense of self, in this case of the national self, is predicated on an oppositional or even an adversarial other, then a *different* difference is required to shore up the border between self and other (Fig. 8). I would therefore argue that an element of U.S. interventionist foreign policy is an incessant search for the different difference which will consolidate its own imagined community. By this schematic reduction, I do not mean to locate any simplistic notion of "agency" within the American psyche, but rather to suggest why it is that the American nation is currently the most appropriate vehicle for realizing the aims of global capital.

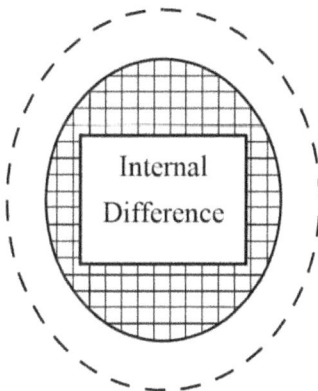

(Fig. 8)

Although it is problematic in some respects, Hardt and Negri's analysis in *Empire* of the logic of the permanent exception by which intervention is justified, remains pertinent, not least for its apparent prescience, written, as it was, prior to the declaration of the war on terror. They write:

> The concept of Empire is presented as a global concert under the direction of a single conductor, a unitary power that maintains the social peace and produces its ethical truths. And in order to achieve these ends, the single power is given the necessary force to conduct, when necessary, "just wars" at the borders against the barbarians and internally against the rebellious. (Hardt and Negri 2000, 10)

It is the logic of the exception, as a kind of deliberate aporia within the normative range of law (Agamben 1998), either domestic or international, which connects the regulation of interior and exterior spaces that I have tried to bring out as an aspect of the post-9/11 era (what Hardt and Negri call "biopolitical production"). The notion of "exceptional circumstances" can be loosely codified as a condition of imminent danger to the existence of the state, but it cannot be made to conform to pre-existing law. Procedural law relies precisely on precedent, but the state of exception is that which exceeds all precedent – as was implied of 9/11 itself. Thus, Hardt and Negri argue that in a new global Empire led by the U.S. there is an assertion of a permanent state of exception which suspends normative law long enough to enable "pre-emptive strikes" or "humanitarian interventions".

Hardt and Negri were writing before 9/11, yet there can be little doubt that the "war on terror" has become the way in which a state of permanent exception has been asserted and maintained (Butler 2004). It has two advantages. Firstly, that of encouraging the paranoia required of a truly panoptical system on the one hand (the terrorist can be the brown-skinned Arab fanatically quoting the Quran, or the innocuous white guy, or even woman, next door); secondly, that of justifying an interventionist foreign policy in the name of the "defence of the realm". The state is licensed to redouble its policing of both external barbarians and the internally rebellious.

One need not go down the conspiracy-theory route so lamentably popular today to argue that 9/11 provided a trope by which to justify increased global as well as local technologies of control. We need not suggest, that is, that the CIA, and not Al-Qaeda, were behind the terrorist attacks, as part of a neo-conservative plot to push the infamous "Project for a New American Century" into overdrive. We can, however, suggest that this project played an important role in the *semiotic* encoding of 9/11.

My argument here is not therefore a radical constructivism which would elide the specificity of 9/11: there *is* a specific and brutal truth of the events of 9/11, but there is also a different kind of truth implicit in its representation which betrays the appropriation of those events to a broader, and pre-existing, agenda. What I have tried to emphasize here is that a necessary corollary to the "Project for a New American Century" is an incessant *internal* nation-building which has increasingly taken the form of a militarization of social life. The concept of terrorism provides the radicalised difference which justifies both this militarization, and the logic of the permanent exception which suspends the juridical sovereignty of both local and international entities, thereby paving the way for the profusion of global conflicts we are witnessing today.

References

Agamben, G. (1998). *Homo Sacer: Sovereign Power and Bare Life.* Stanford: Stanford University Press.

Butler, J. (2004). *Precarious Life: The Powers of Mourning and Violence.* London: Verso.

Enloe, C. (1983). *Does Khaki Become You?: The Militarisation of Women's Lives.* Boston: South End Press.

Foucault, M. (1981). *The History of Sexuality Vol. 1: An Introduction,* trans. Frank Jellinek. Harmondsworth: Penguin.

Freud, S. (2003). *Beyond the Pleasure Principle and Other Writings.* London: Penguin [1920].

Hardt, M., Negri, A. (2000). *Empire.* London: Harvard University Press.

LaCapra, D. (2001). *Writing History, Writing Trauma.* London: Johns Hopkins University Press.

Wright, C. (2002). "Speaking out of the Blue? September 11th as Hate Speech". *Situation Analysis: A Forum for Critical Thought and International Current Affairs,* 1, 1, October, 26-39.

Barbed Wire Whipping Party:
Biographies and Geographies of (Legal) Terror (After 9/11)

David Fraser

A Rough Guide to the Archipelago of (Legal) Terror

Somewhere over Marib province in Yemen, a CIA pilotless Predator drone fires a Hellfire missile into a car holding six suspected Al-Qaeda members, killing them. This action is in clear violation of existing norms of international law, but justified by executive decree of the President of the United States (Downes 2004).

An Israeli aircraft fires two missiles at a car in the Gaza strip, killing Adnan al-Ghoul, a suspected bomb-maker and high-ranking Hamas official. Again in Gaza, an Israeli helicopter attacks and kills Khaled Abu Shamiyeh, in charge of constructing home-made Qassam rockets which were used against Israeli settlements. The spiritual founder of Hamas, Sheik Ahmed Yassin, was also targeted and killed as he left a mosque. Israelis also successfully "eliminated" his successor, Abdel Aziz Rantisi. In Damascus, a car bomb explodes killing Izzideen al-Sheik Khalil, another Hamas official. These targeted killings are again contrary to accepted international law norms, but justified by Israel's executive claims to preventative self-defence (Ben-Yehuda 1997; Nolte 2004; Statman 2004).

Pictures depicting the ritualised and systematic abuse and torture of prisoners in Abu Ghraib by U.S. soldiers are reproduced on television, the internet and in newspapers around the world. The International Red Cross and the FBI both report ongoing prisoner abuse at the detention facilities at Guantánamo Bay. President Bush's current nominee for the post of Attorney General, Alberto Gonzales, and other high-ranking lawyers in the U.S. Department of Justice write legal memoranda justifying abuse of prisoners as long as it falls short of their restrictive definition of "torture" (Gonzales *et al.* 2002).

The interim Iraqi government declares a "state of emergency" just before U.S. and Iraqi troops level the city of Fallujah.

Foreign nationals, identified as terrorist suspects by the British government, sit in the high-security Belmarsh Prison despite a House of Lords decision declaring their imprisonment contrary to international,

European and UK human rights legal guarantees.

All of these incidents of "targeted killings", imprisonment without trial, military assaults and torture can be seen and are justified as the responses of governments to the threat posed by "terrorists" in the aftermath of 9/11. At the same time, leading international lawyers con-demn the actions of various governments and their officials and agents as contrary to accepted and binding norms of the international legal order (Mansell 2004). Competing ideological, rhetorical and legal discourses today place and identify 9/11 as the moment in time when the war on terror began. While some legal scholars have criticized the rhetorical slippage from a discourse of crime and criminality to one of war as unnecessary and dangerous (Hayward and Morrison 2002), the more common view establishes and explains present time, i.e. after September 11, within a framework of an event of world historical moment (Dudziak 2004) and establishes the primacy of "war talk".

What I want to explore in the sections which follow is the possibility of another possibility, one which takes into account the traditional dichotomy of war versus crime as the way in which the legal nature of the war on terror can be understood by asserting the unity of the two, a jurisprudential situation where there are no more "rogue states" because every embodiment of national, lawful sovereignty is by definition a criminal "rogue state" (Derrida 2003, 115-153). This jurisprudence of the "state of exception" seeks to problematize these traditional dichotomous notions (crime/war, legal/illegal) by arguing that we in fact live in a system in which there is a paradoxical third way, in which law appears to destroy itself in order to save itself. I wish to argue that what we in fact find ourselves faced with is a return (if we have ever left) to the jurisprudence of the state of exception or state of emergency, a situation in which the sovereign power uses its legal powers to create an outlaw space populated by individuals and groups who by the force of law are removed from the effective force of law. The law inscribes specialised biographical notes on identified and identifiable bodies and establishes territorial limits in which geographical areas of exception are carved out for the operation of special and specific legal norms.

Some preliminary points about the jurisprudence of the state of emergency need to be briefly emphasized here. The first and most basic assertion upon which I rely is that the new world legal order "post-9/11" is not, in fact or in law, a singular event; it does not mark a new or novel state of being in the legal world. Here we can simply and for the sake of brevity rely on Walter Benjamin's eighth thesis on the philosophy of history:

> The tradition of the oppressed teaches us that the "state of emergency" in which we live is not the exception but the rule. We must attain to a conception of history that is in keeping with this insight. (Benjamin 1968, 257)

Benjamin here is of course referring to the philosophy of Carl Schmitt and to the era of Nazi rule in Germany. As Agamben has established (1998; 1999) and as I have argued elsewhere (2005), modernity and modern law in particular are marked beyond reasonable doubt with the ineffable theoretical and practical practices of the Schmittian exception. In the American context, Sanford Levinson also emphasizes that similar arguments about the essential core value of emergency rule can be found in the writings of Madison and Hamilton (2004). Thomas Jefferson in his revision of the laws of Virginia as it entered the new republic identified at least two categories of legal subject – freed slaves who entered the state or refused to leave it, and a white woman bearing a black child who refused to leave the state within a year – who could be killed but not murdered, the *homo sacer* (1950, 471).

The second and third points which underline and inform my analysis hereafter flow from Agamben's reading of Schmitt, and my own interpretation of Agamben's importance for our current and future jurisprudence. They are inter-related and grounded in the two central elements of the state of law in the state of exception. These are the two key concepts inherent in any appropriate and proper analysis of the state of law in the state of exception. First, as I have just underlined, there is the creation of the new legal subject, the *homo sacer*, the embodied subject of law who can be killed but who cannot be murdered. Thus Agamben describes accurately the way in which the legal order of the state of exception permits (and indeed requires) the physical elimination of a group of legal subjects identified not as the rights-bearing anomic individuals of liberal legalism, but as those who are *homo sacer*.

> Inscribed as a presupposed exception in every rule that orders or forbids something (for example, in the rule that forbids homicide) is the pure and unsanctionable figure of the offense that, in the normal

case, brings about the rule's own transgression (in the same example, the killing of a man not as natural violence, but as sovereign violence in the state of exception). (Agamben 1998, 21)

In the examples with which I began this chapter, one finds the present-day embodiment in legal practice of Agamben's *homo sacer* – the Al-Qaeda suspects travelling through the Yemeni desert; the Hamas officials targeted for elimination by the Israeli government; the citizens and occupants of Fallujah; the internees in Abu Ghraib, Guantánamo and Belmarsh; all are identified as exceptional legal subjects, as the subjects/objects of an exceptional legal regime in which they may be lawfully tortured and killed.

The final basic element which informs this analysis and which is central to our understanding of the juridical regime of exception is that the *homo sacer* always occupies a sovereign space in which the legal state of exception reigns. Foucault identifies the central *nexus* between the creation of a potentially disorderly urban space, the city, with the rise of police and governmentality (2004, 341-370). In the state of exception, these traditional notions of sovereignty which demand – in legal, constitutional and constitutive terms – a territory over which sovereignty must be exercised, continue to exist, albeit in a separately constituted sphere. Spatiality, territory, and governmentality are necessarily coeval concepts and practices (Dicken and Lausten 2002; Flint 2004). This new territory where the exceptional rule is the legal norm is "the camp" for Agamben (1998, 166-180). Again, we can see the ways in which each of the cases which serve as introductory examples here mark individuals as *homo sacer* and then define the territory in which these individuals are found as places and spaces in which the law of exception, the state of emergency, applies. This marks an advance within (post)modern legal rules and practices of governance.

Now in the times and spaces in which we live, the exception can be more precisely limited in its sphere of application. We do not live in Nazi times where the entire nation state was created as a space of exception; we have become more jurisprudentially sophisticated. We can limit the exception by more specifically targeting bodies and spaces. We can create what Derrida identified as the zone or *milieu* in which "rogue states" and individuals live and are "known to the police" (2003, 96-101). The technological advances embodied in Hellfire missiles, operated remotely and fired by drones, combine with the ever more efficient application of the jurisprudence of the state of exception to allow the modern nation state to target and to eliminate its enemies, those lives unworthy of life, without too much inconvenience to ordinary citizens.

The State of Exception: Carl Schmitt, Europe and America

"Sovereign is he who decides the exception" (*Souverän ist, wer über den Ausnahmezustand entscheidet*). These are the words of Carl Schmitt's jurisprudence of the state of exception which have found new purchase in jurisprudential circles since 9/11 (1934, 11). For leading thinkers on the liberal left in the United States in particular, Schmitt's insights into the politics and legality of states of emergency and states of exception pose difficult and troubling issues (Levinson 2004). While these scholars all identify the legal position adopted by the Bush administration in its version of the war on terror as posing fundamental challenges, not to say threats, to liberal democratic visions of the rule of law and human rights, they differ somewhat in the degree of jurisprudential scepticism which they adopt and apply to their analyses of the current situation.

Mark Tushnet, a leading constitutional law scholar of the left, creates a complex reading of the case law of the U.S. Supreme Court in relation to states of emergency in order to conclude that a basic and fundamental strength of American law and democracy resides in its institutional and institutionalised ability to learn from its past mistakes. For Tushnet, American constitutional jurisprudence can be best characterized as an institutional Habermasian dialogue in which the abuses of past declarations of states of emergency become lessons learned by current generations who remain acutely aware of the abusive potential of such legal mechanisms. For Tushnet, forewarned is forearmed (2003).

Kim Lane Scheppele (2004), on the other hand, argues more pessimistically that the United States government has resorted to a state of exception in an almost literal embodiment of the Schmittian legal ideal. Yet she is as optimistic as Tushnet for the legal future of human rights norms. She finds solace in the existence of a countervailing set of juridical norms and practices situated in European and international law and institutions. For her, the Schmittian world of the state of exception, of the world of politics as the inevitable battle between friend and foe (Schmitt 1996) in which legalized repression is a key weapon, has been transformed and transcended by the creation of the post-Auschwitz world legal order.

The real exception for her is the Bush administration's state of exception.

Scheppele in fact and in law offers a romantic and romanticised jurisprudential reading of European legal history, politics and current juridical practice. Putting aside Scheppele's taxonomical error of confusing the "is" and the "ought" in terms of the existence of an international legal order, and putting to one side the complex and never-ending debate over the status of international law as "law", what she fails to recognize is that, while European measures may differ in degree from those adopted under the *USA Patriot Act* and other American measures, there is clear evidence that anti-terror rhetoric in Europe itself has given rise to many of the same criticisms which Scheppele aims at American law and politics. In other words, the "state of exception" is not an American phenomenon, but one which clearly forms a central part of Western (and other) legal systems within modernity (Paye 2004).

At the same time, it is important to note that European authors like Jean-Claude Paye also fall victim to their own bizarre and ironic romanticisms. They make two fundamental and interconnected errors. First, they demonize the United States and give unwarranted primacy to American legal inventiveness. Paye is a classic example of this basic flaw. He asserts, in a completely ahistorical fashion, that various European nations have simply been complicit after the fact with American legal hegemony on the question of the state of exception. In other words, they have followed the American lead instead of, as Scheppele also incorrectly asserts, resisting by establishing a countervailing jurisprudential force. This primary error of ahistorical analysis is compounded by Paye's second failure to engage in another kind of legal historical analysis. He does not examine the real history of the state of exception and of the *homo sacer* outside of the United States.

Had he done so, he would have uncovered the unsettling fact that European and Western legalism, before, during and after the Holocaust, pre- and post-Auschwitz, was centrally implicated in the creation of states of exception as central components of national sovereign legal systems. European legal history, the jurisprudential core of legal modernity, is based on the battle of friend and foe, of collective exclusions and ultimately of Auschwitz as a European, not a German or Nazi, experience (Milner 2004). If we focus only on law "after Auschwitz", when we tell ourselves in an act of collective and legalized forgetting, that we have learned the lessons of the past, when Schmitt was reduced to exclusion and intellectual exile, when the new order of international human rights was created, we find ample proof of the continuous deployment of sovereign legal power over subjects and territories removed from "normal" law.

Torture, mass arrests and deportations, the destruction of civilian populations in the war on terror, all characterized both French democracy's reaction to the Algerian independence struggle in the 1950s and 1960s and the conflicts in the former Yugoslavia thirty years later.

If we step outside the context of war and armed conflict, the underlying normative jurisprudential structures of European and other states of legal exception have not changed. In 2004, the Italian government continued its practice of forcibly rendering refugees from its detention camp on Lampedusa. The so-called *zones d'attente* for asylum seekers in France, the classic "camp" inhabited by the *homo sacer*, continue to experience "republican" intimidation, violence and forced repatriations. Again in 2004, EU foreign ministers, ministers of justice and interior/home ministers met to discuss plans to establish what will be in effect detention centres for refugees and asylum seekers. What is most important about the EU plan is that the camps will be set up outside the sovereign territory of the EU itself, in North Africa (Libya and Tunisia have been mentioned as candidate countries) or elsewhere in Europe (Romania, for example). The sovereign territory and body politic of Europe are defended by the establishment of sovereign and legal zones of exception outside the geographical limits of the EU itself.

Outside of Europe, but still within the European legal tradition, Australia offers the best example of recent invocations of the normative juridical structures of the state of exception and its concomitant and necessary legal re/de/territorialization. By a series of legislative amendments and executive decrees, the government of Australia has proceeded with the creation of "immigration exclusion zones". Under this legal state of exception, the Australians have declared some parts of the nation, consisting of off-shore islands closest to the territory of Indonesia and therefore on the route favoured by "people smugglers", to be "not Australian" for purposes of immigration and/or asylum applications. In other words, a sovereign nation state has exercised its powers to declare a part of its physical territorial space not part of its territory for the express and sole purpose of excluding the Other, the new subject outside the operation of Australian and international law, by the very act of a legal state of physical and ontological exception.

What figure in all of these examples, from legally sanctioned torture and killing by the French in Algeria (then a colony of France), to the conflicts in the former Yugoslavia, to various measures against asylum seekers and refugees, are the two intertwined concepts with which I began this study – the dual creation of a subject Other, the *homo sacer*, to whom the norms of exception apply; and a delimited territory in which the *homo sacer* is enclosed and excluded. The sovereign exception applies, in a new sovereign space, to the subject who has no sovereign protection as a citizen. Again, history and Agamben are instructive and illustrative here:

> And one of the few rules to which the Nazis constantly adhered during the course of the "Final Solution" was that Jews could be sent to the extermination camps only after they had been fully denationalized (stripped even of the residual citizenship left to them after the Nuremberg Laws). (Agamben 1998, 132)

What emerges from the current debates about law and the state of exception, besides the historical ignorance or blindness of participants therein, is the central role which law has always played in the creation of the state of exception, and in the identification and elimination of those subjects who must inhabit the sovereign territories in which the state of exception is the rule. In the final section of this essay, I wish to turn briefly to a slightly fuller examination of this centrality of law in creating a state which many erroneously continue to characterize as one of "nonlaw".

Legal Black Holes: Guantánamo, Belmarsh and Beyond (Law?)

Lord Steyn has famously characterized the detention regime at Guantánamo as "a legal black hole" (2004, 1). By this, Lord Steyn clearly means that executive detention, forced interrogation, mistreatment and possibly torture, with proceedings before a specially constituted military commission, in fact constitute something which is not a "legal" regime as we would know and properly characterize it. For him, the very notion of law requires due process, open and public trials, humane treatment, etc. In other words, law, justice, and human rights are intertwined concepts and necessary conditions each of the other. These are important jurisprudential assertions and the issues raised are clearly of great legal and political moment. Yet, they remain assertions the underlying assumptions of which must be carefully interrogated if we are more fully to comprehend the real stakes at play in the debates over the nature and function of the "state of exception".

At one level, Lord Steyn can be seen to be asserting a simple natural law jurisprudence, one informed by a Radbruchian understanding of "law after Auschwitz" (1946). Here, law must have a substantive content which complies with a basic accepted normative ordering. Law which merely appears in a legal form but which has a normative content offensive to the basic minimal requirements is "not law" (*Unrecht*). At the same time, it may also be possible to support Steyn's claim about the appropriate characterization of Guantánamo Bay by referring simply to a set of domestic and international existing legal norms which are violated by the regime at Camps X-Ray and Delta. Such a position would assert a conjunction of natural law principles and positive law, without the necessity of justifying those principles by reference to an extra-legal moral *Grundnorm*. Unfortunately, space does not allow a more complex and fuller analysis of Steyn's argument here.

What does emerge either from the natural law position or from a legal positivist reading of Lord Steyn's "black hole" position, however, is the basic premise of much jurisprudential debate about the normative character of the "state of exception". Steyn clearly falls into the camp of those who assert that the "state of exception", at least as practised by the Bush administration, is an extra-legal situation. In other words, the "state of exception" is an exception to a normal state of affairs, of government and of governmentality in which law obtains.

In a recent review of the new English translation of Agamben's *State of Exception*, Malcolm Bull (2004) identifies what he sees as an important shift in Agamben's jurisprudence of the state of exception. According to Bull, Agamben has moved from characterizing the state of exception as one which still deeply implicates, and indeed defines law itself to a newer, perhaps more radical position, in which the state of exception is posited as one outside of law altogether. Rather than occupying a position on the threshold of law, where law is at once inside and outside the state of exception, law now, according to this reading of Agamben's reading of the state of exception, is no longer in play within the state of exception. Again, I am unable to fully address the accuracy or indeed the utility of Bull's reading of Agamben. Instead, I shall circumvent the debate at this point by returning to the fundamental insight which unites the Schmittian position with that adopted by Critical Legal Studies in the United States in the 1970s and 1980s, that in reality "law is politics".

I do this not to elide and avoid central questions, but to return to Schmitt and bring him to Guantánamo and Belmarsh. For Schmitt, the political, which always enjoys a state of primacy and which is characterized by a state of war with the enemies of the state/nation/ *Volksgemeinschaft*/ body politic, carries with it, in the exercise of sovereignty, in the sovereign moment of the decision to enter the state of exception, an invaluable premium, perhaps now what we call a *trace* of law. Schmitt divides this political premium into three inter-related juridical and political trumps. First, the declaration of the state of emergency is always an event of governmentality in real space and time. Second, the holder of legal authority, s/he who declares the state of exception, has by the very nature of law, politics and sovereignty, a presumption of legality for any actions relating to the state of emergency. As a necessary consequence of the first two aspects of sovereign power in the state of exception,

> ... even in cases of doubtful legality (1932/36) the directives of the legal holder of state power are directly executable in the immediate instance, even when opportunities for legal challenges and judicial protections are provided. (Schmitt 2004, 32)

This analysis is of vital importance to our understanding of the current state of law and jurisprudence "after 9/11". Just as Auschwitz was a time and place full of bodies and full of law – and full of bodies only because it was full of law (Fraser 1999) – Guantánamo and Belmarsh are equally full of law. This is the insight which we find, ironically perhaps, in Lord Steyn's choice of the metaphor of a "legal black hole". A black hole is not an empty space, not a space from which law is absent. A black hole is a space where matter is so densely packed, so heavily present, that nothing can escape. Guantánamo and Belmarsh and other spaces, other sovereign territories populated by the *homo sacer*, are precisely those sovereign territories in which sovereignty and law reach their plenitude, where there is precisely no escape from law, power and the exception, because there is nothing but law, power and exception.

This becomes clear upon even the most cursory examination of those legal instruments which define existence in these spaces. They are first of all created by sovereign instruments, in the case of Guantánamo, of course, by a treaty between state powers at the end of the Spanish-American war.

They are physically delimited spaces with a series of legal ordering instruments – executive orders, congressional resolutions, Acts of Parliament; and most important for present purposes, and for the third of Schmitt's political premiums, they are spaces in which formal liberal legality exists while at the same time leaving practical room for manoeuvre for the political/legal realities of the state of exception to operate.

If we examine the recent decision of the House of Lords involving foreign nationals subject to indefinite detention at Belmarsh Prison, the situation and appropriate jurisprudential positioning of the (post?) modern state of exception become clear. Thus, in *A and Others v. Secretary of State* (UKHL 56, 2004), the Court was faced with a legal challenge to the regime under which suspected terrorists, all foreign nationals, were detained without trial under section 21 of the Antiterrorism, Crime and Security Act 2001. The government claimed that their detention was warranted on the facts and that the statutory regime under which they were held was a justifiable invocation of the "state of emergency" provisions of the European Convention on Human Rights. Article 15 of the Convention provides that,

> In time of war or other public emergency threatening the life of the nation any High Contracting Party may take measures derogating from its obligations under this Convention to the extent strictly provided by the exigencies of the situation, provided that such measures are not inconsistent with other obligations under international law.

The Court found, by a majority, that the detention of foreign nationals was in violation of the rights of the detainees under the Convention and under the Human Rights Act. At first blush, one can read this case as an embodiment of the principles of liberal legality and of human rights discourse. If it is not inappropriate to reintroduce the metaphor here, the light of the law has been shone into the black hole of detention without trial of the *homo sacer* of Belmarsh Prison. They have been re-incorporated into the body politic and taken into the arms of traditional British justice.

But another reading is also possible. The House of Lords accepted without contention the government's finding that a state of emergency as set out in Article 15 does in fact exist and that the nation is threatened. What they took issue with was whether the other criteria of Article 15 had been met, especially as to measures "strictly provided by the exigencies of the situation". In reality, the government was partly hoist by its own jurisprudential petard because it sought to characterize the detention as an immigration matter, while at the same time agreeing that two of the detainees had in fact been sent to other countries. This was found to be logically inconsistent with its other assertions that detention was necessary, because those being held were international terrorists bent on the destruction of the nation. Similarly, it must also be emphasized here that a central element of the Court's decision was that the actual regime differentiated between nationals and non-citizens, on unlawful grounds of discrimination. If there is a terrorist threat justifying such emergency measures, the Court argued, how can terrorists who are British subjects be treated differently from non-nationals?

This last point is central to our more complete understanding of the role and nature of the state of exception in British and American law today. The detainees remained in Belmarsh Prison, well after the House of Lords reached its decision. The Home Office had announced its intention to continue to hold the "terrorists" in custody. Among the favoured options was a change in the legislation to make it applicable to all terror suspects, British and non-British, thereby removing the discrimination question. The debate here is not about legal black holes in any real sense which might give comfort to those who continue to believe in liberal legalisms. Instead it can be reduced in practice to a debate over the exact make-up of the category *homo sacer*.

Not surprisingly, a similar situation obtains at Guantánamo Bay. A series of cases in Federal Courts have recognized the rights of detainees to make *habeas corpus* claims before competent United States Courts and the U.S. Supreme Court has also recognized the rights of American citizens to due process in the determination of their status as "unlawful combatants" (*Hamdi v. Rumsfeld*, 2004, 124 S. Ct. 2633; *Rasul v. Bush*, 2004, 124 S. Ct. 2686). Yet almost all of the parties to these suits remain in detention. Once again, the courts have accepted the government's assertion of a state of emergency and of an underlying basis for this fundamental claim. The debate centres on the legal margins, on what process to apply to the extraordinary situation, how much law, and what kind of law must be applied in the "state of exception".

Meanwhile, throughout the United States, hundreds if not thousands of individuals, some American citizens, others foreign nationals, were rounded up by immigration officials in the days and weeks which followed September 11. They remain in investigative, immigration detention. They cannot be publicly identified; their lawyers cannot be named; the place of their detention cannot be revealed. These are the new *homo sacer*, nameless, without identities and without any real hope because the law operates on their bodies in this very real sense.

Kim Lane Scheppele is correct when she argues that an emerging international legal order calls into question the Bush administration's war on terror, but she is wrong in all other aspects of her analysis. The new international legal order is this new, transnational gulag archipelago in which torture, like call-centres or manufacturing jobs, is outsourced. This evolving international state of exception, this new juridical order, is an international system of technology, legal cooperation and sovereignty. The CIA flies suspects to countries in which torture is routinely practised, Morocco, Egypt, Azerbaijan, Uzbekistan, Pakistan, in its Gulfstream executive jet, number N379P, owned first by Premier Executive Transport Services Inc. and now by Bayard Foreign Marketing of Portland, Oregon.

The new, jetsetting *homo sacer* is escorted to new places of international cooperation, where s/he can be tortured and killed without being murdered. The technology of easy aeroplane travel, the legal structures which combine a state of exception with normal and lawful aircraft lease arrangements, serve to immunize the body politic by carrying away the contagion to a place where it can be properly dealt with. And all under the watchful eye of the sovereign power of the law. As Schmitt has reminded us, this is the centrality of the intersection of law and politics in the "political premium":

> ... even in cases of doubtful legality (1932/36) the directives of the legal holder of state power are directly executable in the immediate instance, even when opportunities for legal challenges and judicial protections are provided. (Schmitt 2004, 32)

References

Agamben, G. (1998). *Homo Sacer: Sovereign Power and Bare Life.* Stanford: Stanford University Press.

Agamben, G. (1999). *Remnants of Auschwitz: The Witness and the Archive.* New York: Zone Books.

Agamben, G. (2005). *State of Exception.* Chicago: University of Chicago

Press.

Benjamin, W. (1968). "Theses on the Philosophy of History", *Illuminations*. New York: Schocken Books, 253-264.

Ben-Yehuda, N. (1997). "Political Assassination as a Cross-cultural Form of Alternative Justice". *International Journal of Comparative Sociology*, 38, 1, 25-55.

Bull, M. (2004). "States don't really mind their citizens dying (provided they don't do it all at once): they just don't like anyone else to kill them". *London Review of Books*, 26, 24, 3-6.

Derrida, J. (2003). *Voyous*. Paris: Galilée.

Dicken, B. and Lausten, C. B. (2002). "Zones of Indistinction: Security, Terror and Bare Life". *Space and Culture*, 5, 3, 290-307.

Downes, C. (2004). "'Targeted Killings' in an Age of Terror: the Legality of the Yemen Strike". *Journal of Conflict and Security Law*, 9, 3, 277-294.

Dudziak, M. L. (ed.) (2004). *September 11 in History: A Watershed Moment?* Durham, N.C., and London: Duke University Press.

Flint, C. (ed.) (2004). *The Geography of War and Peace: From Death Camps to Diplomats*. Oxford: Oxford University Press.

Foucault, M. (2004). *Sécurité, territoire, population*. Paris: Gallimard Seuil.

Fraser, D. (1999). "Dead Man Walking: Law and Ethics After Giorgio Agamben's Auschwitz". *International Journal of the Semiotics of Law*, 12, 4, 397-417.

Fraser, D. (2005). *Law After Auschwitz: Towards A Jurisprudence of the Holocaust*. Durham: Carolina Academic Press.

Gonzales, A. *et al.* (2002). "Memorandum for John Yoo, Deputy Assistant Attorney General, Office of Legal Counsel, from James C. Ho, AttorneyAdvisor, Office of Legal Counsel, Re: Possible interpretations of Common Article 3 of the 1949 Geneva Convention Relative to the Treatment of Prisoners of War" (1 February 2002); Memorandum for Alberto Gonzales, Counsel to the President, from Jay S. Bybee, Assistant Attorney General, Re: Standards of conduct for interrogation under 18 U.S.C. §§2340-1240A (1 August).

Hayward, K. and Morrison, W. (2002). "Locating 'Ground Zero': Caught Between the Narratives of War and Crime", in Strawson, J. (ed.), *Law After Ground Zero*. London: Glasshouse Press, 139-157.

Jefferson, T. (1950). *The Papers of Thomas Jefferson*. Vol. 1. Princeton: Princeton University Press.

Levinson, S. (2004). "Torture in Iraq and the Rule of Law in America". *Daedalus,* Summer, 5-9.

Mansell, W. (2004). "Goodbye to All That? The Rule of Law, International Law, the United States and the Use of Force". *Journal of Law and Society,* 31, 4, 433-456.

Milner, J. (2004). *Les penchants criminels de l'Europe démocratique.* Paris: Verdier.

Nolte, G. (2004). "Preventive Use of Force and Preventive Killings: Moves into a Different Legal Order", *Theoretical Inquiries in Law,* 5, 1, 111-129.

Paye, J. (2004). *La fin de l'État de droit: La lutte antiterroriste de l'état d'exception à la dictature.* Paris: La Dispute.

Radbruch, G. (1946). "Gesetzliches Unrecht und Übergestzliches Recht", *Süddeutsche Juristen-Zeitung,* 1, 1, 105-111.

Scheppele, K. L. (2004). "Law in a Time of Emergency: States of Exception and the Temptations of 9/11". University of Pennsylvania Law School, *Public Law and Legal Theory Research Paper Series*, Research Paper no. 60.

Schmitt, C. (1934). *Politische Theologie.* Duncker and Humblot: Munich.

Schmitt, C. (1996). *The Concept of the Political.* Chicago and London: University of Chicago Press.

Schmitt, C. (2004). *Legality and Legitimacy.* Durham, N.C., and London: Duke University Press.

Sheehan, C. A. (2004). "Madison v. Hamilton: The Battle over Republicanism and the Role of Public Opinion". *The American Political Science Review,* 98, 3, 405-424.

Statman, D. (2004). "Targeted Killings". *Theoretical Inquiries in Law,* 5, 1, 179-198.

Steyn, J. (2004). "Guantánamo Bay: The Legal Black Hole". *International and Comparative Law Quarterly,* 53, 1-15.

Tushnet, M. (2003). "Defending Korematsu?: Reflections on Civil Liberties in Wartime". *Wisconsin Law Review,* 273-307.

Histories

Las Casas and the Black Legend of Spain[*]

Jeremy Lawrance

As a boy of eighteen Bartolomé de las Casas (1484–1566) was taken by his father to Hispaniola (Haïti-República Dominicana), where he witnessed the early stages of the Spanish conquest of the New World. After twelve years, appalled by his countrymen's treatment of native Americans, he became a missionary and campaigner against slavery. Las Casas's ensuing struggle earned him the title "Protector of the Indians" and an honourable place in the history of humanitarian ideas. This paper discusses how the most powerful of his campaigning works, *Very Brief Relation of the Destruction of the Indies*, gave rise to the Black Legend, the idea that the Spanish empire was uniquely cruel and rapacious.[1] My purpose is to reflect on what bearing this might have on our understanding of the role of the visual in the genre of post-conflict testimony.

Las Casas's narrative covers the fifty years from the first contact between Europeans and Americans in 1492 to the time when he drafted the book in 1542. By then the native population of the West Indies was extinct; *Brief Relation* sets out to document a genocide. Whereas Columbus's fundamental metaphor for the New World had been earthly paradise, Las Casas used another enduring allegory, hell on earth. The symbolic contrast between these two conceits is the inner mainspring of *Brief Relation*, but Las Casas did not set out to write a literary work. He had a political manifesto to put forward (to persuade Prince Philip of Spain to stop granting licences to conquistadors, Prólogo, 71–73); his book was written for this instrumental purpose, not as an end in itself. However, if we expect such a text to be less concerned with literary affect than, say, a novel, we find the opposite; Las Casas is more rhetorical than his purpose seems to warrant, and *Brief Relation* requires reading with the same hermeneutic suspicion-circumspection as any overtly artistic work.

---

[*] Lawrance 2009 is an expanded version of this essay, with further illustrations and more detailed bibliography. I am grateful to the editors for inviting me to republish the paper here in its original form for the wider audience of post-conflict scholars.
[1] *Brevísima relación de la destruición de las Indias*, first published in Las Casas 1552, is henceforth cited as *Brief Relation*, by chapter-heading and page in Las Casas 2007. All translations and emphases are mine. On the Black Legend see Gibson 1971.

In what follows I set Las Casas's work in context, pick apart its contents with the critical mistrust just mentioned, and consider how it was used and abused to produce the Black Legend.

Historical circumstances of *Brief Relation*

Columbus never admitted that he had blundered into the wrong continent – he obstinately went on calling it "the Indies" – but before he died in 1506 he knew something had gone badly wrong with its conquest. On his last voyage in 1503, while marooned for a year in Jamaica by hurricanes, he began to hallucinate and hear voices. As he prepared for death, the horrors of the disaster he had unleashed gnawed at his conscience:

This is no child to give to a stepmother to suckle. I never think of Hispaniola, Paria, or the other lands without tears. [...] They are lying face down; even if they do not die, the sickness is incurable or chronic. Let the man who brought them to this pass come forward with the remedy, if he can. [...]

The whole coast and islands have been plundered, and a great number of people killed. All the days of their life the survivors will never be our friends. [...] I always stated in writing to your Highness that the Indians were the gold and wealth of this place. [...] Once the Indians are lost, the land is lost. [...]

Until now I have wept for others; may Heaven now have pity on me, and earth weep for me. [...] I did not come on this voyage to gain honour or property; I came with sincere intention and true enthusiasm, this is no lie. I beg your Highness to pardon me if I have said anything against your royal will; I am in such anguish and extremity, it is a wonder I have not gone raving mad. (*Relación del cuarto viaje*, in Colón 1992, 499-502)

No longer the heroic *Christophorus*, Christ-bearer, but a harbinger of apocalypse – Columbus's self-image in the Jamaica letter records a journey of disillusion and spiritual disintegration that was no doubt travelled by countless idealistic young Spaniards over the next half century. It epitomizes the real theme of this paper: the trauma that afflicts not losers but victors of conflict. In this respect, as we shall see, Las Casas had little to add.

The psychological speculation of the preceding paragraph will form part of my conclusion about the meaning of *Brief Relation*; here we are concerned with the practical context of Columbus's realization of failure and guilt. The problems were in part institutional: conquistadors carried to the Caribbean methods of economic exploitation developed over centuries of frontier war with Islam, and these proved disastrous to the Taínos, who were unequipped to survive the *encomienda* system of forced labour. Queen Isabel also realized that all was not well; on 23 November 1504, three days before her death, she expressed her disquiet in a codicil to her will bidding her successors to care for the welfare of her American vassals and ensure "they receive no injury to their persons or property and that they are well and justly treated; and *if they have received any injury, to remedy it*" (Isabel I de Castilla 2001, 28).

It is worth laying stress on this conscience-stricken side of Spanish imperialism, in view of what will be said later about the Black Legend. Matters came to a head in Santo Domingo in 1511 when the Dominican friar Antonio Montesinos delivered an Advent sermon in which he denounced the conquistadors to their faces, declaring that they were in mortal sin, and refused them absolution until they repented.[2] When the scandal reached Spain the king submitted the problem to a *junta* or commission of theologians and lawyers with instructions to legislate (Laws of Burgos 1512–13).

Over the next forty years, as conquest engulfed the empires of the Maya, Aztecs, and Incas, a series of such *juntas* subjected the Crown's exercise of its imperial dominion to scrutiny – a process that Lewis Hanke (1949) dubbed the Spanish struggle for justice in the conquest of America. Its intellectual leader was a Dominican friar, Francisco de Vitoria (ca. 1485–1546), professor of theology at Salamanca. In a lecture composed in response to a Crown inquiry in 1539 Vitoria discussed by what law the enterprise of the Indies could be defended (*On the American Indians*, in Vitoria 1991, 231–292). He demolished all eighteen cases constructed by earlier *juntas*, including the most contentious, that Americans fell into Aristotle's category of "natural slaves" because of barbarian practices such as human sacrifice, polygamy, and cannibalism. His verdict, though expressed in the conditional, was stunning:

[2] Our source is Las Casas, *Historia de las Indias*, Bk III, chs 3-7 (1986, III, 10-27), who quotes the sermon: "By what justice do you hold these Indians in such cruel and horrible slavery? [...] Are they not men? Do they not have rational souls? Are you not commanded to *love them as yourselves*?" (ch. 4, p. 13; cf. Mt 22. 36-40).

The conclusion of this dispute appears to be that if all these titles are inapplicable, that is to say if the barbarians gave no just cause for war and did not wish to have Spaniards as princes, *the whole Indian expedition and trade would cease.* (Vitoria 1991, 291)

Vitoria concluded that the Crown should restrict its activities in the Indies to commerce and missionary work. He was by no means the only critic of empire, but he was the most influential; Charles V forbade him to publish his views (they were first printed in 1557), but within the royal council they were discussed and acted upon. What emerged were the New Laws (*Leyes nuevas*) of 1542 banning the *encomienda, requerimiento,* and other abuses.

By that time Vitoria's fellow Dominican Las Casas was already active in imperial politics. He had started out in Santo Domingo in 1502 as a slave-owner and lay cleric. It seems he was little moved by Montesinos's sermon in 1511, though he knew it (n.2, above); at all events, he joined the conquistador Diego Velázquez's "pacification" of Cuba later that year and earned an *encomienda* of slaves. There he witnessed atrocities described in *Brief Relation,* but it was not until three years later, in 1514, that he underwent conversion, released his slaves, and began to petition the Crown. Finally in 1522 he entered the Dominican order to serve as a missionary. Las Casas was no intellectual; he was concerned with action, often at the risk of his life. His campaign involved travel to and fro across the Atlantic, two failed attempts to set up model communities for native Americans, duty as bishop of Chiapas in Mexico, and an endless round of petitions and complaints to the Crown.

Of Las Casas's voluminous works the most notorious is *Brief Relation.* It was written in the run-up to the campaign for the New Laws of 1542, and published ten years later with seven other tracts arising from another famous *junta* (Valladolid 1551) in which Las Casas disputed the question of natural slavery with a lay scholar, Juan Ginés de Sepúlveda (Las Casas 1992). One aim in printing *Brief Relation* alongside the texts of this latter dispute was to bring to public notice the truth of what was really going on in America. When courtiers first heard its tale of atrocities, the shock brought on "a kind of mental fit or faint" (*Brief Relation,* Argumento, 69).

The subsequent fame of *Brief Relation* had little to do with Las Casas's philanthropic aims. Its diffusion was effected by Protestant polemicists who took it up as a weapon to blacken the name of Spain. It was translated into the languages of her imperialist rivals (Dutch, French, English) and furnished with illustrations, the most famous of which, a set of copperplate engravings for a Latin translation published by Théodore de Bry at Frankfurt in 1598, provided an iconography of the Spanish conquest that remains embedded in the popular *imaginaire* to this day. De Bry's *Very True Narration of the Indian Lands Devastated by Certain Spaniards* (Las Casas 1598) played a leading role in spreading the Black Legend.

Analysis of *Brief Relation*

To read Las Casas's book is thus to confront a text that, though written for instrumental ends and in a purposely manipulative style, engineered an unintended response. The stated aim was to secure justice for native Americans; instead, readers construed the book as a hymn of hate against Spaniards. The problem, then, is to understand how *Brief Relation*'s medium so undermined its pragmatic message. I suggest that the contradiction can partly be unlocked by reading the text not as a political pamphlet, but as testimony.[3]

On the face of it there seems little ambiguity about the book's genre; it flaunts every oratorical strategy of forensic diatribe. In the opening chapter Las Casas writes, with characteristic prolixity:

Upon these gentle lambs, endowed with all the aforesaid qualities by their Maker and Creator, the Spaniards fell [...] like most cruel wolves, tigers, and lions ravening with many days' hunger; and in the ensuing forty years up to today they have done, and still do now today, nothing except cut them to pieces, murder them, distress them, afflict them, torture them and destroy them by strange, new, varied, and never seen or read of or heard of manners of cruelty, of which a few will be told below; to such a degree that where once we saw over three million souls on the island of Hispaniola, there are not so many as two hundred natives left. (*Brief Relation*, Descubriéronse las Indias, 77)

This is offered as a documentary record of witness evidence ("we saw"),

---

[3] I use this term because, as Dr Parvathi Kumaraswami pointed out to me, "testimonial" (*testimonio*) is normally reserved for subaltern witness, whereas Las Casas belonged to the colonial class. Her observation serves precisely to pinpoint the paradox of the rhetoric of *Brief Relation*, which evinces a sense of powerlessness we expect of the colonized, not the colonizer.

but we are immediately struck by the style, which is not objective but affective, a language of feeling, not fact. It is marked by overt rhetoric; the three chief devices are, to use the terms Las Casas would have been taught, *superlatio* or *excessus* (exaggeration: "many never seen or read of or heard of manners of cruelty"), *amplificatio* or *tautologia* (accumulation: "tear to shreds, murder, distress, afflict, torture, and destroy", reinforced in Spanish by alliteration and rhyme), and *parabola* (metaphor designed to arouse pathos: the biblical image of innocent lambs and ravening wolves, cf. Ezekiel 22.27, Acts 20.29). Such tropes aim at the passions, not the mind; the chosen tactic is shock – hammering us into submission by sensational hyperbole and inexorable repetition. Despite the attempt to create an air of objectivity with statistics (3,000,000 reduced to 200), the passage is motivated less by an impulse to record facts than by an urgent desire to convince, to engineer a response through subjective emotion. A tell-tale sign of such subjectivity is the careless mistake, writing in 1542, "*forty* years" (Las Casas inadvertently counts from when he himself arrived, in 1502). Even the claim to authority based on personal witness ("we saw") turns out to be figurative: the very rhetoric of autopsy renders this transparent because, however he might have reached a figure of three million inhabitants of Hispaniola, Las Casas could never in any meaningful sense have "seen" it.[4]

Such cumulative strategies of hyperbole have drawbacks, the chief one being the law of diminishing returns. Our sense of fatigue is compounded by the unreadability of the content. Every page of *Brief Relation* – twenty chapters, some 30,000 words – is crammed with descriptions of native Americans being burnt or buried alive, of hands, ears, noses, genitals, or breasts cut off, of babies hacked from their mothers' bellies, fed to dogs, or smashed against stones, of rows of men and women tied together and hung over barbecues or herded into staked pits, hunted with hounds, forced to butcher and eat each other, or worked and starved to such despair that they hang themselves or go mad and kill their children – a ceaseless litany of rape, massacre, and enslavement. Far from building up a cumulative argument, the surfeit of horrors blunts and repels rational response. A case in point is the constant inflation of quantitative data. For Las Casas

---

[4] I do not mean to imply that this invalidates the essential truth of Las Casas's account: the native population of Hispaniola (probably 0·25-0·5 million before contact: see Henige 1978, Zambardino 1978, Livi-Bacci 2003) dropped to 30,000 by 1516, and was effectively extinct by 1542 (Cook 1998, 15-59).

exaggeration is an uncontrollable spasmodic reaction, even though he must know it will be seen through, as when he calls Marién in Haïti (ca 4000 km²) "bigger and richer than Portugal", which at 88,000 km² is larger than the whole of Hispaniola (Los reinos que había en la isla Española, 85). Before claiming that "where we saw over three million souls there are not two hundred", he speaks of "large and infinite islands, all of which we saw had *as high a population* of native inhabitants *as any populated land on earth*", and of a land "as full as a beehive with peoples [...], so it seems God placed in these lands *the whole mass or greater proportion of the whole human race*" (Descubriéronse las Indias, 75). By the end of the chapter he declares that 2000 leagues (11,100 km) of islands round Puerto Rico and ten mainland kingdoms each "larger than Spain" have been left "uninhabited and desolate":

> We will give as a very certain and true count that there have been unjustly and tyranically killed in the said forty years by the said tyrannical and diabolical acts of the Christians more than twelve million souls, men, women, and children, and in truth, that I believe, without I think deceiving myself, that they are more than fifteen million. (Descubriéronse las Indias, 78)

Each overstatement is topped by another, until finally Las Casas cannot resist the futile temptation of pumping up the already wild figures in the course of a single sentence. In the end such language proves self-defeating and needlessly provokes the easiest form of denial. But to question Las Casas's veracity is the opposite of my point. To read his rhetoric as if it were meant to be taken literally is to misrepresent his book's spirit and genre; the defiance of logic in his arithmetic betrays neither insincerity nor mendacity, but a tragic pathology of despair. I contend not that Las Casas lied, but the opposite: namely, that he testified to the truth as he "saw" it.

This brings us back to a trope already remarked as unreliable: the claim to be an eye-witness. Las Casas's statements are constantly bolstered with references to visual autopsy ("we saw", "I saw for myself", "we have seen with our eyes for forty-two years"). He cannot have seen these things; the claim is meant to lend urgency, but when he says "we saw over three million souls" we know the assertion is rhetorical. The phrase is just his emphatic way of stating a conviction; as Michel de Certeau perceived, such appeals to the senses assert "a link to the body" as the only guarantee of "the real that is lost in language" (Certeau 1986, 72, cited by Pagden 1991, 150). Las Casas's insistence on the claim to autopsy, even when it defies reason, is what urges us to take *Brief Relation* not as a *relación* or official report, as its title claims, but as testimony; and this, in turn, justifies its claim to be truthful. At several points Las Casas explicitly presents his text in such a guise: he writes, he says, "as a man with more than fifty years' experience of *seeing at first hand* the evil and the harm", though it was less than forty (Prólogo, 72), and repeats, "I speak with truth from what I know *and have seen* through all this time", though more than half the book is about countries he never visited (Descubriéronse las Indias, 79).

So what had Las Casas witnessed? Not everything he claims, since much of it was not there to be seen, but we can ask a different question: had he ever been present while a native American was butchered, his children stolen, or his wife raped? The answer is yes; we know that from 1503 the teenage Las Casas was given a *repartimiento* of slaves, that he saw the decimation of the Taínos of Hispaniola under Nicolás de Ovando's governorship, and that during the three critical years in Cuba leading up to his conversion in 1514 he was party to atrocities committed by his commander, Diego Velázquez. He tells us of his involvement in these events not only in the first five chapters of *Brief Relation*, but also in greater detail in his huge manuscript *Historia de las Indias* (e.g. Bk II, chs 3–36, in Las Casas 1986, II, 16–134). We might plausibly conclude that *Brief Relation*'s entire unbearable catalogue – which ostensibly covers half a century of atrocity across an entire continent – is really about one man's experience of eleven years in Hispaniola and Cuba.

This last conjecture is suggested by certain disturbing scenes that seem to prize open the hermetic shell of Las Casas's righteous anger and hint at a subliminal guilt – not as a sense of culpability, but as a psychological reaction. For example, describing how *caciques* were executed by being roasted, he states:

> Once *I saw* that, having four or five leaders and lords roasting on these griddles (and I also think there were two or three pairs of griddles where others were burning) and because they were howling so loudly that it was upsetting the captain or keeping him awake, he gave orders for them to be strangled; and the sergeant who was burning them, a man worse than any hangman (I know what he was called and even met his relatives in Seville), not wanting to strangle them, put wooden

bungs in their mouths with his own hands to stop them making a noise, and then stoked the fire under them until they roasted slowly as he wanted. (De la isla Española, 81–82)

This scene, pictured in one of De Bry's dramatic images (Fig. 2), has the hallmarks of first-hand witness; the circumstantial claim, "I know what he was called", unlike the ones examined before, demands to be taken literally. Having needlessly told us he knew the name, why does he not say it? It is his normal practice to refrain from naming "tyrants", but this is usually because they were all too easily identifiable, or (less often) because he did not know them.[5] Here, by contrast, the phrase "I know what he was called" raises – only to evade – a problem of complicity, or rather, of powerless involvement. As usual, Las Casas surreptitiously inflates the statistics ("four *or five*" victims, "two *or three*" other griddles), but if he was present should he not be less casual about the number of victims? The Apostle of the Indies was forced to watch – and does not care to recollect exactly. Yet the mention of the man's relatives in Las Casas's native city of Seville – a unique tactic in *Brief Relation*'s way of proceeding – sounds almost like a threat of blackmail. The throw-away exaggeration in the next sentence, "I *saw all these things* and *infinitely* many others", defuses the tension. Even so, the unmotivated aside, "I know what he was called and even met his relatives", is of a different order and does not read as rhetorical cliché. Generically it belongs to the discourse of testimonial.

A similar example occurs in the fifth chapter, on Cuba:

Seeing themselves dying and perishing without remedy, they all began to flee into the hills, others hung themselves in despair. Husbands and wives hung themselves, and hung their children with them, and as a result of the cruelties of one Spanish tyrant whom I knew more than two hundred Indians hung themselves. Infinite people perished in this way. (De la isla de Cuba, 93)

Illogical hyperbole ("all" – but then "others"; two hundred suddenly "infinite") and excess ("hung" four times) only conspire to lay extra weight on the treacherous un-exaggeration, "a tyrant *whom I knew*": the hint that he could name this man is as unsettling as before. Las Casas knew of a

---

[5] On the "peculiar anonymity" of *Brief Relation* see Las Casas 2006, 51-53.

pitiful thing (entire families, two hundred bodies, hanging from trees or rafters), yet he seems unsure how far to go in denouncing the man responsible; strikingly, he does not here use the words "I saw". For half a sentence his prose goes flat and matter-of-fact. Then, with the next phrase, "Infinite people perished in this way", the bishop takes up his cudgel and goes back to bludgeoning.

Still more revealing is Las Casas's account of a massacre of peaceful Taínos in Jaraguá (southern Haïti). Their leaders were inveigled into a hut and burnt alive, the *cacica* Anacaona hung, and the people put to the sword. He goes on:

> Some Christians, out of pity or greed, succeeded in taking some of the children to protect them from being killed, and put them on their horses' cruppers, but another Spaniard would come up behind and run them through with his lance; if the child was on the ground, another would cut off its legs with his sword. Some of the people managed to escape from this inhuman cruelty to a small island nearby [...]; the governor condemned them all to slavery for having fled the butchery. (*Brief Relation*, Los reinos que había en la isla Española, 86–87; see Fig. 3 & caption)

This massacre at Léogâne occurred during Nicolás de Ovando's governorship in 1503, when Las Casas was nineteen. Other sources make it clear, however, that the commander was not the governor, as *Brief Relation* states, but Diego Velázquez, whom Las Casas later served in Cuba. The mistake is all the more suspicious because, in his account of the episode in *Historia de las Indias*, Bk II, ch. 9, it emerges that Las Casas was involved; he adds to the last sentence about the remnant captured on the island of La Gonâve, "and I got one of them, whom I was given as a slave" (Las Casas 1986, II, 41). Was he one of the Christians who tried to save the children "out of pity or greed"? Not until *Brief Relation*'s next paragraph, talking of the reduction of neighbouring Higüey, does Las Casas mention his own presence, and then in generic terms ("infinite were the people *I saw* burnt alive and cut to pieces and tortured by various novel deaths and tortures, and all those taken alive enslaved", 87).

A clinching example is the account in the same chapter of how, during Velázquez's expedition to Cuba, Las Casas was involved in an unprovoked massacre of unarmed villagers. This is followed by the only passage in which he confesses an actual intervention, when "a few days later", having unwittingly set up another potential atrocity by persuading a group of twenty-one *caciques* to come out of hiding "because they had heard I could be trusted", he found himself having to plead with the captain to spare them from being burnt alive (De la isla de Cuba, 92–93). What we notice, given Las Casas's active role in the episode – the most anguished of his eye-witness scenes – is the way he tells it: despite the first-person pronouns, the style is, for Las Casas, spare and precise, as if his gaze were suddenly driven inwards to the recesses of memory instead of outwards, as it usually is, to gauge the reaction on his reader's face. At the climax, where the passage breaks for a moment from narrative past to historic present (*meten a cuchillo*), he surprises us with a remarkable literary device, a metaphysical conceit (*se les revistió el diablo a los cristianos*, literally "the devil put the Christians on", like clothing):

> Suddenly the Devil got into the Christians, and they begin to put to the sword *in my presence*, without the slightest provocation, more than three thousand souls who were sitting in front of us, men, women, and children. There *I saw* cruelties greater than living men have ever seen or thought to see. (93)

These two sentences read like a key to everything Las Casas wrote; he saw what no normal human being can, in good conscience, live with having seen. The affect of *Brief Relation* lies in passages like this, where emotion brings into play – unselfconsciously in his case – subjective techniques of representation; "I saw" achieves a genuine link with the body.

Brief Relation sets out to show that native Americans and their conquerors were living in a kind of inferno ("I spend my time at this court of Spain trying to rid the Indies of hell", Del Nuevo Reino de Granada, 174). Las Casas said he wrote "in order not to *be guilty, by being silent*, of the infinite loss of lives and souls which these men perpetrated" (Prólogo, 72). The statement makes sense only from the point of view of testimony; the only guilt incurred by the innocent bystander of atrocity is silence.

No one will be inclined to belittle *Brief Relation*'s validity as elegy, as a wreath to the memory of those who died; but to read it with rage in our hearts we must overlook the fact that so much of what it says is not the whole truth. No such cavils are required if we recognize that the text is a record not only of destruction, but of the desolation of those who, like

Columbus and Las Casas, were on the side of the destroyers, and so implicated, however unwillingly, in their guilt. Las Casas's achievement was to chronicle, in his philistine, saintly way, the sensation of his own despair: "a pitiful and heart-rending sight it is to see all this deserted and turned to barren wasteland" (De la isla de Cuba, 94). If *Brief Relation* fails to achieve its declared intention of reportage because its facts are too slipshod, its rhetoric too crude, the text nevertheless wins respect as testimony. Its glaring failure as history is unimportant; its power comes from its subjective truthfulness, from its author's pain.

For Todorov, who dedicated his book "to the memory of a Maya woman devoured by dogs", what matters is not this, but the conquerors' inability truly to *see* the victims; the nub of Las Casas's project was to turn a blind eye to American otherness, to deny difference in the interests of a colonial project of conversion (Todorov 1982, 204–225). Does not such a judgement spring from the same guilty conscience as *Brief Relation* – not as participant, but from the remote throne of impunity? In this respect modern hindsight, however just, may strike us as less authentic than the pitiable confusion of the misguided missionary. Las Casas's perverse hyperboles and cack-handed repetitiveness, so unsuited to realistic description or rational argument, were a fit medium for portraying an eye-witness perception of apocalyptic events. Even his fractured and clumsy syntax, superficially explicable as carelessness or disregard for stylistic embellishment, aptly conveys the subject matter's tortured impact and Las Casas's blinding but noble anger. The literary device of autopsy does not convince in any objective way, but it succeeds, as Pagden put it, in "transmut[ing] the narrative of what he had seen into a mode of experience" (Pagden 1992, xxxiii).

The Black Legend: testimony in two dimensions

It can come as no surprise that *Brief Relation* lent itself to Protestant misrepresentation in the forging of the Hispanophobe Black Legend. It remains ironic, nevertheless, that a colonial enterprise characterized by certain unique manifestations of concern for lawfulness – of which *Brief Relation* was an index – should as a result of Las Casas's efforts have ended up in the popular conception as the most inhumane empire of all time. Though he claimed to write "out of compassion for my native land, which is Castile" (Del Nuevo Reino de Granada, 174), every edition of the work up to 1700 except the first – seventy in a century and a half – was explicitly intended to harm Spain. Las Casas's plea for native American rights was instantly sidelined.[6]

The twisting of Las Casas's message involved little tampering with his words, for, as Samuel Purchas put it, his "zeal flings forth fiery terms and paints out their acts in the blackest ink and most hyperbolical phrases" (Las Casas 1625, 1567); all that was needed to subvert his text was to replace the term "Christians" by "Spaniards".[7] Greater harm could be done in the paratexts, by providing new front-matter, running titles, marginal notes, and illustrations. These manipulations are exemplified by the treatment given to *Brief Relation*'s title-page. The first translation, a Dutch version published anonymously in the Spanish Netherlands (Las Casas 1578), kept the original title but added a prophetic Old Testament epigraph about shepherds who kill their own flock.[8] Over the page, a brief preface explained that the aim in retelling this "lamentable destruction" was to inspire vigilance "that such plagues and wrath of God never befall us". In the tense years after the Spanish Fury at Antwerp (1576) leading up to the Dutch declaration of independence (1581), who could fail to catch the intent of this nationalist rallying cry?[9] The Flemish *predikant* Jakob van Miggrode's French version of the following year was blunter: it changed *Very Brief Relation of the Destruction of the Indies* to *Tyrannies and Cruelties of the Spaniards Perpetrated in the West Indies*, with the subtitle "As a warning and example to the Seventeen Provinces of the Low Countries" and a verse epigraph, "Happy is he who learns to beware from the misfortunes of others"; Miggrode also added a thirteen-page prologue and a sonnet (Las Casas 1579, fols *2–*8ᵛ). Taking his lead, the titles of

---

[6] There is no monograph on *Brief Relation*'s posterity; for various aspects see Gibson (1971, 78-89); Saint-Lu 1978; Alden, Landis *et al.* 1980-88, I-II; Hart 2000; Bumas 2000; the introduction to Las Casas 2000a; Schmidt (2001, 73-122).

[7] This rewording, introduced in Miggrode's French (Las Casas 1579), passed into the English, German, and Latin versions made from it (Las Casas 1583, 1597, 1598, 1620b, 1625, etc.; see caption to Fig. 1). The Barcelona edition (Las Casas 1646), issued as propaganda during the Catalan Revolt, changed "Spaniards" to "Castilians".

[8] Zech 11.4-5 "Feed the flock of the slaughter, whose possessors slay them and hold themselves not guilty; and they that sell them say, "Blessed be the LORD, for I am rich", and their own shepherds pity them not." This was taken from Las Casas's own text (De la Nueva España y Pánuco y Jalisco, 125).

[9] The historical circumstances that motivated the publication of this and each subsequent wave of editions are succinctly noted by Varela (Las Casas 1999, 49-51).

succeeding Protestant editions engaged in spiral proliferation, filling up the type-space with ever more sensational advertisements of the book's content, and underscoring the ethnic dimension by drumming insistently on the word "Spaniards". The second edition of the Dutch *Seer cort verhaal* replaced its biblical epigraph with more bloodthirsty texts, and its sober title with a twelve-line banner, *Mirror of Spanish Tyranny in the West Indies, Wherein Are Told the Murderous, Shameful, and Savage Deeds Practised by the Said Spaniards*, etc. (Las Casas 1596).[10] The German version, translated from Miggrode's *Tyrannies et cruautés* by an anonymous "patriot" and likewise addressed to the Seventeen Provinces as "warning and example", rendered the title as *Truthful Report of the Savage, Abominable, and Inhuman Tyranny of the Spaniards* (Las Casas 1597); Puritan John Phillips' *Tears of the Indians* added sentimental metaphor and an overblown statistic worthy of Las Casas ("above twenty millions of innocent People", Las Casas 1656), while the last English translation of the century doubled "twenty millions" to "above forty" (Las Casas 1699). Such tactics reached their virtuoso peak in the anonymous *Popery Truly Display'd in its Bloody Colours* (Las Casas 1689), where translation became travesty.

These progressive misrepresentations reflect the central dynamic of the Black Legend, its shift from religio-political hostility to ethnic demonization. Miggrode initiated the process by suggesting on his first page that Spanish barbarity was a genetic trait inherited from their "first fathers, the Goths", and "their second fathers, the Saracens"; and though he hastened to deny personal prejudice, the disclaimer was designed to ring hollow.[11] The ethnic slur was immediately picked up in a key text, William of Orange's *Apologie* of 1581: "this cursed race of Spaniards", he intoned, who "in the Indies miserably put to death more than twenty

---

[10] The new epigraphs (Las Casas 1596, fol.[A1]) are: Num 35. 33 "Bloodshed pollutes the land, and atonement cannot be made [...] except by the blood of the one who shed it"; Cicero, *Philippic* XIII.1 "Men who delight in strife, massacre of citizens, and civil war are to be driven from society, removed from the confines of human nature". Both appear intended to encourage violence against Spaniards.

[11] Las Casas 1579, fol.*2-2ᵛ, which reads in the contemporary English translation (Las Casas 1583, fol. *2ᵛ) "Posteritie shall hardly thinke that ever so barbarous or cruell a nation have bin in the worlde, if we had not with our eyes seene it [...]. I confesse that I never loved that nation generally, by reason of their intollerable pride [...]. Howbeit, God is my witness, hatred procureth me not to write these things."

millions of people [...] with such horrible excesses and riots that all the barbarousness, cruelties, and tyrannies which have ever been committed are but sport", came from "the blood of the Moors and Jews" (Willem van Oranje 1581, fols N3ᵛ, F4, and O2). This virulent form of Hispanophobia – the "new discursive knot" that, by slipping into "the mire of ethnic essentialization", chose to link the behaviour of the conquistadors to racial corruption (Griffin 2002, 95) – spread not only to succeeding editions of *Brief Relation*, but into a flood of contemporary anti-Spanish diatribes and pamphlets.

What the Protestant misappropriations of *Brief Relation* shared – besides the effrontery of pretending that Spanish colonists behaved worse than French, German, Dutch, or English colonists – was their urge to drive Las Casas's moral argument about the American conquest back into a Eurocentric rut by discoursing on the evil biologically imprinted in Spanish genes. In one way Las Casas appeared to invite this development. Hand in hand with his carelessness about factual detail went a tendency to oversimplify. His instinct to reject all analysis – to appeal never to the mind, but only to the eye and the pit of the stomach – is nowhere more evident than in his black-and-white contrast between lambs and wolves, "peace-loving, humble and docile Indian peoples who never hurt anybody" and "the irrational greed of those who hold it nothing to [...] kill a thousand million of them" (Prólogo, 72, 73). By this gambit Las Casas reduced both sides to caricature. The cliché of the noble savage has rarely been more naïvely deployed; according to *Brief Relation*, native Americans were God's most gentle creatures, "the most humble, most patient, most peaceful and quiet [...] in the world", too "delicate" to withstand work or illness, their poverty revealing neither barbarism nor underdevelopment but freedom from ambition and greed – an idealization that topples into comedy when Las Casas likens the Taínos' meagre and monotonous diet to the saintly mortifications of the Desert Fathers, or portrays their sleeping on mats and hammocks as a virtuous aversion to the slothful pleasures of the feather bed (Descubriéronse las Indias, 76). As usual, he builds up his exaggeration beyond reason:

> I further affirm that, up to the time when all the multitudinous peoples of that island were dead and destroyed, as far as I can believe and conjecture they did not commit against the Christians a single mortal sin of any kind. (Los reinos que había en la isla Española, 87–88)

This image of the innocent native American falls apart as we read, not merely because the laws of probability and evidence are against it, but because the portrayal, though altruistic, is not disinterested; we sense all too clearly that it is partial, polemical, and paternalistic. Meanwhile, its binary opposite, the image of Las Casas's fellow Europeans, is pushed too far the other way, towards the grotesque. He lists the ferocities of the "tyrants and so-called conquistadors" (Prólogo, 72) without any attempt to understand their behaviour, which for him could only have one motive:

> The reason the Christians have killed and destroyed [...] has been solely because their ultimate aim is gold and stuffing themselves with riches in the shortest possible time and rising to very high estates quite disproportionate to their persons; that is, because of their insatiable greed and ambition. (Descubriéronse las Indias, 78–79)

The "reason" is inane; social climbing and a nose for profit cannot explain the savagery of men who without provocation smash babies' skulls, slow-roast prisoners for amusement, or disembowel pregnant women and feed their babies to dogs – thereby destroying the very people on whom their enrichment depends. Las Casas insults our intelligence with his facile simplification, and then short-circuits questions with mindless epithets: degenerates, subhuman beasts, devils, hellish enemies of God and men.[12] The chronicles of conquest offer few more jejune examples of stereotyping than Las Casas's portrait of his own people, which presents even their table-manners as bestial ("a Christian will consume and destroy in one day what is enough for three [Indian] households of ten persons each for a month", De la isla Española, 80). What is absent from this diatribe, however, is any hint of the Black Legend's defining step-change from moral critique to ethnic essentialization.

In fact, Las Casas's lack of interest in the conquistadors' psychology strikes a modern reader as disturbing, not for any racist tone, but because it seems to show that their behaviour did not strike him as psychotic. He

---

[12] E.g. "feelingless men whom greed made degenerate from being men" (*Brief Relation*, Argumento, 69); "wolves, tigers, lions" (Descubriéronse las Indias, 77); "hellish robbers" (Del reino de Yucatán, 130); "devils from Hell" (Del Nuevo Reino de Granada, 172). Bestial and non-human images occur over thirty times, *infernal*, *diablo*, *diabólico* over fifty; Las Casas suggests at the end that the conquistadors were inspired by Lucifer (Del Nuevo Reino de Granada, 176).

believed, not that torture, burning alive, or slavery (all institutional features of European life at that time) were wrong in themselves, but that their illegal use against an innocent population posed a barrier to evangelization. If this appears to us to miss an essential point about genocide, we may recall that Las Casas cannot have been unaware, at some level, of the insufficiency of his analysis of the conquistadors' motives, as he had participated in their acts. From the perspective of testimony, the analysis could indeed be seen as a subconscious attempt to rationalize traumatic experiences and deep-seated guilt.

More significant for our purpose, however, is the fact that the Protestant editions of *Brief Relation* appeared long after Las Casas's death, and at the moment when "our modern apprehension of 'massacres' began" (El Kenz 2006, 2 & nn.4–5). War, atrocity, and extreme collective cruelty have always characterized human society, but while the number of civilian victims always rises, our threshold of tolerance for such violence has significantly fallen. In this respect the wars of religion of the latter half of the sixteenth century marked a watershed. They were the first to be reported by a full panoply of printed media, in word and image, and the first in which the fate of civilian victims figured as more newsworthy than military campaigns. An index of new sensibility was the banalization of the French word *massacre*, first used in this connection in 1556, general after the St Bartholomew's Day Massacre of 1572, and attested from 1578 in English, where it specifically denoted Catholic atrocities (El Kenz 2006, 2–3 & n.7). The neologism duly figures in the first lines of Miggrode's version of *Brief Relation* (Las Casas 1579, fol.*2 "les Espagnols avoir tué et *massacré* és Indes"), and thereafter in Purchas's précis (Purchas 1613, 751 "Thunders from heaven had need be the voice to utter such hellish and unheard-of *massacres*"), in the title and text of Phillips' *Tears of the Indians* (Las Casas 1656, title & fols.A5ᵛ, A8, *b1, *b2ᵛ, *b7, pp.1, 5, etc.), and throughout *Popery Truly Display'd in its Bloody Colours* (Las Casas 1689, title & 3, 11, 17, etc.).

In this sensitization of the European public to the notion of war crimes a leading role was played by technical advances in the serial printing of graphic images, notably copper-plate engraving. This paved the way to a fresh iconography of atrocity, the baroque theatre of cruelty or visual gallery of massacre (Conley 1990), so named after an early example, Richard Rowlands' *Theatrum crudelitatum* (Verstegan 1587), which Lestringant sees as a Catholic riposte to Dutch and English editions of Las

Casas (Verstegan 1995). The martyrologies that inspired the imagery of these graphic representations of mass violence fed impartially into both Catholic and Protestant propaganda, and thence into illustrations of the American conquest, notably the seventy-two plates of Théodore de Bry's edition of Girolamo Benzoni's *History of the New World* in its translation by the Huguenot Urbain Chauveton (Benzoni 1594–96). It was as a direct spin-off of the success of this last book that *Brief Relation* found its most enduring and influential manifestation, De Bry's illustrated Latin edition with seventeen engravings after designs by the Mannerist artist Joos van Winghe (Las Casas 1598; see Figs 1–4, below). According to its preface the plates were added in response to public demand, and "drawn as lifelike as possible to *make things present* to the reader, which we trust will give [...] honest pleasure" ("Præfatio ad Lectorem", fols *3–[*4]ᵛ). Whether "honest pleasure" is or was intended to be the real effect of the images is a question I consider in a moment, but at any rate they achieved such iconic status that they were subsequently plagiarized (Las Casas 1599), copied (Las Casas 1698), and even issued in comic-strip format (Las Casas 1656, 1699). A striking example of the propagandistic uses to which De Bry's plates could be put is Jan Cloppenburg's *Mirror of Cruel and Horrible Spanish Tyranny* (Las Casas 1620a–b), issued in Dutch and French, in two parts: a reprint of *Brief Relation* (Las Casas 1596/1579), and a parallel account of Spanish atrocities in the Low Countries compiled from Jan Gysius's journal of the Dutch revolt, *Oorsprong ende voortgang der Nederlantscher beroerten* of 1616. A pirated set of De Bry's plates illustrates Las Casas's tale of tortures and murders of native Americans; these are matched by a blood-curdling new set of engravings showing tortures and murders of Dutch Protestants.

Were it not for De Bry's prints, none but specialists would now know of *Brief Relation*. Their imagery, as much as or maybe more than Las Casas's text, accounted for the work's impact in the diffusion of the Black Legend. Self-evidently, however, the role of the visual was here distinct from the one traced out in my previous discussion of eye-witness autopsy in Las Casas's text. Images, like music, may express and arouse emotion more immediately than words; they cannot portray, or be paraphrased in, words. "The creations of painting", declares Plato, "stand as though alive, and yet if you ask them a question they solemnly stay silent" (*Phaedrus* 275e). This silence of art, this "structure of detachment that divides wordless pictures from all language" and resists our impulse to appropriate or "attribute" the image to some external idea, ought to work in the plates' favour; since they cannot of themselves partake in the discursivity of text, they should remain irreducible to the toxic level of anti-Spanish diatribe.[13] Indeed, it is noteworthy that De Bry's preface rejects the discourse of Hispanophobia. Despite following Las Casas in attributing the Spanish "barbarity" to greed, it offers this profound and saving insight:

> If we enjoyed the same freedom and licence as the Spaniards arrogated to themselves in India, with no fear of higher authority to constrain us, there is no doubt we would vie with them in every piece of savagery, cruelty, inhumanity, and injustice. [...] We know there are good and bad men in every nation, [...] and that the vices of a few are not to be imputed to a whole people. [...] Do not just note and deplore the Spaniards' vices, but recognize that the cause and ferment of all those evils is in you too. ("Præfatio ad Lectorem", Las Casas 1598, fol. [*4]ᵛ)

Nevertheless, the "silence" of Van Winghe's images turns out to be illusory, because they are swaddled in surrounding text – not least the prominent headline *Crudelitates Hispanorum* ("cruelties of the Spaniards"). Theoretically irrelevant, such framing texts act in practice as captions, reassigning the engravings to the conceptual frame of ethnic polemic.

Furthermore, to study the atrocious imagery of the plates is to be made aware that their power rests on an appeal to an obscene alliance of three emotions: sadism, horror, and lust. That is to say, they are pornographic in form, method, and effect: the agenda is arousal, not engagement. With his constant subtle injections of the erotic (following established canons of classical nudity and hagiographic representations of martyrdom), Van Winghe does nothing either to resist this categorization or to provide "honest pleasure".[14] The perusal of "hellish and unheard-of massacres", observed Samuel Purchas, Las Casas's most perspicacious contemporary

---

[13] The quoted words are from Elkins (2000, 230-242, at p.235), in his discussion of Derrida's essay on the futility of attempting to re-enact in prose the expressive dynamics of visual art (Derrida 1978, 182: "Dans la peinture, un élément sauvage, irreprésentable, résiste à l'échange entre représentation et discours").

[14] For aesthetic and iconographical analyses of the images see Duviols in Las Casas 2000b, 219-245; Conley 1992; but their patent allusions to religious images of martyrdom and Van Winghe's Mannerist penchant for erotic cruelty and dramatic, artificial poses with outstretched arms and attenuated fingers need little comment.

critic, seems calculated to "astonish the sense of the reader, amaze his reason, exceed his faith, and *fill his heart with horror and uncouth passions*" (1613, 751). No one objects to uncouth passions in a good cause, but this was not a good cause; it was not intended to do native Americans any good, and by inflaming people with hatred of Spaniards it did harm. Art is under no obligation to peddle causes, even good ones; but the objection to this pornographic iconography of atrocity is aesthetic. The incommensurability of art and text works both ways; if textual captions cheapen the artistic force of Van Winghe's images, his visual rendition of *Brief Relation* likewise reduces Las Casas's eye-witness testimony to two dimensions, not just in the literal sense, but by flattening its texture and subtlety, hence overriding its ethical and emotional meaning. Superficially one might argue that the obscenity of the images functions as a visual equivalent of Las Casas's hysterical hyperbole of atrocity, but this proposal is rendered suspect by Conley's acute observation (1992, 110) that the engravings' binary opposition between clothed Europeans and naked Americans in fact codifies ominous ideologies of power and ethnic difference. The coercive force of Van Winghe's visualizations irons out the complexity of Las Casas's attitude to native Americans (from which, by the way, mention of nudity other than the metaphorical is singularly absent). Likewise, the draughtsman erases every trace of the autopsy, the presence of the witness, that (to repeat a phrase quoted earlier) helped "transmute the narrative of what Las Casas had seen into a mode of experience" (Fig. 2 & caption).

As a consequence of all this, the illustrated *Brief Relation* became regressive and, in the hands of its consumers, potentially evil. The commerce between the effects of visual testimony in art and literature does not always have to work in this direction, of course – it is easy to imagine the reverse scenario, of a text more crude and one-dimensional than the corresponding image – but the case of *Brief Relation* may nevertheless draw us to speculate that such works, textual and visual, belonging by nature to quite distinct genres (whether or not we call both "testimony") and operating in separate fields of force, will have disparate, contradictory, and sometimes incompatible effects.[15]

[15] I am grateful to Bernard McGuirk for persuading me to ponder on Las Casas in a post-conflict context; to Dr Christine Ferdinand of Magdalen College, Oxford, and the staff of John Rylands Library, Deansgate, for making consultation of their

Figures

Fig. 1. De Bry, Narratio regionum Indicarum, Plate 1, p.10. Engraving signed "Jodo[cus] a Winghe in[venit]", 11 × 13.5 cm.

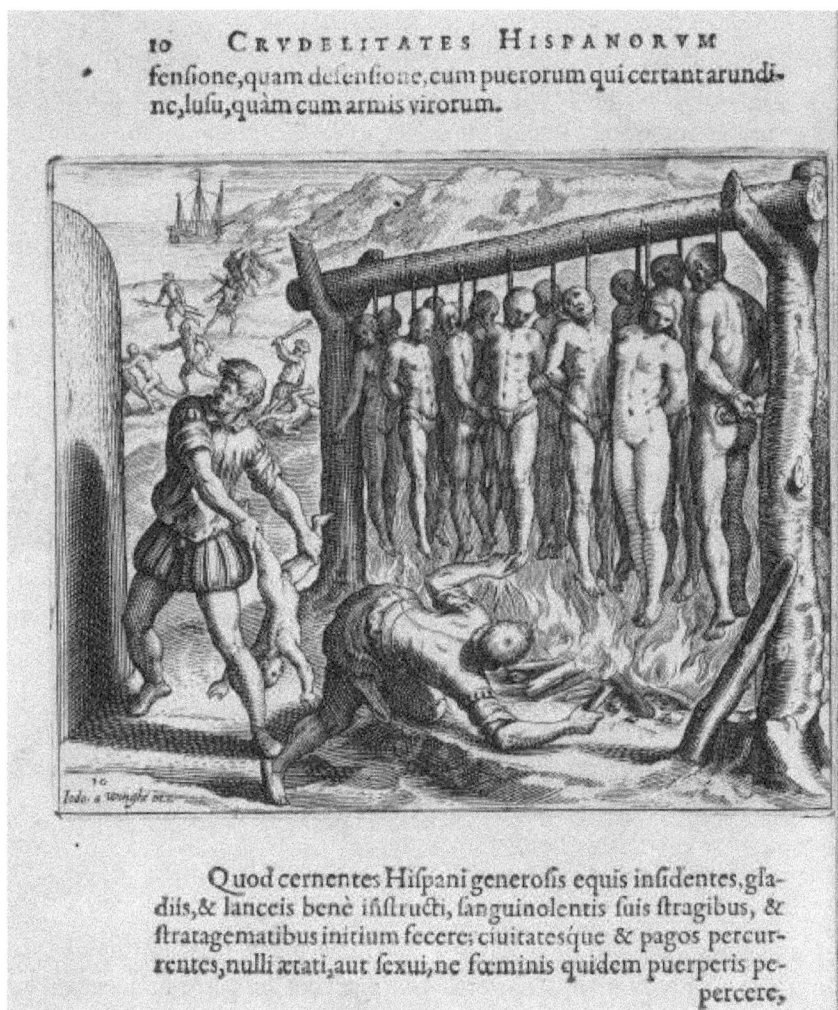

10   CRVDELITATES HISPANORVM

fenfione,quam defenfione,cum puerorum qui certant arundi-
ne,lufu,quàm cum armis virorum.

Quod cernentes Hifpani generofis equis infidentes,gla-
diis,& lanceis bene ififtructi,fanguinolentis fuis ftragibus, &
ftratagematibus initium fecere; ciuitatesque & pagos percur-
rentes,nulli ætati,aut fexui,ne fœminis quidem puerperis pe-
percere,

early printed books so pleasurable; and to Macdonald Daly, Cristina Demaria, and Oliver Noble Wood for helping get the script in despite interminable moping. Special thanks to Gordon Brotherston and his colleagues at the University of Manchester for inviting me to the SPLAS seminar, where these ideas were tossed and gored with generous gusto; their improvements were too many to be acknowledged (except the one mentioned in n.3), but all were greatly valued.

Under the running-title "Cruelties of the Spaniards", this page translates *Brief Relation*, De la isla Española, 81, but is slanted by putting "Spaniards" instead of "Christians", "their" before "slaughters", and adding "cities" (shown in italics):

[Then the Indians took up arms – but what arms, good God!, in] both offence and defence more like children's games with sticks than grown-up weapons. Seeing which, the *Spaniards*, mounted on thoroughbred horses and well armed with swords and lances, began *their* bloody slaughters and campaigns; they swept through *cities and* villages sparing neither age nor sex, not even pregnant women, [slicing them open or hacking them to pieces, like slaughtering lambs penned in sheepfolds. They laid bets on who with one slash could split a man open or decapitate him with a spike or disembowel him; they plucked babies by the heels from their mothers' breasts and dashed out their brains.

Van Winghe chose as the sado-erotic focus of his image a detail on the facing page, apt to inflame Protestant prejudice by its blasphemy ("could the Devil say worse?", Purchas 1613, p.747): "They made long gibbets, hanging them with their feet just off the ground, and then laid firewood, set fire to it, and burned them alive thirteen at a time in honour of our Saviour and the twelve Apostles."

Fig. 2. De Bry, Narratio regionum Indicarum, Plate 2, p.12 (see facing page)

The text translates *Brief Relation*, De la isla Española, 81–82:

> Normally they executed lords and nobles by this death: they made griddles of bars resting on forks and placed a slow fire underneath so that little by little, howling with desperation in this torture, the miserable victims breathed their last. Once I saw four or five of these leaders and lords roasted on these grills, and not far away were to be seen two or three other grills laden with the same merchandise; and because they were [howling so loudly ...] (for the remainder of the story see the quotation on pp. 104-5, above)

Van Winghe's top scene shows punitive mutilations ("those captured alive had both hands cut off; some had them hung round their necks and were told, 'Take a message', meaning, take the news to the people hiding in the hills", 81). The main subject is a torture witnessed by Las Casas while participating in Ovando's conquest of Hispaniola, but despite the text (*Vidi aliquando*, "Once I saw"), Van Winghe does not, here or anywhere else, include the author in the picture.

12 CRVDELITATES HISPANORVM

Hac morte communiter Dominos, & Nobiles mulƈta-
bant. Perticis furca fuffultis craticulas ſtruebant,paruoƈƈ igne
fuppoſito,hi miſeri paulatim,animam,magnis clamoribus,tor-
mentorumƈƈ deſperatione,efflabant.
Vidi aliquando quatuor, aut quinque ex potentioribus
Dominis,his craticulis impoſitos torreri, & non procul duƈ,vel
tres aliæ craticulæ,ijſdem mercibus inſtruƈtæ viſebantur; cum-
que ma-

Fig. 3. De Bry, Narratio regionum Indicarum, Plate 3, p. 17

Van Winghe's drawing illustrates atrocities committed in the Jaraguá region of Haïti, "the marrow and heart or as it were capital of all Hispaniola", in particular the burning alive of Taíno chiefs, the slaughter of their people, and the hanging of the *cacica* Anacaona (*Brief Relation, Los reinos que había en la isla Española*, 86–87):

> Here the governor of the island arrived with sixty horse and a further three hundred infantry (the cavalry alone were enough to ravage the whole island and the mainland), and over three hundred unsuspecting chiefs answered his summons. The governor duped their leaders into gathering in a building of straw and then ordered his men to set fire to it, and they burnt them alive. All the others with their numerous people were run through with lances or put to the sword; as a mark of respect for her rank Queen Anacaona was hanged.

Bias is detectible in Van Winghe's pointed exclusion of any representation of Las Casas's next sentence, to the effect that some "Christians" attempted to protect the children from being killed (see p. 106, above). On the other hand, in *Brief Relation* Las Casas fails to reveal that he participated in the atrocity and was a beneficiary of its outcome; nor does his narrative make clear that Anacaona was imprisoned, tried, and hung a full year later, in 1504. Van Winghe selects moments of the narrative and arranges them in a simultaneous wheel-like composition, "a 'rotative' display of torture in a circle that turns inside of a theatrical [...] space" to create a "theatre of cruelty" (Conley 1992, p.113). This striking device is present in a number of the plates. So too is the eroticization of female victims and contrast of nude *v.* clothed, both replete with overt or covert ideological implications ("Spaniards are clothed while the natives are nude; the effect underscores the relation of power held between the colonizer and the natives, but it also engages prurience in the viewer's relation to the scene. Despite the indictment of the Spanish Catholics, the natives are in fact coded to be below the dignity of the Europeans", Conley 1992, p. 110).

Fig. 4. De Bry, Narratio regionum Indicarum, Plate 13, p.59 (see overleaf)

One of Van Winghe's most haunting images, this represents the Spaniard's use of hunting-dogs to terrorize native Americans: a woman has hung herself and her one-year-old child in despair, but not in time to prevent the dogs from eating the boy alive, "though a friar was able to baptize him before he was quite dead" (*Brief Relation*, Del reino de Yucatán, 127–28). This last sanctimonious detail, well calculated to raise Protestant spleen at what they saw as the hollow casuistry of Catholic ritualism, is satirically portrayed. The foreground shows another "unbelievable savagery" from the facing page (*Brief Relation*, 128):

> In this kingdom, or a province of New Spain, a certain Spaniard out hunting deer or rabbits with his dogs, finding no prey, decided his dogs were hungry; he takes an infant boy from his mother and cuts off his legs and arms in strips with a knife and feeds each dog in turn and then, the strips being eaten, throws the rest of the little body on the ground for all of them.

IN INDIIS PATRATÆ.   59

aliquibus diebus, ad enormia facinora, latrocinia, incarce-
rationes, & maiores contra Deum offensas committendas
reuersi sunt, neq; adhuc cessant, ita vt iam trecenta illa terrae
milliaria,vt dixi,in quibus tanta erat populi frequentia,inculta,
& omnino fere deserta cernantur.

Particulares,saeuidae,&crudelitatis in illa regione patratae,
narrationes,nullus credat.Duas tantùm,aut tres,quae in mente
                    H 2   veniunt,

References

Alden, J., *et al.* (1980-88). *European Americana: A Chronological Guide
to Works Printed in Europe Relating to the Americas, 1493-1776*. 6
vols. New York and New Canaan, CT: John Carter Brown Library.

Benzoni, G. (1594-96). *Americae pars IV [V, VI], sive Insignis &
admiranda historia de reperta primum Occidentali India*, tr. Urbanus

Calveto. 3 vols. Francofurti ad Moenum: Theodorus de Bry (tr. from *La historia del Mondo Nuovo*, Venetia, 1565).

Bumas, E. S. (2000). "The cannibal butcher shop: Protestant uses of Las Casas's *Brevísima relación* in Europe and the American colonies". *Early American Literature*, 35, pp.107-36.

Certeau, M. de (1986). *Heterologies: Discourses on the Other*. Manchester: Manchester University Press.

Colón, Cristóbal (1992). *Textos y documentos completos: Nuevas cartas*, ed. Consuelo Varela with Juan Gil, rev. and enlarged 3rd ed. Madrid: Alianza.

Conley, T. (1990). "Commentary", *Theatres of Cruelty: Wars of Religion, Violence, and The New World*. Newberry Library Slide Set 14, at **http://www.newberry.org/smith/slidesets/ss14.htm**, accessed 17 July 2008.

Conley, T. (1992). "De Bry's Las Casas", in R. Jara, N. Spadaccini (eds.) *Amerindian Images and the Legacy of Columbus*. Minneapolis: University of Minnesota Press, 103-131.

Cook, N. D. (1998). *Born to Die: Disease and New World Conquest, 1492-1650*. Cambridge: Cambridge University Press.

Derrida, J. (1978). *La vérité en peinture*. Paris: Flammarion.

El Kenz, D. (2006). "La mise en scène médiatique du massacre des huguenots au temps des guerres de Religion: théologie ou politique?". *Sens Public: revue électronique internationale*, vol. 2, **http://www.sens-public.org/article.php3?id_article=333**, accessed 2 July 2008.

Elkins, J. (2000). *Our Beautiful, Dry, and Distant Texts: Art History as Writing*. London: Routledge.

Gibson, C. (1971). *The Black Legend: Anti-Spanish Attitudes in the Old World and New*. New York: Knopf.

Griffin, E. (2002). "From *ethos* to *ethnos*: Hispanizing 'the Spaniard' in the Old World and the New". *New Centennial Review*, 2, 69-116.

Hanke, L. (1949). *The Spanish Struggle for Justice in the Conquest of America*. Philadelphia: University of Pennsylvania Press.

Hart, J. (2000). "The example of Spain: French and English representations of the Spanish in the New World", in T. D'haen, P. Krüs eds.) *Proceedings of the XVth Congress of the International Comparative Literature Association "Literature as Cultural Memory", Leiden, 16-22 August 1997*, II: *Colonizer and Colonized*.

Amsterdam: Rodopi, 337-356.

Henige, D. (1978). "On the contact population of Hispaniola: history as higher mathematics". *Hispanic American Historical Review*, 58, 217-237.

Isabel I de Castilla (2001). *El Testamento de Isabel la Católica y otras consideraciones en torno a su muerte: originales conservados en el Archivo General de Simancas y Biblioteca Nacional. Edición facsímil. Estudio*, ed. Vidal González Sánchez. 2 vols. Valladolid: Instituto Isabel la Católica de Historia Eclesiástica.

Casas, Bartolomé de las (1552). *Brevissima relacion de la destruycion de las Indias*. Sevilla: Sebastian Trugillo.

Casas, Bartolomé de las (1578). *Seer cort verhael vande destructie van d'Indien*, [...] *in Brabantsche tale getrouwelick uyte Spaensche overgeset*, [s.l.] [Antwerpen?]: [s.n.].

Casas, Bartolomé de las (1579). *Tyrannies et cruautez des Espagnols perpetrees ès Indes occidentales qu'on dit le Nouveau*, tr. Jacques de Miggrode. Anvers: François de Ravelenghien.

Casas, Bartolomé de las (1583). *The Spanish Colonie; or, Briefe Chronicle of the Acts and Gestes of the Spaniardes in the West Indies, called the Newe World, for the Space of XL. Yeeres*, tr. [from Las Casas 1579] by M.M.S. London: Thomas Dawson for William Broome.

Casas, Bartolomé de las (1596). *Spieghel der Spaenscher tyrannye in West Indien: waer inne verhaelt wordt de moordadige, schandelijcke, ende grouwelijcke feyten die de selve Spanjaerden gebruyckt hebben inde selve Landen*, Amstelredam: Nicolaes Biestkens de Jonghe.

Casas, Bartolomé de las (1597). *Warhafftige Anzeigung der Hispanier grewlichen, abschewlichen und unmenschlichen Tyranney, von ihnen inn den indianischen Ländern* [...] *begangen,* [...] *durch Jacoben von Miggrode den 17 Provincien deß Niderlands zur Warnung und Beyspiel gebracht: jetzt aber erst inß Hochteutsch durch einen Liebhaber deß Vatterlands umb ebenmässiger Ursachen willen übergesetzt*, [s.l.] [Frankfurt]: [s.n.].

Casas, Bartolomé de las (1598). *Narratio regionum Indicarum per Hispanos quosdam devastatarum verissima*. Francofurti: Theodorus de Bry.

Casas, Bartolomé de las (1656). *The Tears of the Indians: Being an Historical and True Account of the Cruel Massacres and Slaughters of Above Twenty Millions of Innocent People Committed by the*

Spaniards in the Islands of Hispaniola, Cuba, Jamaica, &c., as also in the Continent of Mexico, Peru, & Other Places of the West-Indies, to the Total Destruction of Those Countries, tr. John Phillips. London: J. C. for Nath. Brook.

Casas, Bartolomé de las (1689). *Popery Truly Display'd in its Bloody Colours; or, A Faithful Narrative of the Horrid and Unexampled Massacres, Butcheries, and All Manner of Cruelties that Hell and Malice Could Invent, Committed by the Popish Spanish Party on the Inhabitants of West-India.* London: R. Hewson.

Casas, Bartolomé de las (1698). *Relation des voyages et des découvertes que les Espagnols ont fait dans les Indes Occidentales*, tr. Jean-Baptiste Morvan de Bellegarde. Amsterdam: J. L. de Lorme.

Casas, Bartolomé de las (1699). *An Account of the First Voyages and Discoveries Made by the Spaniards in America, Containing the most Exact Relation Hitherto Publish'd of their Unparallel'd Cruelties on the Indians, in the Destruction of above Forty Millions of People: with Propositions Offer'd to the King of Spain to Prevent the Further Ruin of the West-Indies [...]. Illustrated with Cuts.* London: D. Brown, J. Harris, & A. Bell.

Casas, Bartolomé de las (1986). *Historia de las Indias*, ed. André Saint-Lu, Biblioteca Ayacucho 108-10. 3 vols. Caracas: Ayacucho.

Casas, Bartolomé de las (1992). *Obras completas*, X: *Tratados de 1552 impresos por Las Casas en Sevilla.* ed. Ramón Hernández and Lorenzo Galmés. Madrid: Alianza.

Casas, Bartolomé de las (1999). *Brevísima relación de la destruición de las Indias*, ed. Consuelo Varela. Clásicos Castalia 248. Madrid: Castalia.

Casas, Bartolomé de las (2000a). *Brevísima relación de la destruición de las Indias: primera edición crítica (Texto inédito desconocido, de 1542. Texto modificado y añadido, de 1546. Texto remodificado y sobreañadido, de 1552)*, ed. Isacio Pérez Fernández. Bayamón, Puerto Rico: Centro de Estudios de los Dominicos del Caribe.

Casas, Bartolomé de las (2000b). *"La destruction des Indes" de Bartolomé de Las Casas (1552): traduction de Jacques de Miggrode (1579), gravures de Théodore de Bry (1598)*, introd. Alain Milhou, ed. & analyse iconographique Jean-Paul Duviols, revised 2nd ed. Paris: Chandeigne.

Casas, Bartolomé de las (2006). *Brevísima relación de la destruición de las Indias*, ed. José Miguel Martínez Torrejón. Alicante: Universidad.

Casas, Bartolomé de las (2007). *Brevísima relación de la destruición de las Indias*, ed. André Saint-Lu. Letras Hispánicas 158, 15th ed. Madrid: Cátedra.

Lawrance, J. (2009). *Spanish Conquest, Protestant Prejudice: Las Casas and the Black Legend*. Nottingham: Critical, Cultural and Communications Press.

Livi-Bacci, M. (2003). "Return to Hispaniola: reassessing a demographic catastrophe". *Hispanic American Historical Review*, 83, 3-51.

Pagden, A. (1991). "*Ius et Factum*: text and experience in the writings of Bartolomé de las Casas". *Representations*, 33 (Winter), 147-162.

Pagden, A. (1992). "Introduction", in Bartolomé de las Casas, *A Short Account of the Destruction of the Indies*, tr. N. Griffin. London: Penguin, xiii-xli.

Purchas, Samuel (1613). "Of the Spanish cruelties in the West-Indies, and of the perverse conversion of the Indians unto Christianitie", in *Purchas his Pilgrimage; or, Relations of the World and the Religions Observed in All Ages and Places Discovered, from the Creation unto this Present*. London: William Stansby for Henrie Fetherstone, Bk IX, ch. 15, 746-752.

Saint-Lu, A. (1978). "Les premières traductions françaises de la *Brevísima relación de la destrucción de las Indias* de Bartolomé de las Casas", *Revue de Littérature Comparée*, 52, 2-4 (*Hommage à Marcel Bataillon*), 438-449. (Repr. in his *Las Casas indigéniste: études sur la vie et l'œuvre du défenseur des Indiens*. Paris: L'Harmattan, 1982, 159-70.)

Schmidt, B. (2001). *Innocence Abroad: The Dutch Imagination and the New World, 1570-1670*. Cambridge: Cambridge University Press.

Todorov, T. (1982). *La Conquête de l'Amérique: la question de l'autre*. Paris: Seuil.

Verstegan, Richard ("R. V.", pseud. of Richard Rowlands) (1587). *Theatrum crudelitatum haereticorum nostri temporis*. Antuerpiae: Adrianus Huberti.

Verstegan, Richard (1995). *Le théâtre des cruautés (1587)*. Paris: Chandeigne.

Vitoria, F. de (1991). *Political Writings*, ed. & tr. Anthony Pagden and Jeremy Lawrance. Cambridge: Cambridge University Press.

Willem van Oranje (1581). *The Apologie or Defence [...] against the*

Proclamation and Edict Published by the King of Spaine. Delft [i.e. London], [s.n.]: (Tr. from *Apologie ofte verantwoordinghe teghen den ban ofte edict by forme van proscriptie ghepubliceert by den coningh van Spaegnien*. Leiden: Silvius 1581).

Zambardino, R. A. (1978). "Forum: Critique of David Henige's 'On the contact population of Hispaniola'". *Hispanic American Historical Review*, 58, 700-708.

"Le poids des mots, le choc des photos": Conflict and the News Magazines *Picture Post* and *Paris Match*

Nicholas Hewitt

In a retrospective article on news coverage of the Second World War in 1989, the former editor of the photo-journal *Picture Post* from 1940 to 1950, Tom Hopkinson, wrote:

> For about three decades towards the middle of the 20th century, picture magazines were the most popular journalistic source of information and entertainment throughout most of the Western world. This brief spell lasted only from about 1928 to 1960, but during that time their circulation ran into millions; journalists and cameramen were as eager to work for them as they are today for prestigious television programmes. (Hopkinson 1989, 12)

This comment highlights not merely the intrinsic historical importance of the photo-journalism magazines in the decades of the 1930s, 1940s and 1950s, which in the case of *Paris Match* continues until the present, but also the crucial impact upon the entire production of news media: the allusion to television signifies not only an interchange of journalistic staff from the print media to the broadcast media, but also, more broadly, the way in which the news magazines of the inter-war years and beyond established a format for news presentation which influenced profoundly subsequent audio-visual coverage of news and the images which that news utilized. In other words, the ways in which the news magazines dealt with news and, especially, conflict, came rapidly to determine our ways of perceiving news events, what we consider as news, the news agenda, and the filters through which the viewer perceives conflict. In this context, they are a vital ingredient to our understanding of the news agenda of conflict and its subsequent portrayal.

The history of the news magazines, and of modern journalism itself, begins, as Hopkinson recognizes, with a major and permanent technological invention, namely the development in the 1920s of the miniature hand-held camera, the Leica 35mm, invented by Oskar Barnack in 1913, and launched on the market by the new company Leica in 1925.[1] As Hopkinson records, "This transformed the nature of photo-journalism from 'photography by consent' to 'photography by enterprise', or at times 'photography by theft'" (Hopkinson 1989, 12), which paved the way, *inter alia*, for the paparazzi in their search for candid shots of the rich and famous, but also for hitherto unprecedented images of conflict and violence, as illustrated by the early career of Robert Capa (McCabe 1989, 4). It was no coincidence, therefore, that the heyday of photo-journalism in the West should have been the late 1930s, when the West was coming to terms with wars in Abyssinia and Spain, and when the threat of a global war was a virtual certainty. Apart from the daily newspapers, which tended to rely upon textual reports from specialist correspondents, the major source of information, and, especially, visual images of conflict, which had a defining impact on the way in which ordinary people saw conflict, should have been the news magazines: *Berliner Illustrierte*, in Germany, *Life* magazine, founded by Henry Luce in the United States in 1936, and which established itself as an international model for the genre, *Picture Post*, founded in London in 1938, and *Paris Match*, which started life as the more humble *Match* in Paris in 1938.

All these magazines, and their numerous stable-mates, adopted a common format, remarkably similar in their content: articles on, and pictures of, popular film stars, testifying to a recurrent symbiotic relationship between the print media and the audio-visual industry; domestic and general-interest stories, often centred on the lives of ordinary people; science, technology and visions of the future; and, above all, wars and rumours of wars: the staple of the news magazines for the rest of their career. In fact, it is very doubtful if any of these magazines could have survived for as long as they did, and in the case of *Paris Match*, right up to the present day, without the public's interest in conflict and the threat of conflict. As such, the new magazines relied upon a complex reciprocal relationship between editorial concerns and the expectations of the readership, based upon a prurient interest in conflict and fear of its consequences. As such, they laid down a template for news coverage, particularly in its visual form, which influenced indelibly the way in which we perceive and react to conflict through the mass-media.

---

[1] See **http: //www.photoxels.com/history_leica.html**.

This paper proposes to analyze two such news magazines, *Picture Post*, published in London from 1938 to 1959, and *Paris Match*, founded in 1949, the latter of which is still a highly successful, albeit rare, example of the survival of the genre. In both cases, two issues dominate: the role and power of the photographic image of conflict, but also its ability or inability to adapt; and further, the ways in which the potentially contestatory power of the images, together with their attendant written texts, can be acceptable to, or assimilated by, mainstream commercial media publishing. As such, they raise important questions regarding subsequent ways of seeing conflict, together with issues of control and censorship, both overt and covert.

Picture Post

Picture Post was founded in October 1938 by the liberal (but by no means left-leaning) publisher Edward Hulton, and its launch coincided with the Munich Agreement, marking a relationship between the magazine and conflict which was to last until its demise thirty years later. Indeed, such was the interest of the public in the threatening international situation, that, against all the expectations of its staff, it immediately sold out its print run of 750,000 in the South-East alone (Hopkinson 1989, 12; Hopkinson 1948, 47). In fact, as Tom Hopkinson later recorded, it also owed its astonishing success to a combination of a revolution in news photography and an unusually democratic attitude towards its subject matter and its readers. To the question from a distinguished visitor as to what kind of paper *Picture Post* would be, he replied:

> It would be a shock. It would use photographs as they'd never been used before. It would show the lives of ordinary people as they were. It would treat all human beings as of equal dignity and importance. It would show the life of a charlady and the life of a big business boss, without laughing at the charlady or touching its cap at the big boss, the duke, the bishop. It would treat its own method as important – the method of the photograph. If a photograph were good, we'd print it big. We wouldn't mess about with it, write headings over it, or paint plush easels round it – which was the pleasant fancy of the day ... "Would the paper be political?" the visitor asked. Of course it would. All life was political – and would become a lot more so, if we were going to go on at all. (Hopkinson 1948, 13)

It is interesting, incidentally, that Hopkinson uses the word "shock" in his description of *Picture Post*, thus anticipating the slogan of *Paris Match* a year later: "le poids des mots, le choc des photos" ["the weight of words, the shock of photos"].

Good photographers were essential to the success of any news magazine, and *Picture Post* was exceptionally fortunate in recruiting one of the finest news photographers of his day, Bert Hardy, who was one of the first to use a Leica 35mm camera. He subsequently went on to become a distinguished war photographer, covering the bombing of London in 1940, the Normandy invasion in 1944, the Korean War and the French war in Indochina.[2] It was essentially the high quality and dramatic impact of the photographs in *Picture Post*, taken by Hardy and others, which made it a newspaper of record; but it was also an unusual ambition to use photography, not merely to record events, but to shape their future course. As Hopkinson notes:

> It was with the war, and particularly after the fall of France in May-June 1940, that *Picture Post* took photo-journalism into a new element, using photographs not just to record events – at that time there were only disasters – but also to try to influence them. Photo-journalism was to become a weapon. (Hopkinson 1989, 12)

Thus:

> for its first issue of 1941, at the very lowest point of Britain's fortunes, *Picture Post* devoted the whole magazine to "A Plan for Britain", virtually a blueprint for the programme which the Attlee government would carry through. (Hopkinson 1989, 12)

In this respect, the edition of the beginning of January 1944 was typical of the magazine's format and concerns. War coverage was very much to the fore, with photographs of a new phosphorus hand grenade and of Russian snipers on the Eastern Front. There was a more analytical report on the London meeting of the Council of Christians and Jews, at which the Archbishop of Canterbury "expressed his horror at the extermination

[2] See "Bert Hardy", **http://www.spartacus.schoolnet.co.uk/USAPhardy.htm**.

of Jews in Europe" (Edelman 1944, 11). At the same time, *Picture Post* willingly exploited its readership's interest in the cinema and its female film stars with a cover photograph of Betty Grable, and looked towards the post-war future with an enthusiastic project for the urban regeneration of an area of the city of Swansea. Nor was the magazine reluctant to pull its punches in criticism of certain aspects of the conduct of the war, even if, in this case, it used the indirect device of a reader's letter. Under the title "A Czech Girl says 'Amgot' Has Failed", a refugee Czech schoolgirl attacked the military occupation of Italy, in terms which would serve for Iraq sixty years later:

> There has been much discussion lately about the advantages and disadvantages of "Amgot" – the government of occupied territories. The British public has failed to realise that it is not their feelings which should be primarily considered, but the feelings of the peoples living under the yoke of Nazism, who are waiting expectantly for the day of liberation. What do they think of "Amgot"? We believe that they will clamour for the immediate setting up of a democratic government and will turn away with as much contempt from an Allied dictatorship, of however temporary nature this may be, as they did from the Nazi "herrenvolk". "Amgot" is failing: it has not succeeded in gaining the confidence of the conquered peoples, and it is high time we set about finding its successor. (*Picture Post* 1944a, 26)

Further disquiet was expressed over what has become known more recently as "embedded reporting", in this case with reference to British military restrictions on the supply of photographs of the June 1944 D-Day landings. Although the landings had taken place on 6 June 1944, it was not until its issue of 24 June, over two weeks later, that *Picture Post* was able to print photographs of the event. The reason became apparent in an acerbic editorial in the July 15 number, entitled "Where are the Pictures?":

> The British Army in the past few weeks has performed some of the most terrific achievements of its long career. Where are the pictures showing what it has done? Rome fell on June 4. Since then the Allied armies under General Alexander have raced through Italy in a campaign of extraordinary brilliance. Where are the pictures?

Cherbourg fell June 26-27. The dailies printed many excellent pictures of this great American victory. The pictures we should have liked to publish were those of the great tank battles fought by the British and Canadians around Caen and Tilly which had helped to make possible this success. The battle has been raging since June 11. At the moment of going to press we ask again – Where are the pictures? They may come later. They will still have been too late. (*Picture Post* 1944b, 3)

For *Picture Post*, the fault lay squarely with the British military authorities, who, unlike their American counterparts, effectively conscripted news photographers like Bert Hardy into the Army Film and Photographic Unit and had sole power over the release of their work, overruling even the Ministry of Information.

If *Picture Post* owed its phenomenal success and unique relationship with its readership to its photographic coverage of conflict, the post-war period was to prove more troublesome, with a greater reliance on glamour photographs of film stars, coverage of social issues and articles on scientific discoveries and the way of life of the future. When conflict did appear, it was gratefully seized on, as in extensive reporting on the Berlin blockade and airlift and an in-depth series of articles by the proprietor Edward Hulton on the South African Prime Minister Dr Malan and his nascent apartheid regime, concluding "Dr Malan's real fight, it seems, is with the realities of 20th-century life" (Hulton 1948, 24). This measured but critical approach was met with a seven-day delay in distribution of the previous issue on the orders of South African customs.

The liberal image of *Picture Post*, and that of its proprietor, however, was terminally damaged by its coverage of the Korean War in 1950. It shipped out the by now veteran war photographer Bert Hardy, together with the finest foreign reporter of his generation, James Cameron, who had recently joined *Picture Post* from the *Daily Express*. In the South Korean town of Pusan, Cameron came across a "terrible crowd of men", a "grisly mob", starving, beaten and degraded, and about to be led away to mass execution (Cameron 1969, 132-5). As Cameron soon realized:

These prisoners were of course not convicts, nor prisoners of war; they were political hostages of the South Korean administration for whose integrity the United States and Britain and the United Nations were at the moment fighting. They were not North Koreans, but South

Koreans in South Korea, whose crime – or alleged crime, since few of them had been accorded the formality of a trial – was that they had been named as opponents of the Synghman Rhee regime, the one-man oligarchy called with Asian irony the Liberal Party. (*Picture Post* 1944b, 133)

Accordingly, Cameron filed a dispassionate article, fully documented by Hardy's photographs, entitled "An Appeal to the United Nations": "All things considered, it was a journalistic essay of elaborate moderation" (*ibid.*, 146), "which could not possibly be opposed by anyone of goodwill, least of all by a journal of the liberal and humane pretensions of *Picture Post*" (*ibid.*, 145). Someone in a position of considerable influence, however, saw to it that the proprietor, Edward Hulton, was informed of this implicit attack on the Americans, and, in circumstances not unlike the removal of the *Daily Mirror* editor Piers Morgan in 2004 over, as it transpired, bogus photographs of British atrocities in Iraq, Tom Hopkinson was unceremoniously sacked as editor, with the terse announcement: "Tom Hopkinson has been instructed to relinquish the position of editor of *Picture Post*, following a dispute over the handling of material about the Korean War and other matters" (*ibid.*, 147). James Cameron resigned later, but noted that the crisis marked a watershed in the history of the magazine:

> Its proprietor issued yet another statement around which there already clung the scent of defeat: "There is no intention to change the tradition of *Picture Post*," he said, "whereby the staff have full freedom to develop their creative abilities and rely on their own judgement. It is my intention to maintain the political independence of *Picture Post*." In fact, *Picture Post* soon painlessly surrendered all the values and purposes that made it a journal of consideration, before the eyes of its diminishing public it drifted into the market of arch cheesecake and commonplace decoration, and by and by it died, as by then it deserved to do. (*Picture Post* 1944b, 149)

In fact, there were other factors which contributed to the magazine's terminal decline, not least the transfer to television of most of the journalists who had made its reputation in the post-war years, but the episode of the Korean War was undoubtedly crucial.

Paris Match

If *Picture Post* came to grief because it had raised expectations of integrity in its coverage of conflict which it could no longer sustain, *Paris Match* has perhaps owed its survival to a more conservative approach, both politically and editorially. Initially, it came into being the same year as *Picture Post*, 1938, when the press baron Jean Prouvost, who owned the phenomenally successful daily paper *Paris-Soir*, decided to produce a news magazine on the model of *Life*. In one of the press empires which his group had absorbed, there was a weekly sports magazine called *Match*. Prouvost took control of the magazine and immediately changed its format and direction: on 5 July 1938, the new proprietor announced his intentions:

> A partir du jeudi prochain 7 juillet votre hebdomadaire sportif *Match* se transforme, élargit sa formule et devient le grand magazine du sport, des loisirs, de la vie au grand air, de la jeunesse, de l'aventure, de l'héroisme. Il vous donnera chaque semaine une puissante sélection des images de la vie moderne. *Match*, libre, indépendant, dira tout ce qu'il pense... [From Thursday 7 July next your sporting weekly *Match* is changed, has a bigger format and becomes the great magazine, of sport, leisure, outdoor life, youth, adventure, heroism. It will give you every week a powerful selection of images of modern life. *Match*, free, independent, will say what it thinks...] (*Match* 1938, 2; Hewitt 1991, 111-128)

As with *Picture Post*, the new format was immediately successful, taking *Match* to a pre-war circulation of 1,400,000 by October 1939, a feat which owed much to "les événements et la tension internationale" ["events and international tension"] (Boegner 1969, 55). The defeat of France in 1940 and the subsequent occupation put an end to this glittering career, although Prouvost, based in Lyon, was able to launch a replica, called *7 Jours*, which sold 700,000 copies in the Southern Zone alone (*ibid.*, 8). After the Liberation, this success looked rather more ambiguous and Prouvost, who had also served as Pétain's Haut Commissaire de la Presse at Vichy, was tainted with the whiff of collaboration, which seriously delayed his return to mainstream press actvity. In fact, it was not until 1949 that he was in a position to relaunch *Match*, but with the modified title of *Paris Match*.

The delay in re-launching *Paris Match* was in many ways providential. In the immediate aftermath of the Liberation, the market-place was crowded with photo magazines, some of which, like the Communist-oriented *Regards*, dated from the pre-war period, and others of which, like *Le Monde illustré, France-Illustration, Noir et Blanc, Point de vue, Images du monde, Nuit et Jour, Ambiance* and *Radar*, were new (Bellanger *et al.* 1975, 310). In fact, the market-place was not merely crowded, but over-crowded, and most of these titles were unable to withstand the crippling "grève du livre" of 1947 and the major crisis which affected the entire French press from 1949 to 1953 and which led to the disappearance of 137 weekly publications (Faucher and Jacquemart 1968, 220). With its later launch date, its professional experience derived from the pre-war period and the Occupation, and the compelling model of *Life* magazine, *Paris Match* was able to dominate the market over its more fragile and decidedly more old-fashioned rivals. In the 1950s, one of its major competitors, André Beyler's *Radar*, still used engraved line-drawings for its front covers, with the consequence that, whereas the circulation of *Paris Match* continued to rise, that of *Radar* declined from 500,000 to 300,000 between 1952 and 1957, and, despite a belated attempt at a new format, *Radar* disappeared from the scene in 1962 (*ibid.*, 220, 234).

Not, however, that *Paris Match* had things all its own way in the first years of its career: Philippe Boegner recalls that at the end of 1949, circulation was static at 200,000 copies, advertizing was proving difficult to attract, and the entire operation was running at a deficit of 250 million francs (Boegner 1969, 41-2). What saved the magazine was effectively war and death: its coverage of the Korean War and, most importantly, its reporting of famous deaths: Marshall Pétain in 1951, Marshall de Lattre de Tassigny, and King George VI of England, to which *Paris Match* devoted two special numbers, each selling more than a million copies (*ibid.*, 57). Most important of all was its coverage of the final phase of the Indochina War, culminating in the Battle of Dien Bien Phu, in which it raised one of the nurses on the battlefield to the iconic status of "l'Ange de Dien Bien Phu" and established itself as the major source of information, over the cinema newsreels and the still-primitive and embryonic French television.

From the very beginning, *Paris Match* had adopted a formula, essentially derived from *Life* and shared with *Picture Post*, which, as said, it later expressed in the slogan "Le poids des mots, le choc des photos": a clever blend of textual reportage and analysis with dramatic photography. Within this format, its content ranged from the trivial to the portentous, with a marked preference for coverage of war and conflict. The very first number, on 29 March 1949, carried news stories on changes in the Soviet leadership, Winston Churchill's speech to the European Assembly, but led with extensive photographic coverage of the Chinese revolution: "Panique à Shanghai, ruée vers le riz, ruée vers l'or" ["Panic in Shanghai, rice rush, gold rush"]. At the same time, there was a full-page photograph of General Giroud's body lying in state in the Invalides, together with four pages devoted to French domestic politics. Later articles introduced a lighter tone, with stories on French technological advances in the realm of defence, the painter Raoul Dufy, the world-wide impact of Paris fashion, and reviews of films and theatre.

This powerful formula, which has remained broadly unchanged since 1949, was, of course, highly conservative, both explicitly, particularly through the articles of the magazine's political editor Raymond Cartier, and implicitly, in the way in which the "choc des photos" was always effectively neutralized by the mixture of drama and trivia in the format itself and in the perspective offered. *Paris Match* was often compared to a middle-aged Frenchman in slippers looking out of the window of his comfortable apartment at events which might be harrowing in themselves, but which remain safely at one remove. Or, as Roland Barthes comments famously in *Mythologies*, looking at the outside world:

> Voilà le lecteur de *Match* confirmé dans sa vision infantile, installé un peu plus dans cette impuissance à imaginer autrui que j'ai déjà signalée à propos des mythes petits-bourgeois. [Here we have the reader of *Match* confirmed in his or her infantile view of the world, a little more stuck in that impotence to imagine anyone else that I have already referred to in respect of *petits-bourgeois* myths.] (Barthes 1970, 66).

It is no coincidence, therefore, that if *Paris Match* owed its early success and, indeed, survival, to René Coty's Fourth Republic, it should have been able to accommodate itself superbly with de Gaulle's Fifth Republic, in which the "impossibility of imagining anyone else" was reinforced by a celebration of apparent enhanced national pride and international prestige.

In this context, the year 1967 was a good one for *Paris Match*. Not merely did it cover urban riots in the United States, the Cultural Revolution in China, anti-French rioting in Djibouti and revolutionary movements in South America (in which, characteristically, the magazine employed the veteran journalist and adventure-novelist Jean Lartéguy to track down Che Guevara), it also had two major wars: the Six-Day War in the Middle East and the ongoing war in Vietnam, the scene of its previous triumph. In all of these, but particularly in the Middle East and Vietnam, *Paris Match* was able to call upon unprecedented resources, both from its own photographers and journalists and from news agencies. Also, in both wars, the magazine was apparently able to break away from some of the controls of embedded journalism which had restricted the operations of *Picture Post* in World War II and which was to become such an issue in the first, but especially the second, Gulf War.

Thus, during the Six Day War, *Paris Match* could proudly announce that it could put ten correspondents in the field, covering each of the warring camps, reflecting, incidentally, the ambiguous attitude of the French government to the combatants. Nevertheless, the war narrative depends upon a result and, in the same way that *Picture Post* dwelt upon the pathos of the vanquished in World War II, *Paris Match* emphasized scenes of defeat and flight. In Vietnam, at the same time, the coverage is both similar and more nuanced. Again, *Paris Match* prides itself in reporting the war from both sides. Thus, in its number of 25 February 1967, it carries pictures from the photographer Pic with the North Vietnamese in Nam-Dinh and from Marc Riboud on board the USS Enterprise. Similarly, it published pictures by the American photographer Lee Lockwood from Hanoi and stills from a film by Joris Ivens, again in Hanoi. On 28 October, it carried a report on the Vietcong themselves. At the same time, *Paris Match*'s coverage of Vietnam exploits the same narrative of suffering and defeat, but this time exclusively on the American side. Here, the symbolism is clear: the North Vietnamese are depicted either as resilient victims and survivors or as powerful adversaries; the Americans, in contrast, are bogged down in Con-Thien, their very own Verdun, and carried away wounded from the battle of Hill 881. The American predicament is summed up in the photograph of an exhausted and terrified marine at Con-Thien by the American photographer David Douglas Duncan.

Interestingly, in 1967, *Paris Match* was at pains to highlight the role of women reporters in situations of conflict, although often in a curiously subordinate role: the photographer and heroine of the article on the Cultural Revolution, "Une Française chez les Gardes Rouges" ["French woman amidst the Red Guards"], is identified as Suzanne Vincent, "femme du correspondant de l'A.F.P." ["wife of the A.F.P. correspondent"] (*Paris Match* 1967b, 28), whilst one of the main stories from Vietnam concerns the war correspondent Michèle Ray, taken prisoner by the Vietcong, but better known as the former model for Chanel under the name of "Moune" (*Paris Match* 1967a, 45).

In contrast, whilst the work of women reporters is no longer a story, the coverage of the 2003 Gulf War is considerably more limited in its scope. *Paris Match* is at pains to emphasize the suffering wrought on the civilian population of Iraq, but also careful to avoid attributing blame. At the same time, unlike its coverage of the Six Day War and Vietnam, *Paris Match*'s photographs of the American army have a staged appearance which, in group shots, is reminiscent of the earliest days of war photography.

Conclusion

This issue, in its turn, raises an important point regarding the photographic depiction of conflict in general: namely its effectiveness and its ability to evolve. Tom Hopkinson makes a powerful case for the former, and asserts the photograph's superiority over the moving image:

Think back to the Vietnam War, and two pictures come to every mind: the street execution of a Vietcong guerrilla by a South Vietnam police chief; and the little girl running down the road, naked and screaming, her clothes burned off by napalm. Both sequences have been shown many times on television, but it is the still version which makes the lasting impact. The reason is plain. In the filmed version the bullet is fired, and all is over. But in the still photograph his face, distorted by fear of death, is for ever distorted; and the girl, twenty years later, is still running down the road. (Hopkinson 1989, 12)

It is also true that the news photograph, consciously or unconsciously, appeals to experiences derived from our collective visual culture in art history: the celebrated photograph by Robert Capa of the death of a militia-man in the Spanish Civil War, so celebrated that it has been accused of being staged, owes its effect not merely to the drama and pathos of the incident, but also to the allusion to crucifixion. Similarly, the picture of the shocked and grieving student at Kent State University over the body of a fellow student shot in 1970 by the Ohio National Guard, is both the record of an event and a *pietà*.

However, if this is a powerful source for the news photograph's impact, it also raises questions regarding its adaptability. War reporting, and war photography, began in the Crimean War, where, as in the American Civil War, cumbersome equipment and slow film speeds ruled out anything but static, or staged, set-piece shots. In spite of Hopkinson's undoubtedly correct assessment of the technological impact of the Leica, however, even during the World War I, stills from undeniably clumsy movie cameras could achieve the same effect as action photography a generation later. In other words, the aesthetic format was created before the technological means to implement it. It is difficult, indeed almost impossible, to distinguish between frames of advances of troops in World War I and the photographs of similar advances in World War II, just as it is almost impossible to identify photographs of defeat or misery. And, if war photography is curiously impervious to chronology, it is also remarkably non-partisan: the captured British Tommy at Dunquerque, photographed for the German magazine *Signal*, stares at the camera with the same exhaustion and resignation as his American counterpart at Con-Thien in 1967. In other words, in the same way that there are alleged to be only seven basic plots for novels, of which others are merely variants, and only six core jokes, it may well be that photography in conflict follows a similarly restricted pattern, which endows the images with the enhanced power of accumulated memory, but which also contains our perception of conflict within a more limited field than we might normally accept. The line between originality and cliché, or visual shorthand, thus becomes more blurred. However, the role of the news magazines and the invention of photo-journalism in defining the way in which we perceive conflict, and which spills over into all areas of visual culture, becomes more important.

This also, finally, raises questions regarding the relationship between the viewer and the object, and here the issues are complex. On the one hand, the editorial concern of the news magazines must be to disquiet, disturb and galvanize their readers in the wake of the issues raised and portrayed. On the other, as Barthes indicates, there is a more ambiguous process at work: the Western reader, often likened in the case of *Paris Match* to a comfortable bourgeois clad in slippers and looking out from the comfort of his window on the mayhem below, is both challenged and reassured by the images and texts contained in the magazine he is holding. The anguish is compensated by happiness and, for every image of pain and misery, there is a picture of a reassuringly comfortable lifestyle. The news magazines, like their successors in the broadcast media, wove a complicated menu of concern and happiness which constituted a winning formula.

References

Barthes, R. (1970). *Mythologies*. Paris : Seuil, coll. "Points".

Bellanger, C., *et al.* (1975). *Histoire générale de la presse française, IV: De 1830 à 1958*. Paris: Presses Universitaires de France.

Boegner, P. (1969). *Presse, argent, liberté*. Paris: Fayard.

Cameron, J. (1969). *Point of Departure*. London: Panther.

Edelman, M. (1944). "A Good Augury for 1944", *Picture Post*, 8 January.

Faucher, J.-A. and N. Jacquemart. (1968). *Le Quatrième pouvoir: la presse française de 1830 à 1960*. Paris: Special Number of *L'Echo de la Presse et de la Publicité*.

Hewitt, N. (1991). "The Birth of the Glossy Magazines: the Case of *Paris Match*", in B. Rigby and N. Hewitt (eds.). *France and the Mass Media*. Basingstoke: Macmillan.

Hopkinson, T. (1948). "How *Picture Post* began". *Picture Post*, 2 October.

Hopkinson, T. (1989). "When Britain armed itself with a Camera". *The Weekend Guardian*, 11-12 February.

Hulton, E. (1948). "Where is South Africa Going? I talk to Dr Malan". *Picture Post*, 11 December.

McCabe, E. (1989). "Image Makers", *The Weekend Guardian*, 11-12 February.

Paris Match. (1967a). "Notre consoeur Moune ex mannequin de Chanel". 28 January.

Paris Match. (1967b). "Une Française chez les Gardes Rouges", 18 February.

Picture Post. (1944a). "A Czech Girl says 'Amgot' has failed". 8 January.

Picture Post. (1944b). "Where are the Pictures?". 15 July.

Remembering the Future: the Construction of Gendered Identity and Diversity in the Balkans

Patrizia Violi

Memories for the future

In recent years memory has become the object of increasing interest in domains of the human sciences far exceeding the focus of traditional historical research.[1] History has always been, obviously, the discipline that, *par excellence*, deals with the reconstruction and conservation of memories. Today, however, on the geographical map of the academic disciplines, research on memory has multiplied to such a degree that there is even a specific domain recognized as "memory studies". Memory seems to have become an object of study in itself, in accordance with a move towards the "objectification" of various topics that is currently quite popular in our contemporary research landscape. So now we have, besides the well established field of Cultural Studies, also tourism studies, memory studies, and even Holocaust studies.

In this vein, a large number of corpora with memories, life stories, interviews and similar documents have been collected, especially regarding conflict and post-conflict situations, and these are often available on the web. The web is an ideal place to keep trace of a virtually unlimited memory that might well extend to thousands and thousands of individual records, becoming factually, and not only metaphorically, the cultural encyclopaedia of our own civilization.

There is, however, a risk in such an operation, the illusion that the more data, testimonies, or life stories we collect, the more we will be able to "reproduce" the past and thus capture it as an objective, "complete" reality. This, of course, cannot but be an illusion. It is not through a multiplication of records that we will manage to obtain a more precise reconstruction of the past, but rather through an interrogation that, from our present time, is projected into the past, questioning our data from a specific point of view.

In this sense we could say that memories do not represent the past, unless they are put into perspective by a specific hypothesis regarding our

[1] See, for example, Demaria (2006).

own present time, and especially our future. To read the past, and to make sense of it, we need to examine it from the present, while bearing in mind the future. Memories and history can tell us something about our present only with a view towards the future. This is the stance I shall take in the present analysis of a particular collection of memories, an electronic archive of interviews with Kosovan women with different ethnic and religious backgrounds. The analysis of such a corpus will enable us to formulate hypotheses about the construction of gendered identity and difference, and to put forward some ideas on reconciliation practices. In this sense the reading of the past will be, in my perspective, a tool to imagine the future, and how possibly to start imagining a (difficult) future coexistence.

Two hypotheses form the basis for my work: first of all that subjectivity, our own, but also that of the other, is not an ontological entity, defined once and for all, but always the result of a complex net of relations, a place of continuous transformations and reconfigurations, of conflicts and tensions, but also of possible renegotiations. In this perspective *The Other*, in capital letters, is another metaphysical pitfall, that should be dissolved in a multiplicity of different individuals. The second hypothesis, directly connected with semiotic methodology, is that subjectivity can never be captured through an abstract definition, beyond its inscription in some specific form of manifestation, which is always a discursive practice, i.e. one of several textual *genres* in a larger sense, and socially regulated. Not only is every description of subjectivity and otherness partial but, more relevantly from a semiotic point of view, it is also constructed in discourse.

Even more complex is the case of gendered subjectivity, which is the object of the present analysis. Gender is indeed a complex semiotic construction, the result of a social sense-production that, starting from a "natural" attribution of functions based on division by sex, designs a full system of values, competences, life forms, profiling some possible narrative developments for our experience and preventing others.

The Archive "Memory and Culture of Women in Kosovo"
The electronic archive I analyzed includes thirty-four life stories of Kosovar women of different origins – Albanian, Serbian, Roma – collected in the period 1999-2000 in Kosovo and Italy. The project was promoted by the international organization "Women's World", in

collaboration with the Women's Centre of Bologna, which at the time was running a number of projects in Kosovo, and the Schuman Center at the European University Institute in Florence. It is officially signed by Luisa Passerini, Enrica Capussoti and Liliana Ellena, but many more women took part in it, as interviewers, translators, web designers and so on.[2]

The archive includes a description of the original project, a framework and guide used for the interviews, transcripts of the thirty-four original interviews, the biographical data of the women interviewed, three "itineraries" signed by the women who took part in the project regarding the three groups of interviews in Italy: Kosovaro-Albanians, Kosovaro-Serbs, Kosovaro-Roma. In my analysis I shall focus mainly on the two groups of interviews of Kosovaro-Albanians and Serbs, but some brief comments are in order here, too, on the three "itineraries". These indeed represent three autonomous texts, with an obvious framing function relative to the interviews, but at the same time they show the complex, divergent relationship between the subjective voices of the interviewers and those of the interviewees. Interestingly, the two texts devoted to the Albanian and Serb women adopt quite different strategies. While the first, by Silvia Salvatici, is in the first person, centred on the subjective and pathemic experiences of the interviewer, and foregrounding her emotional and even somatic reactions, the itinerary framing the Serb interviews, by Liliana Ellena, is, on the contrary, fairly objective – a kind of historical reportage packed with data. Seen from this point of view, these itineraries play an important role in the construction of the overall sense of the archive: indeed it would be a mistake to think of the archive as merely a container for interviews. On the contrary, the archive is a complex textual object, whose entire sense emerges from the interaction of its various components. In particular, the speaking voices and their different subjectivities have a crucial role here: if the whole site can be seen as a generalized, impersonal enunciator, the singular voices of the interviewers become more specific forms of "delegated enunciators".[3]

Gender and *genre*: women's life stories
The aim of the project – as described by Luisa Passerini on the archive website – is to save and transmit personal and community memories

---

[2] The archive is hosted today by the web site of the Women's Centre of Bologna, at **http: //www.women.it/bibliotecadelledonne/donne_kossovo**.
[3] On this issue see Lorusso and Violi (2004)

related to cultural traditions in historical periods of emergency, such as the Kosovo war. In this perspective it is worth noting that women are taken as the "natural" keepers of community memory, and they are therefore seen as competent subjects endowed with specific knowledge about traditions and everyday life, a kind of "gender competence", so to speak. The interview guide is particularly enlightening in this respect.

In this process, gender competence is both presupposed and simultaneously constructed by the discourse of the archive, in such a way that we could say that the role and function of women in preserving and transmitting cultural tradition – that to which I refer as gender competence – is in part a *genre* construction. More specifically, in the case we are examining, gender representation is the result of a particular textual *genre* in which it is embedded, i.e. the autobiographical life story interview. The life story interview is a highly specific *genre* often used in women's history because it can voice what is generally hidden in official histories, especially everyday knowledge and experiences forgotten by "official" histories of international relations, wars and treaties.

In such a choice we can see the sign of a double valorization: on the one hand the valorization of the "residual" aspects of life, more related to everyday experience, which are generally left at the margins of historical research; on the other hand the valorization of the singular individuals who are part of a collective history, to whom the life story interviews give voice. In our case, "to give voice" is certainly not a metaphorical expression, since life stories were first used in oral history, starting in the 'fifties and 'sixties. On the website of the archive we can find only the transcripts of the interviews, and this is of course an inevitable reduction and flattening of the original richness of the rhythm, intonation and physical substance of real voices. The transcription also loses much of the intrinsically dialogical form of the interview, especially when other people were present during the interview.

Life story is a textual *genre* endowed with specific features. At the level of discourse structure it is characterized by the form of an ongoing discourse, similar to a conversation. In this sense it is a kind of non-planned or incompletely planned form of discourse. Certainly there is a pre-existing script to guide the development of the interview. The guideline does not, however, represent a rigid structure, and each interview has, so to speak, its own life, depending on the situation, the different foci of attention, the attitudes and inclinations of the interviewees and, last but not least, the specific relationship established during the interview. From the very same script, very different discursive elements can emerge. At the level of enunciation, a life story is always a dialogical text, built up around the interaction of at least two voices. Quite often in our corpus, other people are present, having the role of what Goffman (1981) defined as Overhearers.

As far as thematic content is concerned, life stories are mainly focused on everyday life and personal experience, but they are not rigidly structured, and allow a lot of potential for alternative developments, varying considerably depending on the interviewer and the relationship between interviewer and interviewee. As we saw, life story interviews are embedded in a more complex text, the computer archive itself, producing a kind of hierarchy of textual levels and genres. From this point of view, the archive is a complex multi-layered text type that includes different sub-texts: the project, the schema, the itineraries, the interviews, all functioning together as a complex frame for life stories. In a way we could consider the whole archive, with its textual complexity, as a new textual *genre*.

My decision to concentrate mainly on life stories depended on the focus of the present analysis: the construction of gendered identity and difference within a highly specific discursive *genre*. While not believing that gendered subjectivity is *only* a discourse strategy, an effect of meaning inscribed into texts, it is certainly *also* a process, a construction that takes place within discursive practices. In particular the schematic script that guides interviews is quite enlightening on this matter: it is completely focused on personal life, family traditions, domestic habits. In a way, we could say that the script shapes and prefigures at one and the same time a given idea of gender, focusing on some specific aspects of it and predetermining the modalities of expression of gendered subjectivity. This is not a criticism of the interview schema, which will prove to be quite productive, but a way to remind us that discourse form is never "innocent".

Yet life stories are not only the reports of individual lives: they cannot but be read upon the background of a particular socio-historical conflict. Life stories, as a *genre*, include and intertwine both the private experience dimension and the socio-historical dimension of a whole culture and a collectivity. This is what makes them extraordinarily interesting texts from a semiotic point of view, since we can see at work, as in a kind of virtual laboratory, meaning dynamics that belong to a psycho-semiotics of personal experience together with a socio-semiotics of culture. Or, more precisely, a semiotics of *cultures*, since a plurality of many and different cultures inhabit the voices of these women. Gender too can be seen, in this perspective, as a multidimensional category constructed at the same time by personal, individual experience and socio-historical elements. To read these texts one constantly needs to keep in mind how culture affects the construction of that which we are used to calling "subjectivity", and also how individuals may develop very different responses to the same cultural environment. Two general issues are involved in this double movement. The first refers to what I would call the "subjectivization" process: subjectivity should not be seen as something given and organized once and for all, but rather as an ongoing process of construction and transformation. And sometimes a process of deconstruction, as tragically testified in some of our interviews. The second issue is the very complex question of individuality, not often taken into consideration in semiotic research, which is more orientated towards generalization. Life stories reframe the historical dimension at the level of individuals, reading generality explicitly though individual experience. Semiotics has always been concerned with general forms and, in that particular approach, subjectivity has always been taken into account only as a particular textual effect, i.e. as long as it appears as textually inscribed. It was probably only Julia Kristeva who claimed the relevance of individual and unconscious subjectivity as an essential component of the meaning of texts.[4] While Kristeva's work is centred on "feminine genius", materials such as the ones we are considering here suggest a less exceptional reading of women's subjectivity, which is captured in the normality of common, everyday lives.

Individual and collective identities: identification and distance
The identity construction of the individual self emerges in the interviews on the background of two main thematic dimensions: the construction of a collective "us", i.e. the construction of ethnic and religious identities in the two groups of Albanian and Serb women; and the image of the "other", the enemy – the collective "them" – and the representation of the

---

[4] See Kristeva (2001, 2002, 2004) on, respectively, Hannah Arendt, Melanie Klein, and Colette.

conflict.

Identity and conflict appear to be the two semantic isotopies that frame the form of subjectivity in discourse. First of all the individual "I" is profiled in a complex relation with a group – the "us" – that represents the culture of belonging. Such a collective actor is not, however, a homogeneous entity, but a highly stratified reality, where different subcultures and positions coexist with different types of relevance: traditional *vs* innovative, religious *vs* lay, nationalist *vs* more cosmopolitan.

The culture to which the individual belongs is never a singular one, but is the locus of interaction for different forces that place the subject at the centre of a complex, multidimensional network. Consequently, the relations between the "I" and the collective "us" are not univocal or definable once and for all, but appear to be a consequence of a process of mediation between identification and distance. In some cases the "I" becomes completely collapsed into the group, so that each singular identity assumes the full array of collective values of the ethnic identity. In other cases, on the contrary, each singular woman defines herself by her opposition towards her community, and in this case the relation between "I" and "us" becomes one of contrariety.

The second axis of identification (often more powerful than the collective "us" in defining one's own identity) is the relation of the opposition between one community and the "other", the enemy. This is the polemical dimension of the conflict that opposes, as contrary terms, "us" to "them". In the semiotic square these two terms imply two other positions as their logical contradictions, the "not them" and the "not us". In the corpus of our interviews these positions are variously occupied by different actors, for example the European community or international public opinion, NATO troops, the UN representatives, and so on.

Us	Them
Not them	Not us

Different strategies can be found in the construction of the enemy: sometimes it is seen as an indistinguishable whole, sometimes it may present individually differentiated faces, names, biographies. Further-more, it is interesting to see the temporal and aspectual dimension of the textual construction of the enemy: sometimes there is a sudden and punctual transformation of the neighbour into the enemy; sometimes the process has a longer, more gradual growth; sometimes the enemy is seen as historically given since ancient times, according to a durative aspectual perspective. The forms of representation of the other are numerous and variable, concealed behind their apparent univocality, as well as ethnic identity.

Albanian-Kosovan women between archaism and innovation

The interviews from the Albanian-Kosovan group sketch an image of a very archaic society, deeply entrenched within a patriarchal culture, centred on a highly traditional family life. Marriages are arranged by families, and before puberty girls are promised to young boys whom they might not meet or even see before the day of marriage. The level of education is quite poor, especially for girls, who generally stop going to school before high school, and very rarely go to university. Albanian society in Kosovo is characterized by a very strong gender-based division of work; everyday life, too, is organized according to a strict separation of space and time between men and women, who have their different rituals, meeting places and communal activities strictly regulated by gender division. As a result, a fairly strong women's community and women's life parallel men's community and life, often producing a certain degree of freedom within this separated group.

The majority of the women belonging to the Albanian-Kosovan group seems to accept and share the system of values of their traditional culture: they assume without question the authority of the father and the family, which are taken as "natural". Women's subjectivity seems to be inscribed in a non-problematic way in that culture. Notice that this position is also shared by some quite young women, in their forties, and even in their twenties. For this group singular subjectivity (the "I") appears to be syntonic, and in continuity with the "us" of cultural identity of the community, which is not only the extended family, but also the larger Albanian culture whose traditions and habits are widely practised. At the same time, the strong separation of the sexes offers an alternative space for feminine identification, allowing the construction of a "feminine us" within the community. Women have their own separate life, rich in relations and communal activities, from which men are excluded.

The identification with the women's group, however, is always a way of declining a general belonging to a collective identity, more than a claim of feminine autonomy. In other words, among the group of more traditional Albanian-Kosovan women, individual subjectivity seems to disappear in a larger feeling of belonging. We could make the hypothesis that the stronger the agreement with collective traditional values, the more each singular individual inscribes her own subjectivity in a collective form, whether that of Albanian culture as a whole, or that of the more restricted traditional women's community.

Within the Albanian-Kosovan group there is, however, a small minority with a different story. These are women between 30 and 45, with a much higher level of education and, in two cases, with a university degree. Their position is characterized by an explicit distance from, if not an open rebellion towards, the traditions and the values of their community, especially as far as family life is concerned. None of them accepted an arranged marriage, and all chose their husbands outside the traditional community, unknown to, and in some cases not accepted by, the family. Interestingly enough, in these cases a quite different picture of the family appears: we are not facing an extended family, but a nuclear entity, very close to our modern western families, in which the couple plays the dominant role. The role that was occupied by the father and the traditional community is covered here by the couple itself, and identity is found in the new family style, in opposition to both the traditional family and the community of women, which no longer plays a role for emancipated Albanian-Kosovans.

We could synthesize in the following way the different identity structures of the two groups: where traditional culture is still very strong, subjectivity is inscribed in a collectively regulated belonging; the more emancipated, the more educated women are defined within a nuclear couple.

Albanian "us"   Nuclear couple "us"

Dependency   *Autonomy*
Tradition   *Innovation*

Feminine collectiveness   Individual "I"

As far as representation of the enemy is concerned, we notice a difference between traditional and emancipated women in the Albanian-Kosovan group. The more emancipated women are definitely the most radical in their opposition towards Serbs, as if only in the polemic dimension are they able to retrace a sense of belonging to their community that is otherwise lost at the personal identity level. For example, one and the same woman, Manduha, while claiming her own non-traditional choice of a marriage in order to be free from family conditioning, asserts at the same time the absolute impossibility of interethnic marriage because of "psychic impossibility". The conflict here appears to be naturalized, in the sense that it is not attributed to cultural or historical reasons, but to a deeper, more archaic psychic ground, where no possible solutions are available.

Paradoxically, the position of traditional women on this topic is more open: most of them seem to assume that religion is the main reason for the prevention of mixed marriages. In general this group does not express its hostile feelings with the same radical negativity as the emancipated women do. This becomes particularly noticeable in the recall of the traumatic experiences that almost all the Albanian-Kosovan women have suffered during the war, in which most of them lost relatives, even very close ones, and material goods. Remembering these tragic facts, the group of traditional women do not emphasize the pathemic, emotional side of the experience, neither do they insist on the cruelty of the enemy. Quite the opposite: in some cases even some sporadic episodes of humanity are registered, as in the interview with Zijaver, whose husband and elder son were killed by Serbs, but whose younger child was saved because the soldiers were moved by the crying of this little girl.

We could say that, in a way, both the expression of pain and of rage are emotionally "neutralized", and that, in general, feelings of hostility towards Serbs are less predominant. It is as if the more these women have a strong feeling of belonging to their own community, the less they seem to contraposition themselves relative to the other community. On the other hand, the more women are emancipated and the less they identify with their original culture, and thus have an identity that is more individually than collectively based, the more they emphasize the difference of the other as enemy.

How can we interpret such data? We might hypothesize that traditional culture functions as an "emotional container" for individual feelings and reactions: the more people feel they belong to a community that shares the same culture and value systems that they do, the more they are emotionally "contained". Traditional culture operates, so to speak, as an emotional conflict regulator; this is not to say that traditional culture weakens emotional valence, only that it gives it a less individual, more collective, form of expression, inscribing emotions within a common pathemic frame. Whenever such a containing frame is weakened, the more direct and violent becomes the expression of hate and contraposition with the other.

Serbian women: a fragmented culture

A quite different picture emerges from the interviews with Serbian-Kosovan women. First of all, while the Albanian group is a well defined and univocal one, Serbian women do not belong to a unique common culture, and do not share the same sense of ethnic belonging. Rather, we are in the presence of a fragmented constellation of different identities: Kosovan Serbs, Montenegran Serbs, Montenegran non-Serbs, Christian Serbs and even Muslim Serbs. The lack of any univocal communal "we" explains the very weak feeling of belonging to any given community. But another element should also be considered. All the women in this group come from a much more emancipated situation than the Albanian women: the influence of patriarchal structure is much less relevant, and women have always been used to a very high level of freedom, in which girls have the same access to education as boys and in which arranged marriages would not be conceivable. Almost all the women in this group have a university degree, and some among them work for "the internationals", as the KFOR troops are called, as interpreters. A strong awareness of, and possibly pride in, their emancipation is probably the key identity element unifying the group in the face of all other differences: more than an ethnic belonging, they acknowledge a common culture of feminine emancipation that is often asserted as an element that marks a relevant difference with respect to the Albanian community. In a way, although within a very different socio-ethnic context, we find a parallelism here too between emancipation and a weaker feeling of community belonging that we have already observed in the case of the emancipated Albanians. In the case of Serbians, however, in contrast to that of the Albanians, the culture of reference was already highly fragmented and multifaceted.

Perceptions of the conflict

The transformation of relations between the two communities and the starting point of the crisis is perceived in quite different and non-univocal ways. Among the Albanian group there is no common agreement on "when" the conflict started, or in accordance with which temporal sequence it proceeded. In particular it is noticeable how the aspectual dimension of the beginning of the conflict is differently perceived. For some women, the conflict situation has always been so ("since I was a child", says Nushe), in a continual, atemporal opposition in relation to which the actual situation is nothing more than a natural consequence.

On the other hand, many women remember a past of good and reasonably peaceable life together, for some, even excellent and without particular problems, up until 1989 or 1990, but they differ on the modality of the change. While for some women this was a sudden and in some ways inexplicable transformation, others describe a more gradual transition and a progressive deterioration of relations between the two communities.

If the latter is probably the more realistic account of the effective factual reality, it is interesting to notice how widespread and diffused is the subjective perception of a sudden, sharp change. It seems that subjective memory reconfigures continuous processes in the form of discontinuities, with sudden punctual changes instead of progressive transformations. Maybe this is a realistic description of what we subjectively perceive, more than the reality of facts: often we realize all of a sudden that which *has already happened,* and that became real for us only whenever we became conscious of it. According to this hypothesis we would tend to fix, in the reconstruction of gradual events, moments of precise discontinuity, catastrophic points more than durative processes.

Within the Serbian group the most striking feature is certainly the total lack of reflection on the causes of the conflict, or on the concatenation of events and their causal links. They all describe themselves as victims of a discriminating situation, objects of an unfair disparity, both economical and political. Albanians are always represented as more powerful and rich, and are considered totally responsible for the conflict. None acknowledges any responsibility on the Serbian side, nor any form of discrimination against the other community.

There is a high level of agreement on the starting point of the conflict, which is generally localized in 1980, coinciding with the Albanian protests against discrimination and lack of power. Curiously enough, nobody seems to realise the contradiction between those manifestations and the supposed privileged situation of Albanians, and nobody tries to understand the reasons for it. The lack of any analysis of the causes of the conflict, as well as the repression of a possible role on the part of the Serbians, make impossible and opaque any reading of the past.

Distant and close enemies

In the Serbian group, as we saw, a curious paradox seems to characterize the perception of the "other" as enemy: while the description of Albanians collectively considered is extremely conflictual and lacking any understanding, when everyday life is taken into account a very different situation emerges. Most women describe an almost friendly "community life" among the different ethnic groups before the start of the conflict, characterized by good neighbourhood relationships and the absence of tensions. In some cases two almost contradictory descriptions coexist in the same life story, without a solution or continuity. But, at least to some extent, the same shift is present also in the interviews with Albanian-Kosovan women: here too the conflict emerges when women talk in more general and political terms, while in recalling individual, everyday experience a quite different picture appears, more open to the possibility of dialogue.

What appears to be an almost schizophrenic description reveals, at a closer look, less contradictoriness than one would assume. Indeed, the two situations, the conflictual and the friendly, do not refer to *the same contexts*, but to two very different spheres: a public sphere of political and impersonal relations, where there is no direct and immediate personal knowledge, and a private sphere of neighbours and people who are personally known. While the public sphere is dominated by the conflict dimension, the private one, the one of direct interpersonal relations, seems to be more open to a possible, although difficult, contractual dimension. Notice that this not to say that neighbours *did* actually behave in a friendly way, or were any better than the unknown enemies. We know very well that unfortunately this was not the case, and awful crimes were actually committed by people who were very close. Here we are analyzing a discourse world, not the "real" one; in the realm of discourse all these women seem to make a distincton when they refer to the enemy within a dimension of direct personal knowledge, or in a more public, distant form. The latter is dominated by conflict, while the former seems more open to contact. We can summarize the difference in the following square:

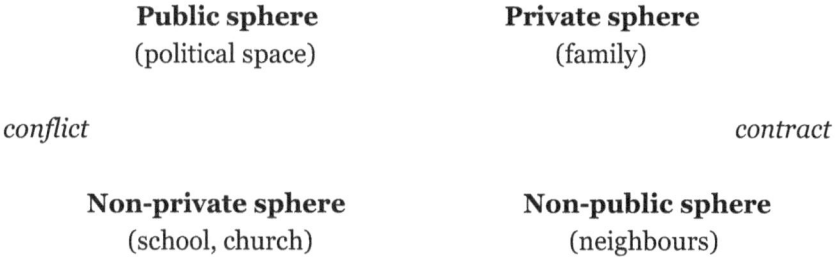

Public sphere (political space)	**Private sphere** (family)
conflict	*contract*
Non-private sphere (school, church)	**Non-public sphere** (neighbours)

We could say that in these interviews, the more the women refer to everyday personal life and individual relationships, the more they seem able to shift from a conflictual to a contractual dimension and to acknowledge the humanity of the other.

If, as I suggested at the beginning, the reading of the past and its memory is meaningful insofar it can help us in (re)constructing the future, what help could such a conclusion offer us in view of a possible future? When directly addressed on this matter, both groups, and in particular the Albanian-Kosovans, are very sceptical when not openly negative towards the possibility of a common future of peaceable cohabitation. However, if my suggestion is correct, we can hypothesize that, when people move from a more public dimension to a more interpersonally grounded one, they may change their perceptions of the other. It is at the macro-level of general political discourse that we find a stronger, more irreducible opposition, while at the micro-level of everyday experience and personal knowledge, a community life is still remembered. This seems an important suggestion for any practical reconciliation work in post-conflict situations, in which the trauma has lacerated the most constitutive structures of social life. In such a perspective, work on life stories may acquire a value that is something more than just a collection of testimonies of collective memory. If subjectivity is also textually and discursively constructed, then a textual *genre* that focuses on individual and personal dimensions of experience may help in the emergence of a freer and less homologated subject than the one inscribed in other discourse forms, from traditional media to historical discourse. And in doing so it may become at least one small contribution to the difficult path of coexistence.

References

Demaria, C. (2006). *Semiotica e memoria: Analisi del post-conflitto*. Rome: Carocci.

Goffman, E. (1981). *Forms of Talk*. Philadelphia: University of Pennsylvania Press.

Kristeva, J. (2001). *Hannah Arendt*. New York: Columbia University Press.

Kristeva, J. (2002). *Melanie Klein*. New York: Columbia University Press.

Kristeva, J. (2004). *Colette*. New York: Columbia University Press.

Lorusso, A.M., P. Violi. (2004). *Semiotica del testo giornalistico*. Bari: Laterza.

The Dialectic of Conflict and Culture:
Leon Trotsky and Less Fortunate Statesmen

Macdonald Daly

It is well known that the phase following the October Revolution in Russia in 1917 (of which Trotsky, my eponymous protagonist, was one of the principal agents), Russia's exit from the Great War at the Treaty of Brest-Litovsk in 1918 (at which Trotsky was the Soviet Union's chief negotiator), and the eventual Soviet victory in the Civil War which ended in 1921 (throughout which Trotsky was the leader of the Red Army), was one of extreme cultural ferment in the new-born USSR. My interest at the time I first engaged with this period was rather narrow: I was concerned with how it affected the future course of Marxist literary and cultural criticism in Western Europe, particularly, such of it as there was, in England. Today I remain interested in what another look at this period can tell us about the way we negotiate the issues of culture and conflict here and now, in an England that is certainly different, but one that, like almost everywhere else, has even less interest in Marxism than was the case in the nineteen-twenties and 'thirties.

The two decades or so after the October Revolution are commonly characterized as a period which began with notable artistic experimentation. There is no need to go into any great detail about these developments here. Let the image reproduced as Figure 1 stand synecdochically for them.

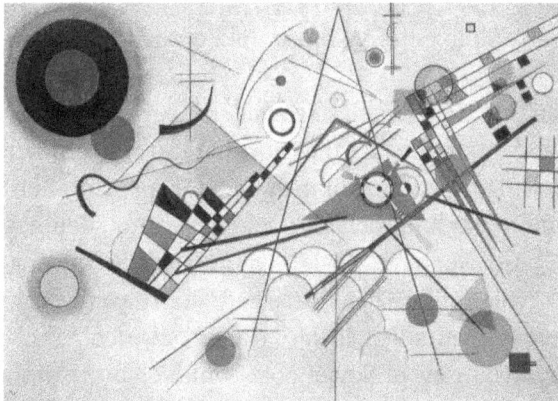

Fig. 1. Wassily Kandinsky, "Composition VIII" (1923)

After the death of Lenin in January 1924 and his supersession by Stalin, this phase of modernist efflorescence gradually turned into its opposite, the rigid, sterile, ideologically slavish practice known, and understandably universally reviled, as Socialist Realism. Let the image reproduced in Figure 2 stand for that.

Fig. 2. Arkady Shaikhet, "A Komsomol Youth at the Wheel" (1936)

I do not dislike this photograph or consider it particularly comparable to the painting, excepting the fact that the obviously experimental painting renders any particular reading of meaning or representation ambivalent while the photograph proclaims its own (no doubt) prescribed obviousness: here we have Soviet youth literally turning the wheel (through a revolution). This perceived shift away from relatively unhindered experimentalism towards enforced ideological dogmatism typifies the received view of Soviet post-conflict culture of the nineteen-twenties and 'thirties, and it is not my intention to challenge that view here, but to indicate what cultural (as opposed to political or military) part Trotsky played in the period. But I also want to articulate, to join up, what I have to say about Trotsky with attention to something closer to home in both place and time.

Whenever one contemplates the dramatic and varied life of someone like Trotsky one cannot help but reflect that contemporary times throw up hardly any examples of his seeming combination of man of action with man of aesthetic inclination and intellectual ability – certainly not in Britain. Here, politicians don't even write their own memoirs, which are ghosted for them (compare Trotsky's *My Life*); at best they produce pulp novels (one thinks of Jeffrey Archer, Douglas Hurd, or Edwina Currie); Gordon Brown, the former Prime Minister, has a little advertised Ph.D. from the University of Edinburgh (1982) and wrote a semi-respectable biography (1986) of James Maxton, the Scottish Socialist labour leader, but it hardly ranks with Trotsky's three-volume *The History of the Russian Revolution*, which was published in English in 1932-33. You have to go back to Churchill before you get anything like that from a British statesman but, although Churchill oversaw a noted multi-volume history (*The Second World War*), he did not also have a lot to say about the state of contemporary literature, art and criticism. Trotsky did: and in what follows I shall compare him unfavourably in this regard to some typical contemporary British Parliamentarians. But before I adjust to these twin foci, I wish to air some more general thoughts, to which I shall return finally, on the relation between conflict and culture.

Trotsky is a proponent of post-conflict culture proper: for him, the culture which might be made possible by the cessation of the conflicts he participated in would be the ultimate triumph over those conflicts. To quote from the introduction to *Literature and Revolution*:

> [...] even a successful solution of the elementary problems of food, clothing, shelter, and even of literacy, would in no way signify a complete victory of the new historic principle, that is, of Socialism. Only a movement of scientific thought on a national scale and the development of a new art would signify that the historic seed has not only grown into a plant, but has even flowered. In this sense, the development of art is the highest test of the vitality and significance of each epoch. (Trotsky 1960, 9)

Coming as it does from the Soviet Commissar of War, that statement seems a refreshingly congenial endorsement of art and its social importance. It is harder to find a name for what contemporary British Parliamentarians see as the relation between conflict and culture. As we shall find out, they largely envisage "culture" (or a certain kind of "culture") as a means of preventing conflict. It would be nicely symmetrical if we could call this "pre-conflict culture", but as, ideally, culture in this view prevents conflict from occurring, there is no "pre-", there is only an "instead of". However, both positions share a certain structural notion of conflict and culture, in which there is a very obvious culture/good, conflict/bad binary opposition.

Thus, neither party would entertain the extremism of the notorious adage, "When I hear the word 'culture' I reach for my gun." Such a statement entirely reverses the terms of the opposition I have just described (it is now culture/bad, conflict/good), and it will come as no surprise that the statement has a Nazi provenance.[1] I flag up the quotation here because we shall hear an echo of it, in significantly modified form, from the mouth of a British noble, a little later. What can we call this attitude except "anti-culture conflict"? It is not uncommon. When certain Islamic groups hear the words "American culture" they may indeed reach for their firearms or their *fatwahs*. Others may harbour a less militant but otherwise similar antipathy. But, again, this is in the realm of the specific. It is very rare to find antipathy to culture *as such* in the abstract, and even philistinism is not quite that (it is simply a failure to see the point of culture in general or specific manifestations of culture in particular: it is not necessarily principled opposition to culture). Likewise, hostility to American culture is hardly ever opposition to that culture *per se*, but it indicates a conflict between cultures – what used to be called "culture clash" – in which formulation, I would point out, the opposition between conflict and culture is in fact dissolved: here, culture is the arena of contestation, or it is what you have conflict over. Thus, for example, you are not meant to be able to procure Coca-Cola in Cuba or Havana cigars in the USA. Of course, one opposition is here abandoned only for another to be instated, *viz*: our culture is good; theirs is bad, let's

---

[1] "Wenn ich 'Kultur' höre, entsichere ich meinen Browning!" is a remark usually attributed to Hermann Göring , but in fact it is a quotation from Hanns Johst's *Schlageter*, a play first performed in celebration of Adolf Hitler's forty-fourth birthday: see Johst (1933).

fight it out, by the pen or the sword or, in the case of my last example, by resort to economic sanctions. But "clash of cultures" is a phrase that seems largely to have dropped out of contemporary parlance, replaced by "cultural difference", a term which attempts to restore all cultures to an equivalence (i.e. non-opposed, non-conflictual), *viz*: we have our culture; they have theirs; they are different, but equal or incommensurable.

The other body of thought I can identify as contributing to this constellation is the Marxist one. It argues that culture, in a capitalist economy, does not deliver us from conflict. We are *always* in conflict, and there will be no true culture until we are beyond conflict. It does not matter what you think of this position. My point is that, logically, it renders the term "post-conflict culture" tautologous. Culture is the reward we shall enjoy only after the cessation of conflict, and conflict is virtually coextensive with capitalism. Not surprisingly, this Marxist note signals the true entry of Trotsky into my discussion.

Literature and Revolution is seen by many as a bizarre and indeed politically irresponsible aberration of Trotsky's. Why? Isaac Deutscher, Trotsky's most famous biographer, sets the scene:

> In the summer of 1922, when he refused to accept the office of Vice-Premier under Lenin and, incurring the Politbureau's censure, went on leave, he devoted the better part of his holiday to literary criticism. The State Publishers had collected his pre-revolutionary essays on literature for republication in a special volume of his *Works*; and he intended to write a preface surveying the condition of Russian letters since the revolution. The "preface" grew in size and became an independent work. He gave to it nearly all his leisure but failed to conclude it. He resumed writing during his next summer holiday, in 1923, when his conflict with the triumvirs, complicated by the expectation of revolution in Germany, was mounting to a climax; and this time he returned to Moscow with the manuscript of a new book, *Literature and Revolution*, ready for the printer. (Deutscher 1959: 164)

In other words, Trotsky failed to seize the political position which might have enabled him to achieve the official adoption of the cultural policies implied by *Literature and Revolution* (had he become Vice-Premier it would have been automatically easier for him to succeed Lenin) and instead absented himself from the intense political fray so that he could adumbrate those very policies. As a political miscalculation, this is second in notoriety only to his later weekend wild duck-shooting trip, taken in November 1923, when Stalin's machinations against him were at their height. The adventure laid him up with a malarial infection that rendered him largely *hors de combat* during the crucial following months, leaving the field virtually clear for Stalin to assume the succession.

Nonetheless, the implied cultural policies of *Literature and Revolution* remain on record. One must remember that a great deal of thinking about literature and criticism in Bolshevik circles was influenced by Lenin's articles on Tolstoy (published between 1908 and 1911), in which, in a manner reminiscent of Marx and Engels on Balzac and Goethe, Lenin argued that Tolstoy overcame the limitations of his own class ideology by transferring his loyalty to the Russian peasantry in the revolution of 1905. The sharp contemporaneousness of Lenin's focus is a feature that Trotsky's book shares; but where he differs from Lenin is in his refusal strictly to align aesthetic judgements with fairly immediate political purposes. The dangers of this Leninist position come to the fore most strongly in Lenin's essay, "Party Organisation and Party Literature" (1905), which with apparent liberality admits that "everyone is free to write and say whatever he likes, without any restrictions", but reserves the quite illiberal right to expel from the Bolshevik Party those whose exercise of this freedom brings them into conflict with the Party line. It is clear in the essay that Lenin's strictures may be applied to creative writers as well as political commentators and interventionists (Lenin 1965, 44-49). Lenin justified such a policy because the Bolshevik Party was a "voluntary association" whose ideological integrity needed to be protected if it was to achieve its historical aims. Once it had achieved those aims, however, and actually become the governing party in 1917, a little later making itself indissociable from the state, such a policy applied to literature was indisputably potentially repressive.

Yet it is perfectly clear that the evaluation of literature according to its political tendency was never originally intended by culture-inclined Bolsheviks to preclude other kinds of evaluation or to necessitate what eventually took place under Stalin – intensifying censorship, rigid prescriptivism for writers prepared to toe the line, and systematic liquidation or geographical banishment of those who were not. In Trotsky's *Literature and Revolution* all the best possibilities of artistic tolerance were promoted alongside the recognition that "it is silly, absurd, stupid to the highest degree, to pretend that art will remain indifferent to the convulsions of our epoch" (Trotsky 1960, 12). Unreservedly suspicious of philistine attempts to reject the achievements of bourgeois art, to impose a "proletarian culture" in its place, and to exercise widespread repression in the cultural field, Trotsky undertook a vigorous and trenchant survey of the contemporary state of Russian literature from his undeniably partisan position as one of the architects of the revolution. Insofar as government was concerned, he stated:

> Our policy in art, during a transitional period, can and must be to help the various groups and schools of art which have come over to the Revolution to grasp correctly the historic meaning of the Revolution, and to allow them complete freedom of self-determination in the field of art, after putting before them the categorical standard of being for or against the Revolution. (Trotsky 1960, 14)

The position may seem characteristically contradictory. Once writers have "come over to the revolution", and once they have been helped to "grasp correctly" its historic meaning, they will be allowed "complete freedom of self-determination". But what if they do not "come over", or what if they do but fail to "grasp correctly" the revolution's "historic meaning", or, even if they do both, what if their allegiance to and "correct" understanding of the revolution later flags or is otherwise found wanting by those who consider themselves empowered to judge? The implications are obviously anxiety-provoking to liberal democratic sentiment. Yet Trotsky's position goes to the heart of the debate about literature and politics. If literature has no political effectivity, but is merely a concern of hobbyists, then it can be left well alone by the state. But if it does indeed have an appreciable role in shaping a society, it would be a foolish government that did not keep an eye on and attempt to control its workings – and, indeed, many liberal democratic governments have imposed censorship and repression precisely out of a recognition of literature's perceived social effectivity. If it happens that the best known cases in the "free world" are to do with the sexual rather than political content of literary texts – from the bowdlerization of Shakespeare to the banning of *Lady Chatterley's Lover* – all that is demonstrated thereby is that liberal governments have considered public discussion or dramatization of sexual mores to be a powerful social force requiring their vigilant control in much the same way as the Soviets came to consider expressions of political "deviance" a threat to October. Inimical as all writers and most readers understandably are to such control, where it is present it is clear that literature is not politically underestimated.

It is simply not true in any case that democratic governments do not prohibit literary texts which depart from what one might call the "party bottom line". How many are aware that Joseph Goebbels, that other notable statesman who was a man of action and a man of aesthetic inclination and intellectual ability, wrote a novel called *Michael* (published in 1929)? The answer is probably not many, because for a long period in modern democratic Germany, particularly during the immediate post-war period of denazification, it was suppressed along with many other thousands of "poisonous" texts (the most well known case is of course Hitler's *Mein Kampf*, whose copyright the state government of Bavaria acquired in 1945, and whose reprinting it thereafter refused to license; it was not published again in Germany until 2016, after the copyright had expired). Largely on account of Goebbels' later actions when in power, rather than its gauche content, the novel was considered not to toe the post-war "democratic bottom line", and few people lost any sleep over its state-sanctioned repression. Closer to home, and closer in time, Edward Bond's anarchic play *Early Morning* was refused a public performance licence as recently as 1968 because, among other things, it depicted Queen Victoria as a lesbian, a murderer and a cannibal.

If these comments enable us to put the somewhat bothersome problem of potential textual censorship and repression on political grounds in brackets, then Trotsky strikes me as the only twentieth century politician of major historical importance who has shown anything like a grasp of the indispensability and potency of cultural production and a willingness, given those propensities and capacities, to encourage it to flourish as freely as possible. One has to remember the tremulous fragility of the October Revolution almost up to the eve of his writing the book, as well as the stormy political environment in which he moved (note his qualification that his remarks applied only to the "transitional period" of the revolution: they were not meant to apply to an established and consolidated state of affairs). It is somewhat easier, in times of peace and plenty, for ruling liberal bourgeois politicians to let artists say whatever they like, not least because, under examination, they ironically turn out, in my view, to be more thoroughgoing materialists than Trotsky ever was. That is to say, whereas the Trotsky who wrote *Literature and Revolution* was the one who argued that the acid test of an economic revolution was whether or not it ultimately delivered in the realm of culture (which in my view, contrary to all popular conception, is the classic Marxist position), the acid test of culture, for liberal bourgeois politicians, is whether or not it delivers in the realm of economics. This latter conclusion I hope to demonstrate in the remainder of this essay, and so I now turn, as promised, to what I have called those "less fortunate" statesmen.

*

Late one evening in the January of 1989, I learned that the familiar and time-honoured term "Cultural Relations" had been replaced in official British political discourse by the phrase "Cultural Diplomacy". I was listening to the BBC radio programme *Today in Parliament*, which reported that the House of Lords had debated a motion calling for increased government funding for the British Council and the BBC's external services (particularly the World Service, which broadcasts to foreign territories world-wide). These are two main agencies of Britain's overseas cultural representation, and both had recently suffered financial cuts in real terms under the Thatcher government. The entire (and entirely astonishing) debate can be found in the official Parliamentary record.[2]

To be fair, some of the noble Lords expressed dislike for the new designation – Lord St. John of Fawsley (then better known as the Rt. Hon. Norman St. John Stevas, Conservative ex-Minister for the Arts) thought that "Cultural Diplomacy" had a "forbidding ring" – but they grudgingly took it up. Lord Bonham-Carter, the Liberal peer proposing the motion, wasted no time in launching a strategic military metaphor, referring within five minutes to the external services of the BBC as "an essential weapon in our armoury". He gave a stirring example of how, shortly before the Falklands War, the BBC's broadcasts to Spain had been

---

[2] *House of Lords Weekly Hansard*, no. 2379, cols. 209-46. Unless otherwise indicated, all quotations in this section are taken from this text.

cut, with the result that Spain's coverage of the War came almost entirely from Argentinian sources. The amount saved by this cut had been £230,000 – "rather less," he ventured, "than the cost of a single Exocet missile". All around Lord Bonham-Carter, parliamentary minds started to whirr into characteristic British warspeakmode. The Earl of Stockton, Director of the Macmillan Publishing Group, which has always profited greatly from the British Council's promotion of British books overseas, said that in supporting calls for increased government funding he was "speaking from the sharp end of the publishing salient" (a salient is a military fortification or line of defences which points outwards). Lord Weidenfeld (another publisher, of Weidenfeld and Nicolson fame) piped up with the idea that cultural diplomacy was "an excellent conduit for reconciliation and peace" in the hostilities he seemed convinced Britain was involved in: "it heals wounds and builds bridges". He ardently hoped that, by the 'nineties, assuming increased funding for the British Council, Britain's involvement in bell-igerence around the globe would be at an end and that our motto would be, "If I hear the word 'gun', I reach for my culture" (a quaint inversion of the Nazi *bon mot* we encountered earlier, although the noble lord wrongly attributed it to Göring because he probably dredged it up from the *Penguin Dictionary of Quotations*). Lord Moore of Wolvercote also hit the target when he repeated what nearly every other peer had said, namely that the universality of the English language gave Britain a ready-made market: "from that base we have various weapons with which to press our cultural offensive".

In this fashion, the Lords harangued the government for two-and-a-half hours, like Generals come back from the field to sort out the bureaucrats who were holding up supplies. It became clear that there was indeed a foreign war of sorts going on, which had to be fought on two fronts. There was the Influence Front, on which a Britain sadly dispossessed of Empire must scramble anew for cultural colonies, in the teeth of fierce competition from the other Western capitalist nations and from the "unfree" world (which then meant Communist countries). The Influence Front had to be secured if Britain was to be successful on the Trade Front, where there was (and no doubt still is and for any foreseeable future always will be) a frenzied struggle going on to flog everything from aeroplanes to zoom lenses in foreign markets.

An obvious instance raised in the debate of how the Trade Front cannot neglect the Influence Front is in the markets created abroad when foreign students educated in Britain return to take up influential positions in their countries of origin. But how can you get people to come and study here when they haven't learned English because the British Council hasn't enough resources to teach them; when they can't hear BBC broadcasts demonstrating how marvellous Britain's culture is, because of poor signals, outdated relay equipment, or sheer absence of a service; when the number of scholarships offered to overseas students is inadequate, and their tuition fees are going through the roof?

And so on. This is where the "civilizing" quality of "British culture" is usually deployed, because, naturally, it would not do to advertise straight out what a commercial coup you stand to effect on foreign nations who allow themselves to fall under your influence. At this point in the debate was heard a tactically evangelical maiden speech by the said Conservative ex-Minister for the Arts. Cultural diplomacy, he averred, is simply "the increase of British influence in the wider world", and yet:

> This increase is not pursued principally for commercial or economic reasons, but because we believe the long, continuous, extraordinarily rich and varied experience of this nation constitutes a unique contribution to the welfare of mankind, and we are therefore under a duty to make it as widely available as possible.
>
> If I were asked what had been this country's three greatest contributions to world civilisation I should reply unhesitatingly: the common law, parliamentary government, English language and literature, and at the heart of all three lies the idea of liberty. I do not believe that we can export our institutions indiscriminately, but by informing people of how they work and flourish, by imparting thoughts about them, we can enhance the chances for freedom elsewhere.

Listening to this on radio – so boundlessly confident was the delivery – one was almost tempted to disregard the strangeness of the argument. Our legal, political and cultural institutions are all about liberty, so we have a duty to press them on everybody else. To force people to be free Britain cannot use gunboats as it used to, so it has to resort to convenient arks such as "English language and literature". We should count ourselves lucky, because we invented English, and know how to use it:

The benefits of the universality of that language are truly incalculable. I often reflect on the extraordinary disposition of Divine Providence that a language spoken originally by a few thousand savages trapped on a fog-encrusted island on the edge of the North Sea should, in the fullness of time, and in the era of communications, become the common language for the entire world [...]

Culture may seem a frail boat to embark on the tempestuous waters of great power and international diplomacy. What has that quiet, nuanced voice to say in the world of telegrams and anger? – I think rather more than one might suppose [...]

Let me say this in conclusion: worldly powers, dynasties, empires rise and fall, culture and learning abide. They are the achievements by which future ages looking back assess the value of previous generations. Power in the 19th century sense has passed from us, never to return. But it has been replaced by something perhaps even more important – influence. Through the dissemination of our culture that influence can be exercised for the good.

This was a hybrid tale of the fertile Noah (the frail boat), delivered in the cadences of Ecclesiastes ("empires rise and fall, culture and learning abide"), told by St. John the Divine. Whatever one's political persuasion, it would be difficult not to admit that the sentence, "What has that quiet, nuanced voice to say in the world of telegrams and anger?" approaches the condition of the poetic. It is arguably two lines of iambic pentameter blank verse. Most of the noble assembly no doubt attended in hypnotized wonderment.

But the proposing Lord (Bonham-Carter) had not asked for poetry: he only wanted cash for the British Council and the BBC. Perhaps he was aware (unlike St. John) that God, actually, was responsible for the confusion of the tongues in the first place (Genesis, xi). At any rate, the only bibliolatry he was interested in was the kind that would profit the Earl of Stockton and Lord Weidenfeld. Sadly, English will not reach foreigners along the effortless route of Divine Providence any more. We have to teach them it. And if we do not, there are American cowboys who will: their Lordships were reminded by Lord Bonham-Carter that "there is a battle going on about the teaching of English English and American English" because, "believe it or not, the Americans claim to be able to speak English":

If you are taught English English you are likely to buy books and other goods from this country: if you are taught American English you are likely to buy books and other goods from the United States of America. Cultural diplomacy is therefore an important commercial consideration and one which should not be forgotten.

This was a blunt and belated formulation of a sense of demise. We may have invented English, but the patent ran out years ago, and we perhaps need to remind ourselves that Britain builds very few boats these days. So, alas, the plea was to no avail. Naturally, in that straitened post-credit-boom heading-towards-the-Thatcher-sunset year of 1989, the cash just was not on the table for Lord Bonham-Carter's cause, no matter how ardently he argued the case for overseas cultural representation being part of the diplomatic service.

It seemed to me at the time, and it still does, that it was a sign of the increasingly frank recognition of the inescapably political nature of cultural work that Whitehall should have accepted the re-designation of "Cultural Relations" to "Cultural Diplomacy". Of course, it always was starkly political, even when it was called "Cultural Relations". But the new term caught on very rapidly in the immediately ensuing years. Perform a search today on Google for "cultural diplomacy" and you will come up with an appreciable number of Masters programmes offered by British and American higher education institutions. Its other recurrent surfacing is in the pages of *Hansard*, the publication of the proceedings of the two chambers of the UK Parliament. For example, as recently as 19 March 2001, there is an exchange like this:

Lord Puttnam: My Lords, is the Minister aware of the fact that in 1995 a conference was held in London under the title "Britain and the World", at which the Foreign Secretary, Mr Cook, the then Foreign Secretary, the noble Lord, Lord Hurd, and the then Prime Minister, Mr John Major, all confirmed unequivocally that cultural diplomacy represented the best value for money in presenting Britain to the rest of the world? Has anything happened in the past six years that would allow Mr Cook to think that that is no longer true?

Baroness Scotland of Asthal: My Lords, absolutely not. It is incredibly good value. Britain's creative sector, including music, design and advertising, generates more than £112.5 billion each year and employs more than 3.3 million people. It is growing faster than the economy as a whole: in 1997-98 it was growing at 16 per cent a year. Exports total £10.3 billion. It is a very vibrant sector, of which we are rightly and justly proud.

This exchange not only demonstrates that British Parliamentarians are impressively telepathic (Baroness Scotland was able to read Robin Cook's mind, despite the fact that he was not even a member of the House of Lords, and thus was not present during this debate): more sinisterly, note how Puttnam's "cultural diplomacy" is simply equated by Baroness Scotland to "Britain's creative sector" and that the only terms in which it is lauded are economic.

Ultimately, such overseas culture-mongering has always been directed towards the process of consolidating the already powerful economic position of Britain in the global economy. Even before the 1989 Parliamentary debate as I have summarized it, the late Sir Anthony Parsons (former Foreign Policy adviser to Margaret Thatcher), had stated this without disguise, and had been quoted with approval by the British Council, in terms which can conclude any case for the thoroughgoing materialism at the heart of the British political establishment:

> It is really dazzlingly obvious. If you are thoroughly familiar with someone else's language and literature, if you know and love the country, the arts, the people, you will be instinctively disposed to buy goods from them rather than a less well-known source, to support them actively when you consider them to be right and to avoid criticizing them too fiercely when you regard them as being in the wrong. (British Council 1988, 7)

*

The juxtaposition of an individual of world renown and his capacious views on literature and culture and their potential for human liberation with a comparatively indifferently talented bunch of unelected politicians and quango-masters mouthing pious nationalist banalities on the relations between trade and commodifiable cultural artefacts is, no doubt, the throw of a loaded dice. Can anyone who truly believes in the social value of culture consider Trotsky the loser from this comparison?

This we can ask even before we draw attention to the ironies which result from the contrast, such as the spectacle of Trotsky, the thoroughgoing communist, recommending what one might call a "regulated free market" approach to culture, while apparently liberal bourgeois lords try desperately to pressgang cultural endeavour into the narrow service of enhanced balance of trade figures, a manoeuvre that makes them seem a little Stalinist, in the sense that Stalin also attempted – much more successfully than they – to extend state patronage to culture as long as it knelt at the feet of narrow economic and ideological dictates.

However, such observations are far from my main purpose in here co-locating these ostensibly disparate attempts to construct and project cultural policies. To juxtapose them may raise questions and prompt conclusions about the general relations between conflict and culture. I suggest that a predictable dialectic of supply and demand is at work between them. Conflicts of the kind that Trotsky and the nascent Soviet Union had survived at the time he was writing were deeply privative. Russia in the years before the Great War was already a materially poor peasant society, whose culture (in the sense of high or artistic culture) was accessible only to a very restricted élite. The War, the February and October Revolutions, and the subsequent Civil War all put culture (in this specific sense) into a suspension even more extreme – who can engage in artistic pursuits or pleasures or enjoy their potentially edifying consequences amidst an absolutely shattered material infrastructure and within a mercurial polity (from which the culturally inclined classes understandably, if they could, tried to escape)? What may explain Trotsky's apparent irresponsibility in turning to literary debates in 1922 was his sense that only with reference to cultural practices and their potential benefits did the privations suffered in the immediately preceding years seem worthwhile: *Literature and Revolution* may have been intended as a timely clarion call (from someone to whom everyone, friend or foe, would certainly have to pay attention) to see the point of it all.

One might feel, by comparison, rather sorry for well-fed-and-feathered politicians plying their trade in times of apparent relative material plenty and peace. Few grand gestures seem possible in such un-Renaissance-like circumstances, when there is an uninhibited plethora of cultural choices and practices to choose from. At best, all that seems possible then to the official political mind is petty calculation. If anything, such a situation seems to lead politicians implicitly or explicitly to turn the important question on its head, to ask what the point of culture is, and to come up with justifications for it which are stultifyingly pragmatic (it wins us friends abroad) or banally economic ("an important commercial consideration and one which should not be forgotten"; "the best value for money in representing Britain to the rest of the world"; "growing faster than the economy as a whole"). Culture is at such a moment even susceptible, as we have seen, to redesignation in econospeak as the "creative sector" to which one can apply income generation figures and with reference to which one can calculate a national contribution to gainful employment.

References

British Council. (1988). *The British Council Overseas Career Service* [British Council staff recruitment brochure]. London: The British Council.

Brown, G. (1986). *Maxton*. Edinburgh: Mainstream.

Brown, Gordon. (1982) *The Labour Party and Political Change in Scotland, 1918-1929*. Unpublished Ph.D. thesis, University of Edinburgh.

Deutscher, I. (1959). *The Prophet Unarmed: Trotsky: 1921-1929*. Oxford: Oxford University Press.

Goebbels, J. (1929). *Michael: ein deutsches Schicksal in Tagebuch-blättern*. Munich: Zentralverlag der NSDAP F. Eher Nachf.

Johst, H. (1933). *Schlageter, Schauspiel*. Munich: A. Langen/G. Müller.

Lenin, V. I. (1965). "Party Organisation and Party Literature". *Collected Works*, vol. 10. Moscow: Progress Publishers.

Lenin, V. I. (2005). *Articles on Tolstoy*. Amsterdam: Fredonia Books.

Trotsky, L. (1960). *Literature and Revolution*. Ann Arbor: University of Michigan Press.

Mimetic Abjection and Animal Metamorphosis: A Benjaminian Reading of Canetti on Kafka

Andrea Borsari

At the crucial juncture of *Kafka's Other Trial* by Elias Canetti, where he advances a reconstruction of the nexus of power and metamorphosis in Franz Kafka, a sequence appears that contains the entire form of the figure that Canetti's anthropology seeks to analyze. It is that passage from a letter to Max Brod, the so-called *Maulwurfsbrief,* or Mole Letter, in which the twenty-one-year-old Kafka (1904) recounts the following peculiar experience:

> While I was out on a walk my dog came upon a mole that was trying to cross the road. He kept leaping at him and wouldn't leave him alone, for he is a young dog, and timid. At first I was amused and I liked especially the mole's excitement [agitation: *Aufregung*] as he looked for a hole in the hard surface of the road, altogether desperately and ineffectually. But then suddenly, when the dog struck him once more with an outstretched paw, he shrieked *Ks, kss,* just like that. And then I thought – no, I did not think anything. I was simply in a state of delusion, because on that day my head was hanging so heavily that in the evening I noticed with amazement that my chin had grown into my chest. (Canetti 1981, 146; 1974, 90)[1]

This account was preceded by one of Kafka's own considerations which refers to this identifying with the mole as to an already achieved metamorphosis: "We burrow through ourselves like moles and emerge out of our vaults of sand all blackened and velvet-haired, with our poor little red feet outstretched for tender sympathy" (Canetti 1981, 146; 1974, 90).

Even Kafka, "the greatest expert on power" [*der größte Experte der Macht*] who does everything "to withdraw [shirk, escape: *sich entziehen*] from power in whatever form it might appear", whose one undertaking is

---

[1] As they refer also to the original texts and, very often, reproduce some words from them in the original language, the quotations from cited works include the reference both to the original texts and, when not English, if available and after a semicolon, to the corresponding English translations.

173

"a tenacious attempt, on the part of a man who was lacking of power" (Canetti 1981, 137; 1974, 80), and whom, in a note from 1947, Canetti defined in this way: "of all writers, he is the only one never to be infected by power" (Canetti 1976, 131; 1985, 99), Kafka here assumes – Canetti comments – the position of the Supreme Being, the *Hohepunkt der Macht*, that elevated point of power that culminates in the *Aufrechtstehen*, whose erect posture is opposed to the horizontal stance of the low-lying animal who shuffles across the ground. Kafka is master and owner of the dog, the elementary level, pre-linguistic of understanding ("verstehen") as an order (Canetti 1980, 335-336; 1973, 351-352), and when he identifies himself for a moment with his obedient extension, he becomes a source of torment and oppression, until the point at which he strikes a mortal anguish ("Todesangst"), until the threat of death – which is the supreme act that for Canetti is foundational to power – until the point at which he feels pleasure in acting this way. Thanks, however, to the absolute control that Kafka wields over him – Canetti notes – he need not fear the dog, his "slave", and is thus capable of carrying out a metamorphosis, transforming himself ("verwandelt") into a mole, and feels ("fühlt") what it means (to the letter: "what it is", "was es ist") "to be a mole" (Canetti 1981, 147; 1974, 91).

If, following René Girard, we can define the Kafka that emerges from the *Letters to Felice*, as reread by Canetti, as an "absolutely hyper-mimetic man" (Girard 2007, 88), then the expression can be understood with a more wide-ranging meaning than that which circumscribes it to the oscillations of mimetic desire in the relationship with Felice Bauer, i.e. even with a meaning that includes the described animal metamorphosis and, in a recursive way, that designates Canetti's interest in the dog and mole as "mimetic". Canetti approaches these according to the mode of ambivalence that Theodor W. Adorno has observed to be at work in Canetti's thinking, in the precise stress on the desired and feared push towards growth ("Drang nach Vermehrung", Canetti 1972, 83) during the reconstruction of human self-preservation from archaic beginnings to contemporary times, and which Axel Honneth (1995) extended in figures to understand the cognitive undertaking both with concern for the representation of the crowd, described by Canetti in the distance of the reflection and alive in the flame of the emotional involvement, and with regards to the analysis of power and the concept of metamorphosis. According to Honneth, this latter one, in particular, presents a formal homology with the ambivalent role taken by "mimesis" in Horkheimer and Adorno's *Dialectic of Enlightenment*, in that it places itself between "strategic guile" and "creative play":

> it connotes a modality of human behaviour that phylogenetically dates back to the archaic impulse for self-affirmation in battle through the rapid assimilation to the environment [...] but, at the end, during the course of the historical development it becomes a potential excess of aesthetic freedom. (Honneth 1995, 123-124)[2]

In the position of the lion's lieutenant that causes the gazelles to flee, the classic example of the primary scene of power and order to flight, the mortal seriousness of flight ("thus Flight is a matter of life and death") "between two animals of different species, one of which threatens the other" (Canetti 1980, 335-336; 1973, 351-352), Canetti summons, through Kafka, the same totemic animal that, in his discourse for Herman Broch's fiftieth birthday (1981; 1987), he had established to be related to the vocation and the task of the writer, who must be "Hund seiner Zeit", the dog, the Hound of his Time, the dog tracker, follower of his time, rather than its subjugator, and the lowest and most humble, the "lowest slave" ("niedrigster Knecht") of the epoch (Canetti 1981, 13, 16; 1987, 3, 6).[3]

That is the same animal whose image provides the privileged medium term to Kafka that allows him to evidence the transfer of the "emotional substance" or content ("emotionelle Gehalt", Canetti 1981, 124; 1974, 65) from the letters to Felice to the literary work, and around which Canetti constructs his precise analysis of Kafka's sinking collapse into *Erniedrigung* (abasement; humiliation, debasement, indignity) and *Demütigung* (humiliation; mortification, abasement, humiliation, indignity) that – straddling both Kafka's literary works and his letters to Felice – takes place.

---

[2] Even if a detailed criticism of Honneth's essay should be out of place here, at least it can be observed that what looks like a weakness there – i.e. Canetti's obstinate attachment to the archaic dimension of human life and to its primary, animal, pre-linguistic level as a way to understand phenomena such as mass and power – results in the actual force of Canetti's work here.

[3] For the "becoming-dog" in Kafka as a "schizo machine" and in connection to Canetti's distinction between mass and mute, see Deleuze and Guattari 1980 and 1987, chapter 1.

Otherwise, in order to illustrate the concomitant movement of the metamorphosis in the small ("Verwandlung ins Kleine") and the elementary *syn-pathos* with the *Gedemütigte* – the "humiliated" on whose side Kafka placed himself ("From the beginning, Kafka sided with the humiliated" (Canetti 1981, 140; 1974, 83) – that accompanies it, Canetti has recourse to the mole, and follows Kafka in the curious sort of perversion of the image that modernity (Shakespeare, Hegel, Marx)[4] had chosen to represent the unconscious intrigue that comes to light and becomes knowledge – like how truth emerges through man's misdeeds and how the conclusion of the historical development becomes visible only in revolutionary understanding – in the figure that fixes the immersion of the creature abandoned to itself in its animal dimension. Here as well, Kafka takes modernity to fulfilment and dissolution, just as in the metamorphosis of other pivotal figures of human self-affirmation: the figure of Odysseus – Ulysses – led to annihilation and to resort to the delusion in presence of the horror brought on by the sirens' silence, and the figure of Prometheus led to oblivion of his own *hubris*, of his punishment, and of the myth itself becoming one thing with the rocks that he is enchained upon – a parable that has been the object of Hans Blumenberg's extended "pensive reflection" (*Nachdenklichkeit*).[5]

"Like a dog" ("wie ein Hund") prostrates, "humbles" ("erniedrigt"), Kafka in front of Felice during a walk in the Berlin Zoo, and produces the most profound, the "deepest humiliation" ("tiefste Demütigung", Canetti 1981, 117; 1974, 52); "like a dog!" rattles K. in the final lines of the *The Trial,* and dies sinking into the shame of the supreme – and final – humiliation ("letzte Demütigung)" (Canetti 1981, 130; 1974, 71-72). Just as the condemned from *In the Penal Colony* is "doggishly" (hündisch) submissive, he looks like a submissive dog, and Block, the tradesman kneeling ("niederkniet") by the lawyer's bedside in *The Trial,* changes "into a sort of dog" ("Art von Hund"), the "image of the dog" always carries the fundamental, the "basic theme of humiliation" ("Grundthema der

---

4 On the history of the mole as a figure, since Shakespeare's *Hamlet,* where it denotes "the spectre of the father, his desire of revenge which makes its way in the young prince's mind", through Herder (the blindness of Enlightenment knowledge) and Kant (the limits of empirical knowledge), to the most famous references in Hegel and Marx, see Bodei 1976 (especially chapter 1).

5 On Blumenberg on Kafka and the aforementioned figures, see Borsari 1999, esp. pp. 156-165, 341-344.

Demütigung") that human beings inflict upon each other (Canetti 1981, 139; 1974, 82). In a few extremely dense pages, Canetti covers nearly the entire corpus of Kafka's work in light of this central theme (Canetti 1981, 137-140; 1974, 79-83) and from *The Judgement, The Metamorphosis, Amerika, The Trial, Letters, The Castle, In the Penal Colony* emerge a continuum of mortification, debasement, and humiliation of bodies, of fathers to sons, of entire families, of hope, of young children and of humanity powerless in the face of dominant instances that are always connoted as superior, in a crescendo that leads Canetti to conclude:

> the submissiveness of those who are sacrificed [of the victims], to whom there never occurs even a dream of an alternative way of life, would make a very rebel out of a person whom the palaver of ideologies – not a few of which have failed – never even remotely touched. (Canetti 1981, 140; 1974, 83)

And today, perhaps, we could even add *especially* those last ones, those who are untouched by ideology.

Those terms that scatter the pages and are used to compose Canetti's reconstruction, and also to define the semantic field of humiliation, are alluded to as "Erniedrigung" and "Demütigung", respectively translated as mortification or abasement, and humiliation. Both recall the spatial direction of lowering, most directly by *Erniedrigung* (lowering, degradation), and the associated verb *erniedriegen* (to lower, to diminish), composed of *niedrig* (low, small, meagre, inferior), and indirectly *Demütigung,* that etymological dictionaries recall to the German capitulation to the Latin *humilitas,* and *humile* from *humu(m)* (earth, low, that which cannot be raised from the ground), and that Grimms' Dictionary returns to the realm of *humiliatio,* of *infractio animi* and of *ignominia.* Hence, the moral sense of both contains the element of diminution, casting-down, of devaluation and debasement, and that of subservience that makes elevation possible, for which the classical source is Matthew 23:12 ("whoever humbles himself shall be exalted") rendered in German by Martin Luther as "wer sich erniedrigt, wird erhöht warden", and, as we shall see, that the Canettian rereading of Kafka transforms into the creatural "precept": "One must lie down with the beasts in order to be set free, or redeemed" or "One must lie down upon the earth among the animals to be saved" ("Man muß sich unter das Getier legen, um erlöst zu werden") (Canetti 1981, 144; 1974, 88).

We are thus presented with a complex of meaning that circumscribes the dejected condition of the soul (Cicero's *abjectio animi*), the state of extreme debasement and misery that, through all of the nuances assessed by the lexicons, is represented by "abjection", the romance expression derived from the Latin *abiectu(m)*, past participle of *abicere,* meaning "to throw away" (*ab*, from, *iacere,* to throw), that in German is translated with a series of interweaving expressions referenced here: *Verworfenheit* [turpitude, abjectness] (substantive from *verworfen*, abject, abandoned, discarded, castaway, past participle of *verwerfen*, reject, condemn, cast away), *Niedrigkeit* (baseness, lowness), *Gemeinheit* (meanness).

For abjection, especially through Georges Bataille and Julia Kristeva, twentieth century thought set forth a theoretical elaboration that, insisting on its constitutive ambivalence, defines it in an initial approximation as: "ambiguous movement of attraction and repulsion through which something intolerable [...] fascinates and repulses the subject at the same time" (Rieusset 1990). Kristeva, among other things, insisted on the implication of a mimetic-identificational propensity within abjection working on the "mimetic logic of the advent of the ego [*du moi*]" ("a territory that I can call my own because the Other, having dwelt in me as *alter ego*, points it out to me through loathing [*dégoût*]") that is contrasted with the primary data of "being separated, rejected, abjected", through the "fragile states where man strays on the territories of *animal*" ("by way of abjection, primitive societies have marked out a precise area of their culture in order to remove it from the threatening world of animals or animalism [*animalité*]") and, in our "personal archaeology", our "earliest attempts to release the hold of *maternal* entity" (Kristeva 1980, 17-18, 20; 1982, 10, 12-13).[6] A relationship in which the communication around "abject things" that rejects a positive definition produces the "principle of contagion", which is mimetic – and mimic – *par excellence*, like the "imperative act of exclusion" that is communicated to the son from the mother thanks to "grimaces" and "expressive exclamations" (Bataille 1970, 217-221).

For Kafka when, in what Canetti calls his "continual confrontation with power" on all sides, to resort to "obduracy" ("Verstocktheit") in order to

---

[6] See the entire first chapter, "Approaching abjection" (Kristeva 1980, 9-39; 1982: 1-31.)

put to it [to the power] a stop and acquire a postponement, a delay, is no longer sufficient. And when the subtle arts of "escape" "withdrawing" ("sich entziehen"), disappear[ance] ("Verschwinden"), and resorting to physical thinness, a kind of "asceticism [...] directed against power" ("Through a bodily diminution, he withdrew power from himself, and thus had less part in it") for which he also felt a sense of contempt ("he despised it") are all demonstrated to be inadequate, another means intervenes; one that Canetti defines as "still more surprising", a true contraction, a "shrinkage" ("Einschrumpfung") that permits him to become "too diminutive" ("zu gering") for it, and escape from those who threaten, while at the same time liberating him from all the despicable "exceptionable means" ("verwerfliche Mitteln") of violence. And so intervenes the *Verwandlung ins Kleine,* the metamorphosis into the little or transformation into something small (Canetti 1981, 145; 1974, 89-90). It is from here that the mole of *Maulwurfsbrief* – the mole letter which is the origin, the genetic place of this unusual aptitude ("ungewöhnliche Begabung") – springs, and it is here where that panoply of very small animals is inserted in which Kafka's most beloved transformations take place ("mit Vorliebe verwandelte;" Canetti 1981, 145-147; 1974, 90-93). Even children are to be considered "usurpers" of the "position of the little"; they are "the false smallness" who only want to become bigger while they submit themselves to injustice and to being overpowered, to that anguish that is so central for Kafka: "fear of superior power", the anguish of being confronted with excessive power, overpower ("Übermacht") in which the only path open is akin to a "consecration of man" ("Heiligung des Menschen") for which "every place, every moment, every trait, every step is serious and important and peculiar to itself". And this produces the transformation into something small: "one changes oneself into an insect, in order to save others from the guilty they incur [by lovelessness and killing]" (Canetti 1981, 103-104; 1974, 35-36).

But, the "small" is exposed in order to translate the relationships of possession and power in terms of smallness and largeness, like what occurs to Kafka when he meets the parents of Felice ("I felt so very small while they stood around me like giants [...] you are theirs, so they are big, you are not mine, so I was small") and when Felice herself was placed in danger when she bowed all the way to him (Canetti 1981, 110; 1974, 43). The "small" is thus exposed to being grasped by the throat ("Griff am Hals") and suffocated, exposed to the *Animalische der Macht,* the animalistic dimension or "animal nature" of power (Canetti 1981, 143; 1974, 87) well noted by readers of *Crowd and Power* (in felines, those "great seizers [*großen Ergreifer*]", power manifests itself in the "highest concentration" [Canetti 1980, 227; 1973, 240-241]), and undergoes the terrible "threat of teeth" [Canetti 1981, 144; 1974, 87], the "most striking instrument of power in man and many animals" [Canetti 1980, 228; 1973, 242]). The greatest contempt imaginable is demonstrated in the destruction of insects, "minuscule creatures" ("winzige Geschöpfe") of complete defencelessness that can be annihilated with impunity, as becomes evident in the threat to crush ("zerquetschen") someone like an insect (Canetti 1980, 225-226; 1973, 239-240).

Kafka, however, persists, and – as we shall see – will persist until the end, in animal metamorphosis. As Canetti notes: "An interest comparable to Kafka's in very small animals, especially insects, is to be found elsewhere only in the life and literature of the Chinese" (Canetti 1981, 147; 1974, 92). For him, they offer two possibilities: "making oneself infinitely small or being so. The second is perfection, that is to say, inactivity, and the first is beginning, that is to say, action" (Canetti 1981, 149; 1974, 94). The act that puts him in contact with small animals will not be the condescension of one who bows towards the floor ("stopping to the earth – writes Kafka – gives one a false, incomplete conception of them"), instead, it will be an oscillating gesture to hold them at eye-level, so that, as Canetti suggests, "this is tantamount to equal status". In making the creatures ("Geschöpfe") larger, like that which occurs to the insect in the *Metamorphosis* and to the "mole-like creature" in *The Burrow*, it is a moment in which, "through the close approach to the animal and the animal's resultant magnification, transformation into something small becomes a more plastic, tangible, credible process" (Canetti 1981, 147; 1974, 92). It will be "at eye-level" ("Augenhöhe") that the protagonist of Kafka's fragments *Memoirs of the Kalda Railroad,* raises the rat that he spears with a knife: "Hanging against the wall in front of me in its final agony, it rigidly stretched out its claws in what seemed to be an unnatural way; they were like small hands reaching out to you" (Canetti 1981, 147; 1974, 91-92). Once again, we return to those "poor little red feet" raised like hands that beg for compassion, and to the mole's cry in *Maulwurfsbrief* where we began – the vehicle of metamorphosis in the little, and the mimetic identification with those subjected to the most profound humiliation, the most literal of mortifications. But the gesture, that posture that approaches overcoming "the guilt of man with regard to the animals" is the exact reversal of that Canettian survivor, whose power is found in staying at the feet in front of the cadaver, and the equivalent of the defensive "assimilation to the dead" that Adorno and Horkheimer had obtained from Roger Caillois' studies on animal mimicry, as well as of the supine position that Kafka recounts to having assumed, stretched out on a boat adrift beneath the Moldava bridges, or, in the joyous tonality (the joy "of being déclassé", "des Deklassiertseins" [Canetti 1981, 159; 1974, 106]) in the ditches between the grass outside of Prague, that so terrorized his office colleagues. If:

> standing upright signifies the power of man over beast – Canetti concludes – and only on the ground, lying among the animals, can one see the stars, which free one from this terrifying [*angsterregenden*] power of man. (Canetti 1981, 144; 1974, 88)

In the project of revising his essay on Kafka from 1934, Walter Benjamin proposed to insert, among other things, the following realization:

> For Kafka, animals were exemplary [or model: *vorbildlich*]. We can read his stories about animals for a long time, without realizing that they aren't actually about men. Perhaps, for him, being animal [*Tiersein*] meant only to have renounced being man [*Menschsein*], for some sort of shame [*aus einer Art von Scham*]. (Benjamin 1980b, 1261)

For Kafka, the creatural dimension associates men and animals, and this is true – as Benjamin had already confirmed in the essay – up to the point at which his "attentiveness" ("Aufmerksamkeit"), the "natural prayer of the soul" that belonged to him "in the highest degree", is able to encompass all of them: "in this attentiveness he included all creatures [*alle Kreatur*], as saints include them in their prayers" (Benjamin 1980a, 432; 2005, 812).

The world of Kafka's ancestors, like "the totem poles of primitive people", returns "down to the animals", to the beasts. "receptacles of the forgotten", and:

> the most forgotten source of strangeness – remembers Benjamin – is our body, one's own body, one can understands why Kafka called the

cough that erupted from within him "the animal" [*das Tier*]. (Benjamin 1980a, 430-431; 2005, 810)

Furthermore, "of all the Kafka's creatures", it is the animals in particular whih dedicate themselves to pensive reflection, that "have the greatest opportunity for reflection" ("Nachdenken") (Benjamin 1980a, 430-431; 2005, 810); the indelible mark of oblivion in Kafka is the deformation imprinted in things, bodies, gestures, and among the gestures of his stories – Benjamin notes – "none is more frequent than that of the man who bows his head far down on his chest" (Benjamin 1980a, 431; 2005, 811).

From theoretical perspectives that are not coincidental and by way of the natural theatre of Benjaminian gestures, we are brought back to the final outcome of creatural metamorphosis between mole and dog, to Kafka's chin dug or "grown into" his "chest" (Canetti 1981, 146; 1974, 90) from which this paradoxical reconstruction of "anthropology of the individual" that Canetti proposed in his research on Kafka has begun. A reconstruction in which, when dealing with human beings' total ignorance of their selves – although "anthropos" is even "considered measure of all things" – he rejects the abstract plane of theories, confiding only in "unimpeded concrete inquiry into particular human beings", in this case, into the "tenacious attempt on the part of a man who was lacking in power [*eines Ohnmächtiges*], to withdraw from power in whatever form it might appear" (Canetti 1981, 137; 1974, 79-80). As Canetti demonstrated, beyond the battle on whose description he based his research, Kafka also had "good moments" that bore stories associated with a sense of spaciousness, movement, and transformation, in the event, "no longer into something small" (Canetti 1981, 162; 1974, 110) – although, as Benjamin sees, the oblivion of guilt of the hunter Gracchus morphs him into a butterfly. And so, beyond the margins of the work that Canetti took into account, Kafka continued to deal with animal metamorphoses and mimetic abjections, of moles, dogs and mice, as those stories from the final years attest, from *Investigations of a Dog* (where dogs appear who walk standing upright), *The Burrow* (where a giant mole reclusively lives in the world of a Canettian paranoiac) and *Josephine the Singer* (in which the creatural destiny converges towards the oblivion as a superior redemption that is shared by all of her brothers). On the other hand, one can also note that in marking a clear break in Kafka's approach from *The Metamorphosis* to

The Trial, some later contribution to literary analysis has made it possible to observe a major complication and evolution in Kafka's take on power, from the complicity of the victim with his executioner, in the first case, to the defendant's final surrender to the overpowering force, in the second, a defendant who has destroyed himself trying "to overthrow the will of the machine of power" (Baioni 1975, 30). And one can note this above and beyond Canetti's intentions that projected a total strangeness and non-involvement in the power upon Kafka, symmetrical and converse to the attraction which Canetti felt in himself, as he declared more than once.

As to Canetti, in the end, it seems that a further research programme has also been traced, a programme that, by overcoming every dichotomous contraposition between a youthful work marked by the "bad" (but for this efficacious in explaining the abysses of evil) and a mature work springing from the conversion to the "good" (but always undermined by too human good intentions), is able to extend the fundamental ambivalence described here – concerning Kafka, the mole, the dog, and the very idea of mimetic abjection which assumes the features of a mark of power as well as of a way to escape it – to encompass Canetti's widest production departing from the obsessive reoccurrence of an exterminated bestiary in order to arrive at the reconstructed centrality in him too of the notion of mimesis that, once connected to imitation and placed in confrontation with the central category of metamorphosis, can now include phenomena like mask, camouflage, simulation, mime, mimicry, the power of images, Bruegel, Michelangelo, Grünewald, and all that which, thanks to them, is still possible to gather in its fulness: "a memory of the dreadful things [*Entsetzen*] that people do to one another" (Canetti 1982, 217; 1990, 230).

(Translated by Brendan Hennessey and Andrea Borsari)

References

Baioni, G. (1975). "Nota introduttiva". In F. Kafka, *La metamorfosi*. Milano: Rizzoli, 11-30.

Bataille, G. (1970). "L'abjection et les formes misérables". In G. Bataille *Œuvres complètes*, vol. 2, *Écrits posthumes 1922-1940*. Paris: Gallimard, 217-221 (and related papers, 437-439).

Benjamin, W. (1980a). "Franz Kafka Zur zehnten Wiederkehr seines Todestages". In R. Tiedemann and H. Schweppenhäuser (eds.), *Gesammelte Schriften*. Frankfurt am Main: Suhrkamp, vol. II.2, 409-

438.

Benjamin, W. (1980b). "Anmerkungen zu Seite 409-438 [Franz Kafka]". In R. Tiedemann and H. Schweppenhäuser (eds.) , vol. II.3, 1153-1276.

Benjamin, W. (2005). "Franz Kafka. On the Tenth Anniversary of His Death". In *Selected Writings*, vol. 2, *1927-1934*. Cambridge, MA: Belknap Press of Harvard University Press, 794-816.

Bodei, R. (1976). *Sistema ed epoca in Hegel*. Bologna: Il Mulino.

Borsari, A. (ed.) (1999). *Hans Blumenberg: Mito, metafora, modernità*. Bologna: Il Mulino.

Canetti, E. (1972). "Gespräch mit Theodor W. Adorno". In E. Canetti, *Die gespaltene Zukunft: Aufsätze und Gespräche*. München: Hanser, 66-92.

Canetti, E. (1973). *Crowds and Power*. Harmondsworth: Penguin.

Canetti, E. (1974). *Kafka's Other Trial: The Letters to Felice*. London: Calder and Boyars.

Canetti, E. (1976). *Die Provinz des Menschen: Aufzeichnungen 1942-1972*. Frankfurt am Main: Fischer.

Canetti, E. (1980). *Masse und Macht*. Frankfurt am Main: Fischer.

Canetti, E. (1981). "Der andere Prozeß: Kafkas Briefe an Felice". In E. Canetti, *Das Gewissen der Worte*. Frankfurt am Main: Fischer, 78-169.

Canetti, E. (1982). *Die Fackel im Ohr: Lebensgeschichte 1921-1931*. Frankfurt am Main: Fischer.

Canetti, E. (1985). *The Human Province*, trans. J. Neugroschel. London: Deutsch.

Canetti, E. (1987). "Herman Broch: Speech for His Fiftieth Birthday. Vienna, November 1936". In E. Canetti, *The Conscience of Words*. London: Picador, 1-13.

Canetti, E. (1990). *The Torch in My Ear*. London: Picador.

Canetti, E. (1991). "Hermann Broch. Rede zum 50. Geburtstag. Wien, November 1936". In E. Canetti, *Das Gewissen der Worte*. Frankfurt am Main: Fischer, 10-24.

Deleuze, G., Guattari, F. (1980). *Mille Plateaux : Capitalisme et schizophrénie*. Paris: Minuit.

Deleuze, G., Guattari, F. (1987). *A Thousand Plateaus: Capitalism and Schizophrenia*, translation and foreword by B. Massumi. Minneapolis: University of Minnesota Press.

Girard, R. (2007). *Evolution and Conversion: Dialogues on the Origins of Culture*, J. C. de Castro Rocha & Pierpaolo Antonello (eds.). London:

Continuum.

Honneth, A. (1995). "Die unendliche Perpetuierung des Naturzustandes. Zum theoretischen Erkenntnisgehalt von Canettis Masse und Macht". In M. Krüger (ed.) (1995), *Einladung zum Verwandlung: Essays zu Elias Canettis "Masse und Macht"*. München: Hanser, 105-127.

Kristeva, J. (1980). *Pouvoirs de l'horreur : Essai sur l'abjection*. Paris: Seuil.

Kristeva, J. (1982). *The Powers of Horror: An Essay on Abjection*, translated by L. S. Roudiez. New York: Columbia University Press.

Rieusset, I. (1990). "Abjection". In A. Jacob (ed.), *Encyclopédie philosophique universelle. Les notions philosophiques – Dictionnaire*. Paris: PUF, vol. 1.

"Entertaining History":
Socialist Realism in Search of the "Historical Past"

Evgeny Dobrenko

> It goes without saying that "everything
> is determined", but history for us is not
> a fetish... (Gorky 1953, 99).

In 1942, during the blockade, a book was published in Leningrad celebrating the twenty-fifth anniversary of Soviet historical studies. In the opening article, academician A. Pankratova (1942, 21) suggested that the ardent response which history arouses in Soviet readers places a burden of responsibility on writers, including historians. But in what sense is the Soviet historian a "writer"? According to Anna Antonovskaya (1938), a historical novelist of the 1930s and 40s, the historical novel should be both entertaining and educational, and the writer should be both an artist and a researcher, armed with the most advanced knowledge. As Mark Serebriansky, author of the first book on the Soviet historical novel comments: "Reappraisal of the historical past is an essential characteristic of the Soviet historical novel. In this sense it has common cause with Marxist historicism" (Serebrianskii 1936, 42). Accordingly, a picture sketched by the historian may differ little in principle from historical painting, novels or films. Yet there is one fundamental difference: in contrast to literature, history cannot be written, but only constantly rewritten.

Consider the many Russian histories of the modern period: Tatishchev's history of the Petrine era, for example, or Slavophile history, the nation-state theory of Russian history from Chicherin to Milyukov, the histories of Ilovaisky or Danilevsky, and others; the list could go on. These all describe the same era. The difference lies in the selection and assessment of events and in the underlying political-historical matrix. One widely held view sees Russian history destroyed by the future-orientated consciousness of revolutionaries for whom the past was the pre-history of mankind; history proper began only with the "salvo from the *Aurora*". Then came the "Great Retreat" in the mid-1930s, when "the unequivocal denial of the old was replaced by the principle of its perpetual modernization" (Kavtaradze 1990, 7). (This denial, we may note, was also a form of "modernization".)[1] Such Sovietological historiography was a mirror-image of the Soviet approach itself, according to which in the mid-1930s the ultra-leftist, nihilistic attitude to the history of the people was rejected and the significance of history "for our state, our party, and the instruction of the rising generation" was recognized (*Kizucheniiu istorii* 1937, 21).

Stalinist historical consciousness entails a discarded model of the revolutionary vision, that of Mikhail Pokrovsky, highly regarded by Lenin, and who, up to his death in 1932, remained the chief Marxist historian of Soviet Russia (Enteen 1978). Pokrovsky reworked Rickert's philosophy of history. No general laws apply to the always unique historical process, and where Rickert proposed "criteria of value" in the selection of historical facts Pokrovsky proposed the "principle of expediency". In other words, "history is politics projected onto the past". And although this formula was subsequently condemned,[2] neither Soviet history nor, indeed, the historical novel or film, could escape it (Gulyga 1974; Wachtel 1994). History was the focus of the struggle for power and to that extent a weapon of political action. In Leninist fashion, Pokrovsky tore down the artificial screens and demystified this aspect of history.

For revolutionary culture, such a foregrounding of the device was fairly typical. For Stalinist culture, on the other hand, the poetics of ideological magism prevailed. Indeed, the dispute with Pokrovsky began with an attempt to conceal the political agenda of the struggle over history. The "Russian turn" of the mid-thirties consisted of a series of actions by the authorities, from resolutions by Sovnarkom and the Central Committee of VKP(b) on the teaching of civic history in schools, to open letters by Stalin, Zhdanov and Kirov concerning "incorrect" publications in journals, or drafts of USSR history textbooks (Brandenberger 2002). Here the Party leadership initiated a direct attack

---

[1] Modernization figured in Soviet criticism by the early 1930s: "Modernization is a basic characteristic of historical artistic works [...] The historical novel is a particularly contemporary novel" (Goffenshefer 1933, 123).

[2] Soviet criticism reacted angrily to the notion of the historical novel as "contemporaneity disguised in historical attire" (Serebrianskii 1936, 146), as understood by Pokrovsky; the historical novel reflected not so much contemporaneity *per se*, as the process of transformation.

on "Pokrovskyism": Pokrovsky had produced bare, abstract outlines, mere schematic sociology; instead a concrete Marxist history must be created in a lively, entertaining form with descriptions of historical figures. In short, history should return to its narrative roots.

The dispute was largely literary: "entertaining history" should illustrate ideologemes as formulated in party invectives. Thus in criticizing a draft textbook on the history of the USSR by the Vanaga group (soon to become "enemies of the people"), Stalin, Zhdanov and Kirov wrote: "The annexationist-colonial role of Russian tsarism, in concert with the Russian bourgeoisie and landowners is not emphasized in this draft ('Russia is the prison of the nations'). The counter-revolutionary role of Russian tsarism in foreign policy from the time of Catherine II to the 1850s and beyond is not emphasized in this draft ('tsarism as international gendarme')" (*Kizucheniiu istorii* 1937, 22).

These were the ideologemes ("international gendarme", "prison of the nations" and so on) to be illustrated in the new "entertaining history", whereas others had to be removed (the Razinshchina and Puchach-evshchina, negative characteristics of "peasant uprisings"). Stalin, Zhdanov and Kirov suggested that modern history should start at the French Revolution, and that the Dutch and English revolutions be moved to the end of the textbook on medieval history. The fundamental axis must be the contrast between the bourgeois and socialist revolutions (*Kizucheniiu istorii* 1937, 25). In short, the Party leadership took it upon themselves to write history, and Stalin can be regarded not only as the author of the *Short Course* history of the Party, but also of the standardized courses on Russian and world history. His hand is easy to recognize in the jury's decisions in the governmental competition for best history textbook (for years 3-4 in middle school). We read that "the authors fill whole pages with pompous rubbish about the happiest country on earth" (*Kizucheniiu istorii* 1937, 33), or that "the majority of authors describe the era of building socialist society in the USSR with exclamation marks, cries of admiration and various moving stories, songs and general characterizations..." (*Kizucheniiu istorii* 1937, 36). This boorish tone undoubtedly belonged to Stalin – only he would have dared to speak in this way of the "happiest country on earth".

This was, of course, not only a literary dispute: it was deeply political. Not only was the manner of writing subject to discussion, but so too were "the principle of value" (Rickert) and "the principle of expediency"

(Pokrovsky) in the selection and assessment of events. The "entertaining" conception of Russian history was not a simple rejection of Pokrovsky's radicalism, or a retreat into earlier Russian histories. Underlying its relationship to the past lay the *principle of continual historical synthesis*.

Dialectical equivalence meant that Soviet ideological doctrine could combine seemingly opposing positions; thus identical phenomena were marked as semantically opposed categories ("proletarian internationalism" turned easily into "rootless cosmopolitanism", "national liberation movements" into "bourgeois nationalism"). As a result, Soviet culture allowed for endless mutation in the succession of "thaws" and "frosts", in which first one pole then another cancelled each other out. These ideological balancing acts were formed historically. Soviet culture was not, of course, the direct continuation of revolutionary culture, but neither was it simply restorative. Rather both elements prevailed simultaneously: frosts are always a recollection of the restoration of the past; in the era of thaws the genes of ardent revolutionaries speak. This characteristic unity yet conflict of opposites endowed Soviet culture with striking stability.

The self-perception of Stalinist culture is consciousness of both legacy and synthesis. It discards nothing, but unifies everything, like an "heir" disposing of all the contradictions of earlier times (Grois 1994, 98). "The socialist era" wrote M. Rozental, one of the main critics of "vulgar sociologism", "must, and will re-shape dialectically the entire history of thought, natural science, and art" (Rozental 1936, 52). This is what defines the historical perspective in Stalinist culture.

All cultures focus attention on certain moments in history in the light of current problems. Certain historical events and eras were always important for revolutionary and then Soviet culture, and reflected enduring problems: historical violence, the cost of revolutionary transformation, the expansion of the state, legitimacy, and so on. The drift of Soviet historical consciousness from the revolutionary outlook to a new synthesis was reflected in an enormous number of books, pictures, novels, plays and films. The dispute with Pokrovsky highlights the new, specifically Stalinist, view of Russian history.

Any optic based on a synthesizing process cannot but be at once composite yet also inconsistent and contradictory. The Soviet model of history is often sketched as follows:

The whole development of humanity was viewed as the workers' emancipation movement, which inevitably led to the victorious Russian proletarian revolution, because all that had gone before it, was, in one way or another, a preparation for October: the beginning of the world revolution, which would put an end to the "world of violence" for the sake of building a kingdom of heaven on earth. And whatever the gaze of the politician, ideologue, artist or simple citizens fell upon came to be viewed in that teleological light and interpreted in that messianic spirit. (Levin 1994, 74)

This viewpoint came not from Stalinist but from revolutionary thinking. In the Soviet text, history becomes more complex: rejecting all previous historical doctrines, whether revolutionary or conservative, Soviet history aimed, so to speak, to combine Pokrovsky with Ilovaisky and Rozhkov with Pogodin. This gave the new history a notorious inconsistency, a kind of historical schizophrenia.

Above all, history in the Stalinist era once again took on a personal dimension. The role of the individual in history was restored and linked to the reformulation of Marxist doctrine, according to which history represented the field of class warfare and permanent conflict between the forces and the relations of production. Pokrovsky summed up this view in the brilliant formula, "Trade capital roamed the land wearing the Cap of Monomakh". Historical individuals had been of no interest to Marxist historians, while for Pokrovsky the Russian princes and tsars were a panopticon and eminent figures, if noted at all, were disparaged. Thus neither the personal qualities of Peter the Great (syphilitic and by the end almost insane, a sadist who tortured his own son, an alcoholic who shut his wife up in a nunnery), nor his works garnered any sympathy. Pokrovsky dismissed the claim that Peter had founded the regular army as an "old prejudice": the *strelsty* had existed before him; Peter's guards were just a gendarmerie; the new naval fleet, constructed from damp timber, was useless; his foreign policy decisions brought nothing but ruin.

As to the role of the individual, Pokrovsky eloquently asserts: "We Marxists cannot view the individual as the agent of history. For us the individual is the instrument through which history acts. Perhaps one day these instruments will be created artificially, just as now we manufacture electrical accumulators" (1929, 13). The Stalinist approach, by contrast, shows reverence for historical personages in keeping with the nature of power in "the era of the cult of personality" (Kammari 1953). This marked a return to a specific historiographic source: Dmitry Ilovaisky, author of school history textbooks in pre-revolutionary Russia, had proposed that dynasties and the court were pre-eminent in history. Thus history was transformed into a procession of princes and tsars and historical events presented as resulting from actions of the Royal family.

History remained just as "entertaining" in the period after Pokrovsky. "Interest in the history of our country", we read in the article "The History of our Motherland and the Tasks of the Soviet Writer", "is increasing rapidly among the general public. It is reflected not only in the many articles commemorating significant historical dates published in *Pravda*, and in the attention devoted by the Party and government to historical education, but also in the interest and warmth with which our Soviet reader greets genuinely creative and historically truthful works of art and literature" (*Znamia* 1937, 249). These works included a great swathe of novels (Serebrianskii 1949; Messer 1955; Petrov 1958; Andreev 1962; Pashuto 1963; Lenobl' 1969; Aleksandrova 1971; Oskotskii 1980), many devoted to the monarchy and military leaders. The historical novel was the most widely read of the so-called "fat books", occupying first place in reader demand (Dobrenko 1997, 130-31). An even more evident personalization occurred in Soviet cinema, with the emergence in the 1930s of the super-genre of the biographical film (Iurenev 1939 and 1949, Dobrenko 2008), which displaced the historical-revolutionary film. Control in cinema was even harsher: Stalin not only worked with submitted scripts, gave directors advice and appointed specific performers, but also supplied the cinematographer with whole programs of development (Khrenov 1994, 176). The films about Alexander Nevsky, Suvorov, Kutuzov, Ushakov and Nakhimov were ordered personally by Stalin. Prestigious historical authors were enlisted. Alexey Tolstoy worked on the script for *Peter the First*, *Minin and Pozharsky* was written by Viktor Shklovsky, *Alexander Nevsky* by Peter Pavlenko, *Pugachev* by Olga Forsh, *Bogdan Khmelnitsky* by Alexander Korneichuk, *Salavat Iulaev* by Stepan Zlobin.

Restored to Russian history via literature and film, tsars, princes and military leaders appear as defenders of Russia, people of unprecedented courage, endowed with wisdom and state-craft. Leaving aside for the moment such famous examples as Alexander Nevsky, Ivan the Terrible, or Peter the Great, a less prominent figure, Ivan III, is worth considering.

V. Iazvitsky's novel *Ivan III, Sovereign of all Russia*, presents him as a genius. By the age of nine he is already incredibly intelligent; sturdy of body and mind, as if he were more than but a lad, those around him never cease to admire his wit and knowledge. At thirteen the "lad" is already taller than his father and cleverer than a grown man. The youthful hero's physique is of fairy-tale proportions: he grows a beard and moustaches and first tastes the "sweetness of love's caresses". ("Can it be that thou art no more than seventeen?" the widow with whom he has a torrid affair inquires.) And this is only the beginning: the reader follows this same tsar for one thousand five hundred pages.[3]

This kind of relationship to historical personages is generally seen to parallel the development of the Stalin and Lenin myths. And although the link between the "new Ilovaiskiism" and the cult of personality is apparent, the conservatism of the Soviet conception of history should not be overestimated. The mechanism of historical synthesis was quite complex, based not on assemblage, but on compartmentalization:

- the tsar's or prince's personality, reverenced if he had fulfilled the will of history by strengthening the state, existed on one plane;
- the historical meaning of the ruler's actions either corresponding to the forward march of history, or resisting it, was evaluated on another plane;
- the masses, who almost always suffered, but whose sufferings were vindicated if the actions were of a progressive character (Ivan the Terrible, for example, or Peter the Great), existed on a third plane.

Thus, instead of the single trade capitalism in Pokrovsky or the lone tsar in Ilovaisky, there were always three main characters in the theatre of Soviet history: The Ruler, Historical Law, and the Masses. The Soviet rewriting of history was a strategy for rebalancing components: the tsars were good, but tsarism was bad; peasant revolts were good, but the rebels themselves did not recognize the real enemy; Tsarist Russia was the prison of the nations, but in joining to itself neighbouring lands, was also progressive; tsarist bureaucracy was bad, but centralization was historically necessary, and so on. Boundaries were defined only to be moved as the moment required, so that the system was open to adjustment, while all the time remaining itself.

[3] See the analysis of Iazvitskii's novel in Pashuto (1963, 109-11).

Emerging from the pragmatics of power, this mechanism for re-shaping history also corresponded ideally to historicizing art. For Hegel the purpose of historical writing lay in the reflection of disharmony, whereas art conveys the harmonization of reality. Stalinist culture erases the boundary between these perspectives. Historical description increasingly serves the aestheticization of history, whilst Socialist Realist art returns to the principles of primitive mimesis. These often contradictory strategies were submitted to Lenin's Theory of Reflection. In historical science as in art, there is a return, on a new level, to prehistory: myth serves to integrate the individual into the natural and social whole. Historical Law was the core of the resulting realm of harmony.

In the Stalin era this programme was reduced to the concerns of the state. Karamzin's conception returned, but on a new level: history was reduced to history of the state, so sharply enhancing the progressiveness attributed to strong, centralizing rulers and underplaying the role of the masses.[4] Accordingly revolts should not be described in too colourful a manner, and attitudes towards figures such as Bulavin, Bolotnikov, Razin or Pugachev could not be unambiguously positive. Pokrovsky had already deprived the "Razinshchina" and "Pugachevshchina" of any aura, maintaining that the Razin uprising was purely a Cossack affair, and that the reasons behind it were economic (the clash of "Cossack" and "Moscow" capital). Nor did he accept the peasant character of either uprising, styling them as "self-activating spontaneous affairs", and maintaining that the peasants under the leadership of Pugachev had wanted only to exterminate the nobles, without seeing their enemy in autocracy. But now the peasant wars were to be viewed differently. They remained a backdrop to the Soviet interpretation of history, but were doomed to failure precisely because they could not but be spontaneous, and lacked a vanguard, though their instructive status was enhanced, and they were seen as more noble.[5] The proletarian revolution, by contrast, succeeded because the Party brought political awareness to the revolutionary movement.

The dialectical approach served to widen the historical horizon, from

---

[4] Konstantin Simonov touched on this in his report at the Second Congress of Soviet Writers. He condemned "turning great people into living monuments". See *Stenograficheskii Otchet Vtorogo Vsesoiuznogo s'ezda sovetskikh pisatelei* (1956, 96).

[5] Pushkin's *Captain's Daughter* was introduced as a school text for this reason.

the demonstration of unity between tsar and people to the vividly painted anti-popular nature of tsarism. Now the scales once again tipped in favour of monarchy.[6] The three re-workings by Aleksey Tolstoy of the play *On the Rack* [*Na dybe*] are typical. The first version was sharply "antiPetrine". Then came motifs displaying reciprocity between Peter and the people until, in the final version, Tolstoy introduces three generations of a peasant family, the Pospelovs, each of whom draws closer to the tsar; they become officers in Peter's Guards, and in the finale a centagenarian Pospelov "grand-dad arriving at communism" (straight out of an industrial novel) appears to share his memories of the Time of Troubles with the tsar.

Dmitry Petrov-Biryukov's novel *The Steppe Frontier* [*Dikoe pole*] is set in the same period, but from the other side: it centres on the Kondrat Bulavin uprising. It turns out, however, that because Bulavin's uprising harms state interests, though sympathetic as a person, he is almost indistinguishable from the traitors surrounding the progressive Russian tsar. From the start Bulavin has doubts: can it be right to plan a conspiracy when the tsar is working so hard to protect the country from the Swedes (Petrov-Biriukov 1946, 122)? Peter is presented as the people's tsar: "I wish to bring the people to reason, not for my own sake, I need but little, but for our great state, for the people themselves" (Petrov-Biriukov 1946, 140, 80-1). Bulavin comes to realize the error of his ways on the eve of his suicide: "One feverish thought after another crept into his sick mind. Like a dreadful vision the powerful figure of Tsar Peter rises up before him. Peter asks sternly, 'Kondrat, why did you raise the sword against me? I want what is good for my people. ... The truth is mine, Kondrat!'" When, after long and tortuous doubts, Kondrat decides to make peace with his enemy, his heart feels lighter, as if a stone crushing him had been lifted (Petrov-Biriukov 1946, 303). The disturbing conclusion follows: "So, the tsar was right. ... I have evidently made a mistake" (Petrov-Biriukov 1946, 306).

Petrov-Biryukov's hero was not the only one to have "made a mistake". In essence the historical novels of the 1930s through to the 1950s devoted to the peasant wars – the status of the uprisings had been enhanced and they were now considered to be wars – contained the same clash in one

---

[6] From the mid-1950s, a reappraisal of peasant wars began and materials illustrating their scale and the terrible cruelty, both in their suppression and of the insurgents themselves, were published (Mazour 1971, 111-23).

way or another.[7] The rebels' struggle was against local oppressors, so that often it seemed that the tsar himself might join them: these good people fight each other only owing to some misunderstanding. The monarchy almost always appears to be liberal-democratic. Thus in Iazvitsky's novel, the dying Ivan III instructs his son Vasily to seek support among the people (1955, 803). Or there is the monologue on the founding of Moscow in Dmitry Eremin's novel, *The Kremlin Hill* [*Kremlevskii kholm*]:

> But in Rus' the ploughmen and craftsmen occupy first place. They raise palaces and temples. They catch bird and beasts, fell timber, reap and sow the fertile corn field, guard the native land from the enemy in times of peril. Glory to them, these people! Intentions both pure and honorable must be with them. Why then has such a lot befallen them? (Eremin 1955, 46)

The further back we travel in the Soviet historical novel, the more we find a people's state. Moving from twelfth-century Moscow to ninth-century Kiev, we witness a strange scene: the *zakup* peasants, living in dire poverty, have risen up against the boyars (never against the prince!) and, during the defence of Kiev against the Pechenegs, a serf (straight out of *The Communist Manifesto*) addresses a boyar: "Begone, boyar ... you have your country, and we, the poor, have ours". Similarly, a fisherman declares (as if he has just read Lenin's *State and Revolution*): "Our peasant freedom is on the point of a spear ... it must be won through force of arms!" A genuine revolution has occurred in Kiev: people stopped bowing to those of rank. But Svyatoslav is chief protector of the people. The peasant farmers call him Father-Prince. Even Dobrogast, the hated boyar felt that something vast and powerful connected him to the Prince.[8] In another novel Dmitry Donskoy toured his principality after the Battle of Kulikovo, declaring in towns and villages that the defeated khan would now receive less tribute, and the people greeted the Prince as a hero and victor (Ezerskii 1941, 117).

---

[7] See Alexey Chapygin's *Roaming Folk* (Guliashchie liudi), Stepan Zlobin's *Stepan Razin* and *Salavat Iulaev*, Vyacheslav Shishkov's *Emelyan Pugachev*, Ivan Le's *Nalivaiko*, Georgy Shtorm's *The Tale of Bolotnikov* (Povest' o Bolotnikove), and others.

[8] As cited in Pashuto (1963, 91), a study comparing the historical novels of the 1940s-50s with historical sources.

In the Stalinist period, Russian history, full of good princes and tsars, became extraordinarily benign, the goodness intensifying the further back we go. On the other hand, the nearer to October, the more criticism is directed at the tsars. The triad "Ruler – Laws of History – People" is again broken, and now the Laws of History work against the Ruler. After Peter, the Romanov dynasty degenerates, culminating in the decay of the imperial court and the destruction of the state. The nineteenth century becomes a history of the three stages of the Russian liberation movement. The Leninist model undergoes the same re-evaluation as the peasant wars, the only difference being that the dialectic of spontaneity/ consciousness is applied not to peasants and Cossacks, but to the Decembrists, *raznochintsy*, and Populists. This shift had its own logic. Insofar as after Peter the state's main purpose was fulfilled, the tsars lost credibility as agents of historical progress. On this model the fervent anti-state thrust of the Russian Revolution is neutralized. Rather, the revolution saved the Russian state from becoming a colony of the European Great Powers. And so the Revolution becomes national-liberationist rather than socialist.

The new model of Russian history attempts to resolve the fundamental problems of the Stalinist era: personal power, rapid economic growth, state centralization and expansion, internal unity, the struggle with internal and external enemies, violence. This problematic is exhaustively explored through the many stories available to Stalinist "entertaining history". And so Soviet historical scholarship, along with the historical novel, play and film, became a historical masquerade, a single great metaphor. Peter the Great serves to represent Bolshevik industrialization, the fight against treachery, and to inculcate the progressiveness of the powerful centralized state. Ivan the Terrible is enlisted to demonstrate parallels with the Stalinist era: just as Ivan IV completed the unification of the country around Moscow and reunited previously occupied lands, Stalin returned what had been taken from Russia; just as Ivan had created the *oprichnina* to strengthen autocracy, Stalin had not faltered before unheard-of terror in the name of a strong, autocratic state, feared by her enemies. The spirit of leaders on the battlefield (Alexander Nevsky, Dmitry Donskoy, Minin, Pozharsky), and military commanders (Suvorov, Kutuzov, Nakhimov, Ushakov) was also conjured up to demonstrate the might of the nation, while the rebel Cossacks and peasants under the command of Bulavin, Bolotnikov,

Razin, and Pugachev demonstrated the historical impossibility of victory in the absence of an organized political vanguard – the Party.

There is no need to go on enumerating participants is this historical masquerade. More pressing is the changing function of history during the Stalinist era. In revolutionary culture, history played a more modest role, the focus being on the creation here and now of a present in the name of the future. But it had not at this stage entirely changed its attire. Hence the images of the Paris communards appeared as a direct projection (Stites 1989, 59-164). The monarchical allusiveness of Stalinist culture could not be directly articulated, however, but was mediated through a complex prism of inverted mirrors. Stalinist culture rejected direct projection not only because the culture concealed its true, restorationist intentions, but also because this type of projection, whether Jacobin or Thermidorean, could not produce dialectical poles for ideological manipulation, but only a straightforward picture which was politically useless.

History, whether in scholarship, literature or cinema, became the patriotic domain of Stalinist culture. Soviet patriotism replaced proletarian internationalism. It did not, however, celebrate the Stalinist era, as is usually thought, but merely created a dialectical terminal in the ideological circuit, through which the current of official creativity could flow.

In considering the shift from revolutionary or Marxist views to Stalinist historiography, let us look first at a few of the "milestones" of Russian history as viewed by the most influential Marxist historian. Contradicting the tradition, which contended that the Polish intervention of the seventeenth century was undisguised aggression, Pokrovsky asserted that the "Time of Troubles" was a bourgeois notion, in reality this was an era of revolts by the lower classes, and the Pretender had relied on support from the Cossacks and the Moscow service class. Pokrovsky, it was later argued, failed to appreciate the nature of the Polish intervention or the heroic struggle for national and political independence waged by the Russian people (Savich 1939, 232), and not only ignored Minin and Pozharsky, but saw no valour either in the Russian irregulars. The poet Alexander Bezymensky expressed this view in an extreme form:

Let us melt down Minin and Pozharsky,
why are they on a pedestal?

....

Big deal they saved Russia,
perhaps it would have been better if they hadn't?

(Dudakov 1993, 218)

Pokrovsky's views on the war of 1812 were similarly anti-patriotic. He saw the Russian nobility, fighting for their "trade capital", as responsible for the war. He blamed commanders afraid of Napoleon's genius and the incompetence of Kutuzov for military failings. The partisan war received the most disparaging evaluation: the people had fought not foreign invaders but pillagers in uniform: "the peasantry, armed with whatever came to hand, rose up against brigands dressed in French, Würtembergian, Westphalian and other uniforms" (Pokrovsky 1924, 567). Pokrovsky's pupil, Pyontovsky (later proclaimed an "enemy of the people"), repeated this assertion, maintaining that the peasantry rose up "in defence of their chickens and geese" (Picheta 1939, 294). Pokrovsky viewed Russian foreign policy in the nineteenth century in a similarly antipatriotic light, claiming, for example, that the Russo-Ottoman war, thanks to Bismarck's machinations, had been advantageous only to Germany in diverting Russia's interests from Europe to Turkey. The Russo-Japanese war was just as meaningless.

Clearly revolutionary culture gave rise to one-dimensional history, which was of no use to the pragmatics of power. This picture was not only, as measured by the principle of expediency, anti-patriotic, but also unsuitable for synthesis, or, in the words of M. Rozental, for the dialectical interpretation of history. Hence all these pictures, in history and literature, were declared "vulgar" ("vulgar economism", "vulgar sociologism", and so on). New requirements were formulated whereby a position might be simultaneously correct and false. An editorial in *Pravda* devoted to Stalin, Zhdanov and Kirov's "Remarks" concerning the draft textbook on the "History of the USSR" stated that the trouble with Pokrovsky and the whole school of Soviet Marxist historians was that "they failed to see the transitions and shifts within the framework of a single formula" (*Pravda* 1936). "Transitions and shifts within the framework of a single formula" precisely defines the principle of historical synthesization shaping the historical dialectic of the Stalinist era: a formula simultaneously both correct and false.

The rejection of Marxist historical doctrine can be approached from two angles: the cultural-ideological and the historical. On the one hand, a flexible bipolar dialectical doctrine allows reinterpretation of historical material in line with current pragmatic needs. On the other, there is the "sublimation" of history into pure politics. In this sense nothing new occurred under Stalinism: just as Pokrovsky rewrote Russian history according to the ideals of the socialist revolution, bringing it into line with Marxist ideas, the Stalinist era returned Russian history to the confines of a new populism and to Soviet patriotism. Political expediency permeated history and aesthetics alike in this period.

Thus the peak of the struggle with "Pokrovskyism", in 1936, coincided with the Socialist Realist revolution in Soviet art. A series of articles expressed the new aesthetic requirements: for opera (the 28 January *Pravda* editorial, "Muddle Instead of Music"), ballet (the *Pravda* editorial of 6 February, "Ballet Trips Up"), painting (the *Pravda* editorial of 1 March, "Concerning Artist-daubers"), and architecture (the 20 February *Pravda* article, "A Cacophony in Architecture"). The Party press naturally, seized upon this theme.[9]

In place of revolutionary "muddle" it was suggested that art and history be given back to the people. A scandal erupted in 1936 concerning the production of Demyan Bedny's *Bogatyrs* at the Tairov theatre. Whether art or history was at issue is difficult to say. In portraying Russians "dozing on their stoves" and implying that "the old Russian culture of woe was stupid" ["Rossiiskaia gore-kul'tura – dura"], Demyan Bedny had in effect followed the same line as Pokrovsky had in history. According to *Pravda*, the play falsified the people's past (no more so, of course, than Aleksey Tolstoy's plays about Ivan the Terrible.) The "Brigands" of Kievan Rus' were portrayed as a revolutionary element, while the legendary *bogatyrs* were ridiculed as drunkards and cowards. The Central Committee rose up in defence of Russian mythology: "The heroism of the Russian people, that *Bogatyr* epic, which is dear to us Bolsheviks too, all the finest heroic traits of the peoples of our own and

---

[9] See the editorials of *Komsomol'skaia Pravda*, 14 February 1936, "Protiv formalizma i 'levatskogo urodstva' v iskusstve"; 4 March, "Vdali ot zhizni"; 18 February, "'Lestnitsa, vedushchaia v nikuda': arkhitektura vverkh nogami"; V. Kemenov's articles in *Pravda*, 6 and 26 March,: "Protiv formalisma i naturalisma v zhivopisi"; and *Literaturnaia gazeta*, 24 February, "O formalistakh i 'otstalom' zritele"; and P. Lebedev's "Protiv formalizma v sovetskom iskusstve" in the sixth issue for 1936 of the journal *Pod znamenem marksizma*, and many, many others.

other countries, have been turned by Demyan Bedny into material for the universal censure of the *bogatyrs*, [...] a slander on the Russian people", which "spits on the people's past" (Kerzhentsev 1936). Clearly the play lacked popular spirit. And so cultural limits were marked out: against abstract art and against left-deviationist censure of the past.

The parallel processes taking place in aesthetics and history reveal an important cultural mechanism: the struggle in aesthetics conducted under the banner of populism, the struggle in history under the banner of historical truth or historicism. If we see in populism the image of the masses as the regime wished to see them, then in historicism we see the image of the past as the regime wished to see it in the here and now. In the later 1930s heroic spirit is inserted into the images of the past, along with statehood and patriotism, with "emphasis on military, heroic themes", as the chief Soviet writer-historian, academician Evgeny Tarle, insisted (*Literaturnaia gazeta* 1940). Pokrovsky's conception of history was condemned for damaging the cause of educating the younger generations in the spirit of Soviet patriotism (Pankratova 1942, 13).

Soviet historians, on the contrary:

strive to show the glorious historical tradition of the Russian people to contemporary generations, the tradition of ardent love for the motherland, and burning hatred for her enemies ... The figures of the great Russian patriots, heroes of the liberation struggle of the peoples of the USSR, must be covered with glory and lovingly preserved for posterity in the works of Soviet historians. (Pankratova 1942, 36)

The historian's task is reduced to museumization of patriots and heroes of the liberation struggle. The pantheon created at the end of the 1930s is confirmed during the war and consecrated in Stalin's speech in Red Square at the 7 November 1941 parade, in which "the great figures of our forefathers", Alexander Nevsky, Dmitry Donskoy, Minin and Pozharsky, Suvorov and Kutuzov, were resurrected. The war gave impetus to the historical novel appealing to the heroic spirit of the past: "history was revealed to us during the war, the pages of books came alive. The heroes of the past rose out of the schoolbooks and came into the dugouts. Who did not experience the events of 1812 as an intimate and real story?" asked Ilya Ehrenburg (1966, 674-75) during the war years. History has been transformed into "a source of light in the dugouts". It is as if the present has brought the past to life, brought it closer, changed it into a sermon on victory (Dobrenko 1993, 297-317). The great wave of literature and feature films about military commanders facilitating this process reached unprecedented heights towards the end of the Stalinist era.[10]

Having dispensed with the Marxist approach to history, Stalinist culture increasingly reworked earlier historical conceptions. The past appears as an intricate mosaic, reconstituted from fragments of previous historical doctrines. Among the most important, undoubtedly, is Mikhail Pogodin's "official populism". Stalinist culture in many respects replicates Pogodin's *History* which is permeated with xenophobia, populism, and strong state power and Pokrovsky now appears on equal terms with Pogodin. The originality of Stalinist historical aesthetics was not the discovery of a new understanding of the past, but the synthesis of fragments of previous ideas.

The entire culture of the 1920s, historical scholarship and novels alike, is permeated with an anti-imperialist view of the incorporation of Russian lands. The most striking literary example was Artem Vesely's novel *Make Merry, Volga! [Guliai, Volga!]*, where Ermak's campaign is portrayed as the work of a band of half-human, half-animal brigands, exterminating the Siberians with gusto.[11] (It is worth recalling here that Marxist scholarship of the 1920s took an extremely critical view of Russian literature, claiming that from Pushkin and Lermontov to Tolstoy, it was permeated with the spirit of imperialism.) In Marxist history annexation was always viewed negatively, while wars of national liberation were justified. In the "Remarks" on the draft USSR history textbook, Stalin, Zhdanov and Kirov see the presentation of USSR history as exclusively Russian as a significant shortcoming. Traditionally the histories of peoples who became part of the Russian Empire entered Russian history only from the time of their annexation. Thus Georgian history proper existed only up to the annexation of Georgia, and was subsequently described as part of Russian history. Now, however, national histories were integrated into Russian history so that David the Builder and Shota Rustaveli, Navoi and Nizami became characters of Russian history,

---

[10] See Kafengauz (1942). Literary historians also stated that, "by the beginning of the war period, the Soviet military-history novel had found its mature form" (Messer 1955, 225).

[11] See Serebrianskii (1936, 77-80). This novel can be contrasted with E. Fedorov's *Ermak*, portraying the subjugation of Siberia in quite a different manner.

alongside Dmitry Donskoy or Archpriest Avvakum, themselves now not only part of Russian, but also Kirgiz, and Armenian history. The appropriation of national histories reaches its peak in the early 1950s, during the "struggle against bourgeois nationalism", when national historians were instructed to employ the concept of the golden age only to describe the period following incorporation (Dobrenko 1993, 364-382). Thus Georgia's golden age of David the Builder and Queen Tamara is moved seven to eight centuries into the future.

Filled with new characters, Russian history was itself subject to another reinterpretation: it now became the history of the friendship of nations. This referred not only to the period of their "union", when Russian "explorers", "navigators", and "discoverers of new lands" are depicted as benefactors of the smaller nationalities, vegetating in the backwoods of history and doomed to extinction (Slezkine 1997), but also to the history of ancient Russia. Thus, in V. Ivanov's *Tale of Ancient Times* [*Povest' drevnikh let'*] we learn that the citizens of ninth-century Novgorod were friends of their neighbours, the Biarmia tribe, bringing them civilization. The military leader of Novgorodians explains their policy in the region around the Dvina as follows: "We must ensure that not one of us out of ignorance wrongs the Biarmians ... do not ever offend them, brothers ... live always with them according to our Novgorod Code". And we witness friendship, the refusal of tribute, fraternization, as if the Russian raids of the ninth century on Byzantium, the Caucasus and the Baltics had never happened. In Ivanov's chronicle-novel the citizens of Novgorod withstand the "Normans" (i.e. Western Europe). The Normans are dirty brigands and sadistic fanatics, destroying all living things. At the same time the Slavs:

> with courage, honour and conscience, having no titles or coats of arms, tournaments, castles or wealthy brides, silently bent their backs to work, suffered and endured all tortures, but with incredible strength of will settled the impassable and almost uninhabited territories of the North-East and the East, continued on to the southern steppes and shaped an enormous state covering a sixth of the entire globe, not through enslavement, but through the labour and friendship of people of all tribes.[12]

---

[12] See the analysis of Ivanov's novel in Pashuto (1963, 90).

The more peace-loving Russian history became, the more the historical model is permeated by internationalism. Here again is the familiar move: where Pokrovsky and Pogodin met a new position emerged in which Pokrovsky's sympathy and Pogodin's disdain towards national minorities are combined. So too in Stalinist historical doctrine the "industrializing" zeal of the revolutionaries meets with an apologia for peasant backwardness. In contrast to an obtuse European peasantry, so Pogodin maintained, the Russian peasant "makes everything for himself, with his own hands; the axe and chisel are substitutes for all machinery". "However many remarkable inventions there are", Pogodin exclaims, "the common man may substitute some wooden mechanism for a hydraulic press ... while another may draw up plans to rival the great Architect" (1874, 5-6).

At the end of the 1940s, Soviet history required the Pogodin spirit, when Russian priorities in science began to be asserted (Dobrenko 1993, 382-390), and the idea of Russian originality and superiority is united with that of advanced industrialism, in accordance with the ideals of industrialization under the Stalinist slogan: "We Must Master Technique!" If Demyan Bedny's famous call for Russians to "get down from the stove" on the eve of the 1930s is reconsidered in the light of the post-war period, it becomes clear that Russians had never actually lain on their stoves, and if they had, then it was because they were not outdated, but were the most technologically advanced stoves ever.

The history of science now moves to the foreground and is hastily rewritten from 1948 to 1950. As before, the revision is carried out in historical scholarship and in a flood of novels, plays, and films about Russian scientific pioneers and explorers: Evgeny Fedorov's *Band of Stone* [*Kamennyi poias*], on the invention of the steam engine by Russian peasants in the 1830s, and his novel *A Great Destiny* (Bol'shaia sud'ba), on the founder of Russian ballet, Vissarion Sayanov's *Heaven and Earth* [*Nebo i zemlia*], on the first Russian aviators, and many others. In film, leading Russian scientists and other cultural heroes filled the post-war screen. Even during the so-called film-drought after the war, pictures were released about Pavlov, Alexander Popov, Zhukovsky, Lomonosov, Michurin, Mussorgsky, Glinka, Rimsky-Korsakov, and so on.

National problems filled the popular imagination and the museum of the revolution turns into the Russian museum. Revolutionary and state culture are covered more thickly than ever with the veneer of Russianness, so that even Lenin's mausoleum is declared, in a peculiar link between cultures, an outstanding example of Russian architecture. This constructivist building is now interpreted as follows: "The populism of the mausoleum's architecture lies not only in its accessibility, that all its forms are intended for the people's consumption, but also in that the formal idiom is comprehensible to the people, that its appearance is rooted in an architectural tradition stretching back to popular architectural design." Shchusev's artistic flair, we learn, and his knowledge of the popular architecture of ancient Rus', all helped in the development of the Lenin mausoleum (Sokolov 1952, 43).

Soviet historical novels, films, drama, and painting are all *history* without a past.[13] The historical genre, especially the novel, became in every sense state-oriented. The state determined its "realistic" texture. Indeed the state was its central character. This was a love-affair of the state with history, the attempt to domesticate the past. The Soviet novel created history as ritual, to use Katerina Clark's (1981) definition, and was drawn to a new form of historicism. Historical concreteness, one of the primary demands of Socialist Realism, was of fundamental importance. "In considering the originality of the historical novel", wrote one Soviet critic, "one could say that in all probability no other form of novel had ever undergone such massive structural-thematic shifts in comparison with the past as occurred here" (*Istoriia russkogo sovetskogo romana* 1965, 338). The Soviet historical novel was the product of a new historical situation, hence the shifts arose.

The discussion about the historical novel in the journal *Oktiabr* in 1936 outlined only in rough the new conception of history. More significant were the results of the polemics. Georg Lukács's conception of the historical novel attempted to unite Marxism's divided world with Hegel's world of wholeness.[14] Lukács's theory, which still remains one of

[13] In Soviet discourse, history and the past merge in the concept of the historical past: "A decisive characteristic of our era is that it is historical, in the most profound sense. Given that tens of millions of people in the Soviet land have undertaken consciously to organize the historical process, to organize their lives around new socialist beginnings ... the transformation of non-historical events into historical ones is happening before our eyes" (Serebrianskii 1936, 149-50, 155).

[14] Lukács's book on the historical novel was written in the USSR in 1936-7; extracts were first published in the journal *Literaturnyi kritik*, 7, 9, 12 (1937); 3, 7, 8, 12 (1938).

the most interesting and profitable, should be understood within the political and ideological context of the Stalinist revolution from which it arose.

In an era when the Marxist sociological, class-based approach to history had been replaced by a traditionalist historicizing national consciousness, that is, as class theory gave way to populism, Lukács's refusal to see the historical novel as a special genre could not but be viewed as a challenge: "The historical novel stands up as a separate genre not because its aims are, in contrast to the freer methods of other types of novel, an exceptional authenticity in the transmission of the past. The historical novel stands up as a separate genre only where the objective or subjective conditions of historical truthfulness in literature have either not yet arisen, or have already long disappeared" (Lukács 1937, 147). This was written in the heyday of the Soviet historical novel, in 1937, when not everyone would have risked saying such things about Stalinist art. Whereas novels set in the present tend, Lukács (1938, 50) suggests, to "correct" the writer's ideological agenda, by contrast "historical material does not resist the writer so much, and adapts to the writer's ideas more easily". In other words, the historical novel was more amenable to ideological manipulation and was mobilized for this purpose. Unsurprisingly this idea was anathema to official criticism, which accused Lukács of positing the "fundamental inferiority of the historical novel" (Serebranskii 1940, 3).

Another feature of Lukács's work was the conspicuous absence of comment on the Soviet historical novel. Lukács's biographers agree that there was an element of hidden attack in this. Soviet historical novels and films of the 1930s revolved around great historical characters. The very titles – Chapygin's *Razin Stepan*, Shtorm's *Tale of Bolotnikov*, Tolstoy's *Peter the First* and so on, and films such as *Alexander Nevsky*, *Minin and Pozharsky*, or *Ivan the Terrible* – already suggest that the course of history is not spontaneous, but organized, with consciousness and expediency, concentrated in the figure of the leader. On the other hand, the role of the masses was also emphasized. This was a romantic conception combining idealization of the hero and the people. Nowhere did Socialist Realism merge with romantic aesthetics more clearly than in historicist art.

Lukács however, suggested that the main characters should not be prominent historical figures, hence he takes Walter Scott as an exemplary author. This argument goes back to the Hegelian opposition between epic literature centred on a great historical figure and modern literature with its prosaic "average" hero: "These were the real national heroes, understood figuratively; the heroes of the life prosaic", Lukács (1938, 64) asserted. Lukács's conception disappeared from the ideological radar during the Stalinist revolution of the 1930s because he did not understand the new dialectic of the "poetry of life itself", which left no room for "prose". In effect, Lukács was not against the historical novel *per se*, but only its biographical variety, at a time when the Soviet historical novel, like the historical film, was dominated by biography.

According to Lukács, drama depicts historical crises, seeks to represent historical laws, and portrays historical heroes. The historical novel, by contrast, should depict the fulness of life in its concrete nature, and must convey the specific flavour of an era. In the second half of the 1930s, when the Soviet historical novel corresponded to the model of historical drama, Lukács's position must have seemed utopian. Indeed, the historical novel in the romantic mode of Scott had already been lost in the USSR at the very time when the heyday of the Soviet historical novel was dawning. These changes were connected to the modernization, pragmaticization, and instrumentalization of history, which reached a pinnacle in the Socialist Realist principle of Party-mindedness.

Throughout Soviet history, attempts were made to reconcile historicism with Party-mindedness (Ivanov 1973, 1976 and 1986). The most direct route was the application of Party-mindedness to the principle of historicism. Party-mindedness could relativize any principle and historicism too was forced to become practically useful to the political requirements of the day. It had therefore to enter the general system of the flexible, dialectically contradictory principles of Socialist Realism, in order to combine truth to life with revolutionary romanticism: "The historicism of Lenin's teaching lies in its scientific understanding of practical historical realities based on the inter-relationship between man and history. Reality must be viewed as the logical continuation of the historical process in its constant development and onward march to the future, whence the chief tendencies of contemporaneity are defined and assessed" (Aleksandrova 1971, 23). This formula is just as valid when reversed: if "the chief tendencies of contemporaneity" are defined and assessed from the point of view of history, then the past must also be defined and assessed from the point of view of "the chief tendencies of contemporaneity": "Socialist historicism is the creative understanding of life based on the communist ideal, the definition of the chief tendencies of the era, promoting the vivid depiction of life in its historical perspective and retrospective, enabling the writer to create the image of the time and the typical hero of the era" (Aleksandrova 1971, 84).[15]

In effect this repeats the formula of Socialist Realism, which demanded "the historically truthful reflection of reality in its revolutionary development", that is, both aspects simultaneously. Becoming Socialist Realist meant, for the historical novel, becoming Party-minded. It was less an internal question of the substance of the historical conception – in the course of the Soviet era this changed many times – than of the capacity for changes demanded from without. Soviet scholars rightly saw the intensity of this process: "By the 1930s we already observe not the different approaches to historicism visible in the creative thought of writers, as in the literature of the 1920s, but different stylistic manifestations within the framework of a single creative method. Even the works of writers on the fringes of the main path of literary development are characterized by a historicism inherent to the creative method as a whole" (Aleksandrova 1971, 85).[16] This "historicism" is a euphemism for the principles of Socialist Realism. Historicism has become party-minded as has the historical novel; like all forms of Socialist Realist literature, it was declared "the most progressive, ideologically advanced novel about the past that world literature had ever seen" (Messer 1955, 296).

The Soviet historical novel's real story was the process of "historical

---

[15] 1920s Soviet criticism asserts: "the historical novel documents the perception of an era and the class which created it and not simply the era which is being described in the novel" (Nusinov 1929, 29). The Stalinist era asserts: "The historical novel's educational significance" consists in "the consolidation of the consciousness of revolutionary historical continuity" (Serebrianskii 1936, 8). Finally, in the 1970s, "heroic experience in national history is subordinated to today's urgent social and moral questions" (Kuznetsov 1977, 91).

[16] It is worth noting that criticism demanded unverifiable historical truth: "The historical novelist does not need to be empirically dependent on historical documents, data, etc. But however free the artist's imagination, *fidelity to historical reality*] is essential" (Serebrianskii 1936, 95). This was a special form of "reality", beyond the scope of empiricism or documents.

synthesization", which forced the historian, writer, director and artist not simply to revise and modernize the past, but to connect the unconnectable. The Stalinist era's discontinuity, ideological overload and non-linear historical viewpoint endowed historical narrative with a dramatic quality, having already dictated the plot. Of course, today, the reason for reading the Soviet historical text, whether scholarship, drama, novel, or film, is neither to discover something about Ivan the Terrible or Emelyan Pugachev, nor even to understand the author's position on events or characters from the past. Their main interest lies in their strategies, the prism they bring to bear on working with the past, and the synthesizing mechanism at work within the revisionist strategies. The originality of the Soviet historical texts is in their barbarous eclecticism. This is their real aesthetic value.

There is more to discover about the era through Stalinist historicizing art than from the totally depoliticized novel of contemporary life. In this culture, the political dramas are played out in the form of allusion in historical novels, films or painting. All the most important actors take to the stage here: the Ruler, History, the People. The choice of genre was, of course, no accident. The historical novel was a profoundly anti-revolutionary genre, appealing to tradition, memory and the "soil". The genre was symptomatic of a crisis in art's relation to the present. But then the Bolshevik approach to art always preferred "timeliness" to contemporaneity. The historical genre was doomed to allusiveness and sterility. On the other hand, Stalinist culture not only sought endorsement in history, as all cultures do, but also required the demonstration of historical rootedness by indirect means, constantly balancing Jacobin and Thermidorean ideas. History really was a "field of dreams", not only enabling the ideological potential of education, literature and art to be tapped, but also giving endless opportunities for ideological fantasizing.

If we turn from Soviet historicizing art to historical scholarship, we see above all that Soviet history has no author. In contrast to the authorial histories of pre-revolutionary and revolutionary times, it is deperson-alized, like all Socialist Realist texts. Soviet history deploys a panoply of ideological clichés which, in the absence of a personal author, unites history into a single whole. The replacement of ideologemes is governed by the principle of Party-mindedness but, as with literature, Party-mindedness was already present in revolutionary culture. Pokrovsky was its active supporter. In one of his last speeches, in December 1931, he continued to urge: "My testament to you is that the 'academic' path is not the way, 'academism' has as a prerequisite the recognition of an objective scholarly discipline that cannot exist. Bolshevik scholarship must be Bolshevik in character."[17]

And although such aggressive anti-objectivism was condemned, the principle of Party-mindedness remained unshakable. The Soviet conception of history underwent the same shift as Soviet aesthetic doctrine, from being class-based towards populism. The class principle, central in revolutionary culture, was replaced by popular spirit by the middle of the 1930s, so depriving history of its former narrative, in which class-determinism was a catch-all definition for motivation. Hence the historical narrative required a new motivating factor. Conspiracy, the idea on which the Stalinist *Short Course* was constructed, became that universal motivating factor. Inscribed in literature and visualized in film, conspiracy became not only the key to understanding the plot, but effectively created the plot around which all action revolved.

These were the processes defining both Socialist Realist and historical doctrine. History became "entertaining", filled with people; it portrayed the past now in realistic images, in "forms of life itself", finding a socialist content and national form. Thus the Soviet conception of history coincides with Soviet aesthetic doctrine, with Socialist Realism. And if borders did exist, they could be defined as internal, on the level of genre. As academician Pankratova observes, history, which "provokes an ardent response in the hearts of readers in the Soviet land", is disclosed most fully in Soviet historicizing art. If this is so, then Soviet history is a genre of Soviet literature, and the Soviet historian is, as Pankratova asserted, merely a breed of Soviet writer. Thus while it was inevitable in the Soviet era that the instructive nature of history would grow sharply, it was also transformed into a key component in the general political-aesthetic project; and by necessity it became, finally, "entertaining".

(Translated by Sarah Young)

---

[17] M.N. Pokrovsky. Istoricheskaia nauka i bor'ba klassov. Vyp. 2, as cited in Iaroslavskii 1940, 9.

References

Aleksandrova, L. (1971). *Sovetskii istoricheskii roman i voprosy istorizma*. Kiev: Izd. Kievskogo universiteta.

Andreev, Iu. (1962). *Russkii sovetskii istoricheskii roman (20-30-e gody)*. Moscow and Leningrad: AN SSSR.

Antonovskaya, A. (1938). Zametki ob istoricheskom romane. *Literaturnaia gazeta* (26 November).

Brandenberger, D. (2002). *National Bolshevism: Stalinist Mass Culture and the Formation of Modern Russian National Identity, 1931-1956*. Cambridge, MA: Harvard University Press.

Clark, K. (1981). *The Soviet Novel: History as Ritual*. Chicago: University of Chicago Press.

Dobrenko, E. (1993). *Metafora vlasti: Literatura stalinskoi epokhi v istoricheskom osveshchenii*. Munich: Otto Sagner.

Dobrenko, E. (1997). *The Making of the State Reader: Social and Aesthetic Contexts of the Reception of Soviet Literature*. Stanford: Stanford University Press.

Dobrenko, E. (2008). *Stalinist Cinema and the Production of History: Museum of the Revolution*. Edinburgh: Edinburgh University Press.

Dudakov, S. (1993). *Istoriia odnogo mifa*. Moscow: Nauka.

Ehrenburg, I. (1966). *Sobranie Sochinenii*, vol. VII. Moscow: Khudozhestvenaia literatura.

Enteen, G. M. (1978). *The Soviet Scholar-Bureaucrat: M. N. Pokrovsky and the Society of Marxist Historians*. University Park and London: Pennsylvania State University Press.

Eremin, D. (1955). *Kremlevskii kholm*. Moscow: Moskovskii rabochii.

Ezerskii, M. (1941). *Dmitrii Donskoi*. Moscow and Leningrad: Gosizdat.

Goffenshefer, V. (1933). "O rodoslovnoi geroev". *Literaturnyi kritik*, 2.

Gorky, M. (1953). *Sobranie sochinenii. v 30-ti tomakh*, vol. XXVII. Moscow: GIKHL.

Grois, B. (1994). "Otstroennaia ideologiia". *Iskusstvo kino*, 10, 95-99.

Gulyga, A. (1974). *Estetika istorii*. Moscow: Nauka.

Iaroslavskii, E.M. (1940). Antimarksistskie izvrashcheniia "shkoly" M. N.

Iazvitskii, V. (1955). *Ivan III – gosudar' vseia Rusi*, vols. IV-V. Moscow: Gosizdat.

Istoriia russkogo sovetskogo romana. (1965), vol. I. Moscow and Leningrad: Nauka.

Iurenev, R. (1939). *Sovetskii istoricheskii fil'm*. Moscow: Goskinoizdat.

Iurenev, R. (1949). *Sovetskii biograficheskii fil'm*. Moscow: Goskinoizdat.

Ivanov, V. V. (1973). *Sootnoshenie istorii i sovremennosti kak metodologicheskaia problema*. Moscow: Nauka.

Ivanov, V. V. (1976). *Leninskii istorizm: Metodologiia i metodika issledovanii*. Kazan: Izd-vo Kazanskogo universiteta.

Ivanov, V. V. (1986). *Istoricheskaia nauka: Voprosy metodologii*. Moscow: Mysl'.

Kafengauz, B.B. (1942). Voenno-istoricheskaia literatura za 25 let. In Volgin, V.P. *et al.* (eds.), *Dvadtsat' piat' let istoricheskoi nauki v SSSR*. Moscow and Leningrad: AN SSSR.

Kammari, M. (1953). *Marksizm-Leninizm o roli lichnosti v istorii*. Moscow: AN SSSR.

Kavtaradze, S. (1990). "'Khronotop' kul'tury stalinizma". *Arkhitektura i stroitel'stvo Moskvy* (Zodchii), 11.

Kerzhentsev, P. (1936). "Fal'sifikatsiia narodnogo proshlogo (O *Bogatyriakh* Dem'iana Bednogo)". *Pravda,* 15 November.

Khrenov, N. (1994). "Dialog kino i literatury v kontekste protivorechii razvitiia kul'tury 30-40-x godov". In A. Bogomolov *et al.* (ed.), *Ekrannye iskusstva i literatura: Zvukovoe kino*. Moscow: Nauka, 164-198.

Kizucheniiu istorii. (1937). Moscow: Partizdat.

Kuznetsov, F. (1977). "Literatura – Nravsvennost' – Kritika". In *Sovremennaia literaturnaia kritika: Voprosy teorii i metodologii*. Moscow Nauka, 52-101.

Lenobl', G. (1969). *Istoriia i literature*. Moscow: Sov. pisatel'.

Levin, E. (1994). "Ekranizatsiia: Istorizm, mifografiia, mifologiia (K istorii obshchestvennogo soznaniia i khudozhestvennogo myshleniia)". In A. Bogomolov *et al.* (ed.), *Ekrannye iskusstva i literatura: Zvukovoe kino*. Moscow: Nauka, 72-97.

Literaturnaia gazeta. 6 October 1940.

Lukács, G. (1937). "Istoricheskii roman i istoricheskaia drama. Stat'ia tret'ia". *Literaturnyi kritik,* 12.

Lukács, G. (1938). "Istoricheskii roman i krizis burzhuaznogo realizma". *Literaturnyi kritik,* 7.

Mazour, A. G. (1971). *The Writing of History in the Soviet Union*. Stanford: Hoover Institution Press.

Messer, R. (1955). *Sovetskaia istoricheskaia proza*. Leningrad: Sov.

pisatel'.

Nusinov, M. (1929). "Zapozdalye otkrytiia, ili kak V. Shklovskomu nadoelo est' golymi formalistskimi rukami i obzavelsia samodel'noi marksistkoi lozhkoi", *Literatura i marksism*. 5, 3-52.

Oskotskii, B. (1980). *Roman i istoriia: Traditsii i novatorstvo sovetskogo istoricheskogo romana.* Moscow: Khudozh. lit.

Pankratova, A. (1942). "Sovetskaia istoricheskaia nauka za 25 let i zadachi istorikov v usloviakh velikoi otchestvennoi voiny". In V.P. Volgin *et al.* (eds.), *Dvadtsat' piat' let istoricheskoi nauki v SSSR.* Moscow and Leningrad: AN SSSR, 3-40.

Pashuto, V. (1963). "Srednevekovaia Rus' v sovetskoi khudozhestvennoi literature". *Istoriia SSSR.*

Petrov, S. (1958). *Sovetskii istoricheskii roman.* Moscow: Sov. pisatel'.

Petrov-Biriukov, D. (1946). *Dikoe pole.* Moscow: Sov. pisatel'.

Picheta, V. (1939). "M. N. Pokrovsky o voine 1812". In B. Grekov *et al.* (ed.), *Protiv istoricheskoi kontseptsii M. N. Pokrovskogo.* Moscow and Leningrad: AN SSSR, 276-302

Pogodin, M. P. (1874). *Sochineniia,* vol. IV. Moscow.

Pokrovskogo. In *Protiv antimarksistskoi kontseptsii M. N. Pokrovskogo.* Moscow and Leningrad: AN SSSR.

Pokrovsky, M. N. (1929). *Oktiabrskaia revoliutsiia.* Moscow: Parizdat.

Pokrovsky. M. N. (1924). *Diplomatiia i voina v tsarskoi Rossii.* Moscow: Krasnaia nov'.

Pravda, 27 January 1936.

Rozental', M. (1936). *Protiv vul'garnoi sotsiologii v literaturnoi teorii.* Moscow: Khudozh. Lit.

Savich, A. (1939). "Pol'skaia interventsiia nachala XVII v. v otsenke M. N. Pokrovskogo". In B. Grekov *et al.* (ed.), *Protiv istoricheskoi kontseptsii M. N. Pokrovskogo.* Moscow and Leningrad: AN SSSR.

Serebrianskii, M. (1936). *Sovetskii istoricheskii roman.* Moscow: Goslitizdat.

Serebrianskii, M. (1940). "K sporam o knige G. Lukacha". *Literaturnaia gazeta,* 10 February.

Slezkine, Y. (1997). "Primitive Communism and the Other Way Around". In E. Dobrenko and T. Lahusen (eds.), *Socialist Realism without Shores.* Durham, NC: Duke University Press, 310-336.

Sokolov, N.B. (1952). *A. V. Shchusev.* Moscow: Gos. Izd-vo po stroitel'stvy i arkhitekture.

Stenograficheskii Otchet Vtorogo Vsesoiuznogo s'ezda sovetskikh pisa-telei. (1956). Moscow: Sov. pisatel'.

Stites, R. (1989). *Revolutionary Dreams: Utopian Vision and Experimental Life in the Russian Revolution.* New York and Oxford: Oxford University Press.

Wachtel, A. (1994). *An Obsession with History: Russian Writers Confront the Past.* Stanford: Stanford University Press.

Znamia. (1937). 10.

Visual and Performance Cultures

After-Images: Trauma, History and Connection in the Photography of Alfredo Jaar

Parvati Nair

Inherent in the notion of post-conflict cultures and questions of testimony is the concept of cultural memory. If in recent years this has become a field of considerable academic focus, then to a large extent this is because of the fracture of memory in the face of conflict, whereby testimony breaks down. Trauma by definition indicates not just the lived conflictive event, but also the subsequent failure of narrative, and hence testimony. In the black hole that ensues, human suffering, questions of justice and historical regard become subsumed and disappear. The discipline of cultural memory has gained momentum from a concern with the Holocaust and its recurrent presentation of this problematic of memory in the face of trauma. Curiously, while the postmemory of the Holocaust continues to command academic focus, other genocides and traumas that have occurred or are occurring in our times all too often remain relegated to academic oblivion.

In his *Memory, History and Forgetting*, Paul Ricoeur (2004) examines the vicissitudes of memory, whereby certain events overtake others in the collective consciousness. Ricoeur traces the links between collective remembering and the forging of historical narrative, showing both to be selective. Equally, he marks the reciprocity between remembering and forgetting, pointing thus to the subcutaneous existence of lost memories, or memories that have fallen short of representation. Historical "knowledge" thus is limited and selective in its inclusion of facts, dependent upon those memories that have gained entry into narrative. At the same time, certain memories are so focused upon that they gain significance that accrues over time. Thus, as a trope of what must not be forgotten and yet falls ever short of adequate articulation, the Holocaust remains today at the forefront of Western collective awareness and hence historical narrative: indeed, so great is its importance that it not only underlines the memory of those absent millions who suffered and died at the hands of the Nazis, but also acts as a key foundational narrative for the modern nation-state of Israel. Ironically, its importance in the collective memory and in the narrative of the nation thus turns it into a key subtext that is aligned to ongoing Zionist action in Palestine. Thus it is that, while the vast majority of conflicts and deaths around the world recede, the memory of certain others can grow over time and mutate, acquiring new signification and political reach. Recent trends in Trauma Studies reveal attempts to move beyond the largely Eurocentric confines of the discipline's origins, linked as it is to Freudian psychoanalysis and a largely Western focus centring on the Holocaust, made more intense since the events of 9/11. Thus, there is relatively little focus on trauma in Jenin or Baghdad, and much more on New York in the twenty-first century, and attempts to understand, represent and politicize the question of trauma remain, with few exceptions, a prerogative of the global hegemony.

To think back to those conflicts and silences that have marked our recent decades and that are in danger of receding into silence, one has only to move slightly beyond the geo-political contours of the West. They are too numerous to list. Think, for example, of the genocide of Armenians at the hands of Turks, never as yet acknowledged by Western powers, of the USSR under Stalin, of the atrocities of Vietnam, of the deaths which occurred during the break-up of the former Yugoslavia, of conflict in Sierra Leone, of the ongoing "war on terror" with its countless concomitant civilian deaths in Iraq and Afghanistan, to name but a few. Think too of the *desaparecidos* of Latin America, the disappeared, who are neither known to be dead nor alive and who can thus neither be mourned nor embraced, whose names hover in the anguished grey zone between life and death. In trying to give voice to the disappeared, the Madres de la Plaza de Mayo struggle to etch the names of their disappeared loved ones over a looming collective neglect. Their voices are small and the forgetting is large.

This chapter will focus on an artwork entitled *The Eyes of Gutete Emerita*, by the photographer and installation artist Alfredo Jaar. My aim is to analyze the ways in which Jaar focuses specifically on trauma in the Rwandan context as a site of silence or forgetting, and unearths within this silence the potential to mobilize politicized responses via his art. There are, not surprisingly, next to no cultural texts that foreground the sufferings of Rwandans, the film *Hotel Rwanda* being an exception. It is curious to note that it has taken fourteen years for a Rwandan to bring out the first "text" on this topic: Gilbert Gatore (2008), who lives in France but is of Rwandan origin, is the first to recount the collective memories of his people. According to an article in *El País* (4 August 2008), he states, though, that he has had to resort to fiction, as so much of the trauma suffered has reverted to silence. The result is that there is as yet insufficient understanding of what really took place. The refusal of memory leaves a historical void.

Through this visual representation that centres upon intensely traumatic events and experiences, Alfredo Jaar taps into the often ignored and unvoiced historical potential in sites of trauma. His artwork intervenes in this silence: it explores the extent to which historical understanding and connection can emerge and be forged from the non-rational and sentient ways in which audiences respond to such representations. Thus, Jaar calls upon an ethics of vision, whereby that pre-discursive moment of encounter with alterity or the *other* via still photography becomes the ground from which to build collective remembering amongst those who did not necessarily live through or witness trauma. In so doing, the photograph becomes the frame within which historical narratives can germinate and collective forgetting can be countered. If the forging of such memory is important, it is so because it aims to challenge, if not override, the larger political context of forgetting that epitomized the global neglect of Rwanda's tragedy. The commitment to representation and memory is thus both an ethical and a political act.

Jaar left his native Chile at the age of twenty-five, seeking respite in New York from the horrors of Pinochet's dictatorship. An architect by training, he managed to elude political scrutiny whilst in Chile, despite showing artwork that exposed the violations of human rights by the prevailing regime. Jaar posits his work against the overriding silence that blankets suffering and loss in contexts that are politically charged and weighted with injustice. While he does not call himself a photo-documentarian – his work bears too obvious an artistic inflection for that and calls instead upon viewers' ability to make tacit connections – nevertheless, Jaar says his artwork is always "project-based", linked to real-life events and focused on building connections or on comm-unicating the lived realities of marginalized events to viewers who are primarily located in the West. As projects focusing on such contexts, Jaar's artwork has a marked social and political dimension. It aims to fill historical gaps by riding the uneven border between global hegemonies and their peripheries. It is the result of a deep engagement between the artist and his chosen contexts and is thus the hybrid result of this prolonged encounter between an artistic drive and a socio-political context. If Jaar is not strictly speaking a documentarian, his work has often followed parallel paths to those of other Latin American photographers working in the field of social documentary, in particular aestheticized photo-documentary, most especially those of the Brazilians Sebastião Salgado and Miguel Rio Branco. He has, for instance, photo-graphed the miners of the Serra Pelada gold mines. Jaar's work centres on military conflicts, political corruption, and imbalances of power between industrialized and developing nations. Subjects addressed in his work include the genocide in Rwanda, gold mining in Brazil, toxic pollution in Nigeria, and issues related to the border between Mexico and the United States. I shall argue in this essay that Jaar's work offers us poignant counter-documentaries to mainstream news images, offering both prolonged meditation on conflict in the crevices and margins of global networks of power and, very importantly, personal testimonies of the latter. In particular, my focus is on his efforts to negotiate the delicate area that lies between the failure of representation in terms of deliberate repression from collective memory and the articulation not of the memory *per se,* but of this absence of historical acknowledgement. In this, he foregrounds the power of visual art to call upon the silent, to frame the invisible and to thus forge a frame for what should have been seen. His focus is dual: if it foregrounds the brutal events that took place, it also highlights the guilt of the West, where these events remain deliberately ignored. By this, I mean that Jaar calls upon the notion of turning a blind eye, whereby the *absence* of what should have been seen and acknowledged is noted and comes into sight.

Perhaps one of the more glaring failures of the collective memory of our times relates to the mass killings that took place in Rwanda in 1994-5. Few realize that the massacres of Rwanda constitute the third genocide of the twentieth century, the first being the rarely recalled one of Armenians by Turks belonging to the Ottoman Empire in 1915 and 1916 and the second the slaughter of Jews by Nazis during the Second World War. If Africa has always remained Europe's marginal "other", then few historical events confirm this invisibility as forcefully as the international neglect that occurred both during and after this genocide. Writing on his country, Juan Tomás Ávila Laurel, a writer and intellectual from Equatorial Guinea, states: "The real international disinterest in the affairs of Equatorial Guinea is the cause of mistaken conceptions about her true situation" (2008). The same holds true for Rwanda.

What occurred in Rwanda was a state-sponsored genocide that was many years in the planning but carried out in no more than a hundred days. As "Hutu Power" extremists incited Hutus across the country to attack the minority Tutsis in a bid to eradicate them, the West turned its back on the bloodshed that was taking place. The ensuing Civil War was savage and intense. During this time, the United Nations withdrew its forces, as the corpses of slain Tutsis, who had been attempting to flee the country, choked the Nyabarongo and other rivers. Within a space of three months, over a million people had died out of an overall national population of eight million. The Hutus targeted Tutsi children in particular, as the aim was above all to wipe out the future of Tutsis and to ensure that the historical memory of this genocide would be forever eradicated. To quote the Indian sociologist Ashis Nandy,

> The massive carnages at Rwanda and Bosnia have taught the students of genocide that the most venomous, brutal killings and atrocities take place when the two communities involved are not distant strangers, but close to each other culturally and socially, and when their lives intersect at many points. When nearness sours or explodes it releases strange, fearsome demons. (2002)

Whilst many agree that intervention from the United Nations may well have stopped the massacres, the latter withdrew the majority of its peacekeeping forces from the country following pressure from the United States and Belgium, a former colonial power in Rwanda. Of the 2,500 United Nations soldiers who had been in Rwanda, only 270 remained. If the world turned a blind eye, it was not because it did not know. Reports were indeed in the press. However, as Elaine Sciolino of the *New York Times* stated, "no member of the United Nations with an army strong enough to make a difference is willing to risk the lives of its troops for a failed central African nation-state with a centuries-old history of tribal warfare" (2004). Closer to home, Simon Hoggart of *The Guardian* stated that "Rwandans are thousands of miles away. Nobody you know has ever been on holiday in Rwanda. And Rwandans don't look like us" (2008). The limited Western intervention that did take place was misleading in its intentions, misinformed by their governments that Tutsis were killing Hutus, French soldiers were dispatched to aid the latter to the further detriment of the Tutsi minority. As Kofi Annan, the previous Secretary-General of the United Nations later acknowledged during a visit to Kigali, "We must and we do acknowledge that the world failed Rwanda at that time of evil. The international community and the United Nations could not muster the political will to confront it" (UN Press Release 1998). Indeed, there was much that the United Nations could have done but did not do. Annan's acknowledgement has done little to place the genocide of Rwanda in the spotlight. While it was somewhat highlighted in the media in 2004, a decade after it occurred, few in the West today have clear details of what took place, quite unlike the Nazi Holocaust.

It is against this backdrop of collective neglect and forgetting that Jaar works. His Rwanda Project spans the years 1994 to 2000 and is the result of a visit made to Rwanda in August 1994. His decision to go to Rwanda to see the situation there for himself was taken as a result of the lack of concern that was prevalent in the United States. When he arrived in Kigali, there was neither water nor power available and very little food. Jaar's first artistic act, later called *Signs of Life,* was to send postcards out of the country with the names of survivors he met: *EMMANUEL RICOGOZA IS STILL ALIVE! CARITAS NAMAZURU IS STILL ALIVE!* Ironically, the postcards all bore images of Rwanda as an idyllic holiday location, bursting with flora and fauna. In the course of his travels around the country, Jaar began to collect stories of survival and to take photographs. A key aspect of his work is the combination of text and image. To quote Sebastião Salgado, "photographs by themselves cannot do very much ... But when you place them next to words, they become so powerful" (personal interview). The effect of Jaar's work lies in the interplay between image and text. Of the twenty-one photographic installations that form Jaar's Rwanda Project, perhaps the best known is the one entitled *The Eyes of Gutete Emerita.* Gutete Emerita witnessed before her own eyes her husband and two sons being hacked to death with machetes as the family attended mass. Jaar met Emerita when she returned to the scene of the massacre to find the bodies of her family.

The artwork consists of a series of slides, the first three containing words that detail the brutal killings of this woman's husband and sons. The last slide dwells solely on her eyes, that look hauntingly out at us. It is after we have registered the horrors that this woman has witnessed, told to us in Jaar's words, that her eyes fall on us. Jaar's work is at once an indictment of the cruelty of what happened in Rwanda and an indictment on the indifference that we, the largely Western viewers and erstwhile uncaring onlookers of Rwanda's tragedy, showed at the time. When we look into them, as Jaar induces us to, we almost see ourselves reflected in the very eyes that had witnessed horror and where the very perpetrators of the murders were once reflected. It was as if, by witnessing the death of her family, Gutete Emerita had become an eye-witness for the whole of Rwanda. In turn, she also became the eyes of a nation that turned to question those who had betrayed her in her time of need.

To look closely at this image of Gutete's eyes is to realize that Jaar presents them to us in the guise of an image that is still within the frame of the negative, film that has yet to be processed. Gutete's eyes remain locked in the box, within the confines of the anteroom of the camera, still repressed from the light of the world and yet filled with the raw colour of pain, a metaphor for her history that has been barred from articulation. In this sense, this is not an image of Gutete's eyes, but in fact an image of the absence that ensues from our refusal to look at her or to dwell on her trauma. What is more, Gutete's eyes become, for us, *the* sole reference points for the trauma she experienced; at the same time, her gaze upon us is the very antithesis of the absence of willing witnesses to Rwanda's horrors. In this sense, Gutete's eyes become a vehicle of trauma, insistently attempting to relay its haunting to those who refused to look or acknowledge. As Barthes says in the opening passage of *Camera Lucida*, "I am looking at the eyes that looked at the emperor" (1982, 3). Barthes thus underlines the fact that photographs bring with them a paradoxical sense both of proximity and distance. They act as windows that link us to what lies around and beyond the subject of the image.

In considering the links between art and trauma, it is important to take note of this distance, for art, as Mieke Bal reminds us, is inevitably belated in its response to the traumatic event (Reinhardt, Edwards and Duganne 2007). Furthermore, the traumatic event can never be repro-duced by art. The photograph is thus unable to represent trauma – for trauma must be seen as the rupture of coherence and rationality that eludes and defies all representational structures and systems, be these linguistic or visual. To quote Cathy Caruth, trauma "is always the story of a wound that cries out, that addresses us in the attempt to tell us of a reality or truth that is not otherwise available. This truth, in its delayed appearance and its belated address, cannot be linked only to what is known, but also to what remains unknown in our very actions and language" (Caruth 1996, 4). Indeed, the artwork itself is the result of the aftershocks of trauma, and as such cannot be seen to engender it in any way. This image of Gutete's eyes is only that – i.e., an image, a re-presentation of eyes that bear the imprint of trauma. By looking into Gutete's eyes, we do not see her. We see only an abstraction of her suffering distilled in her eyes made clear to us by the (con)text. At the same time, the image makes us acutely aware of the impossibility of us ever really knowing her pain or making it ours. When we look into her eyes, we of the global hegemony, we are also looking into the abyss of our collective neglect.

What then, one may well ask, is the point of Jaar's work? To what extent and to what ends can art draw upon trauma to construct a politics for the unvoiced? In what way can an art installation, or even twenty-one art installations, mitigate the losses of a conflict as great as Rwanda's? How can resolution be reached via images and text produced in the aftermath of conflict? Speaking in visual terms, this resolution or clarity that is sought is not one of trauma itself, but of absence, silence and repression, of tacit consent to violence.

In order to understand Jaar's work, we need to seek a conceptual framework within which a nexus between art and experience can be established. In this context, Jill Bennett reminds us that

[T]rauma-related art is best understood as *transactive* rather than *communicative*. It often touches us, but it does not necessarily communicate the "secret" of personal experience. To understand its transactive nature, we need to examine how affect is produced within and through a work, and how it may be experienced by an audience coming to the work. (Bennet 2005, 7)

Crucial here, when exploring the transactive nature of trauma-related art, is the idea of aesthetics, understood as a field that negotiates the sentient with the logical or rational. If such artwork has historical and political value, then this derives from the way in which affective responses to artwork can be translated into conceptual engagement. What is more, in considering the affective or sentient, we need to distinguish it from the sentimental. Jaar's work, in my view, does not seek to arouse sympathy; nor does it seek to foster a sense of identification between us, as viewers, and Gutete, as subject. Indeed, the very fact of her gaze upon us underscores the separation between her and us, for without this space of difference the artwork cannot function. Nor does the photographic installation portend to be anything more than a form of diffusing an account of events. However, it does so, in contrast to dominant media, not by profiling large-scale events in neutral language: one thinks here of commonly heard phrases such as "collateral damage" or, in the context of Rwanda, "a million dead", three words claiming to encompass a million different lives. Instead, Jaar's work diffuses information by deliberately targeting the sentient in viewers. It homes in on the tragedy of a single person and transforms that individual's trauma into one that represents the trauma of an entire people. Furthermore, the point of Jaar's photographic installation is, in fact, to jar the viewer.

Numerous viewers have mentioned the physicality of their responses to Gutete's eyes. David Levi Strauss, for instance, talks of how he felt physically ill and nauseous when he encountered the installation. He states, "I felt dizzy and almost retched. I don't know why this happened, but it did" (Levi Strauss 2003, 97). This response to the artwork via the body is extremely important. It is not an abstract response to an abstract image, but rather a bodily or material response to an abstract image. This materiality of response, the impulse to retch that Levi Strauss felt or the nausea that swept over him, is the stirring of historical and political potential. For politics to be real, and by this I mean experienced, as opposed to thought about or talked about, it needs to be less an ideology encountered conceptually than a lived experience that attacks the neutrality of the viewer and forces a response that is involuntary and non-rational. The artwork that is political affects the viewer despite himself, and not thanks to his preconceptions. Indeed, it is the materiality of bodily or sentient response that then engenders a specific line of thinking. Furthermore, if the viewer is shaken by the artwork, this is not because she or he somehow feels the subject's trauma. In this sense, artwork does not transmit trauma, as such, or convey it, for trauma, by definition, remains elusive to representation and relay. Rather, artworks such as *The Eyes of Gutete Emerita* must be seen as primarily performative. They incite a kind of embodied perception in the viewer, not through the "telling of", but through a sensory assault that shakes the viewer out of her or his complicity. For artworks that speak from trauma can be thought of only in terms of a temporal tension, that of the past traumatic context that produced the work and the relative peace and quiet of the present. In this sense, the artwork does not relay the traumatic experience, but it does convey a mini-shock of trauma generated by this temporal collision. This mini-shock can also be viewed as a mild after-shock, staged with care but material in effect. If it affects the body, then it also affects the mind. It does not convey information or "teach" us anything as such, but it propels us into a mode of uncertainty. Momentarily, but in a very sentient way, the equilibrium of our lives has been upset. We wonder why. As David Levi Strauss states of his response to Jaar's work, "I don't know why this happened."

It is curious to note in this context that trauma is a borderline experience. For the victims of trauma always encounter it in the violence of contact with the world outside, and yet its impact is most acutely felt internally. So too do the temporal contrasts of such artwork present borderlines between what is known and understood and the bewildering silence of what has not been articulated and what transgresses the logic of human understanding. What emerges upon a contemplation of the idea of trauma is the question, "Why?" This borderline is the space of uncertainty from which critical enquiry can emerge. With trauma-related artworks such as this, the viewer first feels the force, not of the experience of trauma itself, but of its million subsequent reverberations that course through the body and force a questioning to explode within the viewer, led thus to conceptualize and interrogate the experience. And in this interrogation lie the stirrings of an ethically and politically necessary articulation of repressed history. These are the after-images that scatter through space, so that personal history is propelled into the wider collective realm across the uneven and unfair divisions of global power: the images or memories both spoken and visualized of Auschwitz, Vietnam, Guantánamo, Abu Ghraib and so many more that repeat in the anterooms of our collective imagination, images that bring with them disquiet.

Cultural representations inevitably lag behind the event. As we dwell here on the idea of testimony in the context of post-conflict cultures, we face a conundrum whereby culture is by definition a field of re-presentation, contestation and struggle, but also, it would seem, inevitably delayed and even removed in its ability to narrate or make sense of conflicts. At the same time, the notion of post-conflict cultures posits the spectral force of past conflicts onto culture in the here and now, somehow complicating temporal experience by drawing the past out and scattering it in the realm of the present. Thus the "post-" indicates not merely that which is posterior, but rather the ricocheting tremor of past moments and events in the present. It indicates the incessant return of shadows and traces that infiltrate memory and identity, all the more forcefully when repressed. It underlines the persistence of sight, even when turning a blind eye. Few cultural media capture this contradiction as well as photography: in always lagging behind the event or the moment, in their interjections into the here and now across space and time, photographs are spectral in their play of absence and presence. For this very reason, they draw into the present shards of memory seized, as Walter Benjamin (2007, 255) stated of the past, "as an image which flashes up at the instant when it can be recognized and never seen again". Thus, photographs are the result of crises, tokens of death and loss that force us to come face to face with our own existential pathos. In this sense, the image is always an after-image, a shadowy trace of that which was or might have been, uncertain and ambiguous, always short of articulation, but also stubborn and persistent. Unfinished and lingering, it is also always uncertain, unresolved, in the interrogative. Despite the brief text that accompanies the image, *The Eyes of Gutete Emerita* does not provide us with historical understanding of Rwanda's tragedy. Instead, what this artwork does is to carve a space within the frame from which a questioning of our silence and our absence may begin.

References

Ávila Laurel, J. T. (2008). "Cuando tu tierra te expulse". Unpublished lecture.

Bal, M. (2007). "The Pain of Images". In M. Reinhardt, H. Edwards and E. Duganne (eds.). *Beautiful Suffering: Photography and the Traffic in Pain*. Chicago: University of Chicago Press, 93-115.

Barthes, R. (1982). *Camera Lucida*. New York: Hill and Wang.

Benjamin, Walter. (2007). *Illuminations*. New York: Shocken Books.

Bennett, J. (2005). *Empathetic Vision: Affect, Trauma and Contemporary Art*. Stanford: Stanford University Press.

Caruth, C. (1996). *Unclaimed Experience: Trauma, Narrative and History*. Baltimore and London: Johns Hopkins University Press.

Cembrero, I. (2008). "Escribir contra el pasado". *El País (Revista Verano)*, 2, 4 August.

Elaine Sciolino, E. (1994). "For West, Rwanda Is Not Worth the Political Candle". *New York Times,* 15 April.

Gatore, G. (2008). *La passé devant soi.* Paris: Editorial Phébus.

Hoggart, S. **www.//query.nytimes.com/gst/fullpage.html?res= 9A00E3DA1F38F936A15756C0A96258260&sec=&spon=&p agewanted=all**, accessed 5 May 2008.

Jaar, A. (2003). *The Eyes of Gutete Emerita*, part of *The Rwanda Project.* Art installation.

Levi Strauss, D. (2003). *Between the Eyes: Essays on Photography and Politics.* New York: Aperture Foundation.

Nandy, N. (2002). "Obituary of a Culture", **www.indiaseminar. com/2002/513/513%20ashis%20nandy.htm**, accessed 8 May 2008.

Ricoeur, P. (2004). *Memory, History, Forgetting.* Chicago and London: University of Chicago Press.

Salgado, S. Personal interview, Gallery 32, London, 10 September 2007.

United Nations Press Release, SG/SM/6552, 6 May 1998. New York: UN Press Office.

Photographs of Suffering: Women and Children Between Stereotypes, the Obscene and the Traumatic

Cristina Demaria

The Testimonial Vocation of Photography: the Image "takes sides"

This study is part of a larger project on photographs which document, and represent, pain and suffering caused by traumas and catastrophes, both natural and man-made.[1] It is, therefore, an explorative reflection which will focus on specific and limited aspects of a broader investigation on the testimonial vocation of photography. I shall attempt to discuss this vocation within a particular and, indeed, complex and fragmented, sub-genre of photography, in its turn defined and transformed by the medium and the context in which it is consumed, that is, photo-reportage once it is produced by, and also produced for, and re-produced on, international humanitarian NGOs' websites. The main aim of the latter is not only to document, to inform their public about the existence and conditions of victims of conflicts, famine, floods, but also to affect the viewers, to move their awareness and conscience in order, possibly, to make them act, do something, such as donating money or subscribing to the organization. How do these pictures affect the – possibly already concerned – viewer? How do they represent traumatized victims? Are there specific visual *topoi*, recurrent poses? And how do they bear witness to the victims' predicaments?

I have selected a sample of photographs from the so-called photo-galleries and photo-essays which constitute many pages of the websites of NGOs such as Amnesty International, Human Rights Watch, The Red

---

[1] It is a project carried out by a group of people from TraMe, a Centre for the Study of Cultural Memories and Traumas of the Department of Philosophy and Communication Studies of the University of Bologna (TraMe 2011). More generally speaking, it must be recalled that the representation of human disgrace does not start with photography, and can be traced back to medieval miniatures that used to illustrate catastrophes such as famine and epidemics, then to Renaissance painting such as those of Bruegel the Elder who pictured beggars, fools, crippled men, up to engravings of gypsies, beggars and of the disasters of war by Jacques Callot and the paintings of Goya.

Cross, UNICEF, Médecins Sans Frontières, Emergency,[2] choosing those which portray women and children, in order to question their peculiar documental nature; also, in order to investigate whether these pictures, besides portraying particular categories of victims, offer a glimpse into their traumas or else enter the realm of the "obscene".

I would like, therefore, to interrogate the many facets of the documental, since to document means to give evidence, to prove, but also to teach, to inform and, possibly, to transform (Solomon-Godeau 1991; see also Criqui 2010). The documentary presents an interpretative structure, an attribute which can be used also to refer to something animated by an exhortative impulse, by a humanistic wish to ameliorate. But to what, then, is the category of documentary opposed, or opposable, to? Expressive? Aesthetic? Abstract? Poetic? And might that which could be called obscene be judged, nevertheless, as documentary? Moreover, is it still the case that what constitutes a proof (of a traumatic event and its aftermath) should not be aesthetically pleasant, even if what is being aestheticized – with the use, for example, of black-and-white photography, of shadows and shades – is something shocking?

These are questions that, in their turn, undermine the complex opposition between witnessing and reporting "reality", and aesthetically re-presenting it. Photography, before the advent of digital technologies, was semiotically defined as an indexical trace,[3] as an evidence of what *has been there*, in front of the camera, a memory trace or, better, a potential trace for both individual and collective memory. The indexical power of photography, along with its status as a form of art, has been the subject of endless debates. Notwithstanding the possibility of manipulation, photographs, especially when they are meant to report, are still

[2] For the purposes of this analysis I considered the websites of Amnesty International, Human Rights Watch, The Red Cross, Médecins Sans Frontières, Emergency and UNICEF. As for the kinds of picture I have considered, they always migrate on the Internet, and are never only on one single website. They can also be found published in different and more traditional media. However, choosing the NGO websites allows me to locate those pictures of trauma in a specific discursive genre, facilitating also a comparative analysis of the corpus.

[3] The debate on the semiotic status of photography is huge and impossible to synthesize: what does it mean for a photograph to be an index? And how does it change in the digital era? Seminal works on this subject have been those of Rosalind Krauss (Krauss 1990; 1993). See also Del Marco and Pezzini (2011); Floch (1986); Mitchell (1986); and Elkins (2007).

considered to produce a "testimonial effect" and affect, the truth of which is probably not about "facts" but about the sharing or the authentication of different experiences: that of the observer, the photographer as a witness, that of the portrayed subject, and that of the viewer. In other words, they also question the opposition between the supposedly objectifying nature of a document such as a photograph and the subjectifying and, ultimately, idiosyncratic stance of the photographic enunciation.

Photography, for Susan Sontag (2003; 1977), is always an image that somebody has chosen, and to frame means to focalize, but also to exclude, to take a side, a position within a scene. One could argue, along with Georges Didi-Huberman (2009; 2010), who revisits Walter Benjamin's position, that every image, notwithstanding the boundaries within which the genre operates, take sides, thanks, also, to its montage, to the enunciative chain in which it is placed, to the series – in our case the other pictures in the gallery, the other images on the website, in which it intervenes, the different contexts through which it travels and is "translated". Nowadays, thanks to the new technologies and the internet, images are very rarely read and interpreted as single texts: they circulate and are manipulated within a complex and multi-layered mediatic intertextuality and intervisuality (Mirzoeff 2002; see also Botler and Grusin 1999), producing every time different affect and effects. In the examples I have chosen, the websites function as a peculiar enunciative *dispositif* which acts back onto the meaning of the single picture, thus contributing to the construction of a more complex discourse on pain and its documentation.[4] I would like to argue, hence, that the privileged place occupied by the work of the documentary within a rhetoric of immediacy starts to show its limits and flows. It is part of a more complex practice of which I shall consider but a very limited and circumscribed example.

Social Photography

The rhetoric of immediacy of a visual document is actually already questioned by the characterization of the broader kind of genre to which the pictures I have selected can be referred, that is social reportage or, better, social photography, a committed form of investigative photo-

[4] Again, see Sontag (2003), but also the work of Luc Boltanski (1992) on how not only photography but also different kinds of media public discourses might adopt diverse strategies, which he calls "topics", of triggering compassion.

graphy which deals with social problems not only to document and report them, but also to denounce them and, possibly, partially to solve them (Christolhomme 2010).[5] The "romantic" critics define social photography as the sensitive eye of history (Mauro 2007), a practice that produces images whose function is not only to portray what is there, but also to focalize our gaze on a reality that very often we want to avoid, or that we are not used to. Its role is to make us *see* people whom otherwise, without its intercession, we would not see. How the "intercession" of this photography works is what is at stake here, that is, its role of mediation between us and the distant, suffering others.[6] Social photography is, therefore, a genre built on the declared goal of changing the limits of our compassion, duties and responsibilities. It is in this sense that the social photographer, again, is someone who takes a side, a side that acquires an ethical dimension, becoming a form of political denunciation and sensitization. He or she does not only desire to render visible what would

[5] The photographers who, so to speak, inaugurated the genre have been Jacob A. Riis (1849-1914), famous for his images of the misery of New York slums, and Lewis Hine (1874-1940), who was, in the first place, a sociologist, notable for his pictures of immigrants arriving at Ellis Island. Equally important was the group of photographers who called themselves the FSA (Farm Security Administration), which lasted from 1935 to 1943, amongst them Dorothea Lange. The FSA was a federal agency whose main objective was that of "informing" public opinion on people's state of indigence and needs. They worked also to legitimate the actions taken by the Roosevelt administration. Another important milestone for the evolution of the genre was the exhibition, *The Family of Man*, alongside its notorious "catalogue", which took place at the Museum of Modern Art in New York in the mid 1950s. One of the slogans chosen by the curators of the exhibition was a quotation from Virgil: "Which region of the world is not full of calamities?". See Cristolhomme (2010).

[6] It goes without saying that social photography has benefited from the technical improvements and progresses that have punctuated the whole history of photography, in particular the history of photography as a means of communication, as a medium: the invention of mobile cameras, of more powerful lenses, etc. Especially in the nineteen-thirties, a transformation of the means of production and of distribution took place which radically changed the market. It is the same period in which the first snapshots are taken, demonstrating the medium's potentiality to render "the eternity of the instant", as Henry Cartier Bresson said; but this is also the period when illustrated magazines underwent a renaissance, with the birth of *Life* and *Picture Post*, in which the first photo-essays were published (similar to the ones we now find on the websites) and the practice of photo-journalism was fully developed.

normally remain invisible but also to have it talk back, to give it a voice. In social photography, we find the inscription of the very practice of bearing witness, a pragmatic dimension that will have, of course, to be accepted and welcomed depending on the viewer. It is a dimension that maintains a very ambiguous character, because it is always already inscribed not only in a cognitive process of communication (we want you, the viewer, to know that this is a reality which otherwise you will never see), but also in texts dominated by a will to make people feel, to render the audience sensitive, to change their attitude in a world dominated by an excessive exposure to images. This can cause compassion fatigue (Moeller 1999), that is, the hypothesis that a continual coverage of distant suffering causes audiences, and even journalists themselves, to lose interest even if the suffering continues.

Social photography is a militant practice, the goal of which is to bear witness to the plights of the victims and to participate in their recovery, in the resolution of what has caused them to be victims, in itself an investigation either on a social issue or, also, on the forms of intervention, actions and reactions triggered by this issue, in order to communicate it, its realization depending on a preliminary work of investigation and on the specific social actors and organization involved, adjusted to the fragility of the victims (Christolhomme 2010).

This genre has been labeled also as "straight photography", "humanitarian photography", "concerned photography", straight photography marking the distance – in the history of photography, with pictorialism,[7] that is, from an artistic pictorial-driven way to think of photography as an art detached from the world, and opening the path to social photography, to a concerned and "realistic" method of documenting "reality" with a new medium, as with the seminal picture of the blind woman taken by Paul Strand in 1916 (Marra 2001). In other words, photography began to be looked at as, also, a way to be committed to the "world", most of all, to its documentation. Concerned photography, is a term coined by Cornell Capa (1918-2008) when in 1965 he started, in New York, the International Foundation for Concerned Photography

[7] *Pictorialism* was a photographic trend that developed at the end of the nineteenth century affirming the "artistic" status of photography, comparing it to painting. While in the beginning this comparison gave photography an artistic status, it later showed its limitation, photography being treated as an "imitation" of painting (Marra 2001).

(Christolhomme 2010), in order to sustain the ethical commitment within the practice of photo-journalism: not only to document reality, but to change it through images. Portraying reality and documenting it, in this wide and *cangiante* genre,[8] is therefore mingled and mixed with the already mentioned exhortative impulse that is part of a documentary stance that is not limited to its "concerns" with the production or, better, the spasmodic search of reality effects, with the will to create a specific style. This was already clear in the mid-thirties, at the beginning of this practice when Roy Starker, the director of the FSA, stated:

> Documentary photography is but a way to access things, it is not a technique – its style does not imply a denial of plastic elements, which are and remain the essential criterion of every picture. The "documentary" style gives these elements a frame, a direction: the fineness of lines, the nitidity of image, the use of particular filters, the feeling. All these components, implied in the very vague notion of quality, serve a specific goal: to speak in the most eloquent way about the chosen subjects, and to do it through images. (Mauro 2007, xvii-xviii)

It is quite obvious, then, how social photography maintains what we could label as a narrative aim, even before it starts *speaking*: its gaze is already charged, its subjects and situations selected because of their values and identities. Also quite evident is the way in which its founding values and "ideology" can be compared to those animating NGOs, in themselves institutions that want to give voice to violence and abuses, to intervene in order to help the victims of violence and catastrophes and, possibly, to change people's awareness and sensitivity. In social photography, and in its use by the NGOs, in the way images are organized and exploited, becoming part of complex syncretic texts, there emerges an author, who desires to be involved and committed, who interpellates the audience; who, also, tries, possibly, to create it, to have the image speak to a public that the image is, at the same time, positioning as concerned viewers.

However, be it social, humanitarian or concerned, this kind of photography has a very long and interesting history which we cannot

---

[8] *Cangiante* is one of four canonical Renaissance modes of painting, along with *Unione, Chiaroscuro, Sfumato.*

trace here in its entirety, but which shows how the relationship between human rights and photography is indeed very closely knit. The first American political intervention labelled as humanitarian was indeed provoked by the world-wide circulation of pictures that witnessed the slaughter inflicted by the Belgian King Leopold II on the Congolese people. This circulation was, in its turn, permitted by the invention of a new technology, the Kodak film. From this scandal up to the Universal Declaration of Human Rights the discourse on these rights and their violation finds in photography – in the circulation of the visual experience of atrocity – its point of reference.

The violation of a right comes through a violation of a body, and the medium that can best witness it is photography, that is, a picture that supposedly registers the suffering of a body which has been deprived of its humanity. And in such a history another important group of actors participated, those moral entrepreneurs who took the responsibility of safeguarding human rights, or of alleviating the pain, the NGOs. In other words, photography may retrace, or better, to quote Parvati Nair, "expose" traces that have the power to infiltrate memory and identity. And photography of victims of pain and suffering might underline "the persistence of sight, even when turning a blind eye". Most importantly, their being social does not cancel out their spectral dimension. Nair's argument needs to be quoted at length:

Few cultural media capture this contradiction as well as photography: in always lagging behind the event or the moment, in their interjections into the here and now across space and time, photographs are spectral in their play of absence and presence. For this very reason, they draw into the present shards of memory seized, as Walter Benjamin stated of the past, "as an image which flashes up at the instant when it can be recognized and never seen again". Thus, photographs are the result of crises, tokens of death and loss that force us to come face to face with our own existential pathos. In this sense, the image is always an after-image, a shadowy trace of that which was or might have been, uncertain and ambiguous, always short of articulation, but also stubborn and persistent. Unfinished and lingering, it is also always uncertain, unresolved, in the interrogative. (2009, 34; this volume, 227)

Nair's words are here linked to a single picture she is analyzing, *The Eyes of Gutete Emerita*, which portrays the gaze of a woman who survived the Rwandan genocide, made by the Chilean artist Alfredo Jaar. She is supposedly dealing with a work of art, and not social photography, but is it really the case? Besides the fact that in many NGOs' photo-galleries we do find images signed by photographers who are also considered as artists, my argument is that, when an image bears witness to suffering, the boundaries between social and aesthetic effects are indeed substantially blurred: the social and concerned context represented by the NGOs' discourse does not exclude, in many cases, powerful aesthetic and, also, aesthetic-documental effects guiding our – the viewers' – possible gaze and commitment, forcing us, to go back to the above quotation, to "come face to face with our own existential pathos".

Here we find again one of the questions with which I began: does visual evidence have to be aesthetically unpleasant? Does the very category of document have to be contrasted with that of fiction not as something fake, but as that which has been made, created, adding other *strata* to the palimpsest of the "real"? Further, in this blurring of categories and discourses, what do some of these images tell us, in the end, about the victims' stories and identities, about their position and positioning? How do they re-open their stories or, on the contrary, close them within a fixed, stylized and stereotypical, iconography of suffering?

Designated Victims: Types and Stereotypes

Amongst the hundreds of images available in the already mentioned websites, between images that are variously classified and thematized within photo-essays and photo-blogs,[9] I shall concentrate on two typologies of victims with an initial sort of fixed thematic (and emotional) role: women and children, the victims *par excellence*, the designated ones, even if, as we shall see, they are not the same kind of victims, if we

---

[9] The way the NGOs' websites frame different images in their photo-blogs, photo-essays and photo-galleries is indeed varied: sometimes they are grouped depending on a specific conflict or catastrophe (the earthquake in Haïti, the conflict in Congo) of which they compose a sort of dossier; at other times they are divided following the kinds of subjects depicted: women, children, landscapes, even "nature".

look at their subject and actantial positioning.[10] My analysis, then, does not focus on the particularity of the discourse of a specific NGO, but on the transversal imaginary which is produced by these organizations on these victims, an imaginary which, also, dialogues with the broader imaginary built on the founding images of this genre, as, for example, the following picture made by Dorothea Lange, a member of the FSA in the

nineteen-thirties.

Fig. 1

My intention is, also, to investigate the migration, translation, and transfiguration of semiotic visual models and configurations of the suffering victim: how have these models changed? Is there a sort of iconography that we can re-trace when looking at women and children, or at women with children? Women and children are designated victims because they are those who normally survive, but with no means actually to succeed, with no value left as, depending on specific cultures and ways

[10] This is a narratological category that refers to the role played by a subject – or by an object – of a narrative. It refers to its function in the narrative: is he/she the one who has the agency? Is he/she the one who is the passive object or the active subject? It has to do with the subject positioning every discourse displays.

of life, widows; those who were already fragile, dominated, unconscious, innocent, as children, human beings with no guilt. And the women are direct victims because, in times of conflict and post-conflict, they are raped, they still die in, and of, labour, they spend their meagre existence in refugee camps, deprived of their citizenship, with no water, electricity, no social, cultural and human rights. They are victims since their condition and their silence are very seldom recognized: their wordless state is not simply what adds up to their predicament, but what constitutes them as a victim (Escobar 1997). Women and children, hence, seem to represent, *a priori*, before an image, a photograph, attempts to have them speak, the unarmed, the defenceless, that is whoever has experienced the horror. Horror is a "passion" from which one cannot escape, that dis-figures, dis-faces, the victim, as Adriana Cavarero maintains(Cavarero 2007). The physics of horror has to do with the reaction to a kind of violence which does not merely kill people, but also destroys the uniqueness of their bodies and rages against their constitutive vulnerability. Horror is a violence that undoes the already wounded bodies, and she who is thus "produced" is forever marked by having witnessed her own disintegration. This is why horror is an effect of dis-*figuration* (Cavarero 2007, 17). How are silence and horror eventually "spoken" and visually translated?

The role of the woman as the desperate survivor left alone to contemplate the dead, and having to come to terms with a very uncertain future, emerges quite strongly from the following image, which is complemented by a very long caption. It is a picture signed by Moises Saman for Human Rights Watch (HRW) and it is accompanied by a text which does not refer to what the image depicts, but to the more general context which caused that death and victimized that woman.

INTRODUCTION

Violence erupted on June 10 when hundreds of Uzbeks gathered near a dormitory in the center of Osh, Kyrgyzstan, allegedly in response to recent scuffles between Uzbeks and Kyrgyz. Human Rights Watch researchers working in southern Kyrgyzstan from June 10 to 22 documented the subsequent massive looting and destruction of civilian property and widespread acts of violence by Kyrgyz and Uzbek mobs in the city of Osh and the towns of Jalal-Abad and Bazar-Kurgan. While both ethnic Kyrgyz and Uzbeks fell victim to the violence, Uzbek neighborhoods were particularly affected as mobs of ethnic Kyrgyz, many of them reportedly from villages surrounding the city of Osh, repeatedly attacked Uzbek areas. Photographs by Moises Saman for Human Rights Watch.

Fig. 2

What is rendered explicit is the role of HRW as the *destinant* and the helper (the alternative power) which has sent its "researcher" to document the explosion of violence in Kyrgyzstan, condensed in the picture of a corpse of a young man assisted, probably, by the desolate mother, an image which tells us of the deplorable consequences of war, of the woman alive having survived the fallen. The pictured space, the interior of a house, is also another recurrent figure of this kind of ambience-landscape that surrounds the victims, and of the more general role played by the represented space as an *actant* of the narrative that these texts want to tell. In trying to find how the gaze and the body of such victims have been captured, how their body as destroyed landscapes, as emblems of violence, have been rendered as images (and therefore, the kind of gaze which defines these landscapes and creates such images), I have initially tried to assess, beyond the official classification given by the website (specific tragedies or conflicts, dossiers, topics of the photo-blog), whether there was any recurrent composition of the victims-actors: how they appeared, and in which pose. It is not, of course, a definitive semiotic typology or classification. What is of interest to me is the ways in which such compositions of different subjects and of their relation to the viewer, with other subjects and with the surrounding space, enter particular visual narratives; how the figurative and also figural, metaphorical elements of the image work, the kind of inscribed interpellation they propose and the possible effects they might trigger.

What do we find, then? We find portraits of solitary, lonely women whereby the place and/or the situation surrounding them maintains very little or no relevance, as in this portrait of an old Congolese woman.

Fig. 3

The focalization is on her face and the upper body, on her big, yet knotty and bony, hands, on a single victim enclosed, wrapped up in her desolation. However, her pain is somehow recognized, her dignity, her composure, returned, even restored, by this black-and-white picture. In similar portraits of solitary women we happen to encounter the kind of interpellation inscribed in this image, that is, of the relationship between the viewer and the represented subject: from the point of view of who is seen, frontal, but very seldom open and direct. Often, the gaze slips away, escapes; or it is lost as if in between worlds, dimensions. The portrait of (a? the?) woman could offer us a direct gaze, she could stare into our eyes, and almost does, but it is as if she is not fully present. If there is a gaze, many times it is dazed, befuddled. These are "portraits" of faces which, apparently, defy some of the characteristics of the genre, that is, to reveal, through the eyes, the soul, to glimpse the face as the sign of a revealed nature. Yet, this face is a landscape of suffering and devastation, of a powerlessness that cannot be exchanged symmetrically with the viewer: we are left to contemplate it.

Portraits come in series together with images of women in transit, refugees of war having to abandon their homes, victims of floods or of earthquakes moving into temporary camps. They are pictures of women inside specific ambiences and landscapes, sometimes of women who become the landscape, melt with it, are confused with it, both of them similarly destroyed.

Fig. 4

Fig. 5

Fig. 6

In these three photographs the relationship between the women and the landscape is obviously rather different. In the first image (Fig. 4), whose chromatic nuances are underlined and heavily saturated, the transit is rendered, paradoxically, through a very still image; also, the women are exoticized via the vibrant colours of both the background and their dresses, the colours of Africa. They almost melt with the background, carrying their few belongings: a stylized pose capturing us because of its plastic elements, the inscribed observer at a safe distance. In Fig. 5, the woman in the front maintains a peculiar relationship with the background, of which she is a silent witness, but to which she also belongs, as in the case of the picture featuring the close-up of the old woman (Fig. 6); or, else, she is a desperate witness, embracing its devastation, showing us her own. If, in Fig. 4, pain and suffering are not made explicit, and we encounter a sort of anaesthetization of the trauma obtained thanks to an exoticizing treatment, in the other two the very framing and construction of a space is marked by a burst of signs of the trauma. It is the landscape *with* the woman that has the task to stage the effective and material devastation: the woman's face, body, expression, becoming part of the landscape, a site of inscription of the destruction, the landscape itself a wounded body. With the use of particular figurative *motifs*, a repertoire of figures, a portion of the world is thus being observed: the rubble, ruins and tears thematizing the wound of the body-landscape, the loss of a stable form and configuration, crumbled and fallen. It is, also, a sort of deformation of the aesthetics of the picturesque, of the stability and continuity of forms, proportions and perspectives. Through a plastic stylization of the landscape and its chromatics, the portrayed subjects absorb the emotional tone of the ambience or, rather, as in the last picture of this series, embrace it: look who I am, what has remained of me, of my place.

However, we encounter also women who are taken care of, hospitalized. What is curious is that it would seem that there are fewer images of women taken care of than images of the same kind where the subject is a child, maybe because often violence against women is less visible, or less effective than that exercised at the expense of children?

Another frequent "composition" is that of the woman with a child, many times a direct quotation of the already cited Dorothea Lange's image of a woman and her son. Of this recurrent figure and motif we find many variations, the first being the portrait which explicitly cites the pictorial images of nativity (Fig. 7). This black Madonna is presented even with the halo, her image in black and white and different shades of grey, her eyes staring at us with a calm and dignified expression, the eyes of her undernourished child pointing to the viewer, with a turning of his torn and tiny body. They are two very different gazes: one resigned, the other alive, profound, yet fragile. Here the distortion of the stereotype of nativity, of its configuration, is rendered by the two contrasting glimpses which, as viewer, we are somehow compelled to give back: not a nativity,

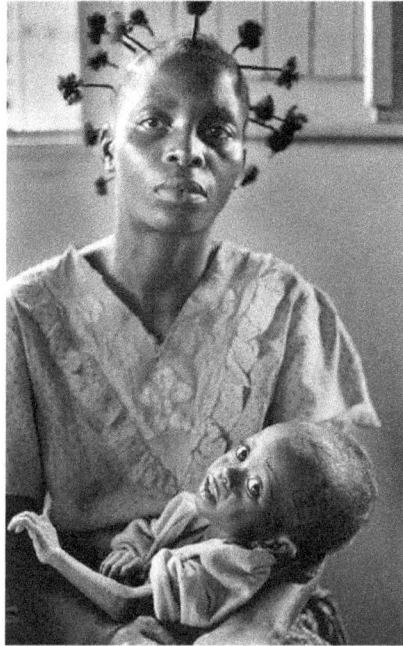

then, but the wish to stay alive.

Fig. 7

Along with this kind of figuration, there are others that portray women as the mothers of wounded children inside a hospital, in a space of care whereby the role of the organization, and of the narrative in which the picture is inscribed, become all the more important: in this case, the one who usually takes care (the woman) is taken care of along with her offspring. In the following image (Fig. 8), though, the place of care is depicted through and with white veiling curtains that mitigate and soften the potential involvement of the viewer. The inscribed observer places us a little bit aside, pointing our gaze to the yellow dress of the mother, the only strongly coloured element of the image, looking at her suffering child. Yet, again, we are not brought inside the picture: the pain is rendered by the position of the body of the child, screened by the thin white gauze.

If we move to the figure of the child, or the children, we encounter photo-galleries that are very often punctuated by the close-up image of the lonely and suffering face of an anonymous black child, contrasted by frequent images, in the following photographs, of the child as being taken care of or who has already been cured and now (he more frequently than she), appears to be serene and, even, looking up at the camera, maybe

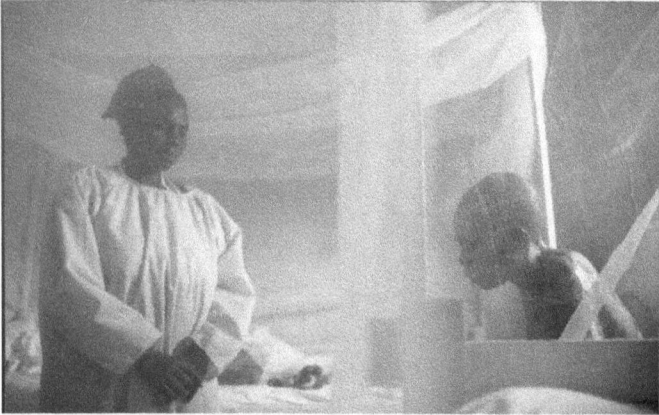

happy.

Fig. 8

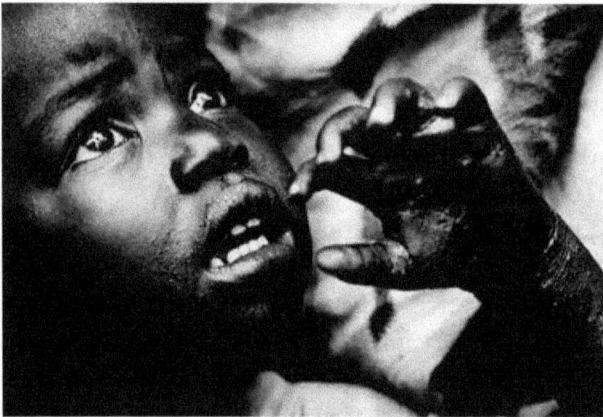

Fig. 9

The contrast between these two images, both present on the websites with different variations, is quite striking, presenting the two stages of a narrative of salvation: the first one existing in an absolute time and space, capturing the face of the innocent and unarmed being whose gaze does not "speak" directly to us, viewers, but to whomsoever is there, to an invisible yet present interlocutor who will have to welcome his request. Fig. 9 is in black and white, with strong and neat chromatic contrast, to stress once again its timeless and eternal demand: not one child, but the child needing help. In Fig. 10, the recovered little child looks at us, spectators, in our turn looking down at him, identifying with the position of the author of the picture, the organization that signs the images with its logo (that of the NGO Emergency). In both cases, we are put in a position of power – that is usually the effect of this kind of camera angle – yet not a negative power to manipulate, but the immense, exhilarating and transcendental power to render, or already having rendered, the defenceless and vulnerable curable, having welcomed his silent request. We witness, from above, his smile: a life over which we still seem to have

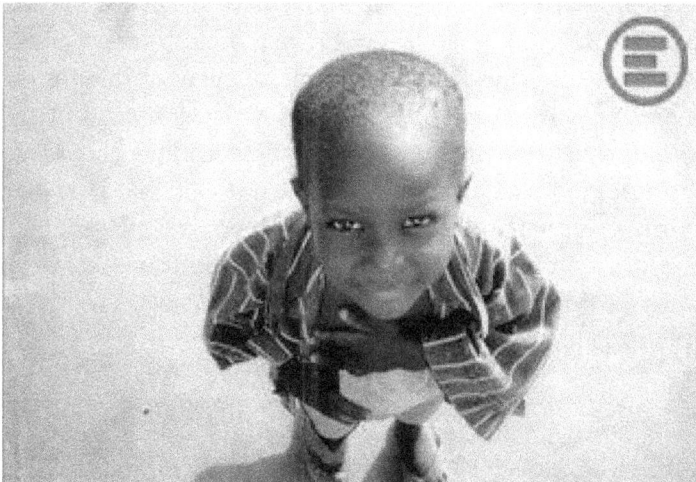

power and control.

Fig. 10

Also in the case of the portrayal of the child, this kind of victim is sometimes surrounded by a destroyed landscape of rubble. But the landscape, the actual physical space of trauma, is less of a frequent figure for children, as if the singularity of the child would prevail over the destruction of the landscape. His/her presence is enough to recall pain. Often, though, we find groups of children, a collective *actant* which interrogates the viewer, frozen in a still pose, diffident, distant, alone, as in the following image from the UNICEF website (Fig. 11). Along with the different plastic and figurative elements of each of these images, is there a particular subject positioning, a narrative value that the portrayed subjects acquire once they are captured in these poses? In other words, is there a configuration underpinning the compositions? In some of the websites on which these images can be found (and in particular in that of Médecins Sans Frontières and HRW) there is no distinction between very different kinds of photographs. The series to which they belong can present an image signed by a very famous author, such as Sebastião Salgado, or Francesco Zizola, world-wide-known photographers, who have directly worked for the NGOs, or have donated their works to such institutions, alongside pictures taken by an amateur, or by one of the volunteers of the organization; black-and-white pictures along with others in colour; there are pictures that would seem to be stolen snapshots, but also, as we have seen, there are demonstrative poses; images that could belong to a coffee-table book on Africa in which the caption alone specifies that the portrayed subjects are victims, and images in which, probably, and I shall soon comment on this, the obscene is *mise-en-scène*. The distinction between authors, styles and the very moment of the picture's production is never made in the photo-gallery of the websites: it looks as if it is of no interest. It looks as if what a single image portrays is not so meaningful: it is the series, the sample (of a condition, of a kind of suffering), that counts, accompanied sometimes by the inscribed authoritative voice of the organization which tries to anchor the possible readings of the image.

Fig. 11

An example of this attitude is the International Red Cross website where, in general, the authorial and interpretative voice of the institution (almost that of an omniscient narrator) prevails, framing the images into tight and specific narratives: what is visible is very much here anchored with what is told, as in the following photograph (Fig. 12), where the caption tells us: "two women ponder on their future". The women are Georgian refugees, their expression not so much pondering but staring into the void, carried by what is happening, flat and lost.

Fig. 12

But in the same series we also find completely different kinds of images, not as flat as the one above. This is the case in the photographs below, built on a play of gazes, the face of an old person mirrored and framed by a window overlooking a place we could not recognize, if it were not for the caption that locates the image in Georgia, just after the conflict with Russia in the summer of 2010 (Fig. 13). The colours are dark and grim, once again the pictured landscape rendering not the trauma but the desolation re-mirrored in the mirrored gaze. Here the pondering is in the image, not in the caption.

Fig. 13

A different case is that of a photo dossier called *Wound*, hosted by the MSF website, dedicated to the never-ending conflict in Congo. The explicit goal of this dossier is to document, of course, but mainly to have the viewer remember the effects of a war nobody is thinking of any longer. In almost all the images black and white dominates, together with an excess of stylization. It is as if, as I anticipated in my opening, the evidence (the document) must be, if not pleasant, at least well-made and constructed. Thus, one could maintain that, when the event is news-worthy (and all the media are covering it), style is of a different kind: the genre of the document is that of reportage, of the stolen risky picture, of the abundance of images. On the other hand, when a situation is lacking attention we have what Luc Boltanski (1992) would probably label as a mixture of the sentimental and the aestheticized modes of possible spectatorship, different topics of the rendering of suffering.[11] In forgotten wars, when there is no wide public debate, no collective enunciative praxis which somehow pre-sensitizes the audience, it is the image with its sublimity, or its obscenity, which talks. "Fiction", in the sense of that which is fabricated, is then not so much a covering, but an un-covering, an un-veiling of what we do not see, but which exists. Appearance works to reveal truth.

---

[11] See note 4. In the sentimental and aestheticized public discourses on suffering, viewers are possibly moved and are pushed to feel compassion through rhetorical strategies centred on emotion and empathy. What is shown and presented to the public are not facts but what Boltanski calls "the heart", via, also, glossy images in which the style acquires a prominent role.

Fig. 14

This is the way which, in this case, an enlarged community of testimony and remembrance is proposed. However, there is more to the image that its plastic and figurative dimensions. In attempting to address how these victims are depicted, it is important to note their narrative roles in the story that the NGO is trying to tell to the audience as its addressee. As already mentioned, the women and the children are not the same kind of victim, and not only for the obvious generational difference, sometimes also a gendered one, even if the child is very often, in these cases, a sort of neutral subject.

A woman seems to be a conscious victim with no power, in the hands of external and alien forces. In some instances, there are images which represent exactly this kind of figure:

Fig. 15

This is a picture used on the Amnesty International website as a cover for the link that, from the home page, directs the visitor to a campaign (and to other images and documents) on "Violence against women". Here it is not the identity of the subjects, or their particular condition, which matters, but their being women in a hostile space: refugees under heavy rain, the umbrella being torn by the wind. Women are subjects very seldom realized as such, that is, as agents, with an agency, with the power to direct their actions. And while the portrait of a solitary woman sometimes tries to give her back some kind of dignity, to re-assign her at least a power of existence (and over her existence), in images in which the space or the landscape prevails, or she/they are seen from the back or, as anticipated, their gaze is lost, the woman seems to play the role of a bridge between us and the represented world. But she is lost, and we lose her. In such examples, the woman appears to act as the object of the image, but not as the object of value, the meaning that is exchanged: in the general discourse of the NGO she is somebody to save (that is, in narratological terms, an object of value), but not in the discourse of the image. There, she is but a left-over of a value, a fragment, an evidence in herself. In some cases, the subject of testimony of somebody else, as in Fig. 16, belonging to the series on the Georgian conflict on the Red Cross website:

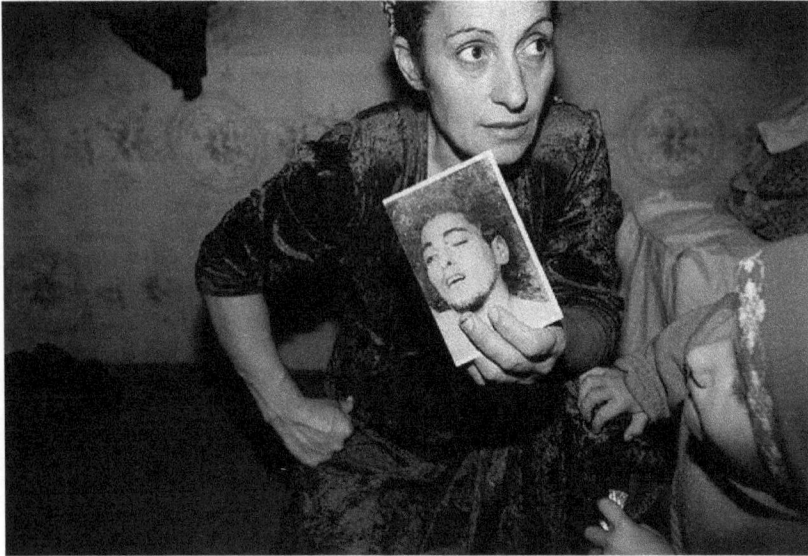

Fig. 16

On the contrary, when the child is portrayed as the innocent and unconscious victim, could it be that his/her image does not constitute the evidence, his/her face the essence of the absolute call for help, since his/her eyes (not always looking at us) result in the *studium*, more than the *punctum*, of the image (to use the terminology of Roland Barthes)?[12] That is what we already, and culturally, recognize, distancing itself from

[12] See Barthes's (1980) seminal work on photography, *Camera Lucida*. The *studium* is what he defines as an interest deprived of intensity. It is what attracts the viewer's attention, triggering his/her curiosity, a field of forces that has cultural connotation. We participate, as spectator of a picture, in something we recognize, that is, the stadium of images composed of figures, expressions, gestures, actions, topics. The *punctum* interrupts the *studium*, it is a wound, an "arrow" that transfixes the observer. It is what (a "point", an element, a sign), in a photograph, *pierces* the viewer.

any sign of trauma, representing the evidence of an evidence that does not shock us, and yet probably should move us, an image of meaningless pain and vulnerability quoted a hundred times?

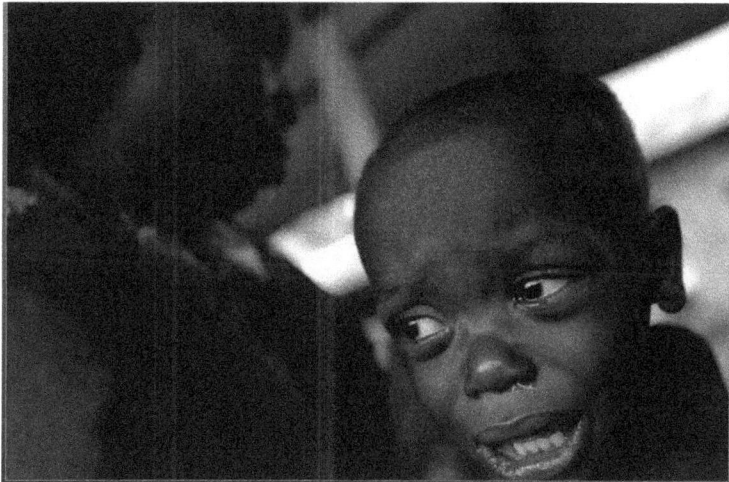

Fig. 17

The child, as an image, seems to play not so much as a subject, but as the object of value that the woman cannot be made to be. He/she is the proposed value, the ultimate value, representing life and/or death; a value the viewer has, of course, to adhere to: life as a potentiality whose exchange value is played in the chain that links the NGO, the images and the viewer and potentially concerned (and not fatigued) viewer-citizens. We are then called to participate in the construction of the very possibility of a subject via the object, in the very possibility of a story and of a value.

The Obscene and the Traumatic
Along with (over) aestheticized images, some of which, if found in another context, would not be ascribed even to the genre of pain, is there still, somewhere, a re-traceable effect of obscenity? Are there pictures that interrupt series of images as does the following one, which looks more like a Benetton advertisement than the portrait of a pregnant young Haïtian woman just after the earthquake which destroyed her country and killed hundreds of people? Pain is here substituted with the pleasure, almost the joy, of being seen, within what Eric Landowsky (1989) would call a *régime de visibilité* (regime of visibility), whereby the viewer finds

herself caught in a malicious play of gazes: I am here and beautiful, I want to be seen. And it does not matter that, in the background, there is not glossy wallpaper but the corrugated iron walls of the hut that is now her

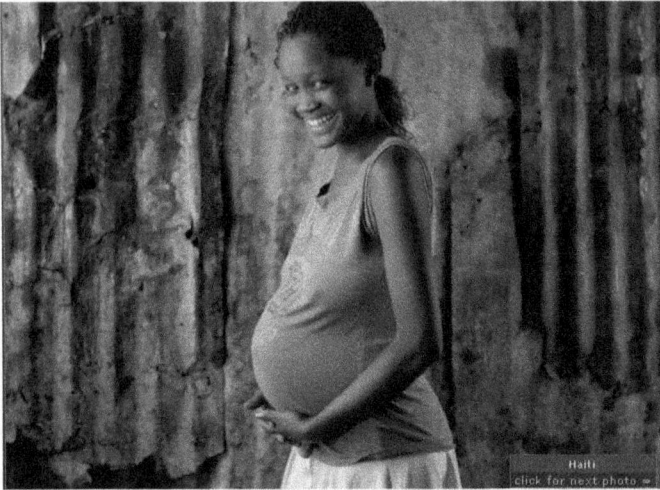

home

Fig. 18

However, what do I mean by obscene? How can we think of it? The obscene (together with pornography) represents what is not proper, appropriate, correct and convenient within a particular moral universe. It is what transgresses and is considered unacceptable for a collective public vision, for a visual morality. And transgression is that thought, expression or act which strays from the straight and narrow, moving beyond conventions; by trans-passing limits, breaking rules, exceeding normative social or cultural constraints, transgression reveals as problematic the everyday negotiations by which both individual and collective identities are formed. However, to judge something obscene and transgressive does not mean to make it disappear. On the contrary, what is valued as obscene is expelled from the channels and the systems of dominant representation only to re-emerge in another place or, better, in the same, but with a specific function. The obscene element functions as the internal exteriority, or, *vice-versa*, as the external interiority, in the eternal game of transgression, which undermines, yet helps to stabilize, every discourse and morality, deciding what is proper. But is the obscene always something that results from a manipulation or, better, from a cultural sanction, to the genre and the practice of the image, and not from the image in itself? Or is the image in itself a non-existent category, especially in the examples I have chosen? And when do we become *voyeurs* looking at these images? Is there such an effect?

The obscene is the perturbing, what disrupts the system of classification, what we cannot understand completely, what we cannot dominate, what makes us lose ourselves, our self-dominance. And to understand does not mean only to comprehend, but also to possess, to recognize and to identify, to be certain of something. In order not to become just bad taste, in order to work as a real perturbing and transgressive element, the obscene must entail the failure (albeit a momentary one) of identification and comprehension processes.

If this is the obscene, then it also refers to an absence, to the failure, too, of the possibility of documenting, to the very possibility of a classified and classifiable memory as a static archive. When effective, the obscene is not disgusting: on the contrary, it allows us not to close our interpretation, it gives us time to meditate. But which of the images I have encountered can have such an effect, or, better, in which could we find a *punctum*, that is, the inscription of at least a fragment of something potentially perturbing, an effect of perturbation that generates an oscillation between figures of the familiar and those of the uncanny?

The obscene, suggests Engle (2009), is what portrays death, always incomplete, yet certain. Violence is not shown, only its effect, and its consequences: a future that is on the point of being accomplished is offered to the view. The obscene regards then a certain rhythm of the image, its aspect, meaning its temporality from the narrative point of view of an inscribed observer: what is it that is going to happen? What has happened and what will continue to happen? And for how long?

The first image overleaf (Fig. 19) is by Sebastião Salgado, and can be found in between some of the glossy pictures I have just shown, its *punctum* representing the lost gaze of the child suspended between life and death, a minuscule body held by the huge hands of a skeletal faceless man. The child is not dead, but he is probably already lost, on the point of disappearing. And this has not yet happened, but it might arrive soon, and that we do not fully know (the website does not provide us with any information): the men are in transit, we do not know from where to where, and it looks like from, and to, a never ending menace.

Below it is another image (Fig. 20), with an aged and consumed woman turning her back to a field of corpses – people killed by cholera in a refugee camp in Congo. If we look at the plastic dimension of the picture, that is, the organizations of its forms, lines, colours and topology, we can detect a plastic rhyme that links her leaning body to the bundled diagonal bodies of the dead ones. We, as spectators, are the only ones having to face death directly: she keeps her eyes closed, the distant people turning their back to the scene. Death has already happened, but, again, it will continue to strike.

Fig. 19

Fig. 20

The next image, on the other hand, is an advertisement (Fig. 21) which uses a photo by Francesco Zizola, commissioned by the Italian branch of Médecins Sans Frontières, and available on their website. The pay-off could be translated as "free examination of your heart"; on the lower side of the image is the number one can use if your heart "functions" and, moved by the picture, you wish to call the NGO to donate money, or time. The verbal text guides the reading in a quite explicit manner, a statement to be read before, and after, looking at the picture: here is the possibility to check your capacity, and your will, to empathize, your ability of and for compassion: how cold can you remain in front of this? The question and, of course, the answer, are left to the viewer, who is put in front of a skeletal body that has lost all of its gender features. The gaze of this young person is transfixed, lightened by a beam coming from above, descending from the upper-left side of the image: it is almost the figure of a mystic who is already in another dimension. Obscene is a body that cannot be controlled any longer, almost already abandoned, that we cannot master, waiting still between life and death. Or is it the use of such a body which is obscene?

Fig. 21

The following (Fig. 22) is an image by the same photographer, part of a dossier he has produced for the same NGO reporting the condition of HIV victims in South Africa. It is the frontal portrait of a mother and daughter, the gender of both actually almost impossible to identify with confidence. From the young one, we get the hallucinated gaze, her proximity to madness. The call of both their gazes is intolerable: it is not a request, it is not a way of saying, here we are, look at us. It is, on the

other hand, an invitation into a horrifying and harrowing world.

Fig. 22

The last image of this study (fig. 23) is very different, also thanks to the caption. We are horrified by this profile which lacks the nose, but the very fact that there is a long text accompanying it, quoting, also, an extract of the collected testimony of the portrayed woman, allows our shock not to become totally perturbing. Here we are back in the realm of the document, of a certain kind of document, with an image that depicts a subject-witness-survivor who decided to act as the evidence of a post-conflict situation (in Rwanda). The living and saved and conscious survivor, the transfigured but controlled body, is acceptable.

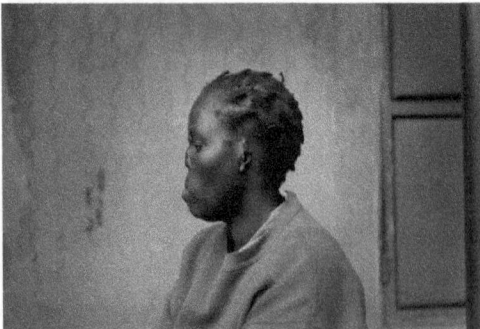

This woman sells vegetables at a local market. She says since the Lord's Resistance Army rebels cut off her nose, ear and upper lip, she has difficulties farming and cannot hear well.

"There's a lot of [government] support for rebels who return. We have been affected [also]. But for those who've done nothing, we get nothing. It's so painful."

Photos by Marcus Bleasdale

Fig. 23

To conclude, one last question. I have discussed the obscene and the perturbing as a possible declination of what Michael Rothberg (2000; see also Caruth 1996) would call "traumatic realism". In these cases it probably still is a document of suffering precisely because of its particular stylization, neither glossy nor direct reportage, but a fictionalization of the real that may capture the trauma. Here we enter another ambivalent dimension, that of the photograph as something in itself spectral and traumatic, as a way to capture time – what has been there, what was there for us to see, and to keep on seeing. Trauma, here, is the unclaimed experience that interrupts the linear continuity of time, the wound that tears apart not only the subject's defences but the possibility of an elaboration. It comes back only as a symptom, shocking us with its obscenity. Photography has been discussed, also, as an "event" that opens up the world, interrupting the sequences and linearity of the time lived and narrated, a possibility that emerges: "photograph not as a frozen moment but as a state of things that photography translates into scenes", whereby our own experience is confronted not with a sequence of connected events, but with an "explosive burst of isolated events" (Baer 2002, 6). This does not mean to deny that photographs beckon viewers to interpret them, triggering narrative impulses, inviting us to make sense by treating each shot as a building-block in a longer story. Yet, this connotative dimension of the photograph "does not entirely drown out the purely deictic statement that each photograph makes. Photographs can capture the shrapnel of traumatic time" (Baer 2002, 6-7).

If we analyze photographs exclusively through establishing the context of their production, we may overlook the constitutive breakdown of context that, in a structural analogy to trauma, is staged by every photograph. Contrasting the commercially viable aestheticization of shock lurking in many pictures of the small sample I have considered, some of these images do manage to move from the act of bearing witness – the mere registration of an event – into how it can be transformed into an act of testimony. In the end, what is seen is not what can be fully owned and known. In the dispossession and radical self-estrangement brought by a trauma, the images, certain images, oscillate between the attempt to bear witness to the unending search for an adequate means of representation, and the self-assuring glossy stereotype, between the performative effect, inciting "a kind of embodied perception in the viewer, not through the 'telling of', but through a sensory assault that shakes the viewer out of her or his complicity" (Nair 2009, 32; this volume, 225), and the confirmation of what we already expect.

References

Baer, U. (2002). *Spectral Evidence: The Photography of Trauma.* Cambridge, MA: MIT Press.

Barthes, R. (1980). *La Chambre claire: Note sur la photographie.* Paris: Gallimard-Seuil. (English translation: *Camera Lucida.* New York: Hill and Wang, 1982).

Boltanski, L. (1992). *La souffrance à distance.* Paris: Éditions Métailié.

Botler, D., Grusin, R. (1999). *Remediation: Understanding New Media.* Cambridge, MA: MIT Press.

Caruth, C. (1996). *Unclaimed Experience: Trauma, Narrative, and History.* Baltimore and London: Johns Hopkins University Press.

Cavarero, A. (2007). *Orrorismi ovvero della violenza sull'inerme.* Milan: Feltrinelli.

Christolhomme, M. (2010). *La Photographie sociale.* Arles: Actes Sud.

Criqui, J-P. (ed.) (2010). "L'image-document, entre realité et fiction", *Les carnets du bal,* 1.

Del Marco, V. and Pezzini, I. (eds.) (2011). *La fotografia: Oggetto teorico e pratica sociale.* Rome: Edizioni Nuova Cultura.

Didi-Huberman, G. (2009). *Quand les images prennent position.* Paris: Les Éditions de Minuit.

Didi-Huberman, G. (2010). *Remontages du temps subi : L'oeil de l'histoire, 2.* Paris: Les Éditions de Minuit.

Elkins, J. (ed.) (2007). *Photography Theory.* New York and London: Routledge.

Engle, K. (2009). *Seeing Ghosts: 9/11 and the Visual Imagination.* Montreal and Kingston: McGill-Queen's University Press.

Escobar, R. (1997). *Metamorfosi della paura.* Bologna: Il Mulino.

Floch, J-M. (1986). *Les Formes de l'empreinte.* Perigueux: Fanlac.

Krauss, R. (1990). *Le Photographique.* Paris: Éditions Macula.

Krauss, R. (1993). *The Optical Unconscious.* Cambridge, MA: MIT Press.

Landowski, E. (1989). *La société réflechie.* Paris: Seuil.

Marra, C. (2001). *Le idee della fotografia : La riflessione teorica dagli anni Sessanta a oggi.* Milano: Mondadori.

Mauro, A. (2007). *Diritti Umani: Cultura dei diritti e dignità della persona nell'epoca della globalizzazione – Documenti fotografici.* Turin: UTET.

Mirzoeff, N. (ed.) (2002). *The Visual Culture Reader*. New York and London: Routledge.

Mitchell, W. J. (1986). *Iconology: Image, Text, Ideology*. Chicago: University of Chicago Press.

Moeller, S. (1999). *Compassion Fatigue: How the Media Sell Disease, Famine, War and Death*. New York and London: Routledge.

Nair, P. (2009). "After-Images: Trauma, History and Connection in the Photography of Alfredo Jaar". In C. Demaria and M. Daly (eds.) (2009), *The Genres of Post-Conflict Testimonies*. Nottingham: Critical, Cultural and Communications Press, 24-35.

Rothberg, M. (2000). *Traumatic Realism: the Demands of Holocaust Representation*. Minneapolis: University of Minnesota Press.

Solomon-Godeau, A. (1991). *Photography at the Dock: Essays on Photography, History, Institutions, and Practices*. Minneapolis: University of Minnesota Press.

Sontag, S. (1977). *On Photography*. New York: Anchor Books.

Sontag, S. (2003). *Regarding the Pain of Others*. London: Penguin.

TraMe (2011). *La forma e l'impronta del dolore: Percorsi nella fotografia della sofferenza*. E/C, 7/8, 157-177. At **www.ec-aiss.it/monografici/7_8_fotografia/7_laboratorio_sei.pdf**, accessed 20 April 2012.

Claudia Di Girólamo and Rodrigo Pérez's *Aquí están*: Little Resistances in the Context of the Fortieth Anniversary Commemoration of the Military Coup in Chile

María José Contreras Lorenzini

In 2013 Chile commemorated the fortieth anniversary of the military coup that ended Salvador Allende's government and began Augusto Pinochet's dictatorship. Throughout 2013 we witnessed an explosion of practices and discourses revolving around our recent past: a plethora of seminars, talks and academic classes; an abundance of acts and homages took place, while in the field of the arts, theatre plays, films and documentaries were produced and broadcast. Public and private museums featured exhibitions related to the last 40 years. Even TV channels scheduled fiction series and documentaries that had as their backdrop precisely the dictatorship years. As Isabel Piper (2013, 1018) states, all of a sudden everyone was talking about the dictatorship: "numerous social actors (movements, organizations and institutions) that on this occasion – as if they did not want to be left out of this trend – organized acts, seminars, film series, issues of journals, cultural gatherings, etc., related to the coup and the dictatorship".[1]

In the context of the fortieth anniversary commemoration, one of the most active fields in the production and circulation of practices and discourses on memory was the arts. Creative expressions have played a very important role both during the dictatorship and in the post-dictatorship, managing to articulate meanings that were marginalized, erased and written out of political and academic discourses (Richard 1998). In the post-dictatorship context, the arts' main role has been one of resistance to official memory, unveiling what has not been said or proposing idiosyncratic and expressive forms to criticize the modes of articulation of hegemonic memory. This critical trend was consolidated in the context of the fortieth anniversary, where, as Caterina Preda (2013, 51) reveals, a series of works of art dealing with memorialization emerged: "Rooted in the dictatorial past [they] raise topics and subjects associated with that very past, unresolved during democracy".

---

[1] Unless otherwise indicated, all translations are my own.

Fig. 1. José Sosa reading Salvador Allende's last speech.
Museo de la Memoria y los Derechos Humanos.

In this effervescent climate, the project *Aquí están* (Here They Are) emerges as an interesting practice for several reasons: first, it is an action that articulates the political by using artistic strategies of intervention. *Aquí están* proposes a complex game between levels of production, reception and circulation of memories that stands out among other works presented in the context of the commemoration. The expressive resources that come together in this intervention are multiple and are mutually nourished: *Aquí están* works with testimonial word, visuality and performativity. This marks a big difference from the great majority of the commemorative artistic pieces that worked within strict disciplinary frameworks, following the modes of expression and canons of each artistic discipline (visual arts, theatre, dance, cinema, documentaries, etc.). On the other hand, the intervention has an intergenerational aspect that proposes an ongoing and necessary discussion on how the memory of the dictatorship is transferred to new generations. All in all, the dialogue (or the dispute) between the stage of the Museo de la Memoria and *Aquí están* presents two modalities of the commemorative work: on the one hand, the "museumification" of memory; on the other, the less ambitious but always effective creation of a contextual and local practice of memory.

Aquí están: **From Testimonial Word to Visual Representation and Performativity**

On 11 September 2013, the artistic intervention *Aquí están* was carried out in the Museo de la Memoria y los Derechos Humanos in Santiago, Chile. The intervention stemmed from the actress and theatre director Claudia Di Girólamo, who, thinking about the emblematic black-and-white photographs of the *detenidos desaparecidos* (missing detainees) as a way of representation, wondered:

> what would these people be like if portrayed alive, with hope, with strength, with beliefs. I asked myself what the detained and disappeared would be like if they were to be painted and portrayed by the youngest members of their families, grandchildren and great-grandchildren. And who could tell them what these people were like. I obviously thought about the relatives of the detained and disappeared: mothers, fathers. (Di Girólamo in Insunza 2013)

Fig. 2. The paintings by girls and boys displayed in the forecourt of the Museo de la Memoria y los Derechos Humanos.

Di Girólamo designed a complex device in order to raise and elaborate this "vital" characterization of the detained and disappeared in an artistic way. First, family testimonies were collected; in a second stage, these testimonies were read to the younger members of the families of the detained and disappeared: girls and boys listened to tales about relatives whom they had never met. Then, the kids were asked to paint a portrait based on the stories their elders told them. The pictures turned out to be colourful, vital portraits that included distinctive objects that represented the life experience of the detained and disappeared: "full of colour, sun, the football team they liked, the places they liked to go to" (Di Girólamo 2013a). The paintings were exhibited in the Museum's forecourt, from 11 to 16 September 2013.

On the evening of 11 September 2013 the project concluded with a final event named *Aquí están* (Here They Are).[2] The event was designed and directed by Di Girólamo in collaboration with the theatre director Rodrigo Pérez, who called on thirty actors and actresses to read the testimonial narratives to the public at the fortieth anniversary commemoration of the Chilean state coup. The testimonies were adapted in order to include solid data regarding the circumstances of their forced disappearance (Di Girólamo 2013b). That evening, little by little, the forecourt began to fill with people: families, elderly persons, youngsters and kids. The guests sat on the floor, in the bleachers, waiting to see what was going to happen. Suddenly the performers moved forward to the centre of the forecourt, where several chairs formed a spiral. Each one carried a white handkerchief, a red carnation and a printed sheet of paper. They sat on the chairs and waited. The court was in complete silence. Gradually the people in the audience left their position as spectators and advanced towards the forecourt to sit in front of some of the actors and actresses, who, paper in hand, read the testimonies provided by relatives of the *detenidos desaparecidos*. This intimate reading of the testimonies ran for a couple of hours, after which some of the artists sat in front of the microphone to read the testimonies. The audience listened attentively, silently, emotionally. Towards the end of the afternoon, a renowned national actor, José Sosa, showed up dressed as Salvador Allende, with his distinctive spectacles and a three-coloured sash across his chest. The silence turned sepulchral. Sosa sat in front of the microphone and read the speech which Salvador Allende uttered moments before dying during the bombing of La Moneda Palace. The actors held their white handkerchiefs high. "¡*Viva Chile! ¡Viva el pueblo! ¡Vivan los trabajadores!*" ["Long live Chile! Long live the people! Long live the workers!"] recited Sosa, while dozens of people in the forecourt answered, yelling with great spirit: "¡Viva!"

---

[2] *Aquí están*. Original idea: Claudia Di Girólamo. Co-direction and dramaturgy: Claudia Di Girólamo and Rodrigo Pérez. Researcher: Ximena Faúndez. Co-researcher: Bárbara Azcárraga. Research assistants: Esteban Olivares, Ignacio García, Manuela Maturana and Diego Urra. Induction and family communication: Raffaella Di Girólamo. Artistic supervisor: Fernanda Di Girólamo. Artistic assistant: Francisco San Martín. Production: Teresita Di Girólamo.

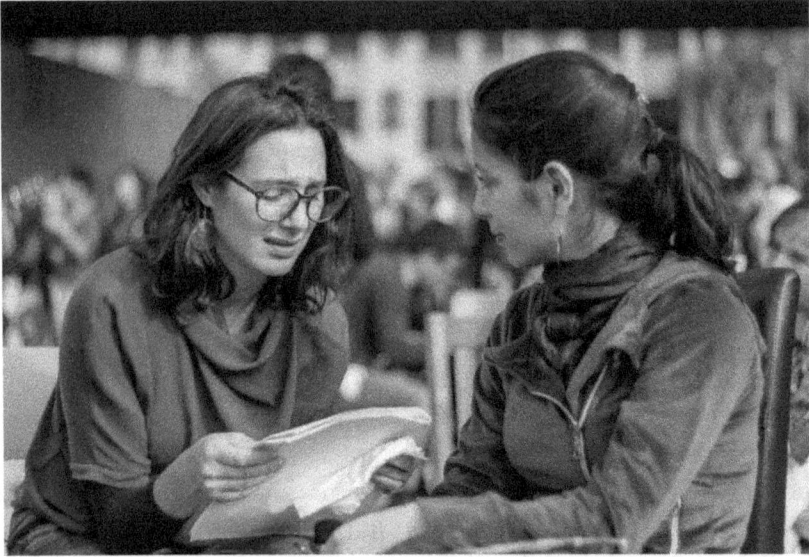

Fig. 3. First phase of *Aquí están*. Testimonial narratives are read.
Museo de la Memoria y los Derechos Humanos

Mediations and Translation Processes

It is well known that every testimony is a construction which, as Giorgio Agamben (2002, 153) states, is played out within the borders of what can be expressed: the testimony is only capable of translating the presence of an absence, the impossibility of speech, there where the impossibility comes to life through the possibility of speaking. The translation of an absence is even more axiomatic in the case of the testimonies of the detained and disappeared. When testimonies are used in artistic practices, their condition of impossibility is reinforced: the artistic work based on testimonies implies a battle in which the experience is subdued to fit the rules both of narrative and of aesthetics, while trying to overcome the situation where the borders between what is real and the textual-artistic simulacrum become blurred.

Generally speaking, artistic manifestations that are based on testimonies work in the awareness of the reality effect they produce, and try to complicate and question notions such as authenticity, rather than establishing truths (Martin 2013; Forsyth and Mergson 2009). What is at stake in such pieces is not what is "real" but the "reality effect" they may produce. *Aquí están*, on the contrary, installs itself, in a rather naïve way, on the level of truthfulness, concealing the enunciation tracks and presenting the testimonies as if they were the direct recounting of a reality. On the Museum's web page, *Aquí están* is defined as a testimony rescue (Museo de la Memoria 2013), an idea which Di Girólamo reinforces in different instances. The project promotes the idea that the tribute rescues "the" memory, as if there were just one memory, and as if this could be exhumed and shared in the final performative event. Without any problematization of the categories of reality, authenticity or veracity, *Aquí están* achieves the dissimulation of the number of mediations entailed in a collaborative and collective construction of memories which are arranged from the present and, thus, are plagued by mediations and translation processes.

A first level of mediation is the testimony provided by the adult relatives. The act of the relatives of the disappeared giving testimony not only responded to the translation of personal experience into verbal language, but also to the framework imposed by the creative process itself. Unlike other kinds of testimonies, this narrative was raised with a specific methodology that defined its content, tone and type. First, those testifying were instructed to piece together a tale for the children, focusing on the lives of their loved ones, being warned that they would later be read in front of an audience (Insunza 2013). These instructions constitute a framework that significantly shapes the discourse. Then, the research assistants proceeded to cross-examine the relatives of the detained and disappeared, according to particular guidelines: they would begin with physical appearance and then move on to ask what they liked to do, how they behaved, etc. The relatives spoke while the assistants took notes, performing another undeniable selection of the testimonial material. This form of testimonial compilation implies a high level of mediation which results in a narrative which is a co-construction that emerges from the interaction between the one testifying and the examiner. Far from being a "salvaged" truth, this enunciative framework produces a testimony that is strongly marked by the communicational interaction of the present.

The translation of testimonies into portraits is a further level of mediation, a mediation that could be defined as inter-semiotic, as it translates verbal discourse into a visual configuration. In my opinion, this is one of the merits of the project, because it opens up a whole new perspective by admitting that the children's re-elaboration of memory is not restricted to the verbal. The portrait, like the testimony, is not made in a "free way", but it too responds to a clear framework defined by the authors' view of the piece. For instance, all children use standard materials, and, as Insunza's (2013) video shows, each boy and girl is given a small mannequin that guides the portrait, imposing a mimetic figurative pattern of the human body. The simple act of providing a scale figure of a human body demonstrates that the directors were looking for a certain degree of figurativeness in the portraits that could clearly connect the narrative to the portrait.

It is interesting to note that, although the majority of the portraits were in fact figurative, some strayed from this framework, proposing more abstract paintings. In a radio interview Di Girólamo assesses the abstract elements as "strange", revealing her expectation of figurativeness. "The portraits are truly beautiful, that is, they are spectacular if they weren't so painful; they are really stunning, full of colours, of sun, with the football team [the detained and disappeared] liked ... the places they liked to visit, so then we have the representation of the countryside, or the city or the house, or nothing; or, suddenly, there are places that are quite abstract or very strange where they locate them" (Di Girólamo 2013a). The preference for the figurative responds ultimately to the prevalence of narrativity over visuality, and may, I think, be on account of the director's theatrical training, which implies in one way or another a strong link with the word.

Fig. 4. Reading of the testimonial tales. *Aquí están.*
Museo de la Memoria y los Derechos Humanos

In the encounter with the public a new mediation process occurs, which passes by way of the voices, the corporeality and subjectivities of the actors and actresses. The vast majority of the actors and actresses participating in *Aquí están* worked in television and so were well known to the general public. This generates a game of mediations that entails not only the framework imposed by the artistic practice, but also an interaction with mass media, such as television. The public recognition and the fame of the actors and actresses participating in the event cannot but influence the reception of the event, which ceases to be one characterized by the "greatest possible simplicity" (Di Girólamo 2013b) and acquires the tones of a spectacle.

Fig. 5. Actor Héctor Noguera reads one of the testimonies at the microphone. Museo de la Memoria y los Derechos Humanos

But the presence of renowned actors and actresses not only spectacularizes the action, it also facilitates an emotional bond, the affective tuning with the public, as well as the identification processes with the public. Because of the pre-established relationship with the actors and actresses (mediated by television), the narratives resonate with greater familiarity, facilitating the affection of the participant. As affirmed by Fisher-Lichte (2008), mutual interaction in live performances occurs with more promptness and effectiveness when a previous emotional circuit exists. Like an already existent path, this allows the emotional and corporeal bond to be more seamless. The inclusion of well-known television faces in this event subverts its own limitations: the public comes waiting to meet their favourite artists, who use this very influence as a seductive and affective tool in order to ease the communicability of the testimonies.

Aquí están therefore proposes a device that is full of mediations, which is the reason why it cannot be considered as the mere rescue of a "forgotten memory", as its promise of veracity claims. It is precisely these translations and aestheticization processes that make *Aquí están* such an interesting intervention. What is highlighted here is precisely the abundance of simultaneous and consecutive layers of mediation that are combined in the mobilization of memories, establishing itself as an emblematic example of the procedures and operations of memorialization in and by the arts.

Girls and Boys as Subjects of Memory

One of the main things at stake in *Aquí están* is the transmission of testimonies from the older generations to the younger, creating a dialogue between generations. Di Girólamo herself states, "Each family went through a process of memorization both personal and collective so as to bring their relatives back to life in their everyday things" (Di Girólamo 2013a). The procedure designed by Di Girólamo to generate the narratives, portraits and the final event is articulated around the idea of the transmission of a family memory that is not known or that requires a certain kind of repair.

The concern over the exchange and re-elaboration of memories across generations was established as one of the recurrent issues in the context of the fortieth anniversary commemoration of the coup. One of the factors that presumably explains the persistence of this issue is the generational turnover that happens over four decades and allows society to overcome the cultural trauma's latency period. That latency period of cultural trauma is no doubt related to the generational relay: forty years after the coup, the generations born under democracy begin to gain importance, even in the political arena. As Aleida Assmann (2010, 41-42) states:

Social memory does not change gradually but undergoes a perceptible shift after periods of around 30 years when a new generation enters into offices and takes over public responsibility. Together with its public presence, the new generation will authorize its own vision of history. The change of generations is paramount for the reconstruction of societal memory and the renewal of cultural creativity.

For the first time, and with great insistence, the question of how the younger generations understand the period of the civil military dictatorship (what they know, what their stance on it is and how they link it to the present) arose in different cultural, artistic and academic fields. The questions concerning the processes of transmission, activation and mobilization of memories seek not only to understand how that memory travels through the generations, but also to unveil the current politics of memory, which are reflected in the way the dictatorship period is taught in schools, in the way what is divulged by the media is actually grasped by the boys and girls of today, and how families tackle topics regarding the violent past.

The Museo de la Memoria y los Derechos Humanos was one of the institutions that most enthusiastically echoed the preoccupation with the intergenerational transmission of memories in the context of the fortieth anniversary commemoration of the coup. In fact, almost all the emblematic projects carried out by the Museum in 2013 had young people and children as protagonists. Its director at the time explained the reasons why the Museum embraced this curatorial line:

Memory cannot remain cloistered in the victims who lived through the traumatic experience, or in their relatives. The transition toward all their contemporaries and from one generation to the next is vital to accept the lessons of that painful past as part of a common body, so as to guarantee the "never again". (Brodsky 2013, 7)

The study of so-called intergenerational (Reyes 2009; Assmann 2010) or trans-generational (Scapusio 2006) memories has established itself as one of the preferred topics in memory studies. Undoubtedly one of the most relevant contributions to the conceptualization of the procedures of memorial transference through generations is the notion of postmemory offered by Marianne Hirsch (1997, 2012). As the author warns, the prefix "post-" does not directly point to a temporal gap, but to the effects that the memory elicits: postmemory is that memory which transmits consequences and implications for the present day to the generations that were not direct witnesses of past events. One of the most important theoretical innovations in the notion of postmemory is the idea that the transmission of these experiences is emotionally rooted in the bodies and behaviours of the young; postmemory is, after all, an affective and embodied memory which is transferred beyond verbal discourse (Hirsch 2012). Hirsch proposes that the mediators of postmemory are the narratives as well as the photographs, the objects and the mediating behaviours that set up a constant process of intertextuality and mutual translation which results in the construction of an indirect, more fragmented memory, which challenges the possibilities of a narrativity that exceeds the scope of words. From this viewpoint, the relationship between postmemory and the past would not be mediated by the witness's narrative, but by the imagination, projection and creation that propel other kinds of semiotic artifacts.

Fig. 6. *Aquí están*. Museo de la Memoria y los Derechos Humanos

Hirsch's interest in the processes of imagination and cultural performance is extremely useful for analyzing the artistic intervention *Aquí están*, which proposes a device that at almost all levels incorporates postmemorial work. One first phase, the workshop, was organized in order to collect the testimonial narratives of the adults and to provide a creative space for the kids' portraits. The workshop is a protected event (both because of the time devoted to it, and because of the constant psychological advice the participants received) in which the older and younger relatives could meet, confront each other and participate together in the posmemorial working through.

The workshop succeeds in dislocating the perception of a certain generational uniformity, eradicating the notion of generations as communities in which a common memory exists. The workshop does not consider adults and children as distinct collectivities that need to be confronted, but rather installs an inter-subjective and dyadic bridge that allows a collaborative working-through for the reconstruction of postmemories.

A second instance of postmemorial reconstruction in *Aquí están* ensues in the final event, in which the work carried out in the intimacy of the workshop was displayed in the forecourt before the gaze and presence of the spectators. When the actors and actresses read the narratives to "whoever wants to listen" (Pérez in Insunza 2013), a projection of private stories onto public space took place, contributing to the creation of a wider postmemory. The anchoring in personal and family stories invested these memories with affects that, when communicated in the public sphere, facilitated processes of identification. As Hirsch (2012, 33) suggests, postmemorial work "strives to reactivate and re-embody more distant political and cultural memorial structures by reinvesting them with resonant individual and familial forms of mediation and aesthetic expression". In this way, postmemory can persist even when all the eye-witnesses and their direct descendants are no longer present. The movement from private to public is also enacted in the performative action itself, which moved from the intimacy of the initial reading, through the declamation of the testimonies at the microphone, and concluded with Salvador Allende's emblematic speech. It is remarkable how the intervention uses precisely the transition from private to public as a vehicle for a more communal and shared cultural memory.

Aquí están accomplished an outstanding political re-definition of the category of childhood by envisioning girls and boys as subjects endowed with voice and body, capable of receiving memories, but also with the ability to establish a diachrony with future generations, positioning them as memory subjects. From the very first instances, the project considered the younger generations not only as recipients of memory, but as agents of it. Although in the first instance the adults were the ones who told the tales which the girls and boys "received", the work that followed dealt precisely with positioning these girls and boys as co-agents of a memory that, rather than being "transmitted", must be reconstructed collaboratively. The generation that did not live through the dictatorship personally became, then, a generation that is capable of re-elaborating and mobilizing a memory which they did not experience. It is unusual for children to be called upon as legitimate political subjects in the construction of memories, or in this case, postmemory. The younger members of the families that suffered the disappearance of a relative acquire in this context a radical role in the responsibility that the mobilization of memories requires for the future. The children can demand their right to memory and, at the same time, become political subjects responsible for keeping that memory alive.

Micro-resistances against the Museumification of Memory

Aquí están took place in the Museo de la Memoria, probably the most emblematic place in the construction of a national narrative about the dictatorship. The contrast between the museumification of memory and the commemorative procedures of *Aquí están* was evident and significant. As Andreas Huyssen (1995, 16) puts it, the museumification of memory is a sort of antidote to the acceleration that characterizes late global capitalism, allowing it to "fulfill a vital anthropologically rooted need under modern conditions: it enables the moderns to negotiate and to articulate a relationship to the past", a trend moved and sustained by mass culture and neo-liberalism. Unlike the enshrinement of memory which the Museum exercises, *Aquí están* was played out within the intimacy of inter-subjective interactions. The artistic gesture of Di Girólamo and Pérez echoed the feminist statement that asserts that what is private is political, bringing to a hegemonic space intimate and minimal stories of the victims' relatives that are not always validated as significant memories. As a collaborative aesthetic practice, *Aquí están* proposed an alternative way to activate non-official stories, offering alternative means of political commitment. *Aquí están* was ultimately a sort of ritual of acknowledg-ment, where what is at stake is not the consolidation of a single memory, but the possibility of re-constructing a collective memory that turns out to be fragmentary, unstable, dynamic and multiple. This was accomplished by the construction of a temporality in progress that occured in the context of the performative gathering. The simultaneous situation of production and reception of memories intensifies collective forms of construction that favour processes of recognition and belonging to the provisional and transient community which this coexistence constructs. *Aquí están* constructed, then, a magnificent game of temporalities that involved all the participants as subjects of memory. When performing this manoeuvre, a responsibility towards the past is transferred between generations but, more importantly, a responsibility regarding the future that looms as a shared horizon is constructed.

Aquí están was a form of action, collaboration and resistance whose political effectiveness lay in the expansion of the responsibility toward the future. Its range was that of "small scale resistances" (Bal 2011), understood as micro-resistance that does not operate at the level of greater social structures (like the museum), but is situated in the intimate and at times minimal space of inter-subjective relationships, where what is relevant is the dialogue, the mutual listening, companionship and solidarity. And that is exactly what *Aquí están* offered: as Di Girólamo (in Insunza 2013) said, it made it possible "for the people to connect emotionally with the detained and disappeared and to question, once again: Where are they?"

References

Agamben, G. (2002). *Remnants of Auschwitz: The Witness and the Archive*. New York: Zone Books.

Assmann, A. (2010). "Re-framing memory: Between individual and collective forms of constructing the past". In K. Tilmans, F. van Vree, and Winter, J. (eds.), *Performing the Past: Memory, History, and Identity in Modern Europe*. Amsterdam: Amsterdam University Press.

Bal, M. (2011). "Heterochrony in the act: The migratory politics of time". *Thamyris/ Intersecting*, 23, 211-238.

Brodsky, R. (2013). "Presentación". In Centro de Estudios de la Niñez OPCION (eds.), *Los ruidos del silencio: Los niños, niñas y adolescentes hablan a cuarenta años del golpe militar en Chile*. Santiago: Lom, 5.

Di Girólamo, C. (2013a). Claudia Di Girólamo invitó a participar de la intervención *Aquí están*. Radio ADN interview, 5 September. At **www.adnradio.cl/noticias/sociedad/claudia-di-girolamo-invito-a-participar-de-la-intervencion-conmemoracion-Aqui-estan/20130905/nota/1964521.aspx**, accessed 22 September 2016.

Di Girólamo, C. (2013b). "Claudia Di Girólamo lidera montaje con 30 actores". *La Tercera*, 47, 6 September. At **http://papeldigital.info**

/lt/2013/09/06/01/paginas/047.pdf, accessed 26 September 2016.

Fischer-Lichte, E. (2008). *The Transformative Power of Performance: A New Aesthetics*. London: Routledge.

Forsyth, A., and Mergson, C. (2009). *Get Real: Documentary Theatre Past and Present*. Basingstoke and New York: Palgrave Macmillan.

Halbwachs, M. (1992). *On Collective Memory*. Chicago: The University of Chicago Press.

Hirsch, M. (1997). *Family Frames: Photography, Narrative, and Postmemory*, Cambridge, MA: Harvard University Press.

Hirsch, M. (2012). *The Generation of Postmemory: Writing and Visual Culture After the Holocaust*. New York: Columbia University Press.

Huyssen, A. (1995). *Twilight Memories: Marking Time in a Culture of Amnesia*. London: Routledge.

Insunza, P. (2013). *Aquí están*. Intervención/conmemoración/11 de septiembre 2013. Video on DVD. Santiago: Museo de la Memoria y los Derechos Humanos.

Martin, C. (2013). *Theatre of the Real*. New York: Palgrave Macmillan.

Museo de la Memoria (2013). Página web Museo de la Memoria. At **http://ww3.museodelamemoria.cl/exposiciones/aqui-estan/**, accessed 19 September 2016.

Piper Shafir, I. (2013). "La conmemoración como búsqueda de sentido". *Pléyade*, 11, 1-11.

Preda, C. (2013). "Arte de memorialización 40 años después del golpe de estado". *Tiempo Histórico*, 6, 49-62.

Reinelt, J. (2009). "The Promise of Documentary". In A. Forsyth and Megson, C. (eds.), *Get Real: Documentary Theatre Past and Present*. Basingstoke: Palgrave Macmillan, 8-21.

Reyes, M. J. (2009). "Generaciones de memoria: Una dialógica conflictive". *Praxis*, 15, 93-104.

Richard, N. (1998). *Residuos y metáforas: Ensayos de crítica cultural sobre el Chile de la transición*. Santiago: Cuarto Propio.

Scapusio, M. (2006). "Transgeneracionalidad del daño y memoria". *Revista Reflexión Derechos Humanos y Salud Mental*, 32, 15-19.

Genres of Testimonies/Genres of Reconstruction

Giving Memory a Future:
Narrating Post-apartheid South Africa

Roger Bromley

Whatever its critics have had to say about its role and effectiveness, the South Africa Truth and Reconciliation Commission (TRC) – set up by the National Unity and Reconciliation Act – has exercised an incalculable influence on political, social and cultural forms in the post-apartheid period. There are those who would question whether the society can, even yet, be described as "post-apartheid" but it is nevertheless true that an extensive range of cultural activity has produced a number of attempts to generate a new set of discourses in narrative forms which are designed to create a radically different political imaginary in the country. As many commentators have noted, the predominant discursive medium of the TRC was a set of complex, multiple and contested narratives in which conflicting voices, hidden and silenced for many years, for the first time made a bid for a symbolic presence in a social order which had denied their existence for so long. Although the TRC involved a significant amount of empirical enquiry and expert, in-depth investigation, what figured most prominently in its public manifestations at different venues throughout the country, and on television and radio, were, mostly, individual and community narratives of violence, humiliation and exclusion brought about by the social division of the political grammar of Afrikaner hegemony. Truth commissions can and do change the frame of public discourse and public memory, but how long it might take to change the affective and material base of a society is another issue.

I take as my starting point, Njabulo Ndebele's argument that the TRC brought about the "restoration of narrative" and the need for cultural forms to participate in what he calls a "rediscovery of the ordinary" after an apartheid era dominated by a concern with "the extreme, the distorted and the extraordinary". The concept of restorative, resurrective or reparative narrative will be linked with what have been identified as three principal characteristics of restorative justice: acknowledgement, reparation, and reconciliation (Villa-Vicencio and Verwoerd 2000, 73). My focus will be on a range of cultural texts which in some way or other are concerned with the theme of the possibilities and, perhaps, impossibilities of reconciliation, and the struggle to liberate identity, time and space from the agencies and paradigms of oppression. It will be argued that stories do not simply describe or relate but are also actually constitutive/reconstructive of something new. As Bakhtin said, "Truth is not born nor is it to be found inside the head of an individual person, it is born between people collectively searching for truth, in the process of their dialogic interaction" (quoted in Phelps 2004, 69).

A range of texts will be examined for their potential as cultural resources, as projects of anamnesis in post-violence society, critical memory narratives. The narratives act as a framework and a methodology by which a society recalls the past and places it in a dynamic and formative relationship to the interpretation of the present (Feldman 2004). Arguably, in South Africa a point had been reached beyond which society could not narrate itself. As Aletta Norval has said, apartheid functioned "as a signifier of closure" (Norval 1998, 259). The post-conflict texts will be examined as part of new directions in narrative procedures, objects and solutions working against structures of forgetfulness and deniability. In Ricoeur's wonderful phrase, the search will be for cultural forms which can "give memory a future". The narratives will not simply be explored in terms of their content but will also be analyzed from the point of view of the need for forms which extend, defamiliarize and subvert existing liberal-rationalist paradigms – multi-dimensional, challenging, and radical explorations of the relationship between power, discourse and the symbolic. Above all, as Teresa Phelps has cautioned, there is the need to be wary of any template "that calls for a certain kind of story, a certain kind of process", something which the TRC did not always manage to avoid, and "be brave enough to trust stories to be tools of disruption" (2004, 128).

Framing my discussion will be two comments, one from Martha Minow's book *Between Vengeance and Forgiveness*, where she warns of the complexities of responding to collective violence:

> I do not seek precision here; nor do I mean to imply that we can wrap up these issues with analysis or achieve a sense of completion … no response can ever be adequate when your son has been killed by police ordered to shoot at a crowd of children; when you have been dragged out of your home, interrogated, and raped …; or when your brother who struggled against a repressive government has disappeared and left only a secret police file, bearing no clue to his final resting place. Closure is not possible. Even if it were, any closure would insult those whose lives are forever ruptured. (Minow 1998, 4-5).

The second comment is from Ismail Mahomed, the Deputy President of the Constitutional Courts of South Africa:

> The granting of amnesty is a difficult, sensitive, perhaps even agonizing, balancing act between the need for justice to victims of past abuse and the need for reconciliation and rapid transition to a new future; between encouragement to wrongdoers to help in the discovery of truth and the need for reparations for the victims of that truth; between a correction in the old and the creation of the new. It is an exercise of immense difficulty interacting in a vast network of political, emotional, ethical and logistical considerations. (Prager and Govier 2003, 265)

As an enemy, it has been said, is someone whose story you have not heard, and dialogue is the recognition that the other is human, this essay has as its focus post-apartheid narratives which have emerged from within Afrikaner culture or are related to it, a culture which was extremely predictable and protective, as well as being insular and insulated. It considers the challenge of producing *inclusive* narratives which extend to both the terrorized *and* the previous agents of terror in new forms of co-existence in the social domain of language and memory.

In speaking of what has been called the culture of state-orchestrated terror, I am taking as read that this involves the production of fear, distrust and suspicion in the general population and that the main forms of state terror are arbitrary detention, unfair trial, torture, political murder or extrajudicial executions, and "disappearance". Seldom have these acts been carried out by monsters or psychopaths but "within a set of practices, discourses and ideologies ... as a way to deploy power within differential social and political relations, or as a means to buttress themselves and to maintain power" (Nagengast 1994, 11). One of the functions of state terror is to render helpless and humiliated those who oppose its repressive policies, to remove the dissenting individual from their "belonging" and attachment in all senses of the word – to family, to community, and to humanity itself. Terror disempowers, immobilizes, silences and isolates its "others". Legal, political and sensory deprivation combine to dominate and abuse, to remove the possibilities of language and communication. One of the tasks of reconstruction and recovery after such terror is to reconstitute society in terms of *mutuality*, not as some kind of abstract or woolly process but as a form of political action itself. In this context, forgiveness is not simply a personal act but is, as Arendt has argued, inherently *political*, in that it seeks to re-associate the individual with their *belonging,* to make possible a return to the presence of others. What seems irreversible, irreparable – the "bleeding wound" of severe trauma – is brought into language, given public form, shaped into narrativity. As Susan Brison argues:

> The communicative act of bearing witness to traumatic events not only transforms traumatic memories into narratives that can then be integrated into the survivor's sense of the self and view of the world, but it also reintegrates the survivor into a community, re-establishing bonds of trust and faith in others. (Brison 2002, xi)

Brison develops a view of the self which she describes as fundamentally *relational* and it is this which I wish to stress throughout; that that which is capable of being undone/unmade by violence can also be re-made in connection with others.

Terror "murders" time and space – coordinates of humanity – by *arrest* and *confinement*; forgiveness is a means of re-entering time and reclaiming space. Terror is predicated upon utter passivity – at the level of the person and the polity – whereas forgiveness can become a form of activity, the promise of action, which empowers both individuals and communities to enter into mutuality with a plurality of others. Forgiveness dismantles the potentiality of terror, and the memory of terror, to exercise continuing domination and impunity over the experience of the oppressed. Remembrance, mourning and, ultimately, forgiveness can become acts of *solidarity* which can restore and renew subjectivity, human connection and agency. Forgiveness reconnects the victim(s) with the time of the present, with the space of the human, and re-establishes structures and conditions for the possibility of meaningful activity smashed by state terrorism. In Arendt's formulation, "the possible redemption from the predicament of irreversibility – of being unable to undo what one has done ... is the faculty of forgiving" (in Griswold 2008, xv).

What I have described is what Elaine Scarry, in *The Body in Pain* (1985), calls "unmaking", the uncreating of the human through torture specifically and terror more generally, objectification and appropriation – non-whites under apartheid were treated simply as objects. Physical pain, she says, is language-destroying, and it also functions to undermine capacity and agency. She adds that it also deconstructs the victim's voice and systematically unstages its personal, cultural and social development. All power over language, capacity and agency is vested in the terrorizing regime; its power is performative. The refusal to recognize or credit the worth of the dissident, to sever her or him from the social and temporal, produces in the oppressor what Scarry calls "a swelling sense of territory" (a phrase which neatly captures De Kock's memoir discussed later). This aptly summarizes the deterritorialization of the oppressed, the violated, the "dissolved". Monopoly, exclusion, and detention all confer voice, world and self on the appropriative, repressive regime. Powerlessness is produced not simply by focusing upon individuals but also on their families, friends, and associates. In this way fear is made manifest and sustained.

How in post-conflict societies people respond to the consequences of repression and violence is partly a matter of "enabling dialogues" (Jackson 2002), narratives of reciprocity and mutuality. State terrorism isolates and segregates and, as Primo Levi says, "It did not matter that they might die along the way; what really mattered was that they should not tell their story" (Levi 1988). Telling a story implies sociality, the presence of another, inter-subjectivity, and the possibility of exchange – all denied in detention. One of the effects of state terrorism is to reduce its oppressed to "a life without speech and without action ... literally dead to the world; it has ceased to be a human life because it is no longer lived among men [sic]" (Arendt, quoted in Jackson 2002, 39).

One of the aims of state terrorism is the production of a people without its own narratives. It is equally true that the active process of storying can be both empowering and restorative and that, as Kubiak argues, "to disrupt narrativity ... is to disrupt body and mind, to induce a kind of madness –not merely to interrupt the story, or cause us to question the outcomes, or challenge our beliefs and suppositions" (Kubiak 2004, 297). This is precisely one of the effects of terrorism, this disruption of body, mind and narrative. As Certeau says, "Stories map out a space which would otherwise not exist" (quoted in Humphrey 2002, 17). One of the primary cultural tasks of post-conflict recovery is this mapping out of spaces which had not previously existed or which had been obliterated, as "deprived of narratives ... the group or individual regresses toward the disquieting, fatalistic experience of a formless, indistinct and nocturnal totality" (Certeau, quoted in Humphrey 2005, 24).

As I have said, I want to consider the challenge of producing inclusive narratives which extend to both the terrorized *and* the previous agents of terror in new forms of co-existence in the social domain of language and memory. If dehumanization, powerlessness and removal "from the universe of moral obligation" (in Ruth Fein's phrase) are experiences of the victim, how can narrative enable a dialogue between victim and former victimizer? How can they come to share basic values, acknowledge each other?

Earlier, I spoke of the victim's loss of voice, self and world, of a life stripped bare and deemed not worthy of life, utterly contracted. In order to recover voice, self-extension into the world, and content (in both senses of the word) from a memory of absence and suffering, as primary, secondary, or tertiary victim, a narrative of *presence,* expression and projection is necessary: a narrative which extends, acknowledges and includes the former persecutor(s) if a society is going to change. There is a need to overcome dis-identification and indifference, the negation of world and word characteristic of the oppressive regime. The split selves of terror have to come together in, what Miroslav Volf (1996) calls the "embrace" – literal or metaphorical – a mutual and equal positioning in time, space and story. The body without story has to inhabit, humanize and own its space, initially, and then open and extend this to the former persecutor. It is both a process of extension and of overcoming of the distance, separation, denial and disclaimers of the perpetrator of the former regime of power.

Something that Andre Brink, the Afrikaner novelist, said is useful in the context of restoring/restorying South Africa:

One might even say that unless the enquiries of the Truth and Reconciliation Commission are extended, complicated and intensified in the imaginings of literature, society cannot sufficiently come to terms with its past to face the future. (Brink 1998, 30)

This is a valuable starting point for thinking about post-apartheid narratives because the period since 1990 has seen a proliferation of narratives of testimony – memoirs, confessions, apologies, fictions – which seek to confront the ideological dimensions of apartheid – to locate its contexts of intelligibility – by textualizing it in a variety of ways. Common amongst these is the rite of passage narrative, like *Country of My Skull,* a personal account of the TRC hearings by the Afrikaner poet and broadcaster Antjie Krog, published in 1998. She says two very pertinent things for my argument in relation to the testimony of those who had inflicted the brutalities of the system: "Week after week, from one faceless building to another, from one dusty, god-forsaken town to another, the arteries of our past bleed their own particular rhythm, tone and image. One cannot get rid of it. Ever" (Krog 1998, 37) She also says, "How do I live with the fact that all the words used to humiliate, all the orders given to kill, belonged to the language of my heart" (Krog 1998, 238). What Krog is articulating is complicity, passive in many cases but also, of course, very active in the different forms of governmentality. Afrikaans – the language, it was claimed, given by God as he also gave South Africa to the Afrikaner – was the language of Afrikaner nationalism and of separate development. At the core of this nationalism was what Krog calls the "second narrative" of the TRC: "After six months or so, at last the second narrative breaks into relief from its background of silence – unfocused, splintered in intention and degrees of desperation. But it is there. And it is white. And it is male" (Krogg 1998, 56). It is this "second narrative" which forms the basis of this essay, with a particular emphasis on constructions of pathological masculinity, texts which may be seen as part of what Ndebele (1998, 24) calls "an informal truth and reconciliation process under way among the Afrikaners" .

I want to comment briefly on Mark Behr's *The Smell of Apples* (1993, Afrikaans; 1995 English), and Eugene de Kock's *A Long Night's Damage: Working for the Apartheid State* (1998), and then concentrate upon Pumla Gobodo-Madikizela's *A Human Being Died That Night: A South African Woman Confronts the Legacy of Apartheid* (2003), based partly on interviews with de Kock in 1997-8 in his maximum security prison cell. As Krog points out, the second narrative is white and male, hence the sub-title of Gobodo-Madikizela's text takes on added significance; the legacy being confronted is not only racial but gendered: she says that it was only when apartheid had ended that was she able to think of herself as *South African* rather than just someone who came from South Africa, which gives yet another dimension to the confrontation and the sub-title. All of these narratives form part of what Njabulo Ndebele described in his "Memory, Metaphor and the Triumph of Narrative":

And so it is that the stories of the TRC seem poised to result in one major spin-off, among others: the restoration of narrative. In few countries in the contemporary world do we have a living example of people reinventing themselves through narrative. (Ndebele 1998, 27)

As Michiel Heyns comments, "narrative also serves as a means of reinvention for those people who inflicted the sufferings of which the victims speak" (Heyns 2000, 44).

The Smell of Apples (1995) has aroused a lot of attention because in 1996, its author, Mark Behr, confessed to having been a spy for the South African government for four years when he was a student at Stellenbosch University – the epicentre of Afrikaner nationalism. His confession, seen by many as pre-emptive, self-serving and foreclosing, has led to his vilification in many circles. My concern, however, is with the novel and its structural doublings – the dual time-frame of 1973 and 1988, its overt and covert narratives, and its constant mirrorings. Behr has said the following about his choice of an eleven-year-old boy as narrator:

> The child's voice could, I felt, succeed in accusing the abusers while at the same time holding up the mirrors. I hoped, and doubted, that the text would show how one is born into, loved into, violated into discrimination and how none of us were, or are, free from it. But to do so I needed a voice that would seem not to seek pardon or excuse, in a language different from the adult's which invariably contains in it ... a corrupt and corrupting formula. (Behr 1997, 120)

It is a rite of passage from innocence (ignorance?) to experience, a looking-back in order to give memory a future. It is a projective text also in which apartheid *as a discursive identity formation* is staged and performed, and seen as constituted in negativity. This novel, along with so many of the Afrikaner narratives, is written in what Fanon calls that "zone of occult instability", a time of reflection and examination, a prelude to the creation of a new national imaginary: a process of re-signification.

The banality and cruelty of everyday apartheid is seen through this bi-focal narrative – the dad-worshipping young boy on the threshold of puberty and, later, the frightened professional soldier engaged in an illicit war on the borders of Angola, both emasculated and sacrificed on the altar of a deeply corrupt ideology of masculinity. Krog speaks at one point about "The *manne* ... The Afrikaans *manne*. Those who call their sons '*pa se ou rammetjie*' or '*my ou bul*' ['Dad's little ram' or 'my old bull']" (Krog 1998,

90). The father in *The Smell of Apples* calls his son "my little bull".

In the novel, we are introduced to a model Afrikaner family – physically attractive, successful ("Dad" is a Major-General in the SADF), exemplary in every respect. Through this middle-class family is reflected patriarchal capitalism, militarization of the state, Christianity, nationalism, misogyny, masculinist ideology, homophobia, the tyranny of conformity and complicity, and the casual, thoughtless and, often, brutal racism of apartheid. The faultlines/fissures of the systemic authoritarianism are evidenced in the fear and paranoia of the family, its performative rigidities (they are their roles), active complicity with the regime, its moral corruption (the father sodomizes the boy's best friend) and hatred of liberalism and communism. As Cheryl Stobie has said, "the novel highlights the contradictions, rationalizations, slippages, and inconsistencies in constructing myths and ideologies about race, nation, religion, masculinity, gender and sexuality" (Stobie 2008, 76).[1]

Both *The Smell of Apples* and, to a certain extent, *A Human Being Died that Night*, could be seen as texts of mourning. In an essay called "The Inability to Mourn – Today" by Margarete Mitscherlich-Nielsen, which focuses upon post-Nazi Germany (Mitscherlich-Nielsen 1989), she speaks of character deformations, mystifications, mis-information, denials and repressions which have persisted in post-1945 Germany, and of traditions of authority and obedience, all of which could be said to have characterized the mentalities which sustained apartheid and its culture of deception and self-deception. Mitscherlich-Nielsen describes the ability of a person to mourn as meaning

> that he [*sic*] is able to part with open eyes not only from lost objects but also from lost attitudes and thought patterns ... The work of mourning, a process of leave-taking, is the prerequisite for being able to think new thoughts, perceive new things, and alter one's behaviour patterns. (Mitscherlich-Nielsen 1989, 408)

Metaphorically speaking, the novel has to re-situate the lost objects and lost attitudes through closed eyes (the naïvety of the narrator) in order to part from them with open eyes, although it would also be naïve to claim

---

[1] A full analysis of the novel will not be attempted here as I am concerned only with its representative or symptomatic features. Two detailed readings of the text can be found in Stobie (2008) and Barnard (2000).

that the leave-taking is ever really complete as, despite the structural changes, many white South Africans continue to live in enclaves of privilege with many of the "lost attitudes" still intact.

The Smell of Apples is an attempt in the form of a cultural fiction to understand and explain apartheid ideology; it is also a process of leave-taking, an act of deconstruction. By engaging with the figure of Eugene de Kock, Gobodo-Madikizela is similarly conducting a process of mourning – for the lives of those de Kock destroyed and for his destructive life – and a leave-taking; not forgetting apartheid but resituating it reflexively. Both texts seek to re-realize a defensive, de-realized world. By writing his novel and by her confronting of de Kock, Behr and Gobodo-Madikizela, respectively, are carrying out a process of mourning in so far as they are acknowledging and recognizing perpetrators of evil in a regime which produced a "crime against humanity", and using their texts as modes of reparation, apology almost. They challenge the values and convictions of a system and of individuals who made it function. In the novel, the technique of using the "innocent" perspective of the child narrator enables all those beliefs and actions lived out as positives to be seen inversely, and at a distance, as negatives. It is both a learning and an unlearning process in which delusional ideologies are located in lived experience, memorized, so to speak, and interrogated. The insider stands at a distance and becomes a critical outsider – textually, *The Smell of Apples* is both, simultaneously. What was perceived from the inside as a normative, moral community is detached from its deep cultural and ideological anchorage and shown as immoral, if not amoral. The narrative exceeds its immediate sphere of reference and temporality and becomes reflexive. Afrikaner self-idealization and power (also manifested in *A Long Night's Damage*) are punctured and revealed in their arbitrariness and contingency. For many, of course, the text may well have been seen as an act of betrayal which, given Behr's spying activities, renders it very complex.

What Mitscherlich-Nielsen calls "emotional anti-Communism" is a refrain which runs through *The Smell of Apples* and *A Long Night's Damage*, and justifies contempt for all forms of liberalism, dissent and resistance, and helped to sustain a totalitarian culture of command and obedience (there is a prominent link with a Chilean general at the time of the coup of 1973 in *The Smell of Apples*), something which, in the novel, is modelled in and by the idealized family, although fissures do appear at intervals throughout the text which check the authoritarianism and narcissism momentarily. If, at a stretch, the de Kock memoir could also be seen as an act of mourning, then it is only over the loss of his own "narcissistic self-worth", for "anyone who mourns ultimately for himself, for his own loss of worth, and national ideals – anyone, that is, who does not mourn for others, for love objects or for the victims of his opportunism or fear – cannot be interested in atoning" (Mitscherlich-Nielsen 1989, 420). Gobodo-Madikizela engages in a dialogue with de Kock and his social, cultural and political formation, and elicits signs of sensitivity and self-awareness which approximate to atonement at times; certainly, a different man emerges from their exchanges than the one in his self-serving memoir.

Both the novel and the memoir need to be seen in gendered terms also. The defensiveness of the father in the novel and of de Kock underlines what Mitscherlich-Nielsen says about paranoia combined with physical violence being the "affair of men" (Mitscherlich-Nielsen 1989, 425). As a Freudian psychoanalyst, she, not surprisingly, locates male aggression in terms of initial father/son rivalry (seen in both texts), the fear of retaliation and castration, thus making violence in a sense pre-emptive and projective, driven by a fear of being destroyed. Hence, she says, the construction of an "armament mentality" (literally and metaphorically) and "the search for enemies, anti-Communism, anti-Semitism" (both featured in the novel) are "etched more deeply into a man's bones than a woman's" (Mitscherlich-Nielsen 1989, 425). Whether this is true or not, apartheid, coordinated by its *Broederbond*, was a deeply patriarchal system predicated upon a militarized and masculinist ideology. Eugene de Kock embodied these values in many ways and it is part of Gobodo-Madikizela's task to engage with, and probe, the gaps and breaks in this armature in order to explore the "human" in the man.

The Smell of Apples is a text of repetition, a rehearsal of core tropes in the narrative of apartheid, not in order to produce a performance as such but, rather, a "de-performative" act of mourning in which lost objects and signifiers are recalled to memory, not for the purposes of recovery but of discovery, revision and displacement. The camouflaged and the covert are brought into the light as a supplement to what Yael Danieli calls the "fourth narcissistic blow" (in Dietrich and Shabad 1989, 456-7). She cites Freud's speculations about Copernicus's blow to humanity's narcissism (no longer the centre of the universe), Darwin's second blow (superiority to the animal world questioned) and adds Freud's "psychological blow" (the limits to human consciousness). Danieli describes Nazi Germany as delivering the "ethical blow" by undermining the belief "that the world we live in is a just place in which human life is of value, to be protected and respected" (in Dietrich and Shabad 1989, 456). I do not wish to make banal comparisons between Nazi Germany and apartheid, except to say that a system which de-humanized the majority of its population on the grounds of race and colour and was deemed a "crime against humanity" also compounded this "ethical narcissistic blow" by challenging notions of morality and of the human.

What *The Smell of Apples* does is to bring its suave, elegant and articulate characters – the respectable, public face of apartheid – into the company of Eugene de Kock, its covert, secretive underside, thus "exposing the potential boundlessness of human evil and ugliness" (in Dietrich and Shabad 1989, 457). What Behr and Gobodo-Madikizela achieve in their different texts is to integrate this "ethical narcissistic blow" with an expanded concept of humanity which recognizes, acknowledges, and mourns an *inclusive* evil, part of shared humanity, rather than consigning it to categories of the abnormal and of the "moral monster".[2] As Primo Levi said of the concentration camp guards at Auschwitz: "These were not monsters" (quoted in Griswold 2008, 75). While acknowledging extremes of behaviour, these are not distanced from "us" but are seen as representative of a set of dominant and prevailing currencies of power. In other words, agency is not discounted – the naïve narrator of the novel chooses to become a professional soldier in an illegal war.

The malice which characterized the apartheid regime was brought out by a dominating illusion of white limitlessness which repressed or denied its need for other people by effectively eliminating its majority population from the realm of meaningfulness. Flahault (2003) argues that the tension between limitlessness and dependency upon others is constitutive of self-construction and, by extending it to the political, I am arguing, by analogy, that the apartheid's regime guiding illusion was that this tension or conflict could be resolved by totalizing legislation which rendered its power limitless and immune to hostility and antagonism – itself a process of stunning naïvety. The years of struggle against the regime, and its recourse to imprisonment, assassination, border wars, torture and

---

[2] Griswold (2008, 72-76) argues convincingly that the "moral monster" label is distracting and misleading because it discounts agency and takes evil acts outside of the scale of a human relationship.

censorship of course revealed the logical/ideological absurdity of "separate development", its core misconception and generalized self-idealization. It is the "what is not said" of both novel and memoir that registers in both narratives this ineluctable tension.

With the exception of an exculpatory narrative like *A Long Night's Damage*, one of the achievements of the "second narrative" has been to produce texts like *The Smell of Apples*, Rian Malan's *My Traitor's Heart*, (2000), Jeanne Goosen's *We're Not All Like That* (1992), and *A Human Being Died that Night* (2007; not that the author is an Afrikaner, of course) which are capable of moving in and out of the system which framed them – the medium which gave their lives meaning and identity, however ambivalently – by producing complex and multi-accented accounts of perpetrators, in the broadest sense of the term, and the regime as a whole.

De Kock's *A Long Night's Damage: Working for the Apartheid State* ("as told to Jeremy Gordin") is, in sharp contrast to the dialogical narrative of *A Human Being Died that Night*, very much a monological narrative, an almost totally unreflective text: a banal, tedious and lengthy enumeration/accumulation of his "contacts" (murders) as a member of the SAP, and latterly as commander of C10 (Vlakplaas), the notorious interrogation centre for "enemies of the state". The book is also a staging of (per)formative moments in de Kock's career. He was, in his own words, a "senior official of the state", as described by Gordin, but chose to style himself as "a foot soldier" when it came to naming and blaming his superiors whose orders he was "merely" carrying out. The detail is allowed to pile up almost as a barrier to reflection as well as being the source material for an indictment. Throughout the text, de Kock occupies the moral high ground, a figure of moral rectitude with an inflated sense of his own superiority and observing strict professional codes ("where I would have to do everything myself"; all those around him are seen as weak in discipline, naïve in strategy), and reveals a rigid, narcissistic personality lacking in empathy – brutalized and maladjusted (literally), with severely blunted emotions, superior to all around him, and addicted to command/control and the power it brought him: a man of action (his words). It is a self-serving and self-exonerating "confession", not in terms of crimes committed (which are honestly and freely admitted) but of limited liability or agency (he comes over as an automated, robotic figure).

Narrated through the medium of a guileless, honest "I", there is a knowingness and constructedness, a defensiveness mixed with self-justification and pride. The text re-frames the self through a number of discursive strategies, almost in the form of a disclaimer. In many ways, it is a pre-emptive discourse, tracing a psychological stereotype, staking a claim for a particular identity for the addressee, as well as naming and blaming all his superiors. It is not clear who this addressee might be but de Kock had made an amnesty application (1200 pages long in May, 1997) to the TRC and he would presumably have anticipated a hearing at a later date. Gordin's "Afterword" expresses the hope that de Kock will be given amnesty, so the book can be seen as tendentious, a form of advocacy. Christopher Browning in *Ordinary Men* (1998) warns of the need to approach perpetrator testimony with caution in terms of its reliability or truth-telling capacity, as there is likely to be an agenda. Unlike other comparable testimonies, de Kock's does not attempt to minimize his involvement in the murders but he seriously limits his own responsibility and culpability.

Efforts at the trial in 1995 (he was sentenced in 1996 to two life sentences and 212 years in prison) to prove that de Kock was suffering from PTSD, inconclusive articles which explore the possibilities of his being "abnormal", and expert evidence that he was not psychopathic, leave us with a sense of a man deep inside the culture of the apartheid state, praised and decorated for his countless number of killings. In clinical terms not unstable, perhaps, but certainly possessed of a narcissistic personality driven to habitual violence by what might be called a severe cultural/relational disorder: "Evil is socially enacted and constructed. It does not reside in our genes or in our soul, but in the way we relate to other people" (Baumeister 1997, 375) or, as Bauman puts it: "Cruelty is social in its origin much more than it is characterological" (Bauman 1989, 116). De Kock was also deep inside a sub-culture of secrecy, power and masculinity. As Foster *et al.* argue, "The message in explaining human conduct is that situational forces take precedence over dispositional tendencies" (2005, 56) but, at the same time, the latter cannot be removed from the account, nor can agency, as de Kock emerges as, in Goldhagen's term, a very "willing executioner" ("merely the executioner", Gordin says disingenuously at one point) with powerful negative emotions towards those "others" he regarded as being outside his moral community, the world of Afrikaner nationalism. At one point in *Country of My Skull*, Krog refers to a conversation she had with a South African psychiatrist, Dr Sean Kaliski, who told her about the ways in which forms of extreme violence (carried out by people like de Kock) had been legitimated by the apartheid regime and made part of a normative structure:

> And the basis was not a fear of Communism, Kaliski says. "We believed black people were not human; they were a threat, they were going to kill us all, and then waste away the country until it was nothing but another African disaster area". He talks about a recently published book, *Bad Men Do What Good Men Dream*. While some men were out killing black people, many whites were busy dreaming of a life without black people: separate laws, separate amenities, separate churches, separate homes, separate towns, separate countries... (Krog 1998,140)

These comments do not excuse, or even explain, a person like de Kock, but they do place his actions, the carrying-out of what he considered his professional duties, in a very clear ideological framework shared by a considerable number of his white compatriots, and the repetition of the word "separate" (by Krog) semiotically produces the addictive effect of such beliefs. The "good men and women" of *The Smell of Apples* do not only dream of this separateness but they live it unquestioningly while the "bad men" (like de Kock) guarantee its security and continuity.

The text of de Kock's memoir is shaped by the perceived negative effects of African decolonization (the African disaster areas just referred to), paranoia about liberalism and communism, and a determination to defend his "country": not South Africa as such but Afrikanerdom. Certain stylistic usages do provide evidence of some reflexivity, e.g. "terrorist" in quotation marks, "so-called", "alleged" etc., plus some confessional utterances, and comments such as "all its black members were exceptional" to show he is not a racist – as long, that is, as the blacks remain under (his) white command. In the late 1980s, he even joined the Inkatha Freedom Party (IFP), which the security forces were then supplying with ammunition and weapons, on the basis, presumably, that they presented no threat to the dream of separateness. Although the book is styled as "told to Jeremy Gordin", a South African journalist, it is never clear whether the reflexive concessions are de Kock's or Gordin's, as no details are given of the ways in which the book was produced – apart from the fact that it was based upon six-and-a-half hours of interviews (in January, 1997, and presumably recorded) – or how much coaching or coaxing/prompting was involved. What is revealed is a life lived in camouflage (as in *The Smell of*

Apples), covert, the life of a scrupulously obedient and willing bully, the noble loner, above pettiness, faction, gossip and jealousy, and corruption. He styles himself, more than once, as a crusader hunting the Saracens. There is a very significant use of "I" throughout and very little use of "we". A sense of "entitlement" also emerges in the text; that, somehow, he had the right to eliminate the "enemy".[3] We learn a lot about "what" he was but almost nothing of "who" he was.

Aletta Norval, in *Deconstructing Apartheid Discourse* (1996) argues that the closures set up by apartheid hegemony – accompanied by a need to dominate and regulate/legislate – could only be brought about by constant differentiation from a series of "others": those not truly Afrikaners, from Jews, from liberals, English-speaking whites, and above all perhaps, from communists. There is a recurring need to refine and define authenticity – *volkseie* – (that which is the "own" of the volk) – and she notes that in the 1970s and 1980s there was a proliferation of those considered to be "enemies of the state". This also led to increasing self-regulation and surveillance of others for evidence of impurity and laxity. In *Exclusion and Embrace*, Miroslav Volf (1996) speaks of the will to purity as a foundation for exclusion.

A number of the testimonies at the TRC, and subsequent narratives produced by victims, represent stages in which trauma, anger and vengefulness lived out in condensed/confined, deeply disturbed spaces and worlds are re-positioned, negotiated and give way to, if not forgiveness in each case, at least the decision to refrain from revenge. In the angry, vengeful phase each victim, or victims, mimics to a greater or lesser extent a reversal of the pain suffered in confronting the now-powerless persecutor. Transformation and exchange, in each case, however minimal in some respects, was liberating, restorative.

Each was enabled to re-enter the temporal, create her/his own space and inhabit again the world of the relational. They were able, in some but not all cases, to change their interpretation of what had happened and simultaneously create a zone of detachment from the past and of attachment to the present and the future. The limits and boundaries of the contracted, powerless world were transcended.

---

[3] The concept of entitlement is discussed in *The Theatre of Violence* in terms of "the right of my spatial freedom over the spatial freedom of others" and "inattention to others' reactions, showing little or no concern for victims, a lack of empathy" (Foster 2005, 68-70).

One remarkable example of forgiveness is given by Gobodo-Madikizela in *A Human Being Died that Night* when she describes the meeting of two widows with the murderer of their husbands, Eugene de Kock. One of the women, Pearl Faku, said that she was "profoundly touched by him":

> I couldn't control my tears. I could hear him, but I was overwhelmed by emotion and I was just nodding, as a way of saying yes, I forgive you. I hope that when he sees our tears, he knows that they are not only tears for our husbands but tears for him as well … I would like to hold him by the hand, and show him that there is a future, and that he can still change. (Gobodo-Madikizela 2003, 14-15)

The key words here are, to emphasize my earlier points, "forgive", "future" and "change", and there is also the allusion to "embrace", the touching of the hand. De Kock's actions as one of the prime architects of destruction under apartheid came close to the "unforgivable" in the sense Derrida (2001) uses it. There were several other such extraordinary acts of forgiveness during the TRC hearings, including the granting of forgiveness to her murderers by the parents of the white American student, Amy Biehl, killed in 1993. Apparently, each time such an action occurred, Desmond Tutu would call for silence "because we are on holy ground". I may disagree with Tutu as to the source of the "holy", but I have no doubt that forgiveness in the context of murderous regimes is a numinous excursion, a transcendent project which exceeds, goes out beyond boundaries.

At least in South Africa there were/are survivors able to story, whereas the reality of the Holocaust, as Dori Laub reminds us, "extinguished philosophically the very possibility of address, the possibility of appealing, of or turning to, another" (in Jackson 2002, 50). The *possibility of address* is central both to forgiveness and narrative as each is predicated upon exchange and affectivity. In the process, as Michael Humphrey states, "empathy moves to recover the victim as 'subject', displacing terror's emphasis on the victim as object" (Humphrey 2002, 112). We are here in the realm of the ethics of compassion. Those disrupted rhythms described earlier are partially restored as, Canclini suggests, "the very act of narration itself can be culturally understood as a social space created to defend against terror" (in Humphrey 2002, 112) and, as Taussig argues, "narrative fills the space of terror to populate it, to create meaning against the abject void" (quoted in Humphrey 2002, 112).

These narratives may reproduce some of the conditions experienced under terror itself, full of silences, ellipses, fragments, echoes, and the failure of language, and remain resistant to preferred or dominant narratives. The challenge, as Gobodo-Madikizela sees it, is "no longer *whether* victims can forgive 'evildoers' but whether we – our symbols, language, and politics, our legal, media, and academic institutions – are creating the conditions that encourage alternatives to revenge" (Gobodo-Madikizela 2003, 118).

A Human Being Died that Night, with its mode of interrogation and investigation, embodies a response to this challenge for transition, modelling in its eclectic forms the kind of surpassing creativity called for. It produces the "rupture [of] unilinear constructions of historical knowledge in order to dispute specific sites of subjectivity" (Dipiero 1993, 111). One of the sites disputed is the comforting stereotype of the "monstrous" perpetrator, and the book's subtitle stresses the need for *confrontation* in its most active and positive sense, to come face to face with, to border upon and against, and to disrupt, the past in the form of one of its most extreme configurations, its highest profile prisoner (perhaps in more than the literal sense in so far as de Kock could be seen as someone in thrall to, imprisoned by, and rendered deeply vulnerable by/to, an idea of himself incarnated in Afrikaner nationalism). The empathy of the text is part of its restorative, inclusive effect – the open-eyed process described earlier with reference to *The Smell of Apples* – starting out from conflict but arriving at the possibility, however limited, of confluence.

A Human Being Died that Night refuses easy closure, and there is a residue of ambiguity and ambivalence in each chapter with unresolved, perhaps irresolvable, issues. Despite Gobodo-Madikizela's epilogue, in which she says that society must embrace those, like de Kock, who see and even lead on the road of shared humanity ahead, the book still leaves questions as to whether de Kock's apparent remorse was brought about by his two life sentences, his quest for pardon, and total loss of power, or was the product of reflection and a profound re-interpretation of his past. The trust and empathetic understanding articulated by the writer throughout the book, and its complex exploration and negotiation of the processes of forgiveness in which she eschews simple or sentimental answers, do suggest that humanity has to be wide enough to embrace even those figures who embodied terrorism in its most merciless form and sought to eliminate and annihilate "face" and silence voice. The discussion which follows, based upon Levinas, will make this clearer, hopefully.

Gobodo-Madikizela's book reminds us that, in our necessary focus on the testimony of the victim in post-conflict societies, we need also to "suffer" (in the sense of allow) the perpetrator's address, that of the other "other" – Levinas's face-to-face encounter in which one is being claimed. Adriana Cavarero, in *Relating Narratives* (2000), has said that each one of us is narratable by an "other", and this is what Gobodo-Madikizela is doing in this book for de Kock, producing a narratable self which his own book fails to do, I would argue. In getting close to the man described in South Africa as "prime evil", Gobodo-Madikizela also recognizes in the form of the book's historical, psychoanalytical and cultural excursuses how her representations can only ever be speculative and *approximate* in all senses of the word, including the spatial, as the book is based upon personal interviews in his high security prison. The work is close and attentive but ultimately incapable of rendering in any precise terms "the scene in which the other is to be confronted".

A Human Being Died that Night is an act of witnessing, an exposure, a submission, even, to one who was not powerless, or a victim of history, but knowingly used his power to attack the *integrity* of others – the fragmenting of voice, self and world referred to earlier. The book is an attempt – a necessary attempt for giving memory a future – to rehabilitate through narrative a figure of destruction who absented himself voluntarily from a shared notion of humanity in order to render other humans without signifying power. As Russell Daye argues, "The combination of moral judgement of wrong and empathy for the wrongdoer's humanity may be rare, but it is this combination that can lay the groundwork for the reconstruction of human community" (Daye 2004, 21). It is this combination of judgement with empathy which characterizes the work in its search for a dialogical truth and its tentative steps towards a form of renewal. In a sense, and to paraphrase Levinas, she offers the book metaphorically as a symbolic form of representative or generic suffering (as third party or proxy of/for all his victims) as an address of the other who persecuted her fellow South Africans. In the process, the persecutor's malice and malevolence are, if not understood, transcended by the address of the symbolic persecuted and, above all, contextualized – her touching of what he later tells her was his trigger-hand marks this "embrace". In Levinas's words the book is "liable to answer for the persecutor". Revealed as a powerless figure, his feet manacled, with his former hatefulness now shown in its utter futility, de Kock finds himself addressed by the persecuted, someone who in his Afrikaner masculinist ideology would have been doubly hated/feared – black and a woman.

The hateful is revealed as now pitiful as the book takes apart de Kock's *intentional* life, and bears witness to it as a delusion. In the process, hatred is replaced by pity in so far as suffering (in its symbolic form of the representative interviewer/writer) continues to address the annihilator who is coerced almost into articulation and reflection by having to listen to his persistent interlocutor. By pitiful, Levinas means compassion and grief: "one is moved by the harm another suffers for the sake of that other" (Hatley 2000, 159). It is almost as if Gobodo-Madikizela's interviews are designed to re-enact those Vlaakplas interrogations de Kock would have conducted, as a way of vicariously re-staging the harm caused in order to act out the *responsibility* the sufferer has for the persecutor, the liability "to answer for the persecutor" (Hatley 2000, 159).

In the terms used by Levinas, in answering one's persecutor, one is called to a patient enduring of that suffered by apartheid's victims, whose very endurance is also symbolically an offering back of that suffering to their persecutor for the sake of that persecutor – out of a unique vulnerability we all (sufferer and persecutor) have to the other. What that patient endurance offers to that other is a re-enactment of the exposure to the suffering inflicted upon his victims that reveals its *shamefulness* (Hatley 2000, 160); it is a remembering, an anamnesis.

As Hatley argues, the "enduring of a specific act of persecution is an explicit moment of revelation in which the other who persecutes is invited to find his or her way back to *animation and createdness, to soul and heart*" (2000, 160, my italics). I would stress this in particular because animation and createdness were designedly beaten out of victims, along with their soul and heart, areas of affect. At the same time, it is implied, the persecutor also lost all contact with these same qualities, and became emotionally anaesthetized. So, the victim bears witness to the persecutor by offering him the possibility of confronting the shamefulness of what he has wrought. Symbolically, suffering under apartheid gives a chance for the persecutor to be addressed in a manner that breaks through his delusions about the false priority attached to his or her previous identity and intentions, now revealed as arbitrary and contingent. The persecutor is offered another way of seeing the relationship between the other and himself, as well as the other and all the other others subjected to apartheid. If, as Tutu has said, *ubuntu* teaches us that we are all implicated in each other's humanity, then, as Alan Block argues, "In our encounters in the world when we stand face-to-face with the Other, we are not ourselves, but our *responsibility*. Perhaps the significance of our memories is the attachment they make for us to humanity" (Block 2002, 43). Paraphrasing Levinas at one point, Block says that the recognition of God occurs in the encounter with the other, and it is an ethical encounter. Coming from a very different perspective, I would risk saying that the recognition of the *human* occurs in the encounter with the other.

In his discussion of Paul Celan, Hatley (2000, 160) shows that condemnation rather than forgiveness, or at least the refusal of the act of vengeance, leaves victims "enmeshed within the plot of violence that the other's persecution has already instigated". For Levinas, "in persecution, one passes 'from an outrage undergone to the responsibility for the persecutor'". In what Levinas calls "expiation", resistance to the other's persecution "is articulated *otherwise* than as a violence countering violence". The distance between persecutor and persecuted – the very premise of the former's power – is closed and made proximate. In each of the works I have cited, the suffering is borne witness to – directly or indirectly – not forgotten or denied, but *memorialized* without any guarantees that the victim will not be untouched by the destruction, even though outrage has been overcome. Nothing of the suffering is obliterated or forgotten but nor is persecution any longer embodied in trauma as one's defining identity – it is carried as a memory into the future but not as a burden of/in the past; vulnerable maybe, but no longer victim, with forgiveness as the resource with which to cross the boundary between exclusion (that of persecuted and persecutor) and embrace. Forgiveness is both a form of witness and an act of reclamation; it reclaims victim, suffering, and perpetrator. It is also a gift which reveals the extent of the human capacity for grace. Forgiveness becomes a means of recoding trauma and re-activating the possibility of coming into narrative.

References

Barnard, R. (2000). "*The Smell of Apples, Moby-Dick* and apartheid ideology". *Modern Fiction Studies*, 46, 1, 207-226.

Bauman, Z. (1989). *Modernity and the Holocaust*. Cambridge: Polity Press.

Baumeister, R. F. (1997). *Evil: Inside Human Violence and Cruelty*. New York: W. H. Freeman.

Behr, M. (1995). *The Smell of Apples*. London: Abacus.

Behr, M. (1997). "Living in the Fault Lines". *Security Dialogue* , 28, 115-122.

Block, A. (2002). "'If I Forget Thee...Thou Shall Forget': The difficulty of difficult memories". In M. B. Morris and J. A. Weaver (eds.), *Difficult Memories: Talk in a (Post) Holocaust Era*. New York: Peter Lang.

Brink, A. (1998). "Stories of history: Re-imagining the past in post-apartheid narrative", in Nuttall and Coetzee, 29-42.

Brison, S. J. (2002). *Aftermath: Violence and the Remaking of the Self*. Princeton: Princeton University Press.

Browning, C. R. (1998). *Ordinary Men: Reserve Police Battalion 101 and the Final Solution in Poland*. London: Penguin.

Cavarero, A. (2000). *Relating Narratives: Storytelling and Selfhood*. London: Routledge.

Danieli, Y. (1989). "Mourning in Survivors and Children of Survivors of the Nazi Holocaust: The Role of Group and Community Modalities", in Dietrich and Shabad, 427-460.

Daye, R. (2004). *Political Forgiveness: Lessons from South Africa*. New York: Orbis.

De Kock, E. (1998). *A Long Night's Damage: Working for the Apartheid State*. Saxonwold: Contra Press.

Derrida, J. (2001). *On Cosmopolitanism and Forgiveness*. London: Routledge.

Dietrich, D. R. and Shabad, P. C. (eds.) (1989). *The Problem of Loss and Mourning: Psychoanalytic Perspectives*. Madison, CT: International Universities Press.

Dipiero, T. (1993). "A discourse of one's own". In B. Readings and B. Schaber (eds.), *Postmodernism across the Ages: Essays for a Postmodernism that wasn't Born Yesterday*. Syracuse, NY: Syracuse University Press, 109-137.

Driver, D. (2006). "South Africa: Under a new Dispensation?" *Eurozine*, 1-6.

Feldman, A. (2004). "Memory Theatres, Virtual Witnessing and the Trauma-aesthetic". *Biography*, 27, 1, 163-202.

Flahault, F. (2003). *Malice*. London: Verso.

Foster, D., Haupt, P., and De Beer, M. (2005). *The Theatre of Violence:*

Narratives of Protagonists in the South African Conflict. Oxford: James Currey.

Gobodo-Madikizela, P. (2003). *A Human Being Died that Night: A South African Woman Confronts the Legacy of Apartheid*. New York: Houghton Mifflin.

Goosen, J. (1992). *We're not all like that*. Cape Town: Kwela Books.

Griswold, C. L. (2008). *Forgiveness: A Philosophical Exploration*. New York: Cambridge University Press.

Hatley, J. (2000). *Suffering Witness: The Quandary of Responsibility after the Irreparable*. New York, Albany: SUNY Press.

Heyns, M. (2000). "The whole country's truth: Confession and narrative in recent white South African writing". *Modern Fiction Studies*, 46, 1, 42-66.

Humphrey, M. (2002). *The Politics of Atrocity and Reconciliation: From Terror to Trauma*. London: Routledge.

Jackson, M. (2002). *The Politics of Storytelling: Violence, Transgression and Intersubjectivity*. Copenhagen: Museum Tusculanum Press.

Krog, A. (1998). *Country of my Skull*. Johannesburg: Random House.

Kubiak, A. (2004). "Spelling it out: Narrative typologies of terror". *Studies in the Novel*, 36, 3, 294-301.

Levi, P. (1988). *The Drowned and the Saved*. New York: Simon and Schuster.

Malan, R. (1991). *My Traitor's Heart*. London: Vintage.

Minow, M. (1998). *Between Vengeance and Forgiveness: Facing History after Genocide and Mass Violence*. Boston: Beacon Press.

Mitscherlich–Nielsen, M. (1989). "The inability to mourn – today". In Dietrich and Shabad, 405-426.

Nagengast, C. (1994). "Violence, terror and the crisis of the state". *Annual Review of Anthropology*, 23, 109-136.

Ndebele, N. (1998). "Memory, metaphor, and the triumph of narrative", in Nuttall and Coetzee, 19-28.

Norval, A. (1996). *Deconstructing Apartheid Discourse*. London: Verso.

Norval, A. (1998). "Memory, identity and the (im)possibility of reconciliation: The work of the Truth and Reconciliation Commission in South Africa". *Constellations*, 5, 2, 250–265.

Nuttall, S. and Coetzee, C. (eds.) (1998). *Negotiating the Past: The Making of Memory in South Africa*. Oxford: Oxford University Press.

Phelps, T. G. (2004). *Shattered Voices: Language, Violence, and the Work of Truth Commissions*. Philadelphia: University of Pennsylvania Press.

Prager, C. A. L. and Govier, T. (eds.) (2003). *Dilemmas of Reconciliation: Case and Concepts*. Waterloo, Ontario: Wilfrid Laurier University Press.

Scarry, E. (1985). *The Body in Pain: The Making and Unmaking of the World*. Oxford: Oxford University Press.

Stobie, C. (2008). "Fissures in apartheid's 'Eden': Representations of bisexuality in *The Smell of Apples* by Mark Behr". *Research in African Literatures*, 39, 1, 70-80.

Villa-Vicencio, C. and Verwoerd, W. (eds.) (2000). *Looking Back, Reaching Forward*. Cape Town: University of Cape Town Press.

Volf, M. (1996). *Exclusion and Embrace: Theological Explorations of Identity, Otherness and Reconciliation*. Nashville: Abingdon Press.

The Spaces of Post-conflict:
From Void to Reconstruction in Literature and Film on the Spanish Civil War

Tomás Albaladejo

Conflict and Post-conflict, Time and Space

The relationship between conflict and post-conflict is vitally connected to historically and culturally specific time and space. Post-conflict can be considered to be a part of conflict, mainly because conflict does not stop after it or, at least, does not stop for one of the groups involved in conflict. If none of the groups is defeated, conflict can continue into post-conflict, but if there are "winners" and "defeated", post-conflict can contain the features of conflict, as a notional enlargement of it. Time is the category which organizes the set consisting of conflict and post-conflict as a series of different temporalities, with past and present working as stages in which relations between human beings of different ideologies and political positions are habitually placed. Space is another category of conflict and post-conflict, because human relations are generally situated in a set of cultural and social spaces. The same space can be understood, ideologically, as different spaces according to historical time and circumstance. Hence, one can refer to a post-conflict situation formed by some spaces organized temporally, without excluding simultaneity whenever it is perceived to have taken place.

The post-war period of the Spanish Civil War is a paradigmatic post-conflict case. The conflict of ideologies and human beings continued, indeed, has continued, for many years after the end of war on 1 April 1939. The Spanish post-war covers a long period, the end of which is difficult to determine. This post-conflict period can be viewed and explained as a consistent period of time that can be divided into several stages rooted in identifiable cultural and social spaces. As a hypothesis, two such spaces can be distinguished within the Spanish post-war: (a) a first space characterized by void and the lack of public and collective memory of the civil war. This is a space of oblivion, although there is material reconstruction; and (b) a second space characterized by the appearance of a collective memory and the beginning of the reconstruction of life together.

In the following pages, the said spaces are understood and shaped focussing on cultural production, that is, from the point of view of the relation between authors and their works and the underlying historical and political context. My case studies do not belong to the militant and strongly ideologized cultural vein of the Francoist regime, where one can find novels such as *La fiel Infantería* [*The Loyal Infantry*] (1943) by Rafael García Serrano (1983) or the film *Raza* [*Race*] (1941) by the film-maker José Luis Sáenz de Heredia (Pavlović 2009, 66-73), from the novel *Raza* (1942) by Jaime de Andrade – Francisco Franco's pseudonym. Albeit this strand can be taken into account as a perspective stressing the regime's position regarding history and society, one would require a specific study centred on it which considers some of its features, such as the opposition to reconstruction. My interest, however, is in literature and film written and produced in Spain outside and beyond the fascist strand (Rodríguez Puértolas 2008).

Void and the Expression of Silence

This first cultural space is connected to authors living in Spain, not in exile, who describe and show the ostensible void of inaction cum emptiness of Spanish society in general and of any private let alone social life in particular in the post-war period. It consists of works in literature and cinema by authors who did not support the Francoist regime; these are mainly authors and film-makers who might have offered or could have represented a supposedly neutral or objective position within Spain, but who were compelled to remain silent, as a consequence of what I have termed that "void" which is not silence, *per se*, but rather the effect of silencing meaningful post-conflict expression. These individuals were not defenders of the Francoist regime and if their voices were not raised overtly against it, that was because of the repressive time and place in which they lived and performed. They might have intended, or meant to offer, some supposedly objective view of reality, although such an aim was difficult to fulfil. The role of censorship was decisive in imposing such so-called void and silence, whence the continuous effect of imposed oblivion in post-war literature and film. The censors have the support of the political power to cut, to interrupt or to modify literary communication in such a way that they control the literature and discourse of critical positions in order that no one can subvert the totalitarian dominion over society. This is well recognized as a tool of power in dictatorship.

The expression of void is opposed to the views provided and the works produced by exiled authors who could write and publish in freedom, without the censorship of the Francoist regime. The expression of void could be considered as a means of internal opposition to dictatorship, but sometimes the said void implies an absence of memory or, at least, the manifestation of an apparent lack of any discourse of memory and of rituals, texts, and other markers that might attempt to interrogate the past. This void does not exclude the possibility of reconstruction in the post-conflict from a material perspective. Memory is only apparently cancelled by void and its resultant silence; for memory can be shown to survive and to continue to exist despite its public cancellation.

Carmen Laforet's *Nada* [*Nothing*] is a novel published in 1945 which represents, in its very title, the idea of void, continuously manifested throughout the text:

> ¡Cuántos días sin importancia! Los días sin importancia que habían transcurrido desde mi llegada me pesaban encima, cuando arrastraba los pies al regresar de la Universidad. Me pesaban como una cuadrada piedra gris en el cerebro. (Laforet 2008, 97)

> [How many days without importance! The days without importance which had passed since my arrival weighed on me when I dragged my feet along coming back from the University. They weighed on me like a heavy square stone in my brain.][1]

Void is represented as nothingness within a suffocating atmosphere in post-war Barcelona, where the main character of the novel, a girl from another Spanish city, is living at her relatives' home while studying for her university degree. The days lacking importance are a big weight in post-war everyday life for people who do not want to remember the Civil War, and cannot speak about it while trapped in a sad environment. The past Civil War is a curtain, but the novel does not deal with it, even though there are characters who speak about it:

> La abuelita hablaba también, como siempre, de los mismos temas. Eran hechos recientes, de la pasada guerra, y antiguos, de muchos años

---

[1] All translations are my own.

atrás, cuando sus hijos eran niños. (Laforet 2008, 98)

[Granny also talked, as ever, about the same topics. They were recent events of the past war and old ones of many years ago, when her sons were children.]

The novel *Nada* is a first-person narrative, and the grandmother's voice, together with the voice of another character, produce a feeling of void in the narrator, who becomes dozy:

En mi cabeza, un poco dolorida, se mezclaban las dos voces en una cantinela con fondo de lluvia y me adormecían. (Laforet 2008, 98)

[Both voices got mixed up inside my head, a little sore, in an old tune with a background of rain, and made me sleepy.]

The difficulty of seeing and understanding the background of the Civil War in the early post-war is but one component of the space associated with lack or weakness of memory, and the spreading of a generalized or actual oblivion. Nevertheless, the expression of void and silence may still constitute a subtle way of rendering the Civil War powerfully present in the post-war period.

Another significant novel of the post-war is Luis Martín-Santos' *Tiempo de silencio* [*Time of Silence*], finished in 1960, and first published in 1961, with parts of the text falling victim to censorship. The first complete edition of this novel was published in 1981. The title of Martín-Santos' novel is a manifestation of void in post-conflict: although the novel was not written in the early post-war, it deals with the post-war period:

Es un tiempo de silencio [...] Por aquí abajo nos arrastramos y nos vamos yendo hacia el sitio donde tenemos que ponernos silenciosamente a esperar silenciosamente que los años vayan pasando y que silenciosamente nos vayamos hacia donde se van todas las florecillas del mundo. (Martín-Santos 1997, 284)

[It is a time of silence [...] Down here we drag ourselves and are going towards the place where we have to stay silently to wait silently for years to pass and for us to go silently towards the place where all little flowers of the world eventually go.]

The action of *Tiempo de silencio* is situated in 1949 (Labanyi 1985, 15), ten years after the end of the Civil War, and hence it portrays the atmosphere of the space of the post-war in which post-conflict is a silent version of conflict and, consequently, everything is dominated by silence. The reiteration of "silencio" and "silenciosamente" in the above extract points to the denial of discourse in the primary cultural and political space of post-conflict.

Cinema, too, is not without the enactment of void in post-conflict. Several films were made after the Spanish Civil War by film-makers who did not agree with Francoist ideology, but could not fight openly against it because of political repression and censorship. This is the case of one of the best and most well-known (as well as most critical) films of the Spanish post-war, *Bienvenido, Mister Marshall* [*Welcome, Mister Marshall*] (1952) (Pavlović 2009, 119), a film by Luis García Berlanga. *Bienvenido, Mister Marshall* strongly criticizes Franco's regime and its relationship with the USA and the Marshall Plan, which never arrived in Spain. In the same way, in the film, the Americans do not stop at Villar del Río, a little Castilian town transformed into an Andalusian town in order to reach the highest possible level of Spanish conventional picturesque appearance, so that the visiting Americans would like it and enjoy it. The success of this film is linked to its subtle criticism of Francoist internal policy. *Bienvenido, Mister Marshall* represents the attitude of that first post-war space, where there is a lack of memory regarding the past conflict, and where oblivion of the real conflict dominates the post-conflict. García Berlanga's film is a sample of void *vis-à-vis* the post-conflict and is a manifestation of the negation of memory in the film, though the film-maker himself was well aware of the post-conflict situation. His film *El verdugo* [*The Hangman*] (1963) (Pavlović 2009, 113 ff.) can also be situated in a similar suspended space of post-conflict oblivion.

Writers and film-makers sharing the above-mentioned characteristics of the first space of post-conflict did their best to portray the void imposed upon contemporary Spanish society, as far as was possible within the Francoist State. Hence, one could refer to the position of some writers and film-makers as one of enclave, since they were aware of the real situation of post-conflict in the post-war period and were surrounded by the official apparatus which maintained dictatorial power and conditioned every social and cultural sphere including, not least, the representation of post-conflict. However, because they lived in an enclave-Spain, they could not express their awareness openly. The will to reconstruct is present in this phase and in the first space of post-conflict yet it is disappointed because of the predominant political control. Spanish society did not lack, but rather hid, memory as it fosussed on oblivion and void for the sake of survival. Memory was thus cancelled and, of course, could not be manifested by those writers who lived in Spain yet were not followers of the Francoist dictatorship. They were able to show, despite everything, and however indirectly, the pervasive void and consequent silence that characterized the post-conflict socciety.

Thus, post-conflict can be considered to be expressed by means of silence and void in works created within the borders of Spain, with obvious differences in relation to the works created by exiled authors and published abroad, without the control of the Francoist regime. The titles of Carmen Laforet's *Nada* and Luis Martín-Santos' *Tiempo de silencio* are significant of the oxymoron constituted by the expression of silence, by the words and images of silence and void, which fill the emptiness of a society in a post-conflict period.

The Francoist regime's consciousness of the demonized if rarely characterized *enemy* is present, nevertheless, during the first space of post-conflict.[2] It is mainly an internal enemy, although there is a stereotyped external enemy, too, and this "Godless", "anti-Christ" and "anti-Spain" external enemy is considered to be sinisterly connected to the internal one. Hence, all those writing in Spain and who criticize the regime in any manner are viewed and treated as internal enemies with undeniable associations with the external enemies. This compels writers and film-makers to produce works in which silence as an expression of the post-conflict void is their only available tool for criticism.

Memory and Reconstruction of Life Together

The second space of the long post-conflict of the Spanish Civil War begins with Franco's death in 1975 and the ensuing *Transición*, the political transition from dictatorship to democracy (Soto Carmona 1998; Albaladejo 2003). One of the features of this stage is that official political censorship disappears, although one can consider that there are always different forms of censorship in societies, from economic or social entities.

[2] For the concept of *enemy* as opposed to *friend* in the constitution of the political, see Schmitt (1998 [1932], 49-66), Moreiras (2000, 126 ff.) and Curtis (2006, 111-132).

Memory, understood as rethinking the past and its multiply complex and buried memories, is one of the topoi and tools of reconstruction. If oblivion cultivates void and silence, and consequently forces that which is implicit upon literary and film creation and communication, memory is the basis of the thinking of all possibilities in perceiving society, and of thinking in the field of political and social ideas. Without memory there is no chance for the reconstruction of relationships in a plural society in post-conflict, and memory is the tool for defeating the oblivion and suspension of historical situations in which the conflict continues to live in a post-conflict situation defined by the pre-eminence of the winner over the defeated. Memory arises in the middle of a previous oblivion manifested by silence, and encourages the reconstruction of a wounded society via the breaking of the silence and the seeking of expressed support for a new life together for a people ideologically confronted as a way to end post-conflict and, consequently, conflict itself. It is a space of hope as to a new joint life for all members of a society divided by the past conflict, and even divided by the post-conflict situation which has enlarged and exacerbated the experience of conflict over time.

This second, notably contrastive, cultural and political space is the stage which contains the Spanish *Transición*, but it must be recalled that it also contains the first years after the process of transition, during the arduous consolidation of democracy in Spain. It will be remembered, too, that there was an attempted coup on 23 February 1981, with the kidnapping of the members of the Parliament and the government for many hours in the palace of the *Congreso de los Diputados*, the Lower House of the Chamber of the Spanish Parliament. Hence, the years of memory and reconstruction are far from homogeneous because there was overt instability at the beginning and relative stability and consolidation of democracy only afterwards.

A significant novel of this second space is Javier Cercas's *Soldados de Salamina* [*Soldiers of Salamis*], published in 2001. This novel is based on a fact, the escape of Rafael Sánchez Mazas, a falangist writer who was a prisoner of the Republican army; he was shot in a collective execution ("*fusilamiento*"), but he was not hurt and succeeded in passing off as dead, also managing to escape with the help of some young countrymen ("*los amigos del bosque*" ["the friends of the forest"]) of the Northern province of Gerona on the south side of the Pyrenees, who had deserted from the Republican army near their home in the Catalan forests. The plot is not only focused on Rafael Sánchez Mazas, but also on an unknown Republican soldier who saw him when he was hidden amid foliage and decided not to shoot him. An important part of the novel is the search for this soldier among the Spaniards exiled in France. The unknown soldier had been identified by the well-known *pasodoble* "Suspiros de España" [Sighs of Spain] he sang when he was a guard of the Nationalist prisoners. Cercas' novel is a combination of reality – Rafael Sánchez Mazas did exist, the Chilean writer Roberto Bolaño appears as a character in the novel, and there are many other real characters – and fiction,[3] which becomes jointly fiction according to the law of semantic maximum of the theory of fiction (Albaladejo 1992, 52-63). Cercas put this combination at the service of reconstruction, with the support of memory. Sánchez Mazas is the main focus of this novel, like the writer Andrés Trapiello, whose opinions about the Falangist writer are taken into account by Cercas:

Dice Andrés Trapiello que, como tantos escritores falangistas, Sánchez Mazas ganó la guerra y perdió la historia de la literatura. La frase es brillante y, en parte, cierta, o por lo menos lo fue, porque durante un tiempo Sánchez Mazas pagó con el olvido su brutal responsabilidad en una matanza brutal; pero también es cierto que, al ganar la guerra, quizá Sánchez Mazas se perdió a sí mismo como escritor. (Cercas 2001, 140)

[Andrés Trapiello says that, like so many falangist writers, Sánchez Mazas won the war and lost the history of literature. The sentence is brilliant and partly true or, at least, it was partly true because for some time Sánchez Mazas paid with oblivion for his brutal responsibility in a brutal slaughter; but it is also true that, by winning the war, Sánchez Mazas perhaps lost himself as a writer.]

The author stresses Spanishness, which is revealed in the scene in which

---

[3] Javier Cercas' last work is a chronicle novel, *Anatomía de un instante* [*Anatomy of an Instant*] (2009) about the above-mentioned putsch of 23 February 1981, which can be connected with the New Journalism and with its precedent, the non-fiction novel or testimony novel *Operación Masacre* [*Operation Massacre*] published in 1957 by the Argentinian writer Rodolfo Walsh (2003). See Martínez Arnaldos and Pujante Segura (2012) for *Anatomía de un instante*. Equally relevant are Martín Cerezo and Rodríguez Pequeño (2011).

an unknown Republican soldier sings the *pasodoble "Suspiros de España"* (Cercas 2001, 121-122), some verses of which evoke exile:

> Tierra gloriosa de mi querer,
> tierra bendita de perfume y pasión,
> España, en toda flor a tus pies
> suspira un corazón.
> Ay de mi pena mortal,
> porque me alejo, España, de ti,
> porque me arrancan de mi rosal.
> (Cercas 2001, 49)

> [Glorious land of my love,
> blessed land of scent and passion,
> Spain, a heart sighs
> in every bloom at your feet.
> Oh my deadly sorrow,
> because I am moving away from you, Spain,
> because I am being pulled out of my rose bush.]

The separation from the country expressed in this song is not voluntary, but forced by an external agent. This *pasodoble* is recurrent throughout the novel and works as a link between different attitudes and views of the Spanish situation of war and conflict, as well as of post-conflict.

The last novel by Antonio Muñoz Molina, *La noche de los tiempos* [*The Night of Times*] (2009) can be placed in this second space, that of memory and reconstruction. This novel offers a realistic and critical view of the Spanish political and social situation during the months preceding the beginning of the Civil War and the first months of it; it is set in Madrid, although it is also valid for other places in Spain. The hero, Ignacio Abel, an architect with Republican and socialist ideas and a member of the Socialist Party and the socialist trade union linked to the Socialist Party, represents many Spaniards who desired social progress and the modernization of Spain, but did not agree with certain undemocratic behaviours which acted against freedom. Ignacio Abel left a village in the Sierra de Guadarrama in order to go to Madrid when the Spanish army of Morocco was rebelling. If he had remained in the nationalist zone, where his family's villa was, he would surely have been executed or imprisoned, and was about to be executed when the *milicianos* searched for him at his home in Madrid, but was saved at the wall where he was to be shot. Here agin, the combination of fiction and reality contributes to the literary and human strength of Molina's novel.

One of the features of creation of memory and reconstruction of the second space is that its authors are not conservative, but generally leftist or democratic. They defend an active role of memory in the reconstruction of a divided society. This is the case with the great film-maker Luis García-Berlanga, too. The author of *Bienvenido, Mister Marshall* directed the film *La vaquilla* [*The little cow*] within the second phase of post-conflict. The script of *La vaquilla* was finished by Berlanga in 1956, although he had written a first version of it in 1948, but he could not make this film in those years of the first phase of post-conflict. This was because the Republican army and the Nationalist army were shown with humour in the film, which would have been censored. However, the second space was absolutely suitable for the film, and it was finally produced in the eighties. *La vaquilla* was premiered in 1985; it presents the war's front line on which the Republican and the Nationalist armies faced each other, and a bullfight that takes place in the no man's land which separates the lines of the conflicting armies. The little cow, which will die in the end, is an allegory of Spain, which dies while Spaniards are fighting against themselves. The Spanishness of the characters of both armies is stressed, and the bullfight as allegory is at the service of this idea, because everybody, Republicans and Nationalists alike, are fond of it. Besides, bullfighting is presented in the film as a typical tradition of Spaniards, in spite of the debate within Spain regarding bullfights.

The cancellation of oblivion as a void opens a broad gate to memory, which fills the void of the precedent space of post-conflict. Thus, it is possible to reach a position in writing and film which contributes strongly to the reconstruction of a wounded society whose life together is yet conditioned during post-conflict by the war that has ended. Literature and film of this second space put great stress on the fact that both parties to the Spanish Civil War were Spanish, and that reconstruction based on memory is a way of putting an end to the long post-war period which had been dominated until the *Transición* by the winners' ideology and power with a Manichaeism consisting of thinking of their own views and ideas as co-extensive with the views and ideas of Spain at large, while the defeated groups' views and ideas would be considered anti-Spanish. One must take into account that the Francoist regime considered that all its enemies were enemies of Spain, by identifying the political regime with the country, as do many other totalitarian regimes. On the contrary, literature and film of this second space had the aim of remembering all those who suffered during war time and the long post-conflict time.

The Revision of Reconstruction

A third space could be distinguished in the complex post-conflict or in post-post-conflict in Spain. It would be a space characterized by the revision of reconstruction, which can be considered as an attempt at the reconstruction of reconstruction. This third space arose when criticism of the *Transición* had been put forward by people asking for its revision in order that the victims of the Francoist regime should receive the acknowledgement they deserved. With this social movement in view, in 2007 the Spanish Parliament passed the Ley de Memoria Histórica (Law of Historical Memory). Regardless of this law and before it, authors like Isaac Rosa had published works which reclaimed the memory of the victims of the defeated; this is the case with his novel, *La malamemoria* [*The bad memory*] (1999), from which his novel *¡Otra maldita novela sobre la Guerra Civil!* [*Another goddamned novel about the Civil War!*] (2007) arises metatextually. These are novels which offer a revision of the reconstruction made in the second space. Memory is also present, but focusing on the defeated of the Civil War. As to films of this third space, one can quote Emilio Martínez Lázaro's *Las trece rosas* [*The Thirteen Roses*] (2008) (Bernárdez Rodal 2009, 61-63). The spirit of the *Transición* is discussed by authors of this third space, which is not always temporally subsequent to the second space. Reconstruction is revised and reconstructed in an attempt to reach a higher level of empathy with the victims of Francoism.

This matter has triggered great controversy in Spain, pitting those who wish to revise the political transition against those who, albeit not supporters of the Francoist regime, argue that the transition process from dictatorship to democracy created a political balance that should be preserved. They claim that maintaining this balance prevents one party from annihilating the other, which is a significant fear in Spain after more than one hundred years of civil wars. The great poet Antonio Machado expresses it in *Proverbios y cantares* [*Proverbs and songs*], from his book of poems *Campos de Castilla* [*Fields of Castile*]:

Españolito que vienes
al mundo, te guarde Dios.
Una de las dos Españas
ha de helarte el corazón.
(Machado 1976, 15)

[God guard you, little Spaniard
who come to the world.
One of the two Spains
will freeze your heart.]

The Role of Memory: Cultural Memory and Cultural Rhetoric

Memory is present even when it is absent (or seems to be absent). Memory is decisive in the second and the third spaces of post-conflict, but it is also important in the first space. The reconstruction of the missing parts of the past is a reconstruction for the whole society, and restores knowledge of events, attitudes and responsibilities, whose cancellation had previously prevented a just life together, because memory is connected to justice (Todorov 2008 [1995]). But memory and oblivion are not exactly opposed (Ricoeur 1999, 53 ff.; Demaria 2006, 25 ff.); memory can control oblivion in a selective view of the past. Hence, memory is important in the first space, too, as its role is that of providing knowledge of the past even when it gives place to oblivion as an instrument for survival. The result of it is void, but a void under the control of a memory which does not want to be active in certain circumstances. Cristina Demaria writes:

L'oggetto stesso della memoria è il risultato di una selezione, dell'intreccio tra memoria e oblio, frutto di processi d'interpretazione, di rimozione e di elaborazione dei lasciti del passato. (Demaria 2006, 43)

[The object of memory itself is the result of a choice, of the framework of memory and oblivion, the outcome of processes of interpretation, the removal and elaboration of legacies of the past.]

Memory is one of the engines which work also to include and welcome in society those members who were pushed into exile. When the post-conflict conditions which prevent exiled people from coming back to their country have ceased to be, many of the exiled travel, but still others remain where they have found a new life. Memory acts then as the link which allows us to connect them to the country of origin and allows them to connect themselves to it (Bromley 2000; Hewitt and Geary 2007). It is a combination of individual memory and collective memory (Demaria 2006, 37 ff.), and it is a case of cultural memory (Erll and Rigney 2009), as Astrid Erll and Ann Rigney suggest:

> [O]ne can note a shift towards understanding cultural memory in more dynamic terms: as an ongoing process of remembrance and forgetting in which individuals and groups continue to reconfigure their relationship to the past and hence reposition themselves in relation to established and emergent memory sites. (Erll and Rigney 2009, 2)

The manifestation of cultural memory in discourses (literary discourses, rhetorical discourses, films and other artistic forms) allows for its sharing and its enlarging in the galaxy of discourses we live by. Literature and film as dealt with by Bernard McGuirk in his book on the war and post-conflict of the Falklands/Malvinas (2007) contribute towards the cultural memory of this conflict and post-conflict, as cartoons do as well (2008). Cultural memory is constructed by a plurality of discourses; it is the result of polyphony (Bakhtin 1968 [1929, 9-63]), as many voices representing a great number of ideas and a plural consciousness constitute its complex producer parallel to the complexity of society.

Cultural imagination, explained by Antonio García-Berrio as follows, is thus shown to be relevant for cultural memory:

> Along with poetic fantasy's vital, essential and existential discoveries, literature has fostered and nourished another special form of the non-anthropological imagination, which I call the *cultural imagination*, an endogamous activity of artistic fabulation in which poetry feeds on the poetic imagination crystallized in privileged mythical moments. (García-Berrio 1992, 347)

This imagination is related to cultural memory, because of its condition of mythical construction. Here memory has an important role regarding its constitution by means of gathering cultural elements and frames and its activation by means of their recollection. Cultural imagination is mapped onto literature by means of cultural memory.

Cultural memory is important in post-conflict situations, because it consolidates a frame which provides consciousness of situation and orientation for individuals in society and for society through individuals. Cultural memory as a set of issues within a structure shared by the members of society is connected to cultural rhetoric (Albaladejo 2009a, 2009b), which maps it into production, communication and interpretation of discourses. Cultural rhetoric activates the intensification of cultural memory by convincing and persuading people as to the role of memory in social life. Polyacroasis (Albaladejo 1998) is inherent to cultural rhetoric and the formation, consolidation and acceptance of cultural memory. The representation of conflict and post-conflict (Grandi 2007; Grandi and Demaria 2008) is characterized by polyacroasis. Representation as mediation between reality or ideas and the interpreters of sign construction (Pitkin 1972; Erll and Rigney 2009) opens new gates to society and interpretation of represented reality and memory by means of discourses as cultural devices rhetorically organized and intensified.

Memory is a tool and a way which leads from void to reconstruction and even to the revision of reconstruction and the reconstruction of reconstruction. Memory, as cultural memory, works as an active treasure of society whose investments are always for a future taking into account the past and the experience of it with the aim of improving people's lives together.

References: Texts

Albaladejo, T. (1992). *Semántica de la narración: la ficción realista*. Madrid: Taurus.

Albaladejo, T. (1998). "Polyacroasis in Rhetorical Discourse". *The Canadian Journal of Rhetorical Studies – La Revue Canadienne d'Études Rhétoriques*, 9, 155-167.

Albaladejo, T. (2003). "Vives' Rhetorical Ideas and the Oratory of the Spanish Political *Transición*: Two Proposals for Political Life". In J. Axer (ed.), *Rhetoric of Transformation*. Warsaw: Centre for Studies on the Classical Tradition in Poland and in East-Central Europe of Warsaw University, 29-39.

Albaladejo, T. (2009a). "La poliacroasis en la representación literaria: un componente de la Retórica cultural". *Castilla. Estudios de Literatura*, o, nueva época, 1-26. At **www5.uva.es/castilla/wp/wp-content/uploads/2009/11/Albaladejo-Tom%C3%A1s.-La-po liacroasis-en-la-representaci%C3%B3n-literaria2.pdf**. Accessed 1 October 2010.

Albaladejo, T. (2009b). "Retórica de la comunicación y retórica en sociedad." In H. Beristaín, and G. Ramírez Vidal (eds.), *Crisis de la historia*. Mexico City: Universidad Nacional Autónoma de México, 39-58.

Andrade, J. de (1942). *Raza*. Madrid: Numancia.

Bakhtin, M. (1968). *Dostoevskij. Poetica e stilistica*. Turin: Einaudi.

Bernárdez Rodal, A. (2009). "De la violencia institucional a la violencia de género: últimas representaciones cinematográficas de la Guerra Civil en el cine español contemporáneo". *Revista Canadiense de Estudios Hispánicos*, 34, 1, 61-75.

Bromley, R. (2000). *Narratives for a New Belonging. Diasporic Cultural Fictions*. Edinburgh: Edinburgh University Press.

Cercas, J. (2001). *Soldados de Salamina*, 6th ed. Barcelona: Tusquets.

Cercas, J. (2009). *Anatomía de un instante*. Barcelona: Mondadori.

Curtis, N. (2006). *War and Social Theory: World, Value and Identity*. London: Palgrave Macmillan.

Demaria, C. (2006). *Semiotica e memoria: Analisis del post-conflitto*. Rome: Carocci.

Demaria, C., and Wright, C. (eds.) (2006). *Post-Conflict Cultures: Rituals of Representation*. London: Zoilus Press.

Erll, A., and Rigney, A. (eds.) (2009). *Mediation, Remediation, and the Dynamics of Cultural Memory*. Berlin and New York: De Gruyter.

Fussell, P. (2003). *Tiempo de guerra: Conciencia y engaño en la Segunda Guerra Mundial*. Madrid: Turner.

Fussell, P. (2006). *La Gran Guerra y la memoria moderna*. Madrid: Turner.

García-Berrio, A. (1992). *A Theory of the Literary Text*. Berlin and New York: De Gruyter.

García Quiroga, D. F., Seear, M. (eds.) (2009). *Hors de Combat: The Falklands-Malvinas Conflict in Retrospect*. Nottingham: Critical, Cultural and Communications Press.

García Serrano, R. (1983). *La fiel Infantería*. Barcelona: Planeta.

Goh, C., and McGuirk, B. (eds.) (2007). *Happiness and Post-Conflict*. Nottingham: Critical, Cultural and Communications Press.

Grandi, R. (2007). "On the Promotion of Conflict: The Media and War". In Goh and McGuirk (eds.), 18-32.

Grandi, R., and Demaria, C. (eds.) (2008). *Marketing e rappresentazione dei conflitti: Media, opinione pubblica, costruzione del consenso.* Bologna: Bononia University Press.

Gill, D. C. (ed.) (2010). *How We Are Changed by War: A Study of Letters and Diaries from Colonial Conflicts to Operation Iraqi Freedom.* London: Routledge.

Hewitt, N., and Geary, D. (eds.) (2007). *Diaspora(s): Movements and Cultures.* Nottingham: Critical, Cultural and Communications Press.

Labanyi, J. (1985). *Ironía e historia en "Tiempo de silencio".* Madrid: Taurus.

Laforet, C. (2008). *Nada* (ed. R. Navarro Durán). Madrid and Barcelona: Espasa Calpe-Destino.

Machado, A. (1976). *Campos de Castilla* (ed. J. L. Cano). Madrid: Cátedra.

Martín-Santos, L. (1997). *Tiempo de silencio*, 41st ed. Barcelona: Seix Barral.

Martín Cerezo, I., and Rodríguez Pequeño, J. (2011). "La narrativa de no ficción (o periodismo literario) y la narrativa policiaca". In A. L. Baquero Escudero, F. Carmona Fernández, M. Martínez Arnaldos, and A. Martínez Pérez (eds.), *La interconexión genérica en la tradición narrativa*, 261-275.

Martínez Arnaldos, M., and Pujante Segura, C. M. (2012). "Anatomía de un instante, de Javier Cercas, como proceso interdiscursivo: ficcional, periodístico y televisivo". *Crisol: Revue du Centre de Recherches Ibériques et Ibéro-Américaines de l'Université de Paris X-Nanterre*, 12.

McGuirk, B. (2007). *Falklands/Malvinas: An Unfinished Business.* Seattle: New Ventures.

McGuirk, B. (2008). "La liberazione degli *animot*. Le vignette di satira politica sulla Guerra delle Falklands/Malvinas. "Humor" e *The If... Chronicles* 25 anni dopo". In Grandi and Demaria (eds.), 227-314.

Moreiras, A. (2000). "Una relación de pensamiento. El fin de la subalternidad". *Tropelías: Revista de Teoría de la Literatura y Literatura Comparada*, 11, 121-142.

Muñoz Molina, A. (2009). *La noche de los tiempos.* Barcelona: Seix Barral.

Pavlović, T. (ed.) (2009). *100 Years of Spanish Cinema.* Malden: Wiley-Blackwell.

Pitkin, H. F. (1972). *The Concept of Representation*. Berkeley & Los Angeles: University of California Press.

Quinn, P. J., and Trout, S. (eds.) (2001). *The Literature of the Great War Reconsidered: Beyond Modern Memory*. Basingstoke: Palgrave Macmillan.

Ricoeur, P. (1999). *La lectura del tiempo pasado: memoria y olvido*. Madrid: Arrecife.

Rodríguez Puértolas, J. (2008). *Historia de la literatura fascista española*. 2nd. vol. Madrid: Akal.

Rosa, I. (1999). *La malamemoria*. Badajoz: Del Oeste.

Rosa, I. (2007). *¡Otra maldita novela sobre la Guerra Civil!* Barcelona: Seix Barral.

Schmitt, C. (1998). *El concepto de lo político*. Madrid: Alianza.

Soto Carmona, Á. (1998). *La transición a la democracia: España, 1975-1982*. Madrid: Alianza.

Todorov, T. (2008). *Los abusos de la memoria*. Barcelona: Paidós Ibérica.

Walsh, R. (1957). *Operación Masacre*. Buenos Aires: Ediciones de la Flor.

References: Films

García Berlanga, L. (1952). *Bienvenido, Mister Marshall*.

García Berlanga, L. (1963). *El verdugo*.

García Berlanga, L. (1985). *La vaquilla*.

Martínez Lázaro, E. (2008). *Las trece rosas*.

Sáenz de Heredia, J. L. (1941). *Raza*.

(Post-)Urbicide: Reconstruction and Ideology in some Cities of Former Yugoslavia

Francesco Mazzucchelli

Introduction: Toward a Semiotics of Reconstruction

In this chapter I shall present some of the results of broader research, which I conducted in 2008, concerning the urban transformations of four cities in former Yugoslavia: Sarajevo, Mostar, Dubrovnik and Belgrade (Mazzucchelli 2010). In that research I analyzed the changes in the processes of representation and auto-representation of identities and collective and shared memories – in other words, the "images", to use the expression of Kevin Lynch (1960) – of those cities after the Yugoslavian wars of the nineties.

My methodology varies: the main theoretical frame refers to semiotics (particularly spatial and urban semiotics) but is "hybridized" with other related perspectives such as cultural geography, urban ethnography and architectural theory. In fact, the subject of my study is heterogeneous as well. On the one hand, I look at the architectonic and urban changes (new projects, architectures, edifices, monuments, plans, but also restoration and reconstruction projects, extending to apparently minor alterations, like toponomy, production/elimination of symbols, apposition/removal/ destruction of commemorative plaques and so on). On the other hand, I carried out a sort of ethnographic investigation: I spent more than three months in those cities for field research, collecting information, conducting interviews, verifying the manner in which "semiotic perception" has changed in certain parts of the city, observing the city's "social life" and some relevant urban practices. The data of my observation were then subjected to a semiotic method of analysis.

In the following pages, I shall focus mainly on the first aspect of my study, that is, the analysis of urban transformations after the post-war works of reconstructions and architectonical restoration. Obviously, cities are not made only of buildings, streets, squares and monuments, but are a "knotty fabric" of practices, "objects" and "discourses" which continually redefine the meanings and identities of their places, like a dynamic text written by many authors, including the people who experience it, who walk in and "use" the city itself; from this point of view, narrowing down the observation, as I will do in this article, to a "bird's-eye perspective" (i.e. looking only at the political choices made at the top which address reconstruction projects and works) and excluding the "street perspective" of the urban practices could be seen as a strong limitation. Indeed, I shall try to demonstrate how a semiotic analysis of an architectonic object (and its transformations) includes an observation of urban processes and practices as well, inasmuch as, assuming that a place can be considered a meaningful and significant "scrap of the world", it contemplates the encompassing of the subjectivities (and their "performances") inscribed in a space and its syntactic and semantic roles.[1] According to this position, a building or a place is not only an "object", but a complex configuration – in other words, a "text".[2]

Moreover, looking at cities from a semiotic point of view means considering the architecture (and all the places which constitute a city) as narrations or, in another word, "narratives" which use space rather than time, as "verbal narratives" do. The subject of this article is then the process of "spatialization of memory" or rather, to better explain it, the processes which transform geographic (in this case, urban) landscapes into "inscapes of national identity" (Bhabha 1994, 143) through the conversion of a "piece of city" in a place of history and identity.[3] This assumption considers the space of a city (and space in general) as a language that can *speak of memory* but, moreover, which can *speak memory* as well. This assumption implies that space possesses a sort of "narratability" which enables spatial narrations of memory.

The cities I analyze have been theatres of war during the nineties: Sarajevo underwent a terrible siege by Serbian paramilitary forces for almost four years (from 1992 to 1995) and nearly ten thousand people died there during the war; Mostar was first attacked by Yugoslavian army in 1992, then, in the following years, was torn by the civil war between

---

[1] For a critical discussion of these theoretical problems see, in particular, Greimas (1976); Hammad (2006); Marrone (2001); Violi (2009a; 2009b).

[2] Semiotics considers text both as a core unity of a cultural universe of a society (and in this sense not only verbal text, but also paintings, architecture and even places can be seen as texts as well), and as a model of analysis (broadly speaking, a consistent configuration of sense, decomposable in units and relations between units). For an elaboration of this conceptual framing, see Marrone (2010).

[3] On the relation between space and collective memory see J. Assmann (1992), A. Assmann (1999); Nora (1984) and Ricoeur (2000).

Bosniaks and Croats;[4] Dubrovnik was heavily bombed by the Yugoslavian Army in 1991; Belgrade was the first European city bombed by NATO, during the humanitarian war in Kosovo in 1999.[5]

The war has left traces of destruction in all these cities, not only on the material surface of the urban landscapes, but also in the collective consciousness and imaginary of these cities, in their "semiotic identities". Indeed, in many instances, these war traces are still present; in other cases they were transformed, removed, or even monumentalized. In any case, one would say that war was and continues to be a strong "stretch of identity" of these cities.

Urbicide: When War Slaughters Cities.

Many have used the concept of *urbicide* to describe this particular way of conducting war, addressed primarily against the city and the values of urban culture it represents. We could define urbicide as a war strategy which aims to destroy the shared identities and memories represented in the urban environment, in other words, to erase the collective memory of the city. In this respect, urbicide is to be considered as a violent practice of de-memorization of the urban landscape (Dell'Agnese and Squarcina 2002).[6]

The term has its origin in the work of Marshall Berman, who spoke of urbicide in relation to the demolitions in the Bronx, New York, which completely changed the neighbourhood's appearance and its historical legacy; the term was then rediscovered by a group of Yugoslav architects (lead by Bogdan Bogdanovic, architect and former mayor of Belgrade during the eighties) and used specifically to explain this distinctive feature of Yugoslav Wars (Ribarevic-Nikolic and Juric 1992). Bogdanovic described urbicide as the "ritual murder of the cities", rooted in the contrast between "city lovers" and "city haters":

> For years I had been developing the thesis that one of the moving forces behind the rise and fall of civilisations is the eternal Manichaean [...] battle between city lovers and city haters, a battle waged in every nation, every culture, every individual. [...] Then came

[4] Here I prefer the term Bosniak to either Bosnian Muslim (which refers only to a religious identity) or Bosnian (referring only to a geographic identity).
[5] For a historiography of Yugoslav Wars, see Silber and Little (1996).
[6] See also Bevan (2006) and Fregonese (2009).

the moment when I realized to my horror that "it" was our day-to-day reality. Together with ritual murder as such I see the ritual murder of the city. (Bogdanovic 1993)

So, according to Bogdanovic, in an "urbicide war" military targets go beyond strategic relevance: the intent of every attack is instead destruction of the cultural landmarks and the cultural heritage, as well as all the places of high collective value. The destruction of the city, Bogdanovic says, aims to eradicate that urban culture grounded on the cosmopolitan, multicultural and liberal culture that characterized many cities in the former Yugoslavia, expressing the conflict between the civilized city environment and the peasant's mentality: a war between city and country.

Following the trail of Bogdanovic's thought, other scholars, such as Stephen Graham (2004) and Martin Shaw (2003), compared urbicide to a form of genocide, inasmuch as it implies a deliberate and systematic destruction of the group's environment. Another scholar, Martin Coward – partly challenging the oversimplification that opposes the cosmopolitanism of cities and urban culture versus the retrograde and conservative rural culture of the countryside – states that urbicide should be framed not necessarily as a genocidal war, but as a specific kind of war, with its own peculiarity, arguing that we should abandon an anthropocentric vision of "political violence against the city". Urbicide should be otherwise understood as a war that assumes the city itself in its materiality to be something to destroy inasmuch as it is the space of heterogeneity and of confrontation with otherness (Coward 2008).

One of the most forceful examples of urbicide is probably the siege of Sarajevo. As with many other cities "murdered by war" during Yugoslav conflicts, Sarajevo, known as the Jerusalem of the Balkans, had always represented an extraordinary historical example of a cultural melting pot and mixed ethnicity. The city itself depicts this plurality very well, with all its mosques, Catholic and Orthodox churches and synagogues coexisting and embodying a particular way of living together.[7]

During the war, Sarajevo was subjected to continuous grenade and bullet fire for four years, and the main targets were libraries, squares, churches, monuments, mosques, places where people used to gather: all the material embodiment of that multiculturalism. The aggressor's aim

---

[7] For a careful history of the city of Sarajevo, see Donia (2006).

was to destroy the unique way the inhabitants co-existed as embodied in the structure of the city, which was perceived as a threat to the nationalist ideology of those who pursued war. And we could say the same for Mostar, Dubrovnik, and also for other cities not listed in my corpus, such as Vukovar. In all these cities the targets were not relevant from a military point of view: the aggressors were not bombing and shelling strategic targets, but the city's cultural identity.

Urban Reconstruction as a City Re-Foundation.

My research focuses mainly, not on the moment of destruction of the cities, but on the post-war phase. The post-war period is in fact a moment of complete redefinition of all value systems (whether epistemic, ethical or aesthetic). It is a catastrophic moment, in mathematician René Thom's definition of the word as well: a moment in which the production of a discontinuity can lead to new forms, new frames; in other words, a "morphogenesis", in direct connection with his obverse, the tendency to "permanence" (Thom 1972). Using this interpretative key, post-war reconstruction can itself be seen as a "catastrophe", consistent and strongly connected to the war intended as a catastrophe itself, in the common sense of the word. Indeed, the projects and the works of restoration, especially in post-war times, strongly reflect the processes of re-definition and re-construction of collective identities, and so they can be considered practices of (re)invention of cultural memory. Moreover, reconstruction affects the urban spaces which – besides being diachronically stratified and then plurivocal and polysemic "texts" – are important places for the definition of our personal and collective "landscapes of memory" and probably the prototypical places for the "staging" of identities and collective memory. So it is possible to read the configuration of the renovated map of identity and memory values directly from the transformation of the city palimpsest.

My aim then is to study the post-war transformation in collective identities by looking at the cities themselves, trying to search for the social and cultural transformations behind the changing urban form, and considering the architectonical and urban reconstructions as spatial narrations. Indeed, urbicide always produces a specular post-urbicide period: on the one hand, this phase is characterized by the restoration of what was destroyed through architectonic reconstructions; on the other hand, we could say that there is a sort of complex semiotic dialogue between the destruction caused by the war and the reconstruction of the post-war period. Moreover, we should not consider the reconstruction as the simple direct opposite of the action of destruction. In fact, even if, as we have seen, urbicide is a practice of de-memorization that wishes to produce oblivion (destroying cultural and social symbols) and reconstruction seems always to be directed to the "re-establishment" of such lost symbols and memory (being thus a "re-memorization practice"), there is what we could call a paradox which connects these two moments. Urbicide also produces a memory through its results (ruins, remains; in other words, traces); reconstruction, while it aims at restoring memory, simultaneously produces oblivion, as a result of the removal of the traces of destruction caused by the urbicide. The common opinion about architectonic restoration considers it a way to preserve memory, to preserve a past neutrally; my hypothesis is that restoration and reconstruction, inasmuch as they treat traces (converting them into signs of memory, history, or even oblivion), constitute a practice of the (re)writing of memory.

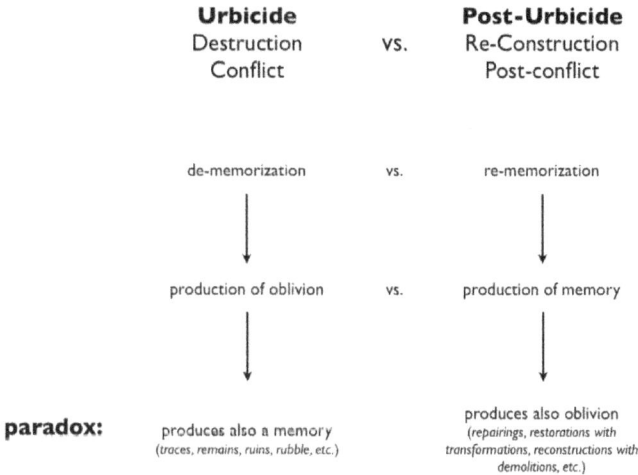

	Urbicide		**Post-Urbicide**
	Destruction	vs.	Re-Construction
	Conflict		Post-conflict

	de-memorization	vs.	re-memorization
	↓		↓
	production of oblivion	vs.	production of memory
	↓		↓
paradox:	produces also a memory (traces, remains, ruins, rubble, etc.)		produces also oblivion (repairings, restorations with transformations, reconstructions with demolitions, etc.)

Sarajevo: the Temptations of Oblivion

Sarajevo still shows today many traces of the war and of the Serbian siege which ended in 1995. But what is the "semiotic destiny" of these traces today? It seems that most of the "signs of war" have been progressively removed from the visible surface of the city through works of restoration and reconstruction, and the demolition of old buildings and construction of new buildings. Hardly a square metre in Sarajevo was untouched: grenade traces, explosion traces, ruins, rubble: the whole city was one big ruin and there was a sort of a continuous "scarification effect" on the entire surface of it. Suddenly, after the war, reconstruction works began to design a new image of the city, and the proof of that is the fact that even today Sarajevo remains one of the capitals of Europe with the most building sites.

However, if you go to Sarajevo today you will still see many ruins and signs of war, although reconstruction is gradually deleting them, apparently not preserving anything that could bring to mind the destruction. Indeed, the way in which reconstructions were (and still are today) conducted has followed various strategies. In the old town centre – the historical district built during the Ottoman period and expanded during the Austro-Hungarian control – the restoration of the historical buildings seems mostly inspired by the principles of a "stylistic reconstruction". The general orientation of these works is directed towards restorations à *l'identique* of the most important Ottoman and Moorish architectures, on the one hand, and of the Austro-Hungarian buildings on the other. And that is not surprising, as the historical heritage of this part of the city is heavily influenced by these two styles. In some cases, the philological accuracy of these restorations is not always impeccable, though. For instance, many restorations should be viewed more as "reconstructions in style" which transform old buildings, giving them a "more Moorish" appearance, but altering the palimpsest of the historical district's stratification.

In other cases there is a clear intention to "redesign" the "memory of the city". One example of this is the "corner spot of Gavrilo Princip". As everybody knows, Gavrilo Princip was a Bosnian Serb who assassinated the Archduke Franz Ferdinand and his wife in Sarajevo in 1914. Before the Yugoslav wars, Gavrilo Princip was considered almost a national hero because he acted on the Yugoslavian nationalist ideals of independence from the Austro-Hungarian Empire. This self-same corner was the place where, after the shooting, the Austro-Hungarian authorities built a monument to commemorate the Archduke who died there. The monument was destroyed a few years after the first kingdom of Yugoslavia was founded in 1918, and the corner was then dedicated to the Bosnian-Serb hero Princip, and his fame has lasted until the Tito period. Thus, the nearby bridge, the *Principov Most* (the "Princip's Bridge"), was named after him. Following the recent war, the bridge was renamed *Latinska Cuprija,* while the museum located just near the spot in front of the bridge, once devoted to Princip, was converted into the "City Museum 1878-1918" (the period of the Austro-Hungarian occupation). The rhetorical change in the narrative of the occupation is well documented in the substitution of the old plaque, which commemorated the figure of Princip and the Austro-Hungarian independence, with a new, more neutral plaque which simply marks the place as the spot where Gavrilo Princip shot Franz Ferdinand, describing the assassination. But the most relevant aspect is that on the pavement at this spot there was a stone representing the footprints of Gavrilo Princip as he was shooting. These footprints were once "revered" by all Sarajevans and were a tourist attraction before the war, but afterwards they mysteriously disappeared. Gavrilo Princip – a Bosnian-Serb but, above all, a Serb – quickly became "too Serbian" for post-war Sarajevo.

There are many instances of this "reductive" trend of removing the symbolic presence of Serbian identity in post-war Sarajevo. The changes in the city's toponomy shows the elimination of many Serbian personalities from the names of streets and places. In the same way, Valter Peric, another pre-war Yugoslav national hero, suffered a similar fate: Peric was a Serbian soldier from Sarajevo fighting for the resistance against Nazi oppression, and his deeds were commemorated throughout the whole of Yugoslavia but particularly in Sarajevo, where he was considered as a sort of "symbol" of the city's unity. Today, his statues and plaques are vandalized and not restored or preserved, in a city centre where, on the contrary, almost everything is restored.

One last example is the plaque commemorating the firing of the Vijecnica, the National Library: this plaque makes abundantly clear that Serbian identity is no longer part of the stretches of identities staged in the urban palimpsest of Sarajevo. In fact, it commemorates the destruction of the library, but speaks of the "Serbian criminals", therefore expressly depicting Serbian people as "aggressors" and, in this way, as an enemy of the city (referring to the present but also to the future, as one may infer from the intention stated in the plaque's exhortation to "remember and warn"). [8]

---

[8] In 2012, after this research was concluded, the restoration of Vijecnica was completed, but controversies still arise about the new function of the building, which will not be a public library anymore, but an administrative office.

But the removal of the traces of war is not always the result of "in-style" restorations of old architectures; indeed, in other cases, it is the outcome of reconstructions of replicas of the most recent buildings destroyed or heavily damaged during war, such as the Parliament and government buildings, or the Unis towers (the "twin towers", which were often shown under fire in all media during the siege). This different "strategy" dominates the outskirts of the historical district which was the "city" of Sarajevo during Tito's regime, with all the most important and representative buildings of government and administration. When they were destroyed during the war, many of these buildings became a media icon of the siege of Sarajevo. After the war, they were reconstructed according to the originals but with new materials (for example, glossy windowpanes instead of the older opaque ones) which have changed the architecture's overall appearance: a sort of "stylistic restoration", but in a "more modern" version which has resulted in the removal of some features which were uniquely Yugoslavian and belonged to the city's socialist period.

This attempt to create a new, modern and "non-socialist" image of the city near the centre is even clearer in some new structures which substitute the damaged architectures with a "hypermodern" style. This is, for example, the case with the new shopping mall built in place of the old Yugoslav mall; or of the former "Museum of Revolution" which is now altered thanks to a project by Renzo Piano. Other significant cases are the old "Tito Army Barracks", which were partially converted into a university (and there is a call for new transformation projects in that complex) and partially demolished (and in its place the new American Embassy is being constructed); and finally, the new building of the *Oslobodjenje*, the main newspaper of Sarajevo (now owned by a large Bosnian corporation). This last example, in particular, is interesting, as the new edifice not only replaces the original architecture, but also deletes the "transformation in ruin" of that building during the war, a ruin which had become in some ways as important as a "monument" for many to remember the tragedy of the war.

Besides the demolition (or the alteration of the visual aspect) of many old Yugoslav edifices, the new civil and residential architecture also testifies to this transition to an architectonic style which breaks with the stylistic tradition of the recent past and, in the case of religious architecture, even with the distant past: the design of the stately mosques situated on the outskirts of the city – huge and monumental – is completely different from the traditional form of the older Bosnian mosques, which were usually small, with only one minaret and meagre outer decoration. So, in conclusion, we can say that we find two main trends in the projects and works of reconstruction and redesign of the image of "post-Sarajevo", depending on the different zones of the city and on the different types of historical heritage subjected to this "spatial rewriting".

In the historical district of the old town, the works are inspired by "*à l'identique* restorations" and stylistic reconstruction producing a strong emphasis on two different components presented as the main "representatives" of the general identity of the city: the Muslim/Ottoman (particularly from a religious point of view) and the Austro-Hungarian (from a historical and cultural point of view). As we have seen, the result of this tendency is the "symbolic expulsion" of Serbian identity from the historical city centre, stressed by the removal of certain distinctive features of the Serb symbolic component within the city's historical palimpsest.

On the outskirts surrounding the centre, there are instead many "replicas" and "remakes", whereas in the suburbs we find an increasing number of new constructions. Here the main tendency is a combination of "hypermodern" design and modernization in the materials of existing buildings reconstructed, with a resultant removal of the "Yugoslav image" of the city built during the socialist period under Tito.

Thus, in the historical district we find a *mise-en-scène* of this kind of auto-representation of a Bosniak (and Muslim) identity through the preservation (which is also a reinterpretation) of the traditional heritage. The business and administrative district near the centre (which was built along the street known as the "sniper alley" during the war and where many of the government buildings were even before the war) is becoming the "new city centre". This is the place where Sarajevo's new image is being designed, an image which breaks either with the socialist past or with the recent war period.

One may ask: where is the memory of the war today in this city still full of ruins but, apparently, "anaesthetized"? Seemingly, there is a sort of subterranean memory, hidden beneath the surface of a city which seems to reject this memory when it shows itself in its devastated urban landscape. Looking at the project of city reconstruction, one would rather talk about a sort of "temptation of oblivion", rather than of memory; there seems to be an attempt to make the memory "harmless" (a memory which still hurts and divides).

Otherwise, there is no cohesive institutional narration of collective re-elaboration of war, and indeed there is a lack of official monuments commemorating the victims. Except for the numerous commemorative tablets inscribed with the names of people who died under Serb fire, scattered throughout the city where the greatest slaughters took place, running paradoxically the risk of being invisible, the only real monument was built in 2009 to commemorate the children who died during the war. However, it was strongly contested by the Serbs, who argued that it was unclear whether only Bosniak children were being commemorated, and so now the message of this monument runs the risk of being interpreted as vague and perhaps even ambiguous.

But this repressed memory abruptly re-emerges in some "heterotopic places", and it is remembered sometimes in mournful ways and, in other cases, through a "translation" into the codes of aesthetics or media languages. So, graveyards, artistic spaces, and even some media representations seem to be the places where the memory of the war is confined (and transformed) today in Sarajevo. One clear example of a reaction against this institutional oblivion (this choice of memory silence) is the so called "roses of Sarajevo". Some people filled many of the numerous holes caused by the grenade explosions with red paint, in order to keep the memory of the war alive and to stage a resistance against it being "deleted" by the reconstructions. This spontaneous "project of memory" aimed to "re-semanticize" (to "give sense" again) to the "de-semanticized imprints" left by war.

Mostar: Challenged Memories, Contested Spaces

Mostar constitutes a similar case of "imposed" forgetfulness, but with some significant differences. The city of Mostar also suffered greatly during the war. First, it was attacked by JNA (the Yugoslav army), and then disputed (when JNA left the battlefield later in 1992) between the Croats (who considered Mostar the capital of *Herceg-Bosna,* the Croat district inside Bosnia, and the Bosniaks, who were besieged in the old city centre built under the Ottoman Empire and whose most famous landmark was the Stari Most, the beautiful old bridge built under Suleiman the Magnificent in 1566. The historical Ottoman district was subjected to severe bombings by the Croats' paramilitary forces and almost razed to the ground. The destruction of the old bridge under the Croats' grenade fire was probably one of the most traumatic events of the whole conflict, both for the *Mostari* (the citizens of Mostar) and in western public opinion.

It was not a surprise then that, after the war, UNESCO promoted a project for the reconstruction of the old bridge as "moral compensation" for the terrible loss; indeed, the bridge was more than a landmark for the *Mostari*. One could say that the bridge was the real "semiotic centre" of Mostar (whose name, by the way, derives from *most*, meaning bridge), a meeting point, a trans-generational monument with which the citizens could identify. It was a symbol of that multiculturalism at the core of the inter-ethnic cohabitation, ever since the Ottoman period, when every religion was allowed and Bosniaks, Croats and Serbs lived together. Even under the socialist regime, Mostar had the greatest proportion of citizens who declared themselves "Yugoslavs" in the census.

Finally, in 2005, the bridge was restored "as it was, where it was", to bring to mind the well-known (and maybe illusory) wording of the stylistic restoration. But the restoration, although it was properly done, has reproduced the paradox of every "in-style" reconstruction, which, in trying to "roll back the hands of time", forgets what has happened in the meantime. And probably this is the main problem of the "new old bridge" of Mostar, appreciated by all the citizens but, at the same time, perceived as a *fake,* and not only because it is, as a matter of fact, a *copy.* Indeed, the problem is not the natural gap which divides the original and the copy, but, more specifically, the fact the new bridge hides something of the old one; that is, to say, its destruction, its temporary and tragic absence.

The reaction to this imposed oblivion has taken form in a small spontaneous monument, probably not planned in the original project: a small stone (of the same material as the bridge, the *tenelja* stone) that bears the words (in English): "Don't forget". So, near the restored old bridge, in the reconstructed *kujundziluk* (the Ottoman historical quarter), this stone re-establishes the memory of the war and makes a "denied memory" come back, the memory which is not displayed in the UNESCO project. Indeed, in Mostar too, as is the case in Sarajevo, the restorations have become the way to impose a forced erasure of every war remembrance, perhaps even more so in the case of Mostar, because it was imposed by the international community, the same international community which is blamed for failing to intervene adequately in the conflict during the war in Bosnia-Herzegovina.

All the UNESCO restoration projects were inspired by a compensatory logic aiming to refund every ethnic group (not only mosques, but also the Catholic Bishop Palace and the Orthodox Bishop Palace were restored). However, as a matter of fact, this choice had the result of a "crystallization" of the ethnic divisions that are still operating in the city, maintaining the two-sided division produced during the war (when the Croat besieger inhabited the western part of the city and the besieged Bosniaks the East). Nowadays there is no real border inside the city and Mostar is governed under a common administration; nevertheless, the street which longitudinally divides the city in two parts, and which was the front line of the conflict, now acts like a "semiotic border" dividing two different Mostars: East Mostar, populated mostly by Bosniaks and Muslims (where the bridge is situated, as well as the old city centre and some new residential zones) and West Mostar (mostly inhabited by Croats).

It is possible to read this internal division in the new architectures (not sponsored by UNESCO) of each part, such as a new mosque (similar to the new ones in Sarajevo, very stately and significantly different from the traditional design of the Bosnian mosques), and a new Catholic church, built on the Croat side near the "border", on the rubble of an old church bombed by the JNA in 1992. The dimensions and the material used (grey concrete) makes the church look very similar to a "bunker" and, moreover, the very tall tower bell (more than eighty metres high) seems to be built to compete, in the urban skyline, with the numerous minarets of the historical city. The monuments commemorating the war on the Croat side feed the internal division and Croat nationalism, celebrating the sacrifice of the Croat soldiers who died during the war (against other *Mostari*). But the most shocking monument is probably the huge Catholic cross (thirty metres high) raised on the Hum mountain (the hill from which the Croats bombed the city) that dominates the whole city, impressing a sort of hierarchy on the balance of the "semiotic forces" fighting in Mostar. It is evident how in Mostar architecture becomes a symbolic language used to mark out a territory and to stage real "semiotic battles" inside the city. However, today you will find in Mostar some elements which "interfere" with this context of conflicting architectonic narratives; one could call them a sort of "symbolic reservoir" which can activate other kinds of memories, the ones suppressed by the "pacified" UNESCO narration.

For instance, the still present ruins have the effect of bringing to life the memory of war, cancelled by the *à l'identique* restoration of the historical heritage. Moreover, there is the partisan and socialist memory, still vivid in many monuments erected under Tito, which is still hardly questioned: while some people (mostly from the older generations) would like to preserve this memory, there are also increasing acts of vandalism against the monuments. In any case, these different memories work out as "narrative interferences": again, a spontaneous memory – Deleuze would call it a *mémoire involontaire* (1964) – that in part contradicts the *mémoire volontaire* of the "institutional memory".

A final example of "contrasting narration" comes from a strange monument, which mysteriously appeared for a short time: a statue of Bruce Lee, the famous actor and martial arts expert. The statue was placed by a group of activists as a provocative symbol with the following inscription: "Alright, we have no more common symbols, let's start finding new symbols to share, whatever they may be". The choice of Bruce Lee was obviously ironic, but not excessively so: he was very popular in former Yugoslavia and was a symbol of the past that everyone could share and understand. The power of this "semiotic experiment" was proven by the fact that the statue annoyed the nationalists on "both sides" and was repeatedly vandalized, to the extent that it ended up being removed. The division within the city is, then, legible through these "conflicting spatial narratives" expressed by different attitudes towards the traces of the past.

Dubrovnik: Preserve to Forget?

During the shelling of the Croat city of Dubrovnik, a Serb general was asked why they were destroying one of the most beautiful places in the world. He answered: "We will rebuild it at the end of the war, more beautiful and more ancient than before" (Vukurevic, quoted by Stefanovic 2004, 73). The general's words may have sounded eery at the time, but the absurd prophecy of the general was destined to be fulfilled: after the war, the restoration works (also sponsored by UNESCO) restored the city to its condition before the war, removing even the smallest sign of conflict. So the ancient Stradun (the main street of the city) and its beautiful renaissance buildings (such as the clock tower and the Dominican Monastery inspired by renaissance and baroque aesthetics) were restored, strictly following the fundamentals of the "as it was, where it was" theory, completely erasing the memory of the war.

Because of the architectonic re-establishment of the historical image of the city of Dubrovnik, a kind of realm "outside time" (and history) has been created, where war is denied. This aesthetic re-interpretation of the past seems to have been used as a substrate for a nationalistic narrative: in this way, the old city centre has become an "urban stage" where it is now possible to exhibit the symbols of the new Croat nation which came about after the dissolution of Yugoslavia, and everywhere you can find national flags and colours.

Hence also in Dubrovnik one could speak of an "anaesthetization" of the traces of war. As in the case of Sarajevo, the only place where what happened is remembered is a "heterotopy": a little memorial located in a hidden room inside a historical palace with its wall covered by the pictures of the citizens of Dubrovnik who died during the shelling and with a small collection of war relics and "heirlooms": a sort of "war variation" of the Croat nationalistic narration that one can find outside in the streets and squares of Dubrovnik.

Belgrade: the Obsession of Memory

My corpus also includes another city which was greatly affected during the Yugoslav conflicts, albeit in a completely different way. As everyone knows, Belgrade was in fact the capital city of Yugoslavia and, during the first phase of the Yugoslav war (1991-1995), its role was solely "directional": from here the Serbian government controlled the JNA and, after the withdrawal of the Yugoslav army, it was here that Milošević planned his project of a "Great Serbia" and continued providing the paramilitary Serbian forces in Bosnia, Croatia and Kosovo with logistic and strategic support. So, at first, Belgrade was not directly struck by the war; instead, it was attacked in the second phase (the "Kosovo war", in which the situation, which had been very tense since the eighties, had worsened in 1996) during the operation "Allied Force" conducted by NATO, to stop the fierce repression of the secessionist movements of Kosovo's Albanians by the Serbian Army.

Can we speak of urbicide for Belgrade as well? Certainly the military attacks against this city had different motivations and "justifications" but, somehow, the NATO attack reproduced the same "urbicidal logic" of every war directed against the urban spaces. During approximately three months NATO's military operations hit several targets even inside the city centre (though NATO always claimed their "strategic relevance") and some of these targets were also important landmarks in the symbolic landscapes of the city. Therefore, I am interested in the way the signs of war left by military attacks in the city of Belgrade have been transformed in the post-war period through the works of reconstruction, and how this transformation has affected the semiotic landscape of the city.

A significant difference, which contrasts with the cities mentioned already, is that in the centre of Belgrade one may still find some ruins of the NATO attack. It is similar to the other cities, but with the difference that, while in Sarajevo and in Mostar the ruins in the city centre are restored or under restoration, here, more than twelve years after the bombings, some of the ruins are plainly visible and no work of reconstruction is planned. There are fewer ruins than in Sarajevo or Mostar, where the presence of relics and traces of shelling and bombings is more pervasive, but here – maybe because they are perceived as a drastic discontinuity inside the urban fabric – the buildings in ruin are more "visible" and they have turned out to become prominent features of the streets in which they are located (Kneza Milosa ulica, one of the most central streets, full of ministers, offices, embassies, etc.).

Some bombed buildings – the Vlada, the government building in Kneza Milosa street and the Usce palace, former building of the "Central Committee of the Communist Party" and, subsequently, among other things, Milošević's headquarters – were quickly repaired, while other edifices, such as the former "Federal Ministry of Internal Affairs" and the Generalstab, the former Army headquarters, both located in Kneza Milosa street, were left in ruins. Another edifice which was struck, the RTS building (the state television offices), was repaired, but a damaged wing was intentionally left in ruins.

It is impossible to ascertain why some of the ruins were left as they were; there may be a lot of sensible reasons, but the fact is that those ruins are actually preserved. In the first example of the "Federal Ministry of Internal Affairs", the ruins are simply there and not repaired and they do not have an important semiotic role, as they are more peripheral. However, in the case of the Generalstab, the unrepaired ruins have assumed a highly symbolic role. This "non-conscious" preservation (a preservation "by inaction") has amplified the semantic value of the ruins and transformed them into a powerful *potential monument*. Indeed, these ruins have become a sort of "natural monument" against NATO, celebrating the "resistance" of the Serbian people against their enemies. This hypothesis is sustained, among other things, by the fact that sometimes they are used as a "scenery" for protests and demonstrations and used as a formidable symbolic resource for the narratives of Serbian nationalists. In some way, the ruined Generalstab takes part (and plays a central role) in the discourse of Serbian nationalism.

The third example (the "refurbished" RTS building) is slightly different inasmuch as in this case the ruins play a more "commemorative" role: they are surrounded by celebratory stones and memorials with the names of the civilians who died in the bombing and, on the anniversary of the attack, some commemorative ceremonies take place there.

All these "non-reconstructed" (and then unintentionally preserved) ruins can be considered examples of "unintentional memory" (*mémoire involontaire*) but, if we take a look at another (older) monument in the historical district we may find a more exact interpretation. The monument in question is the ruined edifice of the National Library bombed by the Nazis in 1941: these ruins, unlike the others analyzed before, have been intentionally preserved as a memorial and a reminder of the Nazi occupation. So it seems that there is a sort of recurrence of the "ruin-form" as a form to recall the past in Belgrade; in this respect, the more recent ruins appear to be a sort of "spontaneous version" of that other institutionalized and monumental ruin.

Therefore, while in Mostar and Sarajevo war ruins operate as "narrative interferences" which may reactivate non-institutional memory, here ruins seem to be "conniving" with a certain nationalistic rhetoric that – maybe accounted for by a lack of a strong politics of memory and then to the absence of a common frame to interpret the events of the war – is today the main interpretative key with which to remember and to code/decode the past. The urban palimpsest of the city is then used as a "repository of traces" and signs of the past that can be recombined in spatial narrations.

In this way the ruin becomes the ceaseless actualization of the "action of the enemy", an event (the aggression against Serbia) that "continues to happen" through those ruins, paralyzing and "blocking" the temporality, bringing it away from the linear time of history to a mythical time, where it commemorates an outside-of-time *epos* of the Serbian people.

Concluding Remarks

This excursion through the transformations in the "memoryscapes" of some former Yugoslavian cities after the war has pointed out how the past is not something inherited but rather "translated" and recombined in narrative configurations: a "discursive construction" which may take the form of spatial (urban and architectonic) texts, practices and objects. In particular, this study maintains the notion of *trace* and its capacity to be used and inserted in those spatial narratives through "semiotic work" on their semantic, axiologic, aesthetic and even epistemic (with regards to the veracity or falsity of the traces) values. The results of this work are the various "effects of memory", different translations of past configurations of signs in a "current" configuration.

I have tried to frame the post-war "actions" of reconstruction and restoration regarding important symbolic architectures and parts of the cities as a peculiar practice of manipulation of past traces and of their transformation into a "commemorative spatial narrative". Far from bringing the past back to the present, the restorations are not only a mode of conservation but also of construction and "invention" – in the sense given by Hobsbawm and Ranger in *The Invention of Tradition* (1983) – of a memory and of a past-in-the-present. Indeed, the notion of "semiotic translation" proposed by Jurij Lotman seems to be more appropriate inasmuch as it considers memory as "a flexible and effective mechanism for the production of new senses" (Lotman 1985), emphasizing the idea that memory works as a "stereotyping device". This not only functions as an archive, but also generates new meanings and new languages, in a dynamic which transforms social meanings, reinterpreting and re-codifying the "texts" (even an architecture can be considered, in this perspective, a text) coming from the past.

Therefore, at the centre of the argument proposed in this study there is the notion of *trace*, an ambiguous element from a semiotic point of view. Indeed, trace has a double nature (Natoli 2005): on one hand it is a *given* (an imprint), on the other hand it is a *sign* (because a trace can be interpreted only while a sign). The Italian historian Carlo Ginzburg argues that traces have a sort of "veracity" on their side that makes them "testify" with a particular "vividness", which Ginzburg denominates as *enargeia* (2006), a feature that, I would add, explains the semantic potential of the trace and the fact that its meanings can be re-constructed and re-interpreted to infinity. On the other hand, traces possess the same contradictory character that Pierre Nora ascribes to the *lieux de la mémoire* (1984): that is, the fact of being *entre histoire et mémoire*, between history and memory; *relics of history* on the one hand, potential *signs of memory* on the other.

At this point, it could be useful, from a semiotic perspective, to distinguish between traces (intended as imprints) and tracks (intended as spatial narrations): according to Umberto Eco (1976), in fact, imprints are not signs, but objects which can become signs, which means that traces can be produced, forged, counterfeited (and in fact there are false traces): an imprint that becomes a sign assumes all the characteristics of the sign, including the fact that it "can tell a lie" (Eco 1976, 7). Therefore, all the processes of transformation of the trace – hiding, (re)discovering, forging, producing and so on – regard the narrative recombination of traces that can be considered then as a chain of traces, or rather tracks: a "selection" of traces, assembled as a spatial narration which selects (erasing and preserving) "chains of traces". The ideological uses and abuses of memory (Ricœur 2000) concern this narrative process of rewriting and recombination of traces in tracks. Semiotically, then, trace is not a given, but a sign that, in order to be interpreted, never occurs alone, but is always assembled in complex configuration of signs (texts).

We can now reinterpret the issue of the relation between memory and spatiality starting from the assumption that memory is a dynamic between preservation and cancellation of traces (conservation versus oblivion): the memory signified (expressed) from a space is always given by a narrative re-organization of some elements of the past (some traces) to the detriment of others. This is a different way of saying that reconstruction is a practice of memory rewriting and that there is always an ethics of memory beyond the aesthetics of a restoration.

What is at stake are the semantic values and their movements in a continuous process of de-semanticization and re-semanticization of traces; this semantic articulation can be shown with the help of a semiotic square (shown on the facing page) which will facilitate the comparison between the different processes of memory in the cities considered. The semiotic square shows the semantic processes triggered by the opposition between strategies of conservation and of cancellation of traces. If we consider memory as a "balance" between conservation and oblivion – the memory is an interaction between "wiping" and "saving", as Todorov (1993, 127) suggests – we can consider the interplay of preservation and cancellation of traces as the basis of every effective process of re-elaboration of collective memory. Similarly, a preservation accompanied by non-deletion, as much as a deletion accompanied by a non-preservation, would lead to different declinations of memory overbalanced towards forms of *obsession* (a sort of "trace fetishism") or forms of *denial* (an unconscious "negation" and repression of memory). The non-deletion plus non-preservation would lead, on the contrary, to a *suspension of memory* (a present outside of time). One could talk about a removal process that seems to take the form of a denial.

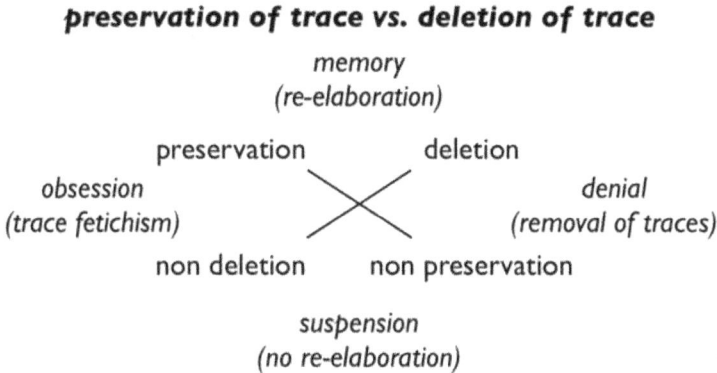

preservation of trace vs. deletion of trace

memory
(re-elaboration)

preservation   deletion

obsession   denial
(trace fetichism)   (removal of traces)

non deletion   non preservation

suspension
(no re-elaboration)

These different dynamics may be found in the cities I have analyzed. In Sarajevo, Mostar and Dubrovnik the traces of war have been (and, in some cases, are being) deleted, although in different ways. In Sarajevo they are gradually disappearing because of the re-design of the image of the city, halfway between a re-discovery (that is also a re-invention) of the historical identities and a fabrication of a new modern "urban style"; in Mostar, as well as in Dubrovnik, on account of the UNESCO restorations of the historical district (but that, in the divided Mostar, is an element of conflict in the interpretation of memory). Nevertheless, in each city the memory of war seems to become "obsessive" when the semantic potential of the war traces, de-semanticized by the restoration, sometimes rise up to the surface as a narrative interference. Similarly, in Belgrade, the presence of untransformed (and not monumentalized) ruins may be read as a non-cancellation and a non-preservation of traces that evolves towards a re-semanticization (and then an unconscious preservation). Here the trace is a spontaneous monument that unceasingly re-presents the war and the bombing, driving towards an obsession of sorts.

Denial on the one hand, and obsession on the other: two coexisting outcomes of unsolved collective traumas. Suspension of memory in Belgrade evolves into an obsession for a "repeating past"; obsession for a future memory in Sarajevo ultimately reinvents the past tradition and neglects the city's history of multiculturalism and "living together"; partial denial of the war memory in Mostar suddenly re-emerges as a battlefield on which the different souls of Mostar can have their fight; oblivion of war in Dubrovnik takes place through the obsession for the rediscovery of a mythological (and then more closely related to nationalism) ancient past. If urbicide is a "war against the city", sometimes reconstruction can become, paraphrasing Clausewitz, "the prosecution of urbicide by other means".

References

Assmann, A. (1999). *Erinnerungräume. Formen und Wandlungen des kulturellen Gedächtnisses*. Munich: C. H. Beck.

Assmann, J. (1992). *Das kulturelle Gedächtnis. Schrift, Erinnerung und politische Identität in frühen Hochkulturen*. Munich: Oscar Beck.

Bevan, R. (2006). *The Destruction of Memory: Architecture at War*. London: Reaktion Books.

Bhabha, H. K. (1994). *The Location of Culture*. London: Routledge.

Bogdanovic, B. (1993). "Murder of the City". At **www.nybooks.com**, accessed September 2011.

Coward, M. (2008). *Urbicide: The Politics of Urban Destruction*. Milton Park: Routledge.

Deleuze, G. (1964). *Marcel Proust et les signes*. Paris: Presses Universitaires de France.

Dell'Agnese, E. and Squarcina, E. (2002). "Urbicidio e smemorizzazione del paesaggio urbano: Vukovar, Dubrovnik, Sarajevo (e Tirana)". In E. Dell'Agnese, E. Squarcina (eds.). *Geopolitiche dei Balcani: luoghi, percorsi, narrazioni*. Milan: Unicopli, 155-173.

Donia, R. J. (2006). *Sarajevo: a Biography*. Ann Arbor: University of Michigan Press.

Eco, U. (1976). *A Theory of Semiotics*. Bloomington: Indiana University Press.

Fregonese, S. (2009). "The Urbicide of Beirut? Geopolitics and the Built Environment in the Lebanese Civil War (1975-1976)". *Political Geography* 28, 5, 309-318.

Ginzburg, C. (2006). *Il filo e le trace: Vero, falso, finto*. Milan: Feltrinelli.

Graham, S. (2004). "Cities, Warfare, and States of Emergency". In S. Graham (ed.). *Cities, War, and Terrorism: Towards an Urban Geopolitics*. Oxford: Blackwell, 1-27.

Greimas, A. J. (1976). *Sémiotique et sciences sociales*. Paris: Seuil.

Hammad, M. (2006). *Lire l'espace, comprendre l'architecture*. Limoges: Pulim Geuthner.

Hobsbawm, E. and Ranger, T. (eds.). (1983). *The Invention of Tradition*. Cambridge: Cambridge University Press.

Lotman, J. M. (1985). *La semiosfera L'asimmetria e il dialogo nelle strutture pensanti*. Marsilio: Venezia.

Lynch, K. (1960). *The Image of the City*. Cambridge, MA: MIT Press.

Marrone, G. (2001). "L'agire spaziale". In G. Marrone, *Corpi sociali: Processi comunicativi e semiotica del testo*. Turin: Einaudi. 287-368.

Marrone, G. (2010). *L'invenzione del testo*. Rome and Bari: Laterza.

Mazzucchelli, F. (2010). *Urbicidio: Il senso dei luoghi tra distruzioni e ricostruzioni in ex Jugoslavia*. Bologna: Bononia University Press.

Natoli, S. (2005). *La verità in gioco: scritti su Foucault*. Milan: Feltrinelli.

Nora, P. (1984). *Les Lieux de mémoire*. Paris: Gallimard.

Ribarevic-Nikolic, I. and Juric, Z. (1992). *Mostar '92: Urbicid*. Mostar: HVO Opcine Mostar.

Ricoeur, P. (2000). *La mémoire, l'histoire, l'oubli*. Paris: Seuil.

Shaw, M. (2003). *War and Genocide: Organized Killing in Modern Society*. Cambridge: Polity Press.

Silber, L. and Little, A. (1996). *The Death of Yugoslavia*. London: Penguin and BBC Worldwide.

Stefanovic, V. (2004). *Milošević: The People's Tyrant*. London: I.B. Tauris.

Thom, R. (1972). *Stabilité structurelle et morphogenèse*. Paris: Interéditions.

Todorov, T. (1993). *Hope and Memory: Lessons from the Twentieth Century*. Princeton: Princeton University Press.

Violi, P. (2009a), "Ricordare il futuro. I musei della memoria ed il loro ruolo nella costruzione di identità culturali". *E/C. Rivista online dell'Associazione Italiana di Studi Semiotici*. At **www.ec-aiss.it**, accessed September 2011.

Violi, P. (2009b). "Architetture della memoria. Il Memorial Hall di Nanjing". *Versus: Quaderni di studi semiotici*, 109-111.

Portugal and its Empire

The Author's Posthumous Condition: War Trauma and Portugal's Colonial War

Roberto Vecchi

> Maybe the inconsolable sadness
> affecting those whose dead dear ones
> lie in the mass grave derives from
> that; they feel the anonymous decay
> could reach them too.
>
> Machado de Assis, *Memórias*
> *póstumas de Brás Cubas*

To the memory of
Carlos Raposo Pereira

One Empire, yet which Conflict?

The problematic nature of the Portuguese imperial configuration, part-icularly with reference to the clash with modernity, is shown by the innovative reflections provided by Boaventura de Sousa Santos (1994) on Portugal's semi-peripheral condition in the complex counterpoint opposing Europe and the Colonies, and with Eduardo Lourenço's (1988) contribution on the contradictory forms distinguishing a country's self-representation with the wane of the colonial experience as a "national hyper-identiy". At the same time, the peculiarities of the Portuguese empire, the longest-lived in Europe, whose collapse dates back to the effective decolonization started in 1975, emphasize in a peculiar way what we have learned from the lesson given by Edward Said in *Culture and Imperialism*: namely, the indissolubility of the terms composing the hendiadys according to which the aesthetic forms produced are indispensable in the comprehension (as a counterpoint) of a historical structure that, as far as the Empire is concerned, would be otherwise condemned to indecipherability (Said 1998, 77). What is important to underline is that the figurations of the Empire, as well as its self-representative narrations, are essential even for a reconsideration of its historical structures. From this point of view, Margarida Calafate Ribeiro summarizes the question in a sharp conceptual image of "empire as imagination of a centre" (2004, 15), synthesizing the ambiguities and knots we run into while thinking over the Portuguese colonial experience. The latter interstitially inscribes itself both on the metropolis (in relation to Africa or to other colonies) and on the side of the subordinate periphery (in relation to Europe), producing a duality that holds on to a massive investment in the imaginary and in processes of representation (the renowned "cultural empire" evoked by Pessoa in *Mensagem*).

An empire configured like this and protracted for five centuries gave birth to a conflict that is no less complex to understand. The "Colonial War" was a ghost war from the beginning (as we shall see later), undertaken by the national movements for the independence of the African colonies against the Portuguese metropolis, depicted as a "multi-continental" nation by official rhetoric and deflagrated between 1961 and 1974 in order to stoke the *salazarista* regime's agony. We could say that it articulated itself as a modern conflict, yet that would be a narrow outlook. More considerable, *de facto*, is the continuity marking a permanent war, dragging on through five centuries of maritime expansion, a real protracted "Colonial War" against which the events that occurred almost fifteen years before the Carnation Revolution are no more than mere epiphenomena.

If, on the one hand, historical reconstruction allows the assumption of a permanent state of belligerence, on the other, the extension of the phenomenon entirely prevents its specific identification. Has the entire colonial and imperial Portuguese history been uninterruptedly marked by a simple embitterment of the conflict or by a recrudescence of the historical stream? The question is not trivial, since it is essential first to define the conflicts engendering post-conflict cultures in order to discuss them; if a lesson can be extrapolated from the facts – including the more recent ones – characterizing our contemporaneity, it is that conflict and post-conflict are linked by a shared complexity, some kind of genealogy – more than a dialectic – which is able to juxtapose its roots and scattered causes, reciprocally enlightening them at the same time. Obviously crises and fractures took place during this wartime continuum. What we conventionally envisage as the "Colonial War" has been one of them, the extreme one, unless we want to attribute to it a special value in relation to the whole period.

Who are the Invisible Casualties of an Unnamed Non-war?
Besides the historical difficulties in extrapolating the specific segment

stressing the Colonial War in Africa between 1961 and 1974, a war whose identity could in some way be guaranteed by the novelties demarcating that phase (nationalist movements, ideologies, international contexts, etc., progressively moulded the conflict), from the historical point of view we have to face a fundamental problem hindering its discussion in terms of war: the lack of a common and shared memory about that experience.

There is still an untied knot: the lack of a history dealing with the Colonial War's last episode, that is the negation of its existence in the historical circumstances which have produced it (for instance, when armed insurrections were represented as mere acts of terrorism) and the ideological revisionism which does the same. It is a fact that not a single official document issued by the past regime ever referred to any Colonial War (obviously during the post World War II phase, characterized by a redefining of imperial policies, Portugal was interested in emphasizing its peculiar nature as a "multicontinental" country existing beyond its European boundaries). At present there is no unanimity, not even about the conflict's name. The term "Colonial War" is ideologically denoted (and often confused as an excrescence of the 1974 revolutionary movement). It is called, with more nostalgic nuances and ideologically marked in the opposite sense, the "Overseas war", or renamed, in a politically correct version, the "African war".

Now, how can there be a post-conflict when the conflict itself is denied? That is why today we can refer to a ghost war, a war whose indelible tracks, such as deaths and mutilations, represent on one side today's witnessed evidence but, on the other, the aporias related to the sociability of memories, to the transposition from personal memories to collective memories, from testimony to history.

As we can see, within the local skirmish, we are facing the representation of one of the great impasses – tragic, we could say – marking our contemporaneity together with the impossible representation of the post-*Shoah* traumatic experience. Once again, Paul Celan's (1980) verse locates, in a figurative way, the tragic aspect inherent in the testimonial act: nobody witnesses on behalf of the witness ("*Niemand zeugt für den Zeugen*", "Aschenglorie"). That is why cultural representations of the war in the Portuguese post-revolutionary context of the second half of the seventies are essentially discussions about the feasibility of representation itself, with a strong critical and meta-critical charge as aesthetic objects. And the growing revisionist-negationist wave is firmly at the heart of the discourses, as testified, for instance, by António Lobo Antunes in the last letter sealing the "alphabet of pain" that is *Os cus de Judas* (1979), explicitly denouncing the revisionism already in progress.

Who are *de facto* the casualties of a war that are not supposed to exist – not even as discourse? What labour is necessary to compensate for its losses, to work out its mourning? This negation, as is easily noticeable, is at least double: as well as the negation that is peculiar to death, it is also the negation of any possible perception – that is, the passage from an individual elaboration to an intersubjective one, of this negation elapsing through the negation of the fact which caused it.

Furthermore, a bio-political reflection can help us to understand the political function of this plural negation, of this negative complex whole. Those taking part in this ghost war, a war dominated by historical phantasmagorias coming from another (imperial) time are close to Giorgio Agamben's definition of *homo sacer*. That is, according to archaic Roman law, a figure devoted to death, or better, along with the amphibological structure peculiar to *sacratio* the *homo sacer* gathers together a double exclusion, since his murder would not be considered a homicide and, at the same time, he cannot be offered in sacrifice, in accordance with the forms prescribed by the rite. The duality on which the concept of *homo sacer* is based – the impunity granted for his death and the prohibition on sacrificing him (Agamben 1995, 81) – contributes, through the "bare life" link, not only to explain the bio-political mechanism distinguishing sovereignty, that is founded on a paradoxical exception, but also to cut out in a more well-defined way the frames of the casualties of an unnamed non-war.

The *sacrae* banned victims are doomed to death, but at the same time cannot be ritually sacrificed by the Power that can perpetuate itself in the negation of war, in the name of the symbolic process whose purpose is the consolidation of the national narration, feeding in this way the imperial illusion that is "Empire as imagination of a centre". The *homo sacer*, this forbidden witness, the living-dead of this unpronounced and unsayable war, is therefore the Colonial War's mute ghost. It roams still unburied, like mortal remains which cannot find their place, in a non-location freezing any chance to complete the labour of mourning.

Cunning and Coincidences of the Posthumous Author in Colonial War Literature

If, as we believe, it is possible to identify a literature running from the void left by the multiple historical negations affecting it, the literary representations of the Colonial War represent, in a figural sense, a literature composed of epitaphs (Ribeiro 2004; Vecchi 2004). This is owing to its connection with an anti-epic and tragic-maritime vision of the sea, but also because of the cultural function carried out by the epitaph as (etymologically) coincident tomb inscription, rising far from the tumulus to symbolize a memory which is transformed into monument even if the remains that caused it are absent (Dahm 2002, 166). Following this sepulchral tradition, from the beginning, Colonial War writing configures itself, in relation to reported facts, as – literally – a posthumous literature.

Actually, this literature's posthumous condition holds a wide-ranging set of connotations and distinctions surpassing the mere literal sense. It is true that, curiously, one of the inaugural works of this peculiar literature assuming the war experience trauma as inspirational matrix is effectively posthumous: I refer to the poetic work of José Bação Leal, who died in Mozambique in 1965 and whose posthumous volume, *Poesias e Cartas*, was published in 1971. In this case the term "posthumous" assumes a wider significance, derived from the cultural relation established by authors representing war with both the horizon of death and the world connected to it. "Post-humous", in fact, is not confined to the primary etymology referring to a son born after his father's death (directly related to its literary sense) or in the dislocation of the graphic etymology singled out by Isidoro de Sevilla, whose definition of *post humatus* can be translated as "something rising after burial". Rather, it belongs to a "constellation" of meanings bearing many cultural values. For that reason, during the classical age, "posthumous" still indicated something close to the end, next to *ultimus, extremus*, or *postremus*. The verb *posthumare*, meaning "to meet later", "to survive" (see Ferroni 1996, 12-15) appeared in medieval times, coming from the Isadorian etymology of *posthumus*.

What prevails in this established constellation is a semantics much broader than the term affecting the posthumous condition peculiar to Colonial War writings. Posthumous seems to point out a supplement, to indicate a further dimension, a "beyond" where something does survive, allowing us to single out, right on the end's edge, a continuity, a heritage (Ferroni 1996, 16); a continuity spurting from fragments, a non-coincidence of something un-concluded, unfinished. That is why posthumous is characterized by a leftover which places itself, culturally both alive and dead, in a further dimension, "after".

The semantic gloss is useful, for it shows the intersection between the constellation of posthumous and another relevant constellation characterizing the representation of war experience: the witness. The latter gathers together some of its multiple facets, since it is made by the *superstes* (survivor) but also by the *auctor*, meaning "somebody connecting two dimensions"; it takes place "after", at the same time constantly assuming the existence of a "before" (Agamben 1998, 15, 138-40). The witness always inhabits a posthumous condition.

In the same way, the epitaph is always necessarily posthumous. We are not simply referring to the posthumous character that we acknowledge in any kind of writing – generally set "after" – for it is distinguished by a further addition, the articulation of a feasible trauma representation.

The literary tradition in Portuguese considers a particular Brazilian novel to offer a lesson about the posthumous condition of literature and its use as a critical device of great import. I refer to Machado de Assis' *Memórias Póstumas de Brás Cubas*. The invention of the "deceased author" exhibits authorship's less evident side, that is a duality immediately introduced by the title, in which the citation is expressed along with Brás Cubas' signature. This peculiarity highlights the subtle non-coincidence marking what are, apparently, coincident – the book by Machado de Assis and the book of Brás Cubas (Baptista 1991, 170). The authorship hides itself behind another shown authorship, looking apparently crossed out. In fact, coincidence reveals itself as an extraordinary arsenal of representations, starting from the fictional resolution, which allows the expression even of what the "experience limit" normally prevents, namely posthumous narration.

So, if there is any possible salvation for what is flowing together with the acts carried out by Colonial War's *homini sacri*, maybe it resides in the conscience of the posthumous, made possible by literature, which is able to represent trauma's irreparably un-performable nature. In this way, writings depicting "life-death" become a "spectre" which gives a shape (identity and space) to other remnants, other ghosts obstinately refusing to dissolve (through the application of this ontological process to the remnants, it is possible to pursue the labour of mourning attached to trauma).

The Tragic's Overflowing Traumas and Posthumous Politics: *Enterrar os Mortos e Cuidar dos Vivos*

The fact that the discourse we have to face is a discourse of mourning, losses and remains (Derrida 2001, 17) is confirmed by the posthumous condition attributed to Colonial War writing and by the ghosts of a history that is hard to discover.

An effective opportunity to think over the elements which have arisen from post-conflict cultural representation – within the problems marking melancholic writing – derives from its re-inscription inside the meta-psychological frame established by Nicolas Abraham and Maria Török (1993). The posthumous author can be defined as a "cryptoforus", the bearer of the inter-psychological tumulus allowing, by incorporation, the elaboration of trauma through the abolition of the metaphoric value affecting the block of reality, aiming towards the opening of the crypt. The latter, according to Abraham's and Török's analysis, acts like a "cemetery keeper" (1993) accompanying visitors to graves or, left to his own devices, setting them on the wrong track. In this way, the cemetery keeper carries out a decisive function as a mediator between the living and the dead, between the remains of trauma and its possible exposition as an object.

Colonial War literature, as a textual spectre referring to another historical spectre, is built upon countless specific characteristics allowing the articulation of a canonical question, starting from its own aporias (its mournful-melancholic track, the testimonial impasse, the instabilities affecting re-writing and conflictual times, etc.) Trying to discover the frame most suitable to contain all of them, to represent them without oversimplifications and maintaining at the same time its strongly problematic roots, we can underline the presence of a tragic matrix which is common to the larger part of the characteristics denoting this kind of literature. I refer to the extremely complex "modern tragic" sphere as a form of differential translation, corrupted by canonical forms belonging to the "ancient tragic" sphere (recovering in this way Kierkegaard's classic meditation; see Kierkegaard 2016).

I will not dwell on a subject of great importance and extreme complexity and hence shall not deepen the perspective from a theoretical point of view (Vecchi 2004, 94-98). It is enough to indicate that a turn towards the tragic provides essential critical devices which are able to report the critical relations joining problematically dialectical – or potentially dialectical – elements such as trauma, the sublime's boundless side related to the traumatic experience and the aporia of the witness, displaying in this way the fracture of the extremes without needing to resort to forced and false reconciliatory syntheses. Elements such as evil, death, trauma and grief put up resistance to representation, remaining inscribed in a dull and silent field that can be depicted only through the tragic aporia of the witness, conceived as a concentration camp survivor, according to Primo Levi's (1986) dramatization.

In Colonial War literature we can notice how the posthumous author has to deal with the same tragic block, pouring down partial facts, traces of experiences, objective coincidences with the – impossible to hold – space belonging to the integral witness – *homo sacer* – who cannot make transitive his excessive experience and, consequently, cannot articulate a symbolization of the scattered and extraneous memories. The construction of a political "heaven of memory" in order to cultivate the memory of huge losses caused by trauma, or better, a passage from the unlimited and overflowing *literality* distinguishing the recollection of the traumatic scene to the figurative and therapeutic *literarity* of representation (Seligmann-Silva 1999, 120), is blocked. Upholding the meta-psychological allegory comparing the author to a "cemetery keeper", according to the vision of history as a trauma which makes reality impossible to access, it is as if the keeper had first to build, map and reconfigure the symbolic territory of death's memory which he is bound to oversee. Only then is he allowed to become a guide to the visitor-readers of the cemetery-text.

It is important to underline the posthumous author's fundamental and tragic dimension on the threshold between life and death, implying an essential role as a mediator between the world beyond the grave and the present which recovers the whole semantic potential inherent in the constellation of the posthumous previously indicated.

It is no coincidence that, in fact, a precocious topic – one that will transversally cover Colonial War's forms and representations defining the author's tragic position – is found, since its first impression of focusing the ghastly scene is related to the trauma caused by a war whose complexity can be rendered only through the category of the absurd.

In the eponymous poem in the volume *Cuidar dos Vivos* (1963) Fernando Assis Pacheco, one among many of the Colonial War's "poets-at-arms" (as far as anti-war is concerned), reconceives the order existing in Lisbon after the tremendous earthquake which occurred in 1755:

Porque é preciso agora	For it is necessary to take care of
cuidar dos vivos, pôr os	the living, to bury the dead: for
mortos no seu lugar: que	they shan't occupy the living's
não tomem o lugar dos	place. Open windows to the sun of
vivos. Abrir janelas ao sol de	May, drink the sun; drink May
Maio, beber o sol, beber	and life
Maio e a vida	

(Assis Pacheco 1992, 13)

This trope is the origin of a structural theme denoting Colonial War's literary canon, a constantly quoted and re-glossed topic: it is present in José Bação Leal's poetry, it is literally transposed in *A Costa dos Murmúrios* by Lídia Jorge (1988), it is fragmented in other texts such as, for instance, *Os Cus de Judas* by António Lobo Antunes, a novel flitting between two dimensions, where unburied dead still remain in the traumatised survivor's memory. Aside from simply glossing Assis Pacheco, we could say that this work is, after all, nothing but the fictional transposition of this verse through a melancholic self.

The reconstruction of the Colonial War literature's characteristic elements according to a tragic version provides a significant critical juxtaposition with that "posthumous" classic tragedy *par excellence* (belonging to the "ancient tragic sphere"): Sophocles' *Antigone*. This is why the crucial question here has to do with both the burial of the dead and a strong concern for the living, a duality that is introduced in terms of tragic conflict from the beginning. Antigone violates the written *nomos* of the *polis*, deciding, after the fratricidal war undertaken by two brothers fighting for power, to bury Polynices' corpse even if Creon, King of Thebes, has condemned it to remain unburied, suspended in the anomic "no man's land", at the mercy of wild animals.

Choosing to follow her family ties, or better, non-written familiar laws, Antigone collides with the *polis*. The price to be paid is the condemnation to be buried while still alive – a significantly dual and tragic condition, we might say – and suicide is the only way out. At this stage it is important to remark that, after his death, it is Polynices, not deserving of the honours attributed to Eteocles, who is degraded to the *homo sacer* condition – not in the sense that he has to be consecrated as a hero, but because he is banned from the public space. Polynices' corpse is de-politicized through the exclusion ratified by the sovereign power. In this way the sovereign power de-consecrates it, excluding it from the sacred space, aiming to erase any trace, any memory of him. For that reason Antigone's act corresponds to a re-consecration of the body (Maj 2003, 57) fulfilled through its redemption from the *sacra* condition in relation to the ban inflicted by the *polis*. This re-politicization takes place through a re-politicization of the brother's corpse, of his mortal remains, countered by the prohibition of public mourning imposed by sovereign laws.

On the contrary, the *polis* promotes the dispersal of the remains and the demolition of memory, leaving mourning unachieved and not even offering a place where the remains could be analyzed from an ontological point of view, or where the loss could be localized. Antigone – apparently a disjunctive figure hindering power (through the relation between gender and an androcentric event such as war) in the conflict between ontology and politics, private and public, privacy and *polis*, body and order – ends up showing the tragic relation opposing the horizon of death and the world of the living: in fact, the relationship existing between "burying the dead" and "taking care of the living" is not disjunctive, as the former becomes the indispensable condition for the latter.

Only by converting trauma into text and burying the remains – even if in opposition to established order – can the posthumous author put an end to the unachieved side of the traumatic experience, which can also coincide with the labour of mourning or with that *"almost* mourning" that is melancholy. The finally achieved past, as observed by Walter Benjamin, gains "the quality to be effectively past and definitely dead" (1997, 111). To take care of the living has a further meaning: the chance to quote the no-longer unachieved past.

Guilt and Cruelty in Colonial War Representations

As we find in Colonial War literature, the modern tragic aspect immediately shows a distinctive fundamental feature in relation to the ancient tragic aspect. As codified by Alessandro Manzoni in a theoretical contribution on modern tragedy (*Lettre à M. Chauvet sur l'unité de temps et de lieu dans la tragédie*, 1823), modern tragedies should re-elaborate the dark side of history. The most evident difference with the "ancient tragic" sphere resides here: history substitutes myth as reality-founding material (Maj 2003, 36). This aspect is evident in "posthumous" narrations of Colonial War experience such as, for instance, *Jornada de África* by Manuel Alegre (1989), a rewriting of the *Sebastianista* myth, whose context is transferred to the present circumstance of Colonial War in Angola. The protagonist Sebastião, sacrificing his life, consciously assumes his ill-omened, tragic fate, a fate that is marked by the eternal return of the myth, and definitively inscribes it – buries it – in history. Such fiction provides a last reflection on an essential theme in modern Colonial War cultural representations, *posthumously* produced by the coloniser culture: does a guilt/innocence tragic paradigm still function in the symbolic reproductions of the losses generated by the conflict? Between the extremes of the twentieth century's biopolitical violence – the *Shoah* being a valid example – we can individuate a sort of catastrophic fall preventing, from an ethical point of view, the assumption of the innocent guilt as conceived by Greek heroes (Agamben 1998, 89-92). In the same way, referring to the Colonial War, the problem cannot be addressed by the simple question, "Who is guilty?", for it is important to understand "which" kind of guilt we are talking about. Is there any objective guilt that is immanent both to colonial experience – to a war provoking the explosion of the colonial system – and to its cultural representations?

Considering the war context, an important connection to be understood in this sense is the one linking the epic (anti-epic, in this case) and the tragic, redefining as well, in some way, the relations existing between tragedy and history. The tragic field becomes a space ethically and politically reflecting the epic's characteristic themes. In her essay on the *Iliad*, Simone Weil (1956) individuates in the action of force the fundamental key to understanding how Attic tragedy represents the real continuation of the epic. The element of force turns human beings into things, not only in a sense related to death, but also in the sense that living human beings can be reduced to nothing because of the cold brutality characterizing war experience, that is, force. Therefore the presence of a destructive historical violence (for instance, against the *polis*, the worst disgrace mankind could conceive) is violating the world beyond the grave and pursuing the total destruction of the enemy. Considering this aspect, we could say that the tragic articulates itself as the reflection both of the ethical side of conflicts and of historical facts (not only because of the presence of two confronting ethical powers, as recognized by Hegel in tragedy). Weil and Benjamin inform us that modern cruelty is marked by a destructive violence. Not even the respect for the dead is spared, for any trace must be erased. Creon's victory prevents Antigone's articulation of the tragic paradigm from functioning.

Facing unrestrained force, objective guilt (the Greek *amartia*), does the tragic assumption of an unconditional guilt on behalf of an innocent – as happens in tragedies – still make sense? Or is it irremediably precluded, as Agamben considers when discussing post-Auschwitz ethics? Among Colonial War novels, *A Costa dos Murmúrios* by Lídia Jorge offers valid help in analyzing this crucial question. Significantly, it is an "obscene" book, or better, a text that is coincidental in relation to the traumatic war scene, being written by a woman about an androcentric experience *par excellence* such as war (paradoxically, this aspect perhaps contributes to making it even more representative). Different kinds of guilt are represented here and in this novel the presence of a tragic matrix in which myths are substituted by history is evident: the most significant example refers to the (fictitious) author of a second writing of the tragic events which have occurred, describing how her husband, a brilliant student of mathematics, is transformed, by the cult of force, into a barbarous murderer showing off, in a pseudo-heroic pose, an enemy's severed head (referring to a genuinely existing picture, fiction is able to incorporate history).

In conclusion, the essential *imperfection* marking the question of the posthumous author probably lies here. In Portugal's Colonial War, historical experience underlies the innocence/guilt tragic paradigm: "heroes" are necessarily both guilty and innocent at the same time but, through the act of writing, they assume the (tragic, because they are aware of its incompletion) responsibility to witness the events. Meanwhile Antigone's horizon – to bury the dead and, consequently, to take care of the living – cannot be realized completely as some corpses will remain unburied forever because of the blind force generated by the modern capacity for human destruction.

The violence against the *homo sacer* is a kind of violence that cannot be represented. Therefore the question is doubly tragic, in the sense that it is founded both on the impossible reconciliation of guilt and on the impossible representation of all the tragic elements involved, that cannot resolve the duality "burying the dead/taking care of the living". In order to provide a representative icon of this problem we could say that the landscape of destruction is simultaneously composed of ruins from which the extraction of any historical meaning is still possible and of debris exclusively referring to destruction, break-up and negativity. So, the author of these precarious representations is forced to assume a posthumous condition in order to represent the dead life of this conflict, the sacrificeable – and dead – victims and the unsacrificeable ones, who keep on persecuting the present like hanging spectres – at least, until there exists a kind of history which is capable of representing, in all its meanings and depths, the tragic dimension of a past otherwise condemned to remain – definitely and radically – *other*.

(Translated from the Portuguese by Jacopo Corrado)

References
Abraham N., and Török, M. (1993). *La scorza e il nocciolo*. Roma: Borla.

Agamben, G. (1995). *Homo sacer : Il potere sovrano e la nuda vita*. Turin: Einaudi.

Agamben, G. (1998). *Quel che resta di Auschwitz : L'archivio e il Testimone*. Turin: Bollati Boringhieri.

Alegre, M. (1989). *Jornada de África*. 2nd ed. Lisboa: Dom Quixote.

Assis, M. (1992). *Obra completa*. Vol. 1. Rio de Janeiro: Nova Aguilar.

Baptista, A. B. (1991). *Em nome do apelo do nome: Duas interrogações sobre Machado de Assis*. Lisboa: Litoral.

Benjamin, W. (1997). *Sul concetto di storia*. Turin: Einaudi.

Celan, P. (1980). *Paul Celan: Poems*. Translated by M. Hamburger. Los Angeles: Persea Books.

Dahm, J. (2002). "Epitaffio". In N. Pethes, J. Ruchatz (eds.). *Dizionario della memoria e del ricordo*. Milano: Mondadori, 166-167.

Derrida, J. (2001). *The Work of Mourning*. Chicago and London: University of Chicago Press.

Postcolonialism and Inter-Identity". *Luzo-Brazilian Review*, 39, 2, 9-43.

Ferroni, G. (1996). *Dopo la fine: Sulla condizione postuma della letteratura*. Turin: Einaudi.

Jorge, L. (1988). *A Costa dos Murmúrios*. Lisboa: Dom Quixote.

Levi, P. (1986). *I sommersi e i salvati*. Turin: Einaudi.

Lobo Antunes, A. (1979). *Os cus de Judas*. Lisboa: Dom Quixote.

Lourenço, E. (1992). *O labirinto da saudade. Psicanálise mítica do destino português*. 5th ed. Lisboa: Dom Quixote.

Maj, B. (2003). *Idea del tragico e coscienza storica nelle "fratture" del Moderno*. Macerata: Quodlibet.

Nun, K and Stewart, J. (2016). *Kierkegaard's Literary Figures and Motifs*.

London: Routledge.

Pacheco, F. A. (1996). *A musa irregular*. Porto: Asa.

Ribeiro, M. C. (2004). *Uma história de regressos: Imperio, guerra colonial e pós-colonialismo*. Porto: Afrontamento.

Said, E. (1998). *Cultura e imperialism: Letteratura e consenso nel progetto coloniale dell'Occidente*. Rome: Gamberetti.

Seligmann-Silva, M. (1998-99). "A história como trauma". *Pulsional*, XI-XII, 116-117, 108-127.

Sousa Santos, B. (1994). *Pela mão de Alice. O social e o político na pós-modernidade*. 7th ed. Porto: Afrontamento.

Vecchi, R. (2004). "Incoincidências de autoras: fragmentos de um discurso não só amoroso na literatura da guerra colonial". *Revista Crítica de Ciências Sociais*, 68, 85-100.

Weil, S. (1956). *Iliad, or Poem of Force*. Wallingford: Pendle Hill.

Intra-Colonialism: Re(p)tiling Angola in J.E. Agualusa's *O Vendedor de Passados/The Book of Chameleons*

Bernard McGuirk

> There where post-colonialism was
> – or is – will intra-colonialism be?

A question of colour

In the canonical lineage of Fyodor Dostoyevsky, and Franz Kafka and, in a swerve towards and away from his own Lusophone literary precursors, João Guimarães Rosa and José Saramago, the Angolan novelist José Eduardo Agualusa deploys in *O Vendedor de Passados/The Book of Chameleons* (2004) a narrator-protagonist prone to be less *porte-parole* than *animot*.[1]

> *Ecce animot*, that is the announcement of which I am (following) something like a trace, [...] assuming the title of an autobiographical animal, in the form of a risky, fabulous, or chimerical response to the question "But me, who am I?" (Derrida 2002, 2)

Jacques Derrida's "announcement" is here appropriated – and (following) "an autobiographical animal" will glide across the surface cracks of my text – in order that I might trace and critically re-contextualize Agualusa's re(p)tiling of history in and on the mosaic of Angolan memory. The eponymous "vendedor", the albino Félix Ventura (future happiness guaranteed?), "is a man with an unusual occupation. If your lineage isn't sufficiently distinguished, he'll change that for you. If your family isn't quite as glorious as you'd like, Félix Ventura can make you a new one. Félix Ventura is a seller of pasts".[2] But who is watching him? Who is telling his tale? Who, or what, is on his tail? Who, or what, sets the plot in (ani)motion? *L'animot juste* or *juste l'animot*?

---

[1] For instance, Fyodor Dostoyevsky's mouse (*Notes from the Underground*), Franz Kafka's beetle (*Metamorphoses*), João Guimarães Rosa's jaguar ("The Mirror") and José Saramago's pachyderm (*The Elephant's Journey*).

[2] This teasing marketing line is provided for the reader of the English translation, *The Book of Chameleons*, by the cover-blurb writer of the Arcadia Books edition of the translation by Daniel Hahn.

The title of the English translation rather lets the catalyst out of the bag, though problematically; for in the shift in the title's emphasis from narratee to narrator(s), there is also a transmogrification from Agualusa's original *lagartixa* or *osga*/gecko to Daniel Hahn's suggestive but translator-*traditore* shading into the perspectives of ever-traducing chameleons. *Il n'y a pas de (mot juste) hors-couleur...*

Intra-colonialism

The continued and continuing structuring of political thought and action in nation states that have gained their independence from former master powers in reaction to but never free from embedded mastering discourses cannot be other than controversial. For what is at stake in the reading and, more pertinently, or riskily, in the writing of, in, and from any supposedly post-colonial condition is the danger of slipping into a perilous repetition, even a misreading, understood as ideological *misprision*; that is, an anxiety-driven re-representation of, and still-terrorized swerve away from, the phantom-laden bin of lapsed imperial histories. If there is a determined or restless concern to escape from the discursive straitjacket of the implications, in a post-colonial context, of Derrida's early insight that "we can pronounce not a single destructive proposition which has not already had to slip into the form, the logic, and the implicit postulations of precisely what it seeks to contest" (Derrida 1978, 280), then the challenge for the novelist addressing an assumedly post-colonial society will be to write supplementarily – in the sense of both after and within – to the spectral discourses of any national literary heritage.

The winning of *The Independent* Foreign Fiction Prize for *The Book of Chameleons*, in 2007, has brought for its author a broader attention that at once highlights both his established reputation in the Lusophone world and the controversial nature of a writing that confronts the legacies of Portuguese colonial power in a manner not easily subsumed under the rubrics of the post-colonial. In Brazil, too, such is the symbiotic pull of the Atlantic relation with a westward-looking if still ostensibly northward-thinking Angola, there has been a noteworthy detection in Agualusa's fiction of pertinent challenges posed in a broader post-imperial southern hemispheric context.[3] Let it be said, however, that it is not the person of

---

[3] Agualusa's novels have come to feature regularly on the syllabus of the Brazilian

the novelist, the figure who infuriates or provokes reaction in the Portuguese-speaking world, which will be the subject of further concern here. Any brouhaha surrounding a writer of growing international renown or notoriety will no doubt be heeded by those who grasp more readily at the context than the thorn-text of Agualusa's ever-prickly narrative relation with Angola's – and Portugal's and Brazil's – discursive histories; whence the option for a Derrida-derived instrument of access to the animotions of *The Book of Chameleons*. While it is to the gecko-voicing of the narrator of *O Vendedor de Passados* – cackler reincarnate of a dandy literatus – that critical attention will be addressed, noted already is the sly slippage from an economy of transformed pasts to the currency of exchanged identities; from the sound of colonizing coinage to the colours of chameleon disguise in the English title's rendering for an international market.[4]

Sic transit gloria (im)mundi as the base looker-on of a reptile/human-human/reptile sphere of action is exploited and explored. From the debased, the abject, might a re-forging of Angola's inheritances be alchemized... true currency or false; stable narrative or fool's gold in the selling of an emergent literature to a world-wide readership.[5] "Tu m'as

---

pre-university examination, the *vestibular*. As to why his Brazilian readers might be trusting the tale and not the teller, see Agualusa's provocative meditation on Brazil's status as colony in footnote 13.

[4] The lure of translation, in the case of the title of this novel, is one with which the author has colluded, as seen in his interview with Paulo Polzonoff, Jr. and Anderson Tepper:

PP/AT: "Do you participate in the process of translating your work from Portuguese?"

JA: "It depends a lot on the translator and the language it is being translated into. With the English translations by Daniel Hahn, I do participate a lot. But this collaboration between the writer and his translator is rare, I think [...] we met twice, and I helped him with a few things. We took a long time to decide on an English title for the book. But the rest was fairly easy. Daniel Hahn is an excellent translator, and also a sensitive creator in his own right – and that seems to me to be the most important quality in this whole process." (Polzonoff and Tepper 2007, 4)

[5] BBC Radio 4, "Today", 4 September 2008: "Luanda is the most expensive capital in the world for expatriates. In oil revenues, Angola is beginning to rival South Africa in terms of regional influence."

donné de la boue et j'en ai fait de l'or"[6] might be heard as one of the many precursor texts that Agualusa's intra-modern narrative echoes whilst the ceiling-seer gecko performs – a complicit *beau de l'air* – the role of mocking interlocutor-witness to the infelicitous ventures of the earthbound Félix:

> "I don't believe it – are you laughing?"
>
> The creature's amazement annoyed me. I was afraid – but I didn't move, not a muscle. The albino took off his dark glasses, put them away in the inside pocket of his jacket, took the jacket off – slowly, sadly – and hung it carefully on the back of a chair [...]
>
> "*Pópilas!*" he exclaimed. "So I see Your Lowness is laughing?! That's quite a novelty..." [...] "You've really got terrible skin, you know that? We must be related..."
>
> I've been expecting something like that. It's like being able to speak. I would have answered him back. But my vocal abilities extend only to laughing [...] Until last week the albino had always ignored me. But since he heard me laughing, he's started coming home earlier [...] we talk. Or rather, he talks, I listen. Sometimes I laugh – this seems enough for him. I get the sense that there's already a thread of friendship holding us together. On Saturday nights – but not always – the albino arrives with some girl. Some of them are scared as they come in [...] trying not to look directly at him, unable to hide their disgust [...] they look around the bookcases for records.
>
> "Don't you have any *cuduro* music, old man?"
>
> And since the albino doesn't have any *cuduro* [...] they end up choosing something with a bright cover, which usually means it's some Cuban rhythm or other. They dance slowly [...] as the shirt buttons come undone, one by one. That perfect skin, so very black, moist and radiant, against the albino's – dry, rough, and pinkish. I watch it all. In this house I'm like a little night-time God. During the day, I sleep. (4-5)

The thread that is to bind the actantial fabric of the novel is not only the affective tug of friendship but also the structuring suture of inverse or inverted perceptions. Félix is seen by the gecko as "the creature"; the gecko

---

[6] The alchemy referred to, and to which I shall return, is the turning of base matter to gold of "L'Invitation au voyage" (Baudelaire 1961, 253-4).

is, in an instant, though it will have to wait for Félix to grant it the dignity of a proper name, elevated to the sovereign albeit ironized status of "Your Lowness", and demeaned by a non-essential but euphemistically expletive epithet, *"Pópilas!".*[7] Bound together in their respectively perceived defectiveness – lack of colour, lack of speech, and a mutually acknowledged lack of status – the companions in mockery sardonically reconstruct the isolated, lonesome, outcast and oft-despised self-identity of the individual judged and thus situated, in a post-conflict Angola, according to perceptions of their skin.

Félix inspires disgust, in the series of black and *mulata* girls and women who pass – or dance – fleetingly through his LP collection, his bedroom and his boredom, as albino, as "old man", and as a cultural throwback to an era prior to the perceived authenticity of the new-Angolan *cuduro*,[8] steeped (blanched?) in an outmoded taste in reading and in records – gaudily sleeved vestiges of a Cuban "or other" cultural imprint of the now-to-be-forgotten anti-colonial wars. The voice of the complicit gecko may be heard to perform dialogically yet differently from those of the itinerant week-end sexual partners that Félix ventures to bring back to his antique book-seller's solitude. Its laughter supplements both Portugal's silence about the colonial wars (prior) and, for Angola, the cacophony (post-; in the 1990s boom) referred to by Mark Sabine as the "potentially therapeutic" and "unprecedented growth in popular publishing and e-publishing, popular music and theatre, television and filmmaking focused on lusophone African culture and history" (Sabine 2009, 254). The vision of the gecko may be seen to supplant the panopticon power of both the colonizing other (Portugal) and the anti-colonial agency of a subsequent, post-1974 alternative, Marxism, and its would-be principal instrument of conversion (Cuba).

Sabine's parallel meditation on Angola's ever-more-rapid shift away from colonizing efforts, literary and otherwise, "to configure the white

---

[7] "Pópilas! Chissa! Possa! Arre! Porra!", undeletedly colonial, post-colonial and, no less, intra-colonial expletives.

[8] *Cuduro* or *Kuduro* is dance of relatively recent vintage which has spread from Angola to Portugal, Brazil and beyond the Lusophone world. Apart from its Afro-rhythms and a characteristic emphasis on the movement of the bottom, the word plays on the Portuguese "cu" and "duro", "ass" and "hard".

male in Africa as a transcendental subject" (Sabine 2009, 266)[9] through recent pop culture and cinema, is both echoed and subverted in Agualusa's exploitation of the albino function. A further inversion of a half-century-old shibboleth text, Franz Fanon's *Peau noire, masques blancs* archiving of white and black as interdependent terms brought into discursive possibility by the binarizing moment of "Empire", underlies the parodic first encounter of Félix Ventura with a mysterious stranger who presents himself as an eager *comprador de passados*, a man in the market for reincarnation. By-product or craft, Agualusa's portrayal of a defining male-to-male exchange will extend as it pastiches standard feminist objections to the gendering, in Africa, of compliant intra-colonialism as being an exclusive or predominantly female enterprise.[10]

Reincarnations… and introducing JB

"*Félix Ventura. Guarantee your children a better past.*" And he laughed. A silent laugh but not unpleasant. "That would be you, I presume? A friend of mine gave me your card."

I couldn't place his accent. He spoke softly, with a mix of different pronunciations, a faint Slavic roughness, tempered by the honeyed softness of the Portuguese from Brazil. Félix Ventura took a step back:

"And who are you?" The foreigner closed the door […] Certain common friends, he said – his voice becoming even gentler – had given him this address. They told him of a man who dealt in memories, a man who sold the past, clandestinely, the way other people deal in cocaine […]

Félix Ventura gave in. There was a whole class, he explained a whole new bourgeoisie, who sought him out. They were businessmen, ministers, landowners, diamond smugglers, generals – people, in other words, whose futures are secure. What these people lack is a good past,

---

[9] Sabine was developing the arguments with respect to Tarzan and the "white hunter" figure as deployed in Landau and Kaspin 2002.

[10] In *Peau noire, masques blancs*, 1952 (*Black Skin, White Masks*, 1967), Fanon suggested that the categories "white" and "black" are interdependent, both emerging as such with Empire and conquest. He focused primarily on black men; feminist critics in particular have reviled and revised his depiction of the role of black women in the apparatus of colony and colonization.

a distinguished ancestry, diplomas. In sum, a name that resonates with nobility and culture. He sells them a brand new past. He draws up their family tree. He provides them with photographs of their grandparents and great-grandparents, gentlemen of elegant bearing and old-fashioned ladies. The businessmen, the ministers, would like to have women like that as their aunts, he went on, pointing to the portraits on the walls – old ladies swathed in fabrics, authentic bourgeois *bessanganas* –, they liked to have a grandfather with the distinguished bearing of a Machado de Assis, of a Cruz e Souza, of an Alexandre Dumas. And he sells them this simple dream.

"Perfect, perfect." The foreigner smoothed his moustache. "That's what they told me. I require your services. But I'm afraid it may be rather a lot of work..."

"Work makes you free..." Félix muttered [...]

"And might I know your name?" [...] Félix insisted [...] "You're right. I'm a photo journalist. I collect images of wars, of hunger and its ghosts, of natural disasters and terrible misfortunes. You can think of me as a witness." [...]

He needed a new name, authentic official documents that bore out this identity. The albino listened, horrified:

"No!" he managed to blurt out. "I don't do things like that. I invent dreams for people, I'm not a forger... And besides, if you'll pardon my bluntness, wouldn't it be a bit difficult to invent a completely African genealogy for you?"

"Indeed! And why is that?!..."

"Well – Sir – ... you're white."

"And what of it? You're whiter than I am..."

"White? Me?!" The albino choked. He took a handkerchief from his pocket and wiped his forehead. "No, no! I'm black. Pure black. I'm a native. Can't you tell I'm black?..."

From my usual post at the window I couldn't help giving a little chuckle at this point. The foreigner looked upwards as though he was sniffing the air. Tense – alert:

"Did you hear that? Who laughed just then?" [...]

"It's a gecko, yes, but a very rare species. See these stripes? It's a tiger gecko – a shy creature, we still know very little about them [...] They have this amazing laugh – doesn't it sound like a human laugh?"

[...] They spent sometime time discussing me, which I found

annoying – talking as if I weren't there! – And yet at the same time it felt as though they were talking not about me but about some alien being, some vague and distant biological anomaly. Men know almost nothing of the little creatures that share their homes. Mice, bats, ants, ticks, flees, flies, mosquitoes, spiders, worms, silverfish, termites, weevils, snails, beetles. I decided that I might as well simply get on with my life (16-18) [...]

"Angola has rescued me for life." [...]

Félix looked up [...] he had an identity card, a passport, a driver's licence, all these documents in the name of José Buchmann, native of Chibia, 52, professional photographer. (38)

A markedly male bonding wreathes the dialogue (cum trialogue) that encourages the initially cautious Félix Ventura to peddle his reading – and his role in the re-writing – of modern-day Angola to an urbane foreign client (soon to be "outed" as José Buchmann). In the post-colonial phase of reconstruction, "a whole new bourgeoisie" must undergo decon-struction, must be de-binarized, must enter that aporia – instead of seeking any verifiable past – which will allow the supplementarity of a falsified story to forge a new Angola. A post-colonial state will play on that *différance* whereby no difference might be traced between inside-outside, intra- and extra-, after-before, pre- and post-, black-white, a blank page or an excess of history. Its trip – "clandestinely, the way other people deal in cocaine" (16) – will consist of a journey into a past-free and timeless present, the chimera of a future construct-country – *un pays superbe/pays de Cocagne* – without ever having to leave home.[11]

Félix thrills and wallows in the "great white trader" role that he plays behind his neither-white-nor-black mask; his skin. Antiquarian book-seller that he would be, albeit divested of the apparel of the economically

---

[11] "Un vrai pays de Cocagne", in the legerdemain of Félix Ventura's artful re-casting of a nation newly hooked on its hallucinogen-history, is re-packaged as a *true* country that can resemble *you*: "Il est une contrée qui te ressemble, où tout est beau, riche, tranquille et honnête, où la fantaisie a bâti [...] C'est là qu'il faut aller vivre, c'est là qu'il faut aller mourir!" Baudelaire's exoticism in the prose poem "L'Invitation au voyage" is played out, it will be recalled, within the confines of "Le Spleen de Paris" (Baudelaire 1961, 253-4). His "Pays singulier, supérieur aux autres, comme l'Art l'est à la Nature, où celle-ci est réformée par le rêve, où elle est corrigée, embellie, refondue" is but one of the precursor tropes to be pastiched by the splenetic fantasy, the Eros-Thanatos risk-taking, of *O Vendedor de Passados*.

dominant male of his father's generation, he traffics still in literary nostalgia amidst the sub-genre of *faux-monnayeur* documentation that has become his daily bread. Ah, would some intra-colonial power the gift but give us to see ourselves as others see us... then might Ventura recognize for what it is his own *branqueamento* – that peculiar brand of skin-lightening which translates the past from a colonizing *Heart of Darkness* to Félix the albino's Art of Lightness.[12] His re-enactment of "L'Invitation au voyage", as a seller of pasts for myriad upwardly mobile fellow citizens, updates the exotic trajectory of an unholy trinity of nineteenth-century *littérateurs* carefully chosen to accompany the cultural alchemy of a virtual if still Jeanne Duval-fixated Baudelaire – Alexandre Dumas, Machado de Assis, Cruz e Souza – because of their long-hidden black imprint on the blank page of a literature of exclusion, the textual apartheid of French, Brazilian... or any other canonic and colonizing culture.[13]

Fleetingly on a high in the artificial paradise of his far-from-simple dream of lineage-and-new-Empire building, Félix soon comes down; and,

---

[12] In a recent and seminal meditation on nationalism and identity, Roberto Vecchi begins with the striking image of "a cartography of horror" and, with particular reference to Lusophone Africa, addresses the problem of events distant not only historically but also and above all spatially, "transoceanic", and in some cases with more than an ocean in between. He speaks of an "elsewhere" of horror that immediately recalls *Heart of Darkness*; an "elsewhere" in which there dwell, however, a present and a proximity very close to home, very much our own and in no way improper or remote (Vecchi 2008, 187) .

[13] On the implications of the colour of Machado de Assis, Cruz e Souza and, by extension, Alexandre Dumas, Agualusa is emphatic: "In my opinion, Brazil is still a country moulded on slavery, the same as Africa. Brazil has an Africa inside itself and at times it pays no attention to it. Here, as in Angola, for example, there exists the figure of the black nanny who passes from one generation to another; there is the house boy brought up as if he were a son but, in truth, he works in the house, without remuneration. Black and poor are conditions which are confused in Brazil. A black élite has not grown up here, as in Angola. People notice this inequality on a day-to-day basis, in the relations between individuals, and even in the culture. Today it is not possible to cite a great black or mestiço Brazilian writer. That is incredible because in the nineteenth-century there were great writers of African descent, such as Machado de Assis and Cruz e Sousa. What is worse, there is not a single great indigenous author, something that is the case throughout the Americas. Until it confronts the problem and does not give greater participation to black people, Brazil will not have decolonized itself. Brazil is a colony" (Agualusa, *Epoca* interview, 2007, my translation).

mutteringly, he ironizes his own racially doctoring enterprise by echoing the anti-*mot*, the obscene lie, the final collusion, of Auschwitz. No poetry... just confession; and the effect is to trigger in his mysterious – possibly East European (via Brazil) – visitor the blurting out of the identity-bereft role of the mere, but no less guilt-ridden, "photo-journalist", the collector of "images of war, of hunger and its ghosts, of terrible misfortunes". Once a witness always a witness, however; and the reader is teased to anticipate that the self-dispossessed stranger, a burdened bearer of *animages*, has come to the new Angola in search of something old and in remembrance of things past... of some unfinished business no longer to be hidden from expression, from view, from memory or from representation.

The discomfited Félix ("Oh, the horror") is so plunged into the loss of his self-possession that he momentarily loses, too, the plot of his own making, his own inventions, his certainty as to his own (perceived) colour. "Can't you tell I'm black?" says the albino. And from within this tension the trialogue is rendered overt... via a chuckle; the "amazing" laughter of identity-deconstruction made manifest. *Et homo faber est* – shaper, moulder, image-maker, factor, *hacedor*... fictionist? But that's another's (short) story; the legacy of one about to be reincarnated. As author, Agualusa will also create his precursors.[14]

Pace animot... for "men know almost nothing of the little creatures that share their homes". Self-obsessedly lost in the game of "But me, who am I?", they are meanwhile narrated by but one of that infinite series of autobiographical animals ("mice, bats, ants, ticks, flees, flies, mosquitoes, spiders, worms, silverfish, termites, weevils, snails, beetles"... and, here, why not?, *geckopidae*) who can say "I might as well simply get on with my life" whilst tell-tailing the "risky, fabulous or chimerical response", or responses, of a felicitous venturer into the company of another re-incarnate J(L)B. José. Bookman par excellence; with one "L" of a difference.

In the actantial sphere of Félix Ventura, of José Buchmann and of the narrating tiger gecko, the possession of their textual status by the shades of Jorge Luis Borges will come ever more overtly to haunt the plot of *O Vendedor de Passados*. Buchmann has the acquired initials of the blind librarian precursor; "Félix and I share a love (in my case a hopeless love)

---

[14] Cf. "El hecho es que cada escritor crea a sus precursores"/"The fact is that every writer creates his precursors", in "Kafka y sus precursores" (Borges 1995).

for old words" (25) muses the gecko; and Félix himself takes on the mantle of a revenant: "The tightly curled hair, trimmed down now, glowed around him with a miraculous aura. If someone had seen him from out on the road, seen him through the window, they would have thought they were looking at a ghost" (23). Interviewed (but trust the tale not the teller; for the text betrays a less restricted, an uncontrollable, a more infectious re-inhabitation), Agualusa says that his gecko-"chameleon is a reincarnation of Borges".[15] Perhaps:

> It's been nearly fifteen years that my soul has been trapped in this body, and I am still not used to it. I lived for almost a century in the skin of a man, and I never managed to feel altogether human either. To this day I have known some thirty geckos [...] But I'd gladly exchange the company of all the geckos and lizards for Félix Ventura and his long soliloquies. Yesterday he confided to me that he'd met an amazing woman. Though, he added, the word "woman" doesn't quite do her justice.
> "Ângela Lúcia is to women what humankind is to the apes."
> "I ought to be charging you overtime, damn it!. Who do you think I am – Scheherezade?..." (40-42) [...]

> But excuse my digression – that's what happens when a gecko starts philosophizing... So let's get back to José Buchmann. I'm not suggesting that in a few days a massive butterfly is going to burst out of him,

---

[15] "PP/AT: *The Book of Chameleons* recalls in many ways the work of the great Argentine writer Jorge Luis Borges. How important has Latin American literature been to your work? JA: I read a lot of Latin American literature when I was younger, especially Borges. His worlds are similar to mine. Gabriel García Márquez once said that when he arrived in Luanda, Angola, in 1977, he saw himself as an African. That part of Africa where he arrived – the old city of Luanda – is a mixed, creole Africa, not so different from the Latin America where he was born and grew up. Evidently, there are a lot of Africas, some of them remote and impenetrable. I found out that I'm a Latin American, too, reading García Márquez and Borges. And I found out that I'm also Brazilian, reading Jorge Amado as a teenager. PP/AT: The novel unfolds from the point of view of a chameleon. Why did you choose such a narrator? Does it owe something to Borges' work? JA: Yes, the book was written in honor of Borges. The chameleon is a reincarnation of Borges – all its recollections are related to actual events in Borges' life" (Polzonoff and Tepper in Agualusa 2007, 1).

beating his great multi-coloured wings. The changes I'm referring to are more subtle. For one thing, his accent is beginning to shift [...] it has a Luandan rhythm to it now [...] to hear him laugh you'd think he was Angolan. (55)

Perhaps not or, at least, not alone.

A Borges-like sequence, a pastiched taxonomy not of the fantastic but of "some alien being[s], some vague and distant biological anomal[ies]", is followed by the narrator's option for neither the shared lineage of the ex-human race (of gecko memory) nor the companionship of fellow lizards but for the role of silent witness cum laughing *animot*-interlocutor of Félix Ventura, of José Buchmann and, not least, of its own alter-ego. *Lagartixa* ("e eu"), too, turns maker of fictions: *castigat ridendo mores... et colores*. All three, albino-black animus, chrysalis-blanched yet potentially "multi-coloured" Angolan, and a "terrible skin[ned]" animator, inherit and re-perform the role of Borges's *El hacedor*: artificer, here, of adopted fictions *qua* the assumed identities of those who buy into the commerce of "the seller of pasts" – a currency, an exchange mechanism (and rate) of memory conceived as coinage and counterfeit bills. All three? Sounds familiar; there where Hegel was will "ipseity" be?

> By means of the chimera of this singular word, the *animot*, I bring together three heterogeneous elements within a single verbal body. (Derrida 2002, 1)

Plus ça change... three in one. Amidst the emerging plurality of a "new" tale of the nation, African, facing West, but resisting the behest of a too-homogenizing "Black" Atlantic identity of popular jargon and populist appeal, echoes the heterogeneity of an intra-Angolan actant. The mixed economy of *O Vendedor de Passados* underwrites the fiction that, there where "new bourgeoisie" peoples' "futures are secure", it is via text, including sold "diplomas", that "a brand new past" will be. It is the happy venture of fiction that "draws up their family tree". Subjectivity *is* heterogeneity; *is* attributable to archi-texture. "But me, who am I?" Anima? No. *Animot*:

> Autobiography, the writing of the self as living, the trace of the living for itself, being for itself, the auto-affection or auto-infection as

memory or archive of the living would be an immunizing movement (a movement of safety, of salvage and salvation of the safe, the holy, the immune, the indemnified, of virginal and intact nudity), but an immunizing movement that is always threatened with becoming auto-immunizing, as is every *autos*, every ipseity, every automatic, automobile, autonomous, auto-referential movement. Nothing risks becoming more poisonous than an autobiography; poisonous for itself in the first place, auto-infectious for the presumed signatory who is so auto-affected. (Derrida 2002, 1).

O tempora, o mores... et colores

At this point a teller is permitted to enter the tale. In a dream sequence, the gecko imagines that Félix confides in him, flick-knife collector and man of inaction reincarnate; again via the gentlemanly intertexts, *à deux*, of JLB, authorizing creator of precursors... and of liars:

> "You invented him, this strange José Buchmann, and now he has begun to invent himself. It's like a metamorphosis... A reincarnation... Or rather: a possession."
>
> My friend looked at me with alarm:
>
> "What do you mean?"
>
> "José Buchmann – surely you're noticed? – He's taken over the foreigner's body. He becomes more and more lifelike with each day that passes and that man he used to be, that night-time character who came into our house eight months ago as though he'd come not from another country but from another time – where is he now?"
>
> "It's a game. I know it's a game. We all know that."
>
> He poured himself some tea and took two cubes of sugar, and stirred it. He drank, his eyes lowered. There we were, two gentlemen, two good friends, wearing white in an elegant café [...]
>
> "So be it," I agreed. "Let's acknowledge that it's no more than a game. So who is he?"
>
> I wiped the sweat from my face. I've never distinguished myself by my valour. Maybe that's why I've never been attracted (speaking of my other life, that is) by the stormy destiny of heroes and rogues. I collected flick knives. And with a pride of which I'm now ashamed I boasted about the exploits of a grandfather of mine who'd been a general. I did befriend some brave men, but unfortunately that didn't

help me. Courage isn't contagious; fear is, of course. Félix smiled as he understood that my terror was greater, more ancient, than his:

"I have no idea. You?"

He changed the subject. He told me that a few days earlier he'd been at the launch of a new novel by a writer of the Angolan diaspora. He was an unpleasant sort of character, professionally indignant, who'd built up his whole career abroad, selling our national horrors to European readers. Misery does ever so well in wealthy countries [...] "In your novels do you lie deliberately or just out of ignorance?" Laughter. A murmur of approval. The writer hesitated a few seconds. Then counter-attacked: "I'm a liar by vocation," he shouted. "I lie with joy! Literature is the only chance for a true liar to attain any sort of social acceptance." Then, more soberly, he added – his voice lowered – that the principal difference between a dictatorship and democracy is that in the former there exists only one truth, the truth as imposed by power, while in free countries every man has the right to defend his own version of events. Truth, he said, is a superstition. He – Félix – was taken with the idea. (67-68)

Ah would some intra-colonial power... It did. JEA as others (his readers, the critics) see him? "But me, who am I?" "Agualusa and I"? "Borges y yo"? "I do not know which of the two is writing this page".[16] "Tiger, tiger"? No. "El otro tigre"? Yes... ("a very rare species"). "It's a *tiger* gecko" and "we *still* know very little about them" [*animot* italics];[17] "this amazing laugh – doesn't it sound like a human laugh?", an anxiety-of-influence, a JLB-echolalic, an other, a nervous, laugh? Laughter that cannot hide that I, geck(anim)o, am also "destined to perish, definitively, and only some instant of myself can survive in him. Little by little, I am giving over everything to him [...] Spinoza knew that all things long to persist in their being: the stone eternally wants to be stone and the tiger a tiger. I shall remain in Borges, not in myself (if it is true that I am someone)" (Borges 1980, 69-70). And the tiger a gecko...? Reincarnation? Or animosity

---

[16] "No sé cual de los dos escribe esta página"/ "I do not know which of the two is writing this page", in "Borges y yo" (Borges 1980, 69-70); my translations of Borges *passim*.

[17] A *tiger* gecko? Leopard gecko, panther gecko, yes, but tiger... "a very rare species" indeed; read between the lines from *El hacedor*'s "El otro tigre"/ "The other tiger" (Borges 1980).

burning bright? Perhaps the funereal dread of the curse of having to remember? Memory as metamorphosed gecko-echo of "Funes el memorioso": "Courage isn't contagious; fear is, of course. Félix smiled as he understood that my terror was greater, more ancient, than his." *Comparationem fingere*: "I was numbed by the fear of multiplying superfluous ge [cko] stures."[18]

Behold the son of man; progeny, too, of *In principio erat verbum*. An inheritor of transcendental "Colony" swerves towards self-identity inseparably from the cadences of intra-colonial discourse, that genre of testimony, in which the *apud*-Ventura performs. The "me who am I?" of the post-colony necessitates not the post-theological echo of proselytizing mono-culture – *Ecce homo* – but the risky, fabulous, or chimerical response *Ecce animot*. There where dictatorship was will democracy, "by vocation", be. Lies must go on. *C'est la vie...*

Just prior to the calculatedly Borges-riddled dream of the differential nineteenth- and twentieth-century "stormy destiny of heroes and rogues", respectively military and literary, in a single-page chapter, "My first death didn't kill me" – a text that mirrors as it distorts the doubling "Borges y yo" original on which it draws – the other "otro tigre" gecko confesses to having considered an alternative to the lie that is life ("woven superstition"), only to be interrupted by the greater lie that is fiction (not "bad at all"):

> Once, when I was in human form, I decided to kill myself [...] I hoped that reincarnation, all that stuff, was no more than slowly woven superstition [...] I thought that the gin in combination with the tedium of a pointless plot would give me the courage to put the gun to my head and pull the trigger. But it turned out the book wasn't bad at all, and I kept reading to the last page [...] I put the pistol to my head, and I fell asleep. (63)

The textual gap after the comma is deliberate; the aporia is unavoidable in the circular ruins of any and all attempts to think from within the post- without acknowledgement of the intra-, the impossibility of not "living", in the new Angola, to spin the yarn, to bear as *animot* the tell-tale tail of

---

[18] *D'après* "me entorpeció el temor de multiplicar ademanes inútiles", "Funes el memorioso"/ "Funes the Memory Man" (Borges 1988).

witness to that afterlife that is the voice, the voicing, of mocked and mocking memory. The coda-imperative of "reading to the last page" is to be the supplement to ever-failing memory as slowly woven fiction comes to the rescue of all-too-fast and irrecuperable history.

The counter-attack

That "literature [might be] the only chance for a true liar to attain any sort of social acceptance" is a perception shared by all who require the services of Félix Ventura; by any who would seek *within* a post-colonial life a fictive identity to be appropriated *from* a preferred colonial memory. Yet the desire that is staged by individuals is played out at a national level not only in the arch-defensive attack on the truth-seekers who, affianced to Plato, would expel fiction-makers from the new Republic of Angola, wishing for an answer to the (1934 or *1984*) provocation – "In your novels do you lie deliberately or just out of ignorance?" – *boutade* of either socialist realist recidivism or dystopian *dirigisme*.[19] "One truth" ideology, confronted with the globalizing falsehood that "every man has [...] his own version", seeks an outlet less transcendental, less religious, than that "the Truth" be "a superstition" – however "taken with the idea" might be a nostalgic and disingenuous Félix.

And so to the unfinished business no longer to be hidden from expression, from view, from memory or from representation. In the overtime of Scheherezadian deferral, the interweaving of her story with his story will divulge why "Ângela Lúcia is to women what humankind is to the apes" not only for Félix but also for the inseparably male plotting that is the actantial tangle of Ventura, Buchmann and the gecko. Seek the supplement. *Cherchez la fff...fiction.*

When Ângela and José come together, the seller of pasts, Félix, prompts in her response to his insouciance a prejudiced reptile-narrator's *apartheid*-adjectival, nay, politically correct, interference:

[19] The "writer of the Angolan diaspora [...] selling our national horrors to European readers" – be it in sly reference to Agualusa himself or to any other unveiler of intra-colonial social structures – will, classically, have to face, and face down, attacks from either post-colonial critics of an unreconstructed 1934 Soviet Writers' Congress bent or Orwellian post-modern gloom-mongers. Amidst the laughter, the timid murmurs of approval.

"Do you two know each other?"

"No, no!" said Ângela, her voice colourless. "I don't think so."

José Buchmann was even less certain:

"Oh, but there are so many people I don't know!" he said, and laughed at his own wit. "I've never been so popular." (73-74)

"I don't think" therefore I am not who I was. "I don't know!" therefore I resist any populism that would hide behind the identity labels of instant recognition. Ângela presses Buchmann not as to *who* he has been but as to "Where?":

"I've spent the last ten years without any fixed home. Adrift across the world, taking photographs of wars. Before that I lived in Rio de Janeiro, and before that in Berlin, and earlier still in Lisbon. I went to Portugal in the sixties to study law, but I couldn't stand the climate. It was too cold. *Fado*, Fátima, football [...] One day a friend gave me a Canon-1, the one I still use today, and that's how I became a photographer. I was in Afghanistan in 1982, with the Soviet troops... in Salvador with the guerrillas... in Peru, on both sides... in the Falklands, again on both sides... in Iran during the war against Iraq... in Mexico on the side of the Zapatistas... I've taken a lot of photos in Israel and Palestine – a lot – there's never any shortage of work there."

Ângela Lúcia smiled, nervous again:

"Enough! I don't want your memories to pollute this house with blood..." [...] The two guests remained [...] Neither spoke. The silence that hung between them was full of murmurings, of shadows, of things [...] dark and furtive. Or perhaps not [...] and I merely imagined the rest. (74-75)

"I am not there where I am the plaything" ["le jouet"] of... my camera.[20]

"But me, who am I?" Am I but my camera? Mere *animage*? If only I could get a shot in sideways... before I am re-narrated, "merely imagined", ani(de)moted to my camera-always-lies reputation, the freeze-frame climate, the bloody pollution, of my photo-reportage, my unwanted memory. Must I, too, become a bookman reincarnate in order to persist in

[20] Cf. "Je ne suis pas là où je suis le jouet de ma pensée"("I am not there where I am the plaything of my thought") (Lacan 1966 , 136).

my being, to compete with the digressions, the interventions, the mediations, the mocking testimony, the authority of that benighted gecko? "*Pópilas!*" No eyelash! I am aware that its eyes are protected by a transparent membrane, cleaned of debris by its long tongue. Not a forked tongue. And when it's caught, it releases its tail, which twitches for a while, allowing it to escape capture... no doubt while, later, it will grow another *tale.* "Little by little, I am giving over everything to him." I don't even know which of us two is writing this page. Damn Spinoza! Damned gecko... whatsisname?

No name? Omniscient but anonymous narrator? Perhaps Félix can help. He sold one to me, "Buchmann"... so why not bequeath an appropriate name, now, to a friend, the confidant of his soliloquies, to a gecko who reincarnates the man who laughs? (Who goes there, Victor?) *Victor ludorum?* ... "Jouet... Lui, Borges"?

As compassion shades the dream-conversation with the Angolan seller of pasts of the reptile pining in reincarnation for the youthful venture to Europe and the dialogical eloquence of its Argentine precursor, let us listen in:

> "I'm a man with no colour," he said. "And as you know, nature abhors a vacuum." [...]
>
> I felt sorry for him:
>
> "In cold countries people with light skin aren't so troubled by the harshness of the sun. Maybe you ought to think about moving to Switzerland. Have you ever been to Geneva? I'd rather like to live in Geneva." [...]
>
> Félix looked at me carefully:
>
> "Sorry to ask – but could you tell me your name?"
>
> "I have no name," I replied quite frankly. "I am the gecko."
>
> "That's silly. No one is a gecko!"
>
> "You're right. No one's a gecko. And you – are you really called Félix Ventura?"
>
> My questions seemed to offend him [...]
>
> "Is this madness?"
>
> I didn't know how to answer him. (79-80)[21]

---

[21] Jouer, lui? Donc moi aussi. Agualusa's text is littered with JLB jokes, not least in the chapter entitled, "Dream No. 4" in which the dream conversation of the aged

The companionable laughter of His Lowliness, sovereign though nameless and wordless, convinces Félix of what happens when one "starts philosophizing" about a nonetheless articulate gecko. In an Apuleian, Erasmian, Bergsonian and particularly felicitous swerve, Ventura geckoes a Roland Barthes's *bon mot*; in the *animot* discourse of Agualusa's novel, his chit-chatting interlocutor demands, deserves, a proper name: "Rire c'est lutter pour être nommé."[22]

I, Eulálio

> The following night Félix asked Ângela Lúcia the same question. First, of course, he'd told her that he'd dreamed of me again. I've seen Ângela Lúcia say very serious things laughing or, on the contrary, adopting a sombre expression when joking with her interlocutor. It's not always possible to tell what she's thinking. On this occasion she laughed at the anxiety in my friend's eyes, greatly increasing his disquiet, but then right away turned more serious and asked:
> "And his name? So did the guy tell you who he is?"
> No one is a name, I thought forcefully...
> The reply took Ângela Lúcia by surprise. Félix too. I watched him look at her as though looking into an abyss. She was smiling sweetly. She lay her right hand on the albino's left arm. She whispered something in his ear, and he relaxed.
> "No," he whispered back. "I don't know who he is. But since I'm the one who dreams about him I think I can give him any name I want, can't I? I'm going to call him Eulálio because he's so well-spoken."
> Eulálio?! That seems fine to me. So Eulálio I shall be. (83)

Subjectivity ("eu") and the speaking voice ("lalia"); whence the articulator is caught but not captured in the act of becoming... never being a fixed form, always potential, ever prone to generate a new tale (trust the tail not the teller?). Eulálio's tap-tapping – between sleeping watchfully and his devouring of multiple little *animaux* – draws Félix into that wisest of friendships which is the echolalia of coming (to laugh) together. Therein,

---

Borges of the Geneva period (1914-1921) provides the intertext for the gecko's tongue-in-cheek advice to Félix.

[22] Cf. "Lire c'est lutter pour nommer" ("To read is to struggle to name") (Barthes 1974, xi).

babelic *ridere* and *ride* wrinkle inseparably into the laughter lines, the ageing skin, the wisdom, of mockery; and the infinite ludics of the mosaic, of tiling, assume the *animot* form of the re(p)tiling:

> It would not be a matter of "giving speech back" to animals but perhaps of acceding to a thinking, however fabulous and chimerical it might be, that thinks the absence of the name and of the word otherwise, as something other than a privation. (Derrida 2002, 2)

Otherwise, I speak (laugh) therefore I am (not) brackets Félix and Eulálio as one and (not) the same: *Ecce homo et animot factus est.*

Out of habit, and out of genetic predisposition (because bright light bothers me), I sleep during the day, all day. Sometimes, however, something will wake me up [...] Perhaps I was dreaming about my father. The moment I awoke I saw the scorpion. He was just a few centimetres away. Motionless. Closed in a shell of hatred like a medieval warrior in his armour. And then he fell upon me. I jumped back, climbed the wall, in a flash, until I was up at the ceiling. I could hear quite clearly the dry tap of the sting against the floor – I can hear it still.

I remember something my father said once when we were celebrating – with only pretend joy, I like to think – the death of someone we disliked:

"He was evil, and he didn't know it. He didn't know what evil was. That is to say, he was *pure* evil."

That's what I felt at precisely the moment as I opened my eyes and the scorpion was there.

[...]

After the episode with the scorpion, I wasn't able to get back to sleep. This meant that I was able to witness the arrival of the Minister. A short, fat man, ill at ease in his body [...] To watch him you'd think he'd been shortened only moments earlier and hadn't yet become accustomed to his new height... He was wearing a dark suit, with white stripes, which didn't really fit and which troubled him [...] [His] sudden camaraderie irritated my friend even more [...] [He] went off to fetch the file he'd prepared. He opened it on the little mahogany table – slowly, theatrically – in a ritual I'd observed so many times. It always worked. The Minister, anxious, held his breath as my friend revealed his genealogy to him:

"This is your paternal grandfather, Alexandre Torres dos Santos Correia de Sá e Benevides, a direct descendent of Salvador Correia de Sá e Benevides, the famous *carioca* who in 1648 liberated Luanda from the Dutch…"

"The fellow they named the high school after?"

"That's the one."

"I thought he was Portuguese! Or a politician from the capital or some colonial; otherwise why did they change the name of the school to Mutu Ya Kevela?"

"I suppose it was because they wanted an Angolan hero – in those days we needed our own heroes like we needed bread to feed us. Though, if you'd rather I can fix up another grandfather for you. I could arrange documents to show that you're descended from Mutu Ya Kevela himself, or N'Gola Quiluange, or even Queen Ginga herself. Would you rather that?"

"No, no. I'll keep the Brazilian. Was the fellow rich?"

"Extremely. He was cousin to Estácio de Sá, founder of Rio de Janeiro." […]

The Minister was astonished:

"Fantastic!"

And indignant:

"Damn! Whose stupid idea was it to change the name of the high school?! A man who expelled the Dutch colonists, an internationalist fighter of our brother-country, an Afro-antecedent, who gave us one of the most important families in this country – that is to say, mine. No, old man, it won't do. Justice must be restored. I want the high school to go back to being called Salvador Correia, and I'll fight for it with all my strength, I'll have a statue of my grandfather cast to put outside the entrance. A really big statue, in bronze, on a block of white marble […] So I'm descended from Salvador Correia – *caramba*! – and I never knew it till now. Excellent. My wife will be ever so pleased." (105-11)

Following scripture into *écriture*, the Minister is confronted by an intra-historical conundrum. "Can a man, merely by taking thought, add one cubit to his…" statue? Can an Angolan (as he spots a different *animot*) change (into) his stripes?

The black-and-white suited politician, ill at ease in his attire but at home in his skin and in his new-found past (post... post-), has many an antecedent in his discovery of the extent to which History with a capital(ist) H inscribes reality with excess... and profit. The sewing into the fabric of memory of the best-fitting minutiae of "historical facts" – in the case of the Fascist Portugal of António Salazar – is replicated in the post-colonial era by an intra-colonialist ploy of writing – or having written for him – that fiction which will be called *The Real Life of a Fighter*. There where History was will his story be; that is, his lie. "Real", "life", "fighter", sobriquets all, "The Minister", "writing his book with a hired hand – the hand of Félix Ventura" (127) – is the butt of Agualusa's set-piece satire of post-colonial intra-colonialism, namely, the appropriation not of the past but rather of the power of the past via mobilized memory. Ventura's sleight of hand, rendered explicit in his amorous boast to Ângela Lúcia, will soon further unveil the Angolan author's unremitting fascination both with Borges as text and with "Borges y yo". Meanwhile, the white rabbit that comes out of the inter-textual hat is more evocative of Lewis Carroll:

> "If you ask me, whenever I hear about something completely impossible I believe it at once. And don't you think José Buchmann is impossible? Yes, we both do. So he has to be for real." (116)

> "You know, that's the first time I've kissed an albino".
> When Félix explained to her what he did for a living – "I'm a genealogist" – which is what he always says when he meets strangers, she became interested at once.
> "Seriously? You are the first genealogist I've met." (117)

Queer egg as he may be perceived to be, the albino's misprision of Humpty Dumpty allows him to perform, in a West African wonderland, the re-writing of history as fiction, genealogy as ingenious ingenuousness, that representation whereby form *is* content. Echoing perhaps the fact that the blind Argentine librarian was once mischievously designated "Ministro de gallinas y conejos" ["Minister of hens and rabbits"] by President Juan Perón, Ventura overtly rewrites Angolan politics as caricature of the exemplary *Buchmann*'s legacy. And so, to bed in "The Minister"... as History beckons:

Félix would sew fiction in with reality dexterously, minutely, in such a way that historical facts and dates were respected [...] We remember other people's memories as though they were our own – even fictional ones.

"It's like the Castle of São Jorge in Lisbon – Do you know it? It has battlements, but they're fake. António de Oliveira Salazar ordered that some crenellations be added to the castle to make it more authentic. To him there was something wrong with a castle without crenellations – there was something monstrous about it – like a camel without humps. So the fake part of the Castle of São Jorge is today what makes it realistic. Several octogenarian Lisboans I've spoken to are convinced the Castle has always had crenellation. There's something rather amusing about that, isn't there? If it were authentic, no one would believe in it."

As soon as *The Real Life of a Fighter* is published, the consistency of Angolan history will change, there will be even more History. [...]

That is the truth that the Minister told Félix. The story Félix had the man tell in his true History [...] He wanted to give the people our-daily-bread. And that is exactly what he did [...] In just two years he himself was named Secretary of State for Economic Transparency and Combating Corruption [...] Today he is Minister for Bread-Making and Dairy Produce. (127-9)

Give 'em this day their daily bread and lead us into temptation – a.k.a. plenty of dough while we milk the system – "driven exclusively by great and serious patriotic motives" (129).

Food for thought? Or just meat and drink to the sick transit of another gravy train *africanus*? *Plus ça* change here for the next station in life on the up-line. "Memory is a landscape watched from the window of a moving train" (139). Intra-colonialism would rattle along, discursive lapses on track, halting not at some recuperable or necessary past (via a Truth Commission, for example) but forever in a present which has moved on, re-tracing, re-mapping, that History in which rewriting is a norm. Until José Buchmann intervenes. When he re-emerges, towards the end of the novel, it is to lift the stone of Angola's recent past. And out crawls Edmundo Barata dos Reis – fetid embarrassment to a post-colonial state that has already forgotten him and his deeds because of pressing and overwhelming needs: to live the post-ideological, intra-economic, "new" nation(alism) that is the globalized (or un-"Black" Atlanticized) actuality of the *cuduro*... hard-assed, hard-headed, hard-faced.

When JB appeared tonight he was accompanied by an old man with a long white beard and wild braids, grey and dishevelled, cascading over his shoulders. I recognized him at once as the old tramp the photographer had been pursuing, for weeks on end, showing him – in that extraordinary image – emerging from a sewer. An ancient, vengeful God, wild-haired, with suddenly lit-up eyes.

"I'd like to introduce my friend Edmundo Barata dos Reis, an ex-agent of the Ministry of State Security."

"Not ex-agent, say rather 'ex-*gent*'! Ex-exemplary citizen. Exponent of the excluded, existential excrement, an exiguous and explosive excrescence. In a word, a professional layabout. Very pleased to meet you." [...]

"I thought you'd enjoy meeting him. This man's life story could almost have been made up by you..." [...]

"I'm-All-Ears. That's what they used to call me. It was my fighting name. I liked it. I liked hearing it. And then – in a flash! – the Berlin Wall collapsed on top of us. *Pópilas*, old man! Agent one day, ex-gent – ex-person – the next." [...]

Two years in Havana, nine months in Berlin (East Berlin), another six in Moscow; his steel tempered, he returned to the solid trenches of socialism in Africa [...] "I used to be a communist..." And he'd keep yelling out – "Yes, I'm a communist, I'm really very Marxist-Leninist!" Even at a time when the official version has begun to deny the country's socialist past [...]

Edmundo Barata dos Reis shrunk back in his chair. He didn't remind me of a God anymore, he didn't remind me of a warrior – he was a dog, humiliated. He stank [...] And instead of replying to Félix's question he addressed himself to José Buchmann, pointing at him... "That laugh – when I hear that laugh, old man, it's as though I'm face-to-face with someone else, from long ago. From another time, an old time. Don't we know each other?" [...]

"And now I wouldn't be able to take it off even if I wanted to. Like a skin to me – you see? I've got a hammer and sickle tattooed on my chest now. That won't come off." (143-6)

To lift the lid on the sewer in which (the cockroach) Barata has been dwelling, ostensibly undetected under the cover of this era of the "official version", restores to *animotion* but one more of that infinite series of "autobiographical animals", the "little creatures that share [men's] homes" and of whom they "know almost nothing" (18). Recall, too, that "nothing risks becoming more poisonous" (Derrida 2002, 1). "But me, who am I?"... In the late chapter, "Love, a crime", "I, Eulálio" delights in narrating the new-found bliss of Félix and Ângela Lúcia:

> Félix turned back to Ângela, and kissed her on the lips. I saw her – with some surprise – closing her eyes and accepting his kiss. I heard her moan. The albino tried to undo her shirt, but she stopped him.
>
> "No. No not that. Don't do that."
>
> She raised her legs elegantly, and slipped off her shorts. Through the shirt that clung to her body you could make out the roundness of her breasts, her smooth belly. Then she turned her body, till she was kneeling over Félix. Her broad shoulders – lovely swimmer's shoulders – made her waist look even slimmer. My friend sighed:
>
> "You're so beautiful..."
>
> Ângela took his head in her hands and kissed him. A long kiss.
>
> It took my breath away.
>
> She takes off the t-shirt. She washes her face, her shoulders, her armpits. I notice a group of dark, round scars on her back, which stick out like insults on her golden velvet skin. I think I can see – in the mirror – just the same marks on her breasts and stomach. (153-4)

But... even indirectly, via the mirror of geckobservation, that "auto-affection" which operates, narratively, "as memory or archive of the living" and would be "an immunizing movement (a movement of safety, of salvage and salvation of the safe, the holy, the immune, the indemnified, of virginal and intact nudity) [...] is always threatened" (Derrida 2002, 1):

> José Buchmann bursts into the room. There's a pistol in his right hand. He's trembling. His voice trembles even more:
>
> "Where is the son of a bitch?"
>
> "You're not coming in!" She explodes: "*Poças!* Where the hell did you come from?"
>
> I can hear the voice of Edmundo Barata dos Reis, shrill, desperate, but only then do I see him [...]

"Girl, this creature has appeared from hell! From the past! From the place the damned come from..." [...]

"Yes, that's right – I've come from the past! And who am I? Well? Tell them who I am!..."

All of a sudden he throws himself forward, knocking Ângela over while lunging for Edmundo – he grabs his neck with his left hand and forces him to his knees. He pushes the end of the pistol-barrel into his neck:

"Tell them who I am!"

"A ghost. A demon..."

"Who am I!"

"A counter-revolutionary. A spy. An agent of imperialism..."

"What's my name?"

"...Gouveia. Pedro Gouveia. I should have killed you back in '77."

José Buchmann kicks at him. One. Two. Three. Four. Five. [...] Edmundo doesn't cry out. He doesn't even try to avoid the blows. The kicks find his stomach, his chest, his mouth. The boots turn red.

"Shit! Shit!"

José Buchmann – or Pedro Gouveia, as you prefer – puts the pistol down on the table [...]

"I never forgot you. I never forgot her either – Marta – young Marta Martinho – passing for some sort of intellectual – poetess, painter and God knows what else. She was pregnant, almost at term, a huge belly. Round. So round. It's as though I can see her now..."

[...] "It happened a long time ago, didn't it? During the struggles..." He gestures towards Ângela – "The girl hadn't even been born. The Revolution was under threat.

"I went off to interrogate the girl. She held out for two days. Then she gave birth to a little girl [...] When I think about it all I see is blood... And Mabeco, a mulatto from the South – he died a while ago, a stupid way to go, stabbed twice in cold blood in a bar in Lisbon, they never found out who did it – Mabeco cut the umbilical cord with a penknife, then he lit a cigarette and began to torture the baby, burning it on the back and chest. And the blood! Masses of blood, and the girl that Marta – her eyes wide like moons – it pains me to dream about it – and the baby screaming, the smell of burning flesh. Even today when I lie down to sleep, the spell is still there, the sound of the child crying..."

"Shut up!"

Félix, a rough shout, a voice I didn't recognize in him [...]

From where I'm watching, from here on top of the cupboard, I can see the top of his head lit up in rage [...]

"Now I'm absolutely certain. It really is you – Gouveia – the factionalist. The other day your laugh almost gave you away. You used to laugh a lot in the faction meetings, before the business with the consul, when your own countrymen handed you over to me. Not in prison, though – you just cried in prison. You cried all the time – boohoo, like a girl... I watch you crying now and I see that nobody Gouveia. Revenge – is that what you wanted?

"No, you need passion for that. You need courage! Killing a man, that's a man's job". And then –

> as
>
> > in
> >
> > > a
> > >
> > > > slow
> > > >
> > > > > dance...

Ângela crosses the kitchen,
Comes to the table,
her right hand picks up the gun,
her left hand pushes Félix away,
she points at Edmundo's chest –
and fires. (157-9)

If revenge – *sans animosité* – is a dish best eaten cold, then Ângela's *sang froid* is still performed in a deferred, a scar-traced, pharmakon-driven, choreography.

In "Choreographies", an interview-dance with Christie McDonald, Derrida responded to her question, "How would you describe woman's place?":

Why should a new "idea" of woman or a new step taken by her necessarily be subjected to the urgency of this topo-economical concern? [...] This step only constitutes a step on the condition that it challenge a certain idea of the locus [*lieu*] and the place [*place*] (the entire history of the West and of its metaphysics) and that it dance otherwise [...] The most innocent of dances would thwart the *assignation à résidence*, escape those residences under surveillance; the dance changes place and above all changes women's movements, and of some women in particular, has actually brought with it the chance for a certain risky turbulence in the assigning of places [...] Is one then going to start all over again making maps, topographies, etc.? distributing sexual identity cards? The most serious part of the difficulty is the necessity to bring the dance and its tempo into tune with the "revolution" [...] an incessant, daily negotiation – individual or not – sometimes microscopic, sometimes punctuated by a poker-like gamble; always deprived of insurance, whether it be in private life or within institutions. Each man and each woman must commit his or her own singularity, the untranslatable factor of his or her life and death. (Derrida and McDonald 1982, 68-9)

It is Ângela Lúcia, challenging Angola's urgent topo-economical concern, in the very market place of private life and institutions where the nation essays its tentative steps of rewriting history – choreographed by Félix as seller of pasts and outed as residence under surveillance by Gouveia alias Buchmann – who makes the decisive move. *Pas... pas*. She it is who brings the dance and its tempo into tune with the "revolution"... and markedly not with the *cuduro* of intra-colonial compromise. Ângela Lúcia, as deprived of insurance in committing her own singularity – her ipseity – as the Archangel Lucifer whose pride her name echoes and her action reflects, triggers a risky turbulence by taking justice into her own hands. Truth without reconciliation... and, certainly, without remedy; but in and with the pharmakon.[23] Félix is left to bury "the narrow body" of the *barata*, latest embodiment of that "*pure* evil" so feared by the gecko since his father's ani-*mot juste* had alerted him to the supplementarity of "celebrating – with only pretend joy – the death of someone we disliked" (105). There where scorpion was will cockroach be?

Et mundus regum...
Edmundo [Barata] dos Reis is dead. Long live Ângela. Viva Angola. Via Ventura. Via Eulálio. Via all bookmen and their [intrusive] *animots*...

> "And did you know that Ângela was your daughter?"
> "Yes, I knew. I left prison in nineteen-eighty [...] That son of a bitch

---

[23] "The *pharmakon* is the movement, the locus, and the play [...] The translation by remedy can thus be neither accepted nor simply rejected" (Derrida 1981, 127; 99).

– Edmundo – had derived great pleasure telling me every time he interrogated me of how he'd killed my wife. He told me they'd murdered the baby too. But it turned out they hadn't killed her. They'd handed her over to Marina, Marta's sister, and she had brought her up [...] I became obsessed [...] I thought that if I killed him I'd be able to look my daughter in the eye [...] I returned to Luanda [...] on the table of my hotel I found a business card of our friend Félix Ventura. *Give your children a better past* [...] Then one evening I waited for him to leave the sewer where he used to hide out, and I slipped down into it. And there, in that filthy hole, I found a mattress, dirty clothes, magazines, Marxist literature and – would you believe it? – a set of archives containing the State Security reports for dozens of people [...] when all of a sudden Edmundo appeared [...] knife in hand. He was laughing [...] He said:

    The two of us, face to face again, comrade Pedro Gouveia – but this time I'm going to finish you off... – and he lunged at me [...] The rest you know. (172-4)

In a pastiche of "and the rest you know" predictability of socialist realist stereotyping presumptions, Agualusa plays with the campaign-poster typicality of Edmundo Barata dos Reis – "I'm the very last communist south of the Equator". His T-shirt is inseparable from his skin, from his tatooed hammer and sickle (146). The easy eponymy of a fallen sovereignty interrupted by the *animot* abjection cockroach of the punning *barata* is a cheap shot at a no-less failed Soviet expansionism. Out of the sewer, with updated notes from the underground, emerges that subverted Marxist other, demon-creature of cyclically Dostoyevskian animation:

If you take, for instance, the antithesis of the normal man [...] it feels insulted [...] and wants to revenge itself [....] The base and nasty desire to vent that spite on its assailant rankles [...] the only thing left for it is to [....] creep ignominiously into its mouse-hole. There in its nasty, stinking, underground home our insulted, crushed and ridiculed mouse promptly becomes absorbed in cold, malignant and, above all, everlasting spite [...] will begin to revenge itself [...] incognito [...] it will suffer a hundred times more than the one on whom it revenges itself [...] But it is just in that cold, abominable half despair, half belief, in that conscious burying oneself alive for grief in the underworld [...] in that acutely recognized and yet partly doubtful hopelessness of one's position, in that hell of unsatisfied desires turned inward, in that fever of oscillations [...] that the savour of that strange enjoyment of which I have spoken lies. (Dostoyevsky 1918, 57-8)

The depiction of the fallen ideologue's ends-and-means, criminal, axial role in the plot of *The Book of Chameleons*, at micro-level, stands in contrast to the macro-economic failure of the nation and the success as fiction-maker and host to Ângela as vehicle of justice of "*o vendedor de passados*", Félix. A venture performed, in collusion, via the silences and the voicings of the albino black and his *animot* interlocutor... but one which still requires a woman to commit her own singularity, the untranslatable factor of her life and death:[24]

"And what about Ângela – did she know you were her father?"

She became a photographer, like me; and, like me, she became a nomad.

A drowsiness came over me, I wanted to shut my eyes and sleep, but I resisted it, sure that if I fell asleep moments later I would awake transformed into a gecko.

"Have you had news from Ângela?"

"Yes, I hear from her. At this moment she should be going down the Amazon on a big, lazy, slowboat [...] I hope she's happy?" (174-5)

---

[24] For recall: "Ângela Lúcia is to women what humankind is to the apes" (40). Not every critic has seen the characterization, or its function in Agualusa's text, as so strongly layered: "Told in short, ironic scenes, *O Vendedor de Passados* is consistently taut and witty. Unfortunately, the novel's violent conclusion, which re-enacts the gruesome fate of the couple who staged the 1977 coup attempt, does not emerge organically from events in Ventura's bookshop; the story's final twists feel imposed" (Henighan 2008, 219). Such a reading of the relationship between fact and fiction, betraying no little animosity towards the mediations that national bookmen bring to international bookshops, hinges on the novel's oblique references (José *et al.*) to the events of 27 May 1977 and a MPLA purge after an attempted coup. Nito Alves, José Van Dúnem and a legendarily beautiful Cita (or Sita) Vales were victims of a prison atrocity still raw in the public conscience of the intra-Angolan national imaginary. Which, *pace* tale-trusters everywhere, is not to say that the thorn-text of another José – E. A. – might not further prick that conscience.

A journey and an escape that Félix and Eulálio already had news of, too. Via a photograph… and an inscription – "In the margin, Ângela Lúcia had written in blue ink: *Plácidas Águas, Pará*" – for, in Brazil now, she is lost to Félix and Eulálio but for her *carte postale*… the missive that, always, may not arrive but that, in this instance, contains a clue to the framing of an inter-continental, intertextual, movement.[25] "And what about Ângela?" Her? Gone to Pará… *Parergon*, as "accessory, foreign or secondary object, supplement, aside, remainder. It is what the principal subject must not become" (Derrida 1987, 54).

After the crime, "the crossing"; Ângela has fled, accessory after the fact, supplement to Angola-Brazil relations, remainder to and reminder of a mosaic of transatlantic shifts, re-enacting toings and froings, emigrations, forced or otherwise, retaking the soundings of an echo chamber of already multiple "crossings", of past and present enslavements in selves journeying towards ipseities (becoming only for principal subjects). The "Black" Atlantic still bears her trace (without signature) but in blue. A binary is diluted, yet an ever-framing Félix still opts for a pin, "a bright, ludicrous green [one], and fixed the photograph to the wall". An ethereally ever blue and green Brazil flags convenient escapism, ostensibly, but Ventura knows, better than most, that any game of colours masks the difference between searching for identities as distinct from ipseities. It's what you do… and she has done. His "eyes filled with tears […] 'I know you want me to forgive her. I'm so sorry my friend, but I can't. I don't think I can do it'" (164). The *pardo*-ing of the sphere of action – a shade of grey – is too much for the African albino's black and white, entrenched, polarity to withstand. Ângela Lúcia's sin of pride, inseparable from revenge, has lost her, to him, forever.

The Borges-haunted Eulálio – "I imagined myself sinking into that silence, blindly, like I used to" (152) – will soon have served, outlived, his purpose in Félix's narrowly superannuated, assigned, residence. After the explosive dénouement, the anxiety-influenced narrator, resisting sleep lest

---

[25] *Plácidas Águas*: placid waters whereby "memory or archive of the living would be an immunizing movement (a movement of safety, of salvage and salvation of the safe, the holy, the immune, the indemnified, of virginal and intact nudity), but an immunizing movement that is always threatened with becoming auto-immunizing, as is every *autos*, every ipseity, every automatic, automobile, autonomous, auto-referential movement"? Or, a cover story for "a certain risky turbulence in the assigning of places"?

he dream, and wake, as a real gecko, settles for his terminal role of being – and penetrating – the animottled skin of Angola and the scarred body of national memory. In echo of "Borges y yo", the narrator, "Eu" and "lália", wills his own and his other's oblivion, a release from the burden of further testimony, from re-narration. "My whole life was an attempt to escape" (172-3), J [L] Buchmann had explained. I wish I had said that...

You will *osga*, you will

"Give your children a better past" had been the slogan of the seller of pasts. Only at the end of the novel, in a newly started diary, does Félix Ventura address his need of a living interlocutor cum witness to his writerly role in the recon/deconstruction of his nation's plausible story. Without an echolalic corroborator, his only resort will be to the painfully less-than-dialogical written or pictorial evidence of a diary or of postcards from afar.

Mythologized sub-Saharan animism will be supplemented by a new Angola-focused anim(ot)ism whereby a haunting if not-so-pure evil catches up with the narrative-for-sale of *O Vendedor de Passados*. "Scorpion" – "I ought to be charging you overtime, damn it! Who do you think I am – Scheherezade?..." – is always, *mot et parole*, already there, sting in the tale of a past that the *osga* Eulálio has heard tap-tapping – and has survived once before. It catches up with (and perishes with, no Scheherezade, *he*) the gecko *animot* that "died in combat, like a hero – who'd never thought of himself as courageous" (179). He got his teeth into the "horrible creature" of the past; the ever-present lurking past and its relationship with the chameleon-coloured laughing witness of a narrative, a dream, constructed, counterfeited before his very eyes.

> This morning I found Eulálio dead. Poor Eulálio. He'd fallen at the foot of my bed, with an enormous scorpion, a horrible creature, also dead, clamped between his teeth. I decided to start keeping this diary today, to maintain the illusion that there's someone listening to me. I'll never have another listener like him, though. He was my best friend, I think. I suppose I'll stop meeting him in my dreams now. And indeed with every passing day, every passing hour, my memory of him becomes more and more like a figure made of sand. The memory of a dream. Maybe I dreamed it all: him, José Buchmann, Edmundo Barata dos Reis.
>
> I'm an animist. I've always been an animist though I've only lately

realized it. The same thing happens to the soul as happens to water [...] Eulálio will always be Eulálio, whether flesh (incarnate) or fish.

I'm reminded of that black and white picture of Martin Luther King speaking to the crowd: *I have a dream...* he really should have said "I *made* a dream". If you think about it there's a difference between having a dream and *making* a dream.

Yes, I've made a dream.

Lisbon, February 13th, 2004. (179-80)

"Finally, I learn to live", as a writer and cultural critic, as "an autobiographical animal". To write, no less than to read, frees us from our spectres.[26]

> *Ecce animot – that is*
> *what I was saying*
> *before this long*
> *digression.*

Jacques Derrida

References

Agualusa, J. E. (2004). *O Vendedor de Passados*. Lisbon: Booket, Dom Quixote.

Agualusa, J. E. (2006). *The Book of Chameleons*. London: Arcadia Books.

Agualusa. J. E. (2007). *Epoca* interview, **www.afirma.inf.br/htm/colunistas/sueli/colunistas2.htm**.

Agualusa. J. E. (2007). Interview with Polzonoff, P. and Tepper, A. *Words Without Borders*, **www.wordswithoutborders.org**.

Barthes, R. (1974). *S/Z*. New York: Hill and Wang.

---

[26] The echoes from Jacques Derrida's meditations on "Je suis en guerre contre moi-même" and "Donner la mort" are taken from *Apprendre à vivre enfin* (Derrida, 2004) and from the last exchange I had with him, in Rio de Janeiro in August 2004, and in Brazil to pursue and to lay some of the ghosts of my present – *pardo* – undertaking. The lesson I ingested is reproduced in *Pensar a desconstução* (McGuirk, in Derrida 2005, 233-44) and in "Derrida Trans(at)l(antic)ated" (McGuirk 2006, 71): "Lire la littérature... c'est une spectrologie... Lire libère les spectres. Mes chants sont méchants".

Baudelaire, C. (1961). *Oeuvres complètes*. Paris: Pléiade.

Borges, J. L. (1980). *El Hacedor*. Madrid: Alianza.

Borges, J. L. (1988). "Funes el memorioso". In *Ficciones*. Madrid: Alianza.

Borges, J. L. (1995). "Kafka y sus precursores". In *Otras inquisiciones*. Madrid: Alianza.

Derrida, J. (1978). *Writing and Difference*. London: Routledge and Kegan Paul.

Derrida, J. (1981). "Plato's Pharmacy". In *Dissemination*. London: The Athlone Press.

Derrida, J. (1982). "Choreographies", interview with C. McDonald. *Diacritics*, 12.

Derrida, J. (1987). *The Truth in Painting*. Chicago and London: University of Chicago Press.

Derrida, J. (2002). Excerpt from "The Animal That Therefore I Am (More to Follow)". *Critical Inquiry*, Winter, 28, 2, **http://criticalinquiry. uchicago.edu/issues/v28/v28n2.derrida.html**.

Derrida, J. (2004). *Apprendre à vivre enfin*. Paris, Galilée.

Dostoyevsky, F. (1918). *Notes from the Underground*. New York: The MacMillan Company.

Fanon, F. (1967). *Black Skin, White Masks*. New York: Grove.

Henighan, S. (2008). *A Report on the Afterlife of Culture* (Windsor, Ontario: Biblioasis).

Lacan, J. (1966). "The Insistence of the Letter in the Unconscious". *Yale French Studies*, 36-37.

Landau, P, Kaspin, D. D. (2002). *Images and Empires: Visuality in Colonial and Postcolonial Africa*. Berkeley: University of California Press.

McGuirk, B. (2005). "Dos *espectros de Marx* aos espectros do mar...". In *Jacques Derrida: Pensar a desconstrução*, ed. E. Nascimento. São Paulo: Estação Liberdade.

McGuirk, B. (2006). "Derrida trans(at)l(antic)ated. Spectres of *mar*... Mythology as Excess in Fernando Pessoa and João Guimarães Rosa". *Versus: Quaderni di studi semiotici*, gennaio-agosto, 41-73.

Nascimento, E. (ed.) (2005). *Jacques Derrida: Pensar a desconstrução*. São Paulo: Estação Liberdade.

Sabine, M. (2009). "Killing and Nostalgia: Testimony and the Image of Empire in Margarida Cardoso's *A Costa dos Murmurios*". In C. Demaria, M. Daly (eds.), *The Genres of Post-Conflict Testimonies*.

Nottingham: Critical, Cultural and Communications Press, 250-77.

Vecchi, R. (2008). "Maudsley e i crimini delle nazionalità". In V. Fortunati, D. Fortezza, M. Ascari (eds.), *Conflitti. Strategie di rappresentazione della guerra nella cultura contemporanea*. Roma: Meltemi.

Capital Topographies from Shore Europe:
In the Wake of Crisis[1]

Rui Gonçalves Miranda

> How can a "European cultural identity"
> respond, and in a responsible way –
> responsible for itself, for the other, and
> before the other – to the double question of
> *le capital*, of capital, and of *la capitale*, of
> the capital?
>
> Jacques Derrida

The writing of space and/or place always involves a certain degree of conflict and violence. Not only has the presumed objectiveness of cartographies veiled numerous economic, political, cultural and sexual agendas, but the tracing of imaginary or projected topographies often reveal the vested interests and desires of (phal)logocentric constructs (national, imperial, economic, cultural) that thus project themselves, draw and are drawn, on(to) their constructed others to fill their own metaphysical vacuity. An imaginary space, where all signs (if any) of conflict are past, ideologically sanitized and politically neutered, is thus projected. The addressing of a general structure of the trace underwriting and undermining these topographies allows us to unveil the writing of otherness as the heightening of the *ipse*, and both reflect and enact political, cultural and economic agendas.

By looking at the case of a country on the western cape of Europe, and taking Europe's imagining of itself as a promontory, after Jacques Derrida, this chapter aims to look at how topographies are both a product and a reflection of conflict, and the ways in which new topographies, often coinciding with those of past imperial imaginary, reappear for the sake of economic efficiency and bearing the demands of free market capitalism. It

[1] The research presented in this chapter was conducted with the support of the *Fundação para a Ciência e Tecnologia* (FCT, Lisbon) (SFRH/BPD/71245/2010).

thus attempts not only to point to the aporetic condition of all topographies (the violence of the *graphein*) but also to the confusion of linguistic with phenomenal reality which enables them to retrace political headings and defuse both European and national exceptionalisms and social and economic injustice.

Traditional national, European identities, or the apparently neoliberal dissolving of identity, which is one more identity still in the siren call of the natural justice of the markets, are not simply an obstacle to be overcome. Addressing these constructs involves a navigation which does not foresee or accept any programmed destinations and which veers through differences and singularities without losing sight and responsibility for the need for shared world values at a time when the spectrality of capitalism is immune to either grand or small narratives (localized and/or heterotopical action) and easily leads to and foments political totalitarianism and/or religious absolutism.

The "incompleteness" of identity does not undermine identity-based social movements. As a matter of fact, as Judith Butler, Ernesto Laclau and Slavoj Žižek remind us in the introduction to the volume *Contingency, Hegemony, Universality: Contemporary Dialogues on the Left*, "[n]o social movement can, in fact, enjoy its status as an open-ended, democratic political articulation without presuming and operationalizing the negativity at the heart of identity" (2000, 2). To address the topographies of post-conflict is not only to acknowledge that conflict is, by definition, never over, but also that acknowledging the "constructedness" of reality (and its possible deconstruction) is the condition for any reconstruction to occur.

To address the topographies of Portugal and Europe by emphasizing space (and spacing) over chronology will thus allow us to tease out the inner (far from unintentional) tensions and the dangers lurking behind the flags of freedom and individualism in the name of an instituted tradition, enlightened and from the Enlightenment. This means to assert the responsibility of not renouncing the spirit of the Enlightenment, precisely by not following it unconditionally, by attending to the exigencies of the *hic et nunc* and to the need not to spread freedom and democracy, but to construct a democracy which is, in Derridan terms, to come.[2]

---

[2] The *to come* of democracy is inextricably linked to the "*hic et nunc* of urgency" (Derrida 2005, 29).

Two days after the Portuguese Government led by the socialist Prime Minister José Sócrates resigned in 2011 in the midst of the national debt crisis, *Financial Times* columnists decided to come to Portugal's rescue. The Lex column proposed that one should think outside the box: Portugal should be annexed to Brazil. The economic environment of the contemporary world makes this manifestly evident: as part of an emerging giant, Portugal would lose prestige but would easily see its chronic economic problems, which the financial and debt crises made evident, rendered insignificant as part of the former colony's thriving economy (Hadas 2011). After having moved the Crown to Rio de Janeiro in 1808 (which became *de facto* the capital of Empire) in order to preserve independence in face of the Napoleonic invasions, it was now left to capital and to operations of the markets to map out a transatlantic flight in order to find a new home. This is but the last reappearance of the naturalized neoliberal dogma that there is (as Margaret Thatcher would put it) "no alternative" (Harvey 2007, 40). The perverse pleasure of this "out-of-the-box" thinking acts as a legitimation of economic theory and "fact" over political action, while constructing a perception of difference between the peripheral unruly states (labelled in the acronym PIGS) and a core Europe which, as the saying goes, starts at the Pyrenees. [3]

In following J. Hillis Miller's meditations on the term "topography" as the textual rendering of space, I am considering all the implications of the "writing" of *topos*, considering both the complexity and the inevitability of such an operation, no *topos* (from the moment it is recognized as place) which is not in one way or another (in Derridan terms) written (see Miller 1995, 1-8). No topographies or cartographies take place outside specific (historical, political, cultural) contexts and no topographies or cartographies fail to contribute towards or imply, as a graft, the marks and margins of a given, albeit constructed, space-time. The inscription of borders and margins in these topographies takes place not despite but because of the dislocation and dispersion, the irreducible "spacing" which both underwrites and undermines "ontopology" (Derrida 2006, 102-103). Much is at play (both at risk and in articulation) in the "writing" –

---

[3] The political acts linked to the economic and political manifestations have once again sanctioned the prejudice against the southern European countries as a valid, distinctive, political category. The nomenclature PIGS (i.e. Portugal, Italy, Greece and Spain) is a reminder that Europe is not a geographical, historical or political concept, but mostly a cultural and economic one.

understood as "extraction, graft, extension" (Derrida 1987, 71) – of the *topos*. This movement of tracing is inseparable from the selections and exclusions operated in the name of identities, which haunt nevertheless the identity constructs of selves and others. As Jacques Derrida states in *Of Grammatology*, "[the] trace must be thought before the entity", although "the movement of the trace is necessary occulted, it produces itself as self-occultation" (1997, 47). He continues to say that "[t]he general structure of the unmotivated trace connects within the same possibility, and they cannot be separated except by abstraction, the structure of the relationship with the other, the movement of temporalisation, and language as writing" (47).

The tracing of imagined cartographies and *t(r)opographies* is far from being specific to Portugal. The imaginary maps that will be addressed are but a particular historical inflexion of the grafting which allows, among other things, "economists" to map out imaginary scenarios in the "flat world of neoliberal utopianism" (see Harvey 2009, 51-76) and "Europeans" to engage in a reconstruction of a "cultural identity" among *perestroika*, democratization, reunification, entry into the market economy, and access to political and economic liberalisms (Derrida 1992, 19-21). This discourse always entails a certain topography:

> I wanted to recall what has *always* identified Europe with a cape or headland [*cap*]. Always, since day one [*depuis toujours*], and this "day one" says something about all the days of today in the memory of Europe, in the memory of itself as the culture of Europe. In its physical geography, and in what has often been called, by Husserl for example, its *spiritual geography*, Europe has always recognized itself as a cape or headland, *either* as the advanced extreme of a continent, to the west and south (the land's end, the advanced point of a Finistère, Europe of the Atlantic or of the Greco-Latino-Iberian shores of the Mediterranean), the point of departure for discovery, invention, and colonization, *or* as the very centre of this tongue in the form of a cape, the Europe of the middle, coiled up, indeed compressed along a Greco-Germanic axis, at the very centre of the centre of the cape. (Derrida 1992, 19-20)

The analysis by Derrida of Paul Valéry's identification of the European cape and persona (its "visage" and its "gaze" [Derrida 1992, 20-21]) establishes a national exceptionalism which was by no means exclusive to France. Fernando Pessoa's description of Portugal as the face of Europe in the opening poem of *Mensagem* (1934) is another illustration of a fusion and confusion of modernity and tradition as a structural element of discourse (Pessoa 2008, 30). Whether during the Portuguese *Estado Novo*'s (New State) modern articulation of the regeneration of the nation (as this essay will address, via the supplementation of overseas provinces, in its appropriation of an also essentially modern sociological discourse on Brazilian society by Gilberto Freyre in *Casa-grande & senzala* [2003, originally published in 1933 and originally translated into English as *The Master and the Slaves*]), or in the present day in the project of saving Portugal's face before the markets, what is often upon the table is a sublimated return to idealized imaginaries and topographies configuring the above-mentioned trinity of "discovery, invention, and colonization".

This topography inscribes a certain teleology, with Europe or Empire, both acting as the return to the capital (the head, the face), as the supplements that both complete and substitute the *ipse*, that capitalize the (political, economic, cultural) investments. The current Portuguese government, elected in 2011, will seemingly paradoxically embrace *la capitale* and *le capital*, national identity and the will of the markets in yet another inflexion of exceptionalism. Rather than think of an annexation to Brazil, the Portuguese Prime Minister, Passos Coelho, will choose the image of the "cabo das tormentas" (Cape of Storms, later renamed the Cape of Good Hope when successful navigation around the Cape and into the Indian Ocean was achieved by Bartolomeu Dias in 1488) as the image of Portugal's destiny when he projects that the goals imposed by the *troika* bailout will be met in 2013 (*Expresso* 2011). As the Minister of Finance, Vítor Gaspar, imagines it, Portugal can now replicate in terms of finance and market capitalism what it achieved in maritime expansion and colonialism:

Mr Gaspar compared his government's challenges to the adventures of Portuguese seafarers in the heyday of his nation's former empire. "When sailors went out to sea in the 16th century, they didn't have absolute control over how they would fare in storms. But they would prepare for them and if they were good sailors they would be successful. We Portuguese have a tradition of being good sailors." (Barber 2012)

This represents more than a rhetorical *topos* and trope; it instigates a rethinking of the limits and the ends of such topographed eschatologies and teleologies, the headlands or capes meaning also the "head or the extremity of the extreme, the aim and the end" (Derrida 1992, 14). This vision evokes other imperial ghosts. As Europe (and its common market) goes through "um mar de incertezas" (a sea of uncertainties]) the opinion of Miguel Relvas, Deputy Prime Minister and Minister for Parliamentary Affairs, is that the Portuguese can take up this opportunity to demonstrate their "adaptability", which allows the Portuguese to be at home in the Americas, Asia or Africas:

"Está na hora e na altura de sabermos aproveitar essa condição natural" dos portugueses, pois "foi também por dificuldades que vivemos à época que nós fomos à vida, à procura de outros mundos e de outros mercados", no século XV. (*Público* 2012)

["It is time to make the most out of that natural condition" of the Portuguese, as "it was also because of difficulties that we were going through at the time that we set off, looking for new worlds and new markets", in the fifteenth century.]

Portugal must "ir à vida" (set out on life) within the context of a nationalist universalism rhetoric that finds in the other a projection of itself. The "outros mundos" (other worlds) e "outros mercados" (other markets) are part of a same economy, that of an adaptability inherited from "navegadores" (navigators), "descobridores" (discoverers), "coloniz-adores" (colonizers). There is something troubling in this unperturbed transposition, this dismissal of differences by articulating them in relation to the needs and projections of an *ipse*. The uncertainties and troubles ("seas" of uncertainties and troubles) are thus projected as natural and inevitable rather than the result of the "systemic risks" of the capitalist system.[4] No other heading is (neoliberally) conceivable. The Portuguese

---

[4] This expression was used in the collective letter sent by eminent economists under the aegis of the British Academy to Queen Elizabeth II in response to a question posed by the monarch in a conference in the London School of Economics in November 2008 (Harvey 2011, vii). As Harvey suggests, the 2008 financial crisis may be unprecedented in scale, but similar crises have affected different parts of the world since neoliberalism took centre stage (see Harvey 2011, 6-10).

government echoes the *rationale* and then reiterates the blind spots in the thinking of the columnists of the *Financial Times* by appealing to the flux of labourers and the attraction of investment by veiling them in historical and affective mythologies, that of the "brother countries", "Lusophone family", etc. This discourse, which promises the end of disturbances, projects and protects the notion of a safe port already envisioned, the end of conflict, is itself, and contrary to appearances, structurally conflictual: it draws and is the drawing of conflict, not only by evoking old colonial space-time but also by projecting a sanitized version of the past as "our" projected future.

Already in the reactionary and conservative view of the *Estado Novo*, however, Portugal was not in need of a home either in Europe or overseas, for it was not a small country:

Figure 1. "Portugal não é um país pequeno" (Portugal is not a small country) (Galvão 1935)

Geographically, this projection implies an absolute view of time and space which leads to the possibility of deterritorialization. The colonial possessions are nothing but space to be added (on the left-hand corner of the image, the total area of the colonial empire is compared to that of different European countries) and calculated in the economy of the country (*país*) within a European context. The country is not small because of its supplements (the territorial space of the colonies) and yet the colonies are not part of the country. They spectrally hover while Portugal seems to remain a part of the Europe it sets the colonies against. But in this topographical act (in the several senses of the word), the supplement is actually the core of Portuguese presentation before Europe. Portugal, as the regime presents it in Europe through Galvão's map, *is* the colonies it inscribes over Europe.

The political and cultural implications of this design go beyond the time span of a particular ideological frame. As is visible in current political discourses, it is not enough to point out the glaringly evident distance between discourse and empirical reality. This writing of space enacts the paradox of *écriture*, the inevitable releasing of spectres that *tracing* entails. The space-time of the metropolis of the "colonial empire" (the phenomenological guarantor beyond mere representation) is shown to be haunted by the selections and exclusions against which it is erected: Europe, on the one hand; the colonial possessions, on the other. Onto(po)logy is indeed a conjuration.

The condition for a Portuguese exceptionalism relies not only on a space-time of its own and on its insular trait as a consequence of its own marginalization in the European context (Lourenço 1994, 13) but also on the absolute view of time and space in which this projection operates, common to a certain European heading, inseparable from a phallic configuration:

Europe is not only a geographical headland or heading that has always given itself the representation or figure of a spiritual heading, at once as project, task, or infinite – that is to say universal – idea, as the memory of itself that gathers and accumulates itself, capitalizes upon itself, in and for itself. Europe has also confused its image, its face, its figure and its very place, its taking-place, with that of an advanced point, the point of a phallus if you will, and thus, once again, with a heading for world civilization or human culture in general. The idea of an advanced point of *exemplarity* is the *idea* of the European *idea*, its *eidos*, at once as *arché* – the idea of beginning but also of commanding (the cap as the head, the place of capitalizing memory and of decision, once again, the captain) – and as *telos*, the idea of the end, of a limit that accomplishes, or that puts an end to the whole point of the achievement, right there at the point of completion. (Derrida 1992, 24-25)

The map of Portugal and the *ultramar* represented as not overseas represents a "full circle", that is, the capitulation of the other before and into Europe as well as capitalization (the accumulation: the arithmetic sum of territory) of the European *eidos*. This projection, at the same time a compensatory mechanism for Portugal (and we shall come to this duplication of the *phallus*), illustrates a chiasmus. The projection of the *ipse* onto the empty space of the colonial territories ("the third empire") simultaneously enacts the folding back of the "non-space" of the overseas territories into Europe and into the European *logos* (the logic of nationalism, territorial expansion, colonialism).[5] Europe and Portugal are a *cap* (cape, head, heading), which cannot leave sight of its origins, which retracts to itself, which does not depart from itself if not to integrate differences in its return and capitalizing the returns.

The reaction of Portuguese elements of government can best be perceived as an illustration of their difficulties in "territorializing" Portugal between its historical and political discursive *loci* of articulation. If Europe is "in a sea of uncertainties" then heading towards the depoliticized Freyrian-inspired "mundo que o Português criou" (world that the Port-uguese created) [6] seems to be the "natural" vocation of the Portuguese, reprising their cultural and historical ties after having contracted to its "original" and "natural" territory.[7]

There is, of course, nothing natural about a territory and its mapping. David Harvey, following David Delaney's meditation, notes how territory, attached to an absolute theory of time and space, became "a device for

[5] Josiah Blackmore brings into his analysis of Portuguese writings on Africa Christopher L. Miller's identification, in the context of French colonialism, of an "Africanist discursive practice" which is born in Europe of European ideas and is a European attempt to fill an empty space called "Africa" (Blackmore 2008, 5-6).

[6] Gilberte Freyre (1900-1987) was a Brazilian sociologist whose theories on the exceptionalism of the Portuguese "integration" in the tropics was instrumentalized by the *Estado Novo* in order to grant a pseudo-scientific legitimacy to the Portuguese colonial possessions (Castelo 1998).

[7] The depoliticization of History is evidenced in seemingly innocuous political statements, functioning as imaginary consensual projections, such as when the President of the Republic, Aníbal Cavaco Silva, suggested in the ceremony honouring the combatants of the Colonial Wars on the fiftieth anniversary of their beginning (15 March 2011) that the young generation of the present should face the economic crisis with the same dedication with which a previous generation fought the Colonial Wars (1961-1974).

simplifying and clarifying something else, such as political authority, cultural identity, individual autonomy, or rights" and how "in order to have this effect, territory itself has to be taken as a relatively simple and clear phenomenon" (Delaney, in Harvey 2009, 172).

What is currently referred to as globalization is linked from its inception to geographical knowledge and to European and Portuguese History: the Tordesillas treaty (1494), in which the kingdoms of Portugal and Spain divided the known world between their global spheres of sovereignty over land and territories, is an early illustration of mapping as a tool which articulates both geographical knowledge and paths of political-economic development. Topographies underwrite a logic of appropriation, demonstrating the inseparability of "inquisitiveness and acquisitiveness" (Mack 2011, 15). If during the Renaissance already the "mapping of the world was crucial to the project of human command over it" (Harvey 2009, 130), it is no less important nowadays.

Harvey calls attention to the specific "forms of territorializing behaviour that arose historically from the seventeenth century on in Europe" which were the object of a process of naturalization (2009, 172). There was, obviously

> nothing natural about this particular form of territorialization or its underpinnings in absolute theories of space and time: it was a social construction and a political achievement. The work of establishing a cohesive relational sense of territorialized national identity, for example, is long, painstaking, and always fragile. (Harvey 2009, 172)

Harvey then goes on to explain the "codification of territorializing behaviours", linked to the rise of the modern state forms (Westphalia, 1648) and to the institution of a system of property rights, which originated in Europe and then spread to the rest of the world through "colonizing practices". The essential construction of fixed "territorial forms" implied an "appeal to the absolute theory of space and time and the invention of practices of representation (mapping and cadastral survey) that confirmed the fixity and lack of ambiguity" (172). This process is inseparable from a "Newtonian and Cartesian mechanical (measurable, calculable) view of the world" (of both [father] Time and [mother] Earth) which also presumes an "absolute version of space and time" (222) and meant that the "relegation of relative and relational dimensions to subsidiary roles was politically assured in Western Europe" (172).

A critique of the "rationality" underlying this process, nevertheless, does not equate to accepting obscurantism and absolutism as "reasonable" stands against neocolonialist practices operated by the "market" under the banner of freedom. [8] On the contrary, one is alerted to the necessity of a constant vigilance for and of reason, as will be addressed later. The invention, discovery and colonization of which the Iberian headland is so proud, is part of a movement of technological advancement and rationality, of a European *logos*, an economy of calculation of which cartographies are but one example. It is, in itself, a de-centering (Lourenço 2004, 57). Later attempts at having the empire function as the "imagination of the centre" (Ribeiro 2002, 136; 151), and of having Africa as a substitute for the loss of Brazil as a colony (2002, 149), attest to Portugal's ongoing capacity to reinvent its past as well as that of others (Lourenço 2004, 71).

Maps perform a political and ideological role and are themselves subject to political and ideological presuppositions. If the Treaty of Tordesillas did not reflect the continuous and ensuing fights for the dominion of sea trade routes and land, and was effectively ignored and/or distorted in the settlement of Brazil, the 1890 rose-coloured map projected the desired dominion of a new "Brazil in Africa" (Ribeiro 2002, 150) by a monarchy eager to ward off political and national decadence (a buzz-word of the elites of the time) by retaining and expanding its colonial enterprise. The map aimed to establish sovereignty and, consequently, to effect possession of the territory between Angola and Mozambique, establishing a colonial space spreading from the Atlantic to the Indic coasts. Based on historical trading links, this claim, mapped in the (in)famous Mapa Cor de Rosa (Rose-Coloured Map) (see facing page) which depicted a projected supplement colonial possession, was set against motions precipitated by the 1884-85 Berlin Conference in the context of the "Scramble for Africa". Portugal's wishful claim was met with an ultimatum by the British Empire, resulting in a severe political crisis.

[8] As David Harvey notes, "the market is predominantly (though erroneously) conceptualized as the harbinger and guardian of individual freedoms" (Harvey 2009, 154).

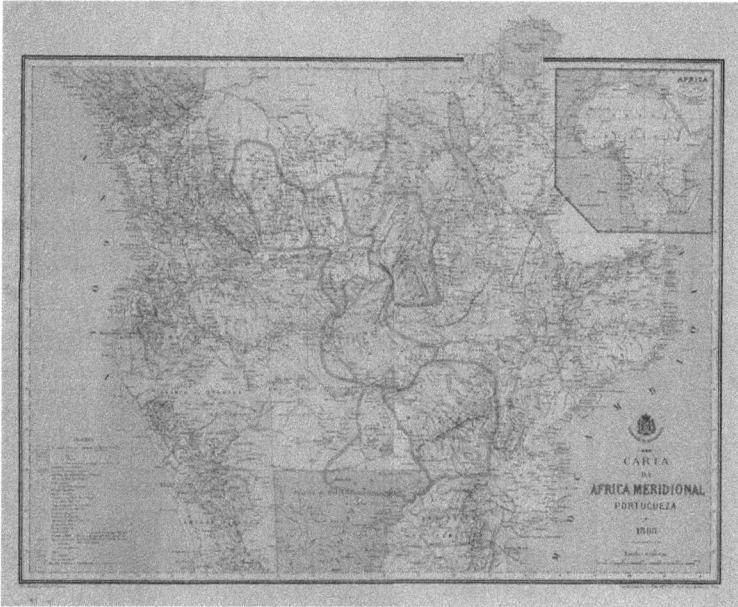

Figure 2. Mapa Cor de Rosa
(The Rose-Coloured Map) (Fres 1886)

> Europe takes itself to be a promontory, an advance – the avant-garde of geography and history. It advances and promotes itself as an advance, and it will have never ceased to make advances on the other: to induce, seduce, produce, and conduce, to spread out, to cultivate, to love or to violate, to love to violate, to colonize, and to colonize itself. (Derrida 1992, 48)

Is there not another possible heading (the "heading of the other", "the other of heading" [Derrida 1992, 15]) beyond the *cap* and the *captain* (Derrida 1992, 13-14)?[9] In *The Other Heading* Derrida registered, among

[9] This would lead one to ponder the framing of possibility, how what is possible or not comes to be construed and instituted. Politics could very well be that "art of the impossible" (see Attridge 2007) framing different possibilities. As Derrida points out, "there is no responsibility that is not the experience and experiment of the impossible" (Derrida 1992, 44-45).

many others, the necessity for a European duty to resist both totalitarian dogmatism (the new anti-capital, and one may add, the resistance to capital) and the capitalist religion (Derrida 1992, 77). In topographical and geographical terms, the consequences are very similar: in the capitalist view, a conception of absolute time and space that accounts for the wit of journalists (reversing the role of the colony-metropolis) and the rhetoric of ministers (the natural adaptability, sons of universalisms); and, when it comes to proclaim both the flatness of the world and its only too-familiar and familial projections of the said Freyrian *"mundo que o Português criou"* (world that the Portuguese created) shrouded in twenty-first century trappings. The image of Portugal in the twentieth century was constructed via the meditation of an imagined perception. Portugal was "proudly alone", a stronghold against capitalism, communism and other internationalisms, pursuing an exceptionalist Portuguese path with the "overseas provinces" configuring a Portuguese economic space. The compulsive imagery of navigators and explorers, the rulers of sea and creators of a new world, the vanguard for culture and commerce, the predecessor of the spreading of European thought and capital, extrapolating from the Mediterranean ("a machine for creating civilization", as Valéry called it (in Derrida 1992, 64) and, effectively, turning the other seas into nothing but "between lands";[10] transforming the others into projections of the self that, however different, can be recuperated into the economy of a self-same, where past and present are articulated as projections of the present. Henrique Galvão's map truly re-presented, in that it both reflected and enacted, Europe, Portugal and its colonies. It exposed and exploited the *ratio* of the representation of colonies (always already) *vis-à-vis* Europe. Galvão's map is a vivid illustration of Paul de Man's definition of ideology as "the confusion of linguistic with natural reality, of reference with phenomenalism" (Man 1988, 363). The *Estado Novo*'s fears that Portugal's abandoning of the "overseas provinces" in favour of myths of European integration would lead to the colonization of the "metropolis" itself, as the ex-Minister during the *Estado Novo* Franco Nogueira stated in 1976 in an interview with Maria João Avilez, are a

---

[10] John Mack notes the need to historicize the sea (Mack 2011, 16-17), additionally pointing out how, historiographically speaking, "the seas are portrayed either as the backdrop to the stage on which the real action is seen to take place – that is, the land – or they are portrayed simply as the means of connection between activities taking place at coasts and in their interiors" (19).

testimony to the *Estado Novo*'s identification of state and nation with empire (Nogueira 2006, 540-541). As Eduardo Lourenço noted, this has had a shockwave effect until the present day: "Consumimos em ficção a ficção em que voluntariamente nos tornámos. Reciclámos os restos imperiais que é o melhor que temos e o único sinal do mútuo reconhecimento" ("We have consumed in fiction the fiction which we voluntarily became. We have recycled the imperial remainders which is the best we have and the only sign of mutual acknowledgement") (Lourenço 2004, 109). As for the Socialist Party's post-1974 election slogan, *Europa connosco* (Europe with us), the "islander mentality" is transversal to political regimes and ideologies (Saraiva 2006, 402).

It is important to recognize how the colonizing topographies addressed, past or present, post or neo-colonially, as a "formation of discourse" (Loomba 1998, 95), leading to violation and love of violation disguised as love, to reproduction of the self-same (trans-, inter-, or intra-nationally) disguised as fruitful insemination of and upon the other. It is crucial to note that the intrinsic violence of the grafting of imperial cartographies goes hand in hand with and is inseparable from both discourses of desire and a philosophical (phal)logocentrism in which not-Europe, the East or the overseas, or even heterogeneity is recognized only to be recuperated and sublimated by the economy of the *ipse*.[11] Luso-tropicalism, as deployed by the New State, provided a pseudo-rational justification of Empire post-1951 (Madureira 2006, 139-142), a manipulable (for internal and international consumption), romanticized and simplistic account of Portuguese colonialism ultimately constructed around the sexual intercourse of Portuguese men with native women (Madureira 2006, 141). The effects of this 1935 (and the 1494, and also 1890) topography must nevertheless be addressed post-1974 (end of dictatorship) and post-1986 (joining the European Economic Community).[12] It is inseparable from an

[11] See Roberto Esposito's *Communitas* regarding the sublimation of heterogeneity in the European tradition of thought on Europe, and on how thinkers such as Hegel and Heidegger have configured the sea as the delimiting site of heterogeneity (see 2010, 107-111). Roberto Vecchi has noted how the sea is eroded in Henrique Galvão's map where the space of this imaginary Portugal confronts that of Europe (2010, 72).

[12] Fernando Arenas insightfully and succinctly emphasizes one of the most enduring contributions of Cláudia Castelo's groundbreaking work *"O modo português de estar no mundo": o luso-tropicalismo e a ideologia colonial*

ipseistic movement that projects Portugal onto Europe and its "others". It is a product of desire for unity, which forces the sublimation of racism, greed, sexual desire,[13] exoticism in a (calculable, justifiable) economy. This economy relies on the effect of "the other", and of "difference from itself", so as to establish the self-sameness of the *ipse*. Otherness and difference operate insofar as they are sublimated in the (phal)logocentric promise of the heightening of the self-same, be it Portugal, be it Europe.

The mock, compensatory topography of the ambiguous claim that Portugal is not small (*Portugal não é pequeno*) in Manuel João Vieira's continuous spoof campaigns for the Presidency of the Republic acts as an obvious parody of Galvão's map, both denouncing the nationalistic and colonialist pseudo-scientific posture and calculations (the sum of the added parts of the overseas provinces) under the erection of a Portugal bigger than itself as well as the nationalistic phallic triumphalism and equally self-centred view of contemporary Portugal ("o império sempre-em-pé" [the always erect empire]). This is obvious in official acts and celebrations as well as in popular culture.[14] It also denounces a serious depoliticization of Portugal as it projects its own fantasies as the image (and mirage) of its self, mechanically and economically repeating itself, not avoiding the duplicates in this mechanicism (the "Left Mozambique", for instance). Vieira's campaign, which had adopted the Shell Oil company

portuguesa (1933-1961) (1998), that of noting that "besides ideologically legitimizing the colonial interests of the Salazar regime, Freyre's theorization also helped perpetuate a mythical image of Portuguese national identity that migrated from his sociological writings to the political field, and eventually to the realms of mentalities with lasting effects still today" (Arenas 2003, 7-8).

[13] As Ania Loomba states, "[t]heories of race were thus also covert theories of desire" (1998, 117).

[14] One example is the scene in Abi Feijó's 1994 lighthearted animation short film *Fado Lusitano*, in which the Portuguese discoverers show the Spanish "*hombres de cojones*" (men of balls) what to do with their "*cojones*", with a Portuguese navigator appearing as the *paterfamilias* of a multi-racial family. Another example took place in that perennial measuring rod of populism and poor aesthetic taste, the Eurovision Song Contest. Portugal's entry in 1989, a song entitled "*Conquistadores*", celebrating the "*ternura, oceanos de amor*" (tenderness, oceans of love) of the Portuguese maritime expansion featured a video clip filmed in historical locations and aboard a ship belonging to the Portuguese Navy (admittedly, a vessel used for the training of navy cadets). It goes without saying that all aspects of performance are saturated with post-imperial mythology and triumphant nostalgia.

logo, would not be indifferent to "the concepts of the machinal, the phallic, and the prosthetic as fundamental features of tele-techno-mediatic-capitalism" (Miller 2009, 126). The above-mentioned evocation of Portuguese adaptability and of the "ties" between ex-metropolis and ex-colonies by the Minister Miguel Relvas is a case in point, as it attempts to provide a supposedly historical and natural alibi for Portugal's capitalist "advancement", as it tries to emulate in capital what it once (supposedly) achieved through colonialism.

Figure 3. "Portugal não é pequeno!", 2004
(Portugal is not small) (Vieira 2011)

This parody reveals the violence and sterility of a masturbatory repetition and projection onto others and the integration of the others of and into an erected phallic prosthetic composite acting as the promise of unity and of an *arkhé* (and, necessarily, *telos*), in the place of a father figure onto which insemination can be traced. Vieira's tracing demonstrates the self-obsessed "constructedness" of ipseistic projections (in official and popular culture alike) by subverting the power of imaginary mappings, such as those of 1492, 1890 or 1935.

However, one would be foolish to think that the topographies traced by the *Financial Times* and the current Portuguese government are not also illustrations of ideology. As such, they reinforce by taking for granted the inescapable grounding (ideological, political) and common ground of the free market in the globalized world. The brave new globalized world is thus presented as the simultaneous object and subject of the markets, the flat globe where space is rendered absolute to the point of imagining new homes for old countries in "tired" Europe. All headings are seemingly determined by "the markets", even and especially when it is repeatedly announced that there is no other heading (no alternative) to cap(ital).

The hope for the "birth of a European public sphere", as was anticipated by Jürgen Habermas and Jacques Derrida in their joint article published on 31 May 2003 (Habermas and Derrida 2005, 4) in the *Frankfurter Allgemeine Zeitung* and in *Libération* simultaneously, following the 15 February demonstrations across Europe in protest against the Bush Administration's War in Iraq, has never been fulfilled. On the contrary, Europe has fallen back on nationalist and xenophobic discourses regarding the peripheries as well as accusations which evoke some of the historical ghosts the European project was meant to conjure. Beyond the dichotomy broached by US Secretary of Defense Donald Rumsfeld between an "Old Europe" and a "New Europe", one should be alert to the problematic and complexities of a shore Europe, the negative remains of a "core Europe" being reimagined and projected as the centre that holds and sustains the peripheries.[15]

Dilma Roussef, the President of Brazil, offered a response of sorts to *Financial Times* columnists with a swerving of her own devising. Speaking in the World Social Forum in Porto Alegre (having declined to participate in the World Economic Forum in Davos), she offered a valid counterpart to the present European governments (and Portuguese) via a political reminder. This is at a time when non-elected bureaucrats have reined in and are now in control of the PIGS of southern Europe, with the role of governments being limited to that of implementing economic measures in order to boost business prospects, what Jacques Rancière terms "[t]he present modesty of the state", which consists in "first of all modesty in

[15] The article by Habermas and Derrida, "February 15, or what Binds Europeans Together: A Plea for a Common Foreign Policy, Beginning in the Core of Europe", was accompanied and followed by several other articles from intellectuals across and beyond Europe. A comprehensive collection of these texts was translated into English (see Levy, Pensky *et al.* 2005).

relation to politics, in other words, hyperbolization of the normal practice of the state, which is to live off the elimination of politics" (Rancière 1999, 136), ends up being fully exposed. [16] In this context, Roussef quoted the Portuguese Zeca Afonso's "Grândola, Vila Morena" (*Diário de Notícias* 2012), the sign for the beginning of the military operations that led to the end of the Portuguese *Estado Novo* and introduced a democracy that eventually joined the EEC. In South America, she noted, "o povo é quem mais ordena" (the people are those who command). The success of Brazil as part of the BRIC, recognized by *Financial Times*, was not achieved because of but rather in spite of the economic policies imposed by the IMF, which Roussef termed "failed recipes" now being applied in Europe.

Roussef's reference and the context in which it was made confront the imaginary topographies in past or present (neo)colonial spaces which are keenly advanced by a (neo)liberal agenda echoed in political speeches and economic commentary. The roles indeed seem to have been reversed, but not as the Lex column imagined it. The citation points to the vacuity of such a drive by harking back to a specific event in the recent history of Portugal to evoke crucial legacies which must always be actualized *hic et nunc* (justice, freedom, democracy). One is reminded undoubtedly of Fredric Jameson's reminder of the necessity to historicize, but it must be added that this is inseparable and indistinguishable from the urgency and indispensability of politicizing.

There is then a sense of urgency still, two decades after Derrida wrote about the necessity of assuming "the uniquely European heritage of the idea of democracy" while recognizing that this idea is never a given, that it "remains to be thought and *to-come*" (Derrida 1992, 78). Perhaps the always already constructed "androcentric positioning of power in the master or head of the household, the sovereign mastery of the lord or seigneur, of the father or husband, the power of the *same*, of *ipse* as the selfsame self" (Derrida 2005, 142) can be deconstructed. This is inseparable from the crisis and a critical position before the topographies which are projected and constructed:

---

[16] David Harvey takes on board Boaventura de Sousa Santos's insight that "the term *governance*, rarely used before 1975, has in recent times become a dominant way to think about and practise politics. The ideology of governance is grounded in ideals of efficiency and rationality of administration, bringing together significant 'stakeholders' (the favoured term) to come up with 'optimal' but 'politically neutral' public policies" (Harvey 2009, 71).

For deconstruction, if something of the sort exists, would remain above all, in my view, an unconditional rationalism that never renounces – and precisely in the name of the Enlightenment to come, in the space to be opened up of a democracy to come – the possibility of suspending in an argued, deliberated, rational fashion, all conditions, hypotheses, conventions, and presuppositions, and of criticizing unconditionally all conditionalities, including those that still found the critical idea, namely, those of the *krinein*, of the *krisis*, of the binary or dialectical decision or judgement. (Derrida 2005, 142)

One must attend to the "deconstructive exigency *of* reason" (Derrida 2005, 142) if one is to respect the spirit of the Enlightenment, that is, veer through tradition and traditions, inherit and, to some extent, disrespect the Enlightenment values while remaining true to their spirit with no foreseeable or programmed heading, attending to the exigencies of *hic et nunc*. To be responsible means to have no headings decided beforehand, but also to consider and respect the logic of other headings, of the "headings of the other" and of "the other of the heading": moving on "to a relation of identity with the other that no longer obeys the form, the sign, or the logic of the heading, nor even of the *anti-heading* – of beheading, of decapitation" (Derrida 1992, 15). Dilma Roussef's discourse navigates against the grain of sedimented mythologies which reinforce Portuguese/European exceptionalism and colonial desires as both a catalyst and a symbolic compensation in the neo-colonial and neoliberal processes and agendas that are underway. It acts as a reminder that in Latin America, Europe and everywhere else in the "global" world, the (re)construction of justice and democracy is, urgently, to come.

Thus, far from allowing neoliberal and neocolonial discourses to pass off as "reasoned" and "reasonable" narratives to which there are no alternatives (in order to push through technocratic, anti-political agendas), one must abandon the (profoundly ideological) proclaimed rationality and reasonability of economic and historical fact over political sentiment, such as Europe's (now constructed as irrational and nonsensical) commitment to the welfare state. There is an urgency to engage with the deconstructive exigency of reason as the condition and the requirement for reconstruction, the possibility for economic, social, political, and cultural justice and democracy.

References

Arenas, F. (2003). *Utopias of Otherness: Nationhood and Subjectivity in Portugal and Brazil*. Minneapolis, MN: University of Minnesota Press.

Attridge, D. (2007). "The Art of the Impossible?". In M. McQuillan, *The Politics of Deconstruction: Jacques Derrida and the Other of Philosophy*. London: Pluto Press, 54-65.

Barber, T. (2012). "Portugal presses on with reforms". *Financial Times*, 1 February.

Blackmore, J. (2008). *Moorings: Portuguese Expansion and the Writing of Africa*. Minneapolis, MN: University of Minnesota Press.

Butler, J., E. Laclau and S. Žižek. (2000). *Contingency, Hegemony, Universality: Contemporary Dialogues on the Left*. London: Verso.

Castelo, C. (1998). *O modo português de estar no mundo: o luso-tropicalismo e a ideologia colonial portuguesa (1933-1961)*. Porto: Afrontamento.

de Man, P. (2001). "Resistance to Theory". In P. Rice and P. Waugh. *Modern Literary Theory: A Reader*. London: Longman, 272-289.

Derrida, J. (1987). "Positions: Interview with Jean-Louis Houdebine and Guy Scarpetta". *Positions*. London: The Athlone Press, 37-96.

Derrida, J. (1992). *The Other Heading: Reflections on Today's Europe*. Bloomington: Indiana University Press.

Derrida, J. (1997). *Of Grammatology*. Baltimore and London: The Johns Hopkins University Press.

Derrida, J. (2005). *Rogues: Two Essays on Reason*. Stanford, CA: Stanford University Press.

Derrida, J. (2006). *Specters of Marx: The State of the Debt, the Work of Mourning and the New International*. London: Routledge.

Diário de Notícias (2012). "Dilma Rousseff diz que o 'povo é quem mais ordena'. At **www.dn.pt/inicio/globo/interior.aspx?content_id=2267763**, accessed 9 October 2012.

Esposito, R. (2010). *Communitas: the Origin and Destiny of Community*. Stanford, CA: Stanford University Press.

Expresso (2011). Em 2013, "Portugal terá 'dobrado o cabo das tormentas'". At **http://expresso.sapo.pt/em-2013-portugal-tera-dobrado-o-cabo-das-tormentas=f695879**, accessed 9 October 2012.

Fres, E. (1886). *Carta da Africa Meridional portugueza*. Lisbon.

Freyre, G. (2003). *Casa-grande & senzala*. Recife: Global.

Galvão, H. (1935). *Portugal não é um país pequeno: superfície do império* colonial *português comparada com a dos principais países da Europa*. Lisbon: Secretariado da Propaganda Nacional.

Habermas, J. and J. Derrida (2005). "February 15, or what Binds Europeans Together: A Plea for a Common Foreign Policy, Beginning in the Core of Europe". In D. Levy, M. Pensky and J. Torpey (eds.), *Old Europe, New Europe, Core Europe: Transatlantic Relations After the Iraq War*. London: Verso, 3-13.

Hadas, E. (2011). "Portugal and Brazil: role reversal". *Financial Times*, 25 March.

Harvey, D. (2007). *A Brief History of Neoliberalism*. Oxford: Oxford University Press.

Harvey, D. (2009). *Cosmopolitanism and the geographies of freedom*. New York: Columbia University Press.

Harvey, D. (2011). *The enigma of capital and the crises of capitalism*. London: Profile.

Levy, D., M. Pensky, *et al.* (eds.). (2005). *Old Europe, New Europe, Core Europe: Transatlantic Relations After the Iraq War*. London: Verso.

Loomba, A. (1998). *Colonialism – Postcolonialism*. London, Routledge.

Lourenço, E. (1994). "Identidade e Memória: o caso português". *Nós e a Europa ou as duas razões*. Lisbon: INCM, 9-15.

Lourenço, E. (2004). "Nós como futuro". *A nau de Ícaro seguido de Imagem e miragem da Lusofonia*. Lisbon: Gradiva, 61-71.

Lourenço, E. (2004). "Portugal: entre a realidade e o sonho". *A nau de Ícaro seguido de Imagem e miragem da Lusofonia*. Lisbon: Gradiva, 55-59.

Lourenço, E. (2004). "Tempo português". *A nau de Ícaro seguido de Imagem e miragem da Lusofonia*. Lisbon: Gradiva, 105-109.

Mack, J. (2011). *The Sea: a Cultural History*. London: Reaktion.

Madureira, L. (2006). "The empire's 'death drive' and the wars of National liberation". *Imaginary geographies in Portuguese and Lusophone-Africa: Narratives of discovery and empire*. Lewiston, Queenston, Lampeter: The Edwin Mellen Press, 135-161.

Miller, J. H. (2009). *For Derrida*. Bronx, NY: Fordham University Press.

Miller, J. H. (1995). *Topographies*. Stanford: Stanford University Press.

Nogueira, A. F. (2006). "Alberto Franco Nogueira: as facturas da opção europeia". In P. C. Ribeiro (ed.), *Portugal como Problema: Século XX, Os Dramas de Alternativa*. Lisbon: Público – Fundação Luso-Americana, IV, 537-554.

Pessoa, F. (2008). *Message*. Lisbon: Oficina do livro.

Público (2012). "Miguel Relvas elogia 'juventude bem preparada' que emigra". At **www.publico.pt/politica/noticia/miguel-relvas-elogia-juventude-bem-preparada-que-emigra-1528045**, accessed 9 October 2012.

Rancière, J. (1999). *Dis-agreement: Politics and Philosophy*. Minneapolis and London: University of Minnesota Press.

Ribeiro, M. C. (2002). "Empire, colonial wars and post-colonialism in the Portuguese contemporary imagination". *Portuguese Studies* 18, 132-214.

Saraiva, A. J. (2006). "António José Saraiva: a "personalidade cultural portuguesa". In P. C. Ribeiro, (ed.) *Portugal como Problema: Século XX, Os Dramas de Alternativa*. Lisbon: Público – Fundação Luso-Americana, IV, 401-416.

Vecchi, R. (2010). *Excepção atlântica: Pensar a literatura da guerra colonial*. Porto: Afrontamento.

Vieira, M. J. (2011). At **www.vieira2011.com/portugal.htm**, accessed 9 October 2012.

**Post-dictatorship times and archives
in Argentina and Chile**

How to Live after Loss?: *Aparecida*, Reparation and Collective Pleasures in Post-Dictatorial Argentina

Cecilia Sosa

Introduction: A Lesson to be Learned?

What is to be learned from traumatic pasts? Can experiences of suffering teach us something about the future? Drawing upon the process that opened up in Argentina after a military regime of terror caused some 30,000 citizens to vanish, infamously known as *los desaparecidos* (the disappeared), I would like to show how different ways of dealing with trauma in the absence of bodies might shed light on different experiences of reparation. I am particularly interested in the idea of "affective reparation" (Eng 2010, 196), because it points towards experiences of loss in which the past is not lost but "worked through" in creative and non-normative ways. In this respect, I propose that a consideration of Argentina's aftermath of trauma might help to delineate the grounds of an ethics that does not rely on individual subjects but rather on the collective ties which have emerged in response to loss. Ultimately, the question that drives what follows is how to illuminate alternative forms of being together in other landscapes affected by trauma and loss. Can the particular ways of contesting violence in post-dictatorial Argentina function as appealing *lessons* in transnational scenarios?

In the introduction to *Specters of Marx* (1994), Jacques Derrida is captivated by a problem: How to learn to live? He reflects that this is not a lesson that one learns from life, or that is thought through in life. Rather, it is something that comes from the dead, or better from the borders between life and death. "Only from the other and by death. In any case from the other at the edge of life", he writes (Derrida 1994, xviii). Here, I would like to consider this problem in the context of contemporary Argentina. Almost forty years after the end of terror, with no bodies to be mourned, the traces of the traumatic past still haunt the lives of the living. In the aftermath of violence, Derrida's queries about potential lessons on how to live delineate an undoubtedly poignant issue.

In 1979, at the height of the military terror, the infamous Military Junta leader Jorge Rafael Videla provided a definition of a disappeared person:

"Le diré que frente al desaparecido en tanto éste como tal, es una incógnita, mientras sea desaparecido no puede tener tratamiento especial, porque no tiene entidad. No está muerto ni vivo... está desaparecido" ("As long as he remains so, I'd say the disappeared is an unknown, as long as he's disappeared he can't be given special treatment, because he has no entity. He's neither dead nor alive... he's disappeared"), he argued during a press conference at the Casa Rosada (Télam 2013). In a terrifying manner, viewed in retrospect, the Military Junta leader's definition seems to echo Derrida's thoughts. To some extent, the disappeared have been assumed to be in a sort of limbo, an infertile terrain that falls beyond the margins of the human. This particular territory could be named, after the meditations of Judith Butler in *Frames of War: When Is Life Grievable* (2009), as an *ungrievable* zone, where bodies do not deserve the right to be mourned as such. Remarkably, Butler also argues that the specific territory between life and death was the realm of kinship (2000). Drawing upon Derrida's and Butler's insights, I would like to propose that Argentina's aftermath of violence also offers the possibility of learning how to live collectively after loss. If so, it is precisely because the experience of terror has managed to challenge the boundaries of kinship while creating affective ties beyond blood.

In order to unpack this intricate set of questions, I propose to focus on *Aparecida* (Appeared) (2015), the autobiographical book written by the journalist Marta Dillon. The book eludes conventional definitions: it could stand as a *memoir*, a novel, a passionate and even playful chronicle, or even as poetry. In any case, *Aparecida* tells the story of Dillon's mother, Marta Taboada, kidnapped in 1976, whose fate remained unknown for decades. Thirty-five years later, her remains were recovered. The title of the book signposts a transition: it names the change from being "an unknown", as Videla was keen to say, to a different form of material reality. I suggest that in this process there was something to be learned. Moreover, I propose that a seemingly minor text can have something to say in relation to kinship, mourning and pleasure, not only in the context of con-temporary Argentina, but also in broader scenarios affected by loss. I suspect that Dillon's book might help illuminate a more inclusive politics of grief for other scenarios. Drawing upon Derrida's impulse, I shall let a *disappeared/reappeared* body weave my thoughts.

Aparecida: A Body/Text

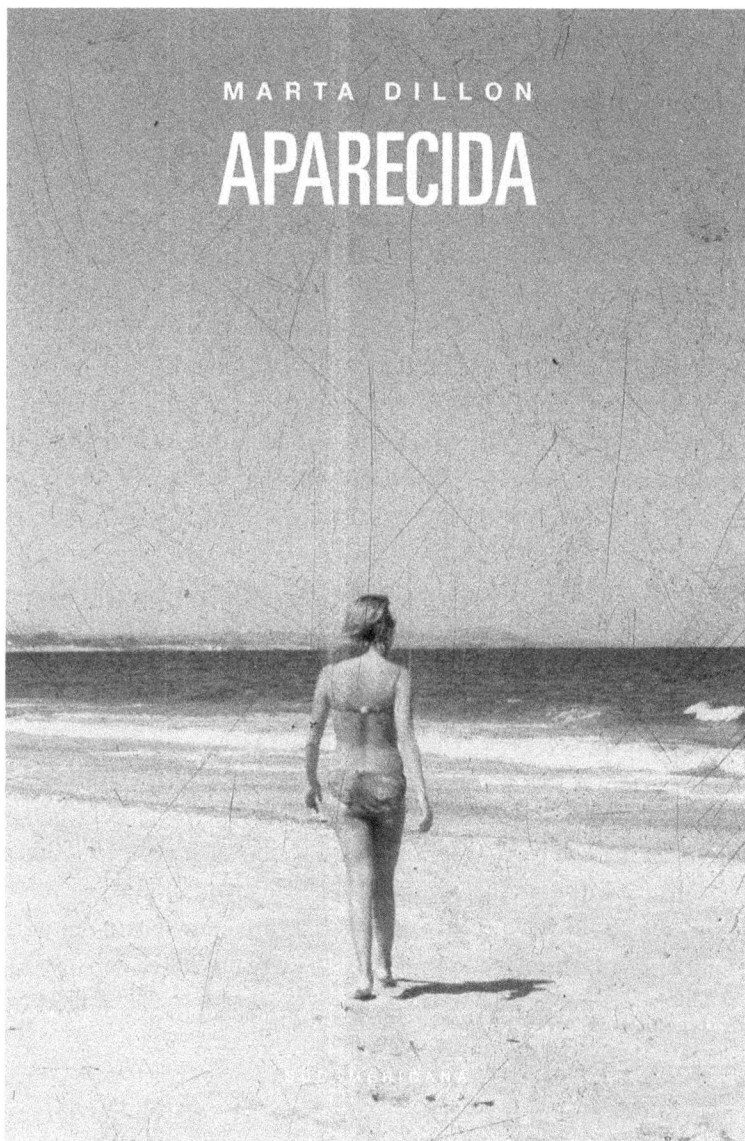

Fig. 1. Book cover of *Aparecida* (2015) by Marta Dillon

What are bodies able to do? And texts? Since the so-called "affective turn", an increasing number of authors, coming from the Humanities, the Social Sciences, Feminist and Queer studies, have proposed to approach cultural texts as forms of "cultural practices" (Ahmed 2004) or "expressive culture"

(Labanyi 2010, 229-230). This approach involves reading literary texts not from the perspective of representation but rather as *bodies* that are able to touch us, hurt us, seduce us; and ultimately *affect* us. Gilles Deleuze has already argued that a body does not define itself for its form or even as a singular subject, but rather "for the affections of those who are capable" (2004, 151).

Taking this invitation on board, I would like to approach *Aparecida* as a particular body/text that can help us to read the intensities of a specific space and time within Argentina's process of mourning; this is the so-called phase of the Kirchner years, the period initiated in 2003 by President Néstor Kirchner and continued under the administration of his wife and widow, Cristina Fernández de Kirchner, until December 2015. What are the intensities that a body can arouse when it makes its way back from the past? What are the circulations of anxieties and rhythms that a set of bones might generate? Thus, my proposal is to read *Aparecida* to examine the politics of memory delineated in a political epoch as powerful as it is controversial. Ultimately, it means reading a book in terms of the intensities of which it is capable while trying to capture the "forms of meaning that are not restricted to the cognitive" (Labanyi 2010, 230).

Marta Taboada was a teacher, lawyer, and activist in the *Frente Revolucionario 17 de octubre* (FR17), Peronist guerrilla group popular in the 1970s. In October 1976, Taboada was kidnapped from her home. In August 2011, her remains were found in a mass grave. As far as the Argentine Forensic Anthropology Team could establish, she had been buried alongside other members of the FR17 who had been killed on a corner of the Buenos Aires suburbs in a clash with the military forces. It was "una muerte sin épica en una esquina oscura de un barrio donde nadie se atrevió a abrir las ventanas" ("an unepic death on a dark neighbourhood corner where no one dared to open the windows"), writes Dillon (2015, 148).

Aparecida is not only an autobiographical book that testifies to more than thirty-five years of searching by a feminist-writer-journalist-daughter. Rather, it shows how an epoch digs up its own past, enters a dialogue with it, and makes of it its most intimate and precious treasure. From the very first pages, Dillon argues that the disappearance of her mother did not belong to her entirely. Rather, Marta Taboada's "return" was also part of "something bigger" (17). More than a personal recovery, her mother became *cosa pública* (a public thing) (Dillon 2015, 197).

Aparecida can be thought of as a public treasure, a body/text that also *does* things. For instance, it delineates the affective cartography of a period, in which anonymous bystanders were also invited to share in grief. In this sense, *Aparecida* can be read as an initiatory passage and also as a process of "affective reparation", which signals an operation of mourning which is as carnal as it is poetic: the return of a body to a community.

A New Stage in the Process of Mourning

Aparecida is a dated text. It was only during the political period that started in 2003 that the experience of loss became visible in a new and undisguised manner. Dillon's book is embedded in the public culture of the Kirchner years, an era that involved a particular way of *being* and *doing* with others, and in which bodies recovered the pleasure of being together.[1] It was also a period in which the past was rewritten and in which many of the symbols that were apparently buried reappeared, like Marta Taboada's body. During that time, grief became both a right and an official duty. This fusion, perhaps oxymoronic, entailed risks and discomforts.

Shortly after taking office, President Kirchner announced: "We are the children of the Mothers and Grandmothers of the Plaza de Mayo".[2] Self-invested as the figure of the son, the President showed how the lineage of the loss did not belong entirely to the "direct victims" – that is, the relatives of the disappeared – but rather could also be inherited by those who were not directly affected by the violence and yet adopted grief as a personal and collective commitment. In an indirect manner, the unspoken entanglement between bloodline victims and truth, which had marked the first decades of democracy, was challenged. Kinship emerged as a brand new political tie.

Kirchner's unexpected death in October 2010 created an unusual momentum in the public affairs of the country. Two disparate experiences

[1] This could be witnessed in the massive demonstrations on the anniversary of the military coup on 24 March every year, the celebrations of the Bicentenary of the May Revolution in 2010, and the impressive mourning rituals in the wake of Néstor Kirchner's death that same year, as well as the demonstrations in support of Cristina Fernández de Kirchner, which continued as an expression of solidarity and resistance even after the official party was defeated by a right-wing economic coalition, led by businessman Mauricio Macri, in December 2015.

[2] This was part of Kirchner's inaugural speech before the United Nations General Assembly on 25 September 2003. See **www.cfkargentina.com/address-by-nestor-kirchner-at-un-general-assembly-2003/**, accessed 7 March 2017.

of mourning eventually intersected. While the government's detractors furtively celebrated indoors, a multitude of supporters cried in the streets, and spontaneously took over Plaza de Mayo to bid farewell to their leader. Thousands of youngsters with apparently no previous political background occupied the front of the scene to pay homage to the public man who had made them "discover the pleasure of politics", as they expressed it.[3] During the communal and highly theatrical procession, the current President and widow, Fernández de Kirchner, received the support of hundreds of mourners who became, somehow, an extended family in grief. The relatives' associations led the mourning rituals. The Mothers brought their scarves to cover the grave. "También era nuestro hijo" ("He was also our son"), they said, evoking Kirchner's inaugural speech. "Huérfanos otra vez" ("Orphans once again"), wailed the Children of the Disappeared. "Era nuestro segundo padre" ("He was our second father"), claimed the young Kirchnerists (*Página/12* 2010).

During those days of sorrow, Kirchner's statement in his inaugural speech acquired an expanded political significance. The mourning rituals showed how the notion of kinship in play did not correspond any longer to that of a traditional family. Rather, a self-fashioned and, to some extent, also joyful community in mourning managed to make visible the unconventional affiliations that emerged in response to grief. The multitudes who were part of the memorials embodied a non-biological conception of kinship. This expanded family in loss, which had been formed in response to the military violence, already circulated throughout Argentine society in different unarticulated forms. Kirchner's death managed to render it visible.

Mourning ultimately empowered individual trajectories. By the time Dillon was writing her book, her partner was Albertina Carri, a talented film-maker whose parents were also kidnapped and murdered during the dictatorship. Together, Dillon and Carri have a son, Furio. Before Kirchner's death, Dillon writes, "Albertina y yo nos sumamos como *hijas* a las endechas desafinadas por la muerte del líder, el presidente que había reivindicado parte de la generación masacrada" ("Albertina and I joined as *daughters* in the out-of-tune dirges for the leader's death, the president who had vindicated part of the butchered generation") (Dillon 2015, 97;

---

[3] Kirchner's death also marked the first public incursion of *La Cámpora* onto the public scene, a mainly youth movement within the official Party which made a cult of the former president's remembrance. See Nassau and Scarpinealli (2011).

my emphasis). To some extent, *Aparecida* embodies a queer, insurgent voice for Argentina's upcoming times. In what follows, I shall explore how this transformation was possible.

A Community beyond Blood

In the wake of terror, the network of organizations created by the victims adopted the form of a peculiar family: mothers, grandmothers, relatives, children and siblings of the "disappeared" conformed to what I have referred to as a "wounded family" (Sosa 2011a, 2013, 2014). All these kin-organizations evoked their biological ties to the missing to make their claims for justice. This particular overlap between kinship ties and groups of victims has marked the human rights landscape in the country. For more than thirty years the evocation of a community of blood functioned as the main instrument of political intervention. Seemingly, only those related to the missing by blood had the authority to demand justice. This misleading overlap between truth and lineage staged a fundamental paradox, which absented from the public scene those who had not been directly touched by violence, and ultimately imposed the status of the injured as the condition of sharing. The Kirchner period changed those unspoken rules. By adopting loss as a question of state, it made room for new narratives that opened the experience of loss to new bystanders.

There is a surreptitious promise underpinning Marta Dillon's book. The promise is framed by Hélène Cixous' voice that inaugurates the book: "Quiero ver con mis ojos la desaparición. Lo intolerable es que la muerte no tenga lugar, que me sea sustraída. Que no pueda vivirla, tomarla en mis brazos, gozar sobre su boca del último suspiro" ("I want to see disappearance with my own eyes. What is intolerable is that death has no place; that it has been subtracted from me. I want to experience it, hold it in my arms, enjoy the last breath on its mouth"). "Enjoy the last breath": as I will further argue, there is an experience of death that reclaims a certain pleasure.

Indeed, the absence of bodies had defined the work of most human rights associations in Argentina for decades to such an extent that it was perceived as "intolerable" that the Madres should brandish the slogan "Return them Alive" (*Aparición con vida*; literally, "Appearance with Life") in the late 1970s. Since then, the recovery of the material bodies was an objective for most of the relatives' groups. Although the finding of the first mass graves in the early 1980s dashed the hopes of recovering the disappeared alive, the Madres' "Return them Alive" slogan remained as a sort of Derridan "impossible claim" which established a common horizon in the struggle for justice. In fact, the "live appearance" could be read as a form of stubborn affection which managed to make linear temporalities disjointed, and shaped the interstices of the politics of grieving for forty years.

During the Kirchner period, however, the feeling of "subtraction" started to be repaired. Not only the so-called "laws of impunity" were ruled to be unconstitutional by the Supreme Court of Justice on 14 June 2005, but pardons were also rescinded.[4] New trials against military personnel recommenced in 2006 and continue today.[5] In addition, the anniversary of the 1976 coup on 24 March was declared a bank holiday and National Day of Memory, and former detention camps were re-opened as spaces of memory. Moreover, during this period, as Cixous' statement anticipates, the experience of loss started to demand some kind of joy. Only in such a context could Marta Taboada's ceremony of reburial taste so much like a strange form of victory.

A Genealogy under Construction

Gabriel Giorgi has analyzed how the bio-politics that operated during Argentina's dictatorship tried to make the disappeared body a form of legal and historical evidence. Giorgi (2014, 198) argues that the military regime attempted to destroy "the bonds of that body with the community". As he writes, the scenes of abduction and forced disappearance which took place during the state terrorism featured the production of "corpses without community" (*cuerpos sin comunidad*). The process not only recalls similar experiences of terror experienced in the Southern Cone as part of the Plan Condor initiative, but also establishes dialogues with different events of disappearance and terror world-wide.

When the Anthropological Forensic Team announced the discovery of Marta Taboada's remains, Dillon still referred to the process as something that was alive, not quite something taking place in the present but rather a sort of continuum with no clear beginning or end. She describes this

[4] In 1986 and 1987 the Full Stop and Due Obedience laws put an end to most prosecutions of military personnel. In 1990, President Carlos Menem "forgave" most of the military officers who had already been condemned.
[5] Almost 1,500 military personnel are involved in cases across the country, as reported by Argentina's NGO, Centro de Estudios Legales y Sociales (CELS).

process using the gerund form *-ing*. "Now it was clear, Mum *is coming back*" (2015, 188; my emphasis). The use of the *-ing* allows readers to experience the resonance of a process that is not finite but ongoing. What is being named, then, is a process of affective reparation which made that re-appearance possible.

Marta Taboada's remains are certainly interrogated by blood: there are genetic and forensic tests, which provide a belated time of death.[6] Yet Dillon makes clear that the body that finally reappears overflows biological certainty. It is a body that has been released from a strictly family economy. Marta Taboada returns not only for a daughter but also "re-appears" in the name of a wider community, which was configured in relation to those bodies that were made to disappear. In this sense, *Aparecida* appoints a community that goes beyond biological ties.

In the acknowledgements, Dillon dedicates *Aparecida* to her brothers ("Santiago", "Andrés" and "Juan"), and also mentions Marta Taboada's grandchildren, who had no opportunity to know her. Dillon also dedicates her book to those "quienes vengan llegando a inscribirse en esta genealogía, a tomar su palabra" ("who are coming to join this genealogy, to take its word"). This is a forthcoming genealogy that names a cast of extended heirs who are not limited to any traditional family. On the contrary, the book ultimately addresses "those who are coming", where the *-ing* form again highlights an ongoing process of transmission – and even of contagion – which takes place in the present. It is to this genealogy "under construction", to this lineage beyond blood, that the book is finally dedicated. Thus, *Aparecida* unravels the affective landscape of a period in which bodies (and texts) reveal their capacity to bring this community to life.

The invitation to Taboada's funeral names a loose and heterogeneous collective of friends and activists. "Lo que quiero es que vengan todos" ("I want all of you to come") (Dillon 2015, 153). Her call was heeded. The mother, grandmother, greatgrandmother, sister, friend, lover, *compañera* was re-buried in an ecstatic ceremony of victorious drums, music and flowers.

---

[6] The Abuelas organization has also relied on genetics in their search for the new-born babies who were taken from their captive parents immediately after birth. A test enabled them to establish the "true identity" of the children with one generation missing.

Memory in Flesh

Marta Dillon's book departs from what has been considered a point of arrival: the discovery of the remains. Right there, *Aparecida* confronts its readers with a morbid, uncanny insistence before the extreme materiality of those findings. The set of bones, which was buried as NN (*ningún nombre*, "no name", or person unknown) and recovered under Marta Taboada's name, is exhaustively described and examined. A feeling of discomfort eventually emerges in front of "una mandíbula loca" ("a crazy jaw") (33) or "una cadera zigzageante" ("a zigzagging hipbone") (57), which through consecutive pages are assessed with impertinent detail. The five pieces of skeleton form a legacy difficult to archive. They speak about something activated, fully charged, almost in the flesh. In this manner, *Aparecida* delineates a way of conceiving of the body in which the boundaries between life and death, the organic and inorganic, and even between culture and nature, are threatened. Dillon's book points towards a zone of uncertain potentialities that delineates a type of memory that waits at the antipodes of representation. Against memorial gestures, *Aparecida* reconstructs a spectacle of matter that is anchored in a practice; a work of mourning that takes place in the present.

Fig. 2. Montage part of the photo essay *Arqueología de la Ausencia* (1998-2000), by Lucila Quieto. Marta Dillon poses in front of a photo showing her mother, Marta Taboada, holding her when she was a baby. Photograph courtesy of the artist.

More than forty years after the military coup, a book telling the story of a disappeared woman begins to grasp the gravity of an absence, which seemed to have been subtracted from the word "disappeared". In doing so, it offers a way of re-politicizing the matter. *Aparecida* contributes to completing a floating sense, as if the very inscription of the word *desaparecidos* had finally been anchored and incarnated – never more literally – in five pieces of bone. While ostensibly focusing on a singular absence, *Aparecida* sheds light on a process that has been written in the plural. Dillon's book functions as an affective force that moves a singular body beyond itself, suggesting the extent to which a body is "always more-than-one" (Manning 2010, 123). It ultimately demonstrates why there have never been heavier bodies than those of the disappeared. This embodied memory in flesh and bone also stands as a quirky *lesson* from Argentina, which can be transferred to other landscapes marked by loss.

Pleasures in Mourning

As already anticipated, the Kirchner years signposted a time in which the experience of mourning claimed a certain pleasure. As Butler (2004, 22) argues, in the act of grief "something about who we are is revealed, something that delineates the ties we have to others, that shows us that these ties constitute what we are". Dillon's book reveals the ambiguous borders on which grief flows from the private to the collective. By countersigning the figure of the injured daughter, *Aparecida* battles at the threshold of kinship, the precise terrain on which blood gives way to more fluid and irregular affiliations. While conceiving of her mother as "a public thing", Dillon introduces a sense of vulnerability that is not merely personal but political. In this sense, *Aparecida* shows how affect – anger, but also empowerment and joy – can forge an alternative sense of community. Far from sinking into despair or melancholy, Dillon's book resonates as a furious cry of victory. Navigating the end of a cycle, *Aparecida* proudly proclaims the secret desires that were hidden in mourning. It demonstrates how grief can also potentially announce forms of exhilaration, effervescence and empowerment. In doing so, it offers a rich example for investigating the entanglement between mourning, kinship and new forms of collective pleasure.

As Dillon recalls, the recovery of her mother's remains overlapped with her wedding with Albertina Carri, director of *Los rubios* (2003). The radiation of conflicting intensities, which tied a wedding to a burial, finds the brides getting rid of conventional wedding outfits. Like twisted versions of "cancan dancers" or "dominatrices with black rubber bras", they opt for dark clothes. Dillon writes: "Esas éramos más nosotras, más lascivas, más dispuestas a usar el luto para bailar clavando los tacos sobre el dolor, obligándolo a aullar de alegría" ("That was more like us, more lascivious, aiming to use mourning to dance and nail highheels into the pain, forcing it to howl with joy") (96). Readers are faced with a provocative, almost oxymoronic image, in which "mourning is forced to howl with joy". I propose that this brilliant figure might be expressive of a poignant, radical and illuminated operation that took place throughout Argentina's last decade, a rhetorical figure that becomes expressive of the affective atmosphere embedded in the Kirchner years. However, it is necessary to investigate first how this tradition was initiated.

A Process of Transference

It was during Kirchnerism that the bereavement jargon of the victims emerged with new intensity. In the previous decades, humour functioned as a sort of "guilty pleasure", a protected and secret treasure among the youngest members of the "wounded family", the Children of the Disappeared. Since the mid-1990s, the descendants gathered in H.I.J.O.S.[7] While continuing the Madres tradition, the question of how to honour the name of the missing already involved a spectral relation to the past: the organization of the descendants not only assumed a retrospective fidelity to their missing parents, but also positioned their members in an endless childhood. In any case, H.I.J.O.S. provided its members with an affective life-world that functioned as a new political family. Being part of the group not only included joining demonstrations and public assemblies, but also parties, camps and journeys. Friendship, politics and sex were tied together. Expelled from conventional structures of kinship, the descendants managed to recreate alternative social ties: the organization functioned as a "family of choice".

At the same time, unspoken distinctions cut across the group. As I have reported elsewhere, these hierarchies were mostly related to the extent to which each member had been affected by state violence (Sosa 2014). The differential levels of infliction installed a regime of ranks inside the group:

[7] H.I.J.O.S. is an acronym meaning "children" in Spanish: "H.I.J.O.S. por la Igualdad y la Justicia contra el Olvido y el Silencio" (Children for Equality and Justice, against Forgetting and Silence).

the more one had been affected by violence, the more "privileged" the status one gained inside the organization. Personal status tended to increase in the cases of well-known disappeared parents. Those who had many disappeared relatives were known as the ones who had *sangre azul* (blue blood).

The discovery of this mischievous internal slang was a turning point in my fieldwork. The ubiquitous code that dramatically defined blood in connection to loss made me aware of a particular sense of humour that had emerged inside the group to cope with loss. It was a dark spirit of the comical, always flirting with death. This particular humour was also animated by a restrictive idea of "us": "Because we suffered, we are entitled to laugh" was the unspoken code. By the mid-1990s, humour functioned as a platform for the descendants to cope with parental absence. It enabled them to mourn through the contagious properties of joy. Yet the only ones entitled to make jokes were the true "orphans". By then, being a direct victim was a strange sort of "privilege".

The period 2003 to 2015 brought new tensions to the memory struggle. If at the beginning of the cycle the "wounded family" received Kirchner's presidential blessing, the same period also promoted more controversial narratives which challenged the official duty to remember while encouraging wider audiences to share in grief. Usually relying on playful and ironic imaginaries, the production of the younger generations brought to light new vocabularies and images, which offered empowering and non-victimizing accounts of trauma.

In 2003, Carri's autobiographical film *Los rubios* inaugurated a playful turn that would be the hallmark of the period. She not only portrayed her disappeared parents through animated toy figures, but also replaced her own figure with that of an actor. The end of the film features the whole documentary team walking off into the sunset. They all wear blond wigs on their heads. The wigs showed how mourning could eventually be transferable. During the Kirchner period, a thrilling list of descendants' productions continued to displace the steady family romance.[8] In his wild

---

[8] For instance, the collective exhibition *Familias Q'Heridas* (2011, Jorgelina Molina Planas, Ana Adjiman, María Guiffra and Victoria Grigera), all daughters of the disappeared; the exhibition *Huachos* (Orphans) (2011), created by an artistic branch of H.I.J.O.S., who described themselves as "orphans scientifically produced by state genocide acts"; and *Filiación* (Filiations) (2013), Lucila Quieto's photographic collection.

autobiographical novella, *Los topos* (2008), Félix Bruzzone, another disobedient son, offers the love story of a descendant of the disappeared and Maira, a transvestite sex worker. Through the character of Maira, who is suspected of being the protagonist's abducted sibling, Bruzzone brings to light a new constellation of desires to "transvest" the purity of the "wounded family". Moreover, in her *Diario de una princesa montonera, 110%* verdad (2012), Mariana Eva Pérez, with both parents missing, pokes fun at the Kirchernist "progressive" politics of memory, depicting the period as "the Disneyland des Droits de l'Homme" (Pérez 2012). Conversely, other contemporaries not "directly affected" by violence, have also followed on this non-normative path.[9] From multiple sides, traditional bloodline ties were estranged, mocked, and even subverted. This process of counter-signature can also be perceived as a mode of transitioning into more expanded forms of kinship (Sosa 2012, 221–33). In all these productions, dark humour was not only a privilege of the victims, but a secret tool to get new audiences involved. Moreover, within these displaced narratives, grief also became a furtive form of "coming out" for the wider society. To some extent, black humour might be considered as a fugitive gift offered to transnational landscapes affected by loss.

The *Guachx* Inheritance and the Feminist Turn

By the end of the Kirchner period, *humor guacho* (orphan humour) experienced another shift. The search for new forms of affiliation also included a feminist, queer turn. *Aparecida* introduces a crucial twist to give a non-normative account of the missing. It sheds light on an incisive and visceral form of feminist humour. In this novel turn, affect works as the "psychic glue", to use David Eng's (2010, 192) expression, a sort of mediation between language and identity, fantasies and history, subjects and subjectivities. It delineates a territory located between life and death, which explicitly looks for alternative forms of kinship. This progressive feminist tone inevitably attaches memory to a gendered body.

"Nuestra fiesta se hizo un deber, una necesidad" ("Our party became a duty, a necessity"), Dillon writes in relation to her wedding (97).

---

[9] I have analyzed the cross-dressing characters of Lola Arias' theatrical production *Mi vida después* (My Life After) (2009) as a gripping example of the "non-affected" position (Sosa 2012, 221-33). In *Cómo enterrar a un padre desaparecido* (2012), Sebastián Hacher, a writer with no missing relatives, adopts the voice of a daughter seeking her missing father.

Aparecida stands as a bloc of sensations that shows the extent to which mourning, pain and pleasure can be secretly entangled. On the eve of her mother's funeral, Dillon laughs: "Nos reímos. Nos íbamos a reír a carcajadas toda la noche. Desde que el entierro tenía fecha, mi cuerpo era la caja de resonancia de unas risas cristalinas que sonaban a cada rato como perlas sueltas de un collar cayendo por una escalera de mármol interminable" ("We laughed. We were going to laugh out loud all night. Since we had a date for the funeral, my body was the soundboard of a crystalline laughter that sounded every few minutes like loose pearls on a necklace falling down an endless marble staircase") (188). This disturbing, uncomfortable laughter speaks about an embodied legacy that largely exceeds Dillon's book. It speaks about a collective laughter in which the traces of the descendant's black humour re-emerge under the orders of an *ad hoc* sisterhood of female friends, ready to act as "wake planners" (187) for Taboada's funeral, and for any body recovered from the limbo of disappearance. Only within this expanded female network that draws upon a shared loss does it become possible to organize "a funeral postponed like a party" (153). To some extent, it could be argued that Taboada's funeral was the last party celebrated in the Kirchner period.

With Pride and Joy

In December 2015, the state's role of protagonist in the process of mourning officially ended. A new government led by businessman Mauricio Macri and a "CEO cabinet" took power (Télam 2015).[10] In the new conservative period, the expanded community in mourning came under threat. 150,000 job cuts were made in public administration, human rights dependencies were squeezed and asphyxiated by the lack of budget, the indigenous activist leader Milagro Sala was detained, becoming "la primera presa política" ("the first political prisoner") of Macri's government (*Página/12* 2016). In this regressive context, it was not surprising that a public servant denied the number of disappeared.[11]

---

[10] President Macri's cabinet has been composed mostly of former executives from private banks and global corporations, including Shell and HSBC.

[11] I am referring to the then Buenos Aires Secretary of Culture, Darío Lopérfido, who had to be removed from his post. Macri himself questioned the long-accepted human rights position on the disappeared. In an interview with *Buzzfeed* he stated: "No sé si son 30 mil o 9 mil, es una discusión que no tiene sentido" ("I don't know if it's 30,000 or 9,000, it's a discussion that makes no sense") (see **www.youtube.com/watch?v=YC8qoSHvJ4U**).

The fiery reaction did not sound like mere support for some sacred numerical convention. Rather, it showed how the weight of a number had become synonymous with struggle.

The constraints imposed by the neo-conservative cycle seditioned a feminist non-normative irruption. In the post-2015 period, the narratives of mourning associated with the dictatorship intersected with a critical anti-patriarchal feminist wave, establishing new urgencies and a new intensity.[12] *Aparecida* foreshadowed this entanglement. It showed how loss could also promote alternative affiliations beyond blood. In so doing, it exposed how memory is not tied to the fixed temporality of duty but rather to untidy narratives that begin time and again with uncertain experiences of body-to-body transmission. Contrary to the official politics of remembering, *Aparecida* envisioned a forthcoming culture of mourning, in which grief and pleasure were knotted together.

Although the conservative cycle threatened the expanded affiliations that had emerged in the 2003-2015 period, the process of transference of grief continued to resonate, open to unexpected iterations and displacements. The current cross-fertilization between memory struggles and the recent feminst irruption also envisions alternative ways of inhabiting the future.[13] An appealing idea of *Matria* (Motherland) seems to be emerging.[14] Somehow, *Aparecida* anticipated this alternative form of feminist power: it imagined "a tribe of *cacicas* [female leaders]" (Dillon 2015, 205), a sisterhood of female friends in which shared mourning acts as the main resonance box. This illusion, maybe this fiction, also included a politics of memory for the generations to come. After all, as Derrida (1994, xx) argues, a non-normative politics of memory will impose further questions for a time that has not yet arrived. In the new context, *Aparecida* becomes a ritual text, almost a wild prayer for the future. In some sense, it

---

[12] The feminist tradition dates back more than a century in the country but has recently been re-energized by the formation of younger groups, including *Ni una menos*, a feminist organization of which Marta Dillon was one of the founding members.

[13] The new feminist wave participated in national and regional gatherings, "los encuentros", mostly linked to the *Ni una menos* organization.

[14] On 19 November 2016, more than 250,000 women took over the streets of Buenos Aires demanding "the end of patriarchy". On March 8, 2017, the local feminist movement took the initiative in a National Women's Strike, which included 44 countries. **www.facebook.com/events/1043905282422378/ permalink/1098350346977871/.**

has become a body-text that fights not to be archived, as it already functions as a space of memory. While moving beyond melancholia, *Aparecida* reminds us of the power of affect to build communities after loss, with blood but also with laughter, forcing pain "to howl with joy". Perhaps this might be the most profound *lesson* from Argentina.

References

Ahmed, S. (2004). *The Cultural Politics of Emotion*. London: Routledge.

Arias, L. (2009). *Mi vida después*. Audiovisual production. Argentina.

Butler, J. (2000). *Antigone's claim: Kinship Between Life and Death*. New York: Columbia University Press.

Butler, J. (2004). *Precarious life: The Powers of Mourning and Violence*. London and New York: Verso.

Butler, J. (2009). *Frames of War: When is Life Grievable?* London and New York: Verso.

Carri, A. (2003). *Los rubios*. Audiovisual production. Argentina.

Clough, P. (2010). "Afterword: The future of affect studies". *Body and Society*, 16, 222-230.

Deleuze, G. (2004). *Spinoza: Filosofía práctica*. Buenos Aires: Tusquets Editores.

Derrida, J. (1994). *Specters of Marx: The State of the Debt, the Work of Mourning and the New International*. New York and London: Routledge.

Dillon, M. (2015). *Aparecida*. Buenos Aires: Sudamericana.

Eng, D. (2010). *The Feeling of Kinship: Queer Liberalism and the Racialization of Intimacy*. Durham, NC and London: Duke University Press.

Giorgi, G. (2014). *Formas communes: Animalidad, cultura, biopolítica*. Buenos Aires: Eterna Cadencia.

Hacher, S. (2012). *Cómo enterrar a un padre desaparecido*. Buenos Aires: Marea Editorial.

Labanyi, J. (2010). "Doing things: Emotion, affect, and materiality". *Journal of Spanish Cultural Studies*, 11, 3-4, 223-233.

Manning, E. (2010). "Always more than one: The collectivity of *a life*". *Body and Society*, 16, 1, 117-127.

Massumi, B. (1995). "The autonomy of affect". *Cultural Critique*, 31, II, 83-109.

Nassau, J., Scarpinealli, L. (2011). "Los jóvenes K conquistaron la plaza".

La Nación. 21 October. At **www.lanacion.com.ar/1319685-los-jovenes-k-conquistaron-la-plaza**, accessed 12 November 2016.

Página/12. (2010). "Con la compañía de los pañuelos". 29 October. **www.pagina12.com.ar/diario/elpais/1-155907-2010-10-29. html**, accessed 7 March 2017.

Página/12. (2016). "Marcha a Plaza de Mayo por Milagro Sala". 18 January. At **www.pagina12.com.ar/diario/ultimas/20-290576-2016-01-18.html**, accessed 18 January 2016.

Pérez, M. (2012). *Diario de una princesa montonera: 110% verdad.* Buenos Aires: Capital Intelectual.

Sosa, C. (2011a). "Queering acts of mourning in the aftermath of Argentina's dictatorship: The Mothers of Plaza de Mayo and *Los Rubios* (2003)". In V. Druliolle and F. Lessa (eds.), *The Memory of State Terrorism in the Southern Cone: Argentina, Chile, and Uruguay.* New York: Palgrave Macmillan, 63-85.

Sosa, C. (2011b). "On mothers and spiders: A face-to-face encounter with Argentina's mourning". *Memory Studies,* 4, 3, 63-72.

Sosa, C. (2012). "Queering Kinship. Performance of Blood and the Attires of Memory". *Journal of Latin American Cultural Studies,* 21, 221-233.

Sosa, C. (2013). "Humour and the descendants of the disappeared: Countersigning bloodline affiliations in post-dictatorial Argentina." *Journal of Romance Studies,* 13, 3, 75-87.

Sosa, C. (2014). *Queering Acts of Mourning in the Aftermath of Argentina's Dictatorship: The Performances of Blood.* London: Tamesis Books.

Sosa, C. (2015). "Affect, memory and the blue jumper: Queer languages of loss in Argentina's aftermath of violence". *Subjectivity,* 8, 358-381.

Télam. (2013). "Videla en 1979: No está muerto ni vivo... está desaparecido". 17 May. At **www.lavoz.com.ar/noticias/politica/ videla-1979-no-esta-muerto-ni-vivo-esta-desaparecido**, accessed 7 March 2017.

Télam. (2015). "Macri presentará un gabinete plagado de representantes de grandes empresas". 7 December. At **www.telam.com.ar/notas/ 201512/129347-macri-gabinete-empresarios-ex-ceo-y-gerentes-de-grandes-empresas.html**, accessed 11 January 2017.

Live to tell

Norma Fatala

> The problem for them, for the real killers, is that I
> never was a policeman. And I lived to tell the tale.
> Carlos R. Moore (Robles 2010)

This essay attempts a sociosemiotic approach to the narratives of survivors of the clandestine centres of detention, torture, and extermination (CCD) that existed in Argentina between 1975 and 1983.[1] The focus of research has been on statements published in "actuality books" (*libros de actualidad*), within the framework of interviews or conversations.[2]

I have referred to the books that make up the corpus as "actuality books" because they are so in many senses; in the first place, because of their very subject. As François Hartog says:

> The imprescriptibility "by nature" of crimes against humanity founds a "juridical atemporality" that can be perceived as a form of the past in the present, of a present past, or, still better, as an extension of the present, considering the present proper to the process. (2007, 234; my translation)

In the second place, every construction of a selective past, as Williams (1997, 137-139) noted many years ago, involves present interests and projects itself into the future.

---

[1] Dating the beginning of state terrorism is quite a controversial matter, as it affects political interests (cf. Tcach 2014). The fact is that there were almost 700 forced disappearances reported before the 1976 military coup, involving not only the Armed Forces (the CDD Escuelita de Famaillá, in Tucumán, began operations in February 1975, in the context of the Operativo Independencia); but also "task groups" formed by policemen and civilians, promoted, protected or tolerated by the state apparatus, which exercised illicit violence in order to terrorize the opposition and the population at large (cf. Robles 2010; Bufano and Teixidó 2015).
[2] Such is the case of *Ese infierno* (That Hell), in which five women (survivors of the ESMA – The Higher Naval School of Mechanics) talk among themselves about their experience in the clandestine camp.

Last but not least, their actuality is confirmed by the *discursive field* (Angenot 1989, 91-93) in which they are produced. In fact, testimonies contained in the books have already been presented before the courts and human rights organizations; but their (re)production in published materials prefigures a broader public and transforms them into a *production of truth* with polemical implications, designed to affect public opinion about the recent past and, therefore, collective memory. Nevertheless, these attempts at documenting barbarism are founded on experience and thus become inseparable from the subjective construction of enunciators. The *enunciation dispositif* (Verón 2004, 173) appears, then, as a document within the document, which offers an entrance into the effects of terror on singular and collective identities.

In order to give a brief report on research involving a very dense corpus and much heartbreaking reading, I shall concentrate on the ethical, subjective and identitarian constructions deployed in and by the narratives.

Telling

According to Mariana Tello (2013), it is common to find in the testimonies of Argentine survivors explicit references to the "unspeakable", "unimaginable" character of concentrationary experience, similar to those present in some classical writings on Nazi camps, such as Primo Levi's or Jorge Semprún's. Nevertheless, the proliferation of testimonies driven by the reopening of trials for crimes against humanity, as well as the abundance of statements in published material, are indicative of an extended *drive to tell*, usually presented as the fulfilment of an ethical command: survivors must make known the truth about state terrorism, for the sake of those who died. However, the straightforward logic of this obligation is but a starting point in a complex tissue of discourse.

Let us return for a moment to the epigraph, which throws light on the *pathos* that runs through the discourse of many survivors. Carlos Raymundo Moore, nicknamed Charlie, was a prisoner in the much feared Intelligence Department of the Córdoba Police (D2) for six years, from November 1974 until November 1980, when he fled to Brazil, where he wrote, in a few days, a very full declaration which he presented to Amnesty International. His statement was based not just on sheer memory but also on the bits of information, written on small pieces of cigarette paper, which he had been able to get out of prison over the years. It could be said, then, that the artisanal and risky collection of information gives credibility to the three propositions included in my short quotation, involving the construction of the adversary ("the real killers"), the description of his own position ("I never was a policeman") and the ethical command ("I lived to tell the tale"). Let me add that, after his first months in prison, Moore was considered a traitor by his former comrades, but in his story (in his *autofiction*, as Robin [1996] would say)[3] he appears as the freelance operator of a huge counter-intelligence scheme that may have saved sixty or seventy lives.[4]

I have chosen this very extreme case because it shows how state terrorism transformed the clichés of political prison in Argentina and triggered new forms of resistance, which rendered fuzzy the clear-cut opposition between the hero and the traitor. It also shows that, after state terrorism, survival required an explanation.

Survival and Suspicion

In terms of the effects of state terrorism on political or social militancy, survival could well apply to a vast number of individuals: those who withdrew into their private lives (internal exiles); those who left the country (external exiles); those who survived prison or clandestine camps. But the dramatic differences, even between the last two cases, impose particular conditions upon the narrative of the experience.

Although there were many deaths in legal prisons (most of them as the result of shootings disguised as attempted escapes or armed confrontations), their numbers (approximately 130 people, according to Garaño and Pertot [2007]) constitute a small proportion of the more than 6,000 political prisoners who occupied the jails from 1974 to 1983. In the case of forced disappearance, the *returning subjects*, as Calveiro (1998) calls survivors from the clandestine centres, are also a small percentage – between five and ten per cent – of those kidnapped.[5]

---

[3] In the terms of Régine Robin (1996, 61-2), *autofiction* does not designate a false or invented story, it rather signals the impossibility of (objective) self-narrative.

[4] The operation consisted of implicating as many prisoners as he could in the take-over of the Military Factory at Villa María by the ERP (10 August 1974), in order to have them legalized, since the military planned to stage an "exemplary" trial of that case (cf. Robles 2010; Carreras 2010).

[5] Although the official number of forced disappearances – that is to say, of those

There are, nevertheless, some differences in situations that should be taken into account. In the first place, the date of *the fall* – that is to say, the date of capture: death was an almost certain fate from the middle of 1975 to the first half of 1977, by which time the political-military organizations – Montoneros and the PRT-ERP – could be said to have been decimated. Afterwards, death became more selective.[6] Casual or unimportant victims of kidnapping could find their way to legal prisons or even to freedom.[7] "Only half of the fifty prisoners that were in La Perla arrived at San Martín [Penitentiary]; the rest were shot", remembers a survivor captured in September 1977 (Mariani and Gómez 2012, 328).[8] Although the figures are shocking, they show the proportional variation in the probabilities of survival.

Nevertheless, the differences underline the status of the long-term survivors, those who were caught in the first stages of state terrorism and outlived their stay in the extermination camps. They were generally put to work on diverse tasks by their captors and thus regained at least the relative possibility of *moving, seeing and hearing*, activities from which the rest of the prisoners were banned. Their living conditions were also better and they were allowed to contact their families and even visit them. Although they were kept under surveillance, they were generally freed long before legal prisoners.

The stigma of collaboration that falls on this group of prisoners depends, then, not only on survival but on this differential treatment. A survivor of the last phase of the dictatorship describes her experience in this way:

> I was questioned by a "broken prisoner" [*un quebrado*]. I know he was a prisoner because I was without the blindfold and I saw him [...] I

that were reported – totals about 13,000 victims, real numbers could easily be double that figure, considering the fact that many claims were never filed because of material impossibility (some families were decimated), ideological differences, fear or ignorance.

[6] ERP (Ejército Revolucionario del Pueblo [People's Revolutionary Army]) was the armed branch of the PRT (Partido Revolucionario de los Trabajadores [Workers' Revolutionary Party]).

[7] Calveiro (1998, 44-45) includes in this category persons kidnapped because they had witnessed illegal proceedings or were relatives or visitors of military targets.

[8] La Perla (12km from Córdoba city) was the largest CCD outside Buenos Aires. It belonged to the III Army Corps.

understand that the contribution of collaborators to Justice is superior to ours, because they worked with the military files and went about the barracks without a blindfold. However, I consider that terror is one thing – saving your life or the lives of your son and husband – and collaborating with the military another. (Mariani and Gómez 2012, 328)

We can see how many questions are interwoven in such a short paragraph: the proof of a particular collaboration; the general traits that would define a collaborator (moving and seeing), and the subtle line that divides giving information under torture from collaborating.

On the other hand, Moore divides the long-term survivors in La Perla into three groups: those who gave information under torture, those who collaborated doing tasks, and those who changed sides (Robles 2010, 208). Here, the line of treachery isolates those who changed sides, that is to say, those who chose to become one of them, while the rest are considered victims, forced to collaborate by extreme violence, but retaining their status as prisoners.

Now, if we put together the second group – those who collaborated in doing tasks – with the superior contribution to justice mentioned in the first quotation, we arrive at the central paradox of the *returning subjects*: survival makes them suspects, but it also transforms them into the only agents who share with the agents of genocide a firsthand knowledge of the clandestine devices of extermination. Their statements, therefore, are the cornerstone of any attempt to achieve "truth and justice", as human rights lawyers understood quite early on. They had to labour, nevertheless, to convince the human rights organizations, mainly composed of relatives of the disappeared, that any expectation of bringing the agents of genocide to justice implied necessarily a symbolic transformation: the *becoming victim* of those up to that point considered traitors.

Knowing

Knowledge seems to be the key to the social reintegration of survivors. But we must look deeper into this harshly acquired competence. If we do, we find that information (collecting, systematizing, communicating data) is at the core of these survivors' trauma, but, at the same time, their only way out of it. In the clandestine camps, they were not only tortured to produce information, but were given the task of analyzing information (for instance, in newspapers) for the military.

On those terms, collecting information against their captors was, as Canetti (1973) would say, the only possible means of *reversal* for human beings subjected to an almost total power. This form of individual resistance gave purpose to survival and helped them regain the human status their torturers had endeavoured to crush: if they had been forced to tell in order to live, they would now, of their own free will, live to tell. Thus, subjection becomes *simulation* and information becomes the gift, the *object of value* which survivors would bring from their descent into hell. However, on the other hand, I must register here some differences that show the multiple nuances of survival. *Simulating* or *acting as if* are recurrent notions in the discourse of survivors, but they frequently refer purely to survival (*Ese infierno* is paradigmatic in this sense). In such cases, the value of information is an afterthought that appears with the return of democracy.

On the other hand, the confluence of simulation and purposeful collection of information anticipates reversal and describes an enunciator who, still in prison, had managed to regain some of his previous competences. In some cases, it is even possible to detect in the statements an undercurrent of self-satisfaction, even superiority, at having outwitted the captors:

> The military made a mistake in letting us live. We are the product of their mistakes. They should have killed us all; but they did not do it and now we are stating what really happened.[9]

Los compañeros (The Comrades), a non-fiction novel written by Rolo Diez, a former militant of the PRT, gives yet another twist to the relation information-survival. Towards the end of the book, an exiled survivor receives a visit from a Party intelligence official who even stays the night at their flat. The survivor and his wife are extremely moved by this gesture of confidence and conciliation. The visitor, who is also the narrator, listens to the survivor's story, including his own collaboration, with remarkable equanimity; but the real object of the visit is to learn if the survivor has any information about the existence of a "filter" (a spy) among the members of

---

[9] Fragment of Piero Di Monti's statement in the trial of Brandalisi *et al.*, quoted in Mariani and Gómez (2012, 98; my translation).

the Party leadership in Córdoba in the seventies – a real and unsolved question that still provokes arguments (Montero 2015).

Narrative Identities

Information, no matter how important, is but a part of the tale. The telling accomplishes other functions, enacting subjects caught in a space-time, producing identities, introducing pathos... In Deleuzean terms, all the properties and qualities of a particular *assemblage* (Deleuze and Guattari 1987, 503-504).

In an article on the incidence of penitentiary treatment upon identitarian constructions of political prisoners and, more precisely, on a classification dreamt up by the last dictatorship which divided "subversive delinquents" into three groups, in which "recoverability" was measured in inverse proportion to resistance,[10] Santiago Garaño (2010, 129) concludes that, in legal prisons, differential grouping contributed, basically among the "irrecoverable" prisoners (G1), to the consolidation of group identities, loyalties and comradeship which, after liberation, allowed the construction of a group narrative that, in large measure, determines "what is memorable and how the experience of political prison is to be remembered" (my translation).

I cannot agree with the almost exclusionary productivity which Garaño assigns to penitentiary power, but I share his view about the importance of collective identification in the feedback on resistance and also about the risk implied in considering the narrative of the prison experience of the

---

[10] a) Group 1: resistant prisoners. Negative attitude: they present traits of irrecoverability. Unruly. They have no symptoms of demoralization. They form groups and exercise leadership. They exhibit a strong ideological foundation and a sense of belonging to the SDB (Subversive Delinquents' Bands).

b) Group 2: undefined prisoner. Their attitudes are not clear or cannot be specified. They exhibit doubt. They require more observation and to be subjected to PA (Psychological Action) in order to be defined.

c) Group 3: ductile prisoners. They do not form groups with the resistant prisoners. They tend to collaborate with the PS (Penitentiary Service) staff. They show symptoms of demoralization. Some of them may make public their rejection or disown ideological positions related to the SDB. They are willing to enter into a process of recovery (*recuperación*). (Special Order No. 13-77 ("Recovery of boarders [*pensionistas*]"). Copy No. 2, Command Zone 1; Buenos Aires, dated July 1977, p.3). Personal archive of a former political prisoner, Córdoba, Argentina, in Garaño (2010: 122-3; my translation).

strongest, "as if it were the same for all political prisoners". Furthermore, I believe it would be even riskier to take the survivors' narratives as the camp experience of all the sequestered, for most of whom self-narration has become impossible.

Both legal and illegal prisoners shared the experience of capture and torture, but the place of detention determined irreparable divergences. According to legal prisoners, death was an ever-present possibility: they could die in torture, they could be "transferred"[11] in order to manufacture an escape shooting, they could be killed as a reprisal for actions carried out by their organizations, or they might simply attract the most brutal punishment from a prison officer.[12] But in clandestine centres, devoid of legal restrictions of any kind, death became almost a certainty.

Even the rudimentary legality allowed by a dictatorial regime made a difference in the conditions of captivity. Although there was a perpetual changing of rules, a moving of prisoners from one penitentiary to another, and all manner of difficulties created for them and their families, their legal status meant a right to a lawyer and, when conditions allowed it, receiving visits, news and packages from relatives, being able to talk to other prisoners, and even maintain collective partisan practices. In their everyday life, legal prisoners were neither blindfolded nor restricted in their mobility by handcuffs, shackles or fetters, as happened in the camps. More important still, even a terrorist state had to account for legal prisoners, but *desaparecidos* had no "entity", as the dictator Jorge Videla said.[13]

---

[11] Taking out prisoners to shoot them or dump them in the sea was euphemistically called "transfer" by the military.

[12] Such is the case of the physician José René Moukarzel, killed on 15 July 1976, in Córdoba's Penitentiary (UP1) (cf. Garaño and Pertot 2007, 208). Moukarzel's wife, Alicia De Cicco, had been killed in December 1975 in the CDD Campo de La Rivera (Córdoba). According to one of La Perla's survivors, interrogation officer Héctor Vergez told them that he had strangled her himself, incensed by the fact that such a beautiful woman would not speak and looked at him with hatred (Liliana Callizo's testimony, *El Diario del Juicio*, 28 May 2012).

[13] "As long as he remains so, the missing person (*desaparecido*) is a mystery. If the man were to appear alive, he would be treated as "x", if appearance confirmed he was dead, he would count as "z"; but as long as he is missing, he cannot have special treatment: a disappeared person has no entity (*entidad*), is neither alive nor dead, is missing. In which case, we cannot do anything" (Jorge R. Videla [1979], in *El*

In the concentrationary regime, besides information, the prime objective of unlimited torture, for an indefinite time, was the destruction of collective identifications, the breaking up of solidarities and loyalties, the reduction of totally helpless individuals to their own resources, which explains the recurrence of the phrase "each one did what he/she could" in different stories. Survival appears, then, as a rather solitary enterprise, a personal experience ruled by the principle of affection, where no abstraction is possible (Calveiro 1998, 131).

I have thought a great deal about the statement of a survivor from La Perla. She says: "The dead have no past, they have memory; I have a past, because I am alive" (Mariani and Gómez 2012, 260; my translation). Inadvertently, perhaps, she has distinguished two problematic fields: the production of collective memory and the coming to terms with one's own past, almost along the lines of the opposition social/individual. But dichotomies, we know, are only heuristic tools. Social and individual fields overlap in real life and, in this case, overlap in the figure of the un-returned subjects, the truly disappeared.

From this point of view, it seems necessary to consider survivors' stories on at least two levels of analysis: one dealing with the *expository* sequences of their narrative, basically consisting of *information* about state terrorist methodology and hard data about the victims and victimizers (names, dates, places...) and another dealing with strictly *narrative* components, basically the configuration of the first-person narrator, his/her pragmatic and cognitive transformations, his/her relation with the other subjects.

The first level, as we have seen, concerns the production of truth, the transmission of an object of value (first-hand knowledge) that, at the same time, reinstates the survivor in the *socius* as a victim of state terrorism. The second has to do with the basic form of getting to grips with one's own past: the construction of what Ricoeur (1996, 147) calls a *narrative identity*, a dynamic identity that exerts a mediating function between the poles of sameness and ipseity, incorporating discontinuities or variations into permanence in time.

In the discourse of survivors, this operation heals the identitarian breach produced by their concentrationary experience and especially by

Día, 17 May 2013; my translation).

torture, which frequently evokes a metaphor of death: "There is no coming back from torture", says a survivor; "I died in La Perla", says another (cf. Mariani and Gómez 2012, 248 and 54; my translation). But the implosion of individual identities also implied a loosening of collective identifications and loyalties, overshadowed by guilt. Self-justification, therefore, plays an important role in the discourse of the returning subjects and filters their recollection of their less fortunate comrades. The dead are, in that sense, delivered into the hands of the living.

Causes and Hazards

Among the long-term survivors there is an almost unanimous assertion of the hazardous character of survival. Collaboration, they argue and even exemplify, did not ensure life. Although they admit to a desire to live, the recognition of survival as an option (in the Sartrean sense) appears as a substantial node of the personal trauma that must remain unsaid. It is possible, nevertheless, to assert that there were prisoners who *chose to die* (Actis *et al.* 2001, 157-158).

The discourse of hazardous survival relies for its reality effect on the description of the irrationality and perversion of the agents of genocide, their internal struggles, their paranoia, and their ravings about their power over life and death... But the reasoning has a sophistic angle because, according to the same stories, there is nothing hazardous in the non-survival of those who refused information or collaboration. These cases, nevertheless, are promptly passed over, in order to reinforce the thesis that everybody said something; in which case, resistance consisted in giving false or useless information or retaining as much information as one could.

As their enunciative stance requires the dismantling of the opposition hero/traitor, "old" prisoners – including those who write scholarly works – find it hard to recount unbreakable resistance and death.[14] Calveiro arrives at an aporetic solution by shifting suspicion onto the dead:

> Among survivors, there are many who resisted torture and surely that first victory helped them to tolerate the hood, the isolation, the pressures and all they suffered until their liberation. (Calveiro 1998, 74; my translation)

[14] There are, of course, exceptions to this rule. Some survivors, like Liliana Callizo, include in their testimonies many instances of death brought about by unbroken resistance.

There are no heroes in a concentration camp:

> The irreducible subject who dies during torture without giving any
> sort of collaboration is the one who comes closest to that notion, but
> there are no proofs of that, there is no exhibition of the heroic deed that
> could be testified to without the shadow of a doubt. Resistance to
> torture is a solitary representation of the tortured before his/her
> torturers. (Calveiro 1998, 129; my translation)

It is easier to find stories of enduring resistance in the testimony of
casual victims or even in the statements of repentant military personnel.
For instance, former sergeant Víctor Ibáñez recalls the torture and death
of a member of the political bureau of the PRT in these words:

> Menna was tortured for months and he never said a thing. I don't know
> how that man could stand it. They would leave him with the automatic
> electric prod on, while the interrogators went to have lunch; and not
> once, but day after day. In the end, he won the respect of the task group
> [interrogators, torturers]. Anyhow, they "transferred" him like
> everyone else. (Almirón 1999, Part II, Chap. XVI; my translation)

It can be noted, though, that the sergeant admires the resistance, but does
not think it very useful, as it did not lead to survival: an un-paradoxical
coincidence with the discourse of some survivors who subtly undervalue
stubborn resistance or open confrontation with the military as a lack of
ability to survive.

Them and Us

If torture was designed to alienate the victim from his/her collective
political identification, being chosen to collaborate or to do tasks
introduced another problematic node: the relationship with the
victimizers. The forced coexistence of kidnappers and kidnapped may have
brought about a mutual process of "humanization" in the perception of the
adversary, as Calveiro (1998, 96-98) puts it; but, according to survivors'
stories, it was a process attended by confusion, fear, distrust and
simulation. Furthermore, this ambiguous closeness drew a line between
the old prisoners and the transitory inhabitants of the extermination
centres, which explains why the relationship of long-term survivors to the
rest of the prisoners is a disturbing aspect of the narratives.

Separation between chosen and not-chosen prisoners becomes quite evident where there were different living quarters, as in the ESMA. In La Perla, where all prisoners shared the same physical space,[15] there was less talk of the human side of victimizers and more emphasis on the human tragedy. Self-narrative encompasses, then, multiple stories which rescue the absent from anonymity: assassinated teenagers, young mothers separated from their just-born children and "transferred" to death, people who met their death in the camp as the result of torture, people each one knew and loved... Stories that construct a *community of suffering*, an aggregate of individuals not devoid of human solidarity, but deprived of a political horizon by sheer terror. Since militancy and partisan discipline seem to have receded to a past prior to capture and torture, the ethical limit is fixed by the command: if someone gets off, he/she must tell what is happening.

Telling the passion of thousands, after having outlived it, is not, however, an easy task. A legitimizing gesture common to most stories consists of the reference to the survivor's conversations with renowned figures who shared captivity in the camp before being assassinated. Besides the obvious importance of attesting to the presence and fate of political and union leaders in the camp, it could be said that as subjects of the enunciated-enunciation (Greimas), quoted as sources of good-will, support and advice, those leaders become the model or ideal reader (Eco) of the survivors' stories: someone who understands the awful exceptionality of forced disappearance and the extreme conditions it imposes on its victims.

Nevertheless, there are inconsistencies that are difficult to surmount, principally as regards the timing of the telling and the (lack of) identification with the non-returned. For instance, some survivors of the ESMA state that they did not attempt to escape or to communicate with the relatives of other prisoners during their outings or even to report the situation to international organizations after being liberated, in order not to harm their *compañeros* (comrades). There is a sort of virtuous reaction against statements presented in Europe as early as 1979 and 1980, directed, we may presume, *at stopping the practice of forced disapp-*

[15] Only in 1978, when there were just five "old" prisoners left, were they taken out of the barracks and allowed to sleep in an office (Mariani and Gómez 2012, 182-184).

earance (cf. Actis *et al.* 2001, 183).[16]

Compañeros, therefore, cannot refer to the blindfolded, immobilized, anonymous numbers who inhabited Capucha and Capuchita, the quarters of the non-chosen prisoners in the ESMA. They can refer only to other members of staff, the group of recoverable prisoners chosen by navy officers. By semantic displacement, the old word has come to describe an entirely new situation, a collective identification built not around ideological principles but around a new value, unthinkable for the militants they used to be: survival. Survival takes the place of ideals in the configuration of an unstable community of long-term prisoners. In the first testimonies, it was usual to find criticisms or even accusations regarding other prisoners' behaviour;[17] but the reopening of the trials has brought about an almost corporate defence of the victim status for everyone:

> I do not agree with some survivors' attitudes in La Perla; but I must acknowledge that all of us were victims of the same destructive system. All of us, without exception, entered as victims and left as victims. (Mariani and Gómez 2012, 186; my translation)

> We have to finish once and for all with the arguments among survivors and concentrate on the real victimizers, who were the military. (Mariani and Gómez 2012, 257; my translation)

The last quotation, I believe, shows clearly the reasoning that underlies these changes: the possibility of achieving justice (i.e., the conviction of the military) merits forgetting some prisoners' weaknesses. Trials appear, then, as the final confrontation (on a purely symbolic level) of survivors and their injurers on an equal footing, that of citizens. In Verón's (1987) terms, it means the discursive construction of the other as an adversary (a *negative other, a counter-receiver*) and the demonstration of his discourse as absolutely false, but, at the same time, it requires anticipating the *destructive reading* of the opponent:

> Of course the military speak ill of us! They do it to defend themselves. They know we are their main enemies and it's easy to understand that

---

[16] According to Calveiro (1998, 125), staff prisoners agreed to keep silent about their experience "until the last of them was set free" (my translation).
[17] Calveiro (1998, 73-76) attempts a classification of prisoners.

they will do everything to discredit us. (Mariani and Gómez 2012, 126; my translation)

Giving testimony on the perverse workings of state terrorism, it seems, not only accomplishes the ethical command so frequently invoked, but it performs *reversal* as well. Contrary to the pious tendency to circumvent the victim's personal feelings on behalf of abstract justice,[18] I would propose that in crimes against humanity, the intensity of personal feelings gives us the measure of the irreconcilable nature of the crimes.

In the discourse of survivors, especially those who collected evidence against their captors, the wish for reversal (for the opportunity of *telling*) justifies and reinforces the drive for survival.

In Sum

From a juridical and social point of view, survivors' testimonies are invaluable; they belong to the category of documents that *change history*, even if they are open (as every discourse is) to different and antagonistic (that is to say, political) readings. As regards collective *memory*, I believe their effects are multiple and heterogeneous and will be better assessed in the long term.

As survivors say, they are the memory of genocide, and their efforts to bring the military to justice for crimes against humanity – a belated answer to the forty years of struggle of the affected families – may impress on the common doxa the virtues of democracy, but it is difficult to predict the scope of reception as half the present population never lived under a military dictatorship and military power is but a shadow of what it used to be.

On the other hand, their fixation on the military was amenable to the administration of memory (and forgetting) operated by Kirchnerist governments, which dated the start of state terrorism to the military coup (24 March 1976), eliding the responsibility of politicians, union leaders, regular police and para-police organizations for illegal repression long before that time. Collective memory, it seems, does not require a working definition of state terrorism.

[18] A witness felt moved to explain that in recognizing the agents of genocide he had deliberately disrespected military rank, not as "revenge" but as "vindication" of himself and his dead comrades (Mariani and Gómez 2012, 181).

Nevertheless, given the present state of discourse, I believe the deeper impact of the survivors' narratives on collective memory may be political, of a negative kind. Survivors proclaim themselves not only the memory of genocide, but also, with scant analysis, the memory of defeat. In order to demonstrate the perversion of the military personnel brought to trial, and to explain their own survival, they produce and reproduce the effects of terror. But in our hedonistic, egotistical times, ruled by self-interest, their survival does not cause moral ripples; while their stories may affect the relatives of disappeared people and a progressive minority, for the general public, torn between clientelism and political disaffection, harassed by economic and labour demands, they just go to prove the unfeasibility of any alternative notion of politics.

References

Actis, M., Aldini, C., Gardella, L., Lewin, M., and Tokar, E. (2001). *Ese infierno: Conversaciones de cinco mujeres sobrevivientes de la ESMA.* Buenos Aires: Sudamericana.

Almirón, F. (1999). *Campo Santo: Los asesinatos del Ejército en Campo de Mayo. Testimonios del ex sargento Víctor Ibáñez.* Buenos Aires: Editorial 21.

Angenot, M. (1989). *1889 : Un état du discours social.* Quebec: Le Préambule.

Anon. (2012). "Megacausa La Perla, 44th day". *El Diario del Juicio*, 28 May. H.I.J.O.S. Córdoba. At **www.eldiariodeljuicio.com.ar/ ?q=content/día-44-28-05**, accessed 20 October 2015.

Bufano, S. and Teixidó, L. (2015). *Perón y la triple A : Las 20 advertencias a Montoneros.* Buenos Aires: Sudamericana.

Calveiro, P. (1998). *Poder y desaparición : Los campos de concentración en Argentina.* Buenos Aires: Colihue.

Canetti, E. (1973). *Crowds and Power.* London: Penguin Books.

Carreras, J. (2010). "Madre noche. Algunas consideraciones sobre el libro de Charlie Moore. At **www.juliocarreras.com.ar/charliemoore - libro.html29/11/10**, accessed 20 September 2015.

Deleuze, G. and Guattari, F. (1987). *A Thousand Plateaus: Capitalism and Schizophrenia.* Minneapolis: University of Minnesota Press.

Diez, R. (2000). *Los compañeros.* La Plata: De la campana.

Garaño, S. (2010). "El 'tratamiento' penitenciario y su dimensión productiva de identidades entre los presos políticos (1974-1983)".

Revista Iberoamericana, 10, 40, 113-130.

Garaño, S. and Pertot, W. (2007). *Detenidos-aparecidos: Presas y presos políticos desde Trelew a la dictadura*. Buenos Aires: Biblos.

Hartog, F. (2007). *Regímenes de historicidad: Presentismo y experiencias del tiempo*. Mexico City: Universidad Iberoamericana, Departamento de Historia.

Mariani, A., and Gómez, J. A. (2012). *La Perla: Historia y testimonios de un campo de concentración*. Buenos Aires: Ed. Aguilar.

Montero, H. (2015). "¿Quién traicionó a Santucho?" *Sudestada*, 14, 136, March-April, 4-17.

Ricoeur, P. (1996). *Sí mismo como otro*. Mexico City: Siglo XXI.

Robin, R. (1996). *Identidad, memoria y relato : La imposible narración de sí mismo*. Buenos Aires: Secr. Posgrado Fac. de Ciencias Sociales/CBC.

Robles, M. (2010). *La búsqueda: Una entrevista con Charlie Moore*. Córdoba: Ediciones del pasaje — Comisión y Archivo Provincial de la Memoria.

Tcach, C. (2014). "La memoria como cuestión de estado". *La Voz del Interior*, 23 March.

Tello, M. (2013). "Narrar lo 'inenarrable', imaginar lo 'inimaginable', comprender lo 'incomprensible': Aproximaciones a las memorias sobre la experiencia concentracionaria desde una perspectiva antropológica". *Eadaem Ultraque Europa*, 9, 14, 211-244.

Verón, E. (1987). "La palabra adversativa: Observaciones sobre la enunciación política ». In E. Verón, L. Arfuch, M. M. Chirico, *et al.* (eds.), *El discurso político : Lenguajes y acontecimientos*. Buenos Aires: Hachette, 12-26.

Verón, E. (2004). "Cuando leer es hacer: La enunciación en la prensa gráfica". *Fragmentos de un tejido*. Barcelona: Gedisa.

Williams, R. (1997). *Marxismo y literatura*. Barcelona: Península/Biblos.

The Closet, the Terror, the Archive:
Confession and Testimony in LGBT Memories of Argentine State Terrorism

Daniele Salerno

State terrorism in Argentina forced LGBT people into hiding or into seeking refuge abroad, and their organizations, such as the Frente de Liberación Homosexual (FLH), were dissolved. In the aftermath of the dictatorship, LGBT organizations drew largely on "the playbook used by the Argentine human rights community" (Encarnación 2016, 109), joining the human rights movement and their struggles for memory and identity in the transitional period.

This essay aims to make a contribution to the study of how LGBT people entered the post-dictatorship memory regime (Crenzel 2008), a topic still neglected in the study of the transition to democracy in the Southern Cone. By mixing different discursive practices stemming both from LGBT transnational political practices (e.g. coming out as militant practice) and from post-conflict and transitional cultures (e.g. oral interviews with witnesses and the public display of past atrocities), how do LGBT people construct the memory of state terrorism, join the human rights movement and consequently reposition their subjectivities?

I will analyze a specific textual object: a section of the Archivo de Historia Oral (Oral History Archive) in Córdoba devoted to the memory of sexual repression. What I argue in the analysis is that the memory archive is a complex enunciative device which, through the oral history interview as a genre and as a discursive practice, allows interviewees to reconfigure their own subjectivity. Passing from the police interrogation and the request for truth in confession during the dictatorship to the narration of their lives and the demand for testimony, the interview as an "interrogation of the subject" resignifies the very act of "coming out of the closet" and of disclosing the truth about the self ("I am gay"/"I was born a male") and state terrorism ("I was imprisoned"/"I was abused and mistreated").

The Ex-D2 as Enunciative Device: The *Palabra* between Space and Document

The Oral History Archive, part of the Archivo Provincial de la Memoria

(Provincial Memory Archive) of Córdoba, is a complex enunciative device (Violi 2014, 116-118) that assembles different semiotic substances (stones, written documents, voices, pictures, etc.) and discursive genres and practices (the museum, the interview, the archive itself), in accordance with the aims and values listed in the provincial memory law that created the archive: to construct, preserve and transmit the memory of the atrocities that occurred during state terrorism, and to develop methodologies and adequate tools for "keeping it alive" in the struggle against impunity and in support of human rights. The Oral History Area was opened in 2007 and today preserves 100 video recorded interviews totalling 186 hours of recording. The aim of the oral history archive is also to give voice to victims, victims' relatives, and survivors in order to understand better the use and meanings of the space of the former D2 (previously a detention centre in the heart of the city).

The museum, the memory archive and, as we shall see, the interviews reframe the place and the stories that are linked to it, trying to invert their axiology and the meaning of certain practices: from a place of human rights violation to a place for the struggle for human rights; from a place to hide atrocities to a place to disclose and report them; from a place where people's identities and lives were hidden, disarticulated by violence and where some began their path towards *desaparición* (Violi 2017) to a place of visibility where the faces, names and stories of the victims are displayed everywhere and where an interview can also function not only as testimony but also as an affirmation of identity, a "right to be, what one is" (Demaria 2017). If we read it as a semiosphere, following Juri Lotman, and within a cultural semiotic perspective (Lorusso 2015), we see how this process of resignification and "repolarization" of discursive practices is in action on different discursive levels, informing different practices and semiotic substances.

The oral history archive now brings together testimonies from different categories of people. As the website says, the interviews are not restricted to political prisoners but also include "trade unionists, students, artists, intellectuals, homosexuals". The political prisoner assumes a central role in the oral archive, which is, however, composed of eleven thematic collections totalling 91 interviews which are currently available and listed on the website.[1]

[1] See **http://apm.gov.ar/apm-historia-oral/**, accessed 28 November 2016.

The setting of the interview includes the interviewee, the interviewer and a cameraman who, although invisible, actively takes part in the construction of the meaning of the interview. The protocol consists of different steps, from a first meeting and pre-interview that help to personalize the questions, to the actual recorded interview. The core of this practice is the reconstruction of the biography which the interviewee assembles by him/herself with the help of the questions, linking the past and the present, what happened and the "un-happened" (the disappointment of what might have been, for example unrealized political utopias) and possible futures (projects and dreams). For this reason, each interview always traces the story of the interviewee from childhood and family origins to the present, although some events (in our case the period of the dictatorship) are often emphasized.

The Archive on Sexual Diversity and Repression
As outlined by Violi (2007, 191; this volume, 145), the autobiographical life story (and oral) interview can be considered as a discursive genre used for "giving voice" to those categories of people marginalized by official historiography. It has been used in particular for giving voice to the so-called "subaltern" (Passerini 1988), producing works that are today considered a watershed in the way we study and investigate the past (e.g. Portelli 1999). This methodology has also been used for reconstructing the history of LGBT people, the most notable example being the oral history project of the AIDS Coalition to Unleash Power (ACT UP), which collects interviews with the militants of the group that, since 1987, has struggled for recognition of the AIDS crisis.

As Omar Basabe (2014) argues in his review of oral history research on Argentine state terrorism, the life story interview is today an important research practice for shedding light on aspects which (political) history and academic research have marginalized in their accounts of the Southern Cone dictatorships of the twentieth century. *Fiestas, baños y exilios: Los gays porteños en la última dictadura*, by Flavio Rapisardi and Alessandro Modarelli, was one of the works that broke the silence on the conditions of LGBT people during the last dictatorship in Argentina. It was inspired in part by oral history methodologies, using first-person testimonies of gay people, framed by the authors' analysis.

It is within this theoretical and methodological framework that we approach the section on the repression of sexual diversity during the 1960s and 1970s, part of the oral history archive of Córdoba, consisting to date of three interviews. The aim of the section is to collect and preserve (*rescatar*) "the voices of those people who were condemned and persecuted for having chosen a different sexuality, during the different democratic and repressive periods that happened in our country". Its goal is "to add new elements to discuss the processes of memory construction through the narratives of those who chose and choose a different way of living their sexuality, outside the normative frames culturally imposed by our society".[2]

The way researchers present the archive and structure the interview is symptomatic both of the way they construct the subjectivity of the interviewee as well as of their initial hypothesis. Firstly, researchers position the interviewees as being outside of hegemonic social frames, by presenting the conflict in this case as being between society at large and non-normative people. Secondly, temporal and historical boundaries of the "last dictatorship" appear blurred: the repression of sexual diversity does not only involve the period of the last dictatorship, but runs with continuities and fractures through recent Argentine history. As we shall see, these two elements are very important and very peculiar, because they reconfigure the *us (victims) vs them (perpetrators)* axis that is typical of post-dictatorship memory: the military and the repressive apparatus during the dictatorship, on the one hand, and militants and those who were imprisoned, tortured and killed by the military, on the other.

The three interviews, all conducted by Damiana Meca and Pablo Becerra, last between two hours and two hours and twenty minutes. What I shall offer in this section is a synthesis of the content of the interviews, while in the next section I shall single out some elements for analysis. To refer to the three interviewees, I shall use their initials: M., H., and D.

M. was interviewed in 2010. Designated as male at birth (given the name Julio César) in 1958 in the province of San Luis, her process of identification as a woman began in childhood and adolescence. In 1976, at the age of 18, M. moved to Buenos Aires where "during the day I was a student and at night I could embody M." The reaction of her mother was to commit her to a psychiatric hospital where transgender and homosexual people normally received electroshock therapy. M. succeeded in avoiding

---

[2] Text available at **http://apm.gov.ar/apm-historia-oral/**, accessed 28 November 2016.

the treatment and was also exonerated from military service on the basis of the 2H (part of the *edictos policiales* [political edicts] against prostitution that were used to imprison gay and transgender people). M. highlights the fact that during this experience what was most striking was to be considered a "sick person" or a "person with disabilities". In Buenos Aires, M. was arrested many times, suffering rituals of degradation, and subjected to what the military called "therapy", i.e. beating (*paliza*, a word that recurs many times in her testimony). Hoping for a better life, M. moved to Córdoba. However, the situation in Córdoba was no different. M. was arrested many times and imprisoned in the D2, where she was also sexually abused. She also remembers her friends, some of them arrested, killed and, one in particular, disappeared. According to M., the return to democracy also marks the birth of *transgéneros* (transgender people) in the public sphere. However, this process was not easy, because of continuities in the repression meted out by the dictatorship and democracy. The event that marked the start of the struggle for rights and recognition was the HIV/AIDS epidemic. M. reflects also on the position that *transgéneros* had in society and in political movements during the dictatorship and also in the transition to democracy. According to M., *transgéneros* were not a "risky group" for the military institution during the dictatorship but were considered "subversive" of public morality. However, out-of-the-closet *transgéneros* and LGBT people were not allowed to take part in political activism.[3] This also happened in the early years of democracy, when discrimination and the impossibility of getting a proper job pushed transgender women into prostitution. The interview ends with an opinion on human rights. M. thinks that, together with the possibility of having a job, human rights dignify people's lives. In order to explain what human rights are for transgender people, M. compares her situation to that of a child with disabilities: "a child with disabilities has an essential right (*derecho esencial*) to education [...] and a particular right (*derecho particular*) to a special needs teacher (*maestra integradora*). Being transgender, we have all the essential rights but we also have particular rights."

[3] One of the slogans of the Montoneros was "No somos putos, no somos faloperos: somos soldados de Perón y Montoneros" (We are not fags, we are not druggies: we are soldiers of Perón and Montoneros), epitomizing their homophobia (Insausti 2015).

Interviewed in 2010, H. was born in 1950 in the province of Córdoba. He was a primary school teacher and lived in Córdoba and Buenos Aires. He is homosexual and started to dress as a woman in adolescence, calling herself Mara. He was imprisoned twice in the D2. Although he adhered to the Peronist Party, he acknowledges that political militancy was forbidden to LGBT people as such. According to H., the HIV/AIDS epidemic helped construct a community and even "an identity", through the work of prevention (often with the help of the Catholic Church), supporting, caring and mourning. However, interestingly, H. makes a distinction between politics and rights, criticizing those movements or parts of the LGBT movement that "mixed" political ideologies – e.g. adhering to a right-wing or a left-wing party – with claims for rights (which from this perspective should be bipartisan). H. highlights the progress in the recognition and quality of life for LGBT people and the success in deconstructing the stigmas and discrimination which the community and individuals suffered. In particular, he remembers the struggle for the abolition of the law that forbade people born as male from dressing as women, the so-called *ropa indebida* (inappropriate clothes).

D. is a gay man and 50 years old. He was interviewed in 2012. The interview starts outside the D2, the place where gay people used to meet in the 1970s (at the corner of Plaza San Martín and 9 de Julio) and where they were arrested and brought to the D2. D. explains how this normally happened, how they were treated and what they were asked, as well as the practices and codes by which gay people recognized each other in the public space. As emerges from interviews (M. also mentions this aspect), gay and transgender people were considered to be a very important source of information, because they were living clandestinely and were familiar with the dimension of the "night". D. explains that, in the world of the prison, gay people were "the lowest of the low", to the point that "the prison guard and the prisoner allied with one another to humiliate 'this other'". D. pushes his discourse to the point of describing the gay prisoner as *preso de los otros presos* (prisoner of the other prisoners). However, he recognizes that, paradoxically, the disgust that the other men expressed (in particular the military) probably saved them from torture. Echoing M.'s words, D. highlights the fact that he did not talk about his experience for many years (25 years of silence with his family) and only talked about the experience of the prison with other gay men through jokes, never approaching the topic directly, since "by joking we could say things that we could not talk about". However, D. is aware that his silence was not due simply to the impossibility of coming out as gay to his family, or to military repression, but also to a sort of "naturalization of injustice": "no la reconocía como injusticia" (I did not recognize it as injustice), he says. Also in D.'s case, the HIV/AIDS epidemic was a pivotal moment in which people had to come out and LGBT associations started to demand recognition and rights. D. confirms that gay people were treated in the same way after the dictatorship, under the presidency of Alfonsín.

The Double Closet and Disclosure: Memory and Subjectivity in the Oral History Interview

My hypothesis is that the oral history interview, as a discursive practice in the framework of the Provincial Memory Archive, works as an important device, allowing people to reconfigure and (re)construct their subjectivity: a truth-telling performance about the self and state terrorism which also allows for the recovery of political agency.

Above all, this happens at the level of the enunciative frame implied in the discursive practice, which transforms confession into testimony.[4] The three interviews take place in the building where M., H. and D. were interrogated and obliged "to confess" their sexuality and gender deviance, who they were and what they did. The interviewer, at another level, does just the same: asks the interviewees where they are from, who their friends and families are and questions about their sexuality. The situation may appear paradoxical: questions which the interviewees are asked may overlap with the interrogation which they were submitted to during their captivity decades ago in the very same place. D. describes the interrogation and the fact that he had to confess his homosexuality and also "who the homosexuals were, where we partied, where we printed pamphlets, the books we read". The oral history genre changes the meaning of the "interrogation of the subject" and the way in which it affects the construction of subjectivities in discourse.

The interrogation of the subject in the place of his/her captivity reframes this practice and its meaning and, in particular, the act of disclosure. These acts, as Cvetkovich (2003) notes, can dramatically alter

---

[4] There is a long debate on confession, sexuality, and the secret that has as its main reference Michel Foucault's theory of sexuality (1976). See on this Cvetkovich (2003), Kosofsky Sedgwick (1990), Bell (1991), and Radstone (2007). On the archive as confessional in transitional cultures, see also Rogers (2016).

their meaning when context, audience, and speaker change. In our case, the oral history interview intertwines different discursive practices that have the act of disclosure as a common feature. First of all, the police interrogation in which the authorities ask for the truth, seek confession about sexuality; second, the "coming out of the closet", the act of gay people disclosing the truth about their sexuality; third, the "life story" genre in which a subject reconstructs the truth about his/her life; fourth, history, the reconstruction of the truth about an institution – the state – and the past of a national community from the perspective of an individual.

The oral history interview brings together these acts of disclosure by transforming confession into testimony and consequently producing a series of semantic transformations thanks to an enunciative "reframing" of the disclosure acts and of the interrogation of the subject. The first transformation is pivotal: to be gay or transgender is transformed from something to be hidden as an illness, source of shame or crime, into something that can be displayed and publicly narrated with dignity. Only this first transformation can open up the possibility of publicly breaking the silence surrounding the other levels and, in particular, surrounding the construction of the memory of state terrorism.

These enunciative shifts make it clear that the LGBT subject was in a sort of double closet. On the one hand, s/he was in the closet as a gay or transgender person. This is particularly evident in the case of D., whose homosexuality was unknown to his family, and in part for M., who had to keep Julio César "alive" during the dictatorship. On the other hand, s/he was in the closet as a victim of the repression instigated by state terrorism. With the return to democracy, LGBT people could not immediately speak of the treatment they had received under the dictatorship: they did not immediately take part in the process of truth-telling and disclosure, the democratic transition and human rights movements. State terror and the secrecy of the clandestine centres that had to be disclosed, along with social homophobia and transphobia in society and the secrecy of the closet acted as if in solidarity, merging into one another.[5]

This explains why these memories are so peculiar and sometimes even uncomfortable for the memory of the human rights movement. While we

[5] On the relation between secrets, self-disclosure and the epistemology of the closet, see Kosofsky Sedgwick (1990).

may consider that the "other", the "persecutor" in the human rights movements' narratives, is mainly the military persecutor and that, temporally, the "end of repression" coincides with the official end of dictatorship, in the three interviews the "other" and the "end" are more blurred and multifaceted.

M., D., and H. agree that the humiliation and repression of LGBT people outlived the dictatorship, in institutions, in the police and in the army, and were a daily occurrence for transgender and gay people. Temporally, this partially disconnects the experience of the dictatorship from the repression of sexual diversity that also continued in democracy.

The "other", "the perpetrator", is much more diverse in these narratives. In different ways, M., D. and H. highlight how as LGBT people their political agency was not recognized by the dissident political movements. Furthermore, as in the case of D., the political prisoner – the central victim-figure in the context of post-dictatorship Argentine memory – may even be represented as perpetrator: the political prisoner and the prison guard might act together to humiliate the LGBT person who was considered an animal or an object. In this sense, the memories of M. and D. may stand at odds in the context of post-dictatorship Argentine memory, as it has been constructed since 1983 (on this see Crenzel 2008).

I want to conclude this brief analysis by looking at how the meaning of being transgender or gay from dictatorship to democracy is re-worked in the narratives. The three interviewees agree that they were treated and defined, literally, as animals. On this topic M. says: "Imagine a corral where there are sheep that recognize each other. Because that was how they made us feel. When you take one which you are going to kill and butcher (*matar y carnear*)". The way LGBT people were arrested on the streets is compared to hunting (*cazería*). In the same way that D. uses the sheep as an animal that signifies the how the repression treated homosexuals, H. says that during the dictatorship a man once told him, "my dog deserves more rights than you".

Together with animalization, the other strategy for depriving LGBT people of agency was to define them as sick, affected by an illness. This reference to the discourse of health/illness is very strong in the three interviews and seemed also to have shaped perpetrators' language of violence (for example, the act of beating was a sort of "therapy"; see on the language of torture Demaria 2006, 135-156). This discursive feature is also the most difficult to overcome.

At the end of her interview, M. tells how important it was when in the 1990s the World Health Organization declared that homosexuality was a free life choice and not an illness. However, talking about the transgender condition, she compares it to that of a disabled person who deserves human rights as particular rights adapted to his/her condition. The way she compares disability to the transgender condition may appear ambiguous. In fact, during the interview the meaning of "disability" oscillates between the past hegemonic meaning that defined disability as illness and a more recent paradigm that defines disability as a(n existential) condition.[6]

D. says: "medicine catalogued us as sick [...] they locked us away and studied us as a strange insect (*bicho raro*)... well, this means being a victim". However, D. argues that "the struggle for civil rights is condensed around the emergence of AIDS" and that the epidemic played a fundamental role in the construction of community, in the appropriation and claiming of memory and identity ("there were many people that had to say: I have got AIDS and I am gay", another instance of the coming out of the closet discourse) and in the struggle for human rights. In this sense, the AIDS epidemic among gay people played a very complex role. On the one hand, it represented a "real" illness that struck LGBT people just after the return to democracy. Its arrival confirmed and reinforced a stigma. On the other hand, it actually represented the moment, according to all three interviewees, in which LGBT people acquired political agency and were reborn as a community and collective subject. Both M. and H., who collaborate together, find that it was in the work of supporting, caring, mourning and prevention that LGBT people were allowed to recover a collective identity and a political agency, as they were also starting to work through the memory of the dictatorship.

It is on this point of the life stories and of collective history, perhaps the point at which gay people were most vulnerable, that the discourse of human rights plays a fundamental role in "dignifying" the life of LGBT people and in enabling them to recover agency. However, the emergence of the discourse of human rights in the middle of the process of recovering political agency happens in an ambiguous way, according to the narrative of M. and H. On the one hand, as already described, M. goes back to the discourse of illness and health to justify human rights for transgender

[6] I thank A. G. Arfini and Juliet Rogers for helping me to clarify this aspect.

people. On the other hand, H. highlights the fact that "Nunca mezclé militancia política y lucha por los derechos humanos" (I never mixed political militancy with the struggle for human rights); it seems that H. separates "politics", conceived as confrontation between parties and political constituencies, from the struggle for human rights, conceived as a struggle for dignity and equality that should be politically bipartisan.

Conclusion

The small corpus of interviews from the Córdoba memory archive is exemplary of how the oral history interview, as a discursive practice, can play a role in the rearticulation of memories and subjectivities in the transitional (and post-transitional) process. In particular, I have shown how the interview transforms, on the enunciative level, the practice of "interrogating the subject" from a form of police confession to a form of testimony. The acts of disclosing the truth about the self and about state terrorism are strictly interconnected, mixing the cultural practices of "coming out of the closet" and truth-telling about the past within the frame of the transitional process.

We can single out some peculiarities of the interviews compared to the hegemonic context of the memory of Argentine state terrorism: the polemical dimension (i.e. the identification of the other as perpetrator) is somewhat more blurred. Society at large may appear as perpetrator, without a clear distinction between the elements of the 1970s' conflict. Even the Montoneros and the political prisoner can appear as perpetrators for LGBT people, something that can make these memories un-comfortable. Furthermore, the time-frame of the repression is broadened, extending well beyond the fall of the dictatorship, fixing a temporality that is slightly different from that of the political history of the country. This resegmentation of the historical temporality of the transition in the accounts I have analyzed can be compared to the broadening of "time frames beyond the dictatorship" (Crenzel 2008, 149) but in a different way: although the beginning of the Alfonsín presidency is still a point of discontinuity, it does not appear as strong as it does in the hegemonic accounts.

Finally, in the interviews the subjects reconstruct their own agency. They do so by deconstructing those knowledge and power systems (medicine, law) that defined the gay and transgender person as criminal or sick, denying them any political agency. The interviewees recognize in some parts that they have interiorized such ideologies. For example, D. speaks of a "naturalization of injustice": he felt like a sick person and that the treatment he received at the hands of the police and the military was natural. However, the reconstruction of political agency and the deconstruction of the systems that defined the LGBT person as sick or criminal appear contradictory in some cases, in particular when the human rights discourse enters the narrative, in a way that is comparable to the role it plays in the hegemonic framework. Human rights organizations restored the humanity of victims and survivors, who were portrayed as immoral and subversive during the dictatorship (which represented itself as a defender of Christian morality and patriotic values), by strongly underplaying their political agency, denying any political connections, and highlighting their individualities and sufferings (Crenzel 2015, 18-19). M. and H. seem to lean towards this strategy. M. used many Christian references to describe "her cross", comparable to Christ's cross, and at the same time compared the condition of a transgender person to the condition of a child with disabilities. H. divides political militancy from the struggle for human rights. So if during the interviews the subjects try to restore their own capacity to act politically, in the end they downplay the reference to political struggle by placing the recognition of human rights on another, perhaps more naturalized, plane, thus neutralizing the potential political and social divisions surrounding the recognition of rights for LGBT people in a society where homophobia and transphobia are still a reality.

References

Basabe, O. (2014). "Relato documental en primera persona como sustento de reconstrucción del historia de la Argentina reciente". In L. Benadiba (ed.), *Otras memorias I : Testimonios para la transformación de la realidad*. Buenos Aires: Editorial Maipue, 19-40.

Bell, V. (1991). *Interrogating Incest: Feminism, Foucault and the Law*. London and New York: Routledge.

Crenzel, E. (2008). *La historia política del* Nunca Más. *La memoria de las desapariciones en la Argentina*. Buenos Aires: Siglo XXI Editores. (English translation: *Memory of the Argentina Disappearances: The Political History of* Nunca Más. London and New York: Routledge, 2011.)

Crenzel, E. (2015). "Toward a history of the memory of political violence and the disappeared in Argentina". In E. Allier-Montaño and E. Crenzel (eds.), *The struggle for memory in Latin America: Recent history and political violence.* Basingstoke: Palgrave, 15-33.

Cvetkovich, A. (2003). *An Archive of Feelings: Trauma, Sexuality, and Lesbian Public Culture.* Durham: Duke University Press.

Demaria, C. (2006). *Semiotica e memoria: Analisi del post-conflitto.* Rome: Carocci.

Demaria, C. (2017). "'Who Needs Identity?': Disappearances and Appearances in Argentina: The Abuelas de la Plaza de Mayo". In A. Sharman, M. Grass Kleiner, A. M. Lorusso, S. Savoini, (eds.) *MemoSur/MemoSouth: Memory, Commemoration and Trauma in Post-Dictatorship Argentina and Chile.* London: Critical, Cultural and Communications Press, 73-92.

Encarnación, O. (2016). *Out in the Periphery: Latin America's Gay Rights Revolution.* Oxford: Oxford University Press.

Foucault, M. (1976). *Histoire de la sexualité I: La volonté de savoir.* Paris: Gallimard.

Insausti, S. J. (2015). "Los cuatrocientos homosexuales desaparecidos: Memorias de la represión estatal a las sexualidades disidentes en Argentina". In D. D'Antonio (ed.), *Deseo y represión. Sexualidad, género y estado en la historia argentina reciente.* Buenos Aires: Imago Mundi, 63-82.

Kosofsky Sedgwick, E. (1990). *Epistemology of the Closet.* Los Angeles: University of California Press.

Lorusso, A. M. (2015). *Cultural Semiotics: For a Cultural Perspective.* Basingstoke: Palgrave.

Passerini, L. (1988). *Storia e soggettività: Le fonti orali, la memoria.* Scandicci: La nuova Italia.

Portelli, A. (1999). *L'ordine è già stato eseguito : Roma, le Fosse Ardeatine, la memoria.* Rome: Donzelli.

Radstone, S. (2007). *The Sexual Politics of Time: Confession, Nostalgia, Memory.* London and New York: Routledge.

Rapisardi, F., and Modarelli, A. (2002). *Fiestas, baños y exilios : Los gays porteños en la última dictadura.* Buenos Aires: Editorial Sudamericana.

Rogers, J. B. (2016). "The archive as confessional: The role of video testimony in understanding and remorse". *Journal of Human Rights Practice*, 8, 1, 45-61.

Violi, P. (2007). "Remembering the future: The construction of gendered identity and diversity in the Balkans". In C. Goh and B. J. McGuirk (eds.), *Happiness and Post-Conflict*. Nottingham: Critical, Cultural and Communications Press, 189-200.

Violi, P. (2014). *Paesaggi della memoria: Il trauma, lo spazio, la storia.* Milan: Bompiani.

Violi, P. (2017). "Disappearance, Mourning and the Politics of Memory". In A. Sharman, M. Grass Kleiner, A. M. Lorusso, S. Savoini (eds.), *MemoSur/MemoSouth: Memory, Commemoration and Trauma in Post-Dictatorship Argentina and Chile.* London: Critical, Cultural and Communications Press, 35-55.

Opposition to the Pinochet Regime:
Two Movies for Two Kinds of Memory

Anna Maria Lorusso

The object of this short essay will be two films, or rather, a television series and a cinema documentary, telling of the period of the Chilean dictatorship and in particular the activities of an institution that has tried to denounce the crimes and to support the victims: the Vicaría de la Solidaridad. The two texts which I refer to are *Los archivos del cardenal* (The Cardinal's Archives), a television series directed by Nicolás Acuña and Juan Ignacio Sabatini[1] and broadcast in 2011 on the national network Televisión Nacional de Chile, and *Habeas corpus*, made in 2015 and directed by Claudia Barril and Sebastián Moreno.

Of course, they are quite different texts, above all generically – a television series and a documentary made for cinema. The comparison of the two emerges spontaneously from the object that both texts, in a very focused and direct manner, confront. First, as I have stated, the Vicaría de la Solidaridad, an organ of the Catholic church, founded on 1 January 1976, under the guidance of Cardinal Raúl Silva Henríquez, which provided legal support (through lawyers) and social support (through social workers) to the victims of the dictatorship's crimes. Being a very prominent organ in the city of Santiago, and closely linked to the Church hierarchy, it enjoyed a special legitimacy that, therefore, made it difficult for the Pinochet regime (which still defended the values of the Church) to attack head on.

We can therefore say that, in a sense, the two films (hereafter, I shall often call them generically "films", with no difference in terms of genre, channel, etc.) recount "the same memory": that of an institution that carried out the very important work of denunciation, resistance, and support for victims of dictatorship. In so doing, they both refer to the same category: that of the archive – the TV series mentioning the archive in the title, the documentary in its development, both visually and verbally (I shall return to this point later). Indeed, one of the most important actions

---

[1] I shall take into account only the first season, that of 2011. In 2014, there was a second season, but it did not have the extraordinary success of the first. I shall not enter here into the reasons for the failure; I am simply interested in reflecting on the "phenomenon" which the first season of the series produced.

of the Vicaría was the work of recording, certifying and storing cases of violation of fundamental rights by the dictatorship. Moreover, both films focus on certain particularly serious cases: the two specific cases on which the documentary centres are those which constitute the subject of the first and last episodes of the series (the discovery of the remains of some missing persons in Lonquén, a town near to Isla de Maipo, where in 1973 fifteen men were arrested and disappeared, the discovery of the remains showing for the first time that the arrests had ended in extra-judicial killings; and the case of the Degollados [the Slit Throat Case], which consisted of the murders of three opposition members in 1985, one of whom was a Vicaría lawyer – the main character of the TV series).

There is no doubt, therefore, that there is substantial convergence in the subject-matter of the two films. However, we wonder if they are really recollecting the same memory. Indeed, perhaps it would seem more accurate to say that they refer to the same events, but with different memories, not because there are conflicting versions – on the contrary, they are quite convergent – but because we are faced with very different ways of remembering: a coherent memory in the case of the series versus a multifaceted and plurivocal memory in the case of the documentary; a narrative and "self-consistent" memory in the series versus an impressionistic and broken memory in the case of the documentary; a modelling memory in the series versus a memory in progress in the case of the documentary. The two films – so different from this point of view – seem to belong to two different cultural epochs, but we know that this is not the case because, as I said, only four years separate them, the series dating from 2011 (and maintaining the same characteristics in 2014) and the documentary from 2015. In the following pages, I shall try to reflect on and clarify with the help of semiotics the differences I have briefly mentioned above.

Fiction/Reality

What the two films put into play in very interesting (and different) ways is, first and foremost, the fiction/reality relationship. We could say, simply, that we have a complete mimesis in the first case and an entirely subjective relationship in the second case, but this is not the only issue at stake. Before making a few observations on this point, I shall give some brief descriptive notes on the two texts.

Los archivos del cardenal is developed along the lines of a detective series. The directors explicitly mention in interviews that they found a model in the American TV series *Law and Order*. Each episode, in fact (there are twelve in the first season), revolves around a case that is discovered by or reported to the Vicaría. The Vicaría, while lending solidarity to the victims involved, investigates and brings to light the violations of rights by the regime. Part of the Vicaría's intervention is a legal action, led by lawyers, to recognize the existence of an offence, whereas the regime wants to normalize and neutralize kidnappings and murders as cases of missing persons or accidental deaths, and as such not prosecutable.

While this legal and social work goes on, there are also several intimate love stories: the "senior" lawyer, who is the main character, is the husband of an anti-regime journalist who was at one point kidnapped and tortured. Their story is a story of resistance and struggle against the regime, together, but it is also a love story and family story. Indeed, also working in the Vicaría is their daughter, a social worker – a beautiful young girl who at the beginning of the story is engaged to a man who chooses the path of armed struggle and who gradually gets close to and falls in love with a young lawyer from Santiago high society. The lawyer has grown up in a powerful family close to the regime and who comes to understand the crimes of the dictatorship and begins working at the Vicaría alongside the "senior" lawyer. We find therefore a real love triangle (the girl with the two alternative models of man: the guerrilla and the more socially acceptable "good guy") which then leads to a happy love story (in which the guerrilla is the one who loses).

This blend of sentimental drama and detection is the main quality of the whole series, and certainly one of the reasons for its commercial success: we are faced with a pop product, albeit aimed at political denunciation (which does not spare us scenes of violence, torture and cruelty). The combination of its commercial quality and its account of the crimes of the dictatorship (perhaps never recounted so clearly to such a wide and general audience) has, indeed, produced side effects at the social and political level. For example, the president of the Renovación Nacional Party, Carlos Larrain, held an extended political committee meeting in La Moneda to express his party's anger at TVN for broadcasting *Los archivos del cardenal*.

What is interesting, though, and I shall return to it, is that throughout the series there is not a single archive image (despite the title *Los archivos del cardenal*): no traces, no documents, nothing from the "real" reality, even in the background of the television screens that sometimes appear. Everything is reconstructed, in some way, *à l'identique*, as if it were real, respecting – with the highest degree of fidelity – the actual characteristics of the facts, while remaining fiction.

Completely different is the case of *Habeas corpus*. The documentary is a sequence of witnesses. One by one, we listen to the various protagonists of the work at the Vicaría de la Solidaridad: lawyers, doctors, social workers, framed sitting, more or less half-length, against a homogeneous background. Each one speaks for a few minutes (and then maybe comes back later), releasing his testimony, telling what their work at the Vicaría was, giving the impression more of an I-I dialogue than of a I-him/her dialogue,[2] with someone asking questions; moments that seem self-conscious, recalling more than "depositions". Among the interviews, to interrupt the sequence, are two types of visual materials: documentary material (several archival files and documentary photographs of the time, some famous, such as the ones of the Estadio Nacional, others less so) and fictional reconstructions, short animations with toy figures, as pictured on the following page.

We could, therefore, simply say that the series is pure fiction, while the documentary is made of documents and testimony, but it is not only this. The thing that seems most interesting to me is the circuit and the *directionality* of the reality/fiction relationship. In the first case, the textual level – the filmic statement – is totally distinct from the plane of reality. As I said, there are no documentary images, all the characters have fictitious names; no media (TV, radio) are included to report reality (as is the case with other TV fictions that are certainly related to this, such as *Los 80*, another Chilean TV series broadcast in 2008). Each episode of the series refers to something real and totally recognizable to anyone who lived through those years, and the main characters work for an institution that really existed, although everything is transposed onto a fictional plane. The film, however, has such a mimetic force – in the setting, in the historical reconstruction of the facts and its protagonists, in the realism of the torture – and exerts it in such a new way (it is the first time one sees

---

[2] I am referring to Yuri Lotman's (1977) distinction between communication "systems I-I" and communication "systems I-he". The first are those that function to stabilize an identity; the second are those that create growth of information, and therefore cultural evolution.

these events with such completeness) as to elevate itself to the *status of document*, and with this "documental force" it returns to reality. We do not, therefore, have a fiction that mixes with reality (as very often happens in contemporary movies and documentaries), but a pure fiction that is so mimetic and so original (and, in this sense, so "foundational") as to become a reference, and in this sense a "document". The level of "referential performance" of *Los archivos* is very strong.

Furthermore, the paths through which the series "merges" with reality are (perhaps not surprisingly) numerous and cannot be neglected. *Los archivos del cardenal* is the core of a series of semiotic productions that together create the *reality effect* of the text. We are faced with the clear case of a "textual galaxy", in which to separate the actual text from the context of circulation and reaction to it would mean to amputate the meaning the text had in Chilean society.

Above all, the film is linked to a site that collects the real cases which the Vicaría worked on. Shortly after the broadcast, two journalists from the Universidad de Chile published a book (Insunza and Ortega 2011) which clearly explains the real cases to which the episodes of the series refer. In this way, real cases and fictional cases begin to go hand in hand, through the website and through the book (and after the completion of the series, the book + DVD box was sold as well). It is very illuminating to note the way in which the book presents the work. The goal of the book is "to reconstruct the real cases that inspired each chapter of the TV series, separating fiction from the facts using the tools of investigative journalism

[...]. So the public who followed the series will know the stories of the men and women who inspired the characters" (Insunza and Ortega 2011, 12-13). These cases were known by a few; the series introduced a dramatization of these events to a wider audience. The book is aimed at those who at the time were not born or have few memories.

The book, in fact, comes from the film. It was the film that set in motion the mechanism of shared consciousness. The two journalists want to separate reality and fiction, but to describe real cases to which they refer, at the beginning of each chapter, to an episode from the film. It is as if the cases themselves have neither readability nor interest for the readers. Before recollecting them, it is always necessary to specify in which episode of the fiction the specific case is. Thus we can say that it is not the fiction that refers to reality, but *the documentation that refers to fiction*.

Moreover, in no way negligible is the event constituted by the last episode. I do not speak in terms of "event" for nothing; the transmission of the last episode represented in fact a genuine shared happening, screened live in the most symbolic and institutional place of Chilean public memory: the Museo de la Memoria y los Derechos Humanos, where someone read out a letter from Estela Ortiz, widow of José Miguel Parada, one of the three actual victims of the macabre Casos Degollados (which is the substance of the last episode), and then, with the credits of the series still running, Manuel García (singer of the soundtrack from the series) with the musician Camilo Salinas and his father Oracio Salinas (director of Inti Illimani) sang "Déjame pasar la vida", the song that closed the series. Therefore, we find in this public event a real collective ritual of participation and *re-enactment*, in which the space (the "theatre" of memory *par excellence*), the text (the staging of memory *par excellence*), and the participants (in some cases directly and personally linked to those events) work together to create an effect of meaning that is anything but fictional, but rather is clearly a political action, in which the representation becomes a discourse in action, and the past of the film becomes the present in the collective ritual. Again, what happens goes from fiction to reality, and it is the reality that seems to "lean on", find inspiration in, fiction (the last episode of the series).

In our second text, *Habeas corpus*, in contrast, "reality" seems to be at the textual level; there is no separation between the level of historical events and the level of discourse on events. On the contrary: the events assume their force throughout the filmic discourse thanks to the density of witness accounts – which stage autobiographical experience, facts, actions, real people – and to the materiality of documents, represented insistently, almost like a visual leitmotif of the film.

The reality of experience and the evidence of the document, however, are not enough to saturate the filmic discourse on memory; on the contrary, they seem to suspend it, if not confuse it, bringing enunciation to silence (with long, empty sound breaks) or to fiction. It is the fictional element that especially attracts the viewer's attention in the film, representing a very strong heterogeneity with respect to all the efforts of *cinéma vérité*. The fictional scene with toy figures, with which the film opens, and which frequently returns (often just after a documentary image), clearly constitutes a suspension of realism, the impossibility of realism in memorial discourse, the unspeakable threshold in the language of reality (and it is no coincidence that these types of image are often placed at the most dramatic moments of the story). There is a constant transition from the document to fantasy.

Therefore, where the first film – certainly more simplistic, more Manichaean and more sentimental – may assume a representative force capable of competing with reality, the second film almost retreats from reality: in the face of its violence, it loses its discursive and expressive power. If in one case the spectator moves from fiction to reality, in the second the movement inscribed in the text seems the reverse: from reality to fiction, or at least to the suspension of realism.

Two Models of Memory

What *Los archivos del cardenal* offers is clearly a model: a memory model, a framework, a master narrative:

> For a trauma to emerge at the cultural level, it is necessary that a social group draw up a new master narrative, whose solidity outlines the reference framework for the enhancement of the trauma itself, in the present and in the future. (Cati 2013: 124)

Each episode has a precise pattern: it corresponds to a narrative unity in which a case emerges at the beginning that catalyses the energies of the characters working at the Vicaría, produces misery and violence (in each episode, there is in fact a moment of brutality – usually in the middle – in which the emotional involvement of the viewer reaches its peak), is intertwined with personal or family worries and inner conflicts, and eventually is resolved, not because it is cancelled but because it is denounced or taken care of. Each episode thus builds a self-contained micro-story, repeating the same pattern in all the other episodes. Overall the series follows a chronological line: it begins with a case from 1973-1975 and ends with a case from 1985, and between one episode and the next a clear evolutionary axis is developed (for example, the passage of the young social worker from one boyfriend to the other, from the guerrilla to the rich lawyer).

At the actantial and actorial level,[3] the dynamic is very stable and defined: the series selects four main protagonists from the Vicaría, the three members of the Pedregal family (the lawyer father, the journalist wife and the social worker daughter) plus the latest boyfriend of the daughter, Ramón Sarmiento. The instance of destination is embodied by the Church (called into question both as institution and as particular actors, such as a priest and a cardinal) and, at a more abstract level, by the ethical consciousness. The polemical axis multiplies the opposing actorial figures: the anti-subject is abstract and invisible (the Regime), but locally, in each episode, the series defines opponents who help the regime to do its job: the torturers, the informers, soldiers of various ranks, the silent connivance of civil society (which is characterized more by a non-doing than by an active doing, but which through its inaction protects the action of the dictatorship). The sanction is always clearly expressed, of course positive but always emotionally dramatic: the work of our players is a good thing, of course, but it is not given and does not end in peace; their work always faces much pain and sometimes fails to save the victims. Particularly significant from this point of view is the end of the first season of the series, based on the Degollados case, where the widow of one of the three victims screams her dissent and her despair.

In this way, the series depicts a highly stable and polarized narrative pattern: there are good people and bad people, defined roles and also defined spaces: the enclosed space of the family (which coincides with that of the Vicaría, with a significant overlap of the place of private solidarity and social solidarity), the dangerous space of the streets, the hidden though common spaces (thus disguised) of torture.

In short, in this series we have memory presenting *exempla*: the cardinal's archives, the archives of the Vicaría, show not only a long string of crimes, but also a long series of counter-measures, the work of those who have risked their lives to oppose the regime. The archive (in the series) is not made of documents but is made of examples. And the exempla, as we know, can be placed in an a-chronic time, are valid forever, have

---

[3] I am referring to the semiotic narrative theory of Greimas (1970).

pragmatic features (relevant endeavours) and ethical and passionate features, which are also conceivable in other contexts. This is why the story of the series is able to offer a model: a script for dictatorship and resistance.

Habeas corpus stages a completely different memory. First of all, we have a plurality of enunciations, with many voices involved in constructing the framework. The entries do not build, do not follow and do not converge on a clear timeline; progressing by leaps, by specific topics, the linearity of the story is further broken by the insertion of documentary images and fictional images which I have already mentioned. In this case, the archive is both visually represented (the files that are framed are those that were used to make up the archive) and verbally represented (some witnesses say explicitly that one of the main actions of the Vicaría involved, from the outset, building up documentation of the crimes of the dictatorship, taking note of all the reports which the relatives of the victims or the victims themselves produced).

Thus the archive in *Habeas corpus* is *work*, and a cognitive work, not a repository. The movie poster summarizes these elements: a desk, a typewriter (a symbolic picture that comes back very often in the film), a phone, some tracking photos.

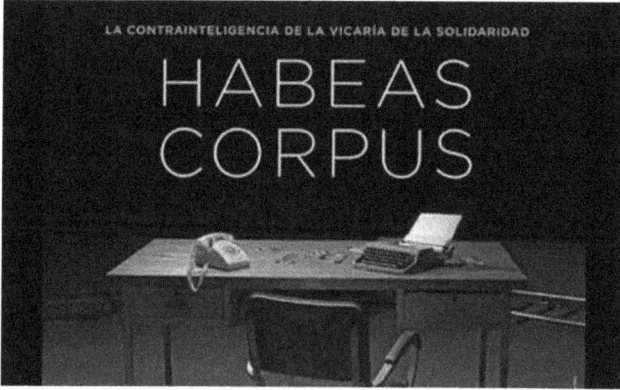

The truth that this archival work builds is not the truth of the criminal detection (made up of investigations, actual actions, raids, interventions), but the truth of lived experience: a testimony truth that is a personal memory. And just as in archival work, the documentary depicts the maximum of fictionalization: current witnesses, on the set of the film, type out the cards of the Vicaría archives, as if today were the past, as if the movie set were the space of the Vicaría. In common, in fact, only the agents: the witnesses are the real workers of the Vicaría.

Faced with this personal memory, the space-time coordinates fade: the stories seem given in an abstract and symbolic space, as in the poster: the time of enunciation (of the witnesses) is intermittent and broken, the enunciation (which witnesses produce) moved to a distant past. We do not have here, however, the timelessness of the "modelling memory" of *Los archivos*; here we find rather a suspended temporality. We do not have the reduction of events to a scheme, such that the pattern can be abstracted from the space-time in which it is given and moved to other contexts. We find, on the contrary, the suspension of all schemes, a "fog effect" in which there is no linear narrative progress, and there are no precise actors, no defined spaces, no precise sanctions.

If *Los archivos* offers us endeavours, *Habeas corpus* provides us with an intense work, with no end and no beginning, an intense activity that – with that typewriter – can go on forever and ever. If *Los archivos* reveals *the episodes* of memory, the other shows rather *its procedures*. One recounts the memory, the other the making of memory. Almost paradoxically, then, it is *Los archivos* – pop production of popular TV – which cuts deep into Chilean culture, down to the political level, rather than *Habeas corpus*. If the archive, according to Foucault (1969), has a regulatory nature, functional in determining the standards by which the community carves out its knowledge about the past, the series can very well determine this canon, becoming a reference script for Chilean public memory.

Reworking (freely) the suggestions by Aleida Assmann (2010), who opposes the category of *canon* to that of *archive*, we could say that the fiction offers a real canon, selecting items, articulating them in a strong narrative and offering them as a model for subsequent readings of the past. Conversely, the documentary proceeds by accumulation, organizes its sequences by themes rather than by narrative patterns, does not offer an orderly model: provides a sum (an archive) of testimonies and documents.

The canon of *Los archivos* is a canon that refers to the real and returns to the real, as we have seen; it knows how and wants to represent it. It believes in the *referential efficacy of fiction*. The *Habeas corpus* archive, conversely, does not know how and does not claim to represent realistically the real. Each witness proceeds solipsistically through his/her memories, metaphorically at his/her desk. Experience and documentation lead to imagination (as what I call toy figures show well). In the first case, we find a realism that I would define as "dramatic realism", while in the second case we find what Rothberg (2002) calls "traumatic realism": a non-representational and non-referential account, which distrusts the possibilities of the "representation of reality".

Unlike Assmann, however, I would not say that the canon of *Los archivos* presents "the past as present", while the *Habeas corpus* archive presents "the past as past". As I said before, in the first case we find a past out of time, an *exempla* gallery that leads to an idea of *historia magistra vitae*. In the second, we find a past rooted in time, a distant time, the subjective time of remembrance that is faced with the limits of speakability, and thus comes to fictional scenes where history, life, days are not present: *not out of time but in the absence of time*, not a gallery of *exempla* but the repetition of some fixed scenes, not *historia magistra vitae* but history as mental experience.

If we were to represent the semantic system that is built around the present/past opposition according to the so-called semiotic square, we would say that the discourse of *Los archivos* has to do realistically with something *not present*, that could happen again; the discourse of *Habeas corpus* has to do with something *not past*, which could continue, at least in the mental and fictional space that is the home of the toy figures or the desk out of time.

Dimension of time

Present	vs	**Past**
Traumatic realism		*Mimetic realism*
Not Past		**Not Present**

Dimension of atemporality

Both texts therefore make memory-building timeless, albeit in one case with a modelling function, and in the other case with an introspective function. In the one case, we are at a tangent to the parable; in the other, to personal recollection: two highly predictable risks, "easy" risks, when memory is still unstable and far from being history.

References

Assmann, A. (2010). "Canon and archive". In A. Erll and A. Nünning (eds.), *A Companion to Cultural Memory Studies*. Berlin and New York: de Gruyter.

Barrios, L. A., and Mateso-Pérez, J. (2015). "Ficción televisiva e historia reciente: El caso de *Los archivos del cardinal*". Paper presented at the XI Jornadas de Sociología de la Universidad de Chile, available online at **http://jornadasdesociologia2015.sociales.uba.ar/wp-content/uploads/ponencias/276.pdf**

Cárdenas, C. (2012). "¿Cómo es representado el pasado reciente chileno en dos modos semióticos?: Reconstrucción de la memoria en *Historia del siglo XX chileno y Los archivos del cardinal*". *Revista Comunicación*, 10, 1, 653-665.

Cati, A. (2013). *Immagini della memoria: Teorie e pratiche del ricordo tra testimonianza, genealogia, documentari*. Milan: Mimesis.

Demaria, C. (2012). *Il trauma, l'archivio, il testimone*. Bologna: Bononia University Press.

Foucault, M. (1969). *L'archéologie du savoir*. Paris: Gallimard.

Greimas, A. J. (1987). *On meaning*. Minneapolis: University of Minnesota Press.

Insunza, A., and Ortega, J. (2011). *Los archivos del cardenal: Casos reales*. Santiago de Chile: Catalonia.

Lotman, Y. (1977). "The dynamic model of a semiotic system". *Semiotica*, 21, 3/4, 193–210.

Palacios, J. M. (2012). "Archivos sin archivo: Sobre el acontecimiento histórico y la imagen de lo real en *Los archivos del Cardenal*". *La Fuga*, 14.

Rothberg, M. (2000). *Traumatic Realism: The Demands of Holocaust Representation*. Minneapolis: University of Minnesota Press.

On the Use and Abuse of History in Post-Dictatorship Argentine Documentary

Adam Sharman

> And even if they themselves are late-born
> – there is a way of living which will make
> them forget it – coming generations will
> know them only as first-born.
>
> Friedrich Nietzsche

Even if we have our suspicions that "memory" will one day become "history", that is, that history is the written record of distant events that were once the stuff of memory, and thus that history and memory have more in common than some are inclined to believe, it is clear that the attention paid to memory in recent times represents a challenge to the notion of history as guardian of the past. Indeed, for some the challenge has been redoubled by "postmemory". Postmemory would seem to be the phenomenon whereby a later generation half-recognizes as another's and half-remembers as its own the experiences of an earlier generation, such that the later generation's connection to the past is mediated by "imaginative investment, projection, and creation" (Hirsch 2012, 5). In post-dictatorship Argentine documentary film-making, postmemory is said to mark a younger generation's "radical break" (Andermann 2012) from an older generation's conventional view of history (and film).[1] The question this study will address is thus simply: is there such a radical generational break in Argentine documentary film?[2] I shall ground my inquiry in an analysis of two films that have a certain "exemplary" status as respective representatives of two kinds, and two generations, of documentary film. Both films deal with the "generation" (their word) of the armed revolutionary groups of the 1970s. The films are David Blaustein's *Cazadores de utopías* (Utopia Hunters) (1995), a "classical" documentary (Ranzani 2016) by the generation of the *guerrilla*, and

---

[1] Hirsch (2012, 6) says that postmemory "reflects an uneasy oscillation between continuity and rupture".

[2] This essay would not have been possible without the generous material and intellectual support of Guillermo Olivera and, above all, Ximena Triquell.

Nicolás Prividera's *M* (2007), a "postmemory" documentary (Andermann 2012) by the generation of the sons and daughters of the armed revolutionaries.

In the two films, personal memory provides the counterpoint to official history. Memory is the testimony of a past existence violently repressed and subsequently subjected to repressive erasure and/or prescriptive forgetting (Connerton 2008). The memory in question is not just individual, but collective. The films record a certain collective memory of the past and are themselves the means to transmit it to new generations, to those who do not remember as such a past they never lived.[3] If the films record the unpleasant truths and suppressed details from the rest of history, they nonetheless exhibit the "liturgical", conservative dimension of remembrance, that is, memory as the ritualistic transmission to future generations of the exemplary path of a (in this case, threatened) group.[4] It is a memory more traditional than *istoria* itself. My point, however, will be that this memory appears not only in Blaustein, where one might expect it, but in Prividera too. *Contra* Borges, the elders create (the memory of) their sequels.

Where one might therefore expect a real difference to open up between the films is in their view of history (their conception of the nature of history, not just their view of the history of the period). For instance, the classical *Cazadores de utopías* gives off a strong "historical sense", the belief, criticized though not dismissed by Nietzsche (if the generational

---

[3] Recalling Plato's distinction between *anamnesis* and *mneme*, Yosef Hayim Yerushalmi (1996, 109, 110) notes that to speak of "a people" remembering a past it never lived is really to say "that a past has been actively transmitted to a present generation" through collective memory. Thus is forged "the *mneme* of the group, the continuum of its memory, which is that of the links in a chain and not that of a silken thread".

[4] According to Yerushalmi, Jewish memory was based on the liturgical transmission of near-mythical events from the Jewish past, the historical detail and accuracy of which were unimportant, since "only those moments out of the past are transmitted that are felt to be formative or exemplary for the *halakhah* [the Hebrew term for path or way] of a people as it is lived in the present; the rest of 'history' falls, one might almost say literally, by the 'wayside'" (113). In contrast, it was modern, critical history ("the faith of fallen Jews") that challenged collective memory, reminding it of unpleasant truths and suppressed details. Yerushalmi's scheme is itself traditional, as history alone (not art, science or documentary film) is critical.

attack on history is "postmodern", it is, before that, irresistibly Nietzschean), that a culture is the inexorable product of history.[5] But even in the much less conventional *M*, "postmemory" is accompanied by an insistent rationalist historicism that paws at the door of the nation. If memory underpins history (no historian could get under way without the basic neurological capacity to remember), it is doubtless less intuitive that history should in any way underpin memory. But that is what Prividera's film, perhaps despite itself, invites us to contemplate.

History Remembered

> One goes so far, indeed, as to believe that he to whom a moment of the past *means nothing at all* is the proper man to describe it.
>
> Nietzsche

"La recuperación de nuestra memoria no podría ser desapasionada ni imparcial" (The recovery of our memory could be neither dispassionate nor impartial). Echoing another beginning, that of *La hora de los hornos*, by those other utopians, Solanas and Getino, David Blaustein's *Cazadores de utopías* (1995) begins with the above epigraph, to the sound of rousing music.[6] Followed by a clip of Evita denouncing "foreign capitalism" and by contrived images of military boots on the march, the film announces that the memory that has been trodden under foot, and that is therefore in need of "recuperation", is that of the "utopia hunters", or the Peronist revolutionary left of the 1970s. This is Blaustein's generation (he was born in 1953). One can imagine a different epigraph: "The recovery of our

---

[5] For Nietzsche (2001, 64), no one would ever do anything of note without the capacity to shrug off the weight of history. But in such forgetting, i.e. the unhistorical, there is necessarily violence: "the unhistorical [...] is the condition in which one is the least capable of being just; narrow-minded, ungrateful to the past, blind to dangers, deaf to warnings, one is a little living vortex of life in a dead sea of darkness and oblivion: and yet this condition – unhistorical, anti-historical through and through – is the womb not only of the unjust but of every just deed too".

[6] See Sonderéguer (2001) for critical responses to *Cazadores* on its release.

history could be neither..." But instead we have *memory*. Where "history" might suggest a residual attachment to official discourse, "memory" announces synecdochically the alternative domain of the witness, more especially of the defeated witness, which is to be granted a dignity at the time denied it by the Argentine state. One of the overriding emotions in *Cazadores* is the simple wish that the story of a "generation" not be so utterly neglected. Some of those interviewed want their experience to be affirmed as a model for the future; many more just want it to be told.[7] In the telling of memory, primacy is not accorded to the classical historian, who claims objective knowledge on the basis of a position external to events, but to the witness, who affirms a truth borne of personal experience and who links it to justice.[8] The recovery of memory, then, has necessarily to be passionate and partial; and its resolution into a phenomenon of knowledge, unendingly problematic.[9]

[7] Blaustein (in Ranzani 2016) says the film was the result of a generational unease at being treated like nobodies during the Menem years (*el ninguneo de los años de Menem*; the verb *ningunear* means to ignore, ostracize, look down on, treat like dirt; *ninguno* means no one, nobody), which seemed to be "condemning the history of our generation to a story of clandestinity and sewers [*cloaca*]. [...] It is the result of a collective feeling that the story [*historia*] of a generation needed to be told". For Beatriz Sarlo (1997), the armed struggle of the period was a generational matter only up to a point. If the politics of the 1970s required youth (robust, unattached, confident enough of their first steps in the adult world to believe themselves right to destroy it), the "juvenilism" on display was "cultural", fatally flawed by a belief in the messianism of Perón. In other words, it was not necessary to be young to be caught up in a youthful politics.

[8] For Nietzsche (2001, 91), objective history is "the silent work of the dramatist", who himself establishes the unity of the plan in the material: "thus [man] gives expression to his artistic drive – but not to his drive towards truth or justice. Objectivity and justice have nothing to do with one another". He cites Grillparzer: "'What is history but the way in which the spirit of man [...] substitutes something comprehensible for what is incomprehensible; imposes his concept of purpose from without upon a whole which, if it possesses a purpose, does so only inherently; and assumes the operation of chance where a thousand little causes have been at work. All human beings have at the same time their own individual necessity, so that millions of courses run parallel beside one another in straight or crooked lines, frustrate or advance one another, strive forwards or backwards, and thus assume for one another the character of chance.'"

[9] "A historical phenomenon, known clearly and completely and resolved into a phenomenon of knowledge, is, for the person who has recognized it, dead" (Nietzsche 2001, 67).

And yet, despite the film's wager on memory and its moving arrangement of memories, *Cazadores* is not antithetical to a traditional view of history. Individual memories are ordered into something resembling a classical historical narrative; here, a reasoned explanation of the actions of the Peronist armed left. The history runs as follows: (1) the need for violence at that moment in history; (2) the *Cordobazo* as the union of workers and students, and the proof that violence was timely; (3) the rise of Third Worldism, indicating that guerrilla militancy chimed with a larger uprising of the oppressed; (4) Perón's blessing of violence; (5) Perón's volte-face regarding guerrilla insurgency, and the attempt by López Rega, and then the Junta, to destroy the revolutionary left. The film ends its history with recollections of torture and of the pursuit by the state of the pursuers of utopia.[10] Memory in the film is closely linked to a desire for historical explanation, an explanation offered from what Blaustein, interviewed on the re-screening of the film in 2016, describes as the perspective of the national-popular movement (Ranzani 2016).[11] If that explanation can be called "Peronist" (there is a moment in the film where Martín Caparrós speaks of Peronism, not as a simple subject, but as the name of a certain collective sentiment), in another sense it can also be called "conventional". History, the film suggests, can be known and explained without too much difficulty. In that same later interview, Blaustein says that he asked his interlocutors in the film not to tell the story from the present (to wit: with all the difficulties posed by historical perspective): "No me cuentes la posmodernidad de Fukuyama [...] necesito reconstruir desde aquel presente, no desde la tontería desde el ahora" (Don't give me Fukuyama's postmodernity [...] I need to reconstruct things from the present of that time, not from the stupid idea of the now).

However, despite its form "giving the impression of a single,

---

[10] Andrés Di Tella's documentary, *Montoneros – una historia* (1994; first shown in 1998), uses a story about one *Montonera* to tell a history of the *Montoneros* as a whole. The film gives a potted history almost identical to that found in *Cazadores* and its historiographical function is further signalled by the appearance of a real historian, Roberto Baschetti. More so than *Cazadores*, it amasses strange recollections of conflicting emotions, such that the exemplary path to follow is much harder to discern.

[11] Jens Andermann (2012, 111) reproduces Gonzalo Aguilar's findings that the memories in question are those of a narrow tranche of the Peronist movement.

homogeneous discourse without contradictions" (Andermann 2012, 110), the film contains much that is not linear, objective history, reflections that betray mixed emotions and confused loyalties. It has the critical function Yerushalmi reserves for modern historiography. The foreign viewer, in particular, cannot easily read off the critical function. Unique, singular experiences are codified in a language, Argentine Spanish, which one will not be certain of having understood. Thus, a former guerrilla describes the group's sense of being the "exclusive owners of violence" and of feeling that, with Cámpora-Perón's victory in 1974, the country's future direction was theirs to determine. A trade unionist recalls how some of his number supported the Triple A in its pursuit of the guerrillas. Unwittingly exemplifying O'Donnell's (2002) seminal thesis on the mass praetorianism of Argentine politics and society, a former fighter speaks of the guerrillas sharing a view widely held by the population as a whole: anyone in the Casa Rosada (i.e. the Presidency) apart from "that woman" (meaning, Isabel Perón).

In addition to telling the story of part of a generation, the recollections of experience serve another purpose in *Cazadores*. They are organized in order to preserve "our memory" as legacy. "Vamos a generar compañeros" (We're going to generate compañeros), one speaker says. As we have seen, *Cazadores'* group memory, such as it is, is not medieval-Jewish: the film has a resolutely non-hierarchical attitude towards its subjects, and accurate historical detail matters, including the detail of unflattering contradictions. Nevertheless, its ending has a liturgical quality. An earlier speaker remarks that, while they might want to alter some of the things they did in order to put right certain mistakes, he would not change the "voluntad de transformación", the will to change things. The final voices are less equivocal. One speaks of the invalidity of the "theory of the two demons" that rose to prominence as a way of explaining the period (the idea that there was a moral equivalence between two equally demonic forces, the state and the *guerrilla*, with everyone else as innocent victim).[12] The other demon, he says (the one opposed to the state), is called "need, equality, law, education, health – [...] it's in those kids in the shanty towns who can't study". It is a poignant refusal of the theory's lazy logic.[13] A former guerrilla reflects that his moment of "protagonism" was in his

---

[12] See Crenzel (2014) for the theory of the two demons, whose existence *qua* theory owes more than a little to the fact that commentators refer to it as such.

[13] Blaustein (in Ranzani 2016) says *Cazadores* was a critical response to the theory.

youth and that it now falls to others. "We gambled with the possibility of happiness," he says, as Serrat's "La Montonera" plays over the top, "and now I'm never going to be entirely happy ever; but I think it was worth it". A woman says that they were looking for "a better world"; others (by no means all; some prefer to speak of the "costs") invoke the key word of the film's title: "utopia". But "utopia" and "a better world" are not the same thing: utopia may be a better world, but a better world does not have to be a utopia. As the earlier speaker says, they wanted the kids from the shanty towns to have an education. No utopia here. And yet the man who never mentions utopia utters the utopian "and now I'm never going to be entirely happy ever". Here the critical function divides. Either its object is the man's naïveté – as though revolution *could have* made him eternally happy (no betrayals, no disappointments, no unhappy sacrifices under the "patria socialista") – or, liturgy and legacy duly accepted, its object is the system that prevents the search for utopia. The latter is monumental memory: necessarily recalling the shared ideals of the great battles of the past, while deceiving by analogies.[14]

The Book of History

—You don't remember anything, do you?
—No.
Nicolás Prividera, *M*

A decade on from the first documentary, Argentina has experienced the epoch-defining 2001 crash, a new government has mobilized the state in matters of memory, intellectuals from the generation of the armed revolutionary groups have opened up the debate on their responsibility for what happened in the 1970s, and the children of the *guerrilla* are behind the camera, one product of which is Nicolás Prividera's *M* (2007) (Prividera was born in 1970).[15] I choose *M* for two reasons: first, because

[14] "How violently what is individual in [the past] would have to be forced into a universal mould and all its sharp corners and hard outlines broken up in the interest of conformity! [...] Monumental history deceives by analogies" (Nietzsche 2001, 69-71).
[15] The key collection on the intellectuals' debate, which dates back to 2004, is del Barco *et al.* (2014). Some of the essays have appeared in translation in the *Journal of Latin American Cultural Studies*, 16, 2, 2007.

of Prividera's importance as a theorist of the new cinema (his meditations gathered together in *El país del cine*), and, second, because of the film's reputation as an instance of "postmemory documentary" (Andermann 2012, 115).

In his excellent study of Argentine cinema, Jens Andermann (2012, 95) traces the emergence of a new type of documentary in which, in Michael Renov's words, "the representation of the historical world is inextricably bound up with self-inscription". Documentary continues to represent history but draws attention to and dramatizes the difficulties posed by any one individual's limited perspective on the world. According to Andermann (2012, 95, 107), Renov associates this shift

> with the shattering of classical-modern documentary's epistemological framework drawn from the social sciences, and based on a belief in the transparency and capacity of optical devices to capture and render "the other" in an objective, unbiased and self-contained fashion. [...] A shift in representations has occurred from the establishing of (juridical, political) truth to its implications in and for the present; that is, a displacement from historical reconstruction to the act of remembrance, however entangled the one still remains with the other.

It is a generational story:

> a radical break has appeared between the "survivors" tales of the generation of 1960s and 1970s political activists and the "secondary witnessing" or "postmemory" of their children who, at the time of their parents' exile, abduction and assassination, were still in their early infancy and childhood. Postmemory, in Marianne Hirsch's influential formulation, is by no means a state of oblivion "after" or "beyond" memory. Rather, it is particular in that its relation with the object of commemoration – here, the struggles of the 1970s and their violent repression – "is mediated not through recollection but through an imaginative investment and creation". (Andermann 2012, 107)

Like *Cazadores*, Prividera's *M* has recollections from the generation of the *guerrilla*; unlike the earlier film, *M* quite literally turns the camera round to concentrate also on the director, that is, on the younger generation's reception of memories that are not its own but that now become its own. Prividera does not receive these memories as a gift handed down intact, but rather sifts, filters and criticizes them. *M* belongs to the genre of documentary investigation – with its 'phone calls, archive visits, and visits to neighbours, contacts and organizations all sustained by Prividera's sharp, at times barbed, commentary. The film is about the investigation as much as it is about the thing being investigated (his mother's disappearance). However, among the shards of memory, the photographs and the home movies, there is a strange reversal, of which one cannot be sure Prividera himself is aware. For unlike the earlier documentary, here it is the *vox populi* of the older generation that ventures an unusual view of history, while the director falls back on the conventional view.

The history of the period is subordinated in the film to the incomplete story of Prividera's mother, who had probably been involved in guerrilla activities. Prividera criticizes the state for failing to take responsibility (his two principal themes are truth and responsibility) for coordinating the efforts to trace the disappeared. Standing in CONADEP, in the Ministry of Justice, he laments the fact that individuals have to bring their little piece of the puzzle (*rompecabezas*) to the table, rather than the state put it together. His watchword is *cruce* (cross, crossing, intersections). There is no cross-referencing, no cross-checking, no joining the dots to establish the truth (is there a "cruce de datos?" [a database]; "si el cruce no está, es imposible" [if there's no cross-checking, there's no chance]). "No hay plano completo de cómo funcionó" (there's no plan of how the whole thing worked), he laments, everything is "muy parcializado" (very fragmented). For entirely understandable reasons (he wants to know what became of his mother, not what the meaning of history is), at this point his view of truth is simple enough: if anyone could be bothered to put all the pieces of the jigsaw puzzle together, the result would be the truth of what happened to his mother, Marta Sierra (the "M" of the title). For the director's younger brother, Guido, the whole business is complicated; for the director, who cuts across him, it is not difficult.

It is not difficult for the older Prividera, because he has a classical view of truth, responsibility and justice: we uncover the truth, they take responsibility, and justice is done. Of these, the key is truth. And it is not a difficult truth, since it could be learned in a history class. How come, he laments, the younger generation knows nothing about its country's history? And, later, talking to an older couple who had been ardent

Peronist militants: don't you think history could have been different if you'd grasped the significance of the Chile coup of 1973? Didn't people know or talk about the Chilean *desaparecidos* or know anything about what had happened in Uruguay? Later still, he has an encounter, to which we are not privy, with one of the leaders of the Juventud Peronista at the time of his mother's militancy. The encounter has sent a shiver down his spine (the man has told Prividera that his mother had "bad luck": "Mala suerte!", he keeps on repeating, disbelievingly, "As if she'd had an accident. As if she'd been struck by lightning"). Andermann (2012, 119-120) discusses the scene at length. Prividera "explicates his and [Albertina] Carri's *political* critique of the survivor generation, while staging in the refracted composition of the shot their impossibility of constructing a stable place of enunciation".[16] Both directors, he argues, are aware of the charges of subjectivity and self-righteousness, but "they counter-attack by exposing – [...] through an aggressive, confrontational interview style, in *M* – the generational abyss motivating these charges". Andermann quotes extensively from Prividera's account of the encounter: the Peronist leader's view that they "fucked up", but that to engage in self-criticism now is to play into the hands of the Right; Prividera's view that "being on the Left is to be self-critical. If you're not self-critical, if you're not critical, you're on the Right"; the man's response, that "you're very subjective in your search".

But Andermann stops short of citing what Prividera says next, which is this: "Es increíble como nadie vio eso. O nadie quiso ver" (It's incredible how no one saw this. Or no one wanted to see it). Prividera continues, facetiously rehearsing the clichéd explanations: "Los vientos de la Historia? Ceguera? Ingenuidad? Estupidez? Un poco de todo" (The winds of History? Blindness? Ingenuousness? Stupidity? A bit of everything). Earlier in the film, he was left almost as apoplectic by one of his mother's collaborators, who, now suffering from cancer, tells him she has been told not to speak of things that will harm her recovery (in fact, she does take part in the film). You can't just say it's a private matter, they were adults, he rails: "tenían uso de la razón" (they had the use of reason). *M* may exhibit the tics and traits of postmemory documentary (the hand-held camera, the absence of a narrator, the absence of music, attention to the

---

[16] Andermann yokes together Albertina Carri, most well known for her lightning-rod documentary *Los rubios* (2003), and Prividera as the flagbearers of "postmemory" documentary.

seemingly insignificant, an apparent scriptless, aleatory quality), but Prividera's stance is a rationalist teleological one. This explains the film's self-righteousness. Why didn't you know? And why didn't you do anything about the situation? *Contra* Nietzsche (2001, 76), for whom life's judgement is always unjust, "because it has never proceeded out of a pure well of knowledge", Prividera's judgement is the righteous stance of the one who knows how the story ended ("It wasn't difficult") and who cannot understand why rational people did not prevent it from happening. Andermann cites an essay by the director published before the release of *M*, arguing that Prividera "goes further in his critique of first-generation memory, reclaiming for his own generation's critique of testimonial discourse the task of recovering historical experience". To which one can only respond: "And even if they themselves are late-born – there is a way of living which will make them forget it – coming generations will know them only as first-born."[17] Prividera, filtered by Andermann: "'The testimonies accumulate – he writes – without helping us to understand better. For some time now, they have ceased to be cathartic [...]. Their multiplication (outside the juridical field) has generated an effect of saturation: a meaningless thicket of experiences of suffering." There are too many memories but a lack of history, he asserts, in the sense of imposing meaning through the construction of critical distance towards the immediacy of experience: 'How can we write the rest of H/history?'"[18]

Yet that is not the end of the generational saga, in which the late-born get to sift through, *but also to order*, the rest, the remainder, the remains

---

[17] Nietzsche (2001, 76): "since we are the outcome of earlier generations, we are also the outcome of their aberrations, passions and errors, and indeed of their crimes; it is not possible wholly to free oneself from this chain. If we condemn these aberrations and regard ourselves as free of them, this does not alter the fact that we originate in them. The best we can do is to [...] implant in ourselves a new habit, a new instinct, a second nature, so that our first nature withers away. It is an attempt to give oneself, as it were *a posteriori*, a past in which one would like to originate in opposition to that in which one did originate: – always a dangerous attempt [...]. But here and there a victory is nonetheless achieved, and for the combatants, for those who employ critical history for the sake of life, there is even a noteworthy consolation: that of knowing that this first nature was once a second nature and that every victorious second nature will become a first".

[18] Prividera's essay is called "Restos" (in *El Ojo Mocho* 20 [2006], p.44). *Restos* means "rest", "remainder" but also "remains" (as in mortal remains). Part two of *M* is called *Los restos de la historia* (*The Remains of History*).

of history.[19] Things turn out, after all, to be difficult. For *M* has another view of truth, which is to say, of history. This other view comes from the older generation. The second half of the film features encounters with people who worked alongside Prividera's mother either at the INTA (the National Institute of Agricultural Technology) or at the adult literacy school. If Prividera's view of truth and history is largely objectivist-teleological, the edited snippets from interviewees hint at a different, discontinuous, relativist view of history. "You see things as they are in a book," one woman says to him, "but history isn't linear"; "it's never total" (*nunca es algo total*). The Peronist couple quizzed about their knowledge (in effect, their ignorance) of the bigger Southern Cone picture of the early 1970s respond to his charge: of course we made mistakes, the woman says, and, yes, we can see that thirty years on; but back then we couldn't..."

M is not a philosophical treatise, so let us not open up a philosophical discussion on situatedness, the circumscription of the human subject by the material and symbolic order that surrounds it. I wish simply to note the coincidence between these witnesses' insights and a perspectivist philosophical view of truth and history (Nietzsche [2001, 101]: "The human race is a tough and persistent thing and will not permit its progress – forwards or backwards – to be viewed [...] as a whole *at all* by that infinitesimal atom, the individual man"). Another woman (it is always the women) says that at moments of terror you don't know who will betray you – anyone could have betrayed your mother; "there are 20,000 conclusions". She does not, I think, mean by this that there is no truth (she says she is more cynical than him and needs only to look into people's eyes to know); she is merely warning against the dangers, despite her own confidence in being able to read people's faces, of taking things at face value: of imagining, for instance (I am extrapolating from her words), that declared political alignments map neatly onto people's actions (it couldn't have been him, he was a Peronist...). At times of terror, you see the worst of humanity, she says. In other words: the only thing that gets in the way of history, truth and memory is people.

---

[19] Section two of Prividera's *El país del cine* makes the history of Argentine film into a generational *family* saga.

Conclusion

M ends on an inconclusive, aleatory note, with images of Prividera's mother from fragments of home movies intercut with images of the director wandering around, agitated and aimless. But this is not before the film has effected a conclusion of sorts. Part of the epilogue takes us to a ceremony at the INTA at which a plaque to Prividera's mother and others is being unveiled. The camera shows us the inscription: "En memoria a Marta Sierra [...] y a todos los compañeros de INTA encarcelados, desaparecidos y cesanteados, reinvindicamos [sic] la lucha de antes, apoyamos la de ahora, acordamos con la futura [...] Nunca más!" (In memory of Marta Sierra [...] and of all the imprisoned, disappeared or laid off INTA compañeros, we sallute [sic] the past struggle, support the current fight, agree with the future one [...] Never again!] Complete with spelling mistake, which adds poignancy, as if it were needed, the monument is the (necessarily) formulaic commemoration of a life and the no less formulaic transmission of a legacy to the future. The memorial pledges future generations to an unknown future struggle, and appears to be a case of the older generation laying down the law to future ones. *Cazadores*, too, does its share of liturgical legacy-making, using and abusing the word "generation" – part accurate descriptor, part strategic mask of differences within. More surprisingly, after all it has said about its members, *M* receives and seems to want to transmit the older generation's legacy. Prividera leans on the formulaic, but not for all that less heartfelt "what might have been" commonplace. Had his mother and "an entire disappeared generation" lived, he says, another life was possible, as was another nation. The statement must remain a truism, as, in light of his criticisms of the older generation's failure to learn the lessons of history, it is unclear what the otherness of that other life, and of that other nation, would have looked like.

Both films are also commemorations of lives. They record memories, before memory passes into history and history is the only one left to remember. Even if, in the case of *M*, the institutional moment has changed (a Government minister responsible for the INTA, and thus directly or indirectly for Prividera's mother's disappearance, is going on trial as the film opens), both films preserve memory as a defence against the evisceration of a life. On one level, then, in neither case can film, as the memory of memory, give up on the traditional history-function, with its attendant values of reason, truth, objectivity. What both films show is that the older generation has an empirical, objectivist view of history *when it is a matter of concrete lives and events*. The older generation knows all too well what happened to the Marta Sierras; it is just that they do not want to, and in many cases cannot, open up a forensic inquiry into what happened. Some are traumatized by having lived the moment, by their responsibility for what happened – and now by being asked, on camera, to recollect. Prividera, from a younger generation, shares this view of history and truth: he simply wants to know what happened to his mother, and he knows someone will have denounced her, someone will have picked her up and someone will have killed her. Memory, history, history, memory: it is a question of truth and justice. On another level, however, *when it is a matter of large historical conjunctures*, at least one member of the younger generation (Prividera) harbours a naïve objectivist historicism, while the older generation has an alternative view of history. Perhaps because the older generation lived the moment without the historical sense. That is to say, members of the generation of the *guerrilla* do not fail, on camera, now, to recollect the moment objectively out of weakness or stupidity, but rather because the historical phenomenon was never *at the time* lived as a simple phenomenon of knowledge, laid out in an instantly graspable, albeit dead, simultaneity. In this instance, it is uncertain that the radicality belongs to postmemory.

References

Andermann, J. (2012). *New Argentine Cinema*. London: I. B. Tauris.

Blaustein, D. (1995). *Cazadores de utopías*. Audiovisual production. At **www.youtube.com/watch?v=7vRydH_dAvY.**

Carri, A. (2005). *Los rubios*. Audiovisual production. SBP.

Connerton, P. (2008). "Seven types of forgetting". *Memory Studies*, 1, 59-71.

Crenzel, E. (2014). *La historia política del* Nunca más. *La memoria de las desapariciones en la Argentina*. Buenos Aires: Siglo Veintiuno Editores.

Dandan, A. (2016). "De vuelta a los dos demonios". *Página/12*, 12 June. At **www.pagina12.com.ar/diario/elpais/1-301566-2016-06-12. html**, accessed 15 July 2016.

Del Barco, O., Belzagui, P. R., *et al.* (2014). *No matar : Sobre la responsibilidad*. Córdoba: Universidad Nacional de Córdoba, Ediciones del Cíclope, Ediciones La Intemperie.

Di Tella, A. (1994). *Montoneros – una historia*. Audiovisual production. At **https://vimeo.com/116316679.**

Hirsch, M. (2012). *The Generation of Postmemory: Writing and Visual Culture after the Holocaust*. New York: Columbia University Press.

Nietzsche, F. (2001). "On the uses and disadvantages of history for life". In D. Breazeale (ed.), *Untimely meditations/Friedrich Nietzsche* Cambridge: Cambridge University Press, 57-123.

O'Donnell, G. (2002). "Modernization and military coups". In G. Nouzeilles and G. Montaldo (eds.), *The Argentine Reader: History, Culture, Politics*. Durham and London: Duke University Press, 399-420.

Prividera, N. (2007). *M*. Audiovisual production. Buenos Aires: Trivial.

Prividera, N. (2014). *El país del cine : Para una historia política del nuevo cine argentino*. Córdoba: Los Ríos Editorial.

Ranzani, O. (2016). "Era una historia que tenía que ser contada". *Página/12*, 22 March. At **www.pagina12.com.ar/diario/ suplementos/espectaculos/5-38336-2016-03-22.html**, accessed 17 December 2016.

Sarlo, B. (1997). "Cuando la política era joven". *Punto de Vista: Cuando la política era joven: Eva Perón, años setenta, democracia, populismo*, 58 (August), 15-19. At **www.ahira.com.ar/revistas/pdv/51/ pdv58.pdf**, accessed 21 February 2017.

Sonderéguer, M. (2001). "Los relatos sobre el pasado reciente en Argentina: Una política de la memoria". *Iberoamericana*, 1, 1, 99-112.

Yerushalmi, Y. H. (1996). *Zakhor: Jewish History and Jewish Memory*. Seattle and London: University of Washington Press.

The Politics of Remembering and Forgetting in the Argentine Education System

Daniel Filmus

> "The question is," said Alice, "whether you
> can make words mean so little."
> "The question is," said Humpty Dumpty,
> "who is to be master – that's all."
> Lewis Carroll

There is a considerable degree of consensus as to one of the principal roles of education systems, namely, that of transmitting from generation to generation the culture of a given society. Such a consensus, however, does not extend to the characteristics pertaining to this process of transmission nor to the social and political functions implied thereby.

For those brought up in the classical tradition of the sociology of education that arose with Émile Durkheim (1991), the culture transmitted through the school system responds to cohesive ideals which allow people to live together in democratic society. These values allow coexistence and mutual respect between citizens on the basis of a general consensus regarding the norms and values that are to govern a society. The said consensus depends on a "neutral" code that, in time, corresponds to a given community and a determinate moment in history. Such a perspective is sustained by the conviction that there exists in the state, and by right, a "national spirit" made up of a collective consciousness which, through state action, must be imparted by schooling to each new generation for it to be fully integrated into society.

A more critical sociology of education, in contrast, conceives of society as non-existent as an organic whole. The social structure is sustained by a profound inequality in the distribution of economic, political and cultural resources. In this model, the contexts and practices of education are never "neutral" and never correspond with some "collective consciousness". They are the result of the dominance of some groups over others, expressed, amongst other ways, through cultural domination. From such a standpoint, the principal purpose of education is to transmit, as legitimate and universal, the culture of dominant groups, which is but one part of culture and therefore *relative* and *arbitrary* (Bourdieu, Passerón 1977; Althusser 1974). From the traditional perspective, both pedagogy and the role of the teacher are directed at unleashing a centripetal force of integration and social cohesion. For a critical-reproductivist sociology, however, the teacher delivers legitimacy, arising from his or her pedagogical actions, to the curricular contexts imposed by the dominant class or group, a part or a slice of culture but also a guarantee of reproducing social inequalities.

Remembering and forgetting, or what is present and absent in the pedagogical design and practice of the curriculum, depends, in Durkheimian terms, on what *society* considers it necessary to include in the intergenerational transmission of culture for the maintenance of order and social integration. From this perspective, the transmission of culture is destined to leave no room for critique but rather to recreate adult mandates. Its objective is the acceptance of an unquestionable legacy (Birgin 2016). In contrast, a critical perspective emphasizes the never neutral political character of the selection of merely a part of the culture and history to be transmitted and, of course, the form to be adopted in this transmission. The strength to be gained by the legitimizing of an unjust social order will depend, in the main, on the capacity of the dominant groups to naturalize, or to attribute some objectivity to, a range of contents and values only sustainable as the defence of their own interests. Thus, critical analysis will detect in instances of "forgetting", in the gaps left in the schooling process, one of the keys to opening up the teaching devices deployed to add symbolic force to the intention of perpetuating the material inequalities of society. Seen thus, it is possible to propose that the reason for the absence from the schooling environment of the history and values of subaltern groups in society (women, native peoples, workers, etc.) and of central social processes or traumatic facts—such as wars and genocides—is not a matter of chance or simply "forgetting". The recent history of Argentina is a clear example of such a tension between remembering and forgetting in the schooling environment, forever linked to the confrontation of vested interests and a politics of antagonisms.

The "Forgotten Ones" in the Argentine Education System

From its earliest phases, the Argentine education system has had as its main objective the integration of a highly heterogeneous population into a Nation and a State under the leadership of a very small section of society that represented the interests of the great landowners and of those who monopolized commerce with the colonial power of the time, the United Kingdom. It was thus that, at the end of the nineteenth century, a strongly exclusivist model in economics and politics, allowing for no mass access to property, participation in politics or upward social mobility, was determined to develop, from the construction of a neutral education system, the ideal mechanism for integrating and modernizing society. In order to achieve this objective, a national curriculum was designed and deployed to exclude from its content and practice an important part of the history, social processes and values involving the great majority of the nation, in particular the original peoples of the land. The construction of the Argentine nation was carried out upon the basis of a Europe-centred culture that marginalized from the school process both the early inhabitants and the popular sectors of society. Without any doubt, however, it was the military dictatorship which governed the country between 1976 and 1983 that took to the most aberrant and unusual extremes the censoring of schooling's contents and materials. The disappearances of individuals that occurred as part of the repressive mechanism of government had as its counterpart the "disappearance" of authors, texts and even school subjects (for example, the prohibition of modern mathematics, set theory and sociology) from the education system. Conscious of the role of education in the development of critical individuals, the military government murdered, persecuted, "disappeared", imprisoned or forced into exile a very great number of teachers. The level of sophistication with which the dictatorship imposed its censorship in schools had no precedents. The swathing prohibition of authors, texts and school subjects was accompanied by an even more efficient system of control: permanent self-censorship. Many teachers chose to exclude from teaching even things that had not been explicitly prescribed, for fear of suffering repression (Filmus and Frigerio 1988).

Democracy is Recovered. But is Memory?

The dictatorship attempted by every possible means to ensure that its actions, particularly in the realm of state terrorism and of its role in the Malvinas conflict, were not revised by the nascent democracy. The "ordered" withdrawal—not by a popular uprising—of the Armed Forces from government generated the conditions by which the military meant to control and tutor the political system over a long period.

The process by which education was democratized, in accordance with what took place throughout the whole country, was not straightforward. The opening up of democracy meant that the grave violations of human rights and state terrorism committed during the dictatorship became public knowledge and that the demands for those guilty to be judged, until then limited only to the organizations of the Mothers and Grandmothers of the Plaza de Mayo and other human rights institutions, eventually multiplied. The government of Raúl Alfonsín took up these demands as its own and as soon as it came to power created a special commission made up of well-known personalities from within Argentine culture to investigate the atrocities committed during the dictatorship. The Comisión Nacional sobre la Desaparición de Personas (National Commission on the Disappearance of Persons) published its stark and profound version of events in an emblematic text for Argentine democracy entitled *Nunca más* (1984). At the same time, the government took the decision to implement a characteristically memorable trial that culminated in the condemnation of the members of the Military Juntas that had controlled the government from 1976 to 1983. The first two years of democratic administration were accompanied in the system of education by the overturning of repressive norms, the elimination of explicit censorship, and the opening up of participatory initiatives in the schools sector. Further, the period saw a gradual inclusion of subjects excluded in the preceding years. Programmes of study and curriculum designs underwent changes and began to include content linked to the crimes committed by state terrorism and to the need for the total enforcement of human rights.

The processes of democratization of public institutions and of the judging of those guilty of state terrorism began to be questioned by sectors of the Armed Forces. Permanent military uprisings against the constitutional order gained their "compensation" through the sanction and application of the Full Stop (1986) and Due Obedience (1987) (*Punto Final* and *Obediencia Debida*) laws and the pardoning of those who had been found guilty (1989). These measures caused the ending of the trials and established the basis for granting impunity to those responsible for genocide. In the education system this process meant a regression in the development in schools of the teaching of "traumatic" subjects and the return to self-censoring. Once again in Argentina there ensued yet another period of "forgetting" of the most painful facts of the country's recent past.

Under the headings of "reconciliation" and "national unity" the possibility that justice might reign was simply diluted. Paraphrasing Yosef Yerushalmi (1998), who, in his book *Los usos del olvido* (*The Uses of Forgetting*), claimed that the opposite term to "forgetting" was probably not "remembering" but "justice", it is possible to suggest that the lack of justice in Argentina was intended to produce a blanket of forgetting. In the education system, the institutionalization of not allowing teaching on the processes of state terrorism and the Malvinas conflict was confirmed in the Federal Education Legislation voted for in 1992. Amongst the obligatory contents that the education system had to deliver in schools, such problematic subjects were not included.

The idea that issues to do with trauma ought not to be brought to attention nor be part of transmitting culture in schools was extended to at least two other dramatic incidents experienced by the country in the 1990s, namely, the most important terrorist attacks which Argentina has suffered in its entire history, those on the Israeli Embassy (1992) and on the Asociación Mutual Israelita Argentina (AMIA) (1994), in which perished, respectively, twenty-two and eighty-five victims. This period, which combined impunity for genocide, the politics of "forgetting" of human rights and the predominance of a neoliberal economic model, ended in the worst manner imaginable. The taking to the streets of the population, with the cry of "que se vayan todos" (all of them must go), provoked the resignation of President Fernando de la Rúa in 2001. The repression of this popular uprising caused fifty deaths and unleashed a political crisis that only began to be resolved with the coming to the Presidency of the Nation of Néstor Kirchner, who won the April 2003 elections.

Argentina Recovers Memory and Seeks Truth and Justice

The government that came to power on 25 May 2003 drastically changed the politics of human rights that had prevailed in the preceding years. In his inaugural address to Parliament, the new president declared that the central axis of his political programme would be that of achieving Memory, Truth and Justice, and proclaimed the legitimacy of the fight against impunity led by the Mothers and Grandmothers of the Plaza de Mayo. Within months, in August 2003, the National Congress approved the project, put forward by the Executive, to repeal the laws of Punto Final and Obediencia Debida. The attempts to throw a blanket of forgetting over the crimes committed were buried under the claim for justice firmly held and advanced by the various human rights organizations.

Two years later, the Supreme Court of Justice declared both these laws unconstitutional, an act which triggered the trials of military and civilian perpetrators of the politics of state terrorism during the period of the dictatorship that had ruled the country from 1976 to 1983. A decade after the start of the trials, more than 2,200 members of the military had been indicted, of whom 660 were found guilty and some 851 were still in the process of being tried.

The Challenge to the Education System in the Transition of Memory

When the new government established the fight for memory, truth and justice as official state policy, the Ministry of Education had to take up the challenge of recovering the work undertaken at the outset of the new period of democracy and extending the measures taken to transmit what had happened during the most traumatic periods of Argentine history.

The challenges faced by the heads of the Ministry of Education and the teams of teachers tasked with the implementation of the policy were by no means easy, given that a broad debate on the issue had been unleashed in society as a whole as well as in the education system itself. In brief, the debate turned on these axes: a) ought schools to transmit the traumatic events of the recent past?; b) how to change legislation to the effect that these subjects be taught in all schools throughout the country?; c) how to guarantee that such a transmission of the facts of history not be reduced to a mere "mechanical reproduction of memory"? In respect of the first question, the Ministry of Education decided to take up the social mandate that had been established in 2003 and to work towards the education system's being able to develop again the conditions that had enabled it to transmit to new generations the memory of traumatic situations that were in the distant past but, in some cases, very close to the present; situations that had often involved exclusion, suffering and death. Thus, schools had to assume the responsibility for working in the classroom with matters of genocide, war, and acts of terrorism that had moved, and continue to move deeply, the conscience of the citizens of Argentina. And, so, education is recovering one of its principal objectives. As Theodor Adorno (1998) wrote, "The pathos (the passion) for schooling, its moral seriousness, stems from the fact that it alone can work immediately, if one takes notice of it, in overcoming barbarity on the part of humanity... I am referring to the extremes, the mad prejudice, the repression, genocide and torture, about which there can be not the least doubt." This perspective, profoundly humanist, stands in counterpoint to the view that the task of education is supposedly neutral, because it stresses the political role of schooling. Yet it does not achieve this aim in a partisan fashion. To stress the political role of and in teaching implies trusting in the capacity of citizens to be brought up with a critical awareness. Citizens ready to avoid the repetition of history and to stop both the rise of dictatorships and the violation of human rights. In support of such a political commitment on the part of schools, Inés Dussel (2001) has proposed the following:

> The transmission of the memory of historic trauma shares the dilemmas of all cultural transmission and of all pedagogical activity, their ethical paradoxes and their political tensions, but it has characteristics that distinguish it from other modes of transmission. In the transmission of memory, it is human suffering that occupies the central and definitive role. Symptomatic of history, these traumatic events carry with them the very limits of representation, the crisis of truth and justice, obliging us to take sides, to explore the politics of transmission.

Yet the debate is not uniquely centred on the different views *vis à vis* the past and the ways of transmitting that legacy (Hassoun 1996), but on the implications that said history sheds upon the present. Each one of these traumatic processes, beginning to be included in the curriculum's design and in schooling practice, weighs upon the decisions made in the present. As Jorge Luis Borges proposed in a prologue of 1968, "history is not a cold museum; it is the secret trap out of which we are formed, that of time itself. In today are our yesterdays." It is not possible to introduce into the classroom content referring to the devastating consequences of conquest and colonization for native peoples without debating the manner in which, today, discrimination and cultural domination are expressed and operated upon the descendants of those peoples. The problem of migration, so present on the public agenda today, is also affected by this discussion. To become conscious of the genocide committed during the military dictatorship obliges teachers and pupils to tackle issues of the day, such as the need to advance in the passing of judgements on those civilians and military personnel guilty of violations of human rights, or the permanent search for identity on the part of children born in captivity and subsequently stolen. The debate on the Malvinas conflict not only needs, as in the case of state terrorism, to be part of the process of judging those responsible for sending to their deaths hundreds of young men and for the violation of the human rights of the soldiers who fought there, but also implies opening further the discussion regarding an unjust international order that allows the United Kingdom to continue usurping a part of Argentine territory after more than 180 years.

Forgetting, or the non-presence of such topics as these in the classroom, exempts the school from the need to locate these facts as part of the pedagogical process and of the intergenerational transmission of culture, distancing the very conflict that invites a reconsideration of that transmission. For to consider that conflict only as a question of past history, without including its implications in and for the present, is a relatively comfortable alternative, thereby suggesting commitment to the project of those who aspire only to fulfil the merest formalities of what is to be expected of "modern" educational programmes. From within the Ministry of Education charged with implementing educational policy from 2003 onwards there arose a different view, one that would link past, present and future.

The second of the aforementioned challenges was limited to the need to ensure that the curricular contents be included in the study programmes of the whole country and, for that objective to be achieved, such contents had to be included in the new National Education Law, in a specific clause that put the obligation to teach these topics at every level of the education system. The debates over the new law took place throughout 2006. More than four million students, teachers and parents participated in this process, along with thousands of community organizations, churches, trade unions, chambers of commerce, universities, graduate associations, etc. Support for the inclusion of topics linked to recent memory and "traumatic" contents was of such magnitude that it halted all resistance in the National Congress, and inclusion was passed by a clear (nearly unanimous) majority in both chambers (Filmus and Kaplan 2012). Thus, article 92 of the National Education Law (No. 26,026) included the stipulation that for all provinces of the nation the following contents be applied in common:

- The exercise and construction of collective memory of the historical and political process that broke the constitutional order and ended by installing State terrorism; with the objective of generating amongst students reflections and democratic feelings and the defence of the Rule of Law and the full application of human rights in accordance with that principle outlined by Law No. 26,061;

- The case for the recuperation of our Islands, the Malvinas, the South Georgias and South Sandwich, in accordance with the principle outlined in the First Transitory Disposition of the National Constitution;
- The acknowledgement of the cultural diversity of indigenous peoples and their rights, in accordance with article 54 of the current law.

In respect of those who participated in acts linked to state terrorism, Law 26,206 (Article 70) is applicable in prohibiting them from carrying out any teaching role.

Thus, the law prescribes concrete mechanisms in order that painful, controversial and complex facts of history and Argentine reality be not only incorporated as teaching material but also absorbed into the everyday reality of classroom experience and the construction of a different future.

Up to this point, we have emphasized the importance of schooling in the irrefutable commitment to transmit fully the history and culture of the country without excluding the dramatic and painful processes of the past and present. We have also summarized some of the legislative mechanisms that underpin and lend "obligatory" character to this transmission. At this juncture we wish to make clear that these processes are necessary but not sufficient for the education system to enhance its task as an effective and total incorporation of social memory into the new generations. The capacity for resistance of schools and practitioners in addressing such complex topics is habitually shown through the mechanizing and formalizing of the methods of transmitting memory. In other words, the school can transmit the experiences of suffering or horror by way of "teaching the memory of memory", ending up by producing "forgetting". Perhaps for that reason there has been and continues to be the most important challenge in tackling the scholarly task of transmitting traumatic experiences: the need to structure a teaching plan that may intensively put the new generations into contact not only with the facts and the contents of memory, but also with the sensations, dramas, sufferings, dreams and illusions of those who lived through them. To transmit the past as do traditional museums or as just some archaeological remains is a form of assuring that it stays stuck in its time and that it "does not loose its demons onto the present" (Dussel 2001).

In his novel *The Name of the Rose*, Umberto Eco puts into the mouth of William, the monk who is searching for the truth, a fascinating reflection on libraries. Speaking to his disciple, Adso, he asserts that a library can provide humanity with all the knowledge that men and women have ever produced, or just the contrary. As is the case with the library in the novel's setting, it can serve to enclose and to ensure that humanity never come into contact with its manuscripts. The art of keeping documents also implies hiding them away (Dussel 2001). A similar phenomenon may be observed in the culture transmitted by schools, which have their own logic, agents and particular cultures. The strategy of formally incorporating certain contents into curriculum designs and subject programmes may also imply that they never reach their intended recipients alive, being conceived of as the mere reproduction of memory. For this reason, it is necessary to complement a politics of inclusion of memory in the school environment with the essential development of pedagogies that ensure that the process of transition itself does not turn into some fixed, dead content but, in contrast, is transformed into a tool designed to establish contact with knowledge, feelings and legacies that focus activities in the present inseparably from constructing the future.

If there is a clear risk in the formalizing or rendering mechanical of a remembering that invites only forgetting, another challenge involved in the transition of memory is its being reproduced as an unquestionable legacy (Birgin 2006). The perspective from which the Ministry of Education introduced the memory programmes was sustained by the idea proposed by Hassoun (1996) regarding what might be considered a "successful transmission". Such would be whatever "offered to the receiver a space of freedom and a base from which to abandon (the past) in order (the better) to rediscover it". As pointed out by Merieu (1998), the transmission of this type of knowledge and awareness cannot be achieved mechanically: "it cannot be conceived as some duplication of the same, as implicit in many forms of teaching. It presupposes a reconstruction, on the part of the subject, of knowledge and awareness that it must inscribe in both that project and in those perceived as contributing to its development." The aim of our teaching task is to provide for new generations both knowledge of social and historical processes and a feeling for them; the pains and the horrors, dreams and hopes through which we have travelled. But if we are to achieve the "successful transmission" suggested by Hassoun, we must also create conditions whereby – with such awareness and feelings – the new generations may decide to travel paths very different to those we have travelled ourselves (Birgin 2016). The meeting point between generations implied in the educational process will surely include new perspectives, new questions posed by those who enter the space of memory for the first time. A successful transmission, if achieved, becomes a process of permanent recreation, depending on the continuing development of the critical faculties of the protagonists involved. This right to question, to re-elaborate upon our legacy, of course includes the right to forget or deny; but now as a right rather than as a result of that absence that imposes the emptiness produced by the lack of memory.

At this point, it is necessary to emphasize that the only possible strategy for incorporating this point of view is through the actions of the teachers involved. Experience shows that no transformation can arrive in the classroom if it is not supported by the willingness to change on the part of teachers and professors. Therefore, the first challenge in counting on them as fundamental to the introduction of these topics into the schooling experience is to invite them to be part of the development of the proposed strategies of inclusion in the programmes of memory and education.

A further and key consideration is the multiplicity of technical and audiovisual support systems available today that allow the transmission of memory through a range of multimedia productions. The setting up of the educational television channel *Encuentro* and of the children's channel *PakaPaka* has become an essential tool for reaching nationwide, with film and television materials, teacher training and access to pupils and students as well as extending contact with the country's communities as a whole. It is also the case that schools have been approached through the arts. Works from the theatre, cinema, literature, exhibitions of the plastic arts, amongst other media, have been privileged instruments in bringing students closer to situations that were very difficult to broach from traditional teaching perspectives and strategies.

The Return to a Politics of Forgetting

Since the coming to power of the government of Mauricio Macri in December 2015, there has been an important shift in the public policies of the nation, pitched at recovering social memory and keeping alive the task of guarding human rights. The new authorities have decided to go into reverse gear on the road taken by the state in respect of the claims of memory, truth, and justice, thereby attempting to delegitimize the struggle of human rights organizations and associations of ex-combatants. They have also tried to turn back the advances achieved thanks to the actions of previous governments. As far as the criminal trials are concerned, there has been a clear attempt to slow down the process, home detention has been ordered for many of the accused and condemned, and there has been a questioning of those judges who adopted a strong line against the genocide of the dictatorship. Furthermore, state support has been withdrawn from such human rights organizations as the Mothers and Grandmothers of the Plaza de Mayo. As for the campaign of delegitimizing appeals for justice, the present government has tried to advance in different directions. All the actions and statements of public officials have focused on throwing into question advances made in the recuperation of public memory regarding condemnation of state activities during the times of the dictatorship.

An example of this attitude has been the series of declarations of the Minister of Culture of the City of Buenos Aires, Darío Lopérfido, who has questioned the emblematic number of 30,000 victims of forced disappearances and has argued that this figure was artificially inflated so that more families might claim the compensation to which they were legally entitled. Over and above that, as Adorno (1998) reminds us, when it comes to genocide, "to point to statistical figures or indeed to haggle over them is already unworthy of being human", and the aim of Darío Lopérfido has been to undermine the authority of human rights organizations. For his part, the Director of National Customs and Excise, Juan José Gómez Centurión, an ex-military officer who rose up against democracy during the government of Raúl Alfonsín, has thrown into question the sentences passed in the trials of the Military Juntas in 1985. He has argued that the actions of the dictatorship were not attributable to a premeditated plan for the extermination of citizens and the disappearance of babies. He has returned to toy with the theory that the violations of human rights were "excesses" the responsibility for which can be ascribed to certain members of the Armed Forces. For its part, attempting to contribute to "forgetting", the government has decreed, ignoring the existing laws, that the public holidays marking the dictatorship (24 March) and rendering homage to the fallen of the Malvinas conflict (2 April) might be moved to other dates with a view to encouraging tourism.

None of these interventions of the Macri government succeeded in their aim. Each one of them prompted a social backlash of great magnitude. The criticism unleashed by his declarations culminated in the resignation of the Minister of Culture Lopérfido, the Director of Customs and Excise had to rectify his position publicly, and the President himself conceded that government also had to take a step back from the attempt to change the date for remembering the dictatorship and the Malvinas victims. But the will to venture further beyond the flaws in the legal system in condemning those guilty for the repressions and genocides of the latest dictatorship became particularly evident when the Supreme Court of Justice decided to apply a reduction in the sentences of those detained for crimes against humanity. With the argument that there ought to be the lightest application of the law to those condemned, the Court ruled on a double counting for each year already served by those detained on the grounds of genocide. The carrying out of this order would have meant that many of those thus condemned might be freed immediately, serving only half of the sentences imposed.

The social indignation arising from this measure, decided on 2 May 2018, was immediate and widespread. The Abuelas y Madres de Plaza de Mayo and other human rights organizations declared very firmly against it whilst at the same time calling for a general mobilization to demonstrate popular rejection of the decision. These organizations announced, "We say never again to impunity, never again to torturers, rapists, kidnappers of children. Never again privileges in respect of crimes against humanity. Never again state terrorism. Never again the freeing of those convicted of genocide. Never again silence. We do not wish to live alongside the bloodiest assassins in our history. We demand memory...". More than half a million people wearing white headscarves, in one of the most important street demonstrations in the history of Argentina, spilled out into the centre of Buenos Aires to reaffirm their commitment to Truth and Justice and to demand the overturning of the ruling. The sheer volume of the protest obliged the National Congress, with unanimity in both Chambers, to approve a Law excluding the benefitting of the "2 x 1" provision for those convicted of crimes against humanity. On 4 December 2018 this same mass movement, in an unprecedented case, forced the Supreme Court of Justice, with the same members who had voted for just the opposite, to revise almost unanimously the earlier error of judgement. Furthermore, the state pressure on the judges did not manage to impede in many cases the process of justice in trials of those guilty for the deaths and disappearances of the dictatorship. A particularly significant case was that of 12 December 2018 which led to the first condemnation of civilians, directors of a multinational company (Ford), for complicity with the military government in the illegal deprivation of liberty and torture of their factory workers.

Another of the strategies of the government directed at discrediting popular memory has been the attempt to equate the demands of the organizations that group together the families of victims of guerrilla actions of the 1970s with those that unite the families of those that suffered state terrorism, such as the Madres y Abuelas de la Plaza de Mayo. In this way, the government is attempting to recuperate the theory of the "2 demons" that would be used to justify intellectually and juridically the genocide committed by the dictatorship. Similarly, the National Government endorsed the requests of the Comisión de Familiares of those detained for crimes against humanity before the Comisión Interamericana de Derechos Humanos (CIDH) for those condemned for genocide to be considered "political prisoners".

In the case of the Malvinas issue, the intention to "forget" began on the very first day of the new government. President Macri became the first ever democratically elected president not to mention the demand for dialogue with the United Kingdom over the sovereignty of the islands in the traditional address which, in Parliament, establishes the new incumbent's mandate. Yet this glaring omission also revealed the wish to relativize the importance of the said demand for negotiation for the Argentine people in bilateral meetings that had already taken place with British authorities as, no less, with multilateral organizations. In a sort of metaphor for the official attempt to remove this subject from the national and international agenda, the Malvinas islands were "forgotten", or left out, in the design of the map of Argentina produced by the Ministry of Social Development.

The strategy of muting demands for dialogue with the United Kingdom for the sovereignty of the Islas Malvinas was evidenced in the agreement signed by deputy ministers of each country on 13 September 2016. Carlos Fornadori and Alan Duncan signed and sealed a document whereby Argentina yields in the face of the claims made by the then British Prime Minister Theresa May, a few days before assuming office, to President

Macri. In this Agreement, unconstitutional in not having been approved by the National Congress, Argentina is committed to "take the appropriate measures in removing all obstacles limiting the economic and sustainable growth of the Islas Malvinas, including trade, fishing, navigation and hydrocarbons". Following this agreement, Argentina is advancing the legitimation of the exploitation of fishing, and the British exploration for hydrocarbons and minerals in the South Atlantic. The same document proposes to implement new air flights from third countries to the Malvinas, discriminating against the flagship Aerolíneas Argentinas and stopping flight departures from that country.

The associations of ex-combatants have considered this agreement to be "the greatest surrender of sovereignty and natural resources in history" (CECIM, La Plata). These same organizations have also strongly criticized the inclusion in the document of a special paragraph on the process of recognizing the identity of those Argentine soldiers interred in the cemetery of Puerto Darwin which had been set in motion by the government of Cristina Kirchner jointly with the International Red Cross. The incorporation of a matter so sensitive for the families of those who lost their lives in combat, in the context of a document that includes economic understandings, suggests that this humanitarian action, owed for the last thirty-five years by the United Kingdom, was used as a counterpart to the ceding of sovereignty on the part of Argentina. In the recent meeting of Theresa May with Mauricio Macri, held in the context of the G20 meeting in Buenos Aires, the agreement advanced, as much in the confirmation of the opening by a foreign airline of a new commercial air route from São Paulo as in the absence of the issue of sovereignty in these conversations.

Another demonstration of the impossibility of putting an end to the memory of gravely traumatic acts in respect and maintenance of human rights has been the recent re-opening on the part of the Cámara Federal de Apelaciones de Comodoro Rivadavia of the case of instances of the torture of ex-soldiers during the Malvinas conflict. This happened in spite of the Macri government having succeeded in identifying a flaw in the Supreme Court's declaration on the matter and in granting impunity to the military torturers. Now, the Cámara Federal, on receiving new denunciations and testimonies, has resolved that such tortures constitute crimes against humanity and, therefore, may not be excluded from the due process of the law. Thirty-six years on, 90 members of the Armed Forces will be judged for alleged homicides, abandonment leading to death, torture, humiliation, and being accessories to crime, threats, antisemitism, etc. This represents another triumph in the people's demand for Memory, Truth and Justice.

As for the rights of indigenous peoples, policies also underwent a profound transformation. The new government vindicated those who had committed genocide against the native populations in order to grab their lands. The Minister of Education, Esteban Bullrich, maintained in a speech that Argentina is facing "a new desert campaign, not with sword but through education" (Bullrich 2016). The Minister brought upon himself the opprobrium of broad sections of society, in particular certain Argentine intellectuals who declared publicly that "it is our right and our duty to demand that education not be left in charge of someone who has vindicated a crime against humanity, both literally and metaphorically" (Rodríguez 2016).

The politics that are fomenting "forgetting" have had corresponding effects in the education system. The new Minister of Education has questioned all national programmes directed at transmitting in schools the social memory of our people and human rights. Thus, the nation has undergone the cancellation, dismantling, or reduction to a minimum of programmes directed at recording state terrorism, the recovery of the identity of the sons and daughters of those who disappeared under the dictatorship, the maintenance of claims to sovereignty over the Malvinas and the implementation of the right to sex education. Particularly grave has been a watering down of policy in the sphere of Intercultural Bilingual Education, given that the National Ministry has been structurally deprived of support for provincial action on this issue. But the aims of government authorities nationally have been to go much further in stopping the function of schooling in respect of transmitting the processes and the traumatic facts that can recuperate memory historically absent from the classroom. Such an objective is but one of the dimensions of a project that is pitched at preventing schools from carrying forward their capacity to develop critical thinking amongst their pupils and students.

This is how the authorities have expressed their policies: the Cabinet Minister Marcos Peña (2016) has stated that "critical thinking taken to extremes has caused great damage to education [...] to maintain a critical thinking leads at the end of the day to the loss of the axis of what is truth". The advisor to the President, Alejandro Rozitchner (2016), has gone further when referring to the role of schools: "critical thinking is a negative value being taught in the nation's schools [...] teachers enjoy saying that they wish their pupils to develop critical thinking as if the most important thing were to be attentive to the traps and pitfalls of society [...] Enthusiasm and the wish to live are more important than critical thinking and objectivity."

All these statements are evidence of what is the ultimate aim of those who propose that "forgetting" return to reign over our schools: to educate young people who lack the capacity to look critically and from their own perspectives at society without either trying or intending to transform it. This stance does not only confront educational policies implemented in the previous period. It also questions the very foundations of the role of education. As Jean Piaget (1980) affirmed, one of the principal objectives of education is "to form minds capable of exercising critique, so that they can test for themselves whatever is presented to them and not accept it simply as that". Only thus will it be possible "not to repeat what other generations have done: to form creative individuals who are inventive, who are discoverers".

Winds of "forgetting" are blowing across Argentina and through its schools. The arm-wrestling between remembering and forgetting is not over and done with, for it is conducted on a daily basis in our classrooms. We trust that the permanent memory of our people, of its teachers and students, fortified by the politics and policies of transmission conducted over the last decade, will prevent this wind from being turned into a storm capable of blowing away and destroying the imperative of "Nunca más" ("Never again") that has risen up from within our history.

(Translated by Bernard McGuirk)

References

Adorno, T. (1988). *Educación para la emancipación: Conferencias y conversaciones con Hellmut Becker (1959-1969)*, ed. G. Kadelbach. Madrid: Ediciones Morata S.L.

Althusser, L. (1974). *Ideología e aparelhos ideológicos de Estado*. Lisboa: Presença.

Birgin, A. (2006). "La apuesta por la igualdad de la enseñanza". Unpublished paper. Encuentro Regional del Programa Integral para la Igualdad Educativa. Bariloche.

Birgin, A. (2016). "El trabajo de enseñar, entre el pasado y el futuro".

Unpublished paper. Buenos Aires.

Bourdieu, P., Passeron, J. C. (1977). *La reproducción: Elementos para una teoría del sistema de enseñanza*. Barcelona: Laia Ed.

Bullrich, E. (2016). "Esta es la nueva Campaña del Desierto, pero no con la espada sino con la educación". *La Nación*, 16 September. At **www.lanacion.com.ar/1938454-esteban-bullrich-esta-es-la-nueva-campana-del-desierto-pero-no-con-la-espada-sino-con-la-educacion**.

Durkheim, E. (1991). "La educación, su naturaleza y su papel". In P. Natorp and J. Dewey (eds.), *Teoría de la educación y sociedad*. Buenos Aires: CEAL.

Dussel, I. (2001). "La transmisión de la historia reciente. Reflexiones pedagógicas sobre el arte de la memoria". In *Memorias en presente. Identidad y transmisión en la Argentina posgenocidio*. Buenos Aires: Grupo Editorial Norma.

Filmus, D. (1988). "Democratización de la educación: Procesos y perspectivas". In D. Filmus and G. Frigerio (eds.), *Educación, autoritarismo y democracia*. Buenos Aires: Miño y Dávila Ed.

Filmus, D. (1996). *Estado, sociedad y educación en la argentina de fin de siglo: Proceso y desafíos*. Buenos Aires: Ed Troquel.

Filmus, D., and Kaplan, C. (2012). *Educar para una sociedad más justa: Debates y desafíos de la Ley de Educación Nacional*. Buenos Aires: Aguilar.

Hassoun, J. (1996). *Los contrabandistas de la memoria*. Buenos Aires: Ed. de la Flor.

Meirieu, P. (1998). *Frankenstein educador*. Barcelona: Laertes.

Peña, M. (2016). "El pensamiento crítico le ha hecho mucho daño a la Argentina". *Clarín*, 9 December. At **www.laopiniondetandil.com.ar/2016/12/09/marcos-pena-el-pensamiento-critico-le-ha-hecho-mucho-dano-a-la-argentina/**.

Piaget, J. (1980). *Psicología y pedagogía*. Barcelona: Ariel.

Rodríguez, C. (2016). "Los repudios a la 'campaña' de Bullrich". *Página 12*, 18 September. At **www.pagina12.com.ar/diario/elpais/1-309683 -2016-09-18.html**.

Rozitchner, A. (2016). Alejandro Rozitchner: "El pensamiento crítico es un valor negativo". *La Nación*, 20 December. At **www.lanacion.com.ar/1968830-alejandro-rozitchner-el-pensamiento-critico-es-un-valor-negativo**.

Yerushalmi, Y. H., *et al.* (1998). *Los usos del olvido: Comunicaciones al Coloquio de Royaumont*. Buenos Aires: Nueva Visión.

Index

www.ingramcontent.com/pod-product-compliance
Lightning Source LLC
Chambersburg PA
CBHW020600270326
41927CB00005B/106